MARYLAND MARRIAGES, 1801-1820

Compiled by
Robert Barnes

Copyright © 1993
Genealogical Publishing Co., Inc.
1001 N. Calvert St., Baltimore, MD 21202
All Rights Reserved
First printing, 1993
First printing in paperback, 2005
Library of Congress Catalogue Card Number 92-83828
International Standard Book Number 0-8063-1373-0
Made in the United States of America

CONTENTS

For Cathy,
Bob and Linda,
JoAnne, Nancy, and Susan

FOREWORD

This volume of Maryland marriage records for the period 1801-1820 was compiled primarily from church records deposited at the Maryland Historical Society in Baltimore and the Maryland State Archives in Annapolis. The records of St. Paul's Lutheran Church in Cumberland were obtained by a visit to the church office, where the staff graciously gave permission for the marriages to be copied. Also included in this volume are marriages recorded in the registers of individual ministers.

As in the two preceding volumes of *Maryland Marriages,* covering 1634-1777 and 1778-1800 respectively, marriages are arranged alphabetically by the groom's last name. Following his name are the date of the marriage and the name of the bride. Also included is any information pertaining to place of origin, parentage, or marital status of either party. In the last column there is a code designation for the source of the marriage followed by a dash and then the page number on which the marriage was found in the record source.

A list of sources used, with their code designation and the location of the records, immediately precedes the list of marriages. The list of sources is followed by a list of published marriage licenses for the years 1801 to 1820. A surname index of brides is given at the end of the book.

Every attempt has been made to spell names exactly as they appear in the original records, so variant spellings should be checked. From time to time the same marriage was recorded in two different records, and there may have been a discrepancy in the spelling of names or in the dates. In all such cases the discrepancies have been noted and the user of the book will have to use his own judgment as to which of the variants is correct.

It was decided not to include any marriage licenses issued by the clerks of the county courts because the licenses of so many counties have already been published. However, the marriage returns of many ministers have been included because they establish that a marriage definitely took place. These returns form a portion of the Scharf Papers and may be found at the Maryland State Archives and at the Maryland Historical Society.

In most church records the marriage entries simply contain the names of the bride and groom and the date of the marriage. Exceptions to this rule may be found in records of the Society of Friends and of many Roman Catholic churches. Marriages recorded in Friends' meetings routinely give the residence of the bride and groom, the names of the parents of both parties, and their places of residence. Marriages in Roman Catholic parishes often give similar information, especially if one or both parties were of French descent. Names of parents, including maiden names of mothers, and former places of residence make it possible to trace the origins of Baltimoreans who came here from France or as fugitives from the slave revolts in Santo Domingo.

The author is extremely grateful to a number of people who helped to make this book possible. His wife and children and daughter-in-law (to whom the book is dedicated) have made this endeavor worthwhile. The late Edna Kanely often gave many helpful suggestions. Cynthia and Ted Miller, Bill and Martha Reamy, and Ed Wright have helped the compiler master the intricacies of the computer and WordPerfect. Pat Czerniewski and Ted Sloane gave material assistance in the compilation of this book. Eileen Perkins, Joe Garonzik, and Michael Tepper of the Genealogical Publishing Company gave much needed editorial assistance. Finally, the staffs of the Maryland State Archives and the Maryland Historical Society were extremely cooperative in locating the records.

LIST OF SOURCES

This list of sources gives the code numbers, the name of the source, and the location of the records. Many marriage license returns filed by Maryland ministers are part of the Scharf Papers which are now at the Maryland State Archives, Annapolis. Photocopies of the marriage returns may also be found at the Maryland Historical Society, Baltimore. Sometimes the original church register was hard to read. In order to ensure accuracy the marriage licenses for the appropriate county were checked. Where information from the county marriage licenses was used it has been placed in brackets. Unfortunately, in a few cases, through an oversight on the part of the compiler, the source was omitted. Although an attempt has been made to identify the source of the marriage, a few items have to bear the designation US for Unidentified Source.

ALLEGANY COUNTY

01 AL - Marriage License Returns of Rev. William Shaw, 1801-1820; Scharf Papers; 01 AL-1 filed 28 Oct. 1794; 01 AL-2 filed 5 1797; 01 AL-3 filed 21 Nov., 1799; 01 AL-4 filed 24 Oct. 1800; 01 AL-5 filed 27 Nov. 1801; 01 AL-6 filed 5 Oct. 1803.

02 AL - Marriage License Return of Rev. William Allen, Presbyterian Minister, 1800; Scharf Papers.

03 AL - Marriages recorded in the Diary of Rev. William Shaw, pub. in DAR Magazine, June-July 1955.

04 AL - Marriage License Returns of Rev. Thomas Larkin; Scharf Papers; 04 AL-1 filed 19 Nov. 1803; 04 AL-2 filed 28 Nov. 1804.

05 AL - Marriage License Returns of Thomas Larkin; Scharf Papers; 0-5 AL-1 filed 26 Nov. 1802; 05 AL-2 filed 26 Nov. 1804.

06 AL - St. Patrick's R. C. Church, Cumberland, Maryland. MSA.

07 AL - Emmanuel P. E. Church, Allegany County. MSA.

08 AL - St. Paul's Lutheran Church, 15 North Smallwood Street, Cumberland, Md. Typed copy of original records at church office.

09 AL - Marriage returns of John Hewley, Prot. Ep. Church, list filed 19 Nov. 1803; Scharf Papers, S-1005, MSA.

10 AL - Marriage returns of John Hewley, Prot. Ep. Church, for Nov. 1803-Nov. 1804; Scharf Papers, S-1005, MSA.

ANNE ARUNDEL COUNTY

01 AA - All Hallows Parish Register; Original Register, MSA.

02 AA - St. Anne's Parish Register; Original Register, MSA.

03 AA - St. James' Parish Register; Original Register, MSA.

04 AA - St. Margaret's Parish Register; Original Register, MSA.

05 AA - Marriage License Returns of Rev. Joseph Wyatt, 1801-1804; Scharf Papers; 05 AA-1 filed 13 Nov. 1801; 05 AA-2 filed 11 Nov. 1802; 05 AA-3 filed 11 Nov. 1803; 05 AA-4 filed 10 Nov. 1804.

06 AA - Marriage License Returns of Rev. John Bloodgood; Scharf Papers; 06 AA-1 filed 27 Nov. 1801.

ANNE ARUNDEL COUNTY, (cont'd).

07 AA - Marriage License Returns of Rev. William Deal; Scharf
Papers; 07 AA-1 filed 9 Nov. 1801 07 AA-2 filed 18
Oct., 1802; 07 AA-3 filed 10 Dec. 1803; 07 AA-4 filed
23 Nov. 1804.

08 AA - Marriage License Returns of Rev. Benjamin Essex; Scharf
Papers; 08 AA-1 filed 25 April 1801.

09 AA - Marriage License Returns of Rev. Joseph Simmons; Scharf
Papers; 09 AA-1 filed 26 Oct. 1801; 09 Aa-2 filed 26
March 1802.

10 AA - Marriage License Returns of Rev. Wilson Lee; Scharf
Papers; 10 AA-1 filed 27 Sept. 1802; 10 A-2 filed 3
Oct. 1803. [See also under Prince George's County]

11 AA - Marriage License Returns of Rev. John Phillips; Scharf
Papers; 11 AA-1 filed 28 March 1803.

12 AA - Marriage License Returns of Rev. Seely Bunn; Scharf
Papers; 12 AA-1 filed 25 Nov. 1802; 12 AA-2 filed after
Nov. 1802.

13 AA - Marriage License Returns of Rev. Daniel Fidler; Scharf
Papers; 13 AA-1 filed 28 May 1804; 13 AA-2 filed 24
Nov. 1804.

14 AA - Marriage License Returns of Rev. John West; Scharf
Papers; filed 26 May 1804.

15 AA - Marriage License Returns of Rev. Greenbury Ridgely,
minister of the M. E. Church; Scharf Papers; 15 AA-1
filed 30 Dec. 1801; 15 AA-2 filed 24 Sept. 1803; 15 AA-
3 filed 6 Nov. 1804.

BALTIMORE CITY AND COUNTY

01 BA - St. James' Protestant Episcopal Parish; Transcript, MHS.

02 BA - Trinity Protestant Episcopal Church; Transcript, MHS.
[See also 37-BA]

03 BA - St. Paul's Protestant Episcopal Church; Transcript, MHS.

04 BA - St. Peter's R. C. Church, 1785-1793: MdHR MF 1510. See
15 BA.

05 BA - First Presbyterian Church, Baltimore; Transcript, MHS.

06 BA - Marriage License returns of Rev. Lawrence McCombs;
Scharf Papers; 06 BA-1 filed 28 Nov. 1801; 06 BA-2
filed 26 Nov. 1802; 06 BA-3 filed 25 Nov. 1803.

07 BA - Marriage Records of First and St. Stephen's United
Church of Christ; Published in the Bulletin of the
Maryland Genealogical Society, 16:67-68, and 20:305-
312.

08 BA - Marriages performed by Rev. Edward Choate, 1808 - .
Transcribed by Jesse Choate Phillips; Published in
History Trails, 7:4, 6, 8.

09 BA - Marriage Register of Rev. Lewis Richards; Photocopy of
register at MHS.

10 BA - Marriage License returns of Rev. Alexander M'Caine, Elder
of the M. E. Church; Scharf Papers; 10 BA-1 filed 23
Nov. 1801.

11 BA - Register of First Methodist Episcopal Church; Vol. 1;.
Original on microfilm, MF 701, at MHS.

12 BA - St. James' Protestant Episcopal Parish, Register, 1814-;
Published in the Bulletin of the Maryland Genealogical
Society, 19 (3) 159-161.

13 BA - Register of First Methodist Episcopal Church; Vol. 2;
Original on microfilm, MF 701, at MHS.

14 BA - Zion Lutheran Church, Baltimore; Transcript, MHS.

15 BA - St. Peter's Roman Catholic/Cathedral Marriages.; Original
register on microfilm, MF.1517, at MSA.

LIST OF SOURCES

BALTIMORE CITY AND COUNTY, (cont'd)

16 BA - Cathedral Marriages; Original register on microfilm, MF.1517, at MSA.

17 BA - Register of East Baltimore Station, Methodist Episcopal Church; Original Register on microfilm MF. M 412 at MSA.

18 BA - St. Thomas' Protestant Episcopal Parish, Baltimore County; Photostat of original register at MHS.

19 BA - St. Peter's Protestant Episcopal Church, Baltimore; Transcript, MHS.

20 BA - Associate Reformed Congregation, Baltimore; Original Register at MHS.

21 BA - New Jerusalem/Swedenborgian Church; Transcript at MHS.

22 BA - First Unitarian Church, Baltimore; Photostat of original at MHS.

23 BA - Marriage License Returns of Rev. Absolom Butler; Scharf Papers; 23 BA-1 filed 18 Oct. 1802; 23 BA-2 filed 1 Oct. 1803; 23 BA-3 filed 20 Oct. 1804.

24 BA - Marriage License Returns of Rev. John Marr; Scharf Papers; 24 BA-1; filed 20 Oct. 1802.

25 BA - Marriage License Returns of John Daniel Kurtz; Scharf Papers; 25 BA-1 filed 1 Nov. 1801; 25 BA-2 filed 20 Nov. 1802; 25 BA-3 filed 4 Nov. 1803; 25 BA-4 filed 12 Nov. 1804.

26 BA - Marriage License Returns of Rev. Lewis Richards; Scharf Papers; 26 BA-1 filed 26 Nov. 1801; 26 BA-2 filed 29 Nov. 1802; 26 BA-03 filed 28 Nov. 1803; 28 BA-4 filed 26 Nov. 1804.

27 BA - Marriage License Returns of Rev. George Roberts; Scharf Papers; 27 BA-1 filed 28 Nov. 1801.

28 BA - Marriage License returns of Rev. William Sinclair; Scharf Papers; 27 BA-1 filed 16 Nov. 1802.

29 BA - Marriage License returns of Rev. John Healy; Scharf Papers, S-5001, MSA; 29 BA-1 filed 28 Nov. 1803. 29 BA-2 filed 29 Nov. 1804;

30 BA - Old Otterbein Church, Baltimore; records published by Paul E. Holdcraft in The Old Otterbein Church Story.

31 BA - St. Patrick's Roman Catholic Church; Marriages, 1806-1815; Original register on microfilm MF. MdHR 1568-1 at MSA.

32 BA - St. Patrick's Roman Catholic Church; Marriages 1815-1820; Original Register on microfilm 1568-2 at MSA.

33 BA - Registers of St. John's Protestant Episcopal Parish, Kingsville; original register, 1768-1816 at MSA.

34 BA - Marriage License Returns of Samuel Coate, minister of the M. E. Church; Scharf Papers; 34 BA-1 filed 19 Nov. 1803; 34 BA-2 filed 16 June 1804.

35 BA - Marriage License Returns of Edward Rockhold; Scharf Papers; 35 BA-1 filed 18 Nov. 1803.

36 BA - Marriage License Returns of Rev. Joshua Wells; Scharf Papers; 36 BA-1 filed 28 Nov. 1803; 36 BA-2 filed 27 July 1804.

37 BA - Trinity Protestant Episcopal Church; Register, 1815 - , at MHS, MS.850 in Manuscripts Division; see also 02 BA.

38 BA - Private Register of Rev. John Keech; handwritten copy in Md. Diocesan Library; contains register for St. John's, Balto. and Harford Counties, 1819-1864, and for Christ Church, Harford Co., 1819- .

39 BA - St. John's German Catholic Church. Records begin 1804. MdHR MF 1584.

LIST OF SOURCES

BALTIMORE CITY AND COUNTY (cont'd)

40 BA - Marriage License Returns of John Bloodgood, filed 30
Nov. 1804 (contains marriages from Calvert, Anne Arundel and Baltimore Counties); Scharf Papers, MdHR S
1005, MSA.

CALVERT COUNTY

01 CA - Christ Protestant Episcopal Church; Transcript copied by
Christopher Johnston at MHS.

CAROLINE COUNTY

01 CR -St. John's Protestant Episcopal Parish Register, 1747-
1853; Transcript at MHS.

CARROLL COUNTY

01 CL - Trinity Evangelical Lutheran Church, Taneytown;
Transcription at MHS.
02 CL - St. Mary's Lutheran and Reformed Churches, Silver Run. -
Transcription at MHS

CECIL COUNTY

01 CE - St. Francis Xavier (Old Bohemia) Roman Catholic Church;
copy of register at MSA; Marriages published in Joseph
C. McCann, History of St. Francis Xavier Church and
Bohemia Plantation, Now Known as Old Bohemia, Warwick,
Maryland, Old Bohemia Historical Society, 1976.

CHARLES COUNTY

01 CH - Trinity Protestant Episcopal Church; Transcription at
MHS.
02 CH - Marriage Returns of Rev. John Brockenbrough, 3 Nov.
1800-16 Nov. 1801; Scharf Papers, Series S-5001, MSA.
05 CH - Records of the Congregations of Upper and Lower Zachiah,
Mattawoman, and St. Mary's (Bryantown); Transcription
at MHS.

DORCHESTER COUNTY

01 DO - Dorchester Parish; Marriages 1801-1820.
02 DO - Dorchester County; Great Choptank Parish. Original
marriage register at MSA, Acc. 312286; also pub. in F.
Edward Wright, Eastern Shore Maryland Vital Records,
1801-1820. Silver Spring: Family Line Pubs., 1986.

FREDERICK COUNTY

01 FR - First German Reformed Church, Frederick; transcript,
1903, at MHS.
02 FR - All Saints Parish' Transcript, by Lucy H. Harrison,
1901, MHS.
03 FR - Zion Lutheran Church, Middletown; Transcript, by Charles
T. Zahn, 1934, MHS.
04 FR - St. John's Roman Catholic Church, Frederick; Transcript,
by Margaret E. Myers, 1967, MHS.
05 FR - St. Joseph's Roman Catholic Church at Emmittsburg,
register on microfilm, MdHR 2832, at MSA.

LIST OF SOURCES

FREDERICK COUNTY (cont'd)

06 FR - Evangelical Lutheran Church, Frederick; Transcript, 1907, by Lucy H. Harrison, MHS. (Marriages, 1811-1820, in Vol. 3, pp. 1315-1331.

07 FR - Unidentified Source.

08 FR - Zion Evangelical Lutheran Church, Middletown Valley. Published in the Bulletin of the Maryland Genealogical Society, 28 (4) 413.

09 FR - Mount St. Mary's Roman Catholic Church, Emmittsburg. MdHR M 2832.

10 FR - Marriage Returns of Rev. Burgess Nelson, Fred. Co.; list filed 13 Nov. 1802; Scharf Papers, Series S-5001, MSA.

11 FR - Marriage Returns of Curtis Williams, filed 8 Oct. 1802; Scharf Papers, Series S-5001, MSA.

12 FR - Marriage Returns of Jonathan Forrest, filed 30 Oct. 1802; Scharf Papers, Series S-5001, MSA.

13 FR - Marriage Returns of Lenox Martin; filed 30 Oct. 1801; Scharf Papers, S-1005, MSA.

14 FR - St. Mark's P. E. Parish, Frederick and Washington Counties. MF M234 at MSA.

15 FR - Record of Marriages: Reformed Congregation of Frederick County, Maryland. Translated by William Hinke. Typescript, MHS. Translator's note: "This translation differs from the copy held by the Maryland Historical Society. It also includes witnesses to the marriage which were not included in the MHS copy."

16 FR - Records of Zion Lutheran Church, Middletown, Frederick County, Maryland, 1781-1826 (Maryland German Church records, volume 2). Translated by Charles T. Zahn. ed. by Frederick S. Weiser. Manchester: Noodle-Doosey Press c.r. 1987. Used with permission of the Carroll County Historical Society.

HARFORD COUNTY

01 HA - Marriage License Returns of Rev. William West; Scharf Papers, MSA. 01 HA-1 filed 30 Nov. 1778.

02 HA - Marriage License Returns of Rev. John Ireland; Scharf Papers, MSA. 02 HA-1 list filed Nov. 1786; 02 HA-2 filed 30 Nov. 1790; 02 HA-3 filed 23 Nov. 1791; 02 HA-4 filed 1 Nov. 1792; 02 HA-5 filed 5 Nov. 1793; 02 HA-6 filed 22 Dec. 1795.

03 HA - Marriage License Returns of Rev. Levy Heath; Scharf Papers, MSA.

04 HA - St. Ignatius Roman Catholic Church; Microfilm M.2849 at MSA.

05 HA - Marriage License Returns of Rev. Benjamin Richardson; Scharf Papers, MSA. 05 HA-1 filed 5 Nov. 1804; 05 HA-2 filed 6 Nov. 1802; 05 HA-3 filed 3 Nov. 1803.

06 HA - Marriage License Returns of Rev. Edmund Rockhold; Scharf Papers; 06 HA-1 filed 25 Oct. 1804.

07 HA - Churchville Presbyterian Church, Churchville. Typed copy of Register.

KENT COUNTY

01 KE - St. Paul's Protestant Episcopal Parish, original register and copy at MSA; see also F. Edward Wright. Maryland Eastern Shore Vital Records, Book 5. Silver Spring: Family Line Pubs., 1986.

02 KE - Shrewsbury Protestant Episcopal Parish Register; Transcript, MHS.

LIST OF SOURCES

KENT COUNTY (cont'd)

03 KE - Chester Parish, Kent County; Photostat of original
register at MHS.

MONTGOMERY COUNTY

01 MO - Marriage License Returns of Rev. William Allen; Scharf
Papers; MSA.
02 MO - Prince George's Parish. Marriages 1806-1813. MdHR M 261.
03 MO - Montgomery Co. Prince George's Parish; Marriages, 1801-
1809. Transcript , by L. H. Harrison, 1890, at MHS.
From 1806 on, the marriages duplicate the entries for
02 MO.

PRINCE GEORGES COUNTY

01 PG - Prince Georges Protestant Episcopal Parish; Original
Register, 1792-1845 at MSA.
02 PG - Unassigned.
03 PG - Marriage License Returns of Rev. William Lee; Scharf
Papers. 03 PG-1 filed 13 Sept. 1803.
04 PG - "Marriage Licenses granted by John R. Magruder and Hugh
Lyon, Taken from an Account Book in the Possession of
Mr. and Mrs. Thomas H. Gibson, 405 Chinquepin St., Port
Gibson, Mississippi. 39150," in DAR Magazine, May
1967, p. 545.

QUEEN ANNE'S COUNTY

01 QA - St. Peter's Roman Catholic Church, Queenstown; Abstracted
from Edward B. Curley's Origins and History of St.
Peter's Church, Queenstown, Maryland, 1637-1976.
02 QA - St. Luke's Protestant Episcopal Parish; Transcript, MHS.

SAINT MARY'S COUNTY

01 SM - St. Andrew's Protestant Episcopal Parish; Trancript, by
Lucy H. Harrison, 1907, MHS.
02 SM - William and Mary Protestant Episcopal Parish; Photostat
of Original Register (now at Prot. Ep. Cathedral,
Washington, D. C.) at MHS.
03 SM - Marriage Register at Newtown, 1799-1801; MPA 171 D. at
Georgetown University Library, Georgetown.
04 SM - St. Mary's Newtown, Roman Catholic; Marriage Register,
1819-1823, MPA 548 E at Georgetown University Library,
Georgetown.

SOMERSET COUNTY

01 SO - Somerset Protestant Episcopal Parish; Transcript, by
Esther Ridgely George, MHS.
02 SO - Coventry Protestant Episcopal Parish Register, 1736-1828,
Transcript, by Mrs. Helen Bowie Clary, 1936, at MHS.
03 SO - Manokin Presbyterian Church; microfilm of original at
MSA; see also F. Edward Wright. Maryland Eastern Shore
Vital Records, Book 5. Silver Spring: Family Line
Pubs., 1986.

TALBOT COUNTY

01 TA - St. Peter's Protestant Episcopal Parish; Transcript, MHS.

LIST OF SOURCES

02 TA - St. Joseph's Roman Catholic Mission, Cordova; Microfilm
M 858 at MSA; see also F. Edward Wright. *Maryland
Eastern Shore Vital Records, 1801-1825, Book 5.*
Silver Spring: Family Line Pubs., 1986.

03 TA - Abstracts from the Diary of Joseph Mosley, S.F.,
recorded from various parishes and missions; compiled
by Rev. Edward B. Carley; Microfilm M 858 at MSA; see
also F. Edward Wright. *Maryland Eastern Shore Vital
Records, 1801-1825, Book 5.* Silver Spring: Family Line
Pubs., 1986.

WASHINGTON COUNTY

01 WA - St. John's Protestant Episcopal Parish, Hagerstown;
Photostat of Original Register, MHS.

02 WA - St. John's Evangelical Lutheran Church, Hagerstown;
Typescript, by Mrs. Louise L. (Warren D.) Miller, 1935,
at DAR Library.

03 WA - Marriage Returns of Rev. John Santee, Cavetown, Washington Co.; list ends 1 Dec. 1804; Scharf Papers,
Series S-5001, MSA.

WICOMICO COUNTY

01 WI - Wicomico County; Stepney Parish. Original Register at
MSA. Marriages also pub. in Wright, *Maryland Eastern
Shore Vital Records, 1801-1825.*

WORCESTER COUNTY

01 WO - Worcester County; Worcester Parish; Original Register at
MSA; also pub. in Wright, *Maryland Eastern Shore Vital
Records, 1801-1825.*

SOCIETY OF FRIENDS

01 SF - West River Meeting; Register published in the *Bulletin of
the Maryland Genealogical Society,* serially, beginning
14(2).

02 SF - Gunpowder Meeting; Marriage Certificates, microfilm
M.1405 at MSA.

03 SF - Pipe Creek Meeting; Transcript, MHS.

04 SF - Cecil Monthly Meeting, Kent Co.; microfilm of original at
MSA; see also Joseph Carroll, *Quakerism on the Eastern
Shore of Maryland,* Baltimore: Maryland Historical
Society), and F. Edward Wright, *Maryland Eastern Shore
Vital Records, Book 5,* Silver Spring: Family Line Pubs.

05 SF - Little Falls Meeting; MF of Records are at MSA: See also:
Hunter C. Sutherland. *The Little Falls Meeting of
Friends, 1738-1988.* Bel Air: the Historical Society of
Harford County, Inc., 1988.

06 SF - Nottingham Monthly Meeting; MF of Records are at MSA; See
also: Alice L. Beard. *Births Deaths and Marriages of
the Nottingham Quakers, 1680-1889.* Westminster: Family
Line Publications, 1989.

07 SF - Northwest Fork Monthly Meeting, Caroline Co.; originals
on MF at MSA; marriages have been published in Wright,
Maryland Eastern Shore Vital Records, 1801-1825, pp.
37-39, and in Kenneth L. Carroll, *Quakerism on the
Eastern Shore of Maryland.*

SOCIETY OF FRIENDS (cont'd)

08 SF - Third Haven Monthly Meeting, Society of Friends;
originals are on microfilm at MSA; marriages have been
published in Wright, Maryland Eastern Shore Vital
Records, 1801-1825, and in Kenneth L. Carroll.
Quakerism on the Eastern Shore of Maryland.

09 SF - Baltimore Monthly Meeting, Marriages, 1794-1817, from
MSA, MdHR M 577; see also Willard Heiss. Maryland
Quaker Records. MHS. After 1807 the records of those
of the Baltimore Eastern District, Soc. of Friends.
(See also 12 SF, below).

10 SF - Sandy Spring Monthly Meeting; Marriages taken from MdHR
M 2250. Membership, 1758-1959. These marriages were
taken from other records and may not be complete.

11 SF - Deer Creek Monthly Meeting. MSA M 609.

12 SF - Baltimore Western District Monthly Meeting, Society of
Friends, See MSA M 577.

US -   Unidentified Source.

PUBLISHED MARRIAGE LICENSES

"Allegany County Marriages, 1794-1847," by Margaret Myers,
Western Maryland Genealogy, 2 (2) 63-ff., and subsequent
issues.

Anne Arundel County, Maryland, Marriage Records, 1777-1877.
Compiled by John W. Powell. Anne Arundel County Genealogical
Society.

"Caroline County Marriage Licenses, 1774-1815." Pub. in Pennsyl-
vania Magazine of History and Biography, 28:209 ff. Repr.
Baltimore: Genealogical Publishing Co., Inc., 1975. See also
Marriage Licenses, 1774-1825. By Raymond B. Clark, and Sara
Seth Clark; St. Michael's: The Authors, 1969.

Cecil County Marriage Licenses, 1777-1840. Baltimore: Genealogical Publishing Co., Inc., 1974.

Dorchester County Marriage Licenses, 1777-1840. By Katherine W.
Palmer. Cambridge, MD: 1960. See also "Marriage Licenses,
1790-1802," in Publications of the Pennsylvania Genealogical
Society Quarterly, 8 (March 1923):252-260.

Frederick County, Marriage Licenses of, 1777-1810. By Margaret
Myers. Westminster: Family Line Publications.

Frederick County, Marriage Licenses of, 1811-1840. By Margaret
Myers. Westminster: Family Line Publications.

Kent County Marriage Licenses, 1799-1850. By Raymond B. Clark,
Jr., and Sara Seth Clark. St. Michael's: The Authors, 1972.

Montgomery County, Maryland, Marriage licenses, 1798-1898. By
Janet D. Manuel. Westminster: Family Line Publications.

Prince George's County Marriage Licenses, 1777-1886, Index of. By
Helen W. Brown. Baltimore: Genealogical Publishing Co.,
Inc., 1973.

LIST OF SOURCES

Queen Anne's County Marriage Licenses, 1817-1858. By Raymond B. Clark, Jr., and Sarah Seth Clark. St. Michael's: The Authors.

Saint Mary's County, Maryland, Marriages and Deaths, 1634-1800. By Margaret K. Fresco. Ridge, MD; The Author, 1982.

Talbot County Marriage Licenses, 1794-1824. By Raymond B. Clark, Jr., and Sarah Seth Clark. Washington: The Authors, 1965.

Worcester County Marriage Licenses, 1795-1865. By Mary Beth Long and Vanessa Long. Westminster: Family Line Publications.

```
(N), (N); Sept. 1807; Barb. Sprigg                  02 WA-84
(N). (N); Aug. 1807; Fanny Newcomer                 02 WA-83
(N), Alexander; 17 June 1804; (N) Beckenbach        15 FR-316
(N), Barnaby; 24 Dec. 1809; Barbara (N) (both black) 15 FR-324
(?)body, John; 21 April 1812; Mary Reynolds         02 WA-94
(?)zner, Peter; June 1807; Mary Hoffman             02 WA-83
Aaron, Charles; 28 Nov. 1811; Dorothy Phillips      01 DO-41
Abbott, William; 21 May 1807 (by Thomas L. Budd); Rachel Conaway
                                                    17 BA-6
Abeart, John; Nov. 1802; Polly Miller               02 WA-73
Abel, Stanfield; 21 Sept. 1815; Ann Sadler          13 BA-22
Abell, Francis; 17 Jan. 1815; Ann Hebb              01 SM-64
Abell, Jonathan; 30 Dec. 1806; Harriet Corwin       02 SM-187
Abercrombie, John; 20 Dec. 1801; Johanna Hibbs      03 BA-411
Abercrombie, Wm.; 28 Sept. 1815; Eliza Knight       13 BA-23
Abernathy, Robert; 6 Nov. 1808; Polly Davis         03 AL-614
Abey, Jacob; 10 April 1806; Sarah Sheppard          14 BA-420
Abraham, Jacob; 30 Dec. 1810; Cath. Schuler         14 BA-428
Abrahams, Wm.; 2 Dec. 1803; Hannah Willey (or Wolley) 17 BA-3
Abram, Jacob; 26 Feb. 1810; Eliza F. Schwartzauer   14 BA-427
Abrams, Abraham; 11 Dec. 1818; Ann Stephens         14 BA-437
Abstheld, Gotfried; 19 April 1807; Cath. Braushott  14 BA-421
Achman, John; 6 Jan. 1802; Kitty Murray             03 BA-412
Acklin, James; 4 Sept. 1808; Nancy Hern             11 BA-13
Ackly (or Ashly or Schly), Benjamin; 21 May 1805; Ann Bussey
                                                    03 AL-613
Adams, (N) (free negro); 1 Jan. 1817; Jenny (N) (free mulatto)
                                                    32 BA-311
Adams, Aaron; 27 Sept. 1804; Mary Sappington        15 AA-3
Adams, Abraham; May 1803; Cath. Snyder              02 WA-75
Adams, Elie; 22 June 1811; Amelia Berry             02 WA-90
Adams, George; 26 Dec. 1808; Sarah Lurby            02 SM-188
Adams, Jacob; 13 Oct. 1816; Nancy Hart              06 FR-1325
Adams, James (age c.23, s. of Solomon and Dorothy Henen Adams);
    16 Nov. 1800; Elizabeth Peake (age c.18, dau. of Peter and
    Sarah Greenwell Peake)                          03 SM
Adams, John; 29 July 1802; Rebecca Johnson          05 AA-2
Adams, John; 2 May 1805; Elizabeth Robinson  (See also 02 BA-35)
                                                    03 BA-493
Adams, John; 11 Nov. 1807; Ann McGrath              15 BA-271
Adams, John; 4 Sept. 1810; Sarah Cooper             13 BA-10
Adams, John; 11 May 1811; Cath. Bence               02 WA-90
Adams, John; 29 April 1813; Rachel Richardson       09 BA
Adams, Joseph; 11 ? Nov. 1818; Ann Trott            17 BA-20
Adams, Philip; June 1816; Barbara Fackler           02 WA-102
Adams, Samuel; 8 Sept. 1801; Nancy Whittington      01 SO-15
Adams, Thomas; c.1802; Margaret Coleman             12 AA-1
Adams, Thomas F.; 10 June 1805; Susannah Fenton     11 BA-6
Adams, William; 23 May 1820; Barbara Uhler          13 BA-35
Aden, Jno.; 15 May 1804; Jane Gold                  14 BA-416
Adelsperger, Michael; 25 April 1820; Louisa Gelwick 05 FR-33
```

Adkinson, Joseph; 20 Dec. 1803 (by Rev. L. W. McCombes); Sally
    Sallowdine (?)   17 BA-3
Adrian, George; 26 Dec. 1802; Mary Kirby   14 BA-413
Adrien, Jaque; 30 Dec. 1819; Clemence Chauche (both free
    blacks)   16 BA-15
Adwood, John Lewis (age c.25, of Mont. Co., s. of James and
    Hannah Jarboe Adwood); 31 Dec. 1800; Theresa Combs (age
    c.28, dau. of William and Millbon Combs)   03 SM
Ady (Edy), Solomon; 1819; Elizabeth McAtee   04 HA
Affayro, (John) Francis; 18 Nov. 1820; Melanie Celamie   32 BA-330
Agelston, (?)ward; Sept. 1807; Elis. (N)   02 WA-83
Agnew, William; 30 Jan. 1812; Mary Ann Hague   09 BA
Aguiton, Henry J. (His Swedish Majesty's Consul and His Imperial
    Russian Majesty's Consulate General, Agent for the State of
    Maryland); 15 Oct. 1813; Eliza Galitren   02 BA-36
Aiken, George; 22 Feb, 1803; Sarah McConnell (widow of John)
                                                           15 BA-178
Aikens, John; 11 April 1817; Margaret Jackson   03 BA-602
Ailer, Jno.; 13 July 1807; Phoebe Peters   14 BA-422
Aimy(?), Edward; 19 Dec. 1819; Harriet Gresham   37 BA-152
Airs, Geo.; 7 Dec. 1805 (by Jno. Bloodgood); Jane Farrall
    (blacks)   17 BA-5
Airs, James; Aug. 1816; Elizab. Robey   02 WA-102
Aisquith, Eli; 11 May 1819; Mary Swain   37 BA-152
Aisquith, Rev. Grandison; 7 Sept. 1819; Charlotte Watts
                                                           19 BA-73
Aitkin, William; 20 May 1816; Nancy Marsling   13 BA-39
Akle, John Philip; 11 July 1803; Rebecca Tivis   03 BA-430
Albach, Christian; 5 Aug. 1804; Cath. Reiner (See also 15 FR-316)
                                                           01 FR-1105
Albach, David; 26 March 1809; Sarah Mayer (See also 15 FR-323)
                                                           01 FR-1105
Albach, William; 24 March 1803; Mary Weaver (See also 15 FR-314)
                                                           01 FR-1105
Albach, William; 24 March 1804; Susan Rothrock (See also
    15 FR-316)   01 FR-1105
Albaugh, Solomon; 3 Sept. 1818; Elizabeth Kantner   06 FR-1328
Alberry, James; 7 Aug. 1806; Ann Myers   03 AL-614
Albers, Salomon Gottlieb; 20 Nov. 1803; Eliza Kipp   07 BA
Albert, Adam; 1804; Marg. Strock (Shrock?)   02 WA-77
Albert, George; April 1806; Sus. Keyser   02 WA-80
Albert, Philip; 4 Dec. 1814; Mary Ann Hardy (both natives of HA.
    Co.)   16 BA-12
Albey, Samuel; 22 Jan. 1818; Mary Travis   02 BA-37
Albright, Jesse P.; 17 Aug. 1815; Mary M. Smallwood   21 BA-8
Alcock, William; 21 May 1801; Ann Botner   03 BA-400
Alden, Benjamin; 3 Nov. 1803; Mary Mitchell (dau. of Peter and
    Barbara Mitchell)   15 BA-189
Alexander, (N); 17 June 1804; (N) Beckinbach   01 FR-1105
Alexander, Archibald; 30 July 1801; Susanna Miller   09 BA
Alexander, Arthur; Feb. 1803; Lid. Mendenal   02 WA-74
Alexander, David; 20 May 1815; Maria Jones   16 BA-19
Alexander, Henry; 6 Jan. 1814; Catherine Ross   06 FR-1320
Alexander, John; 9 June 1810; Eliz'h Gold   13 BA-10
Alexander, Joseph; 9 Jan. 1812; Mary Wallis   02 BA-36
Alexander, Joseph; 20 June 1812; Mary Hargishimer (15 FR-325
    gives date as 21 June 1812)   01 FR-1105
Alexander, Thomas; 7 Dec. 1809; Martha Jeffers   11 BA-13
Alexander, Valent.; March 1820; Rebecca Burgan   02 WA-116
Alexander, William; 28 July 1804; Elizabeth Lazer   15 BA-206
Alexon, James; 29 Jan. 1804; Priscilla Phips   03 AA-120
Alford, John; 23 July 1815; Eliza Holbrook   13 BA-22
All, James; 26 March 1801; Ann Ross   09 BA
Allcorn, James; 16 June 1812; Margaret Dunlavy   09 BA

Allen, Barnes; 23 Feb,. 1809; Mary Erskine   31 BA-56
Allen, David; 22 Jan. 1807; Dolly Norris (colored) 11 BA-10
Allen, Elisha; 16 June 1808; Mary Litchfield   05 BA-235
Allen, George; 20 Aug. 1812; Lovice Owens   06 FR-1318
Allen, Isaac; 10 Jan. 1816; Hannah Clarke   05 BA-239
Allen, James (s. of James, dec., and Rebekah of West Nottingham
    Hund., CE Co.); 12 d, 5 mo., 1802; Esther Pickering (dau.
    of Jesse and Ann also of Little Britain Twp.)   06 SF
Allen, James; 2 Jan. 1819; Elizabeth Curtis   37 BA-151
Allen, John; 19 Dec. 1816; Margaret Watkins   09 BA
Allen, Jno. P.; 29 March 1818; Elize Mooney   13 BA-30
Allen, Joseph; 27 May 1809; Sarah McClinton   03 BA-499
Allen, Robert; 26 July 1812; Mary Ensminger   02 WA-94
Allen, Robert; 23 Dec. 1813; Elizabeth Hopkins   01 BA-11
Allen, Solomon; 15 June 1802; Sarah Deaver   09 BA
Allen, Thos.; 7 June 1804; Eliza Dunging   03 BA-491
Allen, Thomas; 6 June 1817; Susanna Pardy   11 BA-31
Allen, Wm.; 11 May 1807; Jane Spence   14 BA-422
Allen, William; 25 Oct. 1820; Ann Roberts   37 BA-153
Allender, Edw'd.; 23 Dec. 1802; Nacky Enlowes   05 HA-3
Allender, Thomas; 17 Nov. 1803; Sarah Barton   05 HA-1
Allener, Frederic; 3 Nov. 1803; Charity Grimes (see also
    02 BA-33)   03 BA-435
Allenstein, Carl; 14 Aug. 1803; Elis. Schroder   15 FR-315
Allford, John; 26 April 1812; Margt Austin   13 BA-7
Allisen, Heinrich; 17 Aug. 1806; Catharine Benson   07 BA-305
Allison, Robert; 22 Dec. 1810; Eliza Augusta Allender 05 BA-236
Allmey, William; 23 Oct. 1803; Ann Gold   34 BA-1
Allnut, Thomas (son of James and Eliz., both dec.); 29 d, 12 m.,
    1808; Sarah Dare (dau. of Gideon and Elizabeth) 01 SF
Allwell, Nathan; 10 Dec. 1803; Anne Little   05 AA-4
Allwood, Christopher; 10 Dec. 1802; Lorii Blizard   09 BA
Almeda, Joseph (native of Portugal); 11 July, 1814; Teresa Megan
                                                    16 BA-8
Aloysius, Josephus; 8 May 1810; (N) Huberth   39 BA-24
Alsfelt, John; 16 July 1809; Elizabeth Thiels   07 BA-307
Altenderfer, Heinr.; 27 Aug. 1808; Maria Capito   14 BA-424
Alter, Christian; 17 March 1803; Elizabeth Clark   34 BA-1
Alter, Christian; 28 Oct. 1804; Susanna Talbott   03 BA-492
Alter, Fred.; 7 March 1811; Eliz. Lefler   02 WA-89
Alter, George; Aug. 1806; Cath. Hogmire   02 WA-81
Alter, Samuel; Oct. 1813; Polly Bru (?)   02 WA-98
Alterfritz, Jacob; 6 Aug. 1807; Catherine Sackford 31 BA-28
Altwein, Charles; 14 Aug. 1803; Eliz. Schroeder   01 FR-1105
Alvis, Peter M.; 4 Feb. 1819; Sarah Neighbours   11 BA-35
Ambrose, Charles; 28 Jan. 1809; Elizabeth Rose Bertha (?)
                                                    31 BA-55
Ambrose, Rob't; 5 Aug. 1815; Mary Dean   13 BA-22
Amelung, Frederic; 14 Oct. 1812; Sophia Seekamp   14 BA-430
Amery, Thomas; 8 Jan. 1807; Ann Turner   01 CH-5
Amey, Peter; 8 Oct. 1813; Hanna Fainse   14 BA-432
Amich, George; 25 May 1811; Eliz. Schrote   14 BA-428
Amich, Jno. W.; 29 Jan. 1813; Margaret Stall   14 BA-431
Amich, Philip; 3 March 1810; Eliza Berry   US
Amos, Archer; 27 Dec. 1814; Sarah Wayne   11 BA-22
Amos, James; 19 May 1818; Sarah Towson   13 BA-31
Amos, John; 1804; Elizabeth Jarrett   13 AA-1
Amos, Joshua; 10 June 1819; Cathe. Amensether   13 BA-33
Amos, Thomas (s. of William and Susanna, dec.); 11 d. 21 m.,
    1816; Caroline Waters (dau. of Edward and Hannah 09 SF
Amos, William; 20 Nov. 1805; Kitty Crossman   02 BA-2
Amos, William; 31 Oct. 1815; Mary Merchant   13 BA-51
Anderson, Andrew; 11 Jan. 1806; Mary Carson   02 BA-3
Anderson, Archibald; 17 Oct. 1817; Margaret Harvey 17 BA-17

Anderson, Benj'n; 17 Sept. 1818; Ann Camp	14 BA-437	
Anderson, George; 13 Aug. 1818; Martha Hasley	21 BA-9	
Anderson, Gustavus; 13 Dec. 1818; Nancy Batcher	14 BA-438	
Anderson, Henry; 16 Nov. 1802; Mary Aul	03 BA-423	
Anderson, James; 15 Dec. 1820; Maria Williams	11 BA-37	
Anderson, John; 2 June 1803; Anne Miller	03 BA-428	
Anderson, John; 2 Nov. 1808; Catha. Keene	03 BA-498	
Anderson, John; 27 Feb. 1810; Mary Bodley	11 BA-15	
Anderson, John; 11 April 1816; Mary Watson	11 BA-26	
Anderson, Joshua; 31 May 1810; Ruth Towson	11 BA-16	
Anderson, Leonard; 21 Jan. 1812; Rebecca Lucas	09 BA	
Anderson, Michael; c.1804; Rachel Bush	34 BA-2	
Anderson, Michael; 3 Dec. 1818; Christina Folger	37 BA-151	
Anderson, Nathan; 26 Oct. 1816; Mary Rutter	11 BA-31	
Anderson, Nicks.; 23 Nov. 1804; Eleanor Flood	14 BA-417	
Anderson, Nicholas; 27 Sept. 1808; Sophia Marker	14 BA-425	
Anderson, Richard; 2 April 1815; Sally Sindall	09 BA	
Anderson, Thomas; 16 Aug. 1801; Eleanor Taloun	03 BA-404	
Anderson, William; 23 Aug. 1802; Sarah Boyd	03 BA-419	
Anderson, Wm.; 9 April 1808; Mary Ann Lawrence	03 BA-498	
Anderson, Wm.; 19 Nov. 1817; Maria L. Saunders	03 BA-602	

Anderson, Wright (s. of James and Celia); 17 d. 5 mo., 1820;
    Margaret Atwell (dau. of John and Anna)   08 SF

Andre, Gregorius; 4 Jan. 1814; Mary Wright	13 BA-18	
Andrews, Alex'r McKim; 13 Nov. 1815; Louise Byrnes	03 BA-507	
Andrews, Charles; Aug. 1807; Sarah Drury	02 WA-83	
Andrews, Daniel; 2 June 1801; Elizabeth Crate	09 BA	
Andrews, Errickson; 2 May 1820; Cathe. Wilson	13 BA-35	
Andrews, George; 12 Nov. 1810; Jane Fortner	14 BA-428	
Andrews, John; 8 June 1811; Mary Chamberlin	09 BA	
Andrews, John; 13 June 1816; Eliza Curry	13 BA-25	
Andrews, Reuben; 10 Sept. 1818; Ann Barnaby	17 BA-19	
Andrews, Reuben; 7 June 1820; Elizabeth Blades	17 BA-23	
Angel, James; 30 Dec. 1802; Sarah Morris	03 BA-424	
Angelberger, Philip; 13 Oct. 1811; Mary Shroyl	06 FR-1316	
Anspach, Tilghman; 28 July 1805; Bellisa Marshall	03 BA-494	
Anthony, Benjamin; 15 Aug. 1802; Lydia Hill	06 BA-2	
Anthony, Benj'n; 20 Aug. 1805; Mary Hardlin	14 BA-418	
Anthony, Henry; 23 Oct. 1817; Mary Nelson	16 BA-58	
Anthony, Stephen; 15 May 1807; Elizabeth Berryman	02 BA-5	

Anthony, Joseph (son of the late Jacques Anthony and Pindare his
    wife); 10 Dec. 1816; Mary Louisa (dau. of Rodaly) (both free
    blacks)   16 BA-47
Anthony, Moses Abram; 26 Dec. 1805; Katy Ja (?) (blacks)
    17 BA-5

Appel, J. Gotlieb; 26 April 1807; Mary Zieunberg	14 BA-421	
Appleby, Rezin; 18 Feb. 1815; Rosanna Sullivan	13 BA-20	
Appleby, Thos.; 18 May 1807; Margaret Nelson	13 BA-2	
Appledore, William; 27 Dec. 1806; Elizabeth Dorsey	02 BA-5	
Appold, Andrew; 20 Nov. 1817; Margaret Hubbard	09 BA	
Appold, George; 25 Feb. 1813; Margaret Whirl	14 BA-431	
Appold, George; 4 Jan. 1816; Elizabeth Birckhead	11 BA-24	
Arcambal, Felix; 8 Dec. 1818; Louisa Adelaide Figuiere	32 BA-323	
Ardinger, Christian; 9 Feb. 1812; Hannah Bower	02 WA-93	
Ardinger, Philip; 26 Oct. 1815; Kesia Davis	02 WA-100	
Ardy, William; 26 May 1814; Marg't Eaton	13 BA-19	
Arensberger, Joannes; 9 Sept. 1810; Catherine Miers(?)	39 BA-25	

Armand, Francis (widower); 3 May 1801; Margaret Device (widow)
    15 BA-151

Armand, Joseph; 25 April 1816; Nichol Bardet	16 BA-34	
Armat, Christopher; 10 March 1808; Mary E. Hunter	15 BA-260	
Armiger, Jesse; 10 Feb. 1819; Julia Ann Lush	13 BA-34	
Armiger, Leonard; 15 Jan. 1803; Ann Elickson	03 AA-120	
Armitage, Benj'n; 31 Aug. 1805; Ann Edlen	14 BA-417	

Armor, John; 26 Oct. 1815; Mary Stricker   11 BA-24
Armor, Wm.; 8 March 1812; Marg. Fectig   02 WA-93
Armour, David; 13 Oct. 1803; Mary Winchester   03 BA-434
Armour (?), James; 21 Dec. 1815; Susan Askew   11 BA-26
Armour, Thomas; 21 Oct. 1813; Ann Buchman   11 BA-23
Armstrong, Andrew; 23 July 1820; Harriet Bevins   37 BA-153
Armstrong, Daniel; 4 Nov. 1819; Ann Welden   37 BA-152
Armstrong, Henry; 29 Aug. 1818; Emilie Zoe Valette 16 BA-73
Armstrong, James; 3 June 1801; Mary Crabbers   09 BA
Armstrong, Jno.; 5 March 1802; Isabelle McMechen   14 BA-412
Armstrong, John; 14 June 1810; Sophia Everhard   13 BA-10
Armstrong, Robert; 28 Nov. 1820; Eliza R. Glenn   03 BA-605
Armstrong, Thomas; 20 Aug. 1801; Sarah Wolcox   30 BA-108
Armstrong, Thomas; 4 Nov. 1813; Frances Crawford   11 BA-21
Armsworthy, Thos.; 23 June 1814; Elizabeth Hopewell 01 SM-64
Arnet, Cinrie; 17 Aug. 1816; Mary Osnat   32 BA-310
Arnsulty, John Honnore; 27 Aug. 1804; Martha Maurin 09 BA
Arnold, Benjamin; 18 April 1809; Margaret Ramsey   05 BA-236
Arnold, Jno.; 1 Nov. 1803; Charlotte Crabbin   14 BA-415
Arnold, Peter; 13 Dec. 1801; Elizabeth Lynch   03 BA-411
Arnold, Peter; 25 March 1818; Sarah Kelley   11 BA-35
Arnold, Richard; 22 Dec. 1805; Jane Sherbut   03 AA-130
Arnold, William; 5 April 1816 (by Joshua Willey); Sarah Johnson
                                                   17 BA-12
Arquet, Eli; 12 Jan. 1806; Elizabeth Mull   03 BA-495
Arthur (?), John; 20 Nov. 1808; Clemence Thompson 09 BA
Artle, Gorge; 3 Sept. 1820; Catherine Beichel   16 FR-76
Artis, Jeremiah; 10 April 1806; Elizabeth Biscoe   02 SM-187
Artz, David; March 1816; Cath. Hammer   02 WA-101
Artz, Peter; Nov. 1816; Elizab. Heestand   02 WA-102
Artz, Philip; Aug. 1819; Harrot James   02 WA-114
Asbey, Samuel; 11 March 1802; Rebecca Smith   03 BA-414
Ash, George; 29 May 1812; Rebecca Grover   11 BA-19
Ash, John; 3 Oct. 1814; Mary Kendall   13 BA-41
Ashby, William; 26 Feb. 1807; Mary Wilson   03 AL-614
Ashcraft, Thomas; 24 May 1801; Clotilden Cooper   03 BA-401
Ashe, Bernard Diederich; 10 Dec. 1818; Ann Johnson 37 BA-151
Asher, Isaac; 23 Dec. 1802; Elizabeth Barton   09 BA
Asher, William; 27 Aug. 1801; Welthy Galloway   09 BA
Asher, William; 13 Aug. 1803; Eleanor Waller   05 BA-234
Ashley, Abraham; 17 Jan. 1807; Eleanor Schaufel   14 BA-421
Ashley, Wm. H.; 26 May 1810; Mary Craig   13 BA-10
Ashly, John; 19 March 1802; Elizabeth Calvin (?)   05 AA-2
Ashmore, John; 24 Nov. 1801; Elizabeth Cables   09 BA
Ashton, Thomas; 11 Jan. 1815; Ann Spence   09 BA
Askew, Alexander; 10 Dec. 1818; Pamelia Lynch   37 BA-151
Askew, Joseph; 1 March 1803; Elizabeth Hurt   09 BA
Asquith, Robert C.; 25 Sept. 1817; Eleanor E. Winfield 19 BA-72
Assindone (?), Mark (slave of M. Recamier); June or July 1815;
     Elizabeth (N) (slave of M. Recamier)   15 BA-280
Astlin, Joseph; 3 Aug. 1802; Mary Beard   03 MO-118
Atkins, Benjamin; 25 Feb. 1816; Elizabeth Shankel 06 FR-1323
Atkinson, George; 7 Sept. 1803; Mary Dickson   14 BA-415
Atkinson, George D.; 5 Jan. 1816; Henrietta Russum 01 WI
Atkinson, Isaac; 8 March 1801; Eleanor Griffith   09 BA
Atkinson, Isaac (s. of Aaron of Tal. Co.,); 25 d. 11 mo., 1803;
     Esther Edmondson (dau. of James)   07 SF
Atkinson, Isaac; 30 March 1809; Hannah Burnett   01 BA-11
Atkinson, Isaac C.; 4 May 1819; Amelia Stables   05 BA-241
Atkinson, John; 28 Sept. 1806; Rachel Sewell   11 BA-8
Atkinson, John; 10 June 1819 Sabra McComas   17 BA-22
Atkinson, Joseph; 6 Nov. 1803; Mary Cox   02 SM-186
Atkinson, Joshua; 23 Aug. 1801; Ann Johnson   10 BA-1

Atkinson, Joshua; 28 May 1815 (by Joshua Willey); Jemima Rutter
                                                          17 BA-11
Atkinson, Thomas (s. of Aaron and Elizabeth [dec.]); 19 d. 1 mo.,
    1804; Elizabeth Parvin (dau. of Benjamin and Sarah)
                                                          08 SF
Atkinson, Thomas (s. of Aaron and Ann); 20 d. 12 mo., 1810;
    Rebecca E. Bartlett (dau. of Richard and Rebecca) 08 SF
Atkinson, Thomas (of Easton, TA Co., s. of Aaron and Ann, both
    dec.); 15 d., 12 m., 1819; Hannah Hussey (of Balto. Town,
    dau. of George and Rachel, both dec.)   12 SF-74
Atkinson, William; 5 Feb. 1805; Frances Trise   09 BA
Atkinson, William; 21 Jan. 1806; Mary Thompson   03 BA-495
Attwood, John; 13 March 1808; Cathe. Kirkland   13 BA-3
Atwell, Joseph; c.1803; Ann Pritchard   07 AA
Atwell, Robert; 1802; Elizabeth Craig   07 AA-2
Aubb, John; 2 June 1812; Margaret Baer   01 FR-1105
Auchinloss, John, Jr.; 8 April 1812; Matilda Inglis   05 BA-237
Audouin, Louis; 1 July 1810; Sarah Smith   15 BA-280
Aufderheyde, Casper; 10 Sept. 1804; Mary Minick   14 BA-417
Augustin, Dominic; 13 July 1815; Louise Emilie Gill (both free
    col'd)   16 BA-22
Augustin, Sam'l; 11 June 1818; Sophia Myer   14 BA-437
Augustine, George; 1801; Cath. Clopper   02 WA-71
Aulabaugh, Jacob; Aug. 1819; Elizab. Robison   02 WA-114
Auperly, David; 29 Aug. 1819; Christina Kopf   14 BA-439
Austin, Lawless; 5 May 1816; Mary Carter   09 BA
Austin, Purnel; 28 June 1812 (by Rev. Ryland); Amelia
    Hardister   17 BA-9
Austin, William; 19 May 1801; Nelly Clark   01 SO-1801
Austin, William; 26 April 1804; Sarah Reins   09 BA
Austin, William K.; 23 d. 5 mo., 1816; Mary Troth (dau. of Samuel
    and Ann)   08 SF
Auston, Thomas; Dec. 1816; Mary Shurly   02 WA-103
Autrem (or Antrim), Samuel; 26 Aug. 1819; Catherine Merca
                                                        11 BA-36
Auze, Charles (of New York); 14 June 1808; Ann Agnes Martin (of
    Baltimore)   15 BA-263
Avery, Elias; 6 Jan. 1820; Mary Ray   37 BA-152
Avery, Ruben; 4 Sept. 1806; Sarah Puntiny   09 BA
Avril, Aubain; 2 June 1808; Elizabeth Dode   31 BA-42
Avy, Mich'l; June 1820; Elizab. Moyers   02 WA-116
Ayears (?), Samuel; 22 Nov. 1805; Elizabeth Spear   09 BA
Ayme, Francis Samuel (son of Francis Albert Ayme and Marianne
    Bougreau Ayme); 7 Oct. 1802; Charlotte Felicity Guyot (dau.
    of Lewis Guyot and Magd'n Mesquynen Guyot)   15 BA-171
Ayers, William; 2 April 1811; Mary Shimer   03 AL-614
Ayres, Richard; 18 Oct. 1803; Eliz'th Baxter   05 HA-3
B(?), Jno.; 18 Dec. 1805 (by Jno. Bloodgood); Rachel Bracker
    (blacks)   17 BA-5
Babade, Henry; 27 Sept. 1818; Joanna Antoinette Parmentier
                                                        16 BA-74

Babler, Georg; 4 July 1811; Christina Seltzer   07 BA-308
Bachman, Frederic; 1 Sept. 1810; Ann Miles   14 BA-427
Bachtold, Daniel; 9 Nov. 1808; Elizabeth Jordan   09 BA
Backer, Archibald; March 1808; Marty Webb   02 WA-85
Backer, John; Aug. 1807; Marg. Schoffner   02 WA-83
Backer, Nich.; Feb. 1805; Margaret Webb   02 WA-78
Backer, Peter; March 1804; Sus. Otman   02 WA-76
Backer, Peter; May 1806; Cath. Thomas   02 WA-80
Baclor, Jacob; July 1803; Elis. Miller   02 WA-75
Bacon, James; 2 May 1805; Anne Long   03 BA-493
Bacon, James; 27 Feb. 1816; Jane Langworthy   16 BA-32
Bacon, John; 9 April 1801; Ellen Shepherd; (both natives of
    Ireland; 15 BA-150)   03 BA-399

Bacon, William; 7 Oct. 1818 (date of lic.); Mary Todd   11 BA-35
Baden, Nehemiah; 21 July 1817; Frances Eleanor Collins 03 BA-602
Bader, Dominick; 15 June 1802; Eve Hennewalt   15 BA-169
Baer, John; 30 June 1816; Susan Simms   13 BA-25
Baer, John; 9 Feb. 1819; Catherine Delawter   06 FR-1329
Baer, William; 1 Sept. 1812; Harriot Mantz   15 FR-325
Bagwell, Henry; 16 May 1811; Elizabeth Hayes   09 BA
Baichtel, David; 14 June 1812; Susanna Keyser   02 WA-94
Bailey, Anthony; 23 Nov. 1820; Phillis Cheeseman (both were free
     colored persons)   05 BA-243
Bailey, Elijah; (c.1804); Jane Wilson   34 BA-2
Bailey, James (slave); 24 Dec. 1820; Listy Johnson (free woman)
                                                        05 BA-243
Bailey, Samuel; 6 May 1813; Sarah Longwell   09 BA
Bailey, Thos.; 26 Oct. 1802; Mary Campbell   28 BA-1
Bailey, Thomas; 10 Aug. 1820; Anne Maria Catherine Reese
                                                        17 BA-19
Bailey, Walter; 29 Nov. 1804; Sarah Ball   03 MO-119
Bailnley, Robert; 30 May 1804; Julia Carter (see also Buckley,
     Robert)   03 BA-491
Bails, Abner; 24 Dec. 1818; Maria Hirst   06 FR-1329
Baily, Allen (slave); 26 Dec. 1814; Phyllis Butler (free col'd
     woman)   16 BA-12
Baily, Samuel (of Balto. Town, s. of Joseph of Wilmington, DE,
     and dec. w. Elizabeth); 17 d., 1 mo., 1816; Hannah James
     (dau. of Joseph and Mary)   12 SF-51
Baily, William; 27 July 1809; Rachel Preston   01 BA-11
Baine, Martin; 20 Jan. 1816; Sarah Fettes   09 BA
Baizard, Charles Mari; 13 Oct. 1812; Marie Berange, (veuve de
     [widow of] Francois Viberd [Beizarjs?])   15 BA-305
Baker, Benjamin; 19 Feb. 1815; Catherine Maccubbin   03 BA-506
Baker, Christian; 31 May 1810; Mary Minnix   14 BA-427
Baker, George; 14 April 1810; M. Flanagan   30 BA-109
Baker, Frederick; 21 Aug. 1814; Catharina Bergman [or Barkman]
                                                        39 BA-30
Baker, Geo. G.; 12 Sept. 1818; Elize. William   13 BA-32
Baker, Gideon; 25 Sept. 1817; Lydia Hall   17 BA-17
Baker, Henry; 2 Jan. 1820; Nancy Clise   08 AL-3
Baker, Isaac; (c.1804); Lovina Tunis   34 BA-2
Baker, Jacob; 3 June 1801; Mary Catto   15 BA-152
Baker, James; 30 Oct. 1816; Mary Ann Gillespy   17 BA-15
Baker, James; 9 Dec. 1819 (date of lic.); Catherine Anne Green
                                                        11 BA-36
Baker, Jesse; 20 July 1819; Elizabeth Ward   17 BA-22
Baker, John; 15 Sept. 1801; Hannah Smith   14 BA-410
Baker, Jno.; 7 Nov. 1801; Jane Faris   14 BA-411
Baker, John; 22 May 1810; Elizabeth Frantz   08 AL-3
Baker, John; 16 May 1815; Mary Stanford   13 BA-21
Baker, John; Dec. 1819; Mary Spracker   02 WA-115
Baker, Lewis; 8 Jan. 1811; Jane Conn   03 BA-503
Baker, Peter; Nov. 1817; Mary Long   02 WA-107
Baker, Philip; March 1811; Maria Thomas   02 WA-99
Baker, Richard; 2 July 1811; Ann Webb   02 WA-90
Baker, Thomas; 5 March 1805; Sophia Flanagan   11 BA-5
Baker, Thomas; 5 Dec. 1805; Margaret Mark   30 BA-109
Baker (or Parker?), Thos.; 20 April 1817; Mary Elizabeth Mattison
                                                        13 BA-28
Baker, Thomas; 17 March 1819; Elizabeth Smith (See also 02 TA-44)
                                                        01 QA-62
Baker, Wm., Jr.; 20 March 1804; Jane Jones   36 BA-2
Baker, Wm.; 1 March 1809; Anne Marshall   03 BA-499
Baker, William; 7 Mmay 1809; Jane Holebrooks   09 BA
Baker, William; 6 Aug. 1809; Ann Tudor   11 BA-14
Baker, Wrathburn; 17 Nov. 1816; Susan Hutchins   13 BA-27

Balderson, Isaiah; 24 Jan. 1815; Martha Gill   13 BA-20
Balderson, John; 4 Feb. 1816; Nancy Carlin   06 FR-1323
Balderson, Joshua; 1 Feb. 1817; Hannah Gwinn   13 BA-23
Balderston, Hugh (s. of Isaiah and Martha); 12 d. 3 mo., 1802;
     Margaret Wilson (dau. of John and Aliceanna)   09 SF
Balderston, Jonathan (s. of Isaiah and Martha); 1 d, 4 mo., 1808;
     Elizabeth Yarnall (dau. of Ulrich and Martha)   08 SF
Baldwin, Abraham; 26 Oct. 1815; Frances Biddison   09 BA
Baldwin, Edward; 3 Dec. 1801; Mary Marriott   15 AA-2
Baldwin, James; 19 Oct. 1820; Mary Armitage   13 BA-36
Balenger, Samuel; 13 Oct. 1812; Elizabeth Omensetter 11 BA-20
Ball, Daniel; Aug. 1813; (N) Stalcup or Stacy   03 AL-614
Ball (Bull?), Hilary; 4 Dec. 1801; Rachel Keplinger   09 BA
Ball, Jno.; 21 Sept. 1810; Sarah Murray   14 BA-427
Ball, Matthew; 9 Feb. 1802; Elizabeth Athey   03 AL-613
Ball, Walter; 13 Sept. 1815 (date of lic.); Mary Ball 11 BA-26
Ball, William; 11 March 1809; Hanna Jones   14 BA-425
Ball, William; 27 Jan. 1814; Elizabeth Dorsey   11 BA-23
Ballentine, James; 8 July 1801; Ruth Smith   10 BA-1
Balsel, John; 18 Oct. 1801; Elizab. Purnel (15 FR-312 gives
     bride's name as Prunel)   01 FR-1109
Baltzel, William; 16 April 1807; Eliz. Mackenheimer   14 BA-422
Baltzell, Charles; 24 Nov. 1818; Maria V. Ringgold   19 BA-72
Baltzell, Jacob; 23 Nov. 1820; Frances Buchanan   11 BA-38
Baltzell, Thomas; 13 June 1820; Lydia Webster   19 BA-73
Bambach, Johan Henrich; 26 June 1808; Elisabeth Brudy 15 FR-322
Bambach, John Hy.; 26 June 1808; Eliz. Brady   01 FR-1110
Bamberger, John; 28 Aug. 1802; Sally Carter   14 BA-413
Bamer, Henrich; 2 June 1801; Elizabeth Mack (both single)
                                                      01 CL-149
Bandel, Georg; 31 Jan. 1801; Eliza. Boss   14 BA-408
Bandel, Mich'l; 8 March 1805; Rachel Gorman   14 BA-418
Bandel, Wm.; 2 Dec. 1805; Mary Clark   14 BA-419
Bandle, Fred'k; 16 June 1816; Maria Mines   14 BA-435
Bandle, Jno.; 29 June 1813; Justine Barbara Mettee   14 BA-432
Bandson, Peter; 7 Nov. 1803. Mary Egnew   29 BA-1
Bange, Franciscus; 10 Aug. 1809; Catherina Zahner   07 BA-307
Bange, Georg; 22 May 1808; Elisabeth Brungart   07 BA-306
Bange, Lenhard; 14 Oct. 1801; Cath. Snider   14 BA-410
Bangs, Thomas; 2 Dec. 1819; Ann Few   11 BA-36
Banier, Frederic; 3 April 1811; Nancy Bone   14 BA-428
Bank, Cornelius; 18 Oct. 1818; Sarah Schultze   14 BA-437
Bankard, Jacob; 18 March 1813; Mary Rupert   09 BA
Banker, John; 26 Nov. 1807; Henrietta Ogden   03 BA-497
Banks, Jesse; 31 May 1801; Barbara Hagner   09 BA
Banks, Samuel; 20 Oct. 1808; Sarah Hayworth   13 BA-38
Bankson, John C.; 30 March 1819; Sarah Ann Marias   19 BA-72
Banning, Thos.; 26 April 1808; Mary Miller   03 BA-498
Banseck, Christ'n; 31 Oct. 1805; An. Cath. Kelling   14 BA-419
Bantz, Curtius; 31 May 1807; Elizabeth Hildebrand   15 FR-321
Bantz, Gideon; 23 June 1811; Anne M. Sower   06 FR-1316
Bantz, Jacob; 19 Nov. 1804; Cath. Mackenheimer   14 BA-417
Barat, Peter; 12 April 1813; Delila Harrison   13 BA-16
Barban (Barber?), Thomas; 20 April 1806; Elisabeth Cochron
                                                      09 BA
Barber, Thomas; 11 Feb. 1819; Margarite Wellmore   19 BA-72
Barber, William; 8 April 1810; Mary Dorf   15 FR-324
Barbine, Joseph; 5 Nov. 1815; Eliz. Hogan   16 BA-27
Barbine, Sam'l; 31 Dec. 1805; Louise Inglis   14 BA-419
Barclay, Francis; 18 Jan. 1811 (by Rev. Roberts); Eliza Sway
                                                      17 BA-8
Barclay, Francis; 13 April 1818; Rachel Powers   03 BA-603
Barcus, Thomas; 7 April 1814; Patience Ward   08 AL-4
Bard, Jacob; 28 Sept. 1806; Susan Kron   15 FR-319

Bard, Nicol.; March 1807; Mary Shup   02 WA-82
Barger, George; 25 Jan. 1816; Elizabeth Hay   05 BA-239
Barger, Jno.; 6 Dec. 1814; Cath. Amey   14 BA-433
Barghmann, Andreas; 9 Feb. 1804; Rebecca Fischer   39 BA-17
Barhaver, Philip; 19 March 1807; Ann Killman   09 BA
Barkdoll, John.; March 1807; Jane Hable   02 WA-82
Barker, Abraham (of NY, s. of Robert, [late of Kennebunkport, MA]
    and Sarah); 17 d, 8 m., 1809; Priscilla Hopkins (dau. of
    Gerard and Rachel of Balto. Town, dec.)   12 SF-3
Barker, James; 21 Oct. 1804; Mary Lawrence   11 BA-4
Barker, John; 22 April 1819; Kitty Urith Ann White   13 BA-33
Barker, Lewis; 14 Jan. 1808 (by Henry Smith); Ephry Hayes
                                                     17 BA-6
Barker, William; 5 Sept. 1806; Juliana O'Harra   11 BA-9
Barker, William; 16 June 1807; Elizabeth Kent Harris 03 BA-497
Barkley, Ebenezer; 26 July 1804; Ruth Boyer   03 AL-613
Barkman, Daniel; 28 April 1816; Mary Pitinger   08 AL-4
Barkman, John; 14 Nov. 1812; Eliza Gooding   13 BA-17
Barkover, Philip; 19 March 1807; Ann Killman   09 BA
Barkus, John; 12 Sept. 1811; Elizabeth Porter   03 AL-614
Barling, Aaron; 5 March 1812; Rebecca Tucker   05 BA-237
Barling, William; 13 Dec. 1808; Sarah Barling   09 BA
Barlow, Jesse; 19 Oct. 1805; Elizabeth Moore   02 BA-2
Barnard, John; 2 May 1803; Sarah Kennedy (See also 02 BA-32)
                                                     03 BA-427
Barnes, David; 14 Dec. 1819; Mary McNamara   02 DO
Barnes, Henry; 12 May 1820; Nancy Creighton   02 DO
Barnes, John; 2 Jan. 1801; Priscilla Thomas   03 BA-397
Barnes, John; 14 Jan. 1813; Nancy Broadwater   03 AL-614
Barnes, Levin; 27 Dec. 1803; Catherine Shorb (dau. of John and
    Catherine Shorb of Balto. Co.)   15 BA-194
Barnes, Richard; 20 Nov. 1812; Sally M. Denwood   11 BA-20
Barnes, Robson; 5 Dec. 1801; Mahala West   09 BA
Barnes, Thomas; 20 Dec. 1804; Frances McLane   14 BA-417
Barnes, Whiteley; 22 Jan. 1803; Frances Hursten (02 BA-32 gives
    the date as 21 Jan. 1803 and the bride's name as Huiston)
                                                     03 BA-425
Barnett, Jas.; 18 March 1816; Martha Cortly   13 BA-24
Barnett, John; 19 May 1804 (by Rev. L. W. McCombes); Kitty
    Wheeler (?)   17 BA-3
Barney, Daniel F.; 16 May 1802; Elizabeth Humphreys 02 SM-185
Barney, John; 22 Dec. 1801; Clarissa Perill (See also 15 FR-312)
                                                     01 FR-1109
Barnham, Henry; 21 Dec. 1819; Eliz. Rooply   14 BA-439
Barnhart, John; 7 June 1810; Sophia Hough (Slough?) 09 BA
Barnhouse, Richard; 16 Jan. 1816; Jane White   06 FR-1323
Barns, Alexander; 27 March 1801; Jane Stott   02 SM-185
Barns, Ford; 25 Dec. 1806; Elizabeth Dutton   33 BA-41
Barns, John; 27 Feb. 1802; Rachel Walker   10 FR
Barns, William; 1 Jan. 1803; Elisa Blanch   05 BA-233
Barois, Charles; 11 Sept. 1817; Elizabeth Levington 17 BA-17
Baron, Jno.; 28 Feb. 1804; Ann Kimel   14 BA-416
Baroux, James Michael; 5 March 1804; Eliz. Bromfield 02 BA-33
Barr, Benj.; March 1816; Mary Tutweiler   02 WA-101
Barr, David; Nov. 1805; Sus. Reitenhauer   02 WA-79
Barr, David; 17 Aug. 1813; Christina Mantz   06 FR-1319
Barr, Jacob; 23 May 1811; Mary Miller   02 WA-90
Barr, John; 13 Jan. 1811; Betsy Rohrer   02 WA-89
Barr, Peter; Nov. 1818; Nancy Hoffman   02 WA-111
Barrack, John; 13 May 1802; Rebecka Odle   03 AL-613
Barras, Peter E.; 29 Dec. 1806; Kitty Lambeth   03 AA-130
Barrel, Thos.; 8 July 1811; Ann Morford   03 BA-502
Barrett, Edward; 6 May 1819; Mary Bond   14 BA-439
Barrett, John M.; 29 Oct. 1811; Mary D'Healey   03 BA-503

Barrett, Thomas; May 1812 (?); Rachel Phillips   03 BA-504
Barrick, Cornelius, 7 May 1816; Mary Snoke   06 FR-1324
Barrick, Frederick; 2 April 1811; Catherine Cramer   06 FR-1315
Barriere, David; 6 March 1806; Charity Fendall   21 BA-6
Barron, Ellis; 3 Oct. 1817; Mary Forwood   05 BA-240
Barron, Prescott; 15 Jan. 1804; Julia Ridgely   03 BA-490
Barry, Benja. F.; 5 Nov. 1816; Eliza. W. Constable   13 BA-26
Barry, John; 13 July 1810; Rachel Stalcoop   11 BA-15
Barry, Jno. Jones; 6 Feb. 1818; Sophia Ratien   14 BA-437
Barry, Joshua; 17 Feb. 1803; Meriam Chaney   15 AA-2
Barry, Peter; 17 April 1805; Mary Carson   03 BA-493
Barry, Richard; 7 July 1810 (by Rev. Robert Roberts); Mary Ann
    Ledinham   17 BA-8
Barry, William; 17 Nov. 1803; Sarah Dunn   29 BA-1
Bartenslade, Peen; (Nov.-Dec.) 1803; Sarah McCubben   05 HA-1
Bartgis, Benjamin F.; 27 June 1815; Anna Heffner   06 FR-1322
Bartgis, Matthias E.; 23 April 1811; Mary Dertzbach   06 FR-1315
Bartle, George; 28 Nov. 1816; Sophia Gatch   13 BA-27
Bartlett, James; 11 Nov. 1806; Mary Taylor   15 FR-320
Bartlett, John; Sept. 1804 (by John Bloodgood); Ann Gore (See
    also 40 BA)   17 BA-4
Bartlett, John; April 1817; Eleanor Felker   02 WA-104
Bartlett, Joseph, (of TA Co., son of Richard and Rebecca); 20 d,
    6 mo., 1809; Rhoda Matthews, (dau. of Mordecai and Ruth)
                                                        02 SF-110
Bartlett, Sam'l; 20 April 1811; Mary Wineman   14 BA-428
Bartlett, Robert (s. of John [dec.] and Susanna); 22 day, 4 mo.,
    1801; Sarah Fairbank (dau. of James and Elizabeth)
                                                        08 SF
Bartlett, Robert (s. of John and Susanna); 22 d, 2 mo., 1809;
    Elizabeth Shannahan (dau. of Jonathan and Margaret)
                                                        08 SF
Bartlett, Wm.; 22 June 1817; Ally Robertson   13 BA-28
Bartlett, William E. (of Balto. Town, s. of Richard of TA Co. and
    w. Rebecca, both dec.); 20 d., 11 mo., 1816; Mary James
    (dau. of Amos and dec. w. Mary)   12 SF-56
Bartol, George; betw. Sept. 1815 and Oct. 1820; Sarah Bayless
                                                        07 HA
Barton, Asael; 7 Sept. 1802; Sophia Allender   05 HA-2
Barton, James, (of Sussex Co., DE, s. of William and Elizabeth);
    19 d. 12 mo., 1805; Ann Melony (dau. of William and Sophia)
                                                        07 SF-10
Barton, John; 19 Dec. 1809; Susan Duncan   09 BA
Barton, Joseph; 27 Sept. 1801; Alcy Small   03 BA-407
Barton, Joshua; 28 Oct. 1801; Mary Sanders   03 BA-409
Barton, Joshua; 1 April 1815; Mary Lynch   05 BA-238
Barton, Levin (s. of Edward and Ann); 18 d. 1 mo., 1815; Lovicy
    Wright (dau. of Daniel and Sarah)   07 SF-27
Barton, Peter (s. of William and Elizabeth of Sussex Co., DE); 24
    d. 11 mo., 1814; Priscilla Melony (dau. of William and
    Sophia, of Sussex Co., DE)   07 SF-26
Barton, Philip; 3 Feb. 1803; Eliz. Norton (or Horton)   05 HA-3
Barton, Samue; 9 Nov. 1820; Ann Bond   11 BA-37
Barton, Selah; 6 Dec. 1806; Susanna Wright   03 BA-496
Barton, Stephen; June 1806; Sus. Charlton   02 WA-80
Barton, Thos.; Nov. 1805; Elis. Williams   02 WA-79
Barton, Will; Sept. 1807; Patientia Word   02 WA-83
Bartsler(?),Aaron; 22 Nov. 1819; Ann Buckhead   13 BA-33
Bas(?), (N); 12 March 1812; Jean Hart   39 BA-27
Bascadon, Fred; 12 April 1809; Sarah Brane   13 BA-6
Basch, John; 23 April 1818; Catherine Lease   06 FR-1328
Baseman, Thomas; 26 June 1810; Mary Elder   08 BA
Basford, David; 24 Sept. 1818; Cathe. Fowler   13 BA-32
Basil, Robert; 4 Dec. 1802; Mary Hears   15 AA-2

Bassler (?), (Got)lieb; March 1808; Mary Sutton   02 WA-85
Bast, Henrich; 5 June 1808; Susan Windgiegler   15 FR-322
Bast, Valentine (age 72); 6 Dec. 1801; Sidney Mergrin (age 30)
                                                       01 CL-150
Bastian, Andrew C.; 8 Aug. 1816; Barbara Fox   06 FR-1324
Bastian, William; 26 March 1811; Eleanora Dignes   06 FR-1315
Batchelder, Smith; 23 Dec. 1817; Mary Sweeny   14 BA-436
Bateman, Artemas; 5 March 1810; Harriet Ensor   21 BA-7
Bateman, Benjamin; 15 Sept. 1803; Permelia Galloway   34 BA-1
Bateman, Emzi; 13 Sept. 1804 (by Jno. Bloodgood); Catherine Evans
    (See also 40 BA)   17 BA-4
Bateman, Nicholas; 16 March 1815; Constance Decondry   20 BA-222
Bateman, Richard; 23 Dec. 1800; Margaret Wakefield   02 CH
Bates, Jos.; 2 June 1808; Catherine Fringer   13 BA-4
Bates, Wm. H.; 8 Aug. 1815; Eliza M. Boyle   02 BA-36
Battis, Peter; 13 July 1817; Nancy Holliday   17 BA-16
Bauer, Jacob; 1 Aug. 1810; Barb. Niebling   14 BA-427
Bauer, Jno.; 16 May 1811; Harriet Green   14 BA-428
Bauer, Jno.; 30 Aug. 1811; Cath. Wilhelm   14 BA-429
Bauersox, George; 10 Jan. 1804; Sarah Mohler   14 BA-416
Baughman, Andrew; Oct. 1818; Juliet Kuhns   02 WA-111
Baughman, Samuel; 6 May 1813; Mary Gosnel   08 BA
Baum, Sam'l; 18 May 1814; Marg't Ann Scroggs   14 BA-433
Bausman, Benjamin; 18 Jan. 1807; Elizabeth Bauerli   15 FR-320
Bautzel, George; 8 July 1819; Mary Smith   30 BA-109
Bawk?, Henry; 22 Sept. 1816; Antoinette Shearman   17 BA-15
Baxley, James; 12 April 1810; Mary Luke   09 BA
Baxley, Levi; 30 May 1805; Margaret Denesey Burnes   11 BA-6
Baxter, Colin(?); 20 Feb. 1811; Sarah Johns   11 BA-18
Baxter, Isaac, of Phila.; 22 Dec. 1804; Lydia Burgess 15 BA-213
Baxton, John; 6 Oct. 1802; Lydia Dell   10 FR
Bayerele, William; 3 Dec. 1807; Charlotte Mayer   15 FR-321
Bayfield, Jas.; 20 July 1805; Susanna Herman   14 BA-418
Bayley, Edward; 8 Dec. 1814; Elizab. Williams   14 BA-433
Bayley, George W.; 5 Sept. 1818; Mary A. Browning   11 BA-29
Bayley, John; 15 June 1820; Eliza Evans   19 BA-73
Bayley, Winder; 3 Dec. 1818; Drusilla Prickett   17 BA-21
Bayly, Gorden [sic] C.; 15 Oct. 1818; Cassandra Ann Leek
                                                       13 BA-32
Bayly(?); James Walker. See Peredeau(?), James Walker Bayly.
Bayly, John; 12 April 1811; Ann Gannett   06 FR-1315
Bayly, William; 18 May 1812; Sarah Andre   11 BA-19
Bayne, John E.; 18 (Nov.?) 1809; Susanna Clocker   02 SM-188
Bayne (or Byrne), Patrick; 11 Oct. 1801; Mary Howard   09 BA
Bayne, Rev. Thomas; 13 Nov. 1817; Ann Caroline Singleton
                                                       01 TA-328
Beacham, James; 27 June 1814; Rebecca Flanigan   17 BA-10
Beacham, W.; 3 May 1818; Mary Heathcoat   13 BA-31
Beadshais, Joseph; Feb. 1818; Margaret Cossel   02 WA-108
Beales, W.; 24 Oct. 1815; Loisa Pope   13 BA-23
Beall, (?)pton; 1810; Jane Robb (See also 02 MO)   01 PG
Beall, Evan; 7 April 1812; Mary Preston   13 BA-7
Beall, Isaac; 19 Sept. 1807; Rebecca Tomlinson (03 AL-614 gives
    date as 20 Sept. 1807)   06 AL-15
Beall, James; 29 Dec. 1805; Margaret Smith Benson   03 MO-120
Beall, James Alexander; 5 Jan. 1804; Eleanor Culver   03 MO-119
Beall, John W.; 2 Jan. 1810; Rachel L. Lambert   13 BA-9
Beall, Josiah; 3 July 1804; Hannah Read (See also 07 AL-174; 10
    AL)   04 AL-2
Beall, Lewis; 9 July 1801; Eliza Wootton   03 MO-117
Beall, Rezin; 3 April 1802; Sarah Busey (05 AL-1 gives date as 6
    April 1802)   06 AL-8
Bealle, Evan; 8 March 1804; Martha Maria Preston   36 BA-2
Bealmear, Sam'l; 25 Nov. 1802; Priscilla Williams   03 MO-118

Beals, Melzer; 14 May 1820; Eliza Kelly   08 BA
Beam, Conrad; 15 June 1817; Maria Hurst   02 BA-37
Beam, Daniel; March 1817; Sally Garman   02 WA-104
Beam, Elijah; 30 Sept. 1813; Charlotte Christiana Robinson
                                                      05 BA-237
Bean, Charles; July 1818; Lucretia Tarlton   02 WA-110
Bean, George; 9Jan. 1806; Mary Wherrett   02 SM-187
Bean, John; 10 May 1804; Sarah McKay   02 SM-186
Bean, John; 30 Dec. 1805; Ann Lynch   02 SM-187
Bean, Josiah; 25 Oct. 1801; Eleanor Wilson   03 MO-117
Bean, Robert; 27 June 1802; Elizabeth Himson   09 BA
Bear, John; 15 Nov. 1808; Cath. Hoffman (See also 15 FR-323)
                                                      01 FR-1110
Beard, Alexander; 14 Sept. 1803; Mary Ann Blith (See also 02 BA-
     32)   03 BA-433
Beard, George; June 1805; Cath. Boyer   02 WA-79
Beard, Jacob; April 1804; Mary Brunner   02 WA-76
Beard, Jacob; 21 Dec. 1813; Cath. Foy (or Loy)   02 WA-99
Beard, James; Nov. 1813; Elizabeth Ritchy   08 AL-6
Beard, James; 20 April 1816; Mary Lang   32 BA-308
Beard, John; Sept. 1810; Sarah Harry   02 WA-87
Beard, John; 18 Aug. 1812; Martha C. Lambeth   13 BA-14
Beard, Jonathan; 26 Dec. 1805; Harriet Hargrove   02 BA-3
Beard, Nicholas; 3 Sept. 1811; Peggy Beard   02 WA-91
Beard, Nicol.; (June?) 1804; Magd. Fink   02 WA-76
Beard, William; Oct. 1817; Cath. Fiery   02 WA-106
Bearhill, John; 20 July 1818; E. Wensell   30 BA-109
Beasley, George L.; 3 Dec. 1820; Teresa Margerum   16 BA-106
Beattie, James; 24 Feb. 1820; Ann Hewitt Morris   37 BA-152
Beattie, John; 20 Oct. 1811; Sophia Cannon   15 FR-325
Beatty, John; 14 Sept. 1819; Sarah Measel   06 FR-1319
Beatty, William; 27 Nov. 1803; Eleanor Murphy   15 BA-191
Beatty, William A.; April 1808; Elis. Miller   02 WA-85
Beaty, Guy; 20 June 1819; Sarah Fare (widow)   16 BA-83
Beaty, James; 24 April 1806; Catharine Demos   01 BA-10
Beaucham, R'd; 9 Jan. 1809; Euphemia Gordon   03 BA-499
Beauchard, Peter, son of the late Stephen and Jane; 30 Dec. 1805;
     Ann Emmerson, dau. of the late John and Elizabeth 15 BA-233
Beaumont, Pascal; 17 Dec. 1816; Susan Hammet   06 FR-1325
Beausen, Francis, (lawful son of Mathurin Beausen and Mary, from
     Bordeaux, age 24); 19 June 1805; Magdalene Barthe, (dau. of
     the late James Anthony and Elizabeth Barthe, age 19)
                                                      19 BA-221
Beaven, Thomas; 26 May 1817; Mary Logan   11 BA-31
Beaver, Francis; 11 Aug. 1816; Ann M. Crise   06 FR-1324
Beaver, John; 6 Aug. 1807; Nancy Gill   08 AL-6
Bebpel, John; 14 Feb. 1802; Maria Neukammer (both single)
                                                      01 CL-150
Beck, Adam; 26 April 1812; Elizabeth Gilbert   06 FR-1318
Beck, Adolph Emanuel; 28 Nov. 1815; Josephine Calvert 16 BA-28
Beck, John Gotlieb; 28 Jan. 1806; Anne Moody   03 BA-495
Beck, William C.; 28 May 1819; Sarah Matilda McCoy   05 BA-241
Becker, Abraham; 1802; Marg. Partoon   02 WA-72
Becker, Adam; 8 April 1802; Maria Henz (both single) 01 CL-150
Becker, Conrad; 31 May 1803; Cath. Froshauer (15 FR-314 gives
     bride's name as Forschauer)   01 FR-1110
Becker, Joannes; July 1809; Hannah Disney   39 BA-22
Becker, Johan Heinrich; 8 Feb. 1807; Catharine Welsch 07 BA-305
Becker, Peter; 13 March 1808; Elizabeth Wolf   07 BA-306
Reckly, Henry, Jr.; March 1819; Mary Hogmire   02 WA-112
Bedford, Gunning Vansolingen; 28 Feb. 1803; Eliza Deady
                                                      09 BA
Bedford, James; 3 Aug. 1820; Mary Bennett   11 BA-36

Bedford, Wm. Turner; 9 June 1805; Julia Wisham, (dau. of the late
    John Wisham, dec.)   02 AA
Beeberg (or Becberg), Joseph; 24 March 1812; Sarah Frazier
                                                         14 BA-430
Beechus, Louis; 24 Oct. 1813; Charity Castle (both people of
    color)   15 BA-318
Beedle, Augustin; 24 Oct. 1816; Sarah Killum   02 BA-37
Beedle, Thomas; 28 Nov. 1811; Catha. Stewart   03 BA-503
Beem, Richard; 4 Aug. 1801; Elizabeth Duckworth   01 AL-5
Beeman, George; 2 June 1808; Phebe Long   03 AL-614
Beeman, George; 22 June 1820; Barbara Lower   08 AL-6
Beeman (?), Thomas; 27 June 1813; Catharn Wells   03 AL-614
Beemis, Nathan S.; 13 Aug. 1818; Susanna Ashmore   05 BA-240
Beenes, Alan; 7 April 1813; Ellen Barnes   03 BA-505
Beers, David S.; 31 May 1813; Priscilla Cullin   11 BA-23
Behier, Robert; 20 May 1810; Eliz. Frantz   14 BA-427
Behler, Jno.; 22 Oct. 1812; Elizab. Hanes   14 BA-431
Behmer, Peter; 17 April 1804; Elizabeth Ehrhard   15 FR-316
Beimenschneider, Jacob; 26 March 1807; Hanna Casper   14 BA-421
Beinor, Richard; 4 Aug. 1801; Elizabeth Duckworth   03 AL-613
Beiser, Daniel, Jr.; 11 June 1812; Elizabeth Routzang   16 FR-76
Beiser, John; 15 April 1810; Maria Schlosser   15 FR-324
Beisser, Johan; 29 March 1804; Lydia Greber   15 FR-316
Beitel, Phillip; 19 May 1803; Maria Katherine Weisbach   07 BA-680
Bell, Abraham (s. of Richard, dec., and Rachel, of Susquehannah
    Hund., CE Co.); 4 d, 10 mo., 1820; Sarah Trump (dau. of
    Abraham and Jemima of West Nottingham Hund., CE Co.)
                                                         06 SF
Bell, Amos; 19 July 1812; Sarah Murray   21 BA-7
Bell, David; 10 March 1801; Eleanor Weis   04 AA
Bell, Ezekiel; 23 Oct. 1808; Lovey Johnson   13 BA-38
Bell (or Bill), George; 8 Aug. 1802; Rebecca Foster   09 BA
Bell, Jacob; 22 Sept. 1807; Elisabeth Dinteman   15 FR-321
Bell, Jacob; 7 April 1808; Elizabeth Maynes   02 BA-6
Bell, James; 22 May 1814; Marg't Jones   13 BA-19
Bell (or Bill), John; 11 Aug. 1808; Sarah French   09 BA
Bell, John P.; 10 Oct. 1816; Catherine Parks   09 BA
Bell, Peter; June 1817; Julian Lester   02 WA-105
Bell, Richard; 6 Feb. 1810; Sarah Choate   09 BA
Bell, Richard; 26 Dec. 1813; Maria Rhady   07 BA-309
Bell, William; 29 Dec. 1807; Mary Smith   14 BA-423
Bell, William; 18 July 1810; Achsah Smith   13 BA-40
Belsh, James; June 1808; Sus. Timkins   02 WA-85
Belt, Merryman; 9 May 1805; Margaret Whiteford   09 BA
Belt, Robert B.; 28 April 1805; Rachael Giles Deale   03 AA-130
Belt, T. (or L.) Hanson; 7 Oct. 1813; Elizabeth Key Heath
                                                         03 BA-505
Belt, Tobias; 27 May 1802; Sarah Heath   28 BA-1
Beltaken (?), James; 2 Aug. 1812; Anna Hackett   03 KE-14
Bems (Blem? or Blurr?), Andrew; Aug. or Sept. 1811; Elizabeth
    Miller   03 AL-614
Bend, Francis; 17 Sept. 1815; Rebecca Morris   03 BA-507
Bend, Rev. Joseph G. J.; 22 April 1807; Elizabeth B. Claypoole
                                                         03 BA-497
Bendford, Henry; 1 June 1813; Sarah Ann Wilcox   02 WA-97
Bengers, Heinrich; 8 May 1803; Elis. Mayer   14 BA-414
Benix, Samuel; 28 Sept. 1819; Amelia Perrygoy   08 BA
Benjamin, Solomon; 25 July 1809; Catharina Lexee   07 BA-307
Benlor, Richard; 29 April 1819; Susan Eddy   13 BA-33
Bennet, David; 16 Sept. 1813; Charlotte Schultz   15 FR-327
Bennet, George; 5 Dec. 1811; Mary Armour   11 BA-17B
Bennet, James; 24 June 1802; Fanny Flatford   09 BA
Bennet, Matthew; 23 April 1811; Catherine Skerrett   15 BA-287

Bennet, Thomas; 12 May 1804; Nelly Ratlin (See also 02 BA-33)
                                                         03 BA-490
Bennett, Fielding T.; 11 Oct. 1812; Ann Sophia Sharley 31 BA-133
Bennett, John Morris; 25 Sept. 1817; Mrs. M. Thompson 03 BA-602
Bennett, Patrick, (widower); 9 July 1801; Elizabeth McCay,
     (widow)   15 BA-153
Bennett, Patrick, (widower); 17 Oct. 1805; Sally Lilly, (widow,
     of Adams Co., PA)   15 BA-228
Bennett, William; 5 Jan. 1806; Mary Greenwell   02 SM-187
Bennett, William B.; 12 Feb. 1801; Judith Baker   02 SM-185
Benning, William; 2 Jan. 1819; Ann White   05 BA-241
Bennington, James; 7 Oct. 1812; Matilda Auld   13 BA-17
Benno, Sorry; 25 Aug. 1807 (by Henry Smith); Ann Ware 17 BA-6
Bens, David; 2 July 1801; Barbara Glanberger (or Glauberger)
                                                       02 WA-71
Benson, Amos, (son of Benjamin and Hannah); 3 d, 4 mo., 1806;
     Margaret Brown, (dau. of Elihu and Margaret)   02 SF-98
Benson, Amos (s. of Benjamin and Hannah); 11 day, 12 mo., 1806;
     Margaret Brown (dau. of Elihu and Margaret [Brown] Brown)
                                                       05 SF
Benson, Charles; 28 Oct. 1801; Ann Vittel   15 BA-158
Benson, Charles, (widower); 19 May 1806; Ann Eve Barney, (widow)
                                                       15 BA-238
Benson, James; 28 Oct. 1802; Margaret Weaver   06 BA-2
Benson, Levi, (son of Benjamin and Hannah); 11 d, 12 mo., 1806;
     Mary Malsby, (dau. of David and Sarah)   02 SF-104
Benson, Levi (s. of Benjamin and Hannah); 11 d. 12 mo., 1806;
     Mary Maulsby (dau. anf David and Sarah Rees Maulsby)
                                                       05 SF
Benson, Levi, (widower, s. of Benjamin and Hannah); 16 d. 9 mo.,
     1819; Rachel Lancaster (dau. of Jesse and Mary)   05 SF
Benson, Peter; 4 July 1813; Eliz. Ludwig   14 BA-432
Benson, Robert; 14 Nov. 1815 (lic.); Keturah Hayes   11 BA-26
Benson, Samuel; 1 May 1814; Elizabeth Royston   11 BA-22
Bentley, Caleb (s. of Joseph and Mary [Thatcher]); 20 d., 8 mo.,
     1807; Henrietta Thomas   10 SF
Bentley, George; July (?) 1804; Cath. Hoover   02 WA-77
Bentley, John Hunter; 16 Dec. 1819; Jane Forman   16 BA-94
Bentley, Joseph, (son of Ellis and Alice); 26 d, 8 mo., 1812;
     Anna Briggs, (dau. of Isaac and Hannah)   01 SF
Bentley, Joseph (s. of Joseph and Mary [Thatcher]); 6 d., 8 mo.,
     1812; Anne Briggs (dau. of Isaac and Hannah [Brooke])
                                                       10 SF
Bently, Caleb, s. of Joseph and Mary; 26 d, 8 mo., 1807;
     Henrietta Thomas, dau. of Samuel Thomas and Mary 01 SF
Bentz, Friedr.; 5 March 1807; Hanna Gerher   14 BA-421
Bentz, Henry; 8 Feb. 1809; Agnes Stewart   14 BA-425
Bentz, Jacob; 15 Feb. 1814; Elis. Kailer   02 WA-99
Bentz, William; 30 jan. 1817; Elizabeth Metzger   06 FR-1325
Bentzel, Johann; 28 Oct. 1804; Louise Keyser   07 BA
Bentzell, Conrad; 28 Jan. 1805; Ann Holm   03 BA-492
Berck, Henry; 2 July 1809; Cath. Sadler   15 FR-324
Berg, Georg; 5 Nov. 1805; Margaret Krehmer   15 FR-318
Berger, Jacob; 3 Dec. 1807; Mary Candel   15 FR-321
Berger, Johannes; 29 May 1810; Maria Freyer   07 BA-307
Beringer, John; 16 Feb. 1803; Alice White   15 BA-178
Berkley, John M.; 14 Dec. 1815; Mary Stephens   05 BA-238
Bernabeu, Don Juan Joseph, 9son of Don Juan Baptista Berbnabeu,
     Consul of His Catholic Majesty Ferdinand VII); 4 Aug. 1813;
     Ellen Moale, (dau. of the late John Moale)   15 BA-314
Bernard, Alex'r; 17 Oct. 1819; Cath. M. Johannes   14 BA-439
Bernard, Charles; 4 Dec. 1784; Mary White   04 BA-1
Berret, Joseph; 9 March 1801; Mary Eliot O'Donnell   05 BA-236
Berret, Thomas; 22 May 1808; Marg't McKinney   03 BA-498

```
Berroa, Jago; 31 Dec. 1804; Juliane Killeon          15 BA-213
Berry, Christopher M.; 17 March 1816; Mary Meirs     17 BA-12
Berry, Edward; 5 July 1801; Mary Specknel            03 BA-401
Berry, Harry; 10 June 1805; Jane Boyd (02 BA-35 gives the groom's
    name as Henrie and the bride's name as Frances)  03 BA-493
Berry, Horatio; 5 Sept. 1805; Sarah Godman           11 BA-7
Berry, James; 18 Sept. 1817; Henrietta Butler (both free blacks)
                                                     16 BA-56
Berry, John; 4 Jan. 1816; Mahala Neril               17 BA-12
Berry, John; 1 Dec. 1819; Mary Egleston              13 BA-33
Berry, John W.; 8 Feb. 1803; Harriot Dorsey          36 BA-1
Berry, Robert; 11 Feb. 1804; Jane Davey              03 BA-490
Berry, Thomas; 29 Jan. 1809; Ann Foreman             13 BA-5
Berry, Thomas; 6 Jan. 1818; Marg't Appleby           13 BA-30
Bersch, Heinrich; 24 July 1817; Maria Hofman, widow  07 BA-311
Berteau, Peter; 31 Dec. 1807; Emily Bauzamy          15 BA-258
Bertier, Joseph; 17 June 1818; Louisa Vincent        16 BA-69
Bertols, Jno. Fred'k; 30 Nov. 1817; Elizab. Gordon   14 BA-436
Berwick, Daniel; 23 March 1819; Mary Klein           14 BA-438
Bess, Jacob; 27 Dec. 1811; Christine Eberly          15 FR-325
Bessy, Daniel A.; 21 June 1812; Sarah Wilson McMechen 17 BA-9
Betcher, Fred'k; 6 Feb. 1802; Maria Spiers           14 BA-411
Betle, John; 24 June 1820; Marg't Myers              13 BA-35
Betson, Joseph; 26 June 1818; Sarah Funk             14 BA-437
Betteley, John; 20 Sept. 1820; Matilda Miskelly      32 BA-329
Betts, Enoch; 25 March 1819; Elisabeth Bull          37 BA-152
Betts, Franklin; 7 Nov. 1820; Mrs. Ann Davis of CE Co. 03 BA-605
Betts, George W.; 11 April 1811; Eleanor Pindle      09 BA
Betts, James; 4 June 1818; Ann M. Williams           03 BA-603
Betts, John; 14 July 1816; Sarah Ball                13 BA-40
Betty, Samuel; 18 Nov. 1817; Sarah Withington        17 BA-17
Bevard, James; 10 July 1805; Alice Loney Flynn        15 BA-223
Bevens, Allen; 30 Aug. 1802; Mary Dailey             11 BA-3
Bevin, Horatio; 14 Nov. 1815; Jane Myles             05 BA-238
Bevins, James; 23 Dec. 1812; Amelia Andrews          17 BA-9
Biays, Joseph; 22 Oct. 1801; Harriet Gartner         14 BA-411
Bibby, John; 28 Oct. 1802; Julia Todd                01 DO-41
Biddison, Abraham; 29 Nov. 1810; Susanna Burgin      09 BA
Biddison, Daniel; 22 Aug. 1822; Maria Shock          14 BA-434
Biddison, Salem; 6 July 1815; Ann Franklin (notation in the
    record: "received nothing from Biddison")        09 BA
Biddison, Thomas; 12 Sept. 1801; Hannah Lucy         09 BA
Biddle, Abraham; 10 May 1805; Mary Summers           14 BA-418
Biddle, Jesse; 18 Feb. 1815; Eliza Upperman          14 BA-433
B(?)iegler, George; 18 Aug. 1812; Mrs. Yost          02 WA-95
Bier, Henry; 27 June 1815; Maria Ann Watts           06 FR-1322
Bier, Jacob; 9 Nov. 1815; Susan A. Briscoe           03 BA-507
Biers, Jas.; 26 Dec. 1803; Susanna Delcher           04 BA-415
Biggs, James; Oct. 1816; Mary Gilliland              02 WA-103
Bigham, Barney (of Adams Co.); 14 May 1815; Margaret Reilly
                                                     05 FR-11
Bigham, Joseph; Feb. 1805; Elis. Empich              02 WA-78
Bigler, Hugh; 16 Jan. 1801; Margaret McHaffy         03 BA-397
Billingsley, Samuel; 19 June 1805; Cath. Hook (02 BA-35 gives
    bride's last name as Nook)                       03 BA-493
Billington, Wm.; 2 Feb. 1809; Mary Stedikorn         03 BA-499
Billmyer, Gabriel (?); June (?) 1804; Peggy Toby     02 WA-76
Billups, Robert; 29 July 1810; Louisa Wynn           15 BA-281
Binand, David; 14 June 1801; Polly Collins           03 BA-401
Binckle, Jacob; April 1807; Elis. Miller             02 WA-82
Binckle, Philip; Aug. 1806; Jane Locke               02 WA-81
Binebrach, Jacob; Sept. 1817; Susanna Herlinger      02 WA-106
Bingham, Henry; 13 Sept. 1804; Eleanor Chavent (see also 02 BA-
    34)                                              03 BA-491
```

```
Bingham, Robert; 11 Nov. 1815; Mary Potter          11 BA-24
Binkley, Jonathan; Feb. 1818; Esther Simmerman       02 WA-108
Bintzel, Conrad; 8 July 1802; Ann Glenn              14 BA-413
Biomberg, Jean Adolf; 29 May 1820; Jenetta Heuback   14 BA-440
Birch, Wm.; 18 July 1816; Rachel Hands               14 BA-435
Bird, Thomas; 18 Dec. 1811; Mary Fancer              03 BA-503
Bird, William; 19 July 1815 (date of lic.); Ann Merritt
                                                     11 BA-26
Birdsall, Andrew; 13 d., 1 mo., 1813; Lydia Canby (dau. of
     William and Mary)                               10 SF
Birdsall, Andrew M., (s. of Whitson and Rachel); 27 d, 1 mo.,
     1813; Lydia B. Canby, (dau. of Whitson and Mary) 01 SF
Birdsall, William (of MO Co., s. of Whitson and Rachel of Loudon
     Co., VA); 15 d., 4 m., 1818;1 Ruth Hartly (of Balto. Town,
     dau. of Samuel and Lavinia) (See also 10 SF)   12 SF-67
Birgman, Conrad; 12 Jan. 1808; Elizabeth Uyssnel    07 BA-306
Birkhead, Abraham; 26 Sept. 1807; Frances Moales    14 BA-422
Birkholtz, David; 25 March 1802; Eliz. Priestley    14 BA-412
Bisbits (?), John A.; 6 July 1820; Mary Frances (als. Rosetta
     Carr) (both free col'd)                         16 BA-101
Bisch, David; April 1817; Mary Sholl                 02 WA-104
Bischof, Christian; 17 Nov. 1801; Christina Friesen (both single)
                                                     01 CL-150
Biscoe, George Washington; 26 Sept. 1815; Maria Hopewell
                                                     01 SM-64
Biscoe, James; 13 Feb. 1806; Lettitia Chesley        02 SM-187
Biscoe, James; 26 Jan. 1807; Ann Fernandis           02 BA-5
Biscoe, Richard; 24 Dec. 1801; Eleanor Clarke        02 SM-185
Bishop, Elijah; 2 April 1801; Mary Fuller            09 BA
Bishop, Herman C.; 12 July 1809; Cath. S. Johnston   14 BA-226
Bishop, William; 15 Dec. 1820; Eliz. Councill, (both of QA Co.)
     (See also 02 TA-44)                              01 QA-62
Bitmyer, Jacob; 14 July 1801; Mary Smith             09 BA
Bitts, Christ'n; 6 July 1804; Maria Schafer          14 BA-417
Bitts, Stephen; 22 May 1802; Mary King Claiborne     14 BA-412
Bixley, Thomas; 16 Jan. 1802; Rebecca Morrow         14 BA-411
Black, James; 4 Nov. 1805; Jane Croford              09 BA
Black, James; 6 Jan. 1807; Mary Shelhorn             08 AL-8
Black, James; 13 May 1810; Margaret Martin           09 BA
Black, James; 11 April 1816; Jane Patterson          09 BA
Black, John; 25 July 1801; Dorothy Downey            03 BA-403
Black, John; 12 Sept. 1815; Ann Divess               11 BA-25
Black  Richard; 5 Nov. 1818; Margaret Cole           17 BA-18
Black, Samuel; March 1818; Mary West                 02 WA-109
Blackburn, Hugh; 24 Dec. 1810 Elizabeth Maria Vise   15 BA-284
Blackford, James; 24 Dec. 1805; Mary Rains           02 BA-3
Blackford, John; 17 June 1812; Elizabeth Kanode      15 FR-325
Blackguard, Samuel; 28 Aug. 1820; Mary Gorman        16 BA-103
Blackiston, William; 18 Sept. 1808; Ann Price        09 BA
Blackledge, Conway; 24 June 1812; Deb'a Meek         13 BA-14
Blackman, Ivery; 19 Dec. 1816; Elizabeth James Price 17 BA-15
Blades, Peregrine; 24 Aug. 1815; Elizabeth Howard    17 BA-11
Blake, Benjamin; 12 May 1802; Elizabeth Aldridge     09 BA
Blake, Charles; 30 Jan. 1815; Eleanor Blake of QA Co. 01 QA-53
Blake, Charles, Esq. (s. of Charles, Sr.); 30 Jan. 1815; Eleanor
     Blake (dau. of John Sayer Blake and Sarah Collier), both of
     QA Co.)                                         02 TA-43
Blake, James; 8 Oct. 1801; Alphonsa J. A. Carmichael, (dau. of
     William Carmichael of KE Co., MD)               15 BA-155
Blake, Mr. Philemon; 11 May 1805; Sarah Blake, (by virtue of a
     dispensation granted by Rt. Rev. Dr. Carroll) (see also 01
     QA-52)                                          02 TA-39
Blanck, J. Arends; 23 April 1816; Friedericke Hanecke or Hancke
                                                     07 BA-310
```

```
Blas, Christ'n; 27 Feb. 1807; Martha Hill            14 BA-421
Blay, Adam; 30 Dec. 1802; Sabina Summers             03 MO-118
Blay, Jacob F.; 1 June 1807; Mary Longfellow         14 BA-422
Blaybar, Abraham; 7 Nov. 1815; Clara Thompson        03 BA-507
Bleakley, William; 28 Nov. 1801; Eleanor Phelan      15 BA-160
Blentzinger, George; 18 Feb. 1820; Mary Kraft        14 BA-440
Blessing, Michael; 13 Nov. 1817; Christina Long      06 FR-1327
Blick, Wm. B.; 17 Nov. 1818; Mary Ann Feenome        19 BA-72
Bliss, Wm.; 8 Feb. 1813; Ann Riley                   03 BA-505
Blizard, William; 19 May 1802; Ruth Taylor           03 BA-416
Blizzard, William; 8 April 1819; Providence Megee    08 BA
Blomberg. See Biomberg.
Blondel, John H.; 5 Dec. 1812; Aimee Dubois          15 BA-305
Bloodgood, Rev. John; 25 Feb. 1808; Mrs. Ann Inloes  17 BA-6
Bloodsworth, Rizdon; 10 Feb. 1818; Susan Kirwin (01  SO-15 gives
    date as 10 Feb. 1819)                            03 SO
Bloome, Enoch; Nov. 1818; Eve Fantz                  02 WA-111
Bloomingburg, Frederick; 7 Nov. 1806; Sarah Small    09 BA
Blot, Francis; 7 May 1804; Elizabeth Unker           03 BA-490
Blote, William; 10 April 1814; Sarah Griffin         03 BA-505
Blount, Robert; 25 May 1818; Eliza Haughton          13 BA-31
Blubaugh, Stephen; 2 May 1819; Honor Logsdon         06 AL-157
Boarman, Ignatius; 15 April 1805; Mary Kintz         15 BA-217
Bobart, Charles C.; 29 Sept. 1816; Lenorah Green     11 BA-31
Bobbitt, William; 29 Sept. 1803; Mary Bennett        09 BA
Bobst, Daniel; 10 Sept. 1818; Mary Shuck             06 FR-1328
Bocky, Johan; 8 May 1810; Susan Hauser               15 FR-324
Boden, Andrew; 11 Aug. 1803; Mirriam Everson         09 BA
Bodensick, Henrich; 13 Nov. 1803; Sophia Berckmann   07 BA
Bodle, John; 10 Sept. 1816; Eliza Hutton             13 BA-27
Bodler, Thomas; 20 May 1803; Mary Reese              09 BA
Bodley, Chas.; 30 April 1803; Hanna Patten           14 BA-414
Boehm, Chas. G.; 2 May 1811; Eliz. Capito            14 BA-428
Boerstler, Dan'l; Aug. 1807; Marg. Kogler            02 WA-83
Bogal, Sam'l; 30 Dec. 1809; Jane Watts               13 BA-8
Bogener, John; 20 Aug. 1820; Elizabeth Poffenberger  16 FR-76
Boggs, Alexander L.; 11 Feb. 1817; Susan Greer       05 BA-239
Boggs, James; 21 Nov. 1815; Nancy Howard             13 BA-39
Bohn, Charles; 7 Nov. 1819; Caroline Tolpkin         14 BA-439
Bohn, Johannes; 2 Jan. 1810; Rebecca Collins         15 FR-324
Bohn, Michael; 14 Oct. 1804; Magdalene Borger        15 FR-317
Boice, John; 1 Oct. 1807; Eliza Sherry               13 BA-2
Boid, John; 28 July 1818; Marg't Eisler              13 BA-31
Bold, William; 10 Jan. 1808; Elisab. Huggins         14 BA-423
Bolin, John; 31 July 1815; Elizabeth Stevens         11 BA-25
Boling, Simon; 31 May 1812; Sarah Smallwood          13 BA-17
Bolinge, Roger; 21 July 1803; Mary Goddard           34 BA-1
Bolk, Cardo; 15 Feb. 1811; Caroline Storer           07 BA-310
Bollen, Henry; 15 March 1804; Sophia Shultz          03 BA-490
Bollman, Thos.; 8 April 1805; Barbara Raab           14 BA-418
Bolsler, Thos. B.; 15 Sept. 1820; Reba. Vohn         13 BA-35
Bolton, Francis; 23 Oct. 1802; Mary League           09 BA
Bolton, John; April 1817; Eve Isaminger              02 WA-104
Bomers (Borners or Bowers), John; 12 Jan. 1805; Sarah Binnex
                                                     21 BA-6
Bonadey, John; 26 Jan. 1818; Mary Ann Turner         17 BA-19
Bonaparte, Jerome, (brother of the First Consul of France); 24
    Dec. 1803; Elizabeth Patterson, (dau. of William Patterson
    of Balto.)                                       15 BA-193
Bond, Barney; 22 Aug. 1820; Ann Maria Gallop         33 BA-47
Bond, Benjamin; date not given; Rachel Perine        13 BA-38
Bond, Benjamin; 16 Sept. 1804; Mary Perrigoe         09 BA
Bond, Charles; 9 March 1813; Elizabeth Moore         08 AL-10
Bond, Charles; 26 Sept. 1815; Frances Pindell        05 BA-238
```

```
Bond, Edward; 29 March 1804; Mary Chenoweth            23 BA-2
Bond, Emery; 15 July 1815; Ellen Laws                 17 BA-13
Bond, Henry; 28 March 1811; Charity Chenworth         08 BA
Bond, James; 7 June 1803; Margaret Bond               15 BA-183
Bond, James; 4 Sept. 1817; Mary Slaysman              17 BA-17
Bond, James; date not given but c.1808; Nancy Ford    15 BA-38
Bond, John, of Wm.; 27 May 1802; Mary Richardson      05 HA-2
Bond, John T.; 28 Feb. 1806; Sarah Duke               01 CA-68
Bond, Peoly H.; 14 Jan. 1804; Frances Bowers          23 BA-2
Bond, Peter; 23 Dec. 1813; Harriet Walters            08 BA
Bond, Richard; 8 Dec. 1816; Ann Brooks                17 BA-14
Bond, Samuel; 1804; Sally Bond                        13 BA-1
Bond, Samuel; 23 Sept. 1813; Elizabeth Bond           08 BA
Bond, Samuel; 21 July 1816; Isabella Hall             17 BA-13
Bond, Silas (s. of Benjamin and Mary); 4th d., 2 mo., 1807;
     Hannah Kennard (dau. of Ely and Elizabeth, dec., of Fawn
     Town, York Co., PA)                              11 SF-96
Bond, Thomas William; 30 Jan. 1806; Sarah York Scott  23 BA-41
Bonday, James; 29 Feb. 1808; Ann Newton               02 BA-6
Bonnom, George; 3 April 1816; Eliza Geirifan          09 BA
Bonsel, John; 2 June 1819; Mary Everett               13 BA-33
Bonwill, George (of Kent Co., DE, s. of Micael and Mary (dec.) of
     same Co.); 19 d. 3 mo., 1817; Anna Stanton (dau. of Beacham
     Stanton of Caroline Co., and w. Deborah)         07 SF-33
Booker, Lambert; 24 July 1802; Mary Hawsner           03 BA-418
Bookman, Henry; 2 Feb. 1804; Julia Cofenay            14 BA-416
Boom, John; 29 July 1802; Helen Boom                  11 BA-3
Boon, Benjamin; 10 Sept. 1815; Sarah Ringgold         13 BA-22
Boon, James (of Third Haven Mtg); 13 d. 2 mo., 1806; Adah
     Points (Poits or Ports?)                         07 SF-12
Boon, Solomon S.; 8 April 1813; Martha Thompson       06 FR-1319
Boon, Stephen; 27 June 1805; Mary Reed                14 BA-418
Boone, Arnold, (son of Isaiah and Hannah); 28 d., 9 mo., 1808;
     Betsy Shoemaker (dau. of Jonathan and Hannah)    01 SF
Boone, Stephen; 30 Nov. 1815; Elizabeth Merriken      04 AA-97
Boor (or Bohr), Nicholas; 29 June 1806; Rachel Geisinger
                                                      08 AL-10
Boose, Edward; 26 Oct. 1815; Clara Green              11 BA-26
Booth, William; 14 Jan. 1808; Marg't Fitzgerald       03 BA-498
Booth, William; 6 Dec. 1810; Mary Gardner             09 BA
Booze, Zebulon; 9 April 1812; Priscilla Elliott       01 DO-42
Boran, John; 2 June 1803; Betsy Boast                 09 BA
Bord, Georg; Nov. 1803; Magd. Motes                   02 WA-75
Bord, Joh,; Dec. 1802; Maria Russel                   02 WA-74
Borin, Peter; 4 Sept. 1809; Delphine Baden            15 BA-271
Boring, George; 26 April 1815; Ann Artlony (?)        11 BA-24
Boring, Peter; 19 Sept. 1802; Elizabeth Rowles        24 BA
Bose, William; 23 Nov. 1819; Mary Goulding            16 BA-91
Bosely, James; 1 Dec. 1803; Elizabeth McDavid         07 AL-174
Bosick, James; 25 April 1816; Sarah Turner            13 BA-25
Bosley, Amon; 29 April 1813; Rebecca Marsh            11 BA-23
Bosley, Eli; 23 April, 1813; Hannah Tucker            09 BA
Bosley, James; 12 April 1816; Ann Armstrong           11 BA-30
Bosley, James S.; 1 March 1806; Rachel Wollemeyer     14 BA-419
Bosley, Nicholas Merryman; 19 Nov. 1808; Eleanor Addison Smith
                                                      03 BA-499
Bosley, Samuel; 26 Oct. 1803; Elizabeth Talbott       23 BA-3
Bosley, Wm.; 20 May 1801; Elizabeth Stansbury         14 BA-410
Boss, John; 15 Nov. 1812; Marg't Bosley               14 BA-431
Bossecke, Heinr.; 27 Sept. 1807; Elisab. Heide        14 BA-422
Bostic, Wm.; 6 Oct. 1816; Sarah Brown                 13 BA-26
Boston, Isaac; 15 May 1817; Elizabeth Floyd           17 BA-16
Boswell, Alexander; 10 Dec. 1808; Frances Sanders     09 BA
Boswell, John; 10 Feb. 1807; Nancy Walker             09 BA
```

```
Boswell, John; 21 Jan. 1813; Anabella Rouse          13 BA-16
Boswell, John; 15 Feb. 1820; Ellen Butler (both col'd) 16 BA-98
Boteler, Elias; 25 Jan. 1806; Susanna Evitt (15 FR-318 gives
    bride's name as Ebit)                            05 FR
Boteler, Henry; 21 April 1814; Priscilla Robinson    05 BA-238
Boteler, Thomas; 3 Sept. 1801; Hannah Garrott (See also
    15 FR-312)                                       01 FR-1109
Bothons, Richard; 5 Nov. 1811; S. Schutter           30 BA-109
Botner, Jesse; 26 June 1806; Asena Howell            09 BA
Bottor, Francis; 23 May 1802; Mary Frances Dau (both free French
    mulattoes)                                       15 BA-183
Botts, John; 25 June 1818; Ann Miller                05 BA-240
Boulding, Charles D.; 22 April 1819; Mary Gover Wilson 16 BA-81
Boulding, Matthew (bel. to Jno. E. Murry); 26 Dec. 1814; Jenny
    (belonging to Col. Howard)                       16 BA-13
Boult, William; 14 Dec. 1802; Elizabeth Hammett      02 SM-185
Bourbon, Chr.; 18 July 1816; Ann Hook                13 BA-26
Bourjolly, Henry Jerome; 18 Nov. 1811; Mary Conain   31 BA-115
Bourness, William; 4 Jan. 1816; Susanna Garrison     17 BA-12
Bowart, George; March 1807; Marg. (N)                02 WA-82
Bowart, Jacob; 24 Dec. 1812; Cath. Waggoner          02 WA-96
Bowen, David; 14 May 1818; Ann James                 13 BA-31
Bowen, Elijah; 14 March 1807; Catherine Heel (?)     09 BA
Bowen, James; 16 May 1820; Sarah Ann West            11 BA-37
Bowen, John; 31 July 1806; Sarah Surley              15 FR-319
Bowen, John; 19 Dec. 1816; Elizabeth Dalrymple       02 BA-37
Bowen, Nathan; 11 March 1802; Elizabeth P. Bowen     09 BA
Bowen, Pitt E.; 29 Nov. 1810; Mary Bailey            13 BA-11
Bower, Henry; 13 May 1802; Kitty Cole                14 BA-412
Bower, Jacob; 17 Jan. 1813; Elizab. Springer         02 WA-96
Bower, Philip; 18 April 1805; Elisab. Lefebre        14 BA-418
Bowers, John; 30 Sept. 1801; Hannah Willock          03 BA-401
Bowie, Benj'n; 30 Jan. 1814; Eliz. Brenneman         14 BA-432
Bowie, James; 6 Jan. 1809; Ann Christie              02 BA-35
Bowkay, William; March 1818; Cath. Gale              02 WA-109
Bowly, Sam'l H.; 24 Jan. 1816; Sarah Hollins         03 BA-508
Bowly, Wm. Lux; 27 April 1809; Mary Hollins          03 BA-499
Bowman, George; March 1816; Barbara Davis            02 WA-101
Bowman, George; March 1820; Dorothy Stoey            02 WA-116
Bowman, Henry; 3 March 1812; Margaret Stoufer        02 WA-93
Bowman, John; 11 May 1801; Sarah Collins             03 BA-400
Bowman, John; 4 Dec. 1808; Parsilla Madcalf          03 AL-614
Bowman, Joseph; 10 Feb. 1820; Margaret Collins       32 BA-328
Bowser, Henry; Dec. 1820; Christiana Dundore         02 WA-117
Bowser, John; Oct. 1816; Nancy Metz                  02 WA-103
Bowser, Moses; 22 July 1814; Lydia Russell           05 BA-238
Boxell, Robert; April 1819; Patty McDaniel           02 WA-113
Boxley, James; 12 April 1810; Mary Luke              09 BA
Boxley, Thos.; 16 Jan. 1803; Rebecca Morrow          25 BA-2
Boyakin, Stephen H.; 8 Oct. 1801; Rebecca Aderton    02 SM-185
Boyce, Charles; 6 Oct. 1819; Lethe Ann Kelly (widow) 16 BA-88
Boyce, Hugh; 4 Aug. 1801; Jane McLane                03 BA-404
Boyce, Sellas; 4 Nov. 1816; Maria Johnson            17 BA-15
Boyd, Alexander; 15 March 1807; Mary Ann Bowen       31 BA-20
Boyd, Alex'r V.; 13 May 1813; Mary I. Hollingsworth  03 BA-505
Boyd, James; 4 March 1802; Mary Hicks                03 BA-414
Boyd, James; 21 Dec. 1819; Margaret Kane             32 BA-327
Boyd, James P.; 4 Feb. 1808; Ann McHenry             05 BA-235
Boyd, Joseph; 21 April 1810; Mary Hinor              13 BA-12
Boyd, Wm.; 10 Aug. 1806; Margaret Long               03 BA-496
Boyer, Jacob; 31 May 1814; Margaret Nants            09 BA
Boyer, John; 3 March 1816; Maria Stewart             13 BA-24
Boyer, Joseph; 29 Oct. 1811; Sarah Beard             02 WA-91
Boyer, Philip; April 1806; Elis. Thomas              02 WA-80
```

```
Boyers, Samuel; Nov. 1806; Ann Rice                  02 WA-81
Boyers, Solomon; April 1806; Mary Young              02 WA-80
Boykin, Stephen H.; 5 Oct. 1801; Rebecca Adderton    03 SM
Boyle, Daniel; 12 Nov. 1801; Mary Henrietta Brooke   05 FR
Boyle, Jno.; 3 June 1802; Cath. Heger                14 BA-412
Boyle, Joseph; 25 Jan. 1806; Louisa Hagner           14 BA-419
Bozeley, James; 1 Dec. 1803; Eliz'h M'David (See also 10 AL)
                                                     04 AL-2
Brach, Ferdinand; 23 April 1803; Louis[a?] Oler      07 BA-68
Brachley, Peter; 28 Oct. 1810; Sophia Carroll        11 BA-16
Bradberry, Samuel; 15 June 1806; Christiana Gates    17 BA-6
Bradenbaugh, John; 31 Oct. 1803; Priscilla Few       05 BA-234
Braderhouse, Wm.; 5 March 1818; Louise Lanney        03 BA-603
Bradford, George; 26 May 1801; Susanna W. McComas (See also
    03 BA-29)                                        03 BA-18
Bradford, John; 5 June 1817; Margaret Gibson         17 BA-16
Bradford, John; 8 Dec. 1818; Ann Eliza Stricker      05 BA-241
Bradford, Samuel; 25 July 1803; Jane Bond            05 HA-3
Bradford, Wm.; 4 May 1819; Jane Ringgold             19 BA-72
Bradley, James; 20 Sept. 1820; Eliza Muir            03 BA-604
Bradley, Patrick; 28 Oct. 1813; Deborah Flaut        05 FR-5
Bradley, Samuel (slave of J. B. von Kapf); 23 Dec. 1804; Lucy
    Smith (slave of Wm. Jessop)                      03 BA-492
Bradock, John; 23 Feb. 1809; Mary Hilton             15 FR-323
Bradock, William; 25 Aug. 1812; Elizabeth Hilton     15 FR-325
Bradshaw, Richard; 6 April 1819; Ann Maria Beck      13 BA-34
Brady, Edward; 17 July 1820; Elizabeth Brady         16 BA-102
Brady(?), Israel; 18 May 1820; Harriet Moses         37 BA-153
Brady, Samuel; 21 Oct. 1819; Catherine Ann Thomas    11 BA-34
Bragger, Henry (native of Rotterdam); 21 July 1814; Ann Prender-
    ville (widow of the late Garrett Prenderville)   16BA-8
Bragonier, Samuel; 25 May 1811; Eliz. Kohner         02 WA-90
Brahany, James; 10 March 1814; Cecilia Blackney      16 BA-2
Bram, John; 8 Sept. 1815; Catherine Clem             15 FR-318
Bramble, David C.; 16 Jan. 1817; Eleanor Stanley     13 BA-39
Bramley, Thomas; 17 Nov. 1808; Elizabeth Campbell    09 BA
Branch, Alex'r; 10 June 1819; Rebecca McCoy          14 BA-439
Brand, Daniel; 6 Feb. 1805; Mary White               15 BA-215
Brand, David; 11 Jan. 1816; Mahala Mills             13 BA-24
Brand, David; 26 Sept. 1819; Ann Wells               14 BA-439
Brand, Joh.; (Jan.) 1801; Lovisa Deal                02 WA-71
Brand, John; Aug. 1802; Elis. Dederly                02 WA-73
Brand, William; 15 March 1810; Sus. Christina Jungherr 14 BA-427
Brandenberg, Henrich; 15 April 1804; Elizabeth Gebhard 15 FR-316
Brandenburg, William; 17 Sept. 1806; Christina Long  15 FR-319
Brandstatter, Daniel; 1801; Cath. Geiser             02 WA-72
Braner, Heinr.; 6 April 1801; Lena Barrs             14 BA-409
Brannan, Jno.; 27 Aug. 1805; Martha Taylor           14 BA-418
Brannan, John; 27 Oct. 1819; Sarah Hancks            14 BA-439
Brannan, Thomas; 19 May 1803; Juliana Davis          15 BA-182
Brannan, William; 10 Dec. 1807; Rachel Griffin (of Bird River)
                                                     09 BA
Brannock, Edmond; 15 Nov. 1804; Mary Colston         01 DO-41
Branson, Owen (son of David and Elizabeth); 11 d, 14 mo., 1805;
    Hannah Benson (dau. of Benjamin and Hannah) (see also 05 SF)
                                                     02 SF-96
Brant, James; 24 Sept. 1820; Harriet Mitchell        03 BA-605
Brant, Thos.; 30 March 1806; Rebecca Trott           03 AA-130
Brashers, Robert; 7 July 1816; Eliza Lerigan         13 BA-26
Brasley, John; 11 April 1818; Abarilla Adelphia      17 BA-19
Brauer, Frederic; 23 Aug. 1809; Cath. Faus           14 BA-426
Braugh, Thomas; 28 Jan. 1802; Keziah Meekins         01 DO-40
Braun, Ignatius; 1802; Ellis M. Field                02 WA-72
```

Braun, Jacob; 10 Nov. 1816; Maria Anna Whissel   07 BA-310
Braun, Johannes; 11 June 1809; Maria Simon   15 FR-323
Braun, Joseph; 23 March 1802; Margrethe Lohr (both single)
                                                        01 CL-150
Braun, Wm.; 3 Oct. 1812; Mary Mills   14 BA-430
Bray, Edward Smith; 21 Oct. 1810; Catherine Mullen   31 BA-91
Bray, John; 29 Sept. 1803; Julia Philips   14 AA-1
Bray, Joseph; 8 July 1802; Anne Fennel   15 AA-2
Bray, Joseph; 26 April 1804; Elizabeth Brewer   15 AA-3
Brazier, William; 25 July 1805; Elizabeth Saunders   33 BA-41
Bready, Thomas; 31 Dec. 1812; Mary Hatton   17 BA-9
Breese, John M.; 7 June 1813; Harriet Beall   11 BA-21
Breidelbaugh, Valentine; 22 May 1802; Mary Pillic   03 BA-416
Brekenbaugh, Henry; March 1814; Elizab. Gushwa   02 WA-99
Bremerman, Herman; 1 Aug. 1813; Amalia Beerman (nee Schafer)
                                                        07 BA-309
Brenckel, Johannes; 27 March 1803; Elizabeth Ziehler   15 FR-314
Brengel, Peter; 1 May 1803; Cath. Mann   15 FR-314
Brengle, Lawrence; 10 Dec. 1819; Mary Menche   06 FR-1330
Brenneman, George; 2 March 1811; Jane Cherry   14 BA-428
Brent, Robert Young (of Washington City); 4 Jan. 1814; Eliza L.
  Carrere (of Baltimore City)   16 BA-1
Brentlinger, Henry; Sept. 1813; Lydia Tice   02 WA-98
Brentlinger, William; 24 March 1811; Charlotte Foutz   02 WA-89
Breuning, Georg; 25 Nov. 1810; Julian Barcker   07 BA-307
Brewer, Adam; Nov. 1820; Maria Johnson   02 WA-117
Brewer, Daniel; Jan. 1820; Elizab. West   02 WA-115
Brewer, David; April 1820; Sarah Snyder   02 WA-116
Brewer, John; Oct. 1820; Elizab. Fiery   02 WA-117
Brewer, Joseph (son of John and Susan); 16 Feb. 1800; Elizabeth
  Wilmot   02 AA
Brewer, Joseph Newton; 7 Feb. 1802; Mary Birkhead   01 AA-73
Brewer, Lewis; 23 July 1819; Catherine Neppard   07 BA-311
Brewer, Wm.; 27 Oct. 1811; Jane Boyd   13 BA-13
Breyden, Walter; 29 Aug. 1804; Frances Daley   03 BA-491
Brian, Arthur; 5 Nov. 1812; Hetty Lidard   09 BA
Brian, William; 3 Jan. 1819; Catherine Clackner   37 BA-151
Briant, William; 21 April 1815; Susanna Crea   05 BA-238
Brice, Edmund; 17 July 1818; Charlotte Eliza Ann Moss   16 AA-40
Bridges, John S.; 6 Dec. 1815; Catherine A. Capeto   09 BA
Bridgman, Joseph; 13 Oct. 1811; Mary Ebersole   02 WA-91
Briehl, Daniel; 7 Aug. 1820; Mary Miller   14 BA-440
Bright, Martin; 1801; Hannah Stinchcom   06 AA-1
Bright, Nathaniel; 20 Oct. 1803; Sarah Harryman   26 BA-3
Brightnoder, Martin; 27 Feb. 1801; Susanna Myers   02 BA-3
Bringuier, Michael Doravon; 17 June 1812; Elizabeth Louisa Aglae
  Dubourg (of New Orleans)   15 BA-300
Brinkman, Henry; 14 Dec. 1818; Regina Heus   14 BA-438
Brinnum (?), Aaron; 22 Jan. 1800; Eliza Peake   03 SM
Briscoe, Alex'r; 15 Aug. 1809; Mary Wilson   13 BA-8
Briscoe, Philip; 9 March 1814; Ann Spratley   13 BA-18
Brisland, John; 18 Dec. 1815; Eliza Lawson   13 BA-24
Brister, Samuel; 22 Oct. 1807; Margaret Peters   09 BA
Britt, Severn; 21 March 1810; Guiner Leakins [Gaynor Lukens]
                                                        13 BA-12
Brittain, Thos.; 3 Sept. 1806; Mary McGuire   03 BA-496
Britton, John; 17 May 1806; Sophia Jeffery   11 BA-8
Broadrup, George; 26 Jan. 1817; Margareth Burkhardt   06 FR-1325
Broadwater, William; 14 March 1813; Rebeka Green   03 AL-614
Brobeck, Joseph; 16 April 1812; Nancy Yeanivim   02 WA-94
Brock, Thomas; 16 Feb. 1817; Elizabeth Biscop   02 BA-37
Brockett, Peter; 20 Nov. 1817; Mary Butlar   17 BA-17
Brohean, Gotfried; 6 March 1816; Antoinette Shyrman   14 BA-435
Brome, Henry; 23 Feb. 1804; Rebecca Martin   02 SM-186

Bromwell, Jacob; 24 Nov. 1804; Maria Little   11 BA-4
Bromwell, John; 15 Oct. 1801; Rosanna Robson   01 DO-40
Bromwell, William; 9 Nov. 1814; Maria Johns   13 BA-20
Brook, James (negro slave of Henry Nagle); 29 Oct., 1809; Ann
     (free negro)   15 BA-275
Brook, John; 22 June 1815; Mary Traverse (both free col'd)
                                                     16 BA-21
Brook, Samuel (son of John Brook, late of Lancashire, Eng., and
     his wife Mary); 24 d, 6 m., 1812; Elizabeth Cheney (dau. of
     Charles and Hannah Robinson)   01 SF
Brook, William; 27 May 1802; Ann Walker   33 BA-15
Brooke, Robert; 4 Feb. 1819; A. Carolina Fenwick   04 FR-18
Brooke, Roger (s. of Roger and Mary [Matthews]); 1803; Mary
     Pleasants Younghusband   10 SF
Brooke, Roger (son of Roger and Mary); 22 d., 8 m., 1804; Mary
     Pleasants Younghusband (dau. of Isaac and Mary) 01 SF
Brooke, Samuel; 24 d., 6 mo., 1812; Eliza Cheney   10 SF
Brooke, W.; 6 July 1815; Marg't Undutch   13 BA-22
Brookes, John; 3 Feb. 1803; Henrietta Chapman   01 DO-41
Brookhart, David; March 1820; Theresa Funk   02 WA-116
Brooks, Daniel L.; 11 May 1808; Barbara Limes   11 BA-8
Brooks, Geo. W.; 16 April 1816; Rach'l Collins   13 BA-25
Brooks, Isaac; 5 Nov. 1818; Sarah Ann Shuler   17 BA-18
Brooks, James; 18 Aug. 1808; Ann Ashwell   13 BA-4
Brooks, James; 1 May 1816; Biddy McMahon   05 BA-239
Brooks, John; 16 June 1803; Patty Brooks   03 BA-429
Brooks, Jonathan; 12 Oct. 1807; Rosana Curkman   14 BA-422
Brooks, Jonathan; 22 Sept. 1812; Susnana Lambert   14 BA-430
Brooks, Jos. R.; 2 March 1813; Rebecca Todd   03 BA-505
Brooks, Joshua; 20 Feb. 1803; Kelly Gibbons   36 BA-1
Brooks, Rob't; 31 Oct. 1813; Mary Amey   14 BA-432
Brooks, Thomas; 16 Oct. 1807; Rachel Underwood   13 BA-3
Brooks, Wm.; 2 Nov. 1809; Rachel Sincler   13 BA-8
Brooks, William; 12 Jan. 1810; Eliza Field   11 BA-37
Broome, Thomas; 23 May 1805; Elizabeth Todd   03 BA-493
Broone, (?)din; Jan. 1808; Sus. Shank   02 WA-85
Brophy, William; 18 April 1820; Eleanor White   04 FR-19
Brosins, Michael; 21 June 1807; Mrs. Mary Foy   31 BA-25
Brotchey, John; 17 Nov. 1819; Anna Splinter   04 FR-19
Broughton, Noah; 18 Oct. 1810; Catha. Haurner   03 BA-501
Brovenhowl, John; 21 July 1803; Rebecca Ingram   09 BA
Brower, Emanuel; 30 Oct. 1802; Susannah Murray   09 BA
Brown, (N); Dec. 1807; Cath. Lewis   02 WA-84
Brown, Abel; 18 June 1818; Magdalin Purpur   13 BA-31
Brown, Andrew; 16 April 1820; Isabella Boring   13 BA-41
Brown, Benjamin; 6 Oct. 1819; Sarah Kesiah Mullen   16 BA-89
Brown, Caleb (s. of Robert and Dinah of East Nottingham Hund.,
     CE Co., MD); 17 d, 11 mo., 1808; Phebe Johnson (dau. of
     Simon, dec., and Rebecca of Wilmington, DE)   06 SF
Brown, Caleb; 23 Dec. 1819; Ann McLaughlin   16 BA-94
Brown, Christian; 18 Oct. 1818; Mary Derr   14 BA-437
Brown, Christopher; 7 May 1816; Sarah McClure   11 BA-30
Brown, Cornelius P.; 10 Aug. 1819; Catherine Netherman 11 BA-35
Brown, David (s. of David and Elizabeth); 20 d, 9 mo., 1810; Ann
     Birckhead Troth (dau. of William and Elizabeth) 08 SF
Brown, David; March 1817; Elisab. Slusser   02 WA-104
Brown, Edward; 3 Oct. 1807; Jane Boyle   15 BA-254
Brown, Edward; 17 March 1817; Henny Davis   17 BA-16
Brown, Elias; 7 Sept. 1819; Susan E. Brown   18 BA-66
Brown, Emanuel; 29 Aug. 1820; Christina Miller   16 FR-76
Brown, Ezra (s. of Jeremiah, dec., and Anna, of Little Britain
     Twp., Lancaster Co., PA); 10 d, 3 mo. 1802; Hannah Pickering
     (dau. of Jesse and Ann, of same twp.)   06 SF

Brown, Fielder; 5 Nov. 1801; Hannah Heague (See also 15 FR-312)
01 FR-1109
Brown, G. R. A.; 24 Nov. 1812; Caroline (N)   13 BA-15
Brown, Geo.; 12 Sept. 1809; Crecy Carmill   13 BA-8
Brown, George I. (?); 7 March 1810; Esther Allison   05 BA-236
Brown, George; 22 Dec. 1820; Sarah Yoste (See also 16 FR-76)
08 FR-413
Brown, Henry (native of Balto.); 7 Sept. 1811; Marie Bouilon-
gre(?) (native of Paris)   15 BA-290
Brown, Henry; Dec. 1818; Elizab. Knave   02 WA-111
Brown, Jac. S.; 3 May 1810; Emma Lock   13 BA-9
Brown, Jacob; 9 Sept. 1819; Elizabeth Miller   08 BA
Brown, James; 20 Jan. 1803; Ann Leek   03 MO-118
Brown, James; 1804; Rachel Chilton   07 AA-4
Brown, James; 9 Sept. 1805; Catharine Malone   15 AA-227
Brown, James; 10 March 1808; Sarah Gover   13 BA-3
Brown, Jas., Jr.; 18 July 1811; Eliz'h Watson   13 BA-13
Brown, James; 18 June 1812; Ann Tixton   13 BA-9
Brown, Jeremiah (of Little Britain Twp., Lancaster Co., PA); 9
day, 12 mo., 1802; Ann Jones   06 SF
Brown, Jeremiah (s. of Jeremiah and Hannah, dec., of Little
Britain Twp., Lancsaster Co., PAO); 24 d, 8 mo., 1807; Ann
Kirk (dau. of Roger and Rachel of West Nottingham Twp.,
Chester Co., PA)   06 SF
Brown, Jno.; 15 April 1802; Ann Fenton   14 BA-412
Brown, Joh.; 1804; Cath. Sillhart   02 WA-77
Brown, John; 23 July 1804; Sarah Edwards   15 FR-316
Brown, John; Oct. 1806; Elly Tomson   02 WA-81
Brown, John; 17 Aug. 1807; Sarah Newton   11 BA-11
Brown, John; 11 May 1809; Sarah Dalrymple   13 BA-6
Brown, John; 1 Oct. 1812; Susan Freburger   13 BA-15
Brown, John; 31 Aug. 1813; Ann Morris   14 BA-432
Brown, John; 13 June 1816; Mary Allen   17 BA-12
Brown, Jno.; 30 March 1817; Elizab. Smith   14 BA-436
Brown, John; 14 Jan. 1818; Julia Abbott   17 BA-19
Brown, John; 19 Dec. 1819; Eva Ringer (16 FR-76 gives date as 16
Dec. 1819)   08 FR-413
Brown, John; 6 Jan. 1820; Eliza G. Bonsall (see also 02 QA-66)
11 BA-34
Brown, John Carroll; 14 Nov. 1815; Elizabeth Merriken 03 BA-507
Brown, John Dixon; 3 May 1804; Jane Orrick   36 BA-2
Brown, Joseph; 22 April 1802; Frances Davis   09 BA
Brown, Joseph; 30 Aug. 1807; Catherine Wise   15 BA-254
Brown, Joseph; 23 Jan. 1808; Mary Shilling   02 BA-6
Brown, Joseph; 13 Dec. 1809; Ellen Lingham   14 BA-227
Brown, Joshua (s. of Joshua and Hannah); 5th d., 2 mo., 1801;
Sarah Ely (relict of Hugh)   11 SF-82.
Brown, Montillion (s. of Samuel and Ruth of West Nottingham
Hund., CE Co.); 14 d, 5 mo., 1812; Anna Rogers (dau. of
William and Katherine (of East Nottingham Hund., CE Co.)
06 SF
Brown, Morgan; 4 May 1817; Margaret McClain   21 BA-9
Brown, Moses; 31 Dec. 1816; Eliza Williams   13 BA-021
Brown, Nicodemus; 12 Jan. 1817; Eliza Bailey   11 BA-31
Brown, Peter; 8 July 1819; Sarah Gardner   13 BA-33
Brown, Richard Gay; 7 March 1804; Rachel DeFrese (or Depies)
17 BA-3
Brown, Samuel; (of Fred. Co., VA; s. of Isaac and Sarah); 12 d.
12 mo., 1805; Hannah Matthews (dau. of Thomas, dec., and
Ann)   09 SF
Brown, Samuel; 2 May 1809; Charity Brough   09 BA
Brown, Samuel; 2 Oct. 1813; Mary Wheeler ("say Eliza instead of
Mary Wheeler")   03 BA-505
Brown, Sidney; 31 Oct. 1816; Cassy Hews   17 BA-13

Brown, Stephen (s. of Elihu and Margaret); 2nd d., 12 mo., 1813;
    Achsah Warner (dau. of Amon and Ann)   11 SF-110
Brown, Stewart; 17 Sept. 1818; Sarah Muncaster   03 BA-603
Brown, Thomas; 8 Sept. 1801; Harriot (N) (blacks)   03 BA-406
Brown, Thomas; 17 Oct. 1801; Elizabeth Dick   10 BA-1
Brown, Thomas; April 1818; Susanna M'Afee   02 WA-109
Brown, Thomas; 15 Oct. 1820; Sarah Hilton   13 BA-41
Brown, Thos. S.; 15 Aug. 1811; Prisa Dallas   13 BA-13
Brown, William; 19 d. 8 mo., 1802; Jane Ellicott (widow of
    Thomas, late of Bucks Co., PA)   09 SF
Brown, William; 31 Dec. 1807; Rebecca Evans   09 BA
Brown, William (s. of Jeremiah, dec., and Anna of Little Britain
    Twp., Lancaster Co., PA); 24 d, 3 mo., 1808; Esther Kirk
    (dau. of Eli and Susannah of West Nottingham Hund., CE Co.,
    MD)   06 SF
Brown, William; 25 June 1811; Sarah Protzman   02 WA-90
Brown, William; 17 Aug. 1815; Hester Parlet   11 BA-24
Brown, William; 25 April 1816; Susannahn Klise   06 FR-1324
Brown, Zachariah; 24 Dec. 1803; Rebecca Duvall   15 AA-3
Brownell, David; 10 March 1809; Ann Grooms   11 BA-13
Browning, James; 17 Sept. 1818; Mary Eagleston   17 BA-20
Browning, Jeremiah; 5 May 1803; Eliz. Summers   03 MO-118
Browning, Jeremiah; 1804; Rebecca Lane   13 AA-1
Browning, Levi; 8 Aug. 1813; Marg't Sterrett   14 BA-432
Browning, Riston; 11 June 1812; Mary Ann Lee   13 BA-9
Browning, Ritson; 10 March 1803; Ann Scott   34 BA-1
Browning, Wm.; 5 July 1810; Mary Ann Starr   14 BA-427
Browning, Zephania; 23 July 1806; Mary Jones   14 BA-420
Brua, John; March 1819; Amalia Keller   02 WA-112
Brua, Joseph; Jan. 1819; Mary Fiery   02 WA-112
Brubacher, Samuel; 18 May 1809; Barbara Gomer   15 FR-323
Bruce, John; 24 May 1802; Mary Galloway   06 BA-2
Bruce, Robert; 8 Jan. 1807; Ann Scoffield   03 BA-496
Bruce, William; 1 Nov. 1808; Phoebe Cresap   03 AL-614
Bruff, William; 17 Nov. 1804; Sarah Norris   09 BA
Brule, Alexander Mary; 13 Sept. 1809; Mary Teresa Barioteaux
              15 BA-272
Brumbaug, George; April 1807; Louisa Gol(?)   02 WA-82
Brune, Frederic Wm.; 28 Sept. 1805; Ann Clarke   03 BA-494
Brunebaugh, David; Oct. 1805; Eva Keesecker   02 WA-79
Bruner, George; Dec. 1820; Elizab. Faulkwell   02 WA-117
Brunner, Elias; 5 June 1804; Cath. Wolf   15 FR-316
Brunner, George; May 1814; Susannah Staley   06 FR-1320
Brunner, Henry; 16 Aug. 1812; Elizabeth Westenhaver   15 FR-325
Brunner, Jacob; 4 Oct. 1807; Margaret Doll   15 FR-321
Brunner, Valentin; 11 April 1803; Elizabeth Bohrer   15 FR-314
Bruno(?); Joh.; March 1806; Elis. Kreps   02 WA-80
Brunstead, Francis; 23 Dec. 1801; Louisa Ristein   14 BA-411
Brunt, Thomas; 16 Feb. 1811; Ann Tindall   03 BA-502
Brurkburn (Bucklew?), George; 31 March 1803; Sarah Paugh
              03 AL-613
Brushey, Michael; 4 March 1820; Sophia Hartsook   04 FR-19
Bryan, Capt. (N); 19 Jan. 1815; Elizabeth Foard, als. Tate (both
    of QA Co.) (See also 02 TA-43)   01 QA-53
Bryan, John; 13 Sept. 1806; Isabella Montgomery   02 BA-4
Bryan, Jos.; 19 Feb. 1803; Phebe McAllister   14 BA-414
Bryan, Thos.; 6 Nov. 1813; Susan Hooper   14 BA-432
Bryan, Valentine; July 1806; Ann Lambert (see also 01 QA-52)
              02 TA-40
Bryden, Wm.; 22 May 1815; Eliza Goodman   13 BA-21
Brydenstine, Leonhard; March 1804; Elis. Zimerman   02 WA-76
Bryer, Emanuel; 5 Oct. 1809; Margaret Smith   15 BA-274
Bryson, John; 15 Aug. 1802; Margaret Bond   05 BA-233
Buch (Buck), Charles; 19 May 1816; Elisa Hassard   13 BA-25

Buchanan, George; 30 Nov. 1815; Sarah P. Nesbit   14 BA-434
Buchanan, Lloyd; 21 Jan. 1802; Catherine Isabella Stewart
                                                       03 BA-412
Buchenham, Loyd; 30 July 1815; Leah Cranford   08 BA
Buchman, Joseph; 21 Jan. 1820; Mary [Everett]   39 BA-37
Buck, Benjamin; 16 Aug. 1820; Jane Herbert   03 BA-604
Buck, James; 29 Jan. 1815; Eliza Long   13 BA-20
Buck, John; 12 March 1801; Catherine Green   09 BA
Buck, John; 14 Dec. 1814; Anna Forter   30 BA-109
Buck, Samuel; 23 Oct. 1808; S. Curren   30 BA-109
Buck, Thomas; 19 Dec. 1806; Elenor Dickson   30 BA-109
Buckingham, Isaiah; 14 Sept. 1817; Susan McMinn   13 BA-29
Buckingham, James; 29 Feb. 1816; Betsy Ann Brown   17 BA-12
Buckingham, Obadiah; 28 Jan. 1819; Hannah (?)such   08 BA
Buckley, Robert; 30 May 1804; Julia Carter   02 BA-34
Buckman, Jesse; 22 Oct. 1819; Susan Burnham   11 BA-37
Buckman, John; 23 Jan. 1819; Ann Hall   13 BA-32
Buckman, Phineas; 28 Jan. 1810; Catharine Scharf   11 BA-15
Bucks, John; 14 Jan 1816; Mary Weeks   17 BA-12
Bucky, David; 27 Oct. 1812; Elizabeth Kemp   06 FR-1318
Bucky, Michael; 23 March 1806; Cath. Pfeifer   15 FR-318
Buddy, Peter; 28 Jan. 1806; Margaret Hare   14 BA-419
Buffurn, John; 23 June 1807; Jane Keys   05 BA-235
Buhring, Frederick G. Lewis; 18 May 1820; Frances G. Dannenberg
                                                       14 BA-440
Bukhan, James; 26 April 1812; Mary C. Thornton   13 BA-7
Bukley, William; 4 May 1817; Elizabeth Dunnicker   17 BA-16
Bull (or Ball?), Hilary; 4 Dec. 1806; Rachel Keplinger 09 BA
Bull, Jarrett; 22 June 1802; Mary Bo (?)   28 BA-1
Bull, Joshua; Dec. 1804; Letitia Livingston   17 BA-4
Bull, William; 15 Dec. 1803; Polly Hicks   06 HA-1
Bundick, George B.; 25 Feb. 1813; Catherine Dorgan   09 BA
Bunker, Wm.; 23 Nov. 1809; Nancy Chesnut   03 BA-500
Bunting, John; 6 Oct. 1808; Mary Somerville   13 BA-4
Bunting, Joseph; 8 Sept. 1818; Andelia Barnhouse   16 BA-74
Bunton, James; 11 May 1811; Sarah Coale   09 BA
Burcket [Burckel?], Philip; Nov. 1806; Sarah Cramer   02 WA-81
Burdick, John; 29 Jan. 1801; Mary Hall   09 BA
Burditt, Wm.; 16 Feb. 1804; Ruth Fitz[g]erald   03 MO-119
Burdough, David; 9 Dec. 1819; Elizabeth Ratcliff   13 BA-41
Burford, Robert; 28 May 1801; Eleanor Smith   11 BA-3
Burge, William; 24 Dec. 1807; Eliz. Mopps   13 BA-3
Burges, John; 24 Aug. 1801; Mary Mansfield   03 BA-405
Burgess, Enoch M.; 4 May 1806; Sarah L. C. Smith   03 AA-130
Burgess, Jno. (black); 1 Sept. 1814; Elizabeth Williams
                                                       21 BA-8
Burgess, John; 12 Nov. 1819 Unity Gassaway   16 BA-90
Burgess, John H.; 18 Oct. 1812; Marg't Morrison   13 BA-15
Burgess, Joseph; 7 De.c 1809; Ruth Gorsuch   09 BA
Burgess, Thomas; 27 Oct. 1818; Ann Byram   11 BA-33
Burgin, Joseph; 16 April 1809; Deborah Parlet   09 BA
Burgin, Philip; 10 Feb. 1805; Elizabeth Sindle   09 BA
Burgin, Thomas; 15 March 1804; Amelia Parlett   09 BA
Burguine, Augustine; 4 Feb. 1808; Henrietta Wile (?)   31 BA-37
Burk, Ezekiel; 16 Dec. 1802; Sarah Spurr (?)   09 BA
Burk, Francis; 15 Aug. 1811; Sarah Hands   11 BA-17
Burke, Alexis; 6 Oct. 1803; Mary Eliz'th Lingenfelter 09 BA
Burke, Edward D.; 24 March 1805; Mary Johnson   11 BA-5
Burke, George (free black); 24 Jan. 1818; Milley Young (bel. to
    Owen Allen)   16 BA-64
Burke, Isaac; 2 May 1813; Dorcas Sutton   14 BA-431
Burke, James; 21 Sept. 1801; Rebecca Banton   03 BA-407
Burke, Jas.; 18 May 1820; Mary Hawly   04 BA-604
Burke, John; 20 June 1813; Bridget Curley   31 BA-152

```
Burke, John; 28 Nov. 1818; Margaret Nicholson          05 BA-241
Burke, Luke; 26 Sept. 1803; Nancy Smith                14 BA-415
Burke, Michael; 23 Oct. 1801; Rebecca Goods            14 BA-411
Burke, Nicholas; 25 April 1805; Sarah Wright           15 BA-218
Burke, William; 29 April 1807; Mary Powers             15 BA-249
Burkett, Jacob; Feb. 1817; Mary Lefler                 02 WA-104
Burkett, Jacob; 21 July 1811; Cath. Goll               02 WA-90
Burkett, John; Jan. 1818; Elisab. Waggoner             02 WA-108
Burkhard, Lewis; 31 Aug. 1820; Catherine Newport       06 FR-1331
Burkhardt, John; 18 Aug. 1818; Elizabeth Woodward      06 FR-1328
Burkhart, Jacob; March 1819; Elizab. Breckler          02 WA-112
Burkhart, John; 7 March 1816; Rebecca Balzell          06 FR-1324
Burkhart, Peter; 31 Oct. 1813; Mrs. Charlotte Balzel   06 FR-1320
Burklims, John; 26 Nov. 1805; Eleanor Paugh            03 AL-613
Burland, James; 20 July 1820; Ann Stretch              11 BA-38
Burling, Jacob; Dec. 1803; Marg. Saufert               02 WA-75
Burner, Jacob Young; 29 Aug. 1812; Susanna Dickenson   15 FR-325
Burnes, Charles; 23 Jan. 1809; Elizabeth Miller        09 BA
Burnett, Richard; 18 Aug. 1818; Elizabeth McCullough   05 BA-241
Burnham, Edward; 11 May 1805; Elizabeth Bond           09 BA
Burns, Dennis; 12 April 1804; Rachel Bull              09 BA
Burns, John; 14 Sept. 1817; Rach'l Griffith            13 BA-29
Burns, Wm.; 28 May 1819; Jane Needham                  13 BA-33
Burrel, Benjamin; Aug. 1807; Sus. Weiver               02 WA-83
Burrell, A. Albert; 11 March 1813; Cathr. M. Hall      13 BA-16
Burring(?), John S.; 10 Aug. 1818; Nancy Fanning       16 BA-73
Burrman, Henry; 15 June 1809; Barbara Hooks            14 BA-426
Burris, Alexander; 3 May 1806; Mary Smith              17 BA-6
Burrows, Edward; 17 April 1808; Mary Zane              02 BA-6
Burrows, Thomas; 27 April 1820; Elizabeth Winter       06 FR-1331
Burtess, Bernard; 9 Nov. 1817; Margaret Metcalfe       32 BA-316
Burton, Elijah; 31 May 1804; Catherine Eagleston       09 BA
Burton, Elijah; 16 Jan. 1817; Elizabeth Liddiard       09 BA
Burton, James; 5 Oct. 1820; Eleanor Watkins            13 BA-36
Burton, Myers; 18 April 1805; Esther Button            09 BA
Busch, Abraham; 26 Oct. 1807; Catharina Haber, widow   07 BA-305
Bush, Abraham; 11 May 1820; Ann Schmachtenberg         14 BA-440
Bush, Jno.; 26 Nov. 1801; Eliz. Brian                  14 BA-411
Bush, Mark; 24 June 1814; Mary Cadle                   13 BA-39
Bushy, Conrad; 10 Sept. 1801; Rebecca Meyer            14 BA-410
Busk, James; 12 Dec. 1816; Elizabeth Jordan            US
Busk, James; 18 May 1820; Kesiah Parks                 17 BA-23
Busk, John; 20 April 1812; Barbara Murphey             09 BA
Busk, John; 24 Jan. 1816; Mary Weaks                   17 BA-12
Busk (or Husk), John; 24 Dec. 1818; Helen Dobbin       37 BA-151
Busk, Jno. Fred'k; 24 March 1814; Eliz. Benner         14 BA-432
Bussard, Samuel; June 1805; Cath. Kugel                02 WA-79
Bussard, Samuel; 5 Oct. 1812; Mary Delawter            02 WA-95
Bussey, Bennett (of HA Co.); 7 July 1806; Elizabeth Slade
                                                       15 BA-240
Bussey, Edward B.; 20 Dec. 1803; Sarah Howard          05 HA-1
Butler, Absalom; 22 Dec. 1811; Mary Shaw               09 BA
Butler, Clement; 13 Oct. 1802; Mary Ann Foll (free negroes)
                                                       15 BA-172
Butler, George; 6 Nov. 1801; Mary Williams             03 BA-410
Butler, Gideon; 23 April 1816; Sara Stoyer             08 AL-16
Butler, James; 28 Nov. 1802; Ann Green                 36 BA-1
Butler, John; 10 Jan. 1804; Sarah Macatee (both of HA Co.)
                                                       15 BA-196
Butler, Jno.; 11 July 1811; Mary Lynch                 14 BA-429
Butler, Lewis (free negro); 20 Sept. 1804; Priscilla Christie
  (mulatto)                                            15 BA-208
Butler, Ormond F.; 16 Dec. 1813; Eliz'th Bortel        06 FR-1320
Butler, Richard; 6 Feb. 1812; Eliz. Sommer             14 BA-429
```

Butler, Thomas; 24 May 1814; Sarah Clagett   06 FR-1321
Butler, William; 21 April 1806; Julia W. Deal   15 FR-319
Butscher, Josephus; 16 April 1805; Maria Elisabeth Feyge [Phiah]
                                                    39 BA-17
Butt, Edward; Sept. 1816; Eliza. Basehore   02 WA-102
Butt, Hazil; 31 Dec. 1803; Sarah Richards   03 MO-119
Butt, Lewis; 22 July 1804; Henrietta Everton   05 BA-234
Butt, Thomas; May 1805; Barb. Schuck   02 WA-78
Button, George; 29 Oct. 1816; Sarah White   17 BA-15
Butts, Noah; 24 Dec. 1817; Harriot Gentleman   17 BA-17
Butts, Noah; 12 Jan. 1818; Harriott Gentleman   17 BA-19
Buxton, George; 7 Dec. 1802; Mary Ann Traill   03 MO-118
Buzick, John; 10 June 1810; Susanna Burge   03 BA-501
Byrd, Charles; 15 Oct. 1818; Julia Ann Mickle   19 BA-72
Byrne, Gavin; 16 Dec. 1815; Ann Dowling   32 BA-307
Byrne, John; 10 Aug. 1818; Mary O'Neill   16 BA-72
Cable, Jacob; 7 June 1812; Mary Ann Tinges   14 BA-430
Cade, Thomas; 23 Aug. 1812; Sarah Hoover   02 WA-95
Cadle, Thomas; 15 Feb. 1803; Nancy Hall   05 AA-3
Cadue, John (native of Bordeaux, France); 27 April 1812; Mary Ann
    Maillet Lacoste (native of Aux Cayes, St. Domingo)
                                                    15 BA-198
Cadwallader, Rees (of Brownsville, Fayette Co., PA; son of Rees
    and Ruth Cadwallader, both dec.); 27 d, 10 Mo., 1808; Hannah
    Dillon (dau. of Moses and Hannah) (See also 05 SF)
                                                    02 SF-108
Caffrey, John R.; 31 Dec. 1815; Ann Haten   14 BA-434
Caile, Henry; 3 March 1812; Mary Ketero   06 FR-1317
Cain, Aaron; 4 July 1818; Ann Magness   17 BA-19
Cain, Thomas; 4 Nov. 1818; Susanna Hennin   13 BA-40
Calaghan, Peter; 26 Dec. 1805; Mary Ann Carr (both natives of
    Ireland)   15 BA-232
Calbo, Frederic; 16 Nov. 1805; Elizabeth Bowen   03 BA-494
Calder, Wm.; 21 March 1801; Sally Chapman   14 BA-409
Caldwell, Benjamin H.; 19 May 1812; Mary Speake   15 BA-299
Caldwell, James; 27 Sept. 1815; Har[rie?]t Day   13 BA-23
Caldwell, Joseph; 16 May 1816; Mary King   05 BA-239
Caldwin, Joseph; 21 Nov. 1802; Elizab. Francis (See also 15 FR-
    313)   01 FR-1118
Cale, Luther; 25 Jan. 1817/8; Martha Lynch   08 BA
Calef, Samuel; 20 Sept. 1810; Ann Costello   31 BA-90
Calhoun, Hugh; 4 Feb. 1812; Margaret Wilson   09 BA
Calhoun, John; July 1803; Mary Kookess   02 WA-75
Calhoun, William; 11 Aug. 1816; Dorothy Beard   16 BA-40
Callaghan, Burgess (native of London); 14 Sept. 1811; Winifred
    Morgan (native of Ireland)   15 BA-290
Callahan, Joseph; 18 Oct. 1812; Maria Councell, both of TA
                                                    02 TA-42
Callahan, William; 26 Nov. 1805; Ann Cowning   02 SM-187
Callender, George; 10 April 18145; Drusilla Pocock 05 BA-238
Callender, William; 1 Oct. 1801; Elizabeth Callendar 01 TA-315
Callichane, Turbet; 22 Aug. 1809; Nancy Turbet   02 TA-41
Cally, Thomas; 18 Feb. 1818; Mary Herthrop   32 BA-318
Callopy, Timothy; 17 Nov. 1803; Sarah Adreon   21 BA-5
Calwell, John M.; 7 Aug. 1813; Hannah Himbs (Hines?) 11 BA-21
Cameron, Hugh; 12 Feb. 1816; Rachel Walker   11 BA-26
Camp, William; 11 May 1815; Mary Warrick   21 BA-8
Campbell, Mr., of Balto.; 22 May 1820; Ann Dalton (dau. of Mrs.
    McNeale's first marriage)   05 FR-34
Campbell, Dan'l W.; 21 Jan. 1819; Sarah Ann V. B. Jolly
                                                    19 BA-72
Campbell, George; 28 Oct. 1819; Julia Bedford   03 BA-604
Campbell, Hugh; 29 March 1815; Maria S. Death   05 BA-238
Campbell, James; c.1804; Mary Jenkins   34 BA-2

Campbell, James; 15 Nov. 1808; Rebecca Winchester   03 BA-499
Campbell, John; 12 Jan. 1809; Hetty Fitzpatrick   09 BA
Campbell, Sam'l; 26 Dec. 1813; Rhody Steel   13 BA-18
Campbell, Thomas; 10 Feb. 1818; Marg't Joyce   14 BA-438
Campbell, William; 31 March 1812; Rosetta Gray   15 BA-295
Camper, John; 24 Dec. 1815; Catherine Weinenein (?)   09 BA
Campsall, Michael; 22 Dec. 1808; Margaret Long   09 BA
Canada, Mordecai; 13 June 1801; Margaret Brogen   20 BA-410
Canby, Benj.; 24 Sept. 1815; Keziah Rosenberry   13 BA-23
Canby, Joseph; 1820; Sarah Thomas   10 SF
Canby, William (son of William and Mary); 21 d, 9 mo.,   1808;
     Sarah Thomas (dau. of Samuel and Mary)   01 SF
Candler, William; 28 June 1803; Rebecca Ray   03 MO-118
Cann, Thomas; 16 May 1809; Eliz. Norris   01 FR-1118
Cannaday, Hugh; 15 Oct. 1805; Elizabeth Cole   02 BA-2
Cannard, Frank; 29 Aug. 1815; Priscilla Trapnall   14 BA-434
Cannon, Dominic; 27 April 1815; Margaret Smith   16 BA-18
Cannon, Jeremiah; 15 Oct. 1804; Margaret Scharan (both natives of
     Ireland)   15 BA-210
Cantwell, Joseph; 17 March 1816; Mary Dudley   02 BA-36
Capers, Joseph; 20 March 1815; Nancy Chandler   17 BA-10
Capito, Georg; 30 July 1809; Irene Blatin   07 BA-307
Capito, Peter; 2 Oct. 1806; Juliana Keim   14 BA-420
Caples, Jacob; 27 March 1816; Mary Barrett   09 BA
Cappeau, Charles Anthony (lawful issue of Joseph Anthony Cappeauy
     and Ann Magdalenea Charmois [?]); 9 Sept. or Nov. 1814; Mary
     Michael Perdriole (lawful dau. of Michael Alexander
     Perdne[?] and Johanna Melanie Isnardy)   31 BA-184
Cappeau, Joseph; 27 June 1811; Sarah Galloway   11 BA-16
Carback, Elisha; 31 July 1806; Sarah Gardner   21 BA-6
Carback, John; 16 April 1812; Henny Maria Stansbury   09 BA
Carback, Stephen; 9 Feb., 1805; Elizabeth Smith   11 BA-5
Carbeck, Henry; 26 Nov. 1802; Isabella Greatson   06 BA-3
Carberry, John; 8 (?) Feb. 1816; Hannah Richmond   09 BA
Carey, John; 4 Sept. 1817; Elizabeth Cullen   17 BA-17
Carlen, Philip; 23 Dec. 1804; Sarah Willson   03 MO-119
Carlisle, David; 9 March 1813; Elizabeth Stackers   09 BA
Carlisle, James; 3 Jan. 1801; Betsy Forebaugh   14 BA-408
Carlsons, Neils; 22 Feb. 1820; Sophia Hanson   07 BA-312
Carlton, Thomas; 28 Oct. 1806; Mary Pittel (See also 15 FR-319)
                                                         01 FR-1118
Carman, Samuel; 22 Nov. 1804; Elizabeth Hughes (See also 40 BA)
                                                         17 BA-4
Carmer, Henry; 23 June 1808; Maria Banker   02 BA-6
Carmichael, Dougal; 5 Sept. 1801; Mary Jones   03 BA-420
Carmine, Thomas; 14 Nov. 1801; Rebecca Simmons   01 DO-40
Carney, Michael; 15 July 1816; Biddy M'Claskey   32 BA-310
Carnicomb, Jacob; May 1810; Cath. Bower   02 WA-87
Carns, John; 28 Oct. 1805; Mary Jordan   09 BA
Carns, John; 17 July 1817; Elizabeth Snow   02 BA-37
Carpenter, (?)ry; March 1808; Elis. Carpenter   02 WA-85
Carpenter, Allen; 18 March 1806; Sarah Cissell   02 SM-187
Carpenter, Isaac; 18 Dec. 1817; Reba. Willingmyer   13 BA-29
Carpenter, John; June 1818; Mary Eachus   02 WA-110
Carpenter, Nathaniel; 10 July 1807; Margaret Barnes   21 BA-6
Carpenter, Peter; 29 Jan. 1807; Nancy Pindle   09 BA
Carr, Benjamin; 4 Jan. 1803; Mary Denton   03 AA-120
Carr, Benjamin; 16 June 1805; Catherine Welsh   03 AA-130
Carr, Emanuel; 25 Jan. 1816; Mary Ann Reed   11 BA-26
Carr, George; 19 July 1812; Elizabeth Willain   09 BA
Carr, John; 20 Oct. 1801; Honor Bowlin   03 BA-409
Carr, John; 10 May 1804; Sarah Warfield   15 AA-3
Carr, John; 30 Dec. 1806; Mary Armiger   03 AA-130
Carr, John; 4 Sept. 1815; Ann Passiy   13 BA-22

Carr, John; 16 Nov. 1820; (N) Bird (Protestant girl who professed
    to become a Catholic)   05 FR-36
Carr, Joseph; 3 Feb. 1805; Jemimma Caldwell   09 BA
Carr, Jos.; 2 Oct. 1818; Mary Hush   13 BA-32
Carr, Richard; 9 Oct. 1804; Airey Busey   03 AA-130
Carr, Thadeus; 9 July 1810; Eleanor Adelspear   15 BA-281
Carr, Thomas; 27 Feb. 1806; Milcah Merryman   01 BA-10
Carr, William; 5 Jan. 1802; Eleanor Young   09 BA
Carr, William; 6 Feb. 1803; Sarah Murrey   05 HA-3
Carr, William; 13 April 1814; Catherine Austin   16 BA-4
Carr, William; 25 March 1817; Elizabeth Moore   17 BA-16
Carrington, John; 13 March 1814; Betsy Rodgers   11 BA-21
Carrison?, Aaron; 7 Dec. 1803; Henrietta Burton 05 AA-4
Carroll, Aquila; 23 Jan. 1806; Jemima Taylor   09 BA
Carroll, Aquila; 4 April 1816; Ruth Bowen   11 BA-30
Carroll, Benjamin; 15 Dec. 1815; Rachel Clarke   11 BA-25
Carroll, Daniel (of Duddington); 6 Oct. 1808; Ann Boyce
                                                 15 BA-265
Carroll, James, Jr.; 7 Nov. 1811; Achsah Ridgely 03 BA-503
Carroll, John; 30 Nov. 1800; Mary Duvall   15 AA-1
Carroll, John; 21 July 1808; Elizabeth Edwards   13 BA-4
Carroll, John; 13 July 1815; Lucretia Richardson 17 BA-11
Carroll, Matthew; 18 July 1816; Mary Burnett   17 BA-12
Carroll, Michael; 2 June 1820; Mary Connel   04 FR-19
Carroll, R'd; 21 Aug. 1813; Judith C. Riddell   03 BA-505
Carroll, Thomas; 10 Aug. 1809; Ann Cousins   05 BA-236
Carroll, Thomas; 18 Aug. 1812; Dorcas Dulaney (?) 31 BA-130
Carroll, Thos. Henry; 23 June 1814; Juliana Stephenson 03 BA-506
Carroll, William; Nov. 1806; Mary Hose   02 WA-81
Carroll, Wm.; 20 Dec. 1815; Rose McCormick   21 BA-8
Carroll, Wm. (of MO Co.); 16 Dec. 1811; Henrietta Maria
    Williamson   15 BA-294
Carson, Joseph; c.1804; Elizabeth Moore   34 BA-2
Carson, Nathaniel; 16 April 1801; Nancy Specknal 03 BA-399
Carson, Nehemiah; 23 Sept. 1806; Rachel Bull   09 BA
Carson, Robert; 7 Feb. 1805; Nancy Mackran   11 BA-5
Cart, George; 22 May 1801; Eliza Fisher   20 BA-410
Carter, Clement; 3 May 1810; Eliza Tittle   13 BA-9
Carter, Edmund; 1 Feb. 1816; Harriet Barnhart   11 BA-26
Carter, George; 13 June 1803; Alice Tapler   02 SM-186
Carter, Jeremiah (s. of Samuel and Ruth); 22 d, 1 mo., 1817;
    Susan Moore (dau. of Joseph and Mercy)   06 SF
Carter, John; 9 Feb. 1802; Ruth Gorsuch   09 BA
Carter, John; 19 June 1814; Elizabeth Ensor   08 BA
Carter, John; July 1816; Cath. Smith   02 WA-102
Carter, John; 24 Oct. 1820; Eliza Albright   13 BA-36
Carter, Noah; July 1820; Susanna Humrichhouse   02 WA-116
Carter, Peter; 26 May 1816; Ann Kemp   13 BA-25
Carter, R'd; 19 Sept. 1805; Mary Smith   03 BA-194
Carter, Solomon; 1 Dec. 1814; Rebecca Richards   09 BA
Carter, Thomas; 15 Dec. 1812; Nancy Jorden (15 FR-326 gives
    bride's name as Gorden)   01 FR-1118
Carter, Wm.; 25 Sept. 1814; Mary Pell   13 BA-19
Carter, William; 29 June 1815; Mary Wells   09 BA
Carter, Wm. B.; 10 March 1814; Cath. Stevenson   14 BA-432
Cartlet, Nathan; Nov. 1817; Sus. Hendricks   02 WA-107
Cartor, Abel; Sept. 1812; Mary Woolen   03 BA-504
Cartwright, Chas.; 22 April 1802; Mary Dorsey   14 BA-412
Carty, John; 26 Dec., 1802; Margaret Elward   05 BA-233
Carty, William P.; 5 March 1818; Henrietta Waller 06 FR-1328
Caruthers, George; 25 Aug. 1812; Jul. Evans   02 WA-95
Cary, Richard; 21 Oct. 1819; Sarah Togood   11 BA-29
Case, James; 26 Feb. 1807; Eliz. Bowman (See also 02 MO)
                                                 01 PG

```
Casedy, Benjamin; 1 Oct. 1803; Sarah Ravenscraft      03 AL-613
Casey, James; 16 March 1806; Mary Stewart             03 BA-495
Casey, John; 29 May 1802; Margaret Berry              03 BA-417
Casey, John; 15 Dec. 1804; Elizabeth Jane (02 BA-34 gives the
    bride's name as Elizabeth Zane)                   03 BA-492
Casey, John; 7 April 1812; Mary Vickers               13 BA-7
Casey, Rob't; 9 Nov. 1808; Elizabeth Hammond          03 BA-499
Cashell, George; 17 June 1804; Eliz. B. Edmonstone    03 MO-119
Caspari, Jacob; 22 April 1811; Harriet Lepner         07 BA-308
Cass, Otto; 7 May 1816; Elizab. Snyder                14 BA-435
Cassady, Daniel; 21 May 1809; Ann Roach               31 BA-60
Cassady, Francis; 12 April 1818; Mary Baker           11 BA-18
Cassard, Gilbert; 10 March 1811; Sarah Inloes         09 BA
Cassard, Lewis; 14 April 1811; Ann Trumbo             09 BA
Cassey, William; 16 March 1802; Mary Thompson         09 BA
Cassidy, Francis; 28 Sept. 1817; Martha Baker         11 BA-32
Cassidy, Patrick; 26 Aug. 1806; Mary Kilpatrick (both natives of
    Ireland)                                          15 BA-242
Casson, John; 25 July 1820; Caroline Hodskiss         17 BA-23
Castine, Francis; 14 July 1814; Elizabeth Linkins     05 BA-238
Castle, Joseph; 9 May 1802; Ann Matthews              06 BA-2
Castor, Fred.; Sept. 1810; Hannah Beard               02 WA-87
Castover, John; 23 Sept. 1801; Delia Brown            09 BA
Catchell, Clement; 11 March 1804; Matilda B. Mitchell 03 BA-493
Cateby, Richard; 16 Feb. 1804; Jane Silvey            17 BA-3
Catharel, Wm.; 13 Sept. 1807; Eliza Reese             03 BA-497
Cathcart, John; 19 Dec. 1805; Eleanor Hair            11 BA-7
Cathel, W.; 14 March 1814; J. (or S.) McDonald        20 BA-222
Cathell, Clement; 11 March 1805; Matilda B. Mitchel   02 BA-34
Cator, Joseph; 4 April 1805; Hannah Braughn           01 DO-41
Catts, George; 5 Nov. 1815; Letitia Paden             11 BA-24
Catts, Johh; 1 Sept. 18101 Frances Neal               05 BA-236
Caufman, Adam; 24 Feb. 1811; Mary Queen               06 FR-1315
Caufman, Jacob; Dec. 1816; Nancy Painter              02 WA-103
Caufman, James; March 1817; Nancy Palmer              02 WA-104
Caustin, Isaac; 1 Nov. 1812; Susanna Cassatt          11 BA-20
Cavenagh, Bernard; 16 April 1818; Ann McKenna         16 BA-66
Cavilly, Lewis (son of Agnana Cavilly and Clotilde Frare or Fore
    Cavilly, native of Port-au-Prince, St. Domingo); 17 June
    1809; Dorothy Mullen (dau. of Mich'l Mullen and Frances
    Gabrielle Thilliares [?])                         15 BA-169
Cawood, Bernard; 18 Nov. 1809; Ally Galloway          31 BA-70
Ceastel, Samuel; 22 March 1808; Elizab. Ceastel (See also 15 FR-
    322)                                              01 FR-1118
Cecil, Adam; 22 Oct. 1805; Sarah Tool (See also 15 FR-310)
                                                      01 FR-1118
Cel (y)?, Aubraie(?); 16 May 1809; Cecile Gaspar (?)  31 BA-60
Cerry, Benjamin; 24 Nov. 1816; Eliza Biggin           03 BA-508
Cesar, Francis; 20 Oct. 1817; Adele Jacque (both col'd)
                                                      16 BA-58
Cew (?), Jacob; Sept. 1802; Dorrothy Fautz            02 WA-73
Chabat(?), Gabriel; 27 Aug. 1810; Mary Gibbons        31 BA-89
Chaddick, Charles; 26 June 1806; Mary Harris          11 BA-8
Chaffe, Nathan M.; 21 April 1816; Matilda Griffith    09 BA
Chaille, Zachariah; 8 Jan. 1801; Hessy Matthews       01 SO-15
Chalmaneua, Charles Aug'n; 9 Feb. 1809; Ann Dashields 15 BA-268
Chalmers, David; 16 Oct. 1806; Mary Sparrow Clarke    03 BA-486
Chalmers, James; c.1802; Prudence Gough Holliday      10 AA-1
Chalmers, John M.; 5 Sept. 1815 (date of lic.?); Matilda
    Pickett                                           11 BA-26
Chalmers, Philemon; 21 July 1813; Cath. Flanigan      14 BA-432
Chalmers, Timothy; 2 Nov. 1805; Lucy Barton           03 BA-494
Chalmers, Timothy; 18 Feb. 1805; Jerusa Harlow        09 BA
```

Chalmers, W.; 10 Sept. 1811; Sarah Wilson   13 BA-13
Chamberlain, John; 4 Sept. 1806; Rebecka Spencer   03 Al-614
Chamberlaine, Henry; June 1815; Henrietta Eliz'th Gale 01 TA-312
Chamberlaine, James Lloyd; 14 May 1818; Anna Maria Hammond
          01 TA-312
Chamberlain, Thomas; 30 Dec. 1814; Ann Heller   06 FR-1321
Chamberlaine, Robert; 15 Oct. 1801; Kitty Blake (See also
    02 TA-73)   01 QA-43
Chamberlaine, Samuel; 24 Aug. 1814; Arianna Worthington Davis
          01 TA-312
Chamberlin, Philip; 9 May 1819; Eliza. Foster   11 BA-34
Chambers, Campbell; 15 Jan. 1807; Eliz. Clarkson   03 BA-496
Chambers, David; 22 April 1815; Sarah Gardener   03 BA-506
Chambers, Ezekiel F.; 11 Jan. 1817; Sarah Bowers (dau. of James
    and Sarah)   03 KE-13
Chambers, John; 13 Dec. 1801; Ruth Richards   06 BA-2
Chambers, John; March 1806; Mary Cook   02 WA-80
Chambers, Joseph; 19 April 1801; Susanna Weaver   03 BA-399
Chambers, Otho; Jan. 1817; Elizab. Garlinger   02 WA-104
Chambers, William; 15 Nov. 1801; Sarah York, als. Strong
          33 BA-13
Chambers, William (free black); 25 Jan. 1816; Mary Ann Williams
    (col'd slave of M. Devalcourt)   16 BA-31
Chamiller, Joseph; 16 July 1804; Mary Donnell   14 BA-417
Champayne, Henry; 16 Nov. 1819; Rachel Marriott   13 BA-41
Champlin, John; 14 July 1803; Fanny Fishwick   05 BA-234
Chandee, Thos.; 24 May 1810; Ann Park   13 BA-10
Chandler, George; 27 Feb. 1806; Elizabeth Donohue   14 BA-419
Chandler, Samuel V.; 26 May 1819; Harriot Trimble   17 BA-22
Chandley, Thomas; 18 July 1802; Elizabeth Wise   06 BA-2
Chanet(?), John; 4 April 1809; Catherine David McBride (?)
          31 BA-58
Chaney, Cornelius; 27 May 1802; Elizabeth Widderfield 03 BA-417
Chaney, Henry; 12 Dec. 1809; Sarah Crampton   11 BA-14
Chaney, Joseph; 2 March 1802; Sarah Chaney   15 AA-2
Chaney, Joseph; 10 Feb. 1803; Elizabeth Conner   15 AA-2
Chaney, Samuel; 27 Feb. 1806; Delia Everitt   09 BA
Chaney, William; 1804; Sarah Robberts   07 AA-4
Chapman, Job; 11 Jan. 1801; Ann Sykes (see also 01 BA-9)
          18 BA-65
Chapman, Richard; 26 March 1814; Sarah Worley   13 BA-18
Chappell, John G.; 17 July 1817; Rebecca M. Pitt   11 BA-31
Charles, Cannon (s. of Henry of DO Co., dec.); 20 Feb. 1817;
    Amelia Noble   07 SF-33
Charles, Christopher; 16 Oct. 1808; Elizabeth Martin 03 BA-498
Charles, Jacob (s. of Jacob and Eufemy); 22 d, 12 mo., 1802;
    Rachel Wilson (dau. of William and Hannah)   08 SF
Charles, Jean; 27 Nov. 1817; Mary Noel   16 BA-61
Charleys (?), John; 24 Feb. 1807; Sarah Carr   17 BA-6
Charlton, Benjamin; 11 March 1806; Mary Endler   08 AL-18
Chase, Basil; 23 Dec. 1802; Mary Everson   14 BA-413
Chase, John; 17 April 1815; Sophia Cheney   17 BA-11
Chase, Richard; 18 Jan. 1819; Mary Marriott   02 AA
Chase, Wells; 5 April 1814; Amelia Jamison   05 BA-238
Chatard, Peter, M. D. (son of Peter Chatard and Helene Joulain
    Dupuy, natives of Cap Francois, St. Domingo); 29 Dec. 1801;
    Jane Mary Frances Adelaide Boisson (dau. of John Thomas
    Boisson and Adelaide Cornu; native of Cap Francois)
          15 BA-161
Chatfield, Joseph; 3 Oct. 1804; Elizabeth Alderson (see also 02
    BA-34)   03 BA-491
Chattel, Samuel; 17 April 1804; Julia Delavet (02 BA-33 gives
    bride's name as Delivet)   03 BA-490
Chattles, John; 29 March 1816; Ann Fernandis   21 BA-8

Chayman, John; 9 July 1807; Sarah Chalmers   13 BA-2
Chaytor, Daniel; 4 March 1813; Sarah Sewell   17 BA-9
Chelsden, Walter; 17 Sept. 1812; Mary Ann Bond   13 BA-14
Chenoweth, Arthur; 4 April 1811; Anne Clark   03 BA-502
Chenoweth, Thos.; 18 April 1810; Deba. Buckman   13 BA-12
Cherelle, Pierre Louis; 20 (April?) 1815; Marie Claire Leveque
    (both col'd persons)   16 BA-18
Cherry, Edward L.; 23 Dec. 1818; Ann Server   09 BA
Chesley, John; 22 April 1806; Elizabeth Biscoe   02 SM-187
Chesley, John; 18 Feb. 1809; Elizabeth Forrester   31 BA-56
Chesney, Thos. E.; 4 July 1815; Rebecca Gamble   21 BA-8
Chesney, Thos. E.; 8 April 1819; Ann Slye   13 BA-32
Chesnut, Samuel; 8 Dec. 1806; Margaret M'Camel   14 BA-421
Chesnut, Thomas; 16 June 1808; Eliza Gilling   11 BA-12
Chester, Samuel; 16 May 1812; Lettice Rankeman   13 BA-7
Cheston, James; 1 June 1803; Mary Anne Hollingsworth   03 BA-428
Chevalier, Lewis E.; 25 Dec. 1814; Mary Murdock   17 BA-10
Chevanne, Jacques Marie Mareste; 11 Feb. 1804; (bride's name not
    given)   15 BA-199
Chevollan (?), Francis (of Island of Domingo); 15 Jan. 1810;
    Genevise Dela Rue (native of Cap Francois)   15 BA-281
Chids (?), William; 29 Dec., 1803; Rebecca Mays   23 BA-3
Chilcoat, John; 9 April 1815; Eliza. Ensor   13 BA-21
Child, Benjamin; 14 Jan. 1820; Esther Baily   37 BA-152
Child, William I.; 10 June 1819; Sarah Jane Wilson   09 BA
Childs, Cephas; 1812; Ann Clagett (See also 02 MO)   01 PG
Childs, Nathaniel; 14 June 1803; Ann Jessop   09 BA
Childs, Thomas; 11 Feb. 1802; Temperance Inloes   09 BA
Childs, Thomas B.; 30 Oct. 1817; Mary Leach   32 BA-316
China, John; 1 Aug. 1802; Elizabeth Dawson   03 AL-613
Chine, Lewis N.; 9 Jan. 1816; Mary Ann Elliott   17 BA-12
Chinoweth, John; 29 Oct. 1818; M'ry Bond   08 BA
Chittenden, Nathaniel; 16 March 1815; Harriet Smith   17 BA-10
Choat, Elias; 14 March 1811; Barbara Milliron   08 BA
Choate, Job; 13 Sept. 1808; Marg't Adams   03 BA-498
Christ, John; 9 June 1805; Cath. Umford (15 FR-317 gives groom's
    name as Johannes)   01 FR-1118
Christfield, Peregrine; 1 March 1818; Sarah McEntire   14 BA-437
Christhelf, Henry; 29 May 1817; Rachel Daties   13 BA-28
Christman, Frederick; 11 May 1810; Elizabeth Kister   08 AL-18
Christman, George; April 1820; Elizab. Bowers   02 WA-116
Christman, John; 3 Sept. 1805; Elizab. Weethers (15 FR-318 gives
    bride's name as Weathers)   01 FR-1118
Christoph, Edward; 28 Sept. 1807; Sarah Briscoe   08 AL-13
Christopher, Elijah; 10 Oct. 1803; Mary Osburn   14 BA-415
Christopher, James; 25 Aug. 1801; Jane Montgomery   03 BA-405
Christy, Edward; Aug. 1812; Maria Paterson   39 BA-28
Chunn, Charles; 28 April 1801; Jane A. Bowen   02 CH
Church, James; 3 Nov. 1803; Brittianuel (?) Bean   02 SM-186
Church, James; 10 May 1810; Jane Hall   13 BA-10
Church, Jno.; 10 Aug. 1811; Jane Church   14 BA-429
Churchman, Micajah (of BA, s. of Edward of Delaware Co., PA, and
    w. Rebecca); 20 d., 12 m., 1815; Eliza Sinclair (of Balto.
    Town, dau. of John and Elizabeth)   12 SF-47
Churrington, William; 28 May 1803; Margaret Davis   03 BA-428
Chuster, Neal; 22 Nov. 1807; Pegg Bell   11 BA-11
Cindle, Anton; 17 Feb. 1818; Eliz'th Knight   17 BA-19
Ciruel (?), Ludwig; Aug. 1802; Menzi Colwin   02 WA-73
Cissell, Thomas; 3 Feb. 1803; Sarah Hammett   02 SM-186
Clackner, Frederic; 10 April 1811; Elizabe Waddington 03 BA-502
Clackner, Frederick; 14 Feb. 1802; Sarah Cole   03 BA-413
Clackner, Joseph; 18 Jan. 1806; Rebecca Travers   14 BA-419
Clagett, David; 17 Feb. 1801; Sally Odle   03 MO-117
Clagett, Thos.; 12 Jan. 18902; Rachel Offut   03 MO-118

```
Claggett, Amian; 6 Sept. 1804; Margaret Burgess        03 MO-119
Claggett, Eli; 21 Jan. 1816; Mary Grant                13 BA-24
Claggett, Thos. John; 1811; Sophia Martin (See also 02 MO)
                                                       01 PG
Clair, Isaac; 2 April 1809; Mary Lynch                 02 BA-7
Claperton, Jno.; 29 Nov. 1817; Frances Ann Toysen      14 BA-436
Clapp, Enoch; 11 June 1812; Mary Tyson                 13 BA-9
Clapp, Stephen; 10 Aug. 1801; Tamer Fowler             09 BA
Clapsaddle, Jacob; Feb. 1817; Mary Redenauer           02 WA-104
Clapsattle, Jacob; 5 Nov. 1812; Elizab. Brooke         02 WA-95
Clare, John; 4 May 1815; Sarah Wood                    17 BA-11
Claridge, Levin; 31 Dec. 1802; Cath. McDowel           14 BA-414
Claridge, Levin; 25 April 1816; Ann Kilman             17 BA-12
Claridge, Solomon; 27 June 1806; Elizabeth Barnet      02 BA-4
Clark, Augustus; 29 Jan. 1818; Susanna Whiteford       32 BA-318
Clark, Barney; Sept. 1813; Mary Figeley                02 WA-98
Clark, Chancy; 26 Feb. 1819; Cathe. Snowden            13 BA-34
Clark, George; 21 March 1811; Ann Susanna Cobb         15 BA-285
Clark, George; 11 or 12 Aug. 1813; Margaret Joy        31 BA-155
Clark, James; 24 Oct. 1819; Maria Goff                 04 FR-19
Clark, John; 13 Nov. 1806; Martha Thomas               09 BA
Clark, John; 30 Sept. 1817; Agnes Clark (of Great Britain)
                                                       02 BA-37
Clark, John; 29 Oct. 1818; Margaret Humphreys          03 BA-603
Clark, John; 21 Dec. 1820; Jane D. Nichols             19 BA-73
Clark, Joseph; 2 Nov. 1805; Elizab. Rusk               14 BA-419
Clark, Jos.; 19 May 1814; Clarissa Scott               13 BA-19
Clark, Joseph, Jr.; 11 June 1809; Mary Ann Faure       02 BA-7
Clark, Matthew; 13 Nov. 1802; Jennett Flemming         09 BA
Clark, Matthew; Dec. 1818; Rebecca Marg't. Reidenauer  02 WA-111
Clark, Nelson; 4 Aug. 1818; Lucretia E. Thomas         09 BA
Clark, Nicholas; 10 June 1804; Amelia Hall (02 BA-34 give date as
   9 June 1804)                                        03 BA-491
Clark, Patrick; 3 Oct. 1803; Betsy Canary              14 BA-415
Clark, Richard; 30 Nov. 1806; Mary Wells               03 AL-614
Clark, Robert; 4 Jan. 1811; Eliza Lairimore            03 AL-614
Clark, Samuel; 25 June 1801; Mary Anderson             27 BA-1
Clark, William; 1 Nov. 18(?); Elizabeth Abell          01 SM-64
Clarke, Alexander; 4 July 1815; Cassandra Wills        17 BA-11
Clarke, Alfred; 28 Dec. 1806; Ruth Wilson              03 BA-496
Clarke, Andrew; 6 May 1813; Sarah McDugals             14 BA-432
Clarke, Benjamin; 27 March 1820; Massey B. Cooke       17 BA-22
Clarke, Cuthbert; 20 March 1804; Mary Loker            02 SM-186
Clarke, George; 17 Jan., 18(?); Barbary Flower         01 SM-64
Clarke, George Wash.; Sept. 1816; Amelia Jane Hughes   02 WA-102
Clarke, Hooper; 13 June 1811; Rebecca Ingram           11 BA-16
Clarke, Hooper; 14 May 1816; Elizabeth Speake          16 BA-36
Clarke, James; 14 July 1810; Sarah Leaves              03 BA-501
Clarke, James; 23 July 1811; Delade Legrant            09 BA
Clarke, James; 18 July 1816; Elizabeth Herring         02 BA-37
Clarke, John; 12 April 1804; Mary Evans                02 SM-186
Clarke, Joseph; 24 May 1803; Sarah Langley             02 SM-186
Clarke, Joseph; 11 Jan. 1807; Elizabeth Lyon           11 BA-10
Clarke, Joseph; 23 April 1814; Susannah Silence        05 BA-238
Clarke, Thomas; 3 April 1810; Jane Crawford            03 BA-501
Clarke, Zedock; 17 Aug. 1806; Nancy Endler             08 AL-19
Clasly, William A.; 12 Oct. 1819; Eliza. Linthicum     11 BA-37
Classen, Jno.; 10 Oct. 1801; Milda Abell               14 BA-410
Classen, John; 6 Aug. 1806; Elizabeth Gallispey        02 BA-4
Claxton, Abraham (Commanding Lieutenant of the Navy); 27 May
   1819; Joanna Elizabeth Christine Marie Laval         16 BA-82
Clay, George; 18 May 1815; Mary Ann Grove              06 FR-1322
Clayton, Samuel; 24 June 1819; Hannah O'Hara           21 BA-9
Clayton, Samuel C.; 28 Oct. 1816; Eliza W. Thompson    17 BA-15
```

Clayton, Walter I.; 27 June 1812; Sarah Hackett of QA Co.
                                                    03 KE-14
Cleamens, John; 4 Aug. 1815; Elizabeth Winged   13 BA-22
Clean (or Dean), Richard; 2 July 1816; Mary Wolf   13 BA-25
Cleary, Michael; 25 July 1818; Bridget Harkins   16 BA-71
Clein (or Hein), Jacob; Aug. 1802; Hanna Protzman   02 WA-74
Clem, Adam; 3 Sept. 1811; Mary Morningstar   06 FR-1316
Clem, Jacob; 1 Jan. 1815; Eve Morningstar   06 FR-1321
Clemens, Hezekiah; 15 Nov. 1815; Jenny Brown   02 WA-100
Clement, Joseph R.,; 17 April 1804; Mary Levering   09 BA
Clements, Nicholas; 7 Sept. 1801; Elizabeth Musser 10 BA-1
Clemm, John; 8 Aug. 1810; M. Eichelberger   30 BA-109
Clemm, William; 12 July 1817; Maria Poe   03 BA-602
Clemm, William, Jr.; 1 May 1804; Harriet Poe   05 BA-234
Clemstead, Jabed; 11 Sept. 1804; Sarah Kelly (see also 02 BA-
     34)   03 BA-491
Clervana, Thomas; 23 Dec. [prob. 1814 as this is the last entry
     of the year 1814] "1815;" Clare Carter (both free col'd)
                                                    16 BA-14
Clevinger, Geo.; 30 April 1820; Marg't Elliott   13 BA-35
Clifford, Nathaniel H.; 25 July 1816; Sarah Eamorison [sic]
                                                    02 BA-37
Clift, George; 7 April 1810; Elizh. Hines   13 BA-12
Clifton, Arthur; 1 Jan. 1818; Elizabeth Ringgold   16 BA-62
Clifton, Nathan; 12 Feb. 1804; Anny Wright   07 AL-274
Clifton, Nathan; 12 Feb. 1804; Amy Wright (See also 10 AL)
                                                    04 AL-2
Cline, Christian; 19 May 1805; Martha Henry   09 BA
Cline, George; 7 Dec. 1809; Nancy Lawrence   13 BA-8
Clingman, John; 17 March 1803; Sarah Richardson   34 BA-1
Clites, John; 23 Feb. 1812; Christina Reitz   08 AL-20
Clouse, Henry; 9 March 1806; Sarah Fazenbaker   03 AL-614
Clovis, Math.; Dec. 1808; Nancy Bear   02 WA-86
Clunet, John Baptist; 28 Feb. 1810; Aimee Lannay   03 BA-501
Co(?), William; 24 Aug. 1804; Margery Noble (both of Talbot
     Co.)   02 TA-39
Coack, Friederich; 1 Sept. 1809; Elisabeth Scharding or
     Schaneling   07 BA-307
Coad, Joseph; 10 Feb. 1803; Ann Dillaha   02 SM-186
Coale, Daniel; 13 Feb. 1817; Catharine Hagan   21 BA-8
Coale, Selah; 18 Jan. 1810; Sarah Volentine   09 BA
Coale, Skipworth (s. of Samuel and Lydia of HA Co., MD); 17 d. 7
     mo., 1806; Anne Matthews (dau. of George and Sarah)
                                                    09 SF
Coale, Skipwith (H.?); 29 Jan. 1818; Eliza Dugan   03 BA-602
Coale, Thomas; 13 Jan. 1803; Nancy Berry   15 AA-2
Coale, Vincent; 26 May 1801; Eleanor Stewart (See also 15 FR-311)
                                                    01 FR-1118
Coale, William (s. of Samuel and Lydia [Pusey] Coale); 21 d, 6
     mo., 1804; Anna Talbot (dau. of Joseph and Anna) 03 SF
Coats, John; 10 Jan. 1819; Martha Ann Stocksdale   11 BA-33
Cobb, George; 26 Sept. 1816; Harriet Barnes   09 BA
Cobb, Sam'l; 28 July 1812; Eleanor Neale   03 BA-504
Coblentz, Dr. Jacob (s. of Mayor Coblentz); 25 Nov. 1819; Melinda
     Staley   16 FR-75
Coblentz, John; 20 April 1820; Elizabeth Wile   16 FR-76
Coblentz, Philip; 29 March 1803; Elizab. Zimmerman (See also
     15 FR-314)   01 FR-1118
Cobreth, Hezekiah; 14 March 1819; Sarah Surday   13 BA-32
Cochran, Charles; 1 Aug. 1807; Araminta Jackson   03 BA-497
Cochran, Robert; 7 April 1812; Mrs. Margaret Cox   06 FR-1317
Cochran, Robert; 21 Sept. 1816; Mary Ann Prucy   05 BA-239
Cochran, Spencer; 25 April 1811; Mary Giles   06 FR-1315
Cochran, William; 20 Dec. 1804; Deborah Adams   03 BA-492

```
Cochran, William A.; 27 Jan. 1816; Nancy McClellan      20 BA-222
Cockayne, James (s. of Thomas, dec., and Sarah); 19 d,  5 mo.,
    1814; Sarah Dawson (dau. of Elias, of Phila., and Elizabeth)
                                                        08 SF
Cockey, John; 22 July 1802; Ann Beck                    14 BA-413
Cockey, John C.; 6 June 1818; Maria Hoopert             07 BA-311
Cockey, Lewis; 16 July 1812; Helen Dye Wyle             11 BA-19
Cockey, Thomas B.; 9 April 1816; Mary Ann Worthingon    18 BA-66
Cockey, Thomas B.; 10 April 1818; Mary Ann Worthington  11 BA-28
Cockran, Wm. G.; 16 April 1805; Susan McCannon          11 BA-5
Cockrell, Thomas, 22 March 1810; Rebecca Veazey         17 BA-8
Cockshot, Arthur R.; 7 Dec. 1819; Margaret Hook         03 BA-604
Codd, George; 5 Sept. 1802; Mary Kelly                  03 BA-420
Codd, William; 29 March 1810; Ann Tracey                09 BA
Coffield, Henry; 6 Jan. 1820; Bridget Murray            16 BA-96
Coffin, Christopher; 13 Jan. 1817; Mary Morris          17 BA-16
Coffman, Philip; 17 Oct. 1802; Hiccabud Thrift          33 BA-15
Cofroth, William; July 1817; Elizab. Wood               02 WA-105
Coile, Richard; 8 Aug. 1802; Margaret O'Driscoll        03 BA-419
Colbert, Lewin; 15 Jan. 1817; Rebecca Kelly             11 BA-31
Cole, Elza [sic]; 13 April 1815; Mary Simpers           09 BA
Cole, Frederick; 1 March 1818; Rebecca Moran            09 BA
Cole, John; 3 Oct. 1809; Elizabeth Guyther              02 SM-188
Cole, John; 21 Nov. 1816; Susan Wheeler                 11 BA-27
Cole, John; 14 Sept. 1819; Sally Ann Williams           03 BA-604
Cole, Joshua; 12 June 1804; Arey Tipton                 23 BA-3
Cole, Richard; 1 Oct. 1801; Mary Lewis                  09 BA
Cole, Samuel; 14 Feb. 1803; Elizabeth Ninde             03 BA-425
Cole, Samuel; 21 June 1812; Susannah Boston             11 BA-20
Cole, Thos.; 27 June 1802; Ann Fisher                   14 BA-413
Cole, Thomas; 21 Dec. 1809; Ann Taylor                  02 SM-188
Cole, Thomas R.; 22 Sept. 1818; Rachel Barrett          21 BA-9
Cole, William; 2 April 1802; Isabella Salmon            03 BA-415
Cole, Wm.; 21 Jan. 1813; Elizab. Clarke                 14 BA-431
Cole, William; 15 Dec. 1816; Susan Nicoll               03 BA-508
Colehaus, L.; 2 Aug. 1810; A. Geihus                    30 BA-109
Coleman, Gouldsbury; 22 Dec. 1818; Mary Jackson         17 BA-18
Coleman, John; 31 July 1806; Mary Joiner                02 BA-4
Coleman, Philip; 4 Oct. 1808; Judith McAffrey als. Finn
                                                        15 BA-265
Colesee, John; 13 Aug. 1808; Rebec. Schwartz            13 BA-4
Coley, Edw'd; 8 June 1815; Mary Ann Vance               13 BA-21
Collard (?), Peter (age 23, s. of Peter and Mary); 19 May 1806;
    Elizabeth Butler (age 23, dau. of Joseph and Mary)
                                                        31 BA-7
Collenberger, Philip; 2 Oct. 1817; Sarah Brooks         09 BA
Collier, Thomas; Feb. 1818; Sarah Welsh                 02 WA-108
Collette, Andrew; 29 Oct. 1815; Mary Coursey            32 BA-305
Colliflower, Peter; 24 Sept. 1811; Mary Hoover          02 WA-91
Collings, William; 2 April 1819; Malinda Royston        17 BA-21
Collins, Ben'n.; 18 June 1816; Martha Hinson            13 BA-24
Collins, George; 25 Nov. 1802; Charity Stansbury        03 BA-423
Collins, George; 23 Dec. 1804; Mary Thompson            03 BA-492
Collins, George; 8 Aug. 1816; Eliza Pickower            03 BA-507
Collins, Henry; 16 March 1802; Wealthy Thompson         03 BA-415
Collins, John; 23 Dec. 1819; Mary Rollins               13 BA-41
Collins, Jos.; 14 March 1816; Ann Reed                  13 BA-24
Collins, Josias; 8 Nov. 1814; Easy Perk                 13 BA-20
Collins, Michael; 20 Nov. 1819; Sally Nichols           16 BA-91
Collins, Richard; 1 Jan. 1811; Betsy Farden             13 BA-11
Collins, Thomas; 12 Jan. 1812; Sarah Ramsey             11 BA-19
Collins, William; 9 April 1803; Elizabeth Williams      34 BA-1
Collins, William; 22 Oct. 1818; Sarah Parson            11 BA-33
Collins, William; 30 June 1819; Susanna Sherry          17 BA-22
```

```
Collior, William; Feb. 1804; Elis. Heckman            02 WA-74
Collupy (?), William; 2 Jan. 1811; Mary Fitzpatrick   31 BA-94
Colman, Edward; 16 July 1818; Julia Ann Chatterton    17 BA-19
Colmus, Levin; 19 May 1812; Frans. Williams           13 BA-7
Colquhorne, Charles W.; 21 Sept. 1818; Ann Long       03 BA-603
Colson, Levin; 11 Feb. 1802; Sarah Moore              01 DO-40
Colsten, Levin; 29 Nov. 1804; Nancy Porter            01 DO-41
Colston, Levin; 17 Nov. 1818; Ann McFall              02 DO
Colt, Roswell L.; 5 Oct. 1811; Margaret Oliver        05 BA-237
Colvin, John B.; 4 May 1801; Adelina Stewart          21 BA-4
Colwell, Thomas; 1 Oct. 1817; Ellen Po (?)            17 BA-14
Comad, Aquila; 26 March 1818; M. Robison              30 BA-109
Combs, James; 25 July 1804; Ann Farrill (See also 40 BA)
                                                      17 BA-4
Combs, John; 30 April 1816; Basheba Drake             08 AL-21
Combs, Thomas; 12 Feb. 1801; Ann Bahon                15 BA-149
Combs, William; 18 Jan. 1801; Rebecca Price           02 SM-184
Comcy (or Cosin?), Joseph; 20 Aug. 1815; Barbara Keller
                                                      14 BA-434
Comegys, Bartus; 13 Oct. 1818; Eveline Dorsey         19 BA-72
Comegys, Benja.; 16 Jan. 1808; Mary Beck              03 BA-498
Comegys, Cornelius; 1 July 1809; Mary Mayner          11 BA-14
Comegys, William (s. of Cornelius and Elizzbeth, both dec.); 20
    d. 9 mo., 1810; Elizabeth Kinsey (dau. of James Mason and
    Rachel)                                           09 SF
Comphher, Peter; 26 March 1816; Margareth Compher     06 FR-1324
Compton, John; 12 April 1804; Mary Jackson            36 BA-2
Conaway, Addison; 5 Jan. 1804; Eleanor Hyatt          15 AA-3
Conaway, Charles; 23 July 1801; Elizabeth Rummels     15 AA-1
Cone(?) (or Care?), William R.; 1 July 1819; Eliza Maxwell
                                                      20 BA-224
Conely, Thomas; 26 May 1801; Anne Lawler (both natives of
    Ireland)                                          15 BA-152
Confrance, Peter; 18 Nov. 1816; Mary Antoinette Bouguin
                                                      32 BA-311
Conn, Curtis; 25 Sept. 1817; Eliza Seixas (The groom ackn. that
    the following children were begoten by him of Eliza Seixas:
    Mary MAtilda, age 8; Julia Sophia, 7; Richard Anthony, 5;
    William Alexander, 3; and Elisa Ann)             32 BA-315
Conn, Jacob; 15 Aug. 1809; Jane McGlashen             14 BA-226
Conn, James; 5 Feb. 1818; Elleanor Warner             20 BA-223
Connell, Daniel; 23 July 1801; Mary Roberts           15 BA-103
Connell, Daniel; 23 July 1801; Mary Roberts           15 BA-154
Connelly, John; 7 Jan. 1804; Bridget Whelan           15 BA-196
Connelly, Michael; 16 Sept. 1817; Arsain Apollo       06 FR-1327
Connelly, Thomas; 7 June 1804; Mary Weeks             15 BA-203
Conner, Gabrael; Jan. 1818; Mary Reidenauer           02 WA-108
Conner, John; 20 Sept. 1810; Hannah Norris            09 BA
Conner, Richard; 22 May 1820; Esther Albert           06 FR-1331
Conner, Thomas; 2 June 1816; Catherine Dadisman       06 FR-1324
Conner, William; 26 March 1801; Elizabeth West        11 BA-2
Connolly, Henry; 11 June 1801; Sarah Vernum (See also 02 TA-72)
                                                      01 QA-43
Connolly, Michael (widower); 23 Nov. 1813; Mary Reilly (widow)
                                                      15 BA-319
Connolly, William; 22 Aug. 1801; Polly Jackson        01 QA-43
Conolly, William; 22 Aug. 1801; Polly Jackson         03 TA-73
Conoway, John; 25 Oct. 1804; Margery Jordan           09 BA
Conrad, Jno. C.; 31 Dec. 1801; Cath. Steinbeck        14 BA-411
Conrad, Jacob; 5 May 1805; Elizab. Steiner            01 FR-1118
Conrad, James (late of Trinidad); 30 Sept. 1811; Margaret
    Connelly (of New York)                            15 BA-291
Conrad, Jacob; 5 May 1805; Elisabeth Steiner          15 FR-317
Conrad, Theophllus; 8 Dec. 1818; Eunice Morgan        06 FR-1329
```

Conradt, George M.; 2 Nov. 1819; Margareth Fessler   06 FR-1330
Conry, James; Feb. 1803; Henlines Duikes   02 WA-74
Constable, George; 20 Feb. 1814; Sarah Miller   09 BA
Conway, Richard; 5 May 1804; Elizabeth Forman   09 BA
Conway, Robert; 10 Feb. 1803; Sarah McLane   15 BA-177
Conway, Robert; 19 Oct. 1809; Mary Langdon   31 BA-69
Conway, Thomas A.; 26 Jan. 1820; Catherine Rickard   11 BA-37
Conway, William D.; 10 Feb. 1811; Sarah Maltsby   31 BA-97
Conwell, Rezin; March 1812; Nancy Gaines   02 WA-93
Cooch, Zebulon H.; 22 Dec. 1818; Ann Maria Heide   09 BA
Coock, Georg; 23 Sept. 1806; Rebecca Schrein   07 BA-305
Cook, Andrew; 20 Feb. 1816 or 1817; Elizabeth Carr   08 BA
Cook, Caleb; 5 Sept. 1818; Ann Swarin or Swann   11 BA-29
Cook, Dolanson; 11 June 1801; Ann Wherrett   02 SM-185
Cook, Elisha (son of Samuel and Ruth); 18 d, 1 mo., 1804; Lydia
    Pusey (dau. of George and Sarah)   03 SF
Cook (or Koch), Henry; 14 July 1809; Dorothea Dailin   14 BA-426
Cook, Henry; 14 April 1810; Patty Ross (slaves)   05 BA-236
Cook, Jacob; 17 Aug. 1809; Catharine Stubblefield   08 AL-20
Cook, James; 23 Nov. 1805; Sarah Bryan (names appear on list of
    marr. for blacks)   17 BA-5
Cook, James; 5 Feb. 1809; Nancy Constant   08 BA
Cook, Joannes; 6 Feb. 1814; Maria [Weyman]   39 BA-30
Cook, Thomas; 3 Oct. 1805; Eliza Everson   03 BA-494
Cook, Thomas; 23 Dec. 1819; Mary Rankin   11 BA-37
Cook, William (s. of Samuel and Ruth, both dec., of Warrington
    Twp., York Co., PA); 29 d, 11 mo., 1802; Hannah Cutler (dau.
    of Benjamin, dec., and Susannah of Little Britain Twp.,
    Lancaster Co., PA)   06 SF
Cook, William; 16 May 1804; Rebecca Weary (see also 02 BA-33)
                                                        03 BA-490
Cook, William; 24 Oct. 1816; Elizabeth Stansbury   09 BA
Cook, William; 21 Nov. 1819; Ann Biddison   09 BA
Cook, William Isaac (bel. to Robert Walsh); 22 Oct. 1812; Delia
    Powell (bel. to Mr. [?])   15 BA-317
Cooke, George; 21 June 1814; Eller. A. Dall   03 BA-506
Cooke, James; 30 Jan. 1802; Patsy Beeding   03 MO-118
Cooke, John; 30 July 1801; Elizabeth Hinton   15 AA-1
Cooke, John; 23 Dec. 1802; Deborah Hoper [sic]   15 AA-2
Cooke, William; 24 Jan. 1811; Rachel Jones   09 BA
Cookerly, Jacob; 28 March 1820; Sarah Herring   16 FR-76
Cookes, Thos.; 27 Aug. 1818; Ann A. Rose   13 BA-31
Cooley, William; 12 Aug. 1816; Jane Robertson   17 BA-15
Coombes, James; 20 Sept. 1820; Mary Ann Bedford (both slaves;
    marr. with permission of their master, Mr. Gunn)   16 BA-104
Coomes, James; 18 April 1811; Marg't McGlaughlin   03 BA-502
Cooney, Patrick; 1 Nov. 1810; Bridget Costello   31 BA-92
Cooper, Edward; 20 July 1815; Prudence Summerfield   17 BA-13
Cooper, Edward Oakes; 7 March 1816; Mary Bishop   32 BA-307
Cooper, Isaac; 29 Oct. 1816; Matilda Good   16 BA-94
Cooper, James; 24 May 1810; Margaret Anderson   17 BA-8
Cooper, Jno.; 21 Nov. 1803; Cath. Heidelback   14 BA-415
Cooper, John; 25 March 1813; Eliza Wise   13 BA-16
Cooper, John; 23 May 1820; Elizabeth Durham   13 BA-41
Cooper, John M.; 11 Dec. 1806; Ann B. Deaver   11 BA-10
Cooper, Thomas; 6 Dec. 1805; Catherine West   02 BA-2
Cooper, Thomas; 11 Feb. 1813; Elizabeth Southcomb (?)   17 BA-9
Cooper, Wills; 10 Aug. 1809; Catherine Sitler   13 BA-8
Cootee, James; 1806; Betsy Holland (both of Dorset [sic] Co.)
                                                        02 TA-40
Copau, Jean Bernard; 29 Sept. 1812; Maria Francois (both col'd
    from St. Domingo)   15 BA-304

Cope, Jacob (s. of David and Margaret of West Nottingham Twp.,
    Chester Co., PA); 13 d, 6 mo., 1805; Mary Pugh (dau. of John
    and Rachel, dec., of East Notingham Twp., Chester Co., PA)
                                                          06 SF
Copenhaven, Abraham; 8 June 1811; Cassander Wright   11 BA-16
Copper, Thomas; 18 May 1806; Mary Peers   02 BA-3
Corberley, John R.; 23 Jan. 1819; Emerenliana Vincendiere
                                                          04 FR-18
Corbman, Christ.; 30 Aug. 1807; Harriet Tannehill (See also
    15 FR-321)   01 FR-1118
Corbus, Andrew; 26 Jan. 1806; Lydia Taylor   03 AL-613
Corbus, John; 13 March 1804; Elizabeth Trollinger   03 AL-613
Corbus, Michael; 7 Feb. 1805; Mary Tuttle   03 AL-613
Cordery, Shepherd; 2 Feb. 1806; Eliza Kiles   03 AL-613
Cordray, Henry; Sept. 1812; Elizabeth Furlong   03 BA-504
Cornelius, Nicholas; 15 Sept. 1801; Susannah Shane   27 BA-1
Cornish, Edward; 30 June 1816; Betsy Steward   17 BA-13
Cornthwait, John (s. of John and Mary, both dec.); 19 d. 11 mo.,
    1807; Elizabeth Wilson (dau. of David and Jane)   09 SF
Cornthwait, Robert (s. of John and Mary); 3rd d., 1 mo., 1805;
    Aliceanna Wilson (dau. of John and Aliceanna)   11 SF-90
Cornthwait, Thomas; 8 Nov. 1810; Eliza Tharp   09 BA
Corntwhait, William (s. of Robert, dec., and Grace); 18 d. 12
    mo., 1806; Ann Hill (dau. of John and Ann, dec.)   09 SF
Cornwall, Arthur; 9 July 1820; Eliza Knight   17 BA-23
Cornwell, Jos. H.; 26 April 1818; Marg't Parrish   13 BA-30
Corum, James; 21 Feb. 1814; Celia Simmons   01 SM-64
Cosar, Louis; 14 Jan. 1816; Mary (both free blacks from St.
    Domingo)   16 BA-48
Cost, Daniel; 5 April 1801; Mary Fisher   09 BA
Cost, John; 26 Sept. 1811; Benedicta Garrett   06 FR-1316
Cost, Joseph B.; 10 May 1801; Nancy Bentle   3 BA-400
Costello, James I.; 17 Aug. 1815 (date of lic.?); Ann Bull
                                                          11 BA-26
Costigan, Michael; 7 April 1801; Mary Webster   15 BA-150
Costor, Jno. H.; 1 Aug. 1801; Sukey Burley   22 BA-410
Coswell, John; 13 April 1817; Sarah Beete   17 BA-16
Cother, John; 20 Oct. 1807; Elizabeth Brotemarkle   08 AL-21
Cotimore, Richard; 4 April 1816; Nancy Hodgers   03 BA-507
Cottom, Richard; 29 May 1815; Charlotte M. Cochrane   03 BA-506
Couch, Mat.; 18 June 1810; Temperance Deaver   13 BA-12
Coucly, Martin; 31 March 1811; Mary Faherty   15 BA-286
Cough, George; Aug. 1802; Mary Shusst   02 WA-73
Cough, Mat.; 18 June 1810; Temperance Deaver   13 BA-12
Coulson, Patrick; 28 May 1807; Elizabeth LeCount   11 BA-11
Coulson, William; 9 June 1807; Hannah Underwood   05 BA-235
Coulte(?), Henry; 23 Sept. 1802; Anne Clark   05 AA-2
Coulter, David; 1 April 1808; Hannah Relley   09 BA
Coulter, George; 16 July 1819; Isabella McNay   11 BA-35
Coulter, John; 25 Jan. 1820; Deborah Bartleson   20 BA-224
Coulter, Samuel; 7 May 1807; Sarah Parker   13 BA-2
Coulter, William; 7 Aug. 1806; Sarah Humphreys   05 BA-235
Councilman, Jacob; 1 Nov. 1804; Elizabeth Flinn   09 BA
Coupe, Peter; 29 Nov. 1819; Antoinette Gores   16 BA-93
Courcier, Joannes; 13 Jan. 1813; Maria Redgrave   39 BA-28
Coursey, Edward H.; 25 Dec. 1814; Winifred Allen   17 BA-10
Coursey, Henry; 11 Sept. 1803; Helen Murphy (both of Queenstown,
    QA Co.) (See also 02 TA-38)   01 QA-52
Coursey, Isaac; 2 Aug. 1802; Sophia Hipkins   11 BA-3
Courtenay, Henry; 20 Feb.1811; Elizabeth Isabelle Purviance
                                                          05 BA-236
Courtenay, Mathew W.; 30 Nov. 1815; Susan Knott   16 BA-28
Courtnay, William; 14 March 1815; Hannah Maria Weatherburn
                                                          03 BA-506

```
Courtney, Patrick; 10 Jan. 1819; Mary Cane              16 BA-79
Courts, Searson; 19 Nov. 1808; Mary Hoss               14 BA-425
Cously, William; April 1805; Thobitha Lucas            02 WA-78
Coventry, John; 21 Feb. 1808; Amelia Phillips (See also
    15 FR-322)                                         01 FR-1118
Coward, William; 10 Oct. 1801; Ann Baker               09 BA
Cowles, William; 1 March 1814; Margaret Hall           05 BA-237
Cowling, William; 15 March 1810; Ann Kennedy           11 BA-15
Cowman, Gerard (son of Joseph and Mary [Snowden]); 21 d, 3 mo.,
    1816; Elizabeth Wright Poultney (widow of Samuel Poultney,
    and dau. of Joel and Elizabeth [Farquhar] Wright) 03 SF
Cowman, Philip; 18 Dec. 1806; Eliza Shields            03 AA-130
Cox, Benjamin; 2 Aug. 1801; Elizabeth Ants             09 BA
Cox, Daniel (s. of Isaac and Lydia); 23 d, 5 mo., 1811; Ann
    Needles (dau. of William and Elizabeth)            08 SF
Cox, Edmund; 16 June 1805; Eleanor Bond                02 SM-186
Cox, Ephraim; 2 Dc. 1802; Elizabeth Wilson             33 BA-16
Cox, Geo.; 8 Oct. 1812; Eliza C. Hopkins               13 BA-15
Cox, George (son of William and Rachel); 23 d, 1 mo., 1816; Sarah
    Roberts (dau. of John and Rebecca)                 03 SF
Cox, Isaac; 15 Jan. 1820; Ellen Jones                  11 BA-36
Cox, James (age c.30, s. of George and Mary [Stacks] Cox); 15
    Aug. 1801; Mary Redgel (age c.21, dau. of Thomas and
    Anastasia [Micholy] Redgel)                        03 SM
Cox, James; 1804; Eliza Nowell                         13 AA-2
Cox, Jesse; 30 Oct. 1818; Cath. Zieg                   14 BA-438
Cox, John; 25 Jan. 1803; Susanna Gill                  23 BA-2
Cox, John; 10 Aug. 1807; Elizabeth Johns               03 BA-497
Cox, Jonathan; 11 April 1815; Elizabeth Kelly          09 BA
Cox, Jonathan (s. of Joseph and Mary of Upper Proovidence Twp.,
    Montgomery Co., PA); 11 d, 6 mo., 1818; Hannah J. Tyson
    (dau. of Jonathan and Rachel of East Nottingham Hund., CE
    Co.)                                               06 SF
Cox, Joseph; 21 Sept. 1802; Susanna Hogan              03 MO-118
Cox, Joseph; 21 Oct. 1802; Christy Gould               14 BA-413
Cox, Joshua; 26 Aug. 1812; Ann Bailey                  13 BA-17
Cox, Larkin; 9 May 1811; Jane Hardenbrook              09 BA
Cox, Peter; 1 Feb. 1807; Margaret Minchin              15 BA-246
Cox, Samuel; 9 Oct. 1806; Ann Wilson (See also 15 FR-319)
                                                       01 FR-1118
Cox, Samuel; 10 Aug. 1819; Harriet Moore               20 BA-224
Cox, Thos.; 13 Dec. 1803 (CV Co.); Eleanor Strickland  40 BA
Cox, Thomas; 15 May 1817; Eliza Crow                   11 BA-31
Cox, William (son of William and Rachel); 17 day, 11 mo. 1802;
    Ann Shepherd (dau. of Solomon and Susanna [Farquhar])
                                                       03 SF
Cox, William; 9 Sept. 1806; Elizabeth Hopewell         02 SM-187
Cox, William; 16 Dec. 1817; Mary Ann Dawson            03 BA-602
Coxswain, George; 8 Feb. 1817; Mary Andre              03 BA-602
Crabb, Charles; 1811; Mary Summers (See also 02 MO)    01 PG
Crabb, John; 2 June 1812; Margaret Baer                15 FR-325
Craddock, Joseph N.; 30 Oct. 1815; Catherine Williamson
                                                       20 BA-222
Craggs, Robert; 25 Aug. 1801; Susannah Williams        27 BA-1
Craig, Henry; 22 May 1803; Anne Chenoweth              03 BA-428
Craig, John; 23 June 1801; Peggy Smith                 03 BA-402
Craling, John; Aug. 1813; Sarah Wolforth               02 WA-97
Cramblett, Thomas; 27 June 1815; Mary McMechen         13 BA-39
Cramer, Joh.; Feb. 1807; Sus. Miller                   02 WA-81
Cramer, Joh.; March 1807; Sus. Miller                  02 WA-82
Crampton, Joh.; 24 June 1801; Elis. Klopper            02 WA-71
Crandall, Francis; 1802; Susanna Leach                 07 AA
Crandell, Abel; 1804; Eliza Frazier                    13 AA-2
Crandell, Henry; 1804; Ann Woodfield                   07 AA-4
```

```
Crandell, Thomas; 23 Dec. 1813; Willy Hinton         03 AA-131
Crane, Joseph T.; 24 Oct. 1808; Cath. Sapp           14 BA-425
Crangle, Henry; 1 April 1807; Nancy Ball             14 BA-421
Crangle, Henry; 11 Nov.1812; Susan Harford           13 BA-17
Craul, Henry; 1 Oct. 1801; Mary Lewis                14 BA-410
Crausse, Jacob; 18 July 1815; Elizabeth Getier       07 BA-309
Crawford, James; 11 July 1803; Elizabeth McCrary     23 BA-2
Crawford, James; 1812; Cena Gray (See also 02 MO)    01 PG
Crawford, James; 2 May 1817; Isabella Wyer           03 BA-602
Crawford, John; 10 March 1812; Ann Withney           02 WA-93
Crawford, John; 6 Feb. 1816; Margaret Carmichael  32 BA-307
Crawford, Nathaniel; 13 Nov.1800; Elizabeth Figganzer 15 AA-1
Crawford, Thomas B.; 1 Jan. 1807; Elizabeth Athey    03 AL-614
Crawl, Henry; 26 Sept. 1810; Mary Hiss               11 BA-15
Crawmer, Daniel; 28 Jan. 1816; Polly Mumford         06 FR-1323
Crawmer, Helfer; 9 Dec. 1815; Margareth Gosnell      06 FR-1323
Cray, Elias; 7 April 1806; Mary Wallis               09 BA
Creager, Daniel; Feb. 1816; Mary Bower               02 WA-101
Creager, George; 3 Nov. 1805; Mary Salmon            01 FR-1118
Creager, Henry; 21 June 1812; Cath. McDonald         02 WA-94
Creager, Henry; April 1817; Sarah Bowart             02 WA-104
Creagh, John; 13 Nov. 1814; Susanna Black            09 BA
Creiger, George; 3 Nov. 1805; Margaret Salmon        15 FR-318
Creighton, John; Aug. 1819;; Mary Keine, both of Dorset Co.
                                                     02 TA-44
Creighton, Vernal; 24 Dec. 1801; Nancy Keene         01 DO-40
Cremer, Solomon; 10 April 1808; Barbara Cettig (See also
    15 FR-322)                                        01 FR-1118
Cress, John; 15 July 1819; Magdalena Brotemarkle     08 AL-23
Creswell, John; 20 April 1808; Mary Ninde            02 BA-6
Cretcher, John; 30 Jan. 1814; Eliza Malcomb          13 BA-18
Creutzer, Jacob; 9 Nov. 1803; Eliz. Beckenbach (15 FR-315 gives
    date as 9 Oct.)                                   01 FR-1118
Crever, Jacob, Jr.; 20 Oct. 1819; Miss Margaret Deker 07 BA-311
Criner, Joh.; 1801; Elis. Smith                      02 WA-72
Crisfield, Absalom; 8 Nov. 1804; Mary Sly            14 BA-417
Crissingr, Geo.; 16 Aug. 1812; Elizab. Ernst         02 WA-94
Crist, Jacob; 24 Nov. 1812; Catherine Burkhart       06 FR-1318
Crist, Jacob; 29 June 1817; Lydia Norris             06 FR-1326
Cristman, Thomas; 31 Dec. 1812; Susanna Green        09 BA
Critchfield, William; 3 Feb. 1807; Margaret Barkus   03 AL-614
Croan, John George; 25 Aug. 1805; Catha. Strudbiena  03 BA-494
Crocker, Bernard; 7 Jan. 1816; Elizabeth Taylor      02 BA-36
Crockett, George; 19 April 1815; Mary Ann Fulton     05 BA-238
Croft (Krofft), John; 28 May 1820; Arietta Hirsh (or Hush)
                                                     13 BA-41
Croll (Croul), John; 1 Feb. 1811; Catherine Garret   03 BA-502
Cromer, George W; 11 April 1818; Mary A. Burke       11 BA-28
Cromwell, Francis; 14 Jan. 1803; Patience Gaither    36 BA-1
Cromwell, Jacob; 24 Sept. 1814; Helen Knab           13 BA-19
Cromwell, John; 15 Feb. 1803; Marg. Kephard (15 FR-320 gives
    bride's name as Gebhart)                          01 FR-1118
Cromwell, John Cockey; 28 March 1811; Harriot Stitcher 06 FR-1315
Cromwell, Joseph; April 1819; Margaret Zeller        02 WA-113
Cromwell, Mich'l; 14 Dec. 1820; Eliza Wraig          13 BA-36
Cromwell, Moses; 26 March 1809; Barbara Walton       03 BA-499
Cromwell, Oliver; 20 Nov. 1806; Harriet Gebhart (See also
    15 FR-320)                                        01 FR-1118
Cromwell, Richard; 14 Jan. 1817; Ann Stewart         11 BA-27
Cromwell, Samuel (free negro); 26 April 1802; Rachel Lance (free
    mulatto)                                          15 BA-166
Cromwell, William; 5 June 1806; Ann Merriken         11 BA-9
Croneis, Henry; 8 Oct. 1805; Elizabeth Knouff        15 FR-318
```

Croneisz, Jacob; 14 April 1806; Catherine Fonderburg (See also
  15 FR-318)   01 FR-1118
Croney, George; 5 March 1806; Elizabeth Page   02 BA-3
Cronise, Henry; 8 Oct. 1805; Elizab. Knouff   01 FR-1118
Cronley (or Crowley), Sam'l; 31 Jan.1818; Jane Henderson
                                                           14 BA-437
Crook, Charles; 18 Dec. 1804; Charlotte Sellman   03 BA-492
Crook, Dan'l; 4 Feb. 1813; Matilda Eckle   03 BA-505
Crook, Elisha; 16 March 1804; Priscilla Millerman   14 BA-416
Crooks, William; 14 Dec. 1815; Catherine Maxwell   08 BA
Cropper, Stephanus; 24 Jan., 1819; Sophia Ondorf   39 BA-36
Crosedale, George; 25 Nov. 1806; Harriet Gibson   03 BA-496
Crosier, John; 27 March 1801; Anne Eubanks   03 BA-399
Crosmer, Wm. L.; 24 Dec. 1815; Mary Stiegers   14 BA-434
Cross, Benjamin; 25 Dec. 1812; Rachel A. Woodland   03 KE-14
Cross, Jno.; 10 may 1807; Elis. Kraft   14 BA-421
Cross, John; 3 Oct. 1813; Sarah Booth   09 BA
Cross, Michael; 26 Nov. 1816; Ellen Desk   13 BA-40
Cross, Richard; 20 Oct. 1808; Sally Blatchley   09 BA
Cross, Thomas; 2 Feb. 1804; Harriot Howard   15 AA-3
Cross, Trueman; 26 March 1818; Marg't Bohn   14 BA-437
Crosse, Jacob; 13 Nov. 1804; Rachel Merryman   11 BA-4
Crossin, John; 22 May 1814; Maria Dougherty (both natives of
  Ireland)   16 BA-6
Crouch, David; 16 March 1815; Margaret Davis   BA-10
Crouch, John; 12 Jan. 1808 (at New Castle Forest, DE); Mary
  Tygard   01 CE
Crouch, John; 23 May 1813; Elizabeth Nunday   03 BA-505
Crouch, Richard; 5 Aug. 1817; Mary Boussell   17 BA-17
Crouch, Sam'l W.; 5 Dec. 1813; Eliza Purden   13 BA-18
Crous, John; April 1806; Mary Nave   02 WA-80
Crouse, David; 29 Dec. 1808; Nancy Primrose   11 BA-13
Crouse, John J.; 9 June 1811; Mary Cherry   15 BA-287
Croutch, Isaac; 3 Aug. 1815; Phebe Knabbs   11 BA-25
Croutson, Joseph; 15 Oct. 1806; Eliza McKindley   08 BA
Crow, Benjamin; Sept. 1819; Elizab. Lefeber   02 WA-114
Crow, Jacob; 12 Sept. 1811; Margaret Winebrunner   03 AL-614
Crow, John; 15 Dec. 1803; Mary Butler (see also 02 BA-33)
                                                           03 BA-436
Crow, John; 9 Nov. 1809; Jane England   02 BA-7
Crow, Philip; Oct. 1804; Elis. Cruthers   02 WA-77
Crow, Richard B.; 2 Jan. 1816; Rebecca Garret   20 BA-222
Crowl, Joseph; Jan. 1818; Mary Ann Dillehunt   02 WA-107
Crowle, John; 26 April 1810; Jane Bullen   03 BA-501
Crown, John; 1 Dec. 1803; Eliz. Ball   03 MO-119
Crozier, William; 24 Aug. 1815; Ann Maria Fields   17 BA-11
Crugh, Richard; 3 Dec. 1812; Elizabeth Spencer   11 BA-20
Crum, Abraham; Feb. 1819; Mary McDonald   02 WA-112
Crum, John; 9 Feb. 1806; Mary Miller (See also 15 FR-318)
                                                           01 FR-1118
Crum, Nathan; 15 March 1803; Amalia Creager (See also 15 FR-314)
                                                           01 FR-1118
Crump, Alfred; [6] Aug. 1816; Margareta Walter (wid?) Handshue?
                                                           39 BA-32
Cullember, Columbus; 8 Sept 1816; Rebecca Smith   17 BA-15
Cullison, John W.; 24 Feb. 1820; Margaret Mifflin   11 BA-36
Cullum, John; 16 June 1813; Sarah Childs   11 BA-23
Cully, Rob't 31 Dec. 1812; Sally Mowberry   14 BA-431
Culp, Frederich; June 1806; Cath. Coaler   02 WA-80
Culverson, Thomas; 14 Oct. 1802; Elizabeth Sank   03 BA-421
Culverwell, Stephen; 28 Oct. 1801; Rachel Griffith   27 BA-1
Culverwell, Wm.; 4 March 1818; Ann Hemlig   14 BA-437
Cummings, Casper; 17 Aug. 1815; Sarah Bastian   06 FR-1322
Cummings, James; 4 July 1810; Bridget Connelly   31 BA-85

```
Cummings, Robert; 23 Nov. 1819; Alice Shue           11 BA-36
Cummings, Thomas; 26 Oct. 1805; Catherine Ward       02 BA-2
Cummins, William; 21 May 1818; Margaret Adams        11 BA-33
Cunning, John; 24 June 1817; Cathe. Blair            13 BA-28
Cunningham, Alexander; 24(?) Jan. 1804; Elsy Lee     09 BA
Cunningham, Jess; 6 Aug. 1811; Eve Reems             03 AL-614
Cunningham, John; 15 March 1801; Anne Harrison       03 BA-397
Cunningham (Kunningham in original), John; July 1802; Mary
    Rhodes                                           02 WA-73
Cunningham, John; 6 Oct. 1803; Mary Burgan           9 BA
Cunningham, Joseph; Jan. 1801; Nancy Dole (Doll)     02 WA-71
Cunningham, Patrick; 24 Aug. 1809; Ann Morrow        02 BA-7
Cunningham, Walter; 21 June 1804; Cassandra Tuck     01 BA-10
Cupbeach, Justus; June 1804; Barb. Lentz             02 WA-76
Cuphold, Hartman; 1 June 1812; Eliza Hannan          13 BA-17
Curfman, Peter; 31 Oct. 1816; Catherine Stull        06 FR-1325
Curlet, James; 3 Dec. 1812; Elizabeth Grimes         11 BA-20
Curlet, John; 2 April 1812; Ann Rusk                 14 BA-430
Curley, John; 26 Nov. 1814; Elizabeth Carter         06 FR-1321
Curlip, Thomas; 6 May 1813; Sophia Delcher           11 BA-23
Curran, John; 30 Aug. 1808; Leah Brette              13 BA-4
Curran, Moses; 8 Jan. 1818; Mary Doyle               16 BA-63
Curran, Timothy; 21 Feb. 1818; Mary Noone            16 BA-64
Curran, William; 21 Aug. 1810; Nancy Cooke           03 BA-501
Curren, Thomas; 8 Sept. 1810; Sarah Racords          03 SO
Currey, Israel; 22 Sept. 1810; Eliza Eggens          14 BA-227
Curry, Abraham; 20 April 181; Eliz. Shaw             02 WA-89
Curry, John; Oct. 1816; Sarah Kreps                  02 WA-103
Curry, Langley; 2 April 1818; Ester Ann Roberts      11 BA-28
Curtain, James; 7 April 1818; Eliza Josephine Black  32 BA-317
Curtis, John; 3 Jan. 1809; Sarah Adams               13 BA-5
Curtis, Silas; 14 Nov. 1819; Sarah Jambier           11 BA-34
Curts, Robert; 19 Aug. 1809; Mary McMurray           03 BA-500
Curwell, Samuel; 24 Nov. 1801; Fanny Evans           14 BA-411
Custer, Thom.; Jan. 1807; Chath. Brown               02 WA-81
Cutchin, Samuel; 7 April 1814; Nancy Tell            13 BA-18
Cuthever, Sam'l; 5 March 1818; Susan Poorback        13 BA-30
Cuttler, John; 18 Oct. 1807; Alice O'Donnell (widow of the late
    Guelbreth)                                       31 BA-33
Dafft, Edward; 16 Dec. 1805; Mary Cunningham         02 BA-2
Daggett, James; 20 Jan. 1817; Sarah Amest            13 BA-27
Daile, Daniel; 6 July 1815; Eliza Block              03 BA-506
Daley, Daniel; 5 Feb. 1807; Jane Barton              31 BA-18
Daley, Jacob; 16 Sept. 1802; Elizabeth Mountgard     06 BA-2
Daley, James; 17 Nov. 1801; Elizabeth Savington      10 BA-1
Daley, James; 13 Dec. 1815; Rosanna Keens            16 BA-30
Daley, John; 27 Feb. 1805; Mary James                03 BA-492
Daley, Peter; 8 April 1806; Elizabeth Daley          02 BA-3
Daley, William; 11 July 1807; Margaret Daly          31 BA-26
Dall, James; 17 March 1803; Eleanor Laming           03 BA-425
Dallam, William (of Balto. Town, s. of John and Mary of HA Co.);
    24 d., 3 mo., 1813; Sarah Webster (dau. of Isaac and Sarah)
                                                     12 SF-37
Dallis (?), Walter R.; 5 March 1801; Sarah Harman    09 BA
Dalrymple, Wm.; 6 June 1816; M. Augustin             30 BA-109
Dalton, Thos.; 15 April 1811; Mary Miller            03 BA-502
Dalwell, James; 18 May 1820; Sarah Fitzsimmons       16 BA-100
Daly, James (of Concord, Franklin Co., PA); 6 Sept. 1815; Mary
    Jordan (widow)                                   16 BA-26
Daly, John; 13 April 1818; Mary Roach                32 BA-320
Dameron, John; 1 Nov. 1804; Mary Berbine             15 BA-211
Dames, August; 24 Aug. 1805; Diana Bougers           15 BA-225
Dance, Thomas; 5 May 1818; Augusta Temple Sterratt   05 BA-240
Daniel, George S.; 19 Jan. 1805; Sarah Earle         02 SM-186
```

Daniel, Robert; Nov. 1808; Martha Huhney   02 WA-86
Danielson, Rezin; 23 Dec. 1802; Ann Dove   15 AA-2
Dannell, John M.; 11 July 1806; Cathrin Flanagan   11 BA-9
Dannenberg, Fred'k; 21 Oct. 1801; Eliza Kean   14 BA-411
Danner, Abraham; 9 Nov. 1815; Mary Schelly   07 BA-310
Dannesman, Conrad H.; 24 Nov. 1812; Olivia Sophia Yeiser
                                                    14 BA-431
Dannison, Richard; 9 Jan. 1816 (by Joshua Wells); Jemima Parks
                                                    17 BA-12
Danskin, William; 11 June 1801; Margaret Crabben   03 BA-401
D'Arcy, John N.; 27 Jan. 1818; Amelia Didier   03 BA-602
Darden, John F.; 27 May 1817; Mary Moale   37 BA-152
Dare, Ephraim; 21 March 1808; Mary Hay   14 BA-423
Dare, Jeremiah; 17 Feb. 1801; Jane Petterson   11 BA-2
Dare, Thomas C., (of Calvert Co., s. of Gideon and Elizabeth); 19
    d. 5 mo., 1803; Elizabeth Snowden (of Richard. dec., and
    Hannah of PG Co.)   09 SF
Darnal, Ralph; 30 June 1808; Hanna Kohlenberg (See also
    15 FR- 322)   01 FR-1123
Darrell, Sampson; 23 Nov. 1815; Mary Ann Ganteaume 32 BA-306
Dathum, Albin; 11 June 1807; Rachel Booth   13 BA-2
Daub, Valentine; 17 April 1804; Esther Koenig   1 FR-1123
Daub, Valentine; 17 April 1804; Esther Kring   15 FR-316
Daubecourt, Frencia L.; 22 Feb. 1803; Ann Renendet 21 BA-5
Daugherty, David; 17 July 1805; Achsa Winks   14 BA-418
Daunig (?), Antonio; 7 November 1819; Maria Frances Victoire (?)
    Packer   32 BA-326
Davenport, Joseph; 27 April 1816; Susan Reichert   14 BA-435
Davey, William; 18 March 1802; Ann Foules (?)   17 BA-1
Davidge, Francis H.; 4 May 1819; Ann Maria Dorsey   19 BA-72
Davidge, John Beale; 26 Aug. 1819; Rebecca Polk   03 BA-604
Davids, John; 16 May 1810; Rachl Bateman   13 BA-12
Davidson, Abraham; 17 May 1802; Jenny McWhirter   03 BA-416
Davidson, Alex'r. I.; 8 Sept. 1804; Eliza'h Wellman (02 BA-34
    gives the bride's name as Hillman)   03 BA-491
Davidson, Benja. A.; 12 April 1818; Mary Mason   13 BA-30
Davidson, Daniel; 16 Feb. 1802; Sarah McCormick   28 BA-1
Davidson, David; 15 May 1818; Ann Fulton   13 BA-31
Davidson, George; 1 May 1804; Cath. Thomas   03 BA-490
Davidson, George; 5 April 1806; Faithful Pierpoint 14 BA-420
Davidson, James; 5 Nov. 1807; Mary Higinbothom   03 BA-497
Davidson, John; 24 Aug. 1805; Sealy Hill (See also 15 FR-318)
                                                    01 FR-1123
Davidson, Robert; 14 Feb. 1814; Lutitia Kennen   02 WA-99
Davidson, Sam'l; 21 Sept. 1805; Mary Bird   03 BA-494
Davidson, William; 23 April 1801; Elizabeth Barkshire 03 AL-613
Davies, Ephraim; 3 Oct. 1820; Anne Anderson   06 FR-1331
Davis, Alexander; 7 July 1802; Elizabeth Sedgwick   01 MO
Davis, Alexander; 17 Aug. 1815; Mary Becht   06 FR-1322
Davis, Amos; 15 Jan. 1807; Letitia Dimmott   09 BA
Davis, Benj'n.; 1803; Eliz. Trott   07 AA-3
Davis, Benjamin; 8 Oct. 1807; Elizabeth Holbrook   09 BA
Davis, Cadwalader; 20 Aug. 1815; Abigail Davis   11 BA-24
Davis, Caleb; 27 April 1815; Sarah Rowles   13 BA-21
Davis, Charles; 25 Feb. 1817; Molly Willis   01 WO
Davis, David; 29 April 1813; Esther Evans   13 BA-16
Davis, David; 24 April 1817; Mary Shane   02 BA-37
Davis, Edward; 20 May 1819; Mary Ann Clark   13 BA-40
David, Ephraim; Nov. 1808; Elis. Brandner   02 WA-86
Davis, Ezekiel; 17 Dec. 1801; Elizabeth Wells   09 BA
Davis, Francis; July 1803; Ephla Carry   02 WA-75
Davis, Francis; 29 May 1806; Lydia Simpson   03 BA-495
Davis, Henry, Jr.; 4 May 1805; Mary Anne Smith (see also
    02 BA-32)   03 BA-427

```
Davis, Henry; 8 April 1812; Nancy Constantine        03 BA-503
Davis, Jacob; Nov. 1810; Mary Tice                   02 WA-88
Davis, James; 8 Oct. 1801; Susan Lusby               05 AA-1
Davis, James; 16 Feb. 1812; Jemima Phillips          1 DO-42
Davis, James; 9 Jan. 1813; Elizabeth Fitch           09 BA
Davis, James; 29 Oct. 1815; Ann Anderson             13 BA-23
Davis, Jesse F.; March 1820; Elizab. Stine           02 WA-116
Davis, John; 23 Sept.(?) 1810 (by Robert Roberts); Rebecca Willis
                                                     17 BA-8
Davis, John; Aug. 1813; Mary Betz                    02 WA-97
Davis, John; 16 May 1816; Frances Armistead          17 BA-12
Davis, John; May 1818; Elizab. Bowles                02 WA-109
Davis, Joseph; 30 March 1801; Eliza Gold             14 BA-409
Davis, Joshua; 27 May 1806; Mary Beubout             09 BA
Davis, Leonard Young; 2 March 1801; Achsah Worthington 03 MO-117
Davis, Littleton; by March 1802; M. Bell             01 WO
Davis, Luke; 11 Oct. 1807; Mary Duall (See also 15 FR-321)
                                                     01 FR-1123
Davis, Manlow; 20 May 1819; Elizabeth Stinchcomb     13 BA-41
Davis, Peter (widower);19 Nov. 1801; Esther Philippe 15 BA-159
Davis, Richard; March 1820; Eliza Downs              02 WA-116
Davis, Robert; 11 Feb. 1802; Catherine Frenton       15 BA-162
Davis, Robert; 21 Feb. 1805; Darky Wigley            09 BA
Davis, Solomon; 2 Sept. 1804 (by John Bloodgood, in list of
    marriages for blacks); Elizabeth Douglas         17 BA-5
Davis, Thos.; 21 Jan. 1802; Eliz. Bowie              3 MO-118
Davis, Thomas; April 1803; Mary Snyder               02 WA-75
Davis, Thos.; 26 April 1805; Emily Traverse          3 BA-493
Davis, Thomas; 25 Aug. 1805; Jemima Taylor           2 SM-187
Davis, Thomas; 8 March 1807; Keziah Richards         02 BA-5
Davis, Thomas; 12 Sept. 1807 (by Henry Smith); Nancy Jones
                                                     17 BA-6
Davis, Thomas; 15 May 1808; Elizabeth Gorsuch        09 BA
Davis, Thomas; 29 May 1810; Mary Bray                03 AL-614
Davis, Thomas; 20 Nov. 1810; Ann Davis               09 BA
Davis, Thomas; 24 Dec. 1811; Betsy Troot             11 BA-17
Davis, Thomas; 27 April 1812; Prudence Newman        31 BA-135
Davis, Thomas; 4 Aug. 1816; Margaret Ennis           17 BA-15
Davis, Thomas A.; (10 March?) 1804 (by L. W. McCombes); Mary
    (Margaret?) White                                17 BA-3
Davis, Thomas S.; 4 Dec. 1806; Creece Swearingen (See also 04 BA
    and 02 MO)                                       01 PG-97
Davis, Vincent; 28 April 1804; Louise Sophia Tourneau (widow
    Belleville) (both from St. Domingo)              15 BA-201
Davis, Wm.; 28 Nov. 1801; Sarah Simprot              14 BA-411
Davis, William; 20 Nov. 1804; Rachel Rawlings        03 BA-492
Davis, William; 12 Aug. 1817; Sarah Rutter           19 BA-72
Davis, William M.; 22 Oct. 1816; Caroline Gibbons    11 BA-31
Davison, Thos.; 25 May 1815; Isabella McKerlie       21 BA-8
Davy, William; 28 April 1818; Elizabeth Evens        17 BA-19
Dawe, Wm.; 15 May 1809; Susanna R. White             03 BA-499
Dawes, Edward M.;' 11 April 1816; Jane C. Linville   02 BA-37
Dawes, Samuel; 24 Jan. 1804; Mary Ann Lewis          05 AA-4
Dawes, William; 9 Nov. 1813; Ann Wheeler (both res. of HA Co.)
                                                     15 BA-318
Daws, Benjamin; 7 Feb. 1802; Elizabeth Norris        33 BA-13
Daws, James; 9 Oct. 1801; Susan Lusby                05 AA-2
Dawson, James; 22 Aug. 1803; Sarah Eashman (02 BA-32 gives the
    bride's name as Eastman)                         03 BA-433
Dawson, John; 20 Nov. 1804; Cath. Howard             03 BA-492
Dawson, John; 23 Sept. 1806; Anna Hays (See also 15 FR-319)
                                                     01 FR-1123
Dawson, John; 7 Sept. 1807; Parmelia Ravenscroft     03 AL-614
Dawson, John; 21 Jan. 1813; Polly Pesterman          03 AL-614
```

Dawson, Richard (son of Jno. Dawson of Co. Tyrone and Margaret);
    22 d, 1 mo., 1818; Eliza Newlin (dau. of David and Jane)
    (See also 10 SF)   01 SF
Dawson, Theodoier; 10 Feb. 1811; Mary Ravenscroft   03 AL-614
Dawson, Thomas Hammersley (of TA Co., son of Elias and Eliza-
    beth); 3 d, 10 mo., 1810; Edith Matthews (dau. of Mordecai
    and Ruth)   02 SF-114
Dawson, William (of Wm.); 18 Nov. 1806; Rachel Sharpless
                                                          03 AL-614
Dawse, Joshua; 18 July 1816; Ann Shaw   13 BA-26
Day, Cornelius; 30 April 1804; Sarah Deems   14 BA-416
Day, Edward; 11 Jan. 1801; Mary Brown   33 BA-12
Day, Edward (son of John); 6 Aug. 1801; Hannah Wilmer (See also
    33 BA-29)   33 BA-18
Day, Edward; 15 Sept. 1803; Elenor Thornton   15 AA-2
Day, Goldsmith; 27 Dec. 1809; Mary Savory   11 BA-15
Day, James; 16 Feb. 1812; Eliza Ann Kane   03 BA-503
Day, James Maxwell; 6 Dec. 1804; Rebecca Nabb   33 BA-41
Day, Joshua; 12 Nov. 1812; Sarah Dawney   01 BA-11
Day, Levi; 9 Jan. 1817; Elizabeth Johnson   17 BA-16
Day, Nathaniel; 17 Feb. 1803; Ann Brashears   3 AA-120
Dayhoff, Andrew; 18 May 1820; Rebecca Watkins   11 BA-37
Daykle (?), David; Aug. 1810; Susanna Shantzer   02 WA-87
Daymoot, William; 13 Sept. 1818; Ann Howard   13 BA-41
Deady, John; 28 June 1804; Mary Miller   15 BA-205
Deal, George; 19 July 1804; Elizabeth Schunck   15 BA-206
Deal, Henrich; 18 April 1813; Elizabeth Pien (widow)   07 BA-309
Deal, Jacob; 24 June 1807; Christina Deal   14 BA-422
Deal, James; c.1803; Eliza Sherbert   07 AA-3
Deal, Jno.; 19 Nov. 1807; Mary Miller   14 BA-423
Deal, Thomas; 29 Aug. 1811; Eliz. McCoy   02 WA-90
Deale, Frederick; 30 March 1815; Margaret Thomas   16 BA-17
Deale, George; 16 Oct. 1816; Cath. Bomberger   14 BA-436
Deale, Henry; 23 Dec. 1802; Ally Proctor   03 AA-120
Deale, James; 17 Feb. 1805; Mary Franklin   03 AA-130
Dean, Emanuel; 14 March 1801; Martha Price   09 BA
Dean, Godfrey; 20 Jan. 1803; Mary Dunnock   01 DO-41
Dean, John; May 1819; Elizab. Orr   02 WA-113
Dean, William; 17 Jan. 1805; Alice Reynolds (See also 15 FR-317)
                                                          01 FR-1123
Deane, Henry; 26 Jan. 1816; Isabella Orr   02 BA-36
Dear, Alvine; 19 March 1807; Fanny McKinsey   31 BA-20
Dear (?), Joseph; 2 April 1801; Elizabeth Gonneman   09 BA
Deaver, Aaron; 6 Sept. 1804; Honor Welling   03 BA-491
Deaver, Levi; 6 Jan. 1805; Sophia Griffith (See also 15 FR-317)
                                                          01 FR-1123
Deaver, Moses; 27 Dec. 1803; Sally Watts   15 AA-3
de Balke, Cuerdo; 21 July 1812; Maria Defare (Defano?)   07 BA-308
Debarty, Lawrence; 22 June 1802; Rosanna Stop   14 BA-413
Debo, Mahlon; 10 Jan. 1807; Ann Harp   09 BA
DeButts, Elisha; 8 June 1820; Sophia G. Rogers   19 BA-73
De Caindry, Peter D.; 6 June 1801; Theresa Duckkin   22 BA-410
Dechant, Rev. William; 25 Oct. 1808; Rebecca Andree   07 BA-306
Dechart, Peter S.; Dec. 1819; Mary Harry   02 WA-115
Deele, William; 17 Dec. 1803 (CV Co.); Margaret Crandal
                                                          40 BA
Deems, Christopher; 7 July 1801; Ann Sadler   09 BA
Deems, George; 16 Aug. 1811; Mary Roberts   21 BA-7
Deems, Joshua; 11 May 1815; Mary Ann Payne   21 BA-8
Deerbach, Val.; 1 Dec. 1804; Marg. Trumbo   14 BA-417
Deets, George; 13 April 1811; Rachel Clarke   11 BA-16
Deetz, Frederic; 25 July 1816; Cath. Heinling   14 BA-435
Degelvin, John; 8 July 1815; Sarah Grant   11 BA-25
de Gocye, Bartholome; 2 Feb. 1807; Rachel Reed   03 BA-497

DeGraff, John; 31 Dec. 1812; Elisa Walton   31 BA-142
Degraff, Lewis; 18 Dec. 1803; Eliza Lowman   21 BA-5
Degraft, Abraham; 27 Oct. 1812; Amelia Beckley   02 WA-95
DeGroff, Richard; 28 Feb. 1810; Ann Gooding   3 BA-12
Deherigrey, Charles Joseph; 29 Nov. 1817; Theresa Almoide (?)
     Lemaire   32 BA-317
Deil, Christian; 18 June 1816; Sophia Sanders   14 BA-435
Delacour, David; 9 Jan. 1812; Elizabeth Patton   05 BA-237
Delacroze, Jos. Simm Nic. Darene; 1 Oct. 1804; Mary Frances
     Catharine Charlotte Moudet (both from St. Domingo)
                                                         15 BA-109
Delahay, Wm.; 4 April 1811; Jane Amos   21 BA-7
Delany(?), William; 5 Jan. 1812; Julia Milan   31 BA-118
Delaplaine, Joseph; 26 May 1814; Susannah Ott   06 FR-1321
De La Roche, George F.; 23 March 1816; Ann Maria McNulty
                                                         05 BA-239
Delashmutt, Trammel; 19 Aug. 1809; Mary W. Moriarty (See also
     15 FR-324)   01 FR-1123
Delater, Jacob; 21 April 1807; Elizab. Michael (See also
     15 FR-320)   02 FR-1123
Delater, Jacob; 13 Aug. 1813; Sara Ann Brown (See also 15 FR-327)
                                                         01 FR-1123
de la Tullaye, Alexander John (native of Nantes, Brittany; son of
     Henry Lewis Salomon de la Tullaye, and Ann Frances Simeon
     Shlittle Moulin); 14 Oct. 1802; Mary Renee Charlotte
     O'Rourke (native of Laogene in the Island of St. Domingo)
                                                         15 BA-172
Delawter, Geo.; 25 Jan. 1814; Elis. Buzzard   02 WA-99
Delinger, Henrich; 1805; Cath. Cromely   02 WA-77
Dell, W.; 15 Feb. 1816; Eliza Hay   13 BA-24
Dellerhide, George; 4 Nov. 1819; Fanny Stier   17 BA-22
Delly, Gerhard; 22 Nov. 1803; Ann Catherine Fosbinder   14 BA-415
Delmas, Francis; 1 April 1806; Mary Allers (or Walters or
     Watters)   33 BA-41
Delong, David; 30 Sept. 1806; Barbara Brotemarkle   08 AL-26
Delsher, John; (lic. dated 1 April 1813); Elizabeth Kelly
                                                         11 BA-20
Deloste, Francis; 16 April (?) 1812; Rose J. Amel   31 BA-134
De Maugin, Charkles; 25 Jan. 1815; Elizabeth Caldwell   05 BA-238
DeMoss, Thomas; 6 April 1806; Sarah Randall   01 BA-10
Dempsey, John; 18 Jan. 1808; Eliza Gwynn   03 BA-498
Dempsey, John; 24 Oct. 1813; Elizabeth Wiley   31 BA-161
Dempsey, Robert; 15 Dec. 1814; Elizabeth Carman (or Carnan)
                                                         17 BA-10
Demry, William; 28 Nov. 1816; Mary Long   06 FR-1325
Demsey, John; 15 Dec. 1805; Rebecca Gibson   09 BA
Demuth, Henry; 30 April 1818; Barbara Valentine   06 FR-1328
Denby, Wm.; 8 Oct. 1812; Mary Deshon   13 BA-15
Deniau, Jean Montpensier (free Negro); 28 July 1808; Mary Jane
     Fanny (free mulatto)   15 BA-264
Denison, Edw'd.; 20 Feb. 1806; Deb'h Thornburgh   03 BA-495
Dennie, James; 15 June 1812; Harriet Burrow   02 WA-94
Dennis, Edward; 23 Nov. 1816; Catherine Conrod   16 BA-45
Dennison, Edward; 26 Nov. 1812; Eliza Wilson   05 BA-237
Denny, Bartholopmew; 16 Oct. 1811; Peggy Jones   31 BA-112
Denny, Michael; 19 Jan. 1804; Mary Anderson   15 BA-198
Denos, Augustine; 14 April 1811; Eleanorra Curry   13 BA-236
Denoyer, Edward; 28 March 1805; Catherine Longberry   03 AL-613
Dent, Aquila; 17 Oct. 1803; Cath. Thomas (See also 15 FR-315)
                                                         01 FR-1123
Dent, Hezekiah; 18 Jan. 1803; Lareine Milburn   02 SM-185
Denys, Frederick; 18 April 1816; Frances Wheritt (or Wherrell)
                                                         32 BA-307
Depass, George; 7 May 1801; Ida Davis   30 BA-108

Depass, George; 15 Dec. 1801; Ann Barrett   09 BA
Deppish, Caspar; 15 June 1803; Barb. Mumma   14 BA-414
de Ronceray, Charles; 16 April 1816; Margaret Donnelly (dau. of
    Ellinor Donnelly Farrell)   32 BA-308
Derr, John; 7 April 1814; Elizabeth Miller   06 FR-1320
Derr, Peter; 22 Dec. 1803; Cath. Sullivan   14 BA-415
Derrick, Richard; 11 June 1803; Rebeckah Stevenson   34 BA-1
Derry, Henrich; 26 July 1804; Eleanor Yank   14 BA-417
Deschamp, John; 22 Sept. 1818; Rachel Guglean (?)   17 BA-20
Deselen, James; 2 Jan. 1806; Catherine Fulks   01 PG
Deshaye, John; 25 Aug. 1815; Magdalena Raymond   16 BA-24
Deshere (?), John; 14 Dec. 1820; Sarah Guichard   16 BA-106
Deshon, James; 17 Sept. 1816; Ann Roche   21 BA-3
Deshon, John; 11 June 1801; Elizabeth Ray (widow)   15 BA-153
Deslem, James; 2 Jan. 1806; Catherine Fulks   02 MO
Desmangles, Zachariah (son of Andrew Delaforgue Desmangles, and
    Mary Henrietta Hugnot); 22 Oct. 1807; Frances Pujot (dau. of
    Peter [dec.] and Jane [Bedoit?] Pujot)   15 BA-255
Despeau, Elie; 7 Oct. 1813; Eliza Harwood   21 BA-7
Despeaux, John; 29 Jan. 1817; Ann Isabella Ardrey   21 BA-8
Despeaux, Thomas; 11 April 1816; Ann Stevenson   05 BA-239
Dessaven, William; 13 Oct. 1813; Elizabeth Brown   15 FR-327
Detman, Frederick; 18 Feb. 1802; Elizabeth Sutter   03 BA-413
Deutch, Henry; April 1805; Elis. Junes   02 WA-78
de Vattere, Benjamin; 16 May 1815; Jane Lee (both free col'd)
                                                         16 BA-18
Develing, Patrick; 23 Aug. 1818; Ann Mary Moore   32 BA-321
Devenish, Stephen; 3 Dec. 1816; Eliza Ralston   13 BA-39
Devenport, William; Nov. 1808; Nanzi Catlett   02 WA-86
Deveter, Jacob; 26 Jan. 1802; Margaret Angel   15 BA-161
Devine, James; 16 July 1808; Jane Keys   15 BA-264
Devize, Charles (of Cap Francois, Santo Domingo); 27 Nov. 1809;
    Louise Magdalen Rosetta de la Rue   15 BA-276
Devlin, Patrick; 27 June 1805; Eleanor McEnneny   15 BA-222
Devoe, Frederick; 23 April 1812; Mary Rumley   13 BA-7
de von Clot, Wilhelms; 29 March 1810; Catharina Spies   07 BA-307
Devose, Wm.; 22 July 1810; Mary Blount   13 BA-10
Dew, James C.; 29 Sept. 1807; Henrietta Stansbury   13 BA-2
Dew, Wm.; 11 May 1815; Jane Long   13 BA-21
Dewees, Andrew; 21 May 1805; Mary Miles   09 BA
Dewey, Silas; 13 Sept. 1810; Eliza Dowell   05 BA-236
Dewhurst, Greenbury; 26 March 1812; Mary Weaver   14 BA-430
Dewis, William; 22 July 1813; Cathe. Jones   20 BA-222
Dexter, William; 13 Dec. 1804; Eleanor O'Donnell   15 BA-212
De Young, Moses Myer; 4 Jan. 1820; Rachel Joseph   14 BA-440
d'Hebercourt, Lewis Amans (Commercial Agent for the French
    Republic for the State of Maryland; native of Tracy-le-
    Mont,France); 3 Nov. 1803; Margaret Boucharlat (native of
    Cap Francois)   15 BA-190
Dick, Daniel; 22 Dec. 1818; Sarah Leach   14 BA-438
Dick, James; 11 April 1805; Susanna Buck   30 BA-108
Dick, John; 28 Feb. 1808; Elizab. Schraier (or Schreier: 15 FR-
    322)   01 FR-1123
Dick, John; 2 May 1809; Cath. Feagler (See also 15 FR-323)
                                                         01 FR-1123
Dickehut, George; 29 July 1807; Hanna Altherr   14 BA-422
Dickel, Charles; 20 July 1819; Catherine Knabel   30 BA-109
Dickinson, Elisha; 17 June 1812; Mary A. Brady   13 BA-17
Dickerson, John; 18 Sept. 1806; Elizabeth Turnbull (See also 02
    MO)   01 PG
Dickerson, Nathan; 89 Dec. 1801; Margaret Turnbull   03 MO-117
Dickey, Benj'n; 21 Jan. 1802; Mary Griffin   14 BA-411
Dickey, Robert; 19 March 1807; Ann Brown   05 BA-235
Dickhouse, Geo.; 7 July 1819; Louisa Hurds   13 BA-33

```
Dickinson (Dickison), John; 30 May 1816; Elizabeth Auckard
                                                        11 BA-30
Dickmyer, August; 5 Feb. 1808; Rebecca Reese            14 BA-423
Dickson, Robert; 25 Nov. 1802; Lurander Gore            06 BA-2
Didier, Henry; 13 Nov. 1812; Maria Gibson               03 BA-504
Dieffendahl, Joannes; 24 Sept. 1811; Catharina Schilor [Sheeler]
                                                        39 BA-27
Diehl, Johannes; 19 Jan. 1806; Pilgrim Faut             15 FR-318
Diehl, John; 19 Jan. 1806; Philippina Faut              01 FR-1123
Diel, Jacob; 14 May 1802; Cath. Hoetz                   14 BA-412
Diems, Jacob; 13 Aug. 1807; Susanna Grubb               14 BA-422
Dies, Richardson; 17 Dec. 1813; Rachel Landon           03 SO
Dietrich, Jacob; Sept. 1817; Sarah Startzman            02 WA-106
Dietz, Gotlieb; 13 Sept. 1812; Eliz. Fellows            14 BA-430
Diffaren, William; 13 Oct. (1817?); Elizab. Brown       01 FR-1123
Diffenderfer, Charles; 12 Dec. 1816; Ann Milliman       09 BA
Diffenderfer, John; 26 March 1807; Catherine Rogers     09 BA
Diffenderfer, Richard; 28 Oct. 1802; Charlotte Miller (See also
    14 BA-413)                                          25 BA-2
Diggins, Jas.; 26 Nov. 1801; Nancy Campbell             14 BA-411
Diggs, Beverly; 28 June 1810; Maria Ross                17 BA-8
Dilahunt, Thomas; 14 Nov. 1806; Sarah Ayres             11 BA-9
Dill, Jacob; April 1807; Cath. R. (?)                   02 WA-82
Dill, Joshua; 13 April 1817; Mary Klinchard             06 FR-1326
Dill, Wm.; 17 March 1808; Mary Foreman                  14 BA-423
Dillehunt, James; Oct. 1817; Cath. Leckroon             02 WA-106
Diller, Martin; 11 Nov. 1817; Rachael Wolf              06 FR-1327
Dilliagher, Timothy D.; 21 April 1813; Naomye Boyles    31 BA-148
Dillon, Daniel; 8 March 1801; Mary Waits (?)            09 BA
Dillon, Daniel; 20 Feb. 1816; Mary Wheeler              13 BA-24
Dillon, James; 26 May 1801; Mary Hartnell (or Hartnett) (both
    natives of Ireland)                                 15 BA-152
Dillon, James; 16 Jan. 1806; Elizabeth Sinner          09 BA
Dillon, Thomas; June 1803; Mary Stultz                  02 WA-75
Dimmit, Thomas; 6 Dec. 1808; Rebecker Baker             08 BA
Dinsmoor, Thomas; 26 Oct. 1809; Marg. Taylor (See also 15 FR-324)
                                                        01 FR-1123
Dipple, Michael; 22 April 1802; Elizabeth Bell          06 BA-2
Disney, Edw'd G.; 16 March 1819; Eliz. Hall             13 BA-34
Disney, James; 17 May 1810; Martha Sprague              17 BA-8
Disney, John; 18 Sept. 1811; Eliz. Harman               14 BA-429
Disney, John; 19 Oct. 1815; Eliza Watts                 13 BA-23
Disney, Mordecai; 13 May 1813; Sarah Tudor              11 BA-21
Disney, Richard; 1 Aug. 1802; Rachel Disney             15 AA-2
Disney, Richard; 19 April 1804; Regina White            15 AA-3
Disney, Thomas; c.1802; Deborah Williams                12 AA-1
Disney, Wesley; 19 Dec. 1819; Margaret Ann Sanks        11 BA-34
Disney, William (Protestant); 21 Nov. 1802; Mary Moran 15 BA-174
Ditmore, Henry; 17 May 1812; Charlotte Barker           13 BA-7
Diven, John; 2 Nov. 1816; Mary Cross                    11 BA-31
Divers, John; 3 Dec. 1801; Nancy Ford                   09 BA
Divers, John; 3 Jan. 1804; Charity Onion                05 HA-1
Dixon, James; 17 Aug. 1801; Catherine Brown             03 BA-404
Dixon, John; 5 Dec. 1806; Rebecca Bergen                03 BA-495
Dixon, Robert (s. of William and Ann); 2 d, 7 mo., 1802;
    Elizabeth Fairbank (dau. of James and Elizabeth)    08 SF
Dixon, Wm.; 3 Jan. 1804; Fanny Sparrow (free blacks)    03 BA-490
Dixon, William; 6 Dec. 1808; Mary McLean                02 SM-188
Dixon, Wm.; 17 Sept. 1820; Susan Swift                  13 BA-35
Dobbin, John; 16 Jan. 1819; Susan M. Duprey             11 BA-35
Dobler, Jno. Mochael; 15 Nov. 1812; Mary Fietz          14 BA-431
Dodaro, David; 3 Jan. 1802; Eliz. Heintz (See also 15 FR-312)
                                                        01 FR-1123
Dodd, Samuel; Oct. 1817; Cath. Speck                    02 WA-106
```

```
Doddero, Benjamin; 14 Oct. 1819; Mary Dodderso      06 FR-1330
Doerner, John; 10 April 1803; Barbara Dilbus        01 FR-1123
Doerr, Thomas; 10 April 1803; Barbara Steiner       01 FR-1123
Dofe (?), Sebastan; 8 July 1811; Catharine Stofel   39 BA-26
Dohm, John; 16 Nov. 1809; Elizabeth Hartman         07 BA-307
Dolan, Daniel; 4 Oct. 1816; Mary Shurley            16 BA-45
Doland, Wm.; 27 June 1813; Mary Dillon              11 BA-21
Doll, Jacob; Sept. 1807; Magd. Woltz                02 WA-84
Doll, Jacob; 31 May 1812; Mary Myers                01 DO-1123
Domini, Michael; 9 July 1809; Marie Braun           07 BA-306
Dominique, Julien; 10 Feb. 1814; Marie Elizeue (all col'd)
                                                    16 BA-1
Donald, Philip; 12 July 1801; Nancy Preshaw         03 BA-402
Donalds, George; 14 Oct. 1804; Frances Binns        03 BA-491
Donaldson, Hezekiah; April 1818; Sarah Willis       02 WA-109
Donaldson, John; 2 May 1819; Shady Maria Parks      17 BA-22
Donaldson, Samuel Johnston; 8 Nov. 1808; Camilla Almeria
    Hammond                                         03 BA-498
Donaldson, William; 11 April 1815; Catherine Weatherburn
                                                    03 BA-506
Donaldson, Wm.; 27 Nov. 1817; Jane Armstrong        13 BA-29
Donaughy, Henry; 28 May 1815; Bridget Dougherty     16 BA-20
Donekin, William; 17 Aug. 1820; Ann Dowd            32 BA-329
Dongse, Leopold; 25 Aug. 1804; Sophia Hellen        14 BA-417
Donis, Carl; 16 Feb. 1820; Wilhelmina Petri         07 BA-312
Donnell, George; 23 July 1809; Ann Johnston         15 BA-170
Donnelly, Thomas; 2 Aug. 1802; Jane Dodge           03 BA-419
Donnelly, Cornelius; 4 Oct. 1803; Mary Johns        15 BA-187
Donnelly, Daniel; 19 July 1807; Margaret Hyde       15 BA-252
Donnelly, Thomas; 11 Dec. 1816; Elizabeth Carey     11 BA-31
Donock, John; 8 July 1805; Terise Philllips         02 TA-39
Donoho, Barney; 31 Aug. 1820; Eleoner Connolly      32 BA-329
Donoho, Patrick; 23 Feb. 1806; Sarah Thornsbury     15 BA-236
Donohoe, John; 21 Oct. 1803; Catherine Drummond     15 BA-188
Dooble, Henry; March 1819; Susan M. Dill            02 WA-112
Dooble, Jonathan; Oct. 1818; Cath. Palmer           02 WA-111
Doodel, George; 16 Jan. 1803; Eleonor Ryan          01 FR-1123
Doolan, Lawrence; 30 June 1819; Bridget Mullikin    16 BA-83
Dolley, (or McDowell), James; Oct. 1812; Margaret McDonnell
                                                    03 BA-504
Doodel, George; 16 Jan. 1803; Eleanor Ryan          15 FR-313
Dop, George; 14 June 1802; Ann Spencer              15 BA-168
Dorf, George; 20 Nov. 1808; Mary Weber (See also 15 FR-323)
                                                    01 FR-1123
Dorman, Hezekiah; 16 Jan. 1801; Amelia Hayman       012 SO-15
Dorman, Samuel; 17 Oct. 1811; Ann Bishop            11 BA-17
Dorn, Frederick W.; 7 Aug. 1817; Eliza Campbell     13 BA-29
Dorner, Conrad; 10 April 1803; Barbarta Dilbus      15 FR-314
Dorney, Bartholomew; 16 March 1808; Charlotte Rowles 15 BA-260
Dorr, Thomas; 10 April 1803; Barbara Steiner        15 FR-314
Dorrett, Henry; 22 Dec. 1811; Rebecca Belt          11 BA-18
Dorry, Nicholas; 11 May 1820; Mary De Tutrow        37 BA-153
Dorsey, Dr. Archibald; 10 Oct. 1820; Sarah McComas  38 BA
Dorsey, Francis; 28 Nov. 1811; Mary Warter          08 BA
Dorsey, George; 15 Feb. 1811; Mary Stevens          09 BA
Dorsey, Geo.; 5 Feb. 1818; Alice Rowles             13 BA-30
Dorsey, Henry Woodward; 16 June 1807; Rachel Cooke (See also
    02 MO)                                          01 PG
Dorsey, John; 8 Aug. 1816; Elizabeth Stone          16 BA-40
Dorsey, John; 23 June 1818; Harriot Byers           11 BA-32
Dorsey, John Hammond; 30 Sept. 1806; Tilfun (?) York 17 BA-6
Dorsey, Joshua W.; 27 March 1804; Lucetta Plummer   03 MO-119
Dorsey, Mortimer; 1 March 1820; Ann M. Skinner      14 FR
Dorsey, Nicholas; 3 Aug. 1809; Mary Anderson        09 BA
```

Dorsey, Nicholas; 9 June 1818; Eliza C. Long   11 BA-32
Dorsey, Theodore; 24 March 1803; Elizabeth Dorsey   36 BA-1
Dorsey, Thomas; 25 May 1801; Eliz. Worddiwood   03 SM
Dorsey, Thomas B.; 1 Jan. 1805; Sarah Worthington   01 BA-10
Dorsey, Thomas Beale; 28 Oct. 1806; Achsah Brown   09 BA
Dorsey, Vachel; 1 Oct. 1801; Lydia Stringer   03 BA-407
Doruing (?), James; 26 April 1810; Martha Wealy   31 BA-79
Dotter, Adam; 3 April 1809; Susan Langford   02 BA-7
Doub, John; 12 Nov. 1820; Sophia Flight   16 FR-76
Doub, Michael; March 1804; Cath. Stolz   02 WA-76
Doucet, John Baptist; 1 Feb. 1816; Radegonde Turel   16 BA-31
Doughaday, Hugh; 17 March 1803; Elizabeth Oflero   03 BA-426
Dougherty, Alex.; Feb. 1816; Elizab. F. Mackey   02 WA-101
Dougherty, Bernard; 11 Aug. 1809; Elizabeth Curtain   15 BA-271
Dougherty, Daniel; 24 May 1810; Sarah McKinney   31 BA-81
Dougherty, Daniel; 13 June 1819; Ellen Kerney   05 FR-31
Dougherty, Hugh; 2 Feb. 1816; Sarah Duvall   17 BA-12
Dougherty, John; 24 Aug. 1809; Ann Donnelly   02 BA-7
Dougherty, John; 6 July 1814; Susan Thompson   05 BA-238
Dougherty, John; 12 Sept. 1816; Rachel Bates   16 BA-43
Dougherty, John; 31 Dec. 1816; Mary Clogherty   16 BA-47
Dougherty, John; 8 July 1817; Bridget Kenny   16 BA-55
Dougherty, Patrick; 13 July 1806; Jane Davidson   03 BA-495
Dougherty, Patrick; 5 March 1820; Nancy N. Oblenis   06 FR-1330
Dougherty, Samuel; 24 Nov. 1811; Catherine Dougherty (both
     natives of Ireland)   15 BA-293
Dougherty, Theophilus Felix; 30 Oct. 1810; Hannah Young
                                                      15 BA-283
Dougherty, (Th)omas?; Feb. 1808; Mary Holman   02 WA-85
Dougherty, William; 16 Jan. 1802; Amelia Whelan   15 BA-161
Doughty, Thomas; 8 Jan. 1801; Providence Crasins (?) 33 BA-12
Douglas, George; 15 April 1802; Mary Shearman   17 BA-1
Douglas, John; 6 Sept. 1812; Mary Antoinette Ingres   31 BA-131
Douglas, Peter; 17 Oct. 1809; Sarah Everett   09 BA
Dove, Benjamin; 19 Jan. 1813; Elizabeth Clark   09 BA
Dove, Isaac; 21 Dec. 1802; Darkey Hardy   15 AA-2
Dove, Jilson; 1 Nov. 1810; Mary Dugan   13 BA-11
Dove, John; c.1803; Ann Ford   07 AA-3
Dove, Samuel; 6 Feb. 1816; Elizabeth Stallings   03 AA-131
Dowden, James; 1809; Mahala Benton (See also 02 MO)   01 PG
Dowell, John; 26 Dec. 1818; Elizabethg Pardy   17 BA-21
Dowling, Rody; 10 Sept. 1805; Eleanor Kean   15 BA-226
Dowling, William; 29 June 1816; Priscilla Prestman   323 BA-309
Down, Joseph; 19 Aug. 1801; Charlotte Smith   03 BA-404
Downes, William Dickinson; 8 July 1802; Ruth Dunn   03 BA-418
Downey, David; 14 Aug. 1817; Deborah Dorsey   06 FR-1326
Downey, Edmund; 2 Oct. 1810; Maria Herdester   14 BA-428
Downey, James; Dec. 1805; Cath. Wishard   02 WA-79
Downey, Michael; 22 Feb. 1801; Judith McCaffrey (both natives of
     Ireland)   15 BA-148
Downey, William; 8 Oct. 1815; Ellen Rollans   11 BA-24
Downing, Geo. Benjamin; 15 April 1809; Eliza Mulzers 03 BA-499
Downing, John; 15 Feb. 1819; Sarah Tatham   11 BA-34
Downs, Henry; 5 May 1804; Peggy Seth (both of QA Co.) 01 QA-52
Downs, Henry; 5 May 1804; Peggy Sell (both of QA Co.) 02 TA-39
Downs, Isaia; 4 Aug. 1814; Priscilla Ward   13 BA-19
Downs, John; 16 June 1806; Polly Brown   03 BA-497
Downs, Joseph (age c.31, s. of Joseph and Anne [Sanner] Brown);
     19 April 1801; Eleanor Adams (c.21, dau. of Solomon and
     Dorothy [Henning] Adams)   03 SM
Downs, Solomon; 1 July 1807; Orpah Brown   03 BA-497
Downy, Michael; 22 Feb. 1801; Judith McCaffrey (both natives of
     Ireland)   15 BA-149
Dowson, Joseph; 28 Nov. 1809; Susanna Savage   05 BA-236

Doxey, Thomas; 3 Dec. 1801; Ann Bennett   02 SM-185
Doyl, Lago; 26 Sept. 1815; Susannah Colliflower   06 FR-1323
Doyle, John (native of Ireland); 27 Sept. 1804; Catherine Durke
  (of Balto.)   15 BA-209
Doyle, John G.; 23 Dec., 1817; Eliszabeth Hasleton   06 FR-1327
Doyle, Michael; 2 Nov. 1801; Mary Conry   15 BA-158
Doyle, Patrick; 7 Oct. 1805; Margaret Murray   02 BA-2
Doyle, Patrick; 17 May 1807; Rosanna Dunlevy   15 BA-249
Doyle, Stephen; 15 June 1817; Elizabeth Smith (widow) 16 BA-53
Doyle, Thos.; 10 March 1808; Eliza Fisher   14 BA-423
Doyle, William; 28 May 1817; Ann Eickles   11 BA-31
Dracket, Thomas; 28 March 1813; Martha Hynson   11 BA-21
Draft, Christian Fred'k; 10 May 1809; Polly Bicker   14 BA-426
Drapor, Major Smith; 31 March 1803; Maria Moon   13 BA-3
Drawbaugh, John; 25 June 1808; Charity Jacobs   13 BA-4
Dreier, Joseph; 6 June 1816; Catharina Rhode (widow)   07 BA-310
Drekseler, Ignatius; 8 Nov. 1812; Anna Mou..(?).   39 BA-28
Drekseler, Samuel; 30 May 1819; Margareta Buchman   39 BA-36
Dressler, (Ja?)cob; April 1808; Barb. Fare   02 WA-85
Drew, Henry; 24 Feb. 1810; Elizabeth Ringrose   09 BA
Drill, Charles; 5 Dec. 1811; Martha Hackney   06 FR-1317
Driscoll, Dennis; 5 May 1803; Elenor Collins   03 BA-427
Droghan, Thomas; 27 Sept. 1815; Elizabeth Dann   16 BA-27
Droghan, Thomas; 23 April 1816; Jane Dwyer   16 BA-32
Druby, Jacob; Nov. 1817; Mary Weltz   02 WA-107
Druhle, Jacob Adam; 1 April 1819; Caroline Botskin   14 BA-438
Drummond, Jos.; 6 Jan. 1818; Eliza Southeron   13 BA-30
Drury, Henry C.; 27 May 1806; Eliz'th Mills   03 AA-130
Drury, Jerningham; 1801; Sarah Simmons   07 AA-1
Drury, William; 6 April 1806; Margaret Miles   03 AA-130
Dryden, Josa; 9 Feb. 1813; Anna M. Roberts   13 BA-16
Dryden, Samuel; 21 Dec. 1820; Ann Coburn   11 BA-37
Dryden, Thos.; 23 May 1816; Ann Street   13 BA-25
Dubois, James Aime; 16 Jan. 1810; Mary Magdalen (Madeleine)
  Duperalle   31 BA-73
Dubois, Joseph; 28 Feb. 1810; Lanne Casimier   31 BA-75
Dubois, Joseph; 16 April 1818; Josephine Cappeau   32 BA-319
DuBois, Nicholas; 12 May 1808; Agnes McKim   02 BA-6
Dubree, John' 30 March 1820; Rebecca Craig   14 BA-440
Ducatel, Claud Germain (son of Esme Ducatel and Magd'n Lefree,
  his wife; native of Burgundy); 1 April 1807; Magdalen
  Clemence Muloniere (dau. of Joseph Muloniere and Ann
  Gillois; native of Cayes, St. Domingo)   15 BA-247
Duckworth, Aaron; 20 Feb. 1805; Ann Beem   03 AL-613
Duckworth, George; 19 May 1812; Olive Varnham   03 AL-614
Duckworth, Henry; 1 Oct. 1801; Abigail Tichinal   03 AL-613
Duckworth, Mathias; 24 May 1810; Ann Wilson   03 AL-614
Dudderar, Benjamin; 24 Dec. 1801; Rebecca Holton   10 FR
Dudderow, George; March 1806; Sus. Miller   02 WA-80
Dudley, Alndan; 6 Sept. 1805; Mary River   02 SM-187
Dues, Benjamin; 6 March 1803; Ann Greenstead   09 BA
Duff, Wm.; 10 June 1810; Eliza Norris   13 BA-10
Duffer, John; 27 Oct. 1819; Elizabeth Cantwell   01 SO-15
Duffy, John; 4 Oct. 1814; Rachel James   03 BA-506
Duffy, Owen; 12 June 1803; Mary Kelly (widow)   15 BA-184
Dugal, Patrick; 14 Oct. 1801; Margaret Sweeny   03 BA-408
Dugan, George; 8 Nov. 1804; Eliza Chase   03 BA-492
Dugan, George; 2 April 1806; Ann Scheaves   14 BA-420
Dugan, John; 10 Dec. 1816; Susan Allen   17 BA-15
Dugan, William; 18 Nov. 1819; Catherine Steiver   07 BA-311
Duham(?), James; 4 April 1819; Martha O'Bryan   02 TA-44
Duhays, William; 25 Dec. 1803; Sarah More   15 AA-3
Duke, Basil; 11 Nov. 1817; Juliet Wilson   13 BA-29
Duke, John; 19 Sept. 1820; Margaret Hill   13 BA-35

Dukehart, Valerius (s. of Valerius, dec., and Margaret); 17 d. 12
    mo., 1807; Anna Jones (dau. of Robinson, dec., and Mary)
                                                        09 SF
Dukeheart, Thomas; 19 Aug. 1819; Mary Matthews   07 BA-311
Dukes, James; 14 July 1817; Anne Maria Roades, both of Caroline
    Co.   02 TA-43
Dulaney, Joseph; 23 Jan. 1815; Elizabeth Herbst   17 BA-10
Dulany, Andrew; 21 May 1817; Margaret McIntire   05 BA-240
Dulany, Samuel; 6 Oct. 1813; Marg't Mackenheimer   14 BA-432
Duliard, Peter; 3 Jan. 1802; Cath. Esling (widow of Paul
    Esling)   15 BA-161
Dultyg, Henry; 4 Oct. 1812; Cath. Young   01 FR-1123
Dumas, Peter; 10 March 1817; Rose Eulalie Perine Beausamier
                                                       16 BA-51
Dumas, Raymond; 17 Oct. 1816; Elizabeth Genty   16 BA-45
Dumesnil, Peter L.; 21 July 1801; Charlotte Hiat   21 BA-5
Dunbarr, John A.; 7 Jan. 1802; Ann Richardson   02 SM-185
Dunbarr, William; 11 Dec. 1804; Margarert Smith   02 SM-186
Dunbecker, Adam; 29 Janl. 1811; Elizabeth Seumering   07 BA-307
Duncan, Hamilton; 15 April 1804; Hannah Miller   14 BA-416
Duncan, John; 29 July 1806; Catherine King   02 BA-4
Duncan, John; 15 May 1810; Martha Neale   31 BA-80
Duncan, Solomon; 18 June 1818 (date of lic.); Maria Townsend
                                                       11 BA-33
Duncan, Wm.; 3 Dec. 1807; Debby Robinson   03 BA-497
Dungan, Abel L. (or S.); 25 June 1818; Jane Travis   37 BA-151
Dunham, Jacob; 14 June 1801; Elizabeth Cannon   03 BA-401
Dunkan, James; 1 Dec. 1818; Lavina Mackey   03 BA-603
Dunn, Arthur; 15 Dec. 1803; Mary Burke   03 BA-436
Dunn, Johnsee; 5 July 1808; Rebecca Young   11 BA-13
Dunn, Joseph; 11 Oct. 1801; Mary McGowan   09 BA
Dunning, John; 23 March 1809; Maria Magdalene Stock   07 BA-306
Dunning, William; 15 Nov. 1805; Nancy Harry (See also 15 FR-318)
                                                       01 FR-1123
Dunsmore, John; 10 May 18704; Mary Sullivan   29 BA-2
Duplante, Bernard S.; 22 Feb. 1808; Eleanor O'Sullivan 15 BA-259
Duppin, James; 2 June 1808; Flora Adams   02 BA-6
Duprat, George; 18 Nov. 1802; Jeanny (?) Iriney Angeli (free
    mulattoes of St. Domingo)   15 BA-174
Dupuy, David; 2 Dec. 1806; Ann Smith Touron   03 BA-496
Durand, Elie (s. of Andre Durand and Maria Donneau [or Bonneau],
    b. at Mayenne, Diocese of Man, France); 16 Nov. 1820;
    Polynnis Ducatel (dau. of Edmund [and Anne?])   16 BA-105
Durand, John; 7 May 1807; Mary Wire   02 BA-5
Durany, Richard Ferdinand; 17 May 1812; Jane Pettit   14 BA-430
Durbin, John; (7 Nov. 1819?); Mary Winebruner   06 AL-157
Durburow, Daniel; 10 March 1812; Catherine Bratsby   09 BA
Durham, Joshua; 4 July 1816; Mary Varnoe   17 BA-13
Durham, Samuel; 26 April 1809; Marg't Wiley   14 BA-426
Durham, Thomas; 15 July 1802; Polly Chamberlaine   09 BA
Durrow, Samuel; 31 Oct. 1819; Caroline Dinges   13 BA-33
Durst, Henry; 21 Sept. 1806; Cath. Richter (See also 15 FR-319)
                                                       01 FR-1123
Durst, John Felix; 24 Sept. 1812; Fanny Blatner   07 BA-308
Dusablon, Joseph Vallett; 17 April 1816; Mary FIndley 16 BA-33
Duse, Thomas; 20 Aug. 1820; Mary Ann Wilson   13 BA-35
Dushane, John; 9 Feb. 1813; Harriot A. Wilson   13 BA-16
Dushane, Valentine; 5 Feb. 1809; Elizabeth Sindorf   15 BA-267
Dutton, John; 8 June 1819; Sarah Parks   17 BA-22
Dutty, Henry; 4 Oct. 1812; Catherine Young   15-FR 326
Dutweiler, Joh.; Aug. 1805; Peggy Wright   02 WA-79
Duvall, Alvin; 5 May 1811; Nancy Pennington   09 BA

Duvall, Edmund B.; 6 Jan. 1818; Augusta Caroline McCausland
                                                      09 BA
Duvall, Gabriel L.; 12 Dec. 1816; Sophia Deane   06 FR-1325
Duvall, Henry; 20 Jan. 1803; Elizabeth Godman   15 AA-2
Duvall, Isaac; 18 Dec. 1800; Charlotte Blackston   15 AA-1
Duvall, Lewis; 23 Dec. 1802; Mary Perkins   15 AA-2
Duvall, Mareen H.; 6 May 1801; Dorothy Allen   17 AA
Duvall, Marsh M.; 9 Dec. 1813; Mary A. Taylor   11 BA-21
Duvall, Marsham; 25 Aug. 1801; Mary Hyatt   15 AA-1
Duvall, Nathan; 30 Dec. 1807; Elizabeth Glover   17 AA
Duwall, Samuel; 16 Aug. 1807; Mary Allison (See also 15 FR-321)
                                                      01 FR-1123
Dwyer, William; 26 April 1805; Jane Strobridge   09 BA
Dwyer, William; 4 April 1818; Ann Susan Hughes   02 BA-37
Dyer, Barton (of CH Co., age c.25, son of James and Mary [Red-
     mond] Dyer); 3 Jan. 1801; Jane Newton (age c.23, dau. of
     Barnaby and Molly [Greenwell] Newton)   03 SM
Dyer, William; 31 Dec. 1801; Ann March   09 BA
Dysart, Moses A.; 2 Nov. 1818; Ann Goswick   17 BA-18
Dyse, Stephen; 19 Feb. 1805; Adra (?) Payne   02 SM-186
Eacher, Phenies; 12 Jan. 1813; Sarah Goff   02 WA-96
Eachus, Joseph; 4 March 1819; Jane Davis   13 BA-32
Eades, John; 27 Feb. 1806; Jane Hugg (?)   05 BA-234
Eagan, Anthony; 31 Oct. 1813; Lydia French   09 BA
Eagan, Elijah; 19 Aug. 1803; Eleanor Perrigoe   23 BA-2
Eagan, John; 16 May 1816; Jane Sinclair   05 BA-239
Eagleman, Chas.; 6 April 1808; Mary Shaphe   14 BA-424
Eagleston, Benjamin; 23 Feb. 1807; Mary Brooks   14 BA-421
Eagleston, Joseph; 6 Oct. 1818; Jane Edwards   16 BA-74
Eagleston, Joshua; 24 Dec. 1810; (N) Boonz   15 BA-214
Eaglestone, Abraham; 9 July 1801; Elizabeth Branan   10 BA-1
Eaglestone, Abraham; 29 Nov. 1815; Mary Crawford   17 BA-12
Eailer, Con.; 1 July 1816; Elizabeth Kelsie   30 BA-109
Eames, Jas.; 15 Dec. 1803; Eliza Culberson   03 BA-436
Earle, Jesse C.; 26 Aug. 1816; Sarah Stewart   13 BA-29
Early, John; 10 June 1809; Sarah Gilberthorp   01 FR-1126
Early, John; 10 June 1809; Sarah Gelborthoss   15 FR-323
Early, John; 3 Feb. 1813; Mary Fauble (See also 15 FR-326)
                                                      01 FR-1126
Earnest, Charles; 9 Dec. 1809; Sarah Bradshaw   13 BA-8
Earnest, Dr. John; 3 April 1820; Juliet S. Nicholson 19 BA-73
Easterday, Christian; 30 Nov. 1819; Mrs. Elizabeth Burns (See
     also 16 FR-75)   03 FR-59
Easterday, Jacob; 6 March 1817; Rachael House   06 FR-1326
Easton, Levin; 27 Feb. 1801; Druzilla Ricketts   03 MO-117
Easton, Thos. S.; 8 Dec. 1817; Abigail C. Hart   20 BA-223
Eaton, Leonard; 20 Feb. 1804; Mary Palmer   15 FR-316
Eaton, John; 24 Dec. 1807; Eliza Ferguson   13 BA-3
Eaton, Leonard; 20 Feb. 1804; Mary Palmer   01 FR-1126
Eaton, William; 19 Nov. 1812; Mary Keys   05 BA-237
Eaverson, Joseph; 5 Oct. 1820; Isabella Ford   20 BA-224
Ebaugh, Rev. John S.; Sept. 1818; Ann Eliza Kreps   02 WA-110
Ebberts, Joseph; 1 April 1817; Elizabeth McCormick   06 FR-1326
Eberhard, Conradus; 11 April 1811; Christina Decker   39 BA-26
Ebert, Samuel; 3 Oct. 1811; Comfort Wonn   08 BA
Ebert, Valentine; 28 Sept. 1817; Julian Winpigler   06 FR-1327
Eccleston, James; 25 Nov. 1817; Henrietta Martin   02 DO
Eck, Casper; 18 April 1819; Dorothea Reinemeyer   14 BA-439
Eckart, Johan; 30 Jan. 1811; Elizabeth Rhoad   07 BA-308
Eckendorf, Christian; 12 Feb. 1801; Milly Goldenberg 14 BA-409
Eckhard, Anthony; 16 Sept. 1806; Cath. Shickenhelm (15 FR-319
     gives bride's name as Shitenhelm)   01 FR-1126
Eckis, Samuel; 7 May 1816; Catherine Albaugh   06 FR-1324
Eckle, Jacob; 7 May 1812; Eliz. Funk   02 WA-94

Eckles, Samuel; 19 Sept. 1813; Anny Bell   08 AL-30
Eckman, John; 28 Feb. 1816; Mrs. Jane Ellis   06 FR-1323
Edelen, James; 23 Feb. 1804; Eleanor Davis   09 BA
Edelman, Mich'l; 29 Aug. 1819; Sabina Kriesleber   14 BA-439
Eden (or Aden), John; 15 May 1804; Jane Gold   14 BA-416
Eder, Abraham; 1 Jan. 1811; Elizabeth Hill   06 FR-1315
Eder, Jonathan; 2 May 1819; Maria Harman   06 FR-1329
Eder, Solomon; 17 Aug. 1815; Celia Davidson   06 FR-1322
Edgel, Robert; 22 Oct. 1805; Eliz. Brown   14 BA-419
Edgerly, Edward; 6 March 1803; Sarah Parsons   05 AA-3
Edmondson, Hosea; 5 June 1808; Mary Orme   03 MO-121
Edmonson, (N); 5 June 1808; Mary Orme   01 PG
Edmonson, Brook; 11 Sept. 1817; Harriett Fish   06 FR-1326
Edmonston, Franklin; 31 Oct. 1816; Sarah Ann Wray   09 BA
Edmundson, Thomas (son of Thomas and Mary); 18 d, 4 mo., 1803;
     Elizabeth Morsell (dau. of William and Mary)   03 SF
Edward, John; 15 Feb. 1804; Eleanor Cain   03 BA-490
Edwards, Aquilla; 11 April 1816; Mary Foster   17 BA-12
Edwards, Governeur; Oct. 1818; Eugenie Chauche   16 BA-75
Edwards, James; 29 Oct. 1805; Elizabeth Brown   03 BA-494
Edwards, Nathan; 13 Aug. 1801; Sophia Michal   03 AL-613
Edwards, William; 26 May 1801; Anne Ellender   03 BA-401
Edwards, William; 2 June 1801; Mary Allen   11 BA-3
Edwards, William; 19 July 1801; Nancy Berry   03 BA-403
Edwards, William; 21 Aug. 1806; Mary Piercy   01 DO-41
Edwards, William; 7 May 1807; Ann Stewart   09 BA
Efferson, William; 1 July 1804; Elizabeth Heslip   30 BA-108
Egan, James; 2 May 1820; Ann Curtain   03 BA-604
Egerton, Charles C.; 5 Feb. 1807; Jane DuBois   02 BA-5
Egerton, James; 11 Dec. 1804; Elizabeth Chesley   02 SM-186
Egerton, Richard B.; 29 Oct. 1811; Mary Chesley   01 TA-315
Egleston, Jos.; 1 May 1814; Sarah George   13 BA-19
Eglin, William; 15 Jan. 1820; Mary Ann Morgan   17 BA-22
Ehlen, John; 1 June 1815; Mary Olering   14 BA-433
Ehngel, Jno. August; 18 Nov. 1802; Cath. Neiburger   14 BA-413
Ehrlich, Andreas; 8 May 1803; Barb. Rapp   14 BA-414
Eichelberger, George; 11 April 1816; Catherine Meyers   06 FR-1324
Eichelberger, Henry; 29 Jan. 1811; Mary Johnson   06 FR-1315
Eichelberger, Peter; 5 March 1812; Eliz. Gardner   14 BA-430
Eichelberger, William; 30 Dec. 1817; Caroline Genzle   06 FR-1327
Eiler, George; 30 March 1820; Cathrine Smith   07 BA-312
Eilert, John; 14 Nov. 1810; Cathertine Haley/Kaley   07 BA-307
Ekle, Henry; Oct. 1810; Fanny Funk   02 WA-87
Elder, Basil S.; 18 Nov. 1801; Elizabeth Snowden   15 BA-159
Elder, Hilary; 4 Oct. 1807; Patience Stansbury   15 BA-254
Elder, John; 17 Sept. 1802; Rebecka Newmyer   03 AL-613
Elder, John; 23 July 1812; Reba. Wells   13 BA-14
Elderkin, John; 12 Nov. 1816; Esther Chandler   13 BA-40
Elderkin, William G.; 19 July 1815; Margaret Maggs   03 BA-506
Eldrer, Sam'l; 22 Nov. 1804; Wealthy Johnson   03 BA-492
Elizer, Michael; 8 Dec. 1803; Maria Foreman   36 BA-2
Ellen, Johan; 26 Sept. 1811; Anna Maria Braunin   07 BA-308
Ellger, Hartmann; 25 Nov. 1802; Elizabeth Troldenier (widow)
                                                            07 BA-67
Ellhall, Henry; 1 March 1804; Rebecca Stewart   02 BA-33
Ellicott, Evan Thomas; 22 Feb. 1820; Harvey Bond   20 BA-224
Ellicott, James (s. of Andrew and Esther); 18 d. 2 mo., 1807;
     Henrietta Thomas (dau. of Philip William and Eilizabeth,
     dec., of London)   09 SF
Ellicott, John, Jr. (s. of Andrew and Esther); 20 d. 1 mo., 1803;
     Mary Mitchel (dau. of John and Tacy)   09 SF
Ellicott, John (of BA, s. of John and Leah); 19 d. 1 mo., 1814;
     Mary Kirk (dau. of Timothy and Mary, dec.)   12 SF-43
Ellicott, William; 11 Sept. 1804; Elizabeth Barry   03 BA-491

```
Ellidge, William; 1 June 1819; Elizabeth Terry        37 BA-152
Ellingsworth, William; 20 May 1802; Elizabeth Booze   01 DO-41
Elliot, George; 21 Aug. 1806; Mary Beatty             01 FR-1126
Elliot, George; 14 Jan. 1819; Eliza Dillehunt         01 WA-201
Elliot, Jesse; 10 Nov. 1801; Elizabeth Jones          01 SO-15
Elliot, John, Jr.; c.1804; Darcus Shaw                34 BA-2
Elliot, John; 11 Feb. 1820; Amelia Salling            04 FR-19
Elliot, Nicholas; 24 Dec. 1818; Elizabeth Kader       11 BA-34
Elliot, Thomas; 24 Oct. 1802; Mary Tyrrel             26 BA-2
Elliot, Thomas; 9 Nov. 1819; Mary Bizzard             20 BA-224
Elliot, William; 11 Sept. 1804; Elizabeth Barry       02 BA-34
Elliott, Alexander; 1 Nov. 1801; Charity Woodhouse    03 BA-410
Elliott, George; 21 Aug. 1806; Mary Beatley           15 FR-319
Elliott, John (son of William and Mary); 19 d, 12 mo., 1805;
     Rachel Hughes (dau. of Jesse and Elizabeth)      03 SF
Elliott, John; 23 Oct. 1810; Marg't Farrell           03 BA-502
Elliott, John (son of John and Sarah [Milhouse]); 22 d. 1 mo.,
     1818; Elizabeth Russell (dau. of Thomas and Sarah
     [Roberts])                                       03 SF
Elliott, Joseph B.; 6 July 1815; Harriet Shultz       14 BA-434
Elliott, Richard; 26 Dec. 1810; Reba. Gooding         13 BA-11
Elliott, Robert; 7 Aug. 1817; Mary Coffin             05 BA-240
Elliott, Thomas; 1 Nov. 1801; Rachel McCaslin         03 BA-410
Elliott, Wm.; 18 June 1812; Eliz'h Somerville         13 BA-9
Elliott, Zadock; 25 Oct. 1804; Ruth Barnes            03 AL-613
Ellis, Abraham; Aug. 1817; Sarah Couchman             02 WA-105
Ellis, George; 22 June 1806; Martha McClery           02 BA-4
Ellis, John; 30 June 1814; Mary Mackinzie             20 BA-222
Ellis, Thos.; 31 Aug. 1815; Nancy Wilderman           14 BA-434
Elliston, James S.; 23 Oct. 1815; Susan Waddy         17 BA-11
Elliston, John S.; 29 May 1805; Margaret Blackwell    02 SM-186
Ellit, Thomas; 24 Oct. 1802; Mary Sewell              09 BA
Ellmes, Benjamin; 26 Jan. 1813; Elizabeth Lanham      09 BA
Elmore, James; 24 July 1811; Hannah Swindell          11 BA-16
Elms, Samuel; 31 Jan. 1820; Mrs. Rebecca Rainey       37 BA-152
Elville, Elias; 20 Oct. 1803; Elizabeth Burress       03 MO-118
Elvin, William R.; 15 Oct. 1820; Caroline Bogen       06 FR-1331
Elward, John; 15 Feb. 1804; Eleanor Cain              02 BA-33
Ely, Daniel; Aug. 1815; Martha Mobile (?)             06 FR-1322
Ely, David (s. of Thomas and Hannah); 11 d. 11 m., 1819; Abigail
     Pugh (dau. of Jonathan and Esther)               05 SF
Ely, John; 9 Nov. 1816; Mary Hamilton                 13 BA-40
Ely, Thomas; 18 Oct. 1814; Ann Maria Lancaster        01 BA-11
Ely, William; 11 Dec. 1817; Sarah Row                 06 FR-1327
Embree, Merrick (s. of Samuel and Phebe of West Bradford Twp.,
     Chester Co., PA); 4 d, 5 mo., 1801; Lydia Brown (dau. of
     Joshua, dec., and Zillah, of Little Britain Twp., Lancaster
     Co., PA)                                         06 SF
Emerick, Jacob; 20 Nov. 1809; Margaret Rice           08 AL-30
Emerick, John; Aug. 1806; Elis. Smelser               02 WA-81
Emerson, James; 14 Feb. 1801; Mary France             14 BA-409
Emes, Dan'l; 25 Aug. 1805; Patty Harriton             03 BA-494
Emmerson, Andrew; 15 March 1810; Eliz. Clay Carson    14 BA-427
Emmerson, Arthur; 24 March 1812; Sarah Purden         13 BA-6
Emmerson, Thomas; Jan. 1820; Rachel Stoner            02 WA-115
Emmerson, William (s. of Samuel); 20 d, 6 mo., 1803; Lydia
     Register (dau. of John and Esther)               08 SF
Emmet, Abraham J.; 24 May 1810; Jane Moore            15 FR-324
Emmet, William; 6 Dec. 1808; Susanna Shelmann         15 FR-323
Emmit, Abrah. L.; 24 May 1810; Jane Moore             01 FR-1126
Emmitt, William; 6 Dec, 1808; Sus. Shelman            01 FR-1126
Emmons, Thomas; 21 July 1820; Sarah Rogers            01 WA-203
Emory, Peregrine; 8 May 1806; Kitty E. Higson         02 BA-3
Emory, Thomas L.; 13 June 1815; Eliza H. Grant        03 BA-506
```

```
Empech, Jacob; April 1808; Marg. Olwine              02 WA-5
Emzig, Peter; June 1805; Mary Stucky                 02 WA-79
Enders, Adam; 13 Jan. 1801; Nancy Han                01 CL-149
Enders, William; 16 June 1801; Gertraut Blum         01 CL-149
England, Joseph; 3 Nov. 1802; Mary Tippler           10 FR
Engler, James; 31 May 1818; Rachel Jeffers           13 BA-31
English, King; 17 Sept. 1820; Mary Brown (See also 08 FR-413 and
     16 FR-76)                                       03 FR-61
English, Marshall; 24 March 1803; Elisa Davidson     34 BA-1
Ennis, Gregory; 22 July 1819; Elizabeth Pilchard (widow)
                                                     16 BA-84
Ennis, Lucas; 2 Sept. 1802; Ann Cattrell             06 BA-2
Ennis, William; 1 June 1802; Sarah Alwell            03 AA-120
Enoch, Henry; 14 Sept. 1813; Mary Hall               06 FR-1319
Ensey, William; 9 Feb. 1818; Juliann Pierpoint       11 BA-32
Ensminger, Philip; 20 Sept. 1812; Elizab. Stamm      02 WA-95
Ensor, Ab'm; 2 Oct. 1817; Mary Gorsuch               13 BA-29
Ensor, John; 9 Aug. 1810; Elizabeth Lee              11 BA-15
Ensor, Luke; 21 Jan. 1819; Naoma Ensor               08 BA
Ensor, Luke; 4 April 1820; Sarah Ensor               08 BA
Entz, Andrew; 13 Jan. 1820; Sarah Kaufman            30 BA-109
Eperon, Peter Francis, son of Claudius; 15 July 1820; Josephine
     Curvillier                                      39 BA-37
Erb, Jacob; 7 Jan. 1813; Catherine Weigant           02 CL
Erbich (Erlich), Jacob; 28 April 1811; Nancy Henchel 14 BA-428
Erdinger, Peter; Nov. 1808; Sarah Davis              02 WA-86
Erdman, Peter; 6 Nov. 1803; Barb. Shait              14 BA-415
Erig, Jacob; Aug. 1805; Marg. Chesnut                02 WA-79
Erp, Joseph; 8 Dec. 1812; Mary Jones                 09 BA
Erp, William; 26 Oct. 1816; Ann Read                 11 BA-31
Erter, John; 23 Nov. 1806; Catherine Weber (See also 15 FR-320)
                                                     01 FR-1126
Ervin, John; 1801; Molly Baumgartner                 02 WA-72
Escaville, Joseph; 31 Jan. 1819; Sarah Pollard       13 BA-41
Esdall, William; 22 Aug. 1816; Mary Rigby            17 BA-15
Esender, Thomas; 30 Aug. 1807; Catharina Lonsol      39 BA-20
Esmenard, John Baptiste (native of Pilisanne, son of John Baptist
     and Mary Teresa); 30 Aug. 1803; Henrietta Changeux (dau. of
     Peter and Jane Margaret [Osmond] Changeux)      15 BA-186
Esmenard, Jean Baptiste (native of Pellissane, Provence); 2 Aug.
     1816 (in Parish of Loretta, Cambria Co., PA); Zefie Marie
     Bergerac (dau. of Julien and Marie Bergerac, native of
     Bordeaux; recorded in Baltimore)               16 BA-42
Espy, James; 28 May 1812; Margaret Pollard           03 AL-614
Espy, Josiah; 28 April 1812; Maria Murdock           03 AL-614
Etchberger, John; 6 May 1802; Ailsey Fulford         05 BA-233
Etchberger, Wm.; 25 Sept. 1803; Charlotte Cunningham 36 BA-1
Eter, Abraham; 28 Nov. 1804; Susanna Koenig (See also 15 FR-316)
                                                     01 FR-1126
Etzler, John; 16 Aug. 1812; Susannah C. Lock         06 FR-1318
Euboss, Johanes; 6 Nov. 1803; Eleanor Edwards        14 BA-415
Euler, Jacob; 10 April 1805; Margaret Kircher        30 BA-108
Euler, Jacob; 29 Aug. 1812; Rachel Porter            13 BA-17
Eunich, Thomas; 9 April 1815; Margaret Kemp          11 BA-25
Evalt, Edward; 16 Aug. 1803; Anne Lagge (see also 02 BA-32)
                                                     03 BA-32
Evans, Charles; 1 Aug. 1809; Esther Walker           13 BA-8
Evans, Daniel; 6 Jan. 1803; Sarah Clarage            09 BA
Evans, Dan'l; 26 April 1810; Ruth Dew                13 BA-9
Evans, David; 24 Jan. 1815; Maria Poists             13 BA-20
Evans, Geo.; 10 May 1814; Eliza Pugh                 13 BA-19
Evans, Henry T.; 7 Oct. 1819; Ann Cook               11 BA-37
Evans, Hugh; 25 April 1815; Mary Ann Johnson         03 BA-506
```

Evans, Jno. W.; 17 March 1819; Henrietta Crane (blacks)
                                                      19 BA-72
Evans, Joseph; 23 Sept. 1807; Mary Carpenter   14 BA-422
Evans, Joseph; 27 June 1813; Elizabeth Berrett   09 BA
Evans, Joseph; May 1817; Hannah Lincoln   02 WA-105
Evans, Lewis F.; 29 Oct. 1807; Miriam Hunt   13 BA-3
Evans, Rich'd; 31 Jan. 1814; Eliz'th Thomas   01 SM-64
Evans, Sam'l; 1 Oct. 1810; Jane Norris   03 BA-501
Evans, Thomas; 26 Oct. 1818; Elizabeth Fisher   37 BA-151
Evans, William; 5 Sept. 1802; Ann Clarke   02 SM-185
Evans, William; 4 Oct. 1808; Mary Sallsbury   02 BA-6
Evans, Wm.; 6 March 1817; Charlotte Clarke   02 BA-37
Evans, William; 11 May 1817; Charlotte Rennard   17 BA-16
Evens, Edmund (s. of John and Sarah of Devon, Great Britain); 15
    d. 1 mo., 1810; Elizabeth Husband (dau. of Joseph, dec., and
    Mary, of HA Co.)   09 SF
Everet, Abraham Henry; 26 March 1812; Ann Albright   14 BA-430
Everet, Thomas; 13 Dec. 1802; Rebecca Myring   09 BA
Everett, James; 8 Oct. 1812; Agness Reynolds   13 BA-15
Everett, Thomas; 2 Jan. 1817; Elizabeth Burgess   17 BA-15
Everett, Sam'l; 1 Sept. 1811; Ellin Shilling   13 BA-13
Everhart, Jacob; 22 July 1811; Sarah Triplet   03 BA-503
Everson, Joseph; 6 Aug. 1808; Margaret Gatch   13 BA-4
Everwein, Wm.; 17 Aug. 1813; Cath. Gebhard   14 BA-432
Eves, John; 23 June 1818; Anne Grace   17 BA-19
Ewald, Henry; 13 July 1812; Dorothy S. Raab   14 BA-430
Ewalt, Jacob; 9 March 1819; Araminta Pumphrey   13 BA-34
Ewell, Jesse; 23 May 1804 (AA Co.); Rachel B. Weems   40 BA
Ewell, John; c.1804; Margaret Soller   34 BA-2
Ewell, Thomas; 25 Sept. 1802; Ann Spadden   09 BA
Ewen, James; 8 May 1816; Flora Osborne   17 BA-12
Ewerwein, Heinrich; 16 April 1809; Sarah Baxter   07 BA-306
Ewing, David; 3 March 1811; Polly Murphy   06 FR-1315
Ewing, William; 10 Dec. 1801; Lydia Wilson   09 BA
Ewing, William; 21 Nov. 1805; Elizabeth Norrington (see also
    01 BA-10)   33 BA-43
Ewins, Alexander; 4 Nov. 1816; Mary Ann Augustus   17 BA-15
Extreem, Peter; 21 Aug. 1801; Nancy Bartley   14 BA-410
Ezaway, James; 9 Dec. 1819; Catherine Shiply   06 FR-1330
Fachskorn, William; 16 June 1812; Margaretha Craig   07 BA-308
Factenroth, George; 8 March 1814; Elis. Fritz   02 WA-99
Fagan, George; 27 Aug. 1816; Catherine Boley   06 FR-1325
Fagan, James; 11 Dec. 1804; Mary Caton   15 BA-212
Fagin, Daniel; 12 Sept. 1801; Margaret Bolless   27 BA-1
Fague, George; 1 June 1813; Nany Jordan   02 WA-97
Faherty, Bartholomew; 2 May 1804; Mary Staylor   15 BA-202
Faherty, Patrick; 25 April 1814; Bridget Morris (both natives of
    Ireland)   16 BA-4
Faherty, Patrick; 6 Feb. 1815; Mary Claugherty (both natives of
    Ireland)   16 BA-15
Faherty, Thomas; 17 March 1803; Mary Farshar   15 BA-179
Fahs, Casper; 25 June 1806; Mary Haeffler   14 BA-420
Fairall, Erasmus; 30 Jan. 1817; Harriet Woodward   11 BA-31
Fairbairn, Thomas H.; 7 Nov. 1809; Maria Eliza Henry 15 BA-275
Fairbank, James, Jr. (s. of James and Elizabeth); 24 d, 12 mo.,
    1812; Rebecca Dixon (dau. of William, dec., and Ann)
                                                      08 SF
Fairbank, John; 26 Aug. 1802; Blanche Walker   03 BA-419
Fairbank, John; 7 June 1804; Charly (Charity?) Jennings
                                                      15 AA-3
Fairbank, Samuel (s. of James and Elizabeth); 12 d, 8 mo., 1807;
    Mary Dixon (dau. of William and Ann)   08 SF
Fairbank, Wm.; 17 Oct. 1816; Mary Amey   13 BA-26
Faithfull, William; 5 June 1803; Margaret Burke   03 BA-428

Falconer, Peregrine; 1 Nov. 1808; Elizabeth Levy   03 BA-498
Falconer, Abraham Hall; 15 Oct. 1818; Catherine Goff Cantwell
                                                        20 BA-223
Fales, Benjamin; 26 July 1807; Elizabeth Clarke   02 BA-5
Falls, Stephen W.; 14 Dec. 1819; Henrietta Jane Howard 33 BA-47
Falmous?, Martin; 6 Feb. 1809; Mary Davis   31 BA-55
Faner, John; 7 June 1803; Rebecca Klee   15 FR-314
Fanlac, Anthony; 8 Feb. 1812; Mary E. Say   14 BA-429
Fanning, Edward; 23 Dec. 1819; Eliz'th Crane   19 BA-73
Farnandis, Samuel; 4 Oct. 1808; Anne Bowly Stuart   03 BA-498
Farnsworth, Jonathan; 29 Oct. 1811; Ann West   06 FR-1316
Farquhar, Allen (s. of Allen and Phebe [Hibberd]); 22 d. 9 mo.,
    1803; Mary Poulteny (dau. of Anthony and Susanna [Plummer])
                                                        03 SF
Farquhar, Caleb (son of Allen and Phebe [Hibberd]; 23 d. 4 mo.,
    1807; Sarah Poulteny (dau. of Anthony and Susanna [Plummer])
                                                        03 SF
Farquhar, Moses B. (son of William and Mary [Bailey]); 19 d. 5
    mo., 1813; Massey Pusey (dau. of George and Sarah)
                                                        03 SF
Farquhar, William Y. (son of Samuel and Phebe [Yarnall]); 23 d. 5
    mo., 1804; Mary Wright (dau. of Isaac and Eleanor [Parvin])
                                                        03 SF
Farquharson, Charlkes; 14 March 1815; Ann Crossen   09 BA
Farr, John B.; 9 Aug. 1801; Jane Cawood   02 CH
Farrel, James; 1 Aug. 1807; Mrs. Eleanor Maguire (widow of Simon
    Donelly)   31 BA-28
Farrell, Francis; March 1812; Marg't Cross   03 BA-503
Farrell, George; 28 Dec. 1820; Mary Ann Bailey   17 BA-23
Farrell, James; 13 June 1815; Juliana Boyle   16 BA-21
Farrell, James W.; 6 Feb. 1815; Mary Ann Ennis (dau. of Philip)
                                                        32 BA-303
Farren, Neal, of Phila.; 20 Oct. 1817; Ann O'Brien   16 BA-57
Farriny, August; 11 Dec. 1818; Ellen Clouse   14 BA-438
Farrow, Charles; 21 March 1802; Isabella Massey   09 BA
Farry (or Harvey), James; 16 Oct. 1814; Lilly Wiley   17 BA-10
Farthing, James; 6 Oct. 1801; Mary Ott   01 FR-1128
Farthing, James; 6 Jan. 1801; Margaret Ott   15 FR-311
Farver, Jacob; 19 June 1817; Mary Lee   08 BA
Fasenacht, John; 1804; Barb. Warewick   02 WA-77
Fasenacht, John; 3 Sept. 1812; Ros. Wallick   02 WA-95
Fasnacht, Wendel; 4 May 1813; Eliz. Wallich   02 WA-97
Fate, Thomas; 19 Jan. 1807; Elizabeth Gordon   02 BA-5
Faucet, Rowland; 28 Jan. 1805; Sarah Graham   03 BA-492
Fauckler, Jacob; Feb. 1818; Cath. Fishauck   02 WA-108
Fauer, John; 7 June 1803; Rebecca Klee   01 FR-1128
Faulker, Richard; 20 March 1805; Susanna Roberts   02 BA-34
Faulkner, R'd; 20 March 1805; Susanna Roberts   03 BA-493
Fauner, Christian; 24 Oct. 1801; Charlotte Washing   14 BA-411
Fauntz, Jacob; 12 Sept. 1803; Polly Rutter   14 BA-415
Faut, Ernst; 19 March 1806; Elizabeth Kuserick   14 BA-419
Faut, William; 24 Aug. 1806; Magd(alene) Adams (See also
    15 FR-319)   01 FR-1128
Fauvel, John Baptist Gabriel Gouran; 31 Jan. 1813; Sarah Smith
                                                        31 BA-143
Faveer (?), Anthony; 20 Aug. 1816; Jane Delton   14 BA-435
Favorite, Abrah.; 15 Dec. 1807; Elizabeth Shroyack (15 FR-322
    gives bride's name as Shreyack)   01 FR-1128
Feaga, Frederick; 5 Feb. 1815; Elizabeth Fegler   06 FR-1321
Fearroll, Walter; 3 Dec. 1801; Rhoda Danielson   15 AA-2
Federaff, Fred'k. B.; 3 June 1813; Cath. Keilholtz   14 BA-432
Federick, John; 30 April 1809; Catherine Frollinger   03 AL-614
Federman, Philip; 12 Feb. 1809; Lydia Reed   08 AL-33
Feiger, Christian; 18 April 1819; An. Barb. White   14 BA-439

```
Feinour, William; 24 June 1810; Eleanor Hagthrop       31 BA-83
Fell, Elijah; 22 Feb. 1808; Bridget Conner             09 BA
Fell, Joshua; 16 July 1805; Sarah Nicholson            09 BA
Fendall, Edward; 17 Dec. 1811; Frances T. Cockey       09 BA
Fennell, John (a gauger); 29 May 1803; Mary Jordan     15 BA-183
Fenton, Charles; 16 Oct. 1814; Elizabeth Majers        08 BA
Fenton, Eugene; 18 June 1816; Mary Osburne             32 BA-309
Fenwick, Enoch (age c.28, son of Philip and Rebecca [Greenwell]
    Fenwick); 22 Nov. 1800 (by virtue of a dispensation for
    consangunity in the 2nd degree, granted by the Rt. Rev. John
    Carroll, Bp. of Balto.); Jane Greenwell (age c.20, dau. of
    John and Mildred [Neal] Greenwell)                 03 SM
Fenwick, Dr. Martin; 22 Aug. 1815; Ann Louisa Ghequierie
                                                       16 BA-25
Fenwick, Ralph (s. of Wm.); 26 Dec. 1799; Lydia (Smith?) (dau. of
    Jane)                                              03 SM
Ferguson, Benjamin; 24 Aug. 1819; Elizabeth Clark      13 BA-41
Ferguson, David D.; 9 July 1818; Mary Buchanan         11 BA-29
Ferguson, Geo.; 27 Dec. 1812; Ann Johns                13 BA-15
Ferguson, James; 12 Oct. 1813; Catherine Robb          05 BA-237
Ferguson, Joseph; 24 Dec. 1812; Nancy Jones            02 WA-96
Ferguson, William; 17 April 1817; Margaret Craig       05 BA-240
Fermamon, Samuel; 22 Dec. 1803; Charity Kight          03 AL-613
Ferris, John (s., of Nathan and Rachel); 17 d, 11 mo., 1802; Anna
    Gray (dau. of William and Elizabeth)               07 SF-2
Ferris, Josiah; 29 Jan. 1817; Mary McKay               02 BA-37
Ferris, Stephen; 5 July 1820; Mary Jackson (colored)   37 BA-153
Fesler, Godhelph. Chr.; Feb. 1807; Barb. Kring (?)     02 WA-83
Fessler, John; 18 Jan. 1812; Susannah Baer             6 FR-1317
Feyer, Friederich; 8 Dec. 1802; Nancy Church           07 BA-68
Feygele, Peter; May 1805; Elis. Knutz                  02 WA-78
Fiege, George; 19 Nov. 1812; Catherine Trout           06 FR-1318
Fields, James; 20 Oct. 1814; Ann Churcher (?)          16 BA-11
Fields, James (?) M.; 7 Sept. 1819; Sophia Frazier     06 FR-1330
Fields, James; 17 Dec. 1820; Ann Evans                 17 BA-23
Fifer, Fred'k; 6 Dec. 1802; Marg't Grimes              14 BA-413
Fifer, John.; 16 Sept. 1802; Anne Wood                 03 BA-420
Fifer, John W.; 22 May 1817; Mary Tiney                17 BA-14
Fiffell, Joseph; 2 Dec. 1813; Maria (?) Sinsner        14 BA-432
Fige, Friederich; 29 Oct. 1807; Juliana Murray         07 BA-305
Figele, Joh.; Nov. 1803; Marg. Bam (?)                 02 WA-75
Figele, William; Oct. 1803; Sus. Cow                   02 WA-75
Figeley, Peter; Nov. 1807; Nancy Moyer                 02 WA-84
Figely, Henry; 17 March 1811; Polly Ridenour           02 WA-89
Fight, Peter; 1803; Elis. Brua.                        02 WA-76
Fill (or Till?), William; 24 Nov. 1814; Hannah Reese   20 BA-222
Filler, John; 14 March 1819; Mary Tuel                 06 FR-1329
Filler, Solomon; 16 March 1820; Elizabeth Link         06 FR-1330
Finch, Geo.; 3 Jan. 1819; Fanny Blades                 13 BA-32
Finck, Gotfried; 4 Sept. 1806; Susana Maul             14 BA-420
Findal, John; 27 Oct. 1814; Penelope C. D. Cockey      09 BA
Finetell(?), Thomas; 19 March 1807; Margaret Furbay    09 BA
Finigan, John (son of John and Mary); 10 Jan. 1806; Violetta
    Neary (?) (dau. of Peter and Mary)                 31 BA-1
Finkle, Emanuel; 15 Sept. 1818; Elizabeth Gross        06 FR-1328
Finknauer, Henry; 27 May 1819; Marg't Mauer            14 BA-439
Finlay, Samuel; Dec. 1804; Rebecca Bull                17 BA-4
Finlay, William; 14 March 1805; Anna (?)               03 BA-493
Finletter, James; 8 Oct. 1807; Ann Philpot             13 BA-2
Finley, Ebenezer Lewis; 31 Aug. 1819; Eliza White O'Donnell
                                                       03 BA-604
Finley, James; 10 July 1813; Anna Barnes               09 BA
Finley, Thomas; 23 Jan. 1806; Ann Perry Bell           05 BA-234
Finney, Rev. William; 7 Sept. 1815; Susan Correy       07 HA
```

Finney, Rev. William; 10 Oct. 1820; Margaret Irvine Miller
                                                        07 HA
Finnigan, Michael; 22 March 1806; Rosanna McGirk (both natives of
     Ireland)   15 BA-236
Finour, Charles; 3 March 1801; Margaret Maxwell   15 BA-149
Firestone, Michael; 28 Jan. 1812; Susanna Russell   02 WA-92
Firy, Joseph; 20 Feb. 1812; Cath. Rouch   02 WA-93
Fischer, Georg; 26 April 1801; Esther Pfeiffer   01 CL-149
Fish, (N); 1808; Hellen Joy   01 PG
Fish, Allen; 13 June 1811; Ann Monk   11 BA-16
Fish, Hatton; 24 Feb. 1801; Sarah Benton   03 MO-117
Fish, William; Dec. 1808; Hellen Joy   03 MO-121
Fishbaugh, Jesse; 5 Dec. 1804; Elizabeth Sybrae (see also
     03 BA-492)   02 BA-34
Fishbeck, John; 1 July 1809; Lydia O'Bonner (15 FR-324 gives
     bride's name as O'Banner)   01 FR-1129
Fisher, Amos; 24 Dec. 1811; Rebecka Myer   03 AL-614
Fisher, Basel; 19 Oct. 1819; Barbara Ewald   07 BA-311
Fisher, Henry; 29 Jan. 1801; Susannah Swan   11 BA-2
Fisher, Jacob; c.1804; Ann Stevens   34 BA-2
Fisher, James; 16 Feb. 1816; Hannah Massey   09 BA
Fisher, John; 1 June 1809; Ann Young   13 BA-6
Fisher, John; 19 Nov. 1811; Ann Robinson   05 BA-237
Fisher, Jno. J.; 18 Sept. 1807; Elis. Carson   13 BA-2
Fisher, Joseph; 4 March 1801; Rebecca Hammock   09 BA
Fisher, Robert; 21 March 1807; Amelia Alexander   02 BA-5
Fisher, Thomas; 22 Jan. 1807; Mary Ann Shipley   03 BA-497
Fisher, Wm.; 2 July 1801; Rebecca Dalrymple   27 BA-1
Fisher, Wm.; 8 Sept. 1803; Cresey Skidmore (see also 07 AL-274)
                                                       04 AL-1
Fishpaw, Thomas; 15 March 1804; Nancy Rutter   09 BA
Fishpoon, Joseph; 13 Aug. 1801; Sarah Balts   09 BA
Fitch, Daniel; 29 Oct. 1803; Ann Burgoyne   14 BA-415
Fitch, Gideon; 9 Nov. 1815; Mary Ann Lynch   13 BA-23
Fitch, John; 27 Aug. 1801; Catherine Dubridge   03 BA-405
Fitch, Jos.; 23 Jan. 1819; Maria Spedding   13 BA-34
Fitch, Wm.; 14 June 1806; Mary Parlet   14 BA-420
Fite, Andrew; 20 April 1819 (or 1820); Martha Barnett 13 BA-41
Fite, Conrad R.; 2 Dec. 1819; Pamelia Gist   11 BA-32
Fite, Henry; 10 Oct. 1815; Mary P. Worthington   11 BA-24
Fitre (?), William; 29 Nov. 1802; Jane Larew   02 BA-32
Fitz, Robert; 23 Nov. 1809; Rebecca McDowell   09 BA
Fitz, William; 29 Nov. 1802; Jane Larue   03 BA-423
Fitzgarrell, Joseph; 24 Nov. 1818; Elizabeth Mahany   04 FR-18
Fitzgerald, Austin; 15 Nov. 1807; Margaret Walsh   15 BA-258
Fitzgerald, James; 19 Jan. 1820; Clara Victory Candoll 32 BA-327
Fitzgerald, Mich'l; 28 Aug. 1809; Mary Schinge   13 BA-8
Fitzhugh, Henry W.; 12 Oct. 1820; Ellen O. Wilkins   11 BA-36
Fitzhugh, William; 3 March 1818; Maria A. Hughes   01 WA-200
Fitzjeffrey, Richard; 8 March 1805; Eleanor Loury (03 BA-492
     gives her name as Lowry)   02 BA-34
Fitzpatrick, Thomas; 14 Feb. 1802; Mary Dowar (natives of
     Ireland)   15 BA-163
Fitzpatrick, Wm.; 12 July 1802; Charlotte Grogen   14 BA-413
Fixler, Jos.; 28 Oct. 1820; Deb. Starr   13 BA-36
Flachskemp, William; 23 Sept. 1814; Maria Hoffman   07 BA-309
Flaharty, Thomas; 6 July 1817; Nancy Cuney or Currey   03 BA-602
Flaherty, James (widower); 24 Sept. 1805; Mary Duffy (widow)
                                                       15 BA-228
Flaherty, James (son of John and Hannah); 28 Dec. 1805; Mary
     Lawler (dau. of Edward and Judith)   15 BA-233
Flaherty, John (nat. of Ire.); 7 Feb. 1815; Cath. Behner (nat. of
     Balto. City)   16 BA-15

Flaherty, John; 2 Jan. 1817; Hannah Riley   09 BA
Flahery, John R.; 3 Sept. 1820; Rebecca Winnull   04 FR-20
Flanagan, Thomas; 19 Nov. 1816; Anne O'Donell   39 BA-33
Flanagan, Thomas; 20 Nov. 1817; Sophia White   06 FR-1327
Flanigan, Joseph; 20 Aug. 1820; Elizabeth Welsh   05 FR-35
Flaxen, Michael; 8 July 1802; Sarah Halfpenny   09 BA
Fleetwood, William; Feb. 1805; Cathrine Medaira   17 BA-4
Fleming, Caleb; 19 April 1809; Ellen Blummer (See also 15 FR-323)
                                                       01 FR-1128
Fleming, Samuel; 24 Dec. 1829; Elizab. Reynolds   01 FR-1129
Fleming, William; 8 Aug. 1811; Mary Waddell   03 AL-614
Fletcher, Edward; 25 May 1809; Margaret Henry   15 BA-269
Fletcher, George; 12 Nov. 1806; Cath. Black   14 BA-421
Fletcher, Jacob; 17 May 1803; Sarah Murray   14 BA-414
Fletcher, John; 7 Jan. 1813; Catherine Slaughter   09 BA
Fletcher, John; 23 March 1815; Catherine Christ   17 BA-12
Fletcher, John R.; 9 Nov. 1801; Elizabeth Hush   09 BA
Fletcher, Joseph L.; 16 Dec. 1812; Margaret McCubbins 09 BA
Fletcher, Lewis; Nov. 1817; Rebecca O'Neil   02 WA-107
Flin, Owen; 6 May 1819; Jane Boteler   06 FR-1330
Flinn, Charles H.; 8 Oct. 1819; Margaret Lock   01 WA-202
Flora, Christopher; March? 1804; Elis. Oswald   02 WA-76
Flowers, John; 25 June 1808; Elizabeth Watkins   02 BA-6
Floyd, Thomas; 17 Feb. 1814; Lydia Hunt   20 BA-222
Floyd, William; 6 Nov. 1817; Mary Sweeny   17 BA-17
Fluck, John; 5 April 1801; Eliz. Schreyer (See also 15 FR-311)
                                                       01 FR-1128
Fluke, Henry; 21 Nov. 1811; Hannah Castle (See also 15 FR-325)
                                                       01 FR-1129
Foerster, Josephus; Nov. 1807; Esther Harson   39 BA-20
Fogel, Henry; 1 March 1812; Elizabeth Eiler   06 FR-1317
Fogle, Joh.; Sept. 1807; Sus. Bond   02 WA-83
Fogle, John; 15 Sept. 1811; Susannah Smith   06 FR-1316
Fogle, Matthias; 14 Dec. 1813; Catherine Eyler   06 FR-1320
Fogleman, Georg; 5 March 1811; Catherine Ewald   07 BA-308
Fogler, Jacob; 19 March 1811; Catherine Dertzebaugh   06 FR-1315
Fogler, John; 30 March 1813; Susanna Koller   06 FR-1319
Foher, John; 19 Aug. 1816; Bridget Flaherty   16 BA-41
Folan (?), Michael; 18 Sept.(?) 1817; Sarah Lurinburg 32 BA-316
Foley, Priestley; 7 Nov. 1803; Sarah Flemming (see also 03 BA-435)
                                                       02 BA-33
Foley, Timothy; 17 Aug. 1806; Nancy McJustice (age 17 years)
                                                       31 BA-10
Folliard, James; 30 Sept. 1817; Eliza Wasson   13 BA-29
Folsher, John; 14 May 1818; Mary Pendergrass   37 BA-151
Foltz, William; 4 April 1815; Catherine Beyerle   06 FR-1322
Foncett, Jno.; 2 April 1806; Abarilla German   14 BA-419
Fonerden, Adam; 24 Feb. 1803; Easter Marshall   36 BA-1
Foos, John; 6 Aug. 1801; Hannah Cole   15 BA-154
Foquet, Domineque; 25 Feb. 1808; Nancy Grast   13 BA-3
Ford, Ab'm; 7 Oct. 1810; Cathe. Hancock   13 BA-11
Ford, Charles; 21 Jan. 1813; Harrot Fliner   09 BA
Ford, Elias; 11 May 1820; Elizabeth Sarver   11 BA-36
Ford, Geo. L.; 23 July 1812; Lovery Bekskat   03 BA-504
Ford, John; 13 May 1810; Elizabeth Timanus   09 BA
Ford, John; 16 Feb. 1817; Caroline Deye Wyle   09 BA
Ford, Joseph T.; 4 July 1811; Eve Thompson   09 BA
Ford, Mordecai; 20 May 1804; Mary Price   23 BA-3
Ford, Nicholas; 22 Aug. 1807; Eliza Ford   13 BA-2
Ford, Samuel; 28 Sept. 1802; Eleanor Ford   23 BA-1
Ford, Stephen H.; 25 Sept. 1811; Grace Hammond   03 BA-503
Ford, Thomas; Feb. 1820; Mary Winters   02 WA-115
Ford, W.; 22 Nov. 1814; Eliza A. Dorsey   13 BA-20
Ford, Walter; 24 Dec. 1815; Mary Lester   13 BA-24

Ford, William (widower); 30 June 1814; Marg't Foster (widow)
    16 BA-7
Forde, Michael J.; 4 May 1815; Nancy Armstrong   11 BA-25
Fordney, William; 5 Nov. 1809; Susan Jones   11 BA-15
Fordwell, William; 23 Oct. 1819; Lilly Lockerman   13 BA-33
Foreman, Abraham; 3 Dec. 1812; Mary Rowland   02 WA-96
Foreman, Elisha; 19 Dec. 1807; Eliza Driscoll   14 BA-423
Foreman, John; 3 June 1819; Cassandra Burke   17 BA-22
Foreman, Samuel; 9 Feb. 1804; Rebecca Robinson   14 AA-1
Foreman, Thomas; 11 April 1819; Rachel Harris   11 BA-35
Forest, George; 11 Jan. 1820; Ann Hutson   17 BA-22
Forest, Leonard; 15 July 1816; Sarah Stewart   13 BA-26
Forester, John; 12 March 1801; Mary Taylor   11 BA-2
Forguson, Joh.; May 1805; Rachael Williamson   02 WA-78
Forman, Edward; 16 Jan. 1806; Hannah Allan   11 BA-8
Forman, John; 21 Jan. 1804; Ann Marsh   15 AA-3
Forman, Joshua; 21 June 1807; Mary Philips   09 BA
Forman, Thomas; 19 Dec. 1820; Ann Willis   13 BA-36
Formevelt, Jacob; 5 April 1815; Rebecca Gramer   14 BA-433
Fornessen, Henry; Oct. 1817; Polly Gower   02 WA-106
Forney, David S.; 26 feb. 1818; Eliz'th Decker   19 BA-72
Forrest, John; 19 Oct. 1816; Frances Conley   13 BA-40
Forrest, Nich's.; 16 Feb. 1815; Eleanor Dennison   13 BA-20
Forrest, Owen; Sept. 1819; Elizab. Stottlemyer   02 WA-114
Forrest, Solomon; Nov. 1817; Elizab. Wolf   02 WA-107
Forster, (?) miah; Dec. 1807; Mary Webb   02 WA-84
Forster, Francis; 22 June 1806; Sarah Askew   02 BA-4
Forster, Wm.; 28 Aug. 1812; Elizabeth McKnight   21 BA-7
Forsyth, Alexander; 3 June 1809; Hetty Zell   03 BA-499
Forsyth, Wm.; 10 June 1802; Lydia Emmerson   21 BA-5
Forsythe, Isaac; 19 June 1803; Anne Litton   03 MO-118
Fort, Benj.; 18 Jan. 1803; Airey Carrey   21 BA-5
Forte, Thomas; 13 Nov. 1803; Agnes Leuthwaite   05 BA-234
Fortune, Nicolaus; 17 De.c 1807; Anna Borrman (or Burman)
    07 BA-306
Forty, John; 29 Oct. 1803; Sarah Price   05 AA-3
Fosdick, John M.; 16 (or 26) July 1818; Maria McDonnell
    32 BA-321
Foss, George; 10 April 1806; Mary Pouder   30 BA-108
Foss, Jacob; 5 Jan. 1804; Rebecca Priestly   14 BA-416
Foss, Jacob; 2 June 1808; Margaret Ditmore   30 BA-109
Foss, John; 6 May 1804; Anna Henry   30 BA-108
Foss, John; 4 Sept. 1807; Catharine Rigby   13 BA-2
Foss, John; 17 March 1818; Eliza Boggs   13 BA-30
Fossbinder, Dan'l; 1 Nov. 1806; Susanna Butler   14 BA-420
Fossey, John; 25 Aug. 18705; Margaret McClane   15 BA-226
Foster, Francis; 28 June 1817; Barbara Donaldson   03 BA-602
Foster, Isaac; 8 Sept. 1803; Darcus Green   34 BA-1
Foster, James; 1 Aug. 1811; Susan Wehner   11 BA-17
Foster, John; 9 Jan. 1812; Catherine March   15 BA-294
Foster, Jno. M.; 21 Oct. 1816; Louisa Dimmitt   03 BA-508
Foster, Julius C.; 17 April 1810; Martha Hutson   06 AL-18
Foster, Thomas; 20 June 1818; Mary Bent   17 BA-19
Foster, Wm.; 3 Sept. 1812; Louisa Tignal   03 BA-504
Foster, Wm.; 6 Dec. 1812; Mary Raborg   14 BA-431
Foster, Wm.; 1 Feb. 1819; Hanna Schliecker   14 BA-438
Foulke, David; 7 Sept. 1815; Harriet Armstrong   14 BA-434
Fountain, Henry; 29 May 1815; Sarah Good   13 BA-51
Fournin, John; 15 Aug. 1811; Susan Toward   13 BA-13
Fourtnan, Christian; 3 Sept. 1805; Susanna Boyd   14 BA-418
Foust, Philip; 9 May 1811; Elis. Cash   02 WA-90
Fout, Frederick; 17 Nov. 1818; Margareth Silkitt   06 FR-1329
Fowble, Daniel; 9 April 1810; Susanna Roberts   21 BA-7
Fowble, Daniel; 12 Nov. 1811; Anna Bug   30 BA-109

```
Fowble, John; 26 Oct. 1802; Cynthia Algire           23 BA-2
Fowble, Melchor; 15 April 1819; Juliann Bagfoot      08 BA
Fowble, Peter; 21 March 1818; Rebecca Hardister      11 BA-28
Fowler, Abraham; 1804; Mary Stump                    07 AA-4
Fowler, George; 1 Jan. 1801; Elizabeth White         09 BA
Fowler, Henry; 31 Dec. 1801; Nelly (mulatto woman of Lewis Beall)
                                                     03 MO-117
Fowler, George; 7 April 1801; Frances Childs         09 AA-1
Fowler, Jas.; 3 April 1809; Marg't Caldron           03 BA-499
Fowler, James; 12 July 1812; Kitty Fowler            13 BA-17
Fowler, James; Dec. 1818; Mary Inglebrite            02 WA-111
Fowler, John; 19 Nov. 1811; Cath. Lutz               02 WA-92
Fowler, John; 9 Dec. 1813; Hetty Segeser             14 BA-432
Fowler, William; c.1804; Hannah Fonihill             07 AA-4
Fowler, William; 2 Feb. 1818; Deborah Thompson       11 BA-31
Fox, Henry; 16 Nov. 1805; Mary Schwarts              02 BA-2
Fox, John; 14 April 1814; Elizabeth Grushon          06 FR-1320
Foxall, Thomas; 12 July 1810; Mary Cox               09 BA
Foxcroft, James A.; 29 June 1820; Eliza Smith        11 BA-36
Foxcroft, Samuel; 29 Jan. 1818; Susan Brown          13 BA-30
Foxwell, George; 12 April 1809; Cath. Daley          14 BA-425
Foy, John; 30 Dec. 1806; Anna Hawking                07 BA-305
Foy, Michael; Nov. 1819; Elizab. Gilbert             02 WA-114
Foy, Peter; 27 Aug. 1804; Ann Alley                  15 BA-207
Foy, Peter; 1 Nov. 1815; Margaret Butler             32 BA-306
Foye, Frederick; 5 Nov. 1817; Elizabeth Anspach      07 BA-311
Fraley, Leonard; 9 March 1803; Eliz. Stilcher        14 BA-414
Frame, James (s. of Benj. and Elizabeth); 20 d. 3 m., 1816;
    Asenath Farr (dau. of John and Leah)             01 SF
Frame, James M.; 20 d. 3 mo., 1816; Asenath Farr     10 SF
Frampton, Isaac (s. of William and Margaret); 22 d. 1 mo., 1806;
    Deborah Dawson (dau. of Elisha and Lydia of Sussex Co., DE)
                                                     07 SF-11
France, James; 12 Aug. 1819; Margaretta Boyle        20 BA-224
Francis, Ephraim; 15 Sept. 1808; Eliza Jarvis        13 BA-4
Francis, Francis Antonio; 13 Sept. 1806; Jane Smith (widow of
    John Jacob Smith)                                31 BA-12
Francis, John; 12 Nov. 1817; Ellen Cooper            32 BA-317
Francis, John L.; 15 May 1817; Jane Johnson (free people of
    colour)                                          05 BA-240
Francisco, Sam'l; 21 April 1817; Rebecca Pritchett   13 BA-28
Franciscus, John; 2 Feb. 1804; Mary Thompson         09 BA
Franciscus, Wm.; 6 Aug. 1812; Frances Guston         11 BA-20
Franer, Thos.; 6 June 1816; Eliza Weaver             14 BA-25
Frank, Ludwicus; 13 Nov. 1807; Maria Magdalena Klapdore
                                                     39 BA-20
Frank, Ludwicius; 19 [July] 1818; Maria Ritter       39 BA-35
Frank, Luther; 5 June 1806; Margaret Disney          15 BA-239
Frankel, Ludwicus; 13 Nov. 1807; Maria Magdalena Klapdore
                                                     39 BA-20
Frankhausen, George; 8 Dec. 1818; Regina Matthews    39 BA-35
Franklin, George; 9 March 1815; Jullian Essex        13 BA-20
Franklin, James; 14 Oct. 1815; Jane Lane             17 BA-13
Franklin, Thos.; 21 Oct. 1819; Eliza Cochran         13 BA-33
Franklin, James; 19 Nov. 1818; Eliza Dimmitt         08 BA
Franklin, Samuel; 12 Dec. 1818; Louisa Moodie        17 BA-20
Frasier, James; 27 Feb. 1806; Coatney Berry          02 BA-3
Frasier, James; 4 June 1809; Carolina Smith          13 BA-6
Frazier, Charles; 4 April 1820; Helen Tuden          32 BA-328
Frazier, Ezekiel; 28 Nov. 1804; Dorothy Brooks       02 BA-34
Frazier, Ezekiel; 28 Dec. 1804; Dorothy Porter       03 BA-492
Frazier, Harvey; 1 Aug. 1819; Eliza Morris           06 FR-1330
Frazier, Jeremiah; 8 May 1808; Susanna Margaretta McKenzie
                                                     02 BA-6
```

Frazier, Jno.; 2 June 1803; Elizab. Sybrand   14 BA-414
Frazier, John; 18 Jan. 1815; Harriet Armstrong   17 BA-10
Frederic, Michael; 17 Oct. 1801; Christina Gebner   14 BA-411
Frederick, Jacob; 25 Dec. 1817; Mary Ann Derr   06 FR-1327
Frederick, Lawrence; 10 April 1814; Catherine Nussear   16 BA-3
Frederick, Peter; 25 Oct. 1814; Philipine Humel   13 BA-19
Fredericks, John; 21 July 1810; Ruthy Collins   7 BA-8
Freeburger, George; 20 July 1814; Sarah Hutchins   14 BA-433
Freeburger, Hy. E.; 23 July 1812; Sally Hodges   03 BA-504
Freeburger, Johann; 13 May 1804; Nancy (nee Yoice; widow
     Fennell)   07 BA
Freeman, Charles; 30 Sept. 1804 (in list of marriages for
     blacks); Lucy Jones   17 BA-5
Freeman, Charles W.; 15 Oct. 1818; Elvina Brown   13 BA-41
Freeman, Ezekiel; 11 May 1813; Rebecca Price   03 BA-505
French, Barnet C.; 27 May 1802; Permelia P. Burk   09 BA
French, David; 16 Oct. 1811; Martha Anderson   02 WA-91
French, Ebenezer; 20 Feb. 1814; Carolina Hargrove   21 BA-2
French, James; 2 May 1811; Jane Humberstone   03 AL-614
French, John; 24 April 1816; Jane Pennington   17 BA-12
French, John C.; 19 Nov. 1816; Mary Paul   11 BA-31
French, Matt.; 8 April 1813; Cathr. Absley   3 BA-16
French, Nath'l; 17 Aug. 1812; Rachel Baldwin   21 BA-7
French, Nicholas; 23 Sept. 1801; Rebecca Chaney   03 AA-120
French, Otho; 18 Feb. 1802; Eliz. Anderson (See also 15 FR-313)
                                                         01 FR-1128
Fressier, Fabian; 2 July 1812; Mary Noel (slave of Mrs. Leclerc)
                                                         15 BA-301
Frey, Georg; June 1802; Elis. Horker   02 WA-73
Friday, Jno. Henry; 29 Jan. 1812; Hanna Marg. Baughden 14 BA-429
Fridhsy (?), John; 18 May 1806; Barbara Hauer (See also 15 FR-
     319)   01 FR-1128
Frieland, Micajah; 7 Jan. 1813; Mary Sloate   08 BA
Friese, Jno. Fried.; 15 Dec. 1814; Rebecca Prince   14 BA-433
Friese, Philip R. J.; 12 Dec. 1805; Julia G. Avenaux   14 BA-419
Fringer, George; 6 Nov. 1817; Rachel Williams   08 BA
Frisby, Joseph; 12 Dec. 1813; Rachel Welsh   03 BA-505
Frisby, Ric'd.; 12 Aug. 1811; Eliza'h Brown   03 BA-503
Frisby, William; 1 April 1818; Catherine Overe Ruth   02 BA-37
Frise (?), Jacob; March 1807; Cath. Hose   02 WA-82
Frisler, David; May 1805; Christ. Brauchmeyer   02 WA-78
Frizzle, John; 3 June 1813; Mary Varley   17 BA-9
Frizzle, William D.; 6 Sept. 1807; Charlotte Weir   09 BA
Frost, Isah [sic]; 13 Nov. 1806; Sarah Neff   03 AL-614
Frost, James; 27 Jan. 1803; Anne Lord   03 BA-425
Frost, Josiah; 14 April 1812; Margaret McNeer   03 AL-614
Frost, Thomas; 17 March 1803; Fanny Weyman   14 BA-414
Frush, William; 25 Nov. 1819; Rebecker Griffin   08 BA
Fry, George; 16 June 1816; M. Hampshire   30 BA-109
Fry, Peter; Feb. 1818; Mary Hays   02 WA-108
Fryatt, William Th.; 9 Oct. 1816; Susanna Jarboe   05 BA-239
Fryer, Henry; 17 July 1810; Eliz'h Renshaw   13 BA-10
Fuhrman, Charles; 16 Nov. 1813; Margaretha Devinny   07 BA-309
Fulford, Stephen; 9 July 1810; Mary Wilcox   03 BA-502
Full, John; Sept. 1808; Barbara Schafer   02 WA-85
Fuller, George; 27 July 1809; Delila Potter   09 BA
Fulton, James; 2 Feb. 1802; Mary Neilson   28 BA-1
Fulton, James; 2 Feb. 1809; Hannah Amos   01 BA-11
Fultz, Philip; 30 March 1812; Cath. Shafer or Shaster (15 FR-325
     gives bride's name as Schaefer)   01 FR-1129
Fulweider, George; 13 May 1813; Mery Sterett   39 BA-29
Funck, (N); June 1807; Judith Scott   02 WA-83
Funk, David; 21 May 1811; Mary Funk   02 WA-90
Funk, Henry; (Feb.?) 1806; Elis. Good   02 WA-80

```
Funk, John; 13 Feb. 1806; Eliz. Loer                 03 AL-613
Furlong, John E.; 23 June 1817; Elizabeth Dowdle     09 BA
Furlong, Thomas; 18 Aug. 1803; Elizabeth B (?)       15 AA-2
Furry, John; April 1805; Cath. Miller                02 WA-78
Furry, John; April 1805; Barb. Kererkom (?)          02 WA-79
Fuss, John; 23 May 1815; Susanna Rigby               07 BA-309
Fussel, Jacob (son of Bartholomew and Rebecca); 1 d, 12 mo.,
    1814; Clarissa Whitaker (dau. of Joshua and Ruth) (see also
    05 SF)                                           02 SF-127
Fusselbaugh, Wm.; 9 July 1820; Mary Conovan          13 BA-35
Fye, Pollard; 23 Oct. 1819; Elizabeth Madden         17 BA-22
Gaber, David; 21 Feb,. 1805; Mary Beiser             01 FR-1132
Gable, Henry; 26 Sept. 1820; Eliza Sheppard          11 BA-38
Gable, W.; 16 Nov. 1815; Julianna Sherry             13 BA-23
Gabriel, John; 21 April 1816; Ellender Earnest       17 BA-13
Gach, Johannes; 25 March 1806; Eliza Schnoog         15 FR-318
Gach, John; 25 March 1806; Eliza Schnoog             01 FR-1132
Gacle, John H.; 28 Aug. 1806; Ana Mary (?)           30 BA-108
Gadd, Thomas; 29 May 1805; Lucretia Williams         01 DO-41
Gadsby, John; 12 Jan. 1813; Provy Langworthy         03 BA-504
Gafford, Jos.; 21 Nov. 1812; Cordelia Hillon         13 BA-17
Gahuzes, James; 6 Aug. 1809; Ann Spencer             31 BA-65
Gaines, James; 6 April 1815; Ann Hooper              13 BA-21
Gairy, John; 21 Nov. 1802; Rachel Atwell             03 AA-120
Gaither, Henry; 1812; Eliza Worthington (See also 02 MO)
                                                     01 PG
Gaither, John; 24 April 1810; Jane Glover            13 BA-9
Gaither, William S.; 6 Dec. 1812; Letta McCaslin     03 AL-614
Gaither, Zachariah; 1805; Elis. Gerver               02 WA--77
Galand, Jno. Baptist; 4 June 1807; Cath. Kiehnrick   14 BA-422
Galaspey, Patrick; 7 Feb. 1816; Catherine O'Reilly   32 BA-307
Galbraith, Thomas; 18 Dec. 1806; Rosanna Willis      21 BA-6
Galbreath, Gilaspy; 13 May 1805; Alize Gorman        15 BA-219
Gale, Joseph; 16 Oct. 1801; Sarah Jordan (free blacks) 03 BA-408
Gale, Levin; 8 April 1813; Harriet Rebeckah Chamberlaine
                                                     01 TA-312
Gale, William; May 1805; Cath. Malott                02 WA-78
Gallagher, Francis; 12 Oct. 1820; Mary Rynd (Ryan?)  32 BA-329
Gallagher, Hugh; 8 June 1809; Grace McCormick        15 BA-269
Gallagher, James; 23 June 1812; Mary Dennie          15 BA-301
Gallaway, Norman; 10 Dec. 1801; Ann Buckanan         14 BA-411
Gallitin, Dan'l; 25 March 1813; Matilda Maguire      14 BA-431
Gallop, Charles; 22 Sept. 1818; Ann Brown            17 BA-20
Galloway, James; 1 July 1803; Priscilla Strain (see also
    02 BA-32)                                        03 BA-430
Galloway, John; 23 Dec. 1802; Ann Lockard            05 BA-233
Galloway, John; 10(?) July 1817; Mary Little         17 BA-16
Galloway, Moses; 4 Aug. 1803; Rachel Demmitt         09 BA
Galloway, Samuel; 26 Dec. 1816; Tilde Rogers         17 BA-14
Gallup, Thomas; 7 Dec. 1815; Hannah Nicholson        17 BA-12
Galt, Peter; 24 March 1802; Araminta Martin          28 BA-1
Gamble, John; 6 April 1807; Ann Cadron               15 BA-248
Gambrel, William; 3 March 1804; Natie Williams       14 AA-1
Gambrill, John; 22 Aug. 1801; Elizabeth Mark         27 BA-1
Gambrill, John; 9 Dec. 1802; Achsah Sewell           36 BA-1
Gambrill, John; 1 Jan. 1805; Sarah Green             09 BA
Gambrill, Stephen B.; 12 Dec. 1820; Mary Quinn       13 BA-36
Gambrill, William; 6 Jan. 1801; Hariott Fish         15 AA-1
Gambrill, William; 10 Nov. 1803; Martha Peach        15 AA-1
Ganes, Richard; (date not given); Lucy Higher        13 BA-38
Gannon, Absolom; 14 Nov. 1805; Eleanor Evans         11 BA-7
Gannon, John; 18 Jan. 1820; Elizabeth Dempsey        32 BA-327
Gantie, Renet; 12 Oct. 1811; Mary Denos Shields      14 BA-429
```

Gantt, Christopher Lowndes; 19 Sept. 1809; Mary Mewburn
                                                        03 BA-500
Gantz, John; Sept. 1819; Ann Burnhiser   02 WA-114
Gantz, Samuel; July 1810; Mary Linn   02 WA-87
Ganzaw, Jacob; 5 Sept. 1819; Margareth Keller   06 FR-1330
Garber, Joseph; Dec. 1808; Nanzi Hogens   02 WA-86
Garber, Samuel; 18 March 1813; Elizabeth Zipling   06 FR-1319
Gardener, Hezekiah B.; 24 Oct. 1817; Ann Corum   17 BA-17
Gardere, Anthony Hilery; 16 Oct. 1809; Laurette Garrette (people
     of color from St. Domingo)   15 BA-274
Gardiner, Benjamin; 17 Jan. 1805; Susanna Brashears   03 AA-130
Gardiner, Caleb; 16 Oct. 1805; Sarah Raymond   03 BA-494
Gardiner, George; 28 July 1803; Nelly Denny   09 BA
Gardiner, John; 5 Sept. 1801; Sarah Shiply   27 BA-1
Gardiner, Peter; 3 June 1811; Margaret Green   09 BA
Gardiner, Samuel; 16 Aug. 1805; Eleanor Hellen   03 BA-494
Gardiner, Samuel; 31 Dec. 1807; Elizabeth Moren   05 BA-235
Gardiner, Wm.; 14 Jan. 1816; Ann Masser   13 BA-24
Gardner, Francis; 24 May 1817; Ann Foster   17 BA-16
Gardner, George; 11 May 1806; Sarah Stretch   09 BA
Gardner, Isaac; 17 March 1801; Eleanor Baker   09 BA
Gardner, Jacob; 15 May 1803; Elis. Taylor   14 BA-414
Gardner, Joseph; 6 June 1802; Elizabeth Westerly   09 BA
Gardner, Shubael; 5 July 1803; Juliana Larea (02 BA-32 gives date
     as 4 July 1803)   03 BA-430
Gardner, Timothy; 31 Aug. 1805; Elizabeth Moore   09 BA
Garey, Dennis; 19 Sept. 1814; Elizabeth Cooper   17 BA-10
Garey, Gideon; 8 Oct. 1807; Frances Chaney   03 BA-497
Garey, Osborne; 2 or 3 March 1813; Priscilla Sadler   17 BA-9
Garish, Francis B.; 31 Oct. 1815; Elizabeth Stoker   03 BA-507
Garish, Samuel; 7 Sept. 1801; Mary Alder   03 BA-406
Garland, George; 5 April 1804; Mary Marshall   15 BA-200
Garlinger, Jacob; Aug. 1818; Rebecca Benner   02 WA-110
Garnous, William; 5 Jan. 1813; Catherine Bryan   05 BA-237
Garraghly, Peter; 29 May 1817; M. A. Despeaux   02 BA-37
Garret, Robert; 19 May 1817; E. Stouffer   20 BA-223
Garrett, John J.; 28 Oct. 1816; Reba. Price   13 BA-26
Garrett, Johnson; 3 July 1812; Polly Doyle   06 FR-1318
Garrett, Wm.; 8 Oct. 1801; Eleanor Higgins   03 MO-117
Garrettson, Amos (s. of John and Mary [Griest]); 20 d. 4 mo.,
     1802; Mary Talbott (dau. of John and Mary)   03 SF
Garrettson, Aquila; 22 Sept. 1818; Amelia George   11 BA-32
Garrettson, Isaac (of Elkridge, AA Co., s. of Cornelius and
     Hannah); 5 d. 9 m., 1816; Rachel Ely (dau. of Mahlon, dec.,
     and w. Mary)   12 SF-54
Garrettson, Jazer (son of Gareett and Margaret); 18 d. 3 mo.,
     1813; Sarah Poultney Farquhar (widow of Moses Farquhar, and
     dau. of Anthony and Susanna [Plummer] Poultney)   03 SF
Garriques, Robert H. (son of William and Hannah); 22 d. 5 mo.,
     1816; Margaret E. Thomas (dau. of Richard and Deborah)
                                                        01 SF
Garrison, Mason; 15 May 1820; Margaret Ritchie   37 BA-153
Garvin, William; 16 Feb. 1812; Mary Lambert   02 WA-93
Gary, Everet; 1 June 1819; Hannah Galloway   21 BA-9
Gary, Sabrit; 24 Dec. 1816; Rebecca Choate   08 BA
Gash, Peter; 14 Oct. 1806; Mary Binding   02 BA-4
Gashaw, Henry; 29 Dec. 1804; Ann Young   14 BA-417
Gassaway, Henry; 13 Oct. 1807; Rachel Griffith (See also 02 MO)
                                                        01 PG
Gassaway, Nich's; 16 March 1819; Eliza Slucks   13 BA-34
Gatchell, Jeremiah (s. of Nathan, dec., and Elizabeth) of East
     Nottingham Twp., CE Co.; 21 d. 1 mo., 1813; Deborah Brown
     (dau. of Robert and Dinah)   06 SF
Gatchear, Francis; 23 March 1815; Mary Etschberger   14 BA-433

```
Gates, William B.; 13 July 1820; Sophia Hall          17 BA-23
Gather, John; 21 July 1811; Sarah Chaney              13 BA-13
Gatlin, Aquila; 20 Dec. 1804; Mary Owen               03 MO-119
Gaul, Mich'l; 10 Nov. 1814; Eliza Sutton              13 BA-20
Gauline, John B.; 23 Aug. 1804; Mary Shyrock          09 BA
Gawthrop, William (of East Marlboro, Chester Co., PA, son of
    George and Jane); 16 d. 9 mo., 1818; Mary Griffith (dau. of
    Abraham and Rachel)                               02 SF-135
Gaylaner, John; 30 Sept. 1820; Sarah Duvall           13 BA-35
Gear, George; 11 Feb. 1813; Catherine Winpigler       06 FR-1318
Gearhard, Jacob; Jan. 1801; Marg. Albright            02 WA-71
Gearhart, John; 14 Nov. 1811; Polly Carpenter         02 WA-91
Gebhard, George; 3 May 1803; Cath. Doll (See also 15 FR-314)
                                                      01 FR-1131
Gebhardt, John; 27 Dec. 1801; Sarah Hiestland (See also 15 FR-
312)                                                  01
FR-1131
Gebhart, John; 12 Sept. 1805; Ann Downey (Dorse?)     03 AL-613
Gebler, Gotlieb; 1 Aug. 1804; Susi. Madera (See also 15 FR-316)
                                                      01 FR-1132
Geddes, James; 9 Nov. 1820; Sarah Robinson            13 BA-36
Geering, James; Oct. 1810; Margaret Slice             02 WA-88
Geeting, Jacob; 17 Jan. 1819; N. Stufferman           30 BA-109
Gehbers, August; 4 Feb. 1801; Fanny Barkwel           14 BA-409
Gehler, Godfrey; 22 Oct. 181; Mary Ann Crans          13 BA-32
Gehr, Daniel; 14 April 1812; Polly Funk               02 WA-94
Gehr, George; 10 Nov. 1811; Sarah Fisher              02 WA-91
Gehr, Samuel; Aug. 1816; Nancy Hoover                 02 WA-102
Gehret, John; 24 March 1807; Cath. Greims (15 FR-320 gives her
    name as Grims)                                    01 FR-1132
Geiger, Rev. Jacob; 19 Feb. 1818; Catherina Seltzer   07 BA-311
Geisbart, Abraham; 10 May 1814; Mary Stewart          06 FR-1321
Geiser, Heinrich; 1801; Rebb. Young                   02 WA-71
Geisler, Georg; 16 July 1817; Dorothea Kohlhauss      07 BA-310
Geissen, Joannes; 1 April 1806; Maria Greiksler       39 BA-19
Gelbach, Christian; 29 Aug. 1809; Sarah Richards      14 BA-226
Gelbach, John; 31 Jan. 1819; M. Fogel                 30 BA-109
Gelwicks, George C.; 12 Nov. 1807; Mary Nixdorf (See also
    15 FR-321)                                        01 FR-1132
Gembrade, John Francis; 25 Aug. 1807; Catherine Weis  15 BA-253
Gendhard, Xavier; 12 May 1810; Sally Anderson         14 BA-427
Gent, Thos.; 27 April 1803; Margaret Leaf             23 BA-2
Geoghegan, Philemon; 5 Jan. 1804; Betsey Brookes      01 DO-41
Geoghegan, William; 11 Feb. 1802; Sophia Barnes       01 DO-40
Geoghegan, William; 15 Dec. 1803; Martha Geoghegan    01 Do-41
George, David; 18 March 1816; Ann Radruck             08 AL-38
George, James; Dec. 1805; Mary Huston                 02 WA-79
George, John; 10 April 1806; Elizab. Woods (See also 15 FR-318)
                                                      01 FR-1132
George, Luke; 24 Dec. 1807; Margaret Farrell          15 BA-258
George, William; 26 July 1817; Ann Price              11 BA-31
George, William Edmondson (of Balto. Town, s. of Robert and Ann,
    both of KE Co., both dec.); 23 d. 12 mo., 1812; Sarah
    Ellicott (dau. of Jonathan and Sarah of BA)       12 SF-35
Gephart, William; 11 Aug. 1812; Elizabeth Schuck      08 AL-38
Gerard, Amy [sic]; 2 June 1802; Mary Cardrend         14 BA-412
Gerard (Gerass), Peter Johan; 30 June 1817; Maria M. Hagerman
                                                      07 BA-310
Gerhart, Daniel; Feb. 1820; Elizab. Mong              02 WA-115
German, Benjamin; 4 April 1818; Catherine Krebs       11 BA-28
German, Joseph; 1 Feb. 1817; Ann Claire Rey           16 BA-50
German, Mich'll; 13 May 1812; Eliza. (N)              13 BA-16
Gersan, Benj'n; 17 Feb. 1801; Mary Hennan             14 BA-409
```

```
Gerver, Joh.; Jan. 1801; Elis. Weldy                    02 WA-71
Gethard, Henry; 7 April 1811; Catherine Gettich         06 FR-1315
Gettig, Jacob; 9 Feb., 1801; Sus. Mackenheimer          14 BA-409
Gettings, Joseph; 1809; Tabitha Beans                   01 PG
Gettings, Thomas; 3 April 1806; Christiana Perry         01 PG
Getty, James; 2 Dec. 1816; Cath. Quinn                  16 BA-46
Getty, John; 14 April 1801; Eleanor Carey               03 MO-117
Getz, Frederick; 26 Sept. 1816; Maria Habber            07 BA-310
Geyer, Johannes; 30 April 1803; Maria Nuss              15 FR-314
Geyger, Joannes; 23 June 1807; Maria Gruben             39 BA-19
Gibbons, Laurence; 11 (?) June 1814; Mary Jones         11 BA-7
Gibbons, Richard; 6 Dec. 1808; Ruth Johnson             13 BA-5
Gibbons, William; 20 May 1801; Elizabeth Wardell        03 BA-400
Gibbons, William; 4 June 1802; Mary Johnson             09 BA
Gibbs, John; 8 Oct. 1818; Neonora [sic] Pondy           04 FR-18
Gibbs, Thomas; 20 Jan. 1815; Mary Chisholm              03 AA-130
Gibson, Edwin; 26 Dec. 1820; Mary Gallegher             13 BA-36
Gibson, George; 24 Oct. 1807; Elisab. Shilling          14 BA-423
Gibson, Gerrard; 18 Jan. 1813; Harriet Taylor           11 BA-20
Gibson, Gideon, Jr. (s. of William and Hannah [Unckles]); 23 d.
    12 mo., 1802; Hannah Elliott (dau. of John and Sarah
    [Milhouse])                                         03 SF
Gibson, Gideon, Jr. (s. of William and Hannah [Unckles]); 22 d.
    12 mo., 1807; Sarah Elliott (dau. of Wm. and Mary)
                                                        03 SF
Gibson, James; 27 Dec. 1815; Emily Ann Grundy           03 BA-507
Gibson, John; 18 Sept. 1806; Eliza C. Grundy            03 BA-496
Gibson, John; 5 Nov. 1815; Eleanor Rowland              09 BA
Gibson, Jose.; 3 Feb. 1814; Sarah Brown                 13 BA-18
Gibson, Wm., Jr.; 12 Dec. 1811; Sarah Charlotte Hollingsworth
                                                        03 BA-503
Giesy, John; 16 May 1809; Catharine Baltzel             15 FR-323
Giesg, John; 16 May 1809; Cath. Baltzell                01 FR-1132
Gigues, Joseph; 7 Sept. 1802; Mary Magdalen Stall       15 BA-171
Gilbert, Isaac; 3 Aug. 1820; Mary Hershman (See also 16 FR-76)
                                                        03 FR-60
Gilbert, Jacob; Jan. 1801; Christina Schwab             02 WA-71
Gilbert, James; 9 Sept. 1818; Marg't. Hadaway           13 BA-31
Gilbert, Johnston; 7 Jan. 1813; Jemima Mallonee         09 BA
Gilbert, Lyman; 2 Nov. 1815; Margaret Dehoff            11 BA-24
Gilbert, Peter; 16 Aug. 1803; Elizab. Larkin (See also 15 FR-315)
                                                        01 FR-1132
Gilbert, Reubin; March 1818; Maria Norris               02 WA-109
Gilbert, William; April 1820; Magdalena Ludy            03 FR-60
Gilbert, William; c.April 1820; Magdalena Luby          16 FR-76
Gilberthright, William; 23 Aug. 1801; Catherine Rooke   10 BA-1
Gildea, Feliz; 31 July 1810; Mary Zimmers               15 BA-282
Gilder, Michael; 21 Apreil 1811; Ruth Gist             15 BA-286
Giles, John; 22 Sept. 1810; Anna Maria Prentiss         03 BA-501
Gilfort, George; 15 June 1803; Sophia Robinson          14 BA-414
Gilgen, John; 4 May 1806; Catherine Feather             02 BA-4
Gill, Bennett G.; 1 Oct. 1811; Marg't Boile             13 BA-13
Gill, Ezekiel; 6 May 1818; Sarah Ann Jones              11 BA-29
Gill, George; 11 Sept. 1806; Frances Mitchel            02 SM-187
Gill, Jacob; 19 Sept. 1815; Agnes Kempler               14 BA-434
Gill, John; 15 Sept. 1810; Actious Perigo               09 BA
Gill, John B,; 11 Aug. 1816; Prische Herron             13 BA-26
Gill, Joshua; 4 April 1820; Susannah Osburn             08 BA
Gill, Nicholas; 1 Jan. 1803; Mary Ensor                 23 BA-2
Gill, Selmon; 19 Dec. 1813; Margaret Dorret             11 BA-23
Gill, Stephen; 14 Feb. 1805; Elizabeth Canady           09 BA
Gillchrest, Alex'r; 13 June 1816; Eliza Smith           20 BA-222
Gilleron, Lackey; 3 July 1806; Cath. Hagerty (both natives of
    Ireland)                                            15 BA-240
```

Gillet (?), Pierre; 13 Feb. 1810; Louisa Palisier (both free
     people of color)   15 BA-179
Gillet (?), Moses; Dec. 1809; Cordela (N)   08 BA
Gillingham, George; 5 Dec. 1803; Ann Hazle (see also 02 BA-33)
                                                     03 BA-436
Gillingham, George (of Balto. Town, s. of James and Elizabeth);
     18 d. 9 mo., 1811; Miriam James (dau. of Amos and Ann of
     Balto. Town)   12 SF-13
Gillingham, William, (of Balto. Town, s. of James and Elizabeth);
     18 d. 3 mo., 1812; Jane McPherson (dau. of Isaac and
     Elizabeth, dec.)   12 SF-25
Gilly, John; 16 Dec. 1817; Mrs. Sarah Clark   37 BA-152
Gilmor, Robert, Jr.; 1 June 1802; Elizabeth Susanna Cooke
                                                     03 BA-417
Gilpin, Bernard; 17 d. 7 mo., 1807; Letitia Canby Gilbert
                                                     10 SF
Gilpin, Bernard (son of Gideon and Sarah); 26 d. 8 mo., 1808;
     Letitia Gilbert (dau. of Whitson and Mary [Canby])
                                                     01 SF
Gilpin, Elias; 1 Dec. 1801; Lydia Ball   03 AL-613
Gilpin, George; 15 May 1820; Margaret Smith   17 BA-22
Giltz, John; 29 March 1818; Catherine Zimmerman   06 FR-1328
Girado, Pedter; 20 Nov. 1806; Louisa E. Mingare   31 BA-15
Gisebart, Gusebart; 19 Dec. 1811;Hester Padgett   06 FR-1317
Gisehart, Abraham; 1 fewb. 1817; Catherine Knouf   06 FR-1327
Gislebert, Joseph; 14 Sept. 1806; Rodey Zane   13 BA-12
Gist, William; 9 June 1818; Margaret Kipp   11 BA-32
Gitchell, Increase; 26 May 1804; Cassandra Barton (see also
     02 BA-33)   03 BA-490
Gitson, Henry; 2 April 1805; Susannah Lloyd   03 AL-613
Gittinger, Henry; 9 Dec. 1802; Margaret Hooker   23 BA-2
Gittings, Archibald; 30 May 1815; Martha Rumsey   03 BA-506
Gittings, Joseph; 1809; Tabitha Beans   02 MO
Gittings, Thomas; 10 Dec. 1801; Mary Wilmot   18 BA-65
Gittings, Thomas; 3 April 1806; Christiana Perry (See also
     02 MO)   01 PG-97
Gittings, Wm.; 24 March 1806; Mary Sands   14 BA-419
Gladhill, Samuel; 23 July 1811; Sarah Edwards   06 FR-1316
Glan, Robert; 11 May 1802; Elizabeth Hurst   03 BA-416
Glanden, Wm..; 18 Aug. 1811; Magdalena Peacock   02 WA-90
Glasbrenner, (N); April 1808; Elis. Lambert   02 WA-85
Glasgow, W. R.; 13 Dec. 1810; Eliza. Russell   13 BA-11
Glassbrener, (N); Dec. 1807; Christ. Shane   02 WA-84
Glasser, Jacob; 17 March 1803; Mary Harman   14 BA-414
Glattus, Petrus, widower; 23 Nov. 1816 (or 1817); Elizabeth Pauls
     (widow)   39 BA-33
Glenn, John; 25 June 1810; Sarah Davidson   03 BA-501
Glenn, John Washington; 14 April 1803; Elizabeth Watts (see also
     02 BA-32)   03 BA-427
Glenn, Samuel; 20 Feb. 1802; Elizabeth Connoll   03 BA-413
Glenn, Thomas; 18 July 1816; Gartha (?) Colember   17 BA-12
Glenn, William Stoppes; 14 Feb. 1802; Elizabeth Sink 03 BA-413
Glisson, James; 29 Oct. 1801; Esther White (See also 15 FR-312)
                                                     01 FR-1131
Glover, Josias; 16 June 1803; Sarah Hall   34 BA-1
Gobright, Wm.; 25 Sept. 1806; Louisa Norman   03 BA-496
Godefour, Joannes; Dec. 1809; Catherina Fitzemeyer (widow
     Schmaltz)   39 BA-23
Godfrey, Benjamin; 27(?) Nov. 1817; Harriet Cooper 17 BA-17
Godfrey, Henry; 7 July 1818; Sarah Broadmaid   11 BA-29
Godfrey, William; 7 Jan. 1813; Eulalie Maillet Lacosnte (both
     natives of France)   15 BA-306
Godi, Earnst; July 1817; Mary Miller   02 WA-105
Godman, Brutus; 1 Sept. 1803; Margarett Wood   15 AA-2

```
Godshare, Andr.; 10 Jan. 1815; Marg't West              13 BA-20
Godwin, John; 17 Jan. 1817; Elizabeth Hester Hall       02 QA-66
Goetzendanner, Thomas; 10 April 1808; Cath. Bar         01 FR-1132
Gogen (or George), Thomas; 16 July 1816; Sarah Newcomen (?)
                                                        16 BA-39
Gohagan, John; 27 May 1819; Louisa Willson              17 BA-22
Gohoging, Joshua; 10 (or 13) June 1805; Rebecka Bell    11 BA-6
Goinard, John; 6 May 1813; Eugenia Reneaud              31 BA-148
Going, Michael; 12 Feb. 1816; Polly Heinemann           08 AL-39
Gold, Alex'r; 31 Dec.1802; Susan Barber                 14 BA-414
Gold, Chas.; 14 July 1818; Susannah Jackson             16 BA-71
Gold, Joseph; 21 July 1807; Harriet Landre              15 BA-252
Golden, Samuel; 6 Sept. 1804; Dolly Haner               03 MO-119
Golding, Daniel; 18 April 1808; Eliz. Harris (See also  02 MO)
                                                        01 PG
Goldsborough, Cornelius; 15 Sept. 1803; Margaret Green  02 SM-186
Goldsborough, Ignatius; 3 Jan. 1802; Mary Lurby         02 SM-185
Goldsborough, James; 3 March 1818; Mary Pattison        02 DO
Goldthwait, Jas.; 16 Nov. 1802; Mary Johnson            14 BA-413
Goldthwait, Joseph; 16 Nov. 1802; Mary Johnston         25 BA-3
Goldthwait, Joseph; 22 Sept. 1808; Molly Dorsey         03 BA-498
Goldthwaite, Samuel; 15 Oct. 1801; Mary Jamieson        03 BA-408
Goll, Baltzer; Nov. 1810; Merg. Bell                    02 WA-88
Goll, John G.; 14 May 1818; Barbara Kendall             01 WA-201
Gollibert, John Francis; 6 March 1810; Marie Antoinette Chap-
    peau (?)                                            31 BA-76
Gonet, Marcelino; 28 Nov. 1813; Nancy Craycroft         09 BA
Gonnale, William; Dec. 1810; Nancy Vanetre              02 WA-88
Gonsales, Raphael (native of Havanna); 31 Aug. 1804; Rose Parent
    (widow, native of Port-au-Prince, St. Domingo)      15 BA-28
Good, John; Sept. 1818; Margarety Summer                02 WA-111
Good, William; 29 Oct. 1809; Ann Forrest                02 SM-188
Gooden, John; 30 Aug. 1805; Mary Bond                   09 BA
Goodman, Thomas Jefferson; 18 June 1816; Ellen McCarty  16 BA-36
Goodmanson, Peter; 1 Feb. 1820; Marg't Weymeier         14 BA-440
Goodrick, Elijah; 6 (?) 1801; Elizabeth Bateman         02 CH
Goodrick, Elis.; 9 March 1813; Susanna Senseny          14 BA-431
Goodrick, Samuel B.; 9 Aug. 1818;Eleanor Wingate        14 BA-437
Goodwin, Caleb; 21 Dec. 1819; Juliann Bell              17 BA-22
Goodwin, Edward D.; 9 July 1818; Penelope D. Price      03 BA-603
Goodwin, James; 10 June 1802; Rosanna Fisher            15 BA-168
Goodwin, James; 6 Feb. 1808; Elizabeth Combs            02 BA-6
Goodwin, Lyde; 8 Oct. 1801; Nancy Worthington           09 BA
Goodwin, Lyde; 21 Dec. 1813; Elizabeth Augusta Carroll  33 BA-505
Goon, Samuel; 11 Dec. 1807; Mary Wilson                 13 BA-3
Gootee, John; 30 July 1801; Nancy McNamara              01 DO-40
Gootee, John; 14 Oct. 1807; Margaret Todd               01 DO-41
Gordon, Benjamin; 16 July 1811; Margareta O'Donnel      31 BA-111
Gordon, Francis; 21 Jan. 1808; Ann Payne                02 BA-6
Gordon, Henry; Oct. 1808; Eliza. Shmith [sic]           02 WA-86
Gordon, James; 29 Aug. 1802; Catherine Deal             15 BA-170
Gordon, James; 7 Dec. 1803; Mary McCrane (see also 02 BA-33)
                                                        03 BA-436
Gordon, John; 8 March 1802; Elizabeth Dickey            28 BA-1
Gordon, Jno.; 14 Nov. 1807; Clara Hendricks             14 BA-423
Gordon, Joseph; 24 Nov. 1817; Elizabeth Crookshanks     17 BA-17
Gordon, Joshua; 10 July 1807; Charlotte Shisler         21 BA-6
Gordon, Richard; 12 Aug. 1815; Mary Sullivan            17 BA-11
Gordon, Thomas; 21 June 1803; Ann Barnett               01 TA-317
Gore, Samuel, of Jno.; 25 Oct. 1807; Teresa Harding     15 BA-256
Gore, William; 31 Jan. 1801; Mary Jackson               15 BA-148
Goret, Peter A.; 2 Jan. 1801; Elizabeth Deagle          15 BA-148
Gorham, John; 24 Dec. 1805; Sarah Manning               02 BA-36
Gorman (?), Christian; 10 March 1810; Agnes Adam         39 BA-24
```

Gorman, Edward; 11 Aug. 1816; Sarah [O'Connor]   39 BA-32
Gorner, George; 1 March 1801; Barbara Puffentan   01 CL-149
Gorsuch, Abraham; 21 March 1811; Ann James   09 BA
Gorsuch, Elisha; 22 Sept. 1803; Susanna Miller   35 BA-1
Gorsuch, Elisha; 23 Nov. 1817; Barbara Smith   08 BA
Gorsuch, John; 1 Nov. 1803; Nancy Goodwin   03 BA-434
Gorsuch, John; 20 Aug. 1804; Rachel M. Dresser   03 BA-491
Gorsuch, John; 9 April 1812; Mary Ann Slocum   09 BA
Gorsuch, Nicholas; 4 Jan. 1801; Nancy Glenn   09 BA
Gorsuch, Nicholas; 25 Sept. 1803; Susannah Davis   23 BA-2
Gorsuch, William; 3 Jan. 1815; Rebecca Tibbett   09 BA
Gorton, Henry; 2 Oct. 1817; Mary McGavern   13 BA-29
Gorton, Wanton; 10 Jan. 1807; Mary Pentz   14 BA-421
Goshee (?), Peter; 27 June 1816; Sarah Cavanagh (?)   17 BA-12
Goshill, Peter; 29 Aug. 1820; Margaret Baltiste   37 BA-153
Gosick, Joshua; 21 March 1804; Presilla Standiford   05 HA-1
Goslin, Abednego; 18 Jan. 1816; Martha Ann Frew   11 BA-26
Goslin, Ambrose; 14 Aug. 1803; Anna Shaffer (See also 15 FGR-315)
                                                        01 FR-1131
Gosnell, Charles; 9 March 1801; Nancy Shipley   08 BA
Gosse, Jno. Francois; 23 April 1805; Juliana Vergen   14 BA-418
Gossen, Henry; 7 July 181; Dorothy Ridgeway   11 BA-29
Gotham, John; 24 Dec. 1815; Sarah Manning   37 BA-150
Gothe, Ernst; 10 Dec. 1811; Eliz. Hammel   02 WA-92
Gothrop, John; 3 Oct. 1816; Margaret Copes   13 BA-40
Gothrop, Thos.; 15 Aug. 1816; Sarah Spencer   13 BA-26
Gott, Richard; c.1802; Sarah Collison   07 AA-2
Gott, Robert; 8 July 1811; Polly Randall   21 BA-7
Gotzendanner, Thomas; 10 April 1808; Catharina Baer   15 FR-322
Gouer, Adam; 1804; Elis. Beard   02 WA-76
Gouges, Gustavus; 6 July 1811; Marie Josephine Mulomiere
                                                        15 BA-288
Gough, (N) (s. of Ann; 5 Jan. 1800; Rachel (N)   03 SM
Gough, William; 30 Aug. 1808; Rachel Parks   07 BA-306
Gould, Alexander; 20 March 1817; Kitty Rollings   11 BA-27
Gould, John G.; 4 March 1818; Caroline McIlvaine   02 BA-37
Gould, Samuel; 26 July 1811; Mary Ann Parker   03 BA-503
Gould, Samuel; 22 Nov. 1819; Mary Ann Holliday   11 BA-34
Gould, William; 12 May 1808; Mary Ray   09 BA
Gourley, Edward (s. of Emmor R. and Grace H.); 6 d. 1 mo., 1820;
    Mary Beans (dau. of Edward and Mary Ann)   05 SF
Gourlie, Joseph (native of Tarwin[?] in the Division of Geneva);
    20 July 1801; Margaret Webb (of HA Co.)   15 BA-154
Gouty (?), John; 6 March 1818; Anne Williby, both of Caroline
                                                        02 TA-44
Gouty, Thomas; 24 May 1818; Rebecca Smith   02 TA-44
Gowens, George; 24 Oct. 1815; Susan Patterson   06 FR-1323
Gowler, Jacob; 31 Oct. 1815; Polly Stroobe   02 WA-100
Grable, Moses; 11 March 1817; Sarah Wolf   06 FR-1326
Grace, George; 22 Nov. 1808; Abby Remma   11 BA-12
Grace, John; 3 July 1812; Ann Clarke   11 BA-19
Grace, John S.; 4 June 1815; Margaret Caughey   37 BA-150
Grace, Richard; 14 Jan. 1806; Charlotte Clayland   15 BA-234
Grace, Thos.; 4 April 1818; Dorothy Williams   13 BA-30
Gracy, William; 9 Dec. 1801; Eliza Brown   09 BA
Graeber/Gruler, Daniel; 11 Oct. 1812; Nancy Frey   07 BA-308
Graff, John; 11 Oct. 1808; Araminta Greenfield   03 BA-498
Graff, Sebastian; 8 Aug. 1816; Eliza Johnson   02 FR-15
Grafton, William; 23 May 1801; Mary Etherington   09 BA
Graham, August; 26 Oct. 1806; Martha Cock (See also 15 FR-319)
                                                        01 FR-1132
Graham, George; 19 Aug. 1802; Dorothy Whitely   01 DO-41
Graham, Geo.; 1 March 1813; Mary Harris   13 BA-16
Graham, Sebastian; 15 Jan. 1810; Charlotte Salter   09 BA

```
Graham, Thos.; 9 Dec. 1812; Ann Stuber                    03 BA-504
Graham, William; 26 Dec. 1811; Elizabeth Reeder          03 AL-614
Grain, Peter (native of Havre de Grace, France); 1 Oct. 1811; Ann
    Eliza Higinbotham                                     15 BA-291
Grainger, George; 2 July 1816; Anna Lehmann              16 BA-37
Grainger, Mnatthew; 13 Sept. 1804; Sarah Woolfit         09 BA
Granger, Clement; 12 Jan. 1815; Margaret Henry           32 BA-303
Grant, Elijah; 4 Jan. 1816; Ann Meek                     11 BA-24
Grant, Henry; Jan. 1819; Marıa Weckham                   02 WA-112
Grant. Henry; 31 Oct. 1819; Eliza Driscoll               32 BA-326
Grant, Joseph; 18 July 1801; Fanny Brown                 03 BA-403
Grant, Marius; 21 Oct. 1804; Jane Caldwell               15 BA-210
Grant, Patrick; 1 Jan. 1803; Jane Gilmor                 03 BA-424
Grant, Thomas; 17 Nov. 1803; Mary Baxter                 03 BA-435
Grantham, Joh.; May 1805; Nanzi Hodi(page torn)          02 WA-79
Grapevine, Frederick; 17 Jan. 1802; Mary Ryland          06 BA-2
Grashon, Elias; 7 April 1816; Elizabeth Shauk            06 FR-1324
Grass, Francis; 10 Aug. 1815; Maria Banget               14 BA-434
Grate, William; 16 Dec. 1818; Ellen Hills                37 BA-151
Grauel, Benj.; 29 May 1810; Rebr. Palmer                 13 BA-10
Graves, Ebenezer; 30 April 1820; Susanna Flint           09 BA
Graves, Robert; 15 March 1801; Kitty Kelbreath           03 BA-399
Graves, Robert; 29 June 1805; Cath. Rusk                 14 BA-418
Graves, Robert; 23 March 1820; Lydia Humes               17 BA-22
Gray, Abishaw; 30 April 1805; Eleanor Miller             03 MO-120
Gray, Andreew; 23 Feb. 1802; Rebecca Rogers              35 BA-14
Gray, Edw's; 11 June 1804; Bathara Peterson (02 BA-34 gives bride
    as Bathuta and date as 7 June 1804)                  03 BA-491
Gray, Elias; 22 April 1817; Ann McGuire                  17 BA-16
Gray, Enoch (of New Garden Twp., Chester Co., PA); 17 d. 4 m.,
    1811; Mary Hicks (widow of James Hicks of HA)        12 SF-7
Gray, Henry W.; 2 Nov. 1815; Sarah E. Churchman          03 BA-507
Gray, Jacob; 9 Oct. 1810; Ann Jones (free blacks)        03 BA-502
Gray, John (nat. of Md.); 22 Jan. 1807; Sophia Gold (nat. of
    Balto.)                                              15 BA-246
Gray, John; Aug. 1812; Belinda Redmond                   03 BA-504
Gray, Joseph (s. of William and Elizabeth); 21 d, 12 mo. 1809;
    Mary Fairbank (dau. of James and Elizabeth)          08 SF
Gray, Nicholas; 26 Nov. 1807; Henrietta Scoffield        03 BA-497
Gray, Richard; 20 July 1819; Martha Burton               11 BA-34
Gray, Robert; 19 Oct. 1809; Ann Scott                    15 BA-275
Gray, Thomas; c.1801; Margaret Creek                     08 AA-1
Gray, William; 26 Oct. 1802; Eleanor Williams            09 BA
Gray, William; 2 March 1809; Catherine McSherry          15 BA-268
Gray, William; 7 March 1816; Martha Arnold               02 BA-36
Gray, Zacharias; 13 Sept. 1813; Elizab. Hardy (See also
    15 FR-326)                                           01 FR-1132
Grayson, John; 9 May 1816; Martha Wray                   05 BA-239
Grearson, Andrew; 22 Sept. 1818; Ann T. Miller           11 BA-33
Greatfield, John; 25 June 1816; Eliz. Barckly            16 BA-37
Greaves, Thomas; 8 Oct. 1801; Sarah Goldsborough         02 SM-185
Greeker, John; 26 Dec. 1816; Elizabeth Nort              03 BA-508
Green, Andrew; 4 April 1812; Cath. Gardner               14 BA-430
Green, Anthony; 16 Dec. 1813; Eliza Stars                09 BA
Green, Armistead; 11 April 1815; Eliza Harryman          09 BA
Green, Edward; 25 Sept. 1809; Sarah Rage                 15 BA-273
Green, Edward; 24 Feb. 1819; Lydia Ann Sumwalt           13 BA-34
Green, Eli; 5 Nov. 1812; Priscilla Hood                  17 BA-9
Green, Elisha; 17 Nov. 1807; Elizabeth Johnson           17 BA-5
Green, Frederick; 21 Aug. 1803; Ann Jones                02 SM-186
Green, George Whitefield; 12 May 1810; Elizabeth Perrigoy
                                                         09 BA
Green, Henry; 2 July 1801; Ruth Jones                    27 BA-1
Green, Henry; 19 Sept. 1820; Eleanor Danker              13 BA-35
```

Green, Jacob; 23 Nov. 1815; Susanna Miller   08 AL-41
Green, James; 20 Nov. 1804; Jane Horn   03 BA-492
Green, John; 18 Jan. 1801; Hannah Bryan   09 BA
Green, John; 27 April 1806; Nancy Miller (See also 15 FR-319)
                                                      01 FR-1132
Green, John; 15 Nov. 1810 (with lic.); Rebecca Simmes 15 BA-283
Green, John; 27 Nov. 1811; M. Green   13 BA-27
Green, John; 13 April 1817; Mary Boyd   17 BA-16
Green, John, Jr.; 17 Sept. 1818; Elizabeth Working   11 BA-32
Green, Joseph; March 1820; Sophia Davis   02 WA-115
Green, Lewis; 14 March 1815; Eliza Cary   06 FR-1322
Green, Peter; 11 Sept. 1803; Dorothy Cole   30 BA-108
Green, Peter; 16 Oct. 1803; Lydia Trimble   09 BA
Green, Richard; 8 June 1815; Elizabeth Shimer   08 AL-41
Green, Robert; 3 Aug. 1820; Hanna Ann Moss   14 BA-440
Green, Sol (free black); 23 Nov. 1806; Sally Connoway (slave of
   Jas. Ninde)   03 BA-496
Green, Thomas; 2 Feb. 1811; Jane Hill   17 BA-8
Green, Thos. Dickason; Dec. 1813; Ann Kugin (?)   20 BA-222
Green, Vincent; 14 Feb. 1805; Margaret Yeiser   09 BA
Green, Wilford; 13 Feb. 1810; Isabella Carson   03 BA-501
Green, William (free black); 5 Sept. 1801; Rosetta Gorse (free
   mulatto)   03 BA-406
Green, Wm.; 2 April 1807; Sarah Lewis   14 BA-421
Greenan, Michael; 15 Oct. 1819; Ann McNally   16 BA-89
Greenfield, Amos; 21 Sept. 1817; Ann King   11 BA-32
Greenfield, Edward; 27 April 1815; Eliza Adams   03 BA-506
Greenfield, Jno.; 11 Oct. 1814; Susan Lotts   21 BA-8
Greenfield, John; 29 Sept. 1816; Winifred Hall   11 BA-31
Greenway, Edward M.; 21 Jan. 1817; Maria Taylor   05 BA-239
Greenwell, Cam. (?); 11 May 1817; Nancy Queen (both col'd)
                                                      16 BA-52
Greenwell, James, (age c26, son of Clement and Jane [Downbarr]
   Greenwell); 14 May 1801; Elizabeth Wheatley (age c.29, dau.
   of James and Henrietta [Norris] Wheatley   03 SM
Greenwell, W. Enoch; 8 June 1820; Catherine Holtz   04 FR-20
Greenwell, Wilfred; 29 Jan. 1806; Mary Bennett   02 SM-187
Greenwood, Thos.; 10 Nov. 1810; Mary Hill   13 BA-11
Greer, George; 11 May 1803; Mary Hall   03 BA-428
Greer, Samuel; 19 Nov. 1814; Jane Righter   13 BA-20
Greer, Thos.; 26 Dec. 1811; Mary Stiner   03 BA-503
Greetham, Wm.; 29 Nov. 1804; Marg't Weatherburn   03 BA-492
Greg, William; 23 Oct. 1806; Charity Watkins   11 BA-8
Gregg, John; 11 June 1804; Harriet Hall   03 BA-491
Gregion, Jesse; 24 Oct. 1820; Rachel Murphy   13 BA-36
Gregoire, Charles; 29 Oct. 1817; Maria Louise (both free col'd)
                                                      16 BA-59
Gregory, Joseph; 22 Feb. 1815; Nancy Jacobs   17 BA-10
Gregory, Joshua; 8 Feb. 1801; Elizabeth Fell   09 BA
Gregory, Robert; Feb. 1807; Nanzi Stephenson   02 WA-82
Gregory, William; 19 Aug. 1802; Eleanor Carback   03 BA-419
Greiger, George; 7 April 1807; Mary Epler   01 FR-1132
Greives, Ebenezer; 25 Oct. 1804; Rebecca Clarke   09 BA
Grendjean, Abraham; 21 Nov. 1820; Julian Calaway   06 FR-1331
Grenier, Gabriel; 3 March 1816; Annette Caroline Colim Sutaine
                                                      05 BA-239
Greuly, David; 14 April 1817; Ann Kurtz   14 BA-436
Greve, Henry; 14 Oct. 1812; Nancy Pierpoint   21 BA-7
Greves, Francis; 17 June 1810; Mary Wise   17 BA-08
Grewee, William; 31 July 1817; Mary Smith   17 BA-16
Grewthrop (see Gawthrop), Richard; 27 Jan. 1820; Charlotte Young
                                                      03 BA-604
Grice, George; 4 july 1811; Avarilla Sollers   08 BA

Grice (or Gree), John Anthony (native of France); 2 June 1817;
   Ann G. Renaudette   16 BA-54
Grieger, George; 7 April 1807; Maria Fyler   15 FR-320
Grieger, Lewis; 10 May 1808; Susanna Hauer   01 FR-1132
Grieger, Ludwig; 10 May 1808; Susanna Hauer   15 FR-322
Grier (?), John; 16 Feb. 1813; Mary L. Enger   02 WA-96
Griffen, Capt. Thomas; 5 Oct. 1820; Susan Alexander 37 BA-153
Griffer, Heinrich; 28 Oct. 1809; Anna Maria Geiser 07 BA-307
Griffet, John; Jan. 1820; Mary Slacum, (Dorset Co.) 02 TA-44
Griffin, Anthony; 23 Aug. 1814; Ann Fields   16 BA-9
Griffin, George; 9 Sept. 1808; Ann Nichols   02 BA-6
Griffin, Henry; 13 Dec. 1814; Mary Taylor   17 BA-10
Griffin, Jacob; 29 Oct. 1815; Cath. Hahn   14 BA-434
Griffin, James; 17 Nov. 1811; Elizabeth Thompson   31 BA-113
Griffin, Jas. S.; 16 Aug. 1810; Eliz'h Little   13 BA-10
Griffin, Larkin; 23 July 1812; Mary Ennis   03 BA-504
Griffin, Philip; 10 Sept. 1805; Elinor McMullin   11 BA-7
Griffin, Rob't; 28 Nov. 1811; Mary Turner   03 BA-503
Griffin, William; 8 Oct. 1812; Amelia Magness   01 BA-11
Griffin, William; Aug. 1818; Mary Blundell   16 BA-72
Griffith, Amos (s. of Jacob and Lydia); 7 d. 12 mo., 1820; Edith
   Price (dau. of Daniel and Elizabeth)   02 SF-137
Griffith, Greenberry; 10 Feb. 1803; Mary Hair   36 BA-1
Griffith, Henry; 15 April 1813; Jane Mack   11 BA-21
Griffith, John; 19 July 1801; Catherine Master   30 BA-108
Griffith, Joshua; 1 Jan. 1818; Mary D. Blackeney   13 BA-30
Griffith, Martin; 13 Dec. 1803; Bridget Connelly   15 BA-192
Griffith, Mathew; 18 Aug. 1808; Nancy Herbert   21 BA-7
Griffith, Nathan; 20 feb. 1803; Sarah Matthews   09 BA
Griffith, Nathan (s. fof William and Alice) of East Nottingham
   Twp., CE Co.; 17 d. 18 mo., 1818; Mary Kirk (dua. of
   William and Lydia of the same place)   06 SF
Griffith, Samuel Gouldsmith; 2 June 1807; Mary Layfield
                                                    14 BA-422
Griffith, Thomas; 31 March 1807; Rachel Neavez   11 BA-10
Griffith, Thomas; 11(?) July 1814; Ann Murray   16 BA-7
Griffith, Thomas B.; 17 June 1816; Sarah Betts   03 BA-507
Griffith, Thomas D.; 16 Jan. 1817; Elizabeth Waits 11 BA-31
Griffith, Thomas Taylor (son of Abraham and Rachel); 31 d. 5 mo.,
   1815; Rachel Matthews (dau. of John and Martha) 02 SF-129
Griffith, William; 20 Jan. 1803; Susanna Stocksdale 23 BA-2
Griggs, John; 31 May 1818; Frances Fear   37 BA-151
Grim, Andreas; 25 July 1809; Maria Brunner   15 FR-324
Grim, Daniel; 4 Aug. 1803; Sarah Staub (See also 15 FR-315)
                                                    01 FR-1131
Grim, Samuel; 27 May 1819; Rebecca Frazier   06 FR-1330
Grimes, Edward; 12 May 1811; Nancy Ousler   08 BA
Grimes, George; 13 April 1811; Margaret Serjent   14 BA-428
Grimes, James; 1 Feb. 1803; Eleanor Dickenson   05 BA-233
Grimes, James; 29 Oct. 1812; Charlotte Towson   11 BA-20
Grimes, Jno.; 29 Oct. 1803; Eliz. Toast   14 BA-415
Grimes, John; 21 Oct. 1804; Sarah Wilson   05 AL-2
Grimes, Levi; 3 May 1801; Sarah Hoppim   09 BA
Grimes, Owen; 4 Feb. 1819; Martha Kelly   16 BA-80
Grimes, Rezin; 7 June 1804; Sophia Richardson   09 BA
Grimes, Richard; 12 May 1814; Mary Schunck   14 BA-433
Grimes, Stephen; 5 Feb. 1807; Tamar Clapp   09 BA
Grimes, William; 6 May 1817; Sarah Gambrill   17 BA-16
Grimes, William; 21 Sept. 1820; Nancy Hilton   11 BA-36
Grindall, Josiah; 17 Jan. 1818; Ann Lee   16 BA-64
Griner, Ginder; 7 Aug. 1811; Eleanor Kuat   14 BA-429
Gritzner, Frederic; 18 july 1807; Sarah Smith   14 BA-422
Groome, James; 12 Sept. 1802; Eleanor Fish   03 MO-118
Gross, Andres; Jan. 1801; Maria Hummer   02 WA-71

```
Gross, George; 1 May 1813; Cath. Sanders              01 FR-1132
Gross, George; 5 May 1813; Catherine Saunders         15 FR-327
Gross, Jacob; 1801; Barb. Miller                      02 WA-72
Gross, John; 25 July 1815; Ann King                   06 FR-1322
Gross, John (son of Lewis and Catherine); 20 April 1820;
   Elizabeth Worthington (dau. of Henry and Mary)     16 BA-99
Grossnikel, Peter; Aug. 1802; Hannah Gross            02 WA-73
Grosvenor, Thomas P.; 16 March 1815; Mary Jane Hanson 03 BA-506
Grout, Samuel; 1804; Marietta Williams                03 WA
Grove, John; May 1808; Barb. Foltz                    02 WA-85
Grove, Reuben; 7 April 1818; Sophia Ely               06 FR-1328
Grover, Chas.; 7 May 1820; Susan Crook                14 BA-440
Grover, John; 14 April 1803; Ann Smith                09 BA
Grover, Thomas; 11 Aug. 1811; Elizabeth Scarff        09 BA
Groves, George (widower); 8 Nov. 1807; Mary Chamberlain (widow)
                                                      15 BA-256
Groves, George B.; 2 June 1817; Isabella Boyd         05 BA-240
Groward, George M.; 31 July 1813; Ann O'Bryan         11 BA-21
Groym, Wm.; 23 Dec. 1817; Marg't Storey               13 BA-30
Grub, William; 11 Nov. 1819; Elizabeth Sanks          11 BA-36
Grubb, George; 3 Nov. 1812; Margaret Gotwalt          14 BA-431
Grubb, Jacob; 26 Sept. 1802; Susanna Dixon            09 BA
Grubb, Mich'l, Jr.; 23 March 1815; Ann Rutledge       13 BA-21
Grube, Anton; 8 Jan. 1809; Charlotte Messe            14 BA-425
Gruber, Jacob; 3 July 1817; Anna Gruber               07 BA-310
Grunewalt, Joh.; 8 Feb. 1801; Anna Barbara Schuhin    01 CL-149
Grush, Michael; 22 March 1812; Mary Kister            02 WA-93
Grushon, John; 18 April 1815; Elizabeth Baugher       06 FR-1322
Gryer, John; 30 April 1803; Mary Nusz                 01 FR-1131
Grymes, Benjamin; 8 March 1807; Sarah Lowry (See also 02 MO)
                                                      01 PG
Guhe, Miche.; Oct. 1805; Fanny Hoover                 02 WA-79
Guber, David; 21 Feb. 1805; Mary Heiser               15 FR-317
Guibert, Francis; 21 April 1808; Josephine Berry      15 BA-261
Guiesy, Lewis W. H.; 23 Sept. 1809; Mary Hesling      02 BA-7
Guildener, Charles; 13 Nov. 1819; Susan Scheidel      14 BA-439
Guinand, Frederick E.; 7 Jan. 1817; Frances C. Duhon  16 BA-48
Guinevan, Edward; 29 Nov. 1808; Mary Downy            03 BA-499
Guinges, Robert; 22 d. 5 mo., 1816; Margaret E. Thomas 10 SF
Guiton, Benjamin; June 1806; Rebb. Ditto              02 WA-80
Gunby, Elisha; 10 Dec. 1816; Jemima Gunby             17 BA-15
Gunby, Stephen; 16 March 1813; Elizabeth Ann Hague    09 BA
Gunn, James; 26 Nov. 1805; Elizabeth Robb             05 BA-234
Gurberick, Mich'l; 17 July 1811; Rachel Low           13 BA-13
Gurlie, Joseph (of Diocese of Geneva); 20 July 1801; Margaret
   Webb (of HA Co.)                                   15 BA-154
Guthrea, Francis; c.1804; Ann Reed                    34 BA-2
Guthrow, Stephen; 23 April 1804; Juliet Deagle        15 BA-201
Gutlega, Francis; 18 April 1819; Julia Ganetaume      32 BA-325
Gutridge, William; 11 June 1820; Margaret West        02 FR-14
Gutsus (?), John; 7 July 1806; Mary Ann Todd          17 BA-6
Guyton, Henry; Dec. 1805; Sarah Simpkins              02 WA-79
Gwynn, Thomas; 8 Sept. 1807; Jane Murdock             03 AL-614
Gwynne, John Evan; 8 March 1807; Fanny Dent           08 AL-26
Gynappon, Michael; 21 Dec. 1808; Elizabeth Walsh      09 BA
Haage, Frederic; 9 Aug. 1818; Dorothy Shise           14 BA-437
Haas, Henrich; Jan. 1801; Magd. Mengel                02 WA-70
Haber, (N); Nov. 1807; Eliz. Sch(wab?)                02 WA-84
Hablitz (Hublitz), Johan; 12 Oct. 1806; Elizabeth Pott 07 BA-305
Hachenbracht, Henrich; 21 Oct. 1803; Louise Lauterjung 07 BA
Hadaway, Robert; 4 July 1801; Elizabeth Miller        11 BA-3
Haddaway, William; Oct. 1806; Ruth Combs              02 WA-81
Hadder, Jacob; 1804; Cath. Herring                    02 WA-77
Haden, Garrett; 27 April 1820; Nancy Dilliway         14 BA-440
```

```
Haden, Richard; 25 Aug. 1813; Rachel Topper              05 FR-5
Hadley, John; 5 March 1815; Deborah Barnes               17 BA-12
Hadley, Richard; Sept. 1808; Sus. Bryen                  02 WA-85
Hadskis, Samuel Harper; 24 April 1803; Sarah Davey       03 BA-427
Hafekost, Henrich; 9 Dec. 1816; Johanna Levi             07 BA-310
Haff (or Hoff), Wm.; 6 March 1802; Anna Seiler           14 BA-412
Haffer, Joel; 5 April 1806; Mary Zell                    14 BA-420
Hagan (Hagar), Michael; 31 Dec. 1814; Hannah Burke       11 BA-22
Hagemann, Carl; 24 May 1804; Martha Cocheran             07 BA
Hager, John; April 1814; Mary Kaigy                      02 WA-100
Hager, Jonathan; April 1816; Cath. Hogmire               02 WA-101
Hagereis, Michael; Sept. 1820; Nancy Troup               02 WA-117
Hagers, William; 21 Oct. 1818; Jane Lynn                 01 WA-201
Hagerty, Barney; 19 May 1801; Marga't Breniff (both natives of
     Ireland)                                            15 BA-152
Hagerty, John; 4 Feb. 1808; Sarah Dean                   11 BA-13
Hagerty, John, Jr.; 4 June 1812; Ann Deaver              13 BA-7
Hagerty, Levi; 5 June 1820; Rebecca Rockhole             11 BA-36
Hagerty, Samuel; 30 Aug. 1810; Martha Richmond           03 BA-496
Hagner, George; 12 Dec. 1816; Florence Foy               13 BA-39
Hagner, William; 20 March 1813; Ann Miller               13 BA-16
Hagthorp, John; 8 June 1817; Mary O'Donnell              32 BA-312
Hahn, Christian; 3 Aug. 1815; Elizabeth Desper           07 BA-310
Hahn, George; 1 Jan. 1806; Sarah Thomas                  14 BA-419
Hahn, Jno. Adam; 13 Feb. 1801; Milly Stratin             14 BA-409
Hahn, Wm.; 21 Dec. 1820; Susan Gough                     14 BA-440
Hailey, Joseph; 11 June 1801; Ann Connelly               15 BA-153
Hailey, Thomas; 23 July 1801; Susanna Dixton             09 BA
Hain, John; 30 May 1811; Eliz. Mourer                    02 WA-90
Haines, Adam; June 1818; Sarah Tice                      02 WA-110
Haines, David; 12 Dec. 1811; Nancy Armsley               02 WA-92
Haines, Jacob; Dec. 1817; Frances Hersh                  02 WA-107
Haines, Joseph (s. of Isaac and Mary of West Nottingham Hundred,
     CE Co.); 9 d. 9 mo., 1801; Rebecca Reynolds (dau. of Jacob
     and Rebecca, both dec., of the same place)          06 SF
Haines, Nathan (s. of Joseph and Rachel [Cookson]); 23 d. 12
     mo., 1812; Elizabeth Shepherd (dau. of Solomon and Susanna
     [Farquhar])                                         03 SF
Hains, David; Sept. 1807; Nancy Angony                   02 WA-84
Hains, Peter; Jan. 1881; Cath. Hains                     02 WA-108
Hair, James; 16 Dec. 1801; Margaret Weaver               09 BA
Haislett, Joseph; 30 April 1801; Catherine Helfin        15 BA-151
Hakesley (?), John; 25 Aug. 1806; Mary O'Bryan           31 BA-10
Halbert, David; March 1807; Sarah Byron                  02 WA-82
Halbert, John; Aug. 1818; Nancy Monee                    02 WA-110
Hale, John; 31 Jan. 1804; Martha Mays                    06 HA-1
Hales, Randall; 4 Nov. 1802; Ann Taylor                  36 BA-1
Haley, Edward; 26 May 1816; Nancy Slavin                 11 BA-27
Haley, Henry; 27 May 1813; Ann Howland                   11 BA-23
Haley, James; 29 Dec. 1818; Catharine Anderson           17 BA-21
Hall, Andrew; 22 Sept. 1819; Ann Giles Moore             17 BA-22
Hall, Benedict William; 9 June 1812; Mary Calhoun        05 BA-237
Hall, Benedict Wm.; Oct. 1820 Ann Calhoun                05 BA-243
Hall, Benjamin; 2 July 1801; Rachel Ingram (See also 15 FR-311)
                                                         01 FR-1136
Hall, Benj'n; 20 Nov. 1803; Eliz. Candles                14 BA-415
Hall, Caleb, Jr.; 30 March 1815; Sarah Ann Griffith      13 BA-21
Hall, Carter A.; 17 Sept. 1818; Anna M. Diffenderfer     20 BA-223
Hall, Christ.; 3 May 1810; Susan Cole                    13 BA-9
Hall, Elijah; 14 April 1817; Eliza Jones                 17 BA-14
Hall, Francis C.; 26 July 1813; Mary Louisa van Wyck     03 BA-505
Hall, George; 29 Jan. 1801; Mary Cooper                  09 BA
Hall, Henry; 16 Nov. 1820; Charlotte I. Ramsey           05 BA-243
Hall, James; 7 Jan. 1802; Sarah Caples                   24 BA-1
```

Hall, James; 21 Jan. 1808; Eliza Cole   13 BA-3
Hall, Jas.; 5 Oct. 1811; Susanna Cline   14 BA-429
Hall, James; Jan. 1819; Mary Geatch   02 WA-112
Hall, James; 28 May 1820; Jane Sullivan   16 BA-101
Hall, Jesse; 7 July 1819; Mrs. Elizabeth Graham   37 BA-152
Hall (or Hull), John; 7 June 1803; Mary Kelly   09 BA
Hall, John; 25 Nov. 1819; Sarah Williams (col'd)   16 BA-92
Hall, Jno. B.; 12 Oct. 1803; Margaret Voice   14 BA-415
Hall, John Thomas; 20 April 1815; Margaret James; 20 April 1815
                                                     11 BA-24
Hall, Joseph; 25 Feb. 1802; Harriet Ann Sullivan   01 AA-73
Hall, Joseph; 2 Oct. 1806; Eliza Lovely   03 BA-496
Hall, Nelson R.; 8 Dec. 1819; Emily Augusta Swan   11 BA-36
Hall, Richard; 10 Jan. 1802; Eleanor Blake   01 QA-43
Hall, Richard; 6 June 1802; Mary Conaway   15 AA-2
Hall, Richard; 3 Oct. 1811; Elizabeth Gorsuch   08 BA
Hall, Rich'd Motton; 29 March 1804; Eliz Davidson   03 BA-490
Hall, Richard Wilmot; 14 May 1815; Eliza Taylor   05 BA-238
Hall, Shadrack; 15 March 1817; Mary Barrett   21 BA-9
Hall, Thomas; March 1819; Mary Fritz   02 WA-112
Hall, Thomas Bowie; 27 Oct. 1808; Ann Buchanan Pottenger
                                                     03 BA-498
Hall, Walter Tolly; 6 Jan. 1801; Charlotte White Hall, dau. of
     Benedict Edward Hall   33 BA-12
Hall, Wash'n; 16 Sept. 1809; Ann Gwinn   13 BA-8
Hall, William; 8 May 1803; Elizabeth Griffith   06 BA-3
Hall, William; 2 July 1807; Mary Davis   03 BA-497
Hall, William, Jr.; 6 June 1807; Mary Ann Dubert   13 BA-2
Hall, William White; 24 Oct. 1815; Elizabeth Presbury 20 BA-222
Hallen, John C.; c.1804; Elizabeth Bateman   34 BA-2
Haller, Charles; 14 April 1803; Cath. Brunner   11 FR-1136
Haller, George; 14 March 1813; Ann Myers (See also 15 FR-326)
                                                     01 FR-1137
Haller, George W.; 4 April 1815; Wilhelmina Zinstack 06 FR-1322
Haller, Jacob; 3 Nov. 1816; Mary Daddisman   06 FR-1325
Haller, Josua; 4 April 1805; Cath. Han   15 FR-317
Hallor, Joshua; 4 April 1805; Cath. Haen   01 FR-1136
Halls, (N); March 1808; Sarah Halls   02 WA-85
Hallsmith, John; 8 Sept. 1811; Elizab. Binkly   02 WA-91
Halmkiln, Aaron; 6 Feb. 1816; Mary Burns   14 BA-435
Halwadt, Charles (of Balto. Town, s. of Christopher of Exter, Co.
     of Flotko/Flotho, Principality of Menden, in Prussia, and
     wife Elizabeth, both dec.); 20 d. 11 mo., 1811; Sarah
     Frazier (dau. of William of Northeast MM, CE Co., and w.
     Rosey)   12 SF-16
Ham, George; March 1806; Polly Reel   02 WA-80
Hambleton, Edward; 27 March 1806; Priscilla Johnson 01 BA-10
Hambleton, Isaac (of BA, s. of William of Belmont Co., OH and
     Mary); 17 d, 7 m., 1811; Martha Brooks (of Balto. Town,
     dau. of Thomas Brooks of Chester Co., PA, dec., and w. Mary)
                                                     12 SF-10
Hamer, August; 13 April 1815; Jane Munday   14 BA-433
Hamers, Daniel; 2 March 1818; Abarilla Wassan   17 BA-18
Hamill, Patrick; 12 May 1805; Mary Morison   03 AL-613
Hamilton, Frans. S.; 30 April 1814; Ann Murphy   13 BA-18
Hamilton, Henry; Oct. 1819; Mary Hess   02 WA-114
Hamilton, John; 24 Dec. 1805; Anne Morris   03 BA-495
Hamilton, John; 29 March 1812; Catherine Evett (See also
     15 FR-325)   01 FR-1137
Hamilton, John; 26 May 1818; Mary Nicholls   06 FR-1328
Hamilton, Joseph; 8 Aug. 1813; Achsah Lynch   08 BA
Hamilton, Jos.; 12 Oct. 1815; Sarah Kelpan   13 BA-23
Hamilton, Robert Mandevill; 6 May 1813; Mary Ann Armitage
                                                     02 BA-36

Hammacher, Peter; Oct. 1817; Elizab. Krouse   02 Wa-106
Hammel, Georg; Feb. 1803; Barb. Kuntz   02 WA-74
Hammel, Jacobus; 21 Jan. 1812; Catherina Schaeffer (lic.)
                                                     39 BA-27
Hammelton, David (aged 85 years); 1 Dec. 1807; Ann Preston (See
    also 02 MO)   01 PG
Hammen, U!rick B.; 10 June 1817; Maria Hughes   02 BA-37
Hammer, Friderich; 11 June 1807; Margaretha Austin   07 BA-305
Hammer, George; 22 Oct. 1812; Mary Wilderman   14 BA-431
Hammer, Jac.; 12 Sept. 1816; Ann Robertson   13 BA-27
Hammersly, James; 20 April 1819; Sophia Jane Martindale
                                                     13 BA-34
Hammett, Robert; 25 Feb. 1802; Catherine Hebb   02 SM-185
Hammett, Samuel; 14 June 1817; Narcissa Boult   01 WA-200
Hammon, Lloyd; 17 Nov. 1803; Elizabeth Mereweather   03 MO-119
Hammond, Andrew; 29 Nov. 1808; Ritty Thomas   02 BA-7
Hammond, Edward; 24 June 1816; Harriet Wade   02 BA-37
Hammond, Jacob; Aug. 1813; Elizab. Riley   02 WA-98
Hammond, James; 29 Oct. 1803; Grace Anderson   02 BA-32
Hammond, James; 18 April 1808; Matulda A. Richmond   09 BA
Hammond, Philip; 3 March 1814; Julia Ann Hammond   11 BA-23
Hammond, Rezin; 15 Aug. 1816; Ann Mewburn   02 BA-37
Hammond, Rezin; 16 Jan. 1816; Mary Ann Edwards   11 BA-24
Hammond, Solomon; 26 Oct. 1803; Letty Ripper   14 BA-415
Hammond, William; 22 May 1812; Nelly Friend   02 WA-94
Hamond, (N); 1804; Esther Rudledge   02 WA-77
Hamond, (N); Jan. 1808; Soçia. Price   02 WA-84
Hamond, Henry; May 1805; Rachel Williams   02 WA-78
Hampton, William; 1 June 1801; Kitty Murphy   03 BA-401
Hamtranck, John; 16 May 1820; Mary Williamson   16 BA-100
Hanan, Michael; 18 Nov. 1819; Esther Graham   16 BA-92
Hance, James; 9 Jan. 1816; Ann Sweetser   11 BA-24
Hanckey, Jos.; 10 Dec. 1811; Catherine Hanson   15 BA-294
Hancock, Benjamin; 31 March 1803; Sarah Jenkins   05 AA-3
Hancock, Frank; 31 May 1808; Rachel Beal   13 BA-4
Hancock, Jonathan; 14 Jan. 1816; Sophia Stutson   05 BA-239
Hancock, Mich'l; 29 Oct. 1810; Nancy Townsend   13 BA-11
Hancock, Stephen; 8 Oct. 1801; Ann Cromwell   15 AA-1
Hancocke, John; Oct. 1813; Nancy Cook   08 BA
Hand, John; 13 May 1806; Margaret Barton   02 BA-3
Hand, Moses; 20 April 1809; Ann Frazier   11 BA-14
Handle, John; 9 Oct. 1815; Ann Woodville   17 BA-11
Hands, John; 24 Feb. 1803; Aairy [sic] Duvall   15 AA-2
Hands, Nicholas; 27 Feb. 1816; Ruth Hogner   09 BA
Handy, Gen. George; 20 Dec. 1815; Sally Wilson   03 SO
Handy, William A.; 1 Sept. 1818; Elizabeth Kelly   17 BA-19
Handy, William W. (of Balto. Town, s. of Henry of SO and w. Jane,
    both dec.); 22 d. 11 mo., 1811; Elizabeth Tyson (dau. of
    Jesse of Balto. Town, dec., and w. Margaret)   12 SF-19
Hane, Henry; 20 July 1807; Elisabeth McClarey   08 AL-44
Hane, Michael; 26 Nov. 1811; Marg[aret] Bertgis (See also
    15 FR-325)   01 FR-1137
Haney, Chas.; 6 June 1813; Sarah Cramford   14 BA-432
Haney, John; Aug. 1812; Eliza Yandell   03 BA-504
Haney, John; March 1816; Barbara Oderfer   02 WA-101
Haney, Nicholas; 15 Sept. 1803; Sarah Golden   03 MO-118
Hangle, Wm.; 30 June 1818; Ann Pouney (?)   13 BA-31
Hanke, Frederic; 18 Feb. 1813; Charlotte Wilh. Kleinhaus
                                                     14 BA-431
Hanke, Ludwig; 28 May 1816; Louisa Waag   14 BA-435
Hanks, Thomas; 12 or 17 Jan. 1814; Sarah Adams   17 BA-10
Hanna, Isaac; feb. 1820; Nancy Funk   02 WA-115
Hanna, Stephen Balch; betw. Sept. 1815 and Oct. 1820; Mary Ann
    Fulton   07 HA

Hannan, Michael; 6 Jan. 1803; Mary Howell   03 BA-424
Hannon, Nathan; 21 Jan. 1819; Charlotte Burke   16 BA-79
Hanshew, George; 7 Dec. 1815; Nancy Carpenter   06 FR-1323
Hanson, George; 12 Oct. 1817; Harriet Wayson   14 BA-436
Hanson, Henry; 14 Sept. 1815; Mary Rutter   16 BA-27
Hanson, Nathan; 21 Jan. 1819; Charlotte Burke   16 BA-79
Hanson, Oliver; 29 Dec. 1820; Mary Ann Murray   37 BA-153
Hanson, Wm.; 28 April 1808; Ruthy Peters   11 BA-13
Hanson, Wm.; 8 May 1810; Eliz'th Donnovan   13 BA-10
Hanson, Wm. H.; 13 May 1813; Eliza'h Smith   03 BA-505
Hanway, Amos; 15 Oct. 1805; Jane Naylor   09 BA
Hanx, Geo. Jac.; 23 Feb. 1808; Cath. Faubel   01 FR-1137
Hany, James; 25 Jan. 1820; Maria Brown   13 BA-41
Happener, Johan G.; 3 Oct. 1809; Margaret Reeb (?)   15 FR-324
Happener, John; 3 Oct. 1809; Marg. Reeb   01 FR-1137
Harbaugh, Benja.; 11 Dec. 1815; Marg't Reynolds   13 BA-23
Harbaugh, Jacob; 2 Oct. 1815; Ann Richter   13 BA-23
Harden, Samuel; 4 Oct. 1804; Maria Bull   11 BA-3
Hardester, Jno.; 10 Sept. 1818; Eliza Shyrock   14 BA-437
Hardesty, Charles R.; 28 Feb. 1819; Sarah R. Murray   37 BA-152
Hardesty, John; 1803; Agnes Nettles   07 AA-3
Hardesty, William; 23 Dec. 1802; Mary Howard   03 AA-120
Hardesty, William; 3 March 1810; Eleanor Whittington   17 AA
Hardevay, Daniel; 1 Jan. 1807; Clemence Hughes   02 BA-5
Hardin, Isaac; 10 Feb. 1807; Maria Kuch   08 AL-44
Harding, John L.; 30 May 1804; Eleanor Marshall (See also
   15 FR-316)   01 FR-1136
Harding, John L.; 29 March 1820; Eleanor Mantz   06 FR-1330
Harding, Stephen; 21 Aug. 1806; Mary Ann Scott   09 BA
Harding, William; 2 June 1814; Wilhelmina Kohlenberg   06 FR-1321
Harding, Wm.; 24 Feb. 1820; Elizabeth Stewart   16 BA-98
Hardinger, George; 17 Sept. 1816; Anna Rice   08 AL-44
Hardman, Martin; 28 June 1807; Eliz. Neushwanger   01 FR-1136
Hardy, (N); 16 April 1811; (N) Macquety   04 FR-17
Hardy, William; 14 Aug. 1817; Ann Bretton   13 BA-29
Hare, Benjamin; 26 Nov. 1815; Rebecca Trapnall   14 BA-434
Hare, Jesse; 11 Oct. 1810; Cath. Walsh   14 BA-428
Hare, Mark; 12 Sept. 1818; Margaret Bringham   17 BA-19
Hare, William; 8 June 1808; Ruth Sutton   02 BA-6
Harford, John; 27 May 1820; Rebecca Merick   11 BA-36
Harger, William; May 1817; Elizab. Hartman   02 WA-105
Hargood, Henry; 10 May 1801; Elizabeth Turner   03 BA-400
Hargrove, Rev. John; 14 June 1804; Mary Mather   03 BA-491
Harker, James; 10 June 1807; Elizabeth Browning   09 BA
Harker, James; 11 Aug. 1818; Julia Ann McCullen   09 BA
Harker, Jno.; 7 Jan. 1819; Alice Wooden   14 BA-438
Harker, William; 1 Oct. 1808; Elizab. McAllister   14 BA-425
Harking, William; 20 Dec. 1820; Eleanor Lawler   32 BA-331
Harkins, Giles; 22 Dec. 1814; Rosanna Clouse   16 BA-13
Harl, John; 18 Nov. 1809; Susannah Roney   31 BA-70
Harlan, John (s. of Joseph and Hannah Webster Harlan); 29 d. 9
   mo., 1803; Hannah Amos (dau. of William Amos and Susanna
   Howard Amos)   05 SF
Harlan, Joseph (s. of Joseph and Hannah); 29 d. 9 mo., 1803;
   Hannah Amoss (dau. of William and Susanna)   02 SF-85
Harland, Samuel D.; 23 June 1808; Ann Fifer   11 BA-13
Harlow, Winslow; 19 Dec. 1805; Rebecca Osborn   02 BA-3
Harman, Andrew; 28 Dec. 1820; Elizabeth Fairbank   13 BA-42
Harman, Daniel; 28 May 1812; Ann Lowery   11 BA-19
Harman, George; 7 Dec. 1813; Barbara Wilhite   06 FR-1320
Harman, Henry; 8 May 1816; Ann Brown   14 BA-435
Harman, Jacob; 22 Jan. 1804; Nackey Mallet   15 AA-3
Harman, John; 25 July 1809; Mary Hasson   15 BA-270
Harman, Philip; 18 May 1820; Catherine Trulock   13 BA-41

```
Harpe, James; 28 Feb. 1811; Cath. Baker              14 BA-428
Harper, Jacob; July 1802; Mary Fischer               02 WA-73
Harper, James; 18 Oct., 1812; Olly Stirmes (blacks)  15 FR-326
Harper, Robert Goodloe; 7 May 1801 (at Annapolis); Catherine
    Carroll                                          15 BA-152
Harper, Thomnas; 26 Sept. 1811; Sarah Miller (See also 15 FR-325)
                                                     01 FR-1137
Harpper, James; 18 Oct. 1812; Polly Stirmes (blacks) 01 FR-1127
Harpt, Christian; 29 Nov. 1808; Latheysy Ensly       07 BA-306
Harpum, Jonathan; 3 Aug. 1802; Priscilla Himes       09 BA
Harr, Peter; 6 Oct. 1818; Hannah Graham              37 BA-151
Harran, John; 22 Jan. 1806; Nancy Hill               21 BA-6
Harrington, Ezekiel; 19 April 1815; Sarah Ann Steel  09 BA
Harrington, Peter; 30 Oct. 1802; Mary Ford, widow Decarter (both
    natives of Ireland)                              15 BA-173
Harrington, Samuel; 30 Nov. 1819; Mary Lee           11 BA-36
Harris, Benjamin; 14 Jan. 1820; Cloe Worthington (blacks)
                                                     19 BA-73
Harris, Caesar (free negro); 3 Jan. 1808; Nancy (N), (mulatto
    slave of William Wetherall)                      15 BA-259
Harris, Jesse; 20 Oct. 1801; Darkey Norris           13 FR
Harris, John; 4 Sept. 1811; Eleanor McEntire         03 A1-614
Harris, John; 9 Dec. 1815; Mary Henderson            11 BA-26
Harris, John; 27 Nov. 1816; Eliza Penny              13 BA-27
Harris, Joseph; 20 July 1801; Susanna Reader         02 SM-185
Harris, Joseph; Feb. 1807; Sus. Hide                 02 WA-82
Harris, Nehemiah B.; 27 Nov. 1817; Marg't Campbell   13 BA-29
Harris, Oliver; 12 Feb. 1803; Mary Leak              06 BA-3
Harris, Richard; 9 Sept. 1820; Sophia Scott          13 BA-35
Harris, Samuel; 11 Oct. 1810; Eliza Story Conkling   05 BA-236
Harris, Sam'l; 1 Dec. 1811; Mary Warnell             13 BA-14
Harris, Samuel; 13 July 1815; Harriet Munro          17 BA-11
Harris, Samuel; 25 March 1819; Mary Ann Green        11 BA-35
Harris, William; 1809; Matilda Grainger              02 MO
Harris, William; 26 Nov. 1814; Emily Ferrall         21 BA-8
Harris, William C.; 7 May 1818; Mehitable Haggar     21 BA-9
Harris, Willis; 8 April 1814; Susan Vermillion       13 BA-18
Harrison, Benj. H.; 5 May 1812; Maria Enloes         13 BA-7
Harrison, Bill; 19 Feb. 1811; Polly Corkrill, (both of TA)
                                                     02 TA-41
Harrison, Francis; 9 June 1807; Sarah Cook           14 BA-422
Harrison, Henry; 17 Nov. 1818; Mary Sunderland       11 BA-33
Harrison, James; 31 Oct. 1802; Alleyfar Dashiell     03 BA-422
Harrison, James; 21 Jan. 1803; Alleyfor Dashield     02 BA-32
Harrison, James; 26 Dec. 1815; Ann Blades            17 BA-12
Harrison, James; 10 Sept. 1817; (?) Russell Brown    32 BA-314
Harrison, John; 20 Jan. 1807; Eliz[abeth] Hoffman (See also
    15 FR-320)                                       01 FR-1136
Harrison, John; April 1816; Deborah Kendal           02 WA-102
Harrison, John; 21 April 1818; Phillisenner Waltham  17 BA-19
Harrison, Joseph G.; 28 May 1816; Matilda B. Wood    03 AA-131
Harrison, Jos. N., Jr.; 12 Feb. 1817; Rosetta Green  13 BA-27
Harrison, Nicholas; 21 Aug. 1817; Catharine Gray     17 BA-17
Harrison, Oliver; 20 Jan. 1804; Mary Gordon          14 BA-416
Harrison, Peter; 28 May 1816; Bridget Wallace        32 BA-309
Harrison, Robert; 22 July 1813; Sarah Constant       09 BA
Harrison, Samuel; Feb. 1820; Elizab. French          02 WA-115
Harrison, Stephen; 19 Nov. 1815; Ann Greenfield      13 BA-23
Harrison, Thomas; 25 Oct. 1818; Elizabeth Ann Barker 17 BA-20
Harrison, Thomas; 21 Dec. 1818; Elizabeth Ann Barker 17 BA-18
Harrison, William: 10 Dec. 1805; Martha Dent         09 BA
Harrison, William; 9 Oct. 1806; Johanna Thomas       03 BA-496
Harrison, William; 27 Nov. 1806; Mary Miles          17 BA-6
```

```
Harrison, William; July 1812; Sarah Callichan, (both of TA Co.)
                                                       02 TA-42
Harrison, Zephaniah; 12 April 1818; Mary Haller       06 FR-1328
Harriss, Barton; 9 Feb. 1802; Mary Griffith           03 MO-118
Harriss, William; 27 (?) 1809; Matilda Grainger       01 PG-96
Harriss, William (s. of James, Jr., and Celia); 22 d. 5 mo.,
    1811; Mary Kelly (dau. of Ann, dec., and Dennis)  07 SF-18
Harrod, Henry; 7 Dec. 1806; Ann Mounters              02 BA-5
Harrop, Josiah; 5 Feb. 1820; Elizabeth Wilkins        03 BA-604
Harropp, Joseph; 27 Jasn. 1820; Ann (N)               03 BA-604
Harrow, James; 13 July 1809; Rebecca Ellis            02 BA-7
Harry, John; 15 June 1811; Ann Nappett                09 BA
Harry, Richard; 10 Nov. 1803; Charlotte Troutan       36 BA-1
Harry, Will; 25 Nov. 1813; (N) Wolford                02 WA-98
Harryman, Aquilla; 2 June 1803; Sarah Joice           09 BA
Harryman, Aquilla; 18 Oct. 1804; Mary Galloway        09 BA
Harryman, Samuel; 29 Jan. 1804; Elizabeth Wheeler     23 BA-3
Harryman, Thomas; 15 April 1802; Rachel Rowlings      09 BA
Harryman, William; 27 April 1814; Mary M. Yeiser      09 BA
Hart, Benjamin; 4 Dec. 1806; Clemency Taylor          09 BA
Hart, Isaac; 29 June 1819; Mary Carruthers            20 BA-224
Hart, John; 6 Dec. 1818; Elizabeth Dempsey            03 BA-603
Hart, John Peter; 29 Dec. 1814; Hanna Mellinger       14 BA-433
Hart, Joseph; 31 July 1804; Ann Porter                09 BA
Hart, Josias; 22 Dec. 1814; Sarah Garrett             14 BA-433
Hart, Michael; 25 Jan. 1814; Sus. Stokes              02 WA-99
Hart, Robert; 7 April 1804; Margarfe Murphey          02 BA-33
Hart, Valentine; 31 July 1817; Juliann Boyd           11 BA-31
Hart, Valentine; 4 July 1820; Elizabeth Lane          11 BA-38
Hart, William; 12 Nov. 1808; Mary Hush                14 BA-425
Hart, William; 17 Dec. 1807; Elizabeth Wilson         11 BA-12
Hartey, Joseph; 15 Aug. 1809; Sarah McKinsey          09 BA
Hartly, William (of BA, s. of Samuel and Lavinia); 20 d. 12 m.,
    1815; Mary Buckman (of AA Co., dau. of Phineas and dec. w.
    Susanna)                                          12 SF-49
Hartman, George; March 1818; Cath. Miller             02 WA-109
Hartner, Ignatius; 4 June 1816; Anna Maria Hun(arkers?)
                                                      39 BA-31
Hartshorne, Peter S.; 5 April 1814; Sarah Proud       03 BA-505
Hartzog, Jacob Frederick; 6 July 1818; Maria Renaudett
                                                      16 BA-71
Harvey, James; 16 Oct. 1814; Lilly Wiley              17 BA-10
Harvey, James; 2 Sept. 1819; Eliza Uhler              14 BA-439
Harvey, Nacy Wheeler; (date not given, but listed between mar-
    riages of 29 Dec. 1800 and 2 June 1801); Delilah Banister
    (15 FR-311 gives date as May 1801)                01 FR-1136
Harvey, Samuel Dawes; 6 Aug. 1802; Marg't McMechen    03 BA-504
Harwood, Geo.; 30 April 1811; Marg't Hargenhammer     03 BA-502
Harwood, James; 7 Aug. 1815; Mary Elder               05 BA-238
Harwood, Thos.; 1 June 1815; Eliza Wall               13 BA-21
Haskins, Roger; 21 Nov. 1805; Sarah O'Donnell         02 BA-2
Haslet, William; 26 Nov., 1802; Isabella McKim        05 BA-233
Haspelhorn, Ludwig (age c70, widower); 30 Dec. 1801; Rosina
    Woring (age c.30-40, single)                      01 CL-150
Hassell, Thomas; 5 March 1820; Mrs. Elizabeth Ware    37 BA-153
Haswell, John W.; 9 Sept. 1807; Eliza. Madlicoate     11 BA-11
Hatch, Frederic; 8 Sept. 1811; Frances Robertson      03 BA-503
Hatch, Rev. Frederick W.; 9 Aug. 1814; Ann Weatherburn 03 BA-506
Hathaway, John; 6 Sept. 1815; Hariot Stanes           11 BA-26
Hattan, John; 18 Jan. 1807; Anna Maria Bond           11 BA-10
Hatter, Jacob; May 1817; Maria Butten                 02 WA-105
Hatton, Daniel; 3 March 1803; Ann Carback             26 BA-3
Hatton, John; 25 Dec. 1803; Sarah Collings            05 HA-1
```

Hatton, Robert (s. of Joseph and Susanna); 25 d. 5 mo., 1808;
    Lydia Willis Farquhar (wid. of (N) Farquhar and dau. of
    William and Betty Willis)   03 SF
Haubert, Fred'k; 24 June 1810; Eliza'h Rawlings   13 BA-10
Hauck, Jacob; 24 Dec. 1805; Cath. Loh (See also 15 FR-318)
                                                  01 FR-1136
Hauck, Jacob; 4 Feb. 1806; Marg. Getzendanner (See also
    15 FR-318)   01 FR-1136
Hauck, Johannes; 2 June 1801; Maria Schaup   15 FR-311
Hauck, John; 2 June 1801; Mary Schaup   01 FR-1136
Hauer, George; 9 Oct. 1803; Cath. Schelman (See also 15 FR-315)
                                                  01 FR-1136
Haupsch, Johanes; 26 Dec. 1819; An. Barb. Long   14 BA-439
Haupt, Georgius; 20 May 1816; Maria [Doeney]   39 BA-31
Hauptman, Hein.; 20 June 1806; Susanna Benjamin   14 BA-420
Hauptman, Jno.; 2 Dec. 1808; Elizabeth Curtis   14 BA-425
Haus, Wm.; 22 July 1817; Rebecca Hertzog   14 BA-436
Hause, William; 10 Oct. 1805; Sus[anna] Lamar (See also
    15 FR-318)   01 FR-1136
Hauser, Frederick; 15 Jan. 1818; Christian Stoner (See also
    15 FR-327)   01 FR-1137
Haux, George Jacob; 23 Feb. 1808; Cath. Faubel   15 FR-322
Havis, William; 31 May 1808; Alice Benson   15 BA-262
Hawes (Haas), Frederic; 14 Sept. 1815; Cath. Hughes (Yost)
                                                  14 BA-434
Hawkins, Aaron; 30 Sept. 1819; Ann Hawkins   13 BA-41
Hawkins, John; 7 June 1802; Marg't Kirby   13 BA-7
Hawkins, Samuel; 27 June 1819; Sarah Sheppard   11 BA-37
Hawkins, Thomas; March 1805; Susan Burgess   17 BA-4
Hay, Geo.,; 23 Aug. 1808; Margaret Bateman   13 BA-4
Hayden, Dennis; Aug. 1818; Rachel Fowler   16 BA-72
Hayden, Horace; 23 Feb. 1804; Maria Antoinette Robinson
                                                  03 BA-490
Hayes, (?)uel S.; 1812; Anna Rawlins   02 MO
Hayes, Alexander; 9 June 1803; Elizabeth Hamilton   03 BA-429
Hayes, James; 15 June 1809; Sarah Beall (See also 15 FR-324)
                                                  01 FR-1137
Hayes, John; 26 March 1806; Bellinda Riddle   05 BA-234
Hayes, John; 5 July 1813; Mary Calmes   03 AL-614
Hayes, Reverdy; 16 May 1811; Tabithy Fairbairn   05 BA-236
Hayes, Robert; 7 March 1813; Sarah Richardson   02 WA-97
Hayes, Samuel S.; 1812; Anna Rawlins   01 PG
Hayes, Simon; 31 Oct. 1815; Eliza Deakons   13 BA-23
Hayes, William; c.1804; Elizabeth Jarvis   34 BA-2
Hayes, William; 22 Oct. 1818; Jane Moran   09 BA
Hayman, Dan'l; 29 Oct. 1815; Mary Pumphrey   13 BA-23
Hays, Abram; 30 Oct. 1814; Susan Sheets   13 BA-19
Hays, George; 14 July 1807; Mary Kinnear   03 BA-497
Hays, John; 14 April 1811; Elizabeth Eckman   06 FR-1315
Hays, John Otho; 1804; Sophia Fox   03 WA
Hays, Leareen; by 30 Oct. 1802; Millee Forrest   12 FR
Hays, Thomas; 8 April 1802; Elizabeth Jones   33 BA-14
Hays, William; 12 July 1810; Mary Bowman   08 AL-46
Hayward. Isaac (s. of William and Keziah); 20 d. 6 mo., 1816;
    Elizabeth Balderston (dau. of Ely and Esther   09 SF
Hayward, Col. William; 4 Feb. 1806; Arietta M. Lloyd (by license
    and by dispenssation; both of Tal. Co.)   02 TA-39
Hazlehurst, Andrew; 3 Jan. 1805; Frances Purviance   05 BA-234
Head, Richard L.; 9 June 1803; Margaret Stitcher (widow)
                                                  15 BA-184
Heaflick, Jacob; 14 April 1814; Charlotte Grant   05 BA-238
Heairn, John; 20 May 1807; Mary Summers   03 BA-497
Heald, William; 9 May 1815; Hannah Henneman   20 BA-222
Healy, John; 29 Oct. 1806; Susanna Fauning (age 17) 31 BA-14

Heamer, August; 24 Dec. 1803; Margaret Altherr   14 BA-415
Heard, Ignatius; 2 Feb. 1819; Eleanor Herbert   04 SM
Heard, John; 9 April 1820; Mary Moore   32 BA-328
Heard, Joseph; 17 Sept. 1805; Sophia Abell   02 SM-187
Heartley, James; 19 May 1817; Martha Wright   17 BA-16
Hearvy, Edward; 1 May 1803; Elizabeth Wilson   06 BA-3
Heater, George; 22 Dec. 1801; Charlotte Porter   03 MO-117
Heater, John; 13 Feb. 1806; Frances Shook   03 MO-120
Heath, (N); 1 Dec. 1813; (N) Leiger   02 WA-99
Heath, Daniel Charles; 2 July 1807; Elizabeth McKim   02 BA-5
Hebb, William; 6 July 1802; Ann Taylor   02 SM-185
Hebb, William; 21 March 1809; Sarah Bailey   02 SM-188
Hebert, John B.; 6 Nov. 1801; Martha Steel   14 BA-411
Heckrate, Wm.; 11 Dec. 1815; Ann Pinnell   11 BA-24
Hector, Charles; 4 Aug. 1813; Mary Celestine (free blacks)
                                                       15 BA-313
Hedge, Andrew; 29 Jan. 1805; Juliana Lederman   15 FR-317
Hedgh, Andrew; 29 Jan. 1805; Julian Lederman   01 FR-1136
Hedrick, Thomas S.; 7 July 1818; Mary Jupper   20 BA-223
Hedricks, Richard; 26 Nov. 1812; Jula. Edwards   13 BA-15
Heedwohl, Samuel; Oct. 1817; Mary Kable   02 WA-106
Heeter, Frederick; 1811; Mary Porter (See also 02 MO) 01 PG
Heffner, (N); 29 Dec. 1812; (N) Shupp   02 WA-96
Heffner, Jacob; 28 Nov. 1813; Mary Heffner   06 FR-1320
Heffner, Joseph; 6 Feb. 1816; Eleonora Burkhart   06 FR-1323
Heffner, Lawrence; 21 Dec. 1817; Charlotte Heffner   06 FR-1327
Heffner, Michael; 26 April 1817; Margareth Stoll   06 FR-1326
Heflich, Jacob; April 1818; Cath. Mong   02 WA-109
Heflich, Peter; March(?) 1804; Cath. Stover   02 WA-76
Hefner, George; 10 April 1808; Elizab. Hefner (See also
   15 FR-322)   01 FR-1137
Heigh, David; 7 June 1812; Sarah Armstrong   11 BA-20
Heigh, David; 9 Dec. 1819; Harriot Shryer   13 BA-34
Heil, Frederick; 28 Feb. 1805; Maria Gibbs   14 BA-418
Heil, Johannes; 7 Aug. 1804; Elisabeth Elcher   14 BA-417
Heiler, John; 13 Feb. 1806; Frances Shook   01 PG
Heim, Andrew; 25 July 1809; Mary Brunner   01 FR-1137
Heinecke, Frederick; 21 Dec. 1815; Lavinia Wilson   14 BA-434
Heis, Wm.; 3 Nov. 1818; Marg. Konig   14 BA-438
Heisher, Clement; 15 Dec. 1881; Rachel Pundy   04 FR-18
Heislaw, John; 9 May 1804; Sarah Mitchell (See also 25 BA-4)
                                                       14 BA-416
Heiter, John; 13 Feb. 1806; Frances Shock   02 MO
Heldt, John; Jan. 1820; Elizab. Neikirk   02 WA-115
Helmling, Joannes; 26 Dec. 1818; Sophia Slough   39 BA-35
Helmeling, Joseph; 2 (20?) May 1806; Sarah Bathges   39 BA-19
Helms, Adam; 1 Nov. 1803; Elizabeth Madden (see also 04 AL-1;
   09 AL gives date as 29 Oct. 1803))   07 AL-274
Helms, James; 13 June 1811; Mima Duvall   09 BA
Helms, Thomas; 19 Nov. 1801; Mary Ann Maggs   03 BA-410
Hemling, Anthony; 24 June 1807; Sarah Lashly   14 BA-422
Hemp, Henry; 18 May 1817; Elizabeth Keller   06 FR-1326
Hencke, F. Wilhelm; 7 Feb. 1808; Sarah Pew   14 BA-425
Henderson, Benja.; 6 Aug. 1812; Sarah Creswell   13 BA-14
Henderson, Henry; 10 May 1804; Christian McCulloch   14 BA-416
Henderson, James; 15 Dec. 1803; Jane Merley (02 BA-33 gives the
   bride's name as Kerley)   03 BA-436
Henderson, Peter; 29 Oct. 1815; Mary Booth   09 BA
Hendrick, Joshua; Feb. 1813; Sarah Galloway   01 BA-11
Hendricks, Thos.; 6 Aug. 1807; Eliza Myers   13 BA-2
Hendrickson, David (native of N. J.); 30 Nov. 1806; Mary O'Connor
   (widow of the late John O'Connor, native of Ireland)
                                                       15 BA-244
Hendrickson, Daniel; 6 De. 1819; Mary Norwood   19 BA-73

Henerray (?), Dan'l; 22 Dec. 1812; Cath. Fohner					14 BA-412
Heney, Abel; 6 Aug. 1815; A. Hagner					13 BA-22
Henis, Friedrich; 10 July 1814; Mary Kelly					14 BA-433
Henisler, Joseph; 26 May 1806; Mary Parker					03 BA-495
Henkel, Herman; 17 March 1801; Margaret Hale					14 BA-409
Hennesey, John; 15 Feb. 1819; Juliana McCarty					16 BA-80
Hennicain, Thos.; 28 Sept. 1810; Nancy Bryson					14 BA-428
Hennican, Matthew; 15 Oct. 1801; Elizabeth Penn					02 CH
Henniken, John; 18 Feb. 1817; Rebecca Ward					11 BA-31
Henning, Benjamin; 24 Oct. 1805; Eliz. Schartel					14 BA-419
Henning, Bennett; 17 Jan. 1805; Ann Kendrick					02 SM-186
Henning, Frederick; 13 Oct. 1808; Sarah McClelland					02 SM-188
Henning, John; 30 Dec. 1802; Sarah Henning					02 SM-185
Henning, Thomas; 31 Dec. 1805; Priscilla Sword					02 SM-187
Henning, Thos.; 4 April 1813; Hannah Burnett					03 BA-505
Henrich, Isaak; 18 July 1803; Maria Polluck					07 BA
Henry, Abraham; 27 Sept. 1804; Ann Martin (see also 02 BA-34)
					03 BA-491
Henry, Charles; 8 Oct. 1808; Mary Schriner (See also 15 FR-322)
					01 FR-1137
Henry, David; 17 June 1813; Martha Duncan					31 BA-152
Henry, Georg; 27 July 1806; Elizabeth Dick					07 BA-305
Henry, John; 1 Aug. 1801; Elizabeth Downing					10 BA-1
Henry, John; 1804; Nelly Nimmey					02 WA-77
Henry, John; 4 Oct. 1818; Mary Nash (free col'd)					02 DO
Henry, Jno.; 2 Dec. 1819; Sarah Kovy					14 BA-439
Henry, Robert S.; 17 Dec. 1818; Susannah Brotherton					37 BA-151
Henry, Thomas; 7 Oct. 1805; Judith Ennis					11 BA-7
Henry, Thomas; 7 Nov. 1816; June Howard					09 BA
Henry, W. George; 14 Nov. 1819; Elizabeth Fox					02 FR-15
Hensey, Thos.; 14 Jan. 1814; Henrietta Smith					13 BA-18
Henshaw, Robinson J.; 19 Sept. 1820; Marg't E. Waltham 13 BA-35
Henson, Benjamin; 5 Dec. 1805; Martha Jackson					11 BA-7
Hensoner, Wm., Jr.; 22 July 1819; Mary Norton					13 BA-33
Heny, James; 14 Nov. 1805; Jane Savage					08 AL-48
Hepburn, John M.; 14 April 1818; Eliza S. Johnston					05 BA-240
Herald, George Doderich; 23 July 1802; Eliza Pfalzgraf 14 BA-413
Herbert, Charles R.; 6 April 1810; (N) Steinmetz					39 BA-24
Herbert, Jas.; 30 Oct. 1805; Sarah Brady					14 BA-419
Herbert, John; 9 Aug. 1803; Nancy Bosdick					03 BA-432
Herbert, John; May 1817; Rachel Sacket					02 WA-105
Herbert, Joseph; 25 Aug. 1801; Eleanor Jenkins					15 BA-155
Herbert, Stewart; Jan. 1818; Rebecca Doyle					02 WA-107
Herbert, Wm.; 21 Feb. 1804; Susanna Gablet					14 BA-416
Herget, John; 19 April 1810; Barb[ara] Thomas (See also
			15 FR-324)					01 FR-1137
Herley, John; 7 June 1811; Sara Harden					04 FR-17
Herlon, Mich'l; 1 Dec., 1816; Eliza Sanders					13 BA-27
Herman, [Ja?]cob; Nov. 1807; Cath. Arnen					02 WA-84
Herman, George; 13 Dec. 1802; Mary Lisney					14 BA-414
Herman, George; 17 Nov. 1808; Ann Shipley					14 BA-425
Herman, Jno.; 2 May 1806; Mary Haselbach					14 BA-420
Herman, Jno.; 19 Oct. 1808; Mary Fetterling					14 BA-425
Herman, Matthias; 24 May 1804; Dorothea Hoss					14 BA-416
Herman, Peter; 13 March 1811; Mary Herman					14 BA-428
Herman, Philip; 17 April 1802; Sarah Dunkin (or Dankin)
					03 BA-415
Heron, Alexander; 19 Nov. 1818; Ann Heck					20 BA-223
Heron, John; 15 Feb. 1801; Blanchy Imbert, (both of QA Co.)
					03 TA-71
Herr, Conrad; March 1818; Cath. Beagler					02 WA-109
Herr, Joseph; 16 Oct. 1812; Cath. Moudy					02 WA-15
Herrick, Thomas; 11 Oct. 1807; Pheobe Carrothers					15 FR-321
Herring, George; 9 Jan. 1812; Mary Hershberger					06 FR-1317

Herring, John; 11 Jan. 1816; Mary Harget   06 FR-1323
Herris, Robert; 16 Aug. 1806; Kitty Larket (blacks) 21 BA-6
Herron, John; 30 Dec. 1812; Ann Powell   02 BA-36
Herron, Robert B.; 26 June 1802; Jane Crook   09 BA
Hershberger, Henry; 24 April 1817; Juliana Scott   06 FR-1326
Hersbergere, John B.; 14 Sept. 1820; Sarah Wiles (See also
   16 FR-76)   03 FR-100
Hersche, Jacob; Dec. 1803; Marg. Yung   02 WA-75
Hersh, George; April 1820; Sarah Burkhart   02 WA-116
Hershey, John; 13 Aug. 1811; Mary Dewalt   14 BA-429
Hershman, Philip; April 1804; Frany Dornbach   02 WA-76
Herstons, Charles; 29 Feb. 1816; Martha D. Allen   11 BA-26
Hertick, Gabriel; 10 Feb. 1803; Catherine Kelley   15 BA-177
Hertick, Henry; 27 April 1801; Maria Kellen   15 BA-151
Herton, John; 19 Feb. 1815; Mary Waters   06 FR-1321
Heslett, Joseph; 30 April 1801; Catherine Helfin   15 BA-151
Hesong, John; 8 Nov. 1803; Rebecca McMahon (See also 04 AL-1)
                                                    07 AL-274
Hess, Jacob; 2 Dec. 1819; Susan Hurst   11 BA-37
Hess, Jeremias; May 1805; Dorothy Kose   02 WA-79
Hessey, Archibald; 28 Oct. 1813; Mary Ann Martin   13 BA-38
Hessinger, Geo.; Aug. 1810; Barbara Kooch   02 WA-87
Heston, Samuel (of BA, s. of Joseph and dec. w. Phoebe); 21 d.
   10 m., 1812; Rebecca Lownes (dau. of Joseph and Miriam of AA
   Co.)   12 SF-28
Hetherington, John; 31 May 1818; Julian Fulton   13 BA-31
Hetzer, John; 24 Dec. 1811; Eliz. Nitzel   02 WA-92
Heuisler, Ant'y, widower; 3 Feb. 1801; Dorothy Lawrence, widow
                                                    15 BA-149
Heuisler, Anthony, Jr.; 6 March 1804; Margaret Robinson, widow
                                                    15 BA-200
Hewell, Lewis; 5 Oct. 1820; Ann Richardson   13 BA-36
Hewer(?), Thos.; 1 Dec. 1807; Priscilla Boreing   13 BA-3
Hewes, Aaron; 12 March 1809; Elizabeth Boult   02 SM-188
Hewes, Daniel; 12 April 1819; Mary Jones   05 BA-241
Hewes, John (of Balto. Town, s. of Edward of Wilmington, DE, and
   w. Mary); 15 d., 1 mo., 1812; Rachel Thomas Ellicott (dau.
   of Elias of Balto. Town, and dec. w. Mary)   12 SF-22
Heyl, William; 15 June 1806; Mary Louisa Martin   15 BA-239
Heyser, William; 13 Jan. 1813; Sarah Artz   02 WA-96
Hetzeler, Joannes; 10 June 1813; Julia [Fifer]   39 BA-29
Hiants, Christian; 6 May 1816; Mary Gruber   07 BA-310
Hibberd, Allen (s. of Joseph and Jane [James]); 6 d. 1 mo., 1808;
   Rachel Haines (dau. of Nathan and Sophia [Price]) 03 SF
Hibberd, Benjamin (s. of Joseph and Jane [James]); 13 d. 11 mo.,
   1811; Charity Beeson (dau. of Edward and Jane ‡Pugh])
                                                    03 SF
Hibberd, Joseph, Jr. (s. of Joseph and Jane [James]); 15 d. 3
   mo., 1806; Rachel Wright (dau. of Joel and Elizabeth
   [Farquhar])   03 SF
Hibberd, Silas (s. of Joseph and Jane [James]);24 d. 10 mo.,
   1810; Elizabeth Haines (dau. of Joseph and Rachel [Cookson])
                                                    03 SF
Hibbert, Henry; 10 Oct. 1816; Eliz. S. Faulkner   14 BA-436
Hickel, Joseph; 22 Feb. 1807; Ann Becks   14 BA-421
Hickinger, Jacob; 11 June 1815; Christina Wilhelm   08 AL-48
Hickle, Joseph; Sept. 1820; Elizab. Hoffman   02 WA-117
Hickman, Christopher; 16 April 1811; Catherine Ely 06 FR-1315
Hickman, David; 1 March 1808; Jane Sinclair   09 BA
Hicks, Elijah; 14 Nov. 1816; Sarah B. Watts   09 BA
Hicks, George; 25 July 1813; Elizabeth Cole   11 BA-23
Hicks, George; June 1818; Mary Brannon   02 WA-110
Hicks, John; 2 June 1814; Margaret League   09 BA
Hicks, William; 20 June 1816; Mary Ann Rollison   13 BA-40

Hide, Valentine; 18 Aug. 1812; Polly Ropp   06 FR-1318
Hidle, Michael; 11 Oct. 1817; Matilda Meyers   32 BA-315
Hiesh, Charles; 30 May 1814; Catherina Haley   07 BA-309
Higden, Ralph; 14 Aug. 1817; Harriet Prill   13 BA
Higenbaugh, Henry; 8 Nov. 1803; Eleanor Madden   09 AL
Higginbotham, Ralph; 19 Oct. 1815; Sophia Hall   03 BA-507
Higgins, Daniel; 17 April 1818; Honora Carroll   16 BA-66
Higgins, Edward; 2 May 1804; Susanna Grubb   09 BA
Higgins, John (s. of Joseph and Sarah, dec.); 3rd d. 11 mo.,
     1803; Sarah Norton (dau. of Stephen and Sophia) 11 SF-92
Higgins, Robert; Oct. 1818; Lavinia Wherrett   02 WA-111
Higgs, James; 30 June 1818; Cynthia Ann Seaman   01 WA-201
Higgs, Thomas; April 1805; Amelia Duvall   02 WA-78
Highstone, Sol.; 19 Jan. 1817; Ann Duley   13 BA-27
Higinbotham, William; 18 Oct. 1804; Marg't Turner (see also
     02 BA-34)   03 BA-492
Hignault, John; 11 Feb. 1819; Caroline Pritchard   11 BA-34
Higson, George; 2 June 1810; Judith H. Furgerson   21 BA-7
Higson, James; 5 April 1804; Kitty E. Hutchings   21 BA-5
Higson, Thos.; 26 April 1802; Ann Melker   14 BA-412
Hilary, Ambrose; 24 Nov. 1817; Mary Pierre (both free col'd)
                                                       16 BA-60
Hildebrand, John Christian; 25 Sept. 1810; Rebecca Logus
                                                       07 BA-307
Hildebrand, Petrus; 11 Oct. 1810; Martha Durragh   39 BA-25
Hildebrandt, Andreas; 6 Oct. 1807; Catherine Caplern 07 BA-305
Hildt, John; 13 April 1802; Mary Weller   30 BA-108
Hilky, George; 16 Aug. 1814; Barbara Koltz   06 FR-1321
Hill, David; June 1820; Sarah Faulkwell   02 WA-116
Hill, George; 25 April 1819; Margareth Hoffman   06 FR-1329
Hill, Henrich; 1 Nov. 1804; Polly Cling   07 BA
Hill, James; 7 April 1803; Nancy Brian   09 BA
Hill, James; 9 Aug. 1817; Elizabeth Wier   17 BA-17
Hill, Jeremiah; 3 Feb. 1809; Mary Story   02 BA-35
Hill, John; 9 Aug. 1805; Margaret Hickey   03 BA-494
Hill, John H.; 30 Nov. 1809; Nancy Turner   13 BA-8
Hill, John W.; 5 Oct. 1820; Mary Orrok   03 BA-605
Hill, Nathaniel; 21 Nov. 1805; Rachel Clark   11 BA-7
Hill, Nicolas; 3 Feb. 1813; Francesca [Shauk]   39 BA-29
Hill, Richard; 14 Nov. 1809; Hanna McFadan   14 BA-426
Hill, Richard; 30 Jan. 1816; Margaret Drury   03 AA-131
Hill, Stephen; 7 May 1815; Eleanor Shannon   21 BA-8
Hill, Thomas; 8 June 1801; Martha Browning   37 BA-18
Hill, Thos. G.; 30 April 1816; Mary Sleuby   13 BA-25
Hillanderville, Daniel; 29 Feb. 1820; Harriet Warner 19 BA-73
Hillary, Henry; 6 Jan. 1820; Rebecca Ryan   02 FR-15
Hillary, Louis; 5 May 1819; Caroline Barker   16 BA-82
Hilleary, Thos.; 24 Nov. 1803; Sarah Wheeler   03 MO-119
Hilleary, Walter Henry; 1813; Susan Smith (See also 02 MO)
                                                       01 PG
Hillen, John; 29 Nov. 1804; Catherine Reish (?)   04 BA-1
Hillen, Solomon; 23 July 1807; Frances Woodyear   15 BA-252
Hillers, John; 2 June 1801; Mary Spencer   03 AL-613
Hilliard, James; 19 April 1804; Mary Laurence (See also
     15 FR-316)   01 FR-1136
Hillyard, Benj. H.; 25 Feb. 1816; Hart. McNier   13 BA-24
Hilton, John; 16 April 1802; Elenor (?) Jeane (?) Jones (?)
                                                       05 AA-2
Himes, John; 15 Jan. 1812; Sarah Holter   06 FR-1317
Hinds, John; 21 Feb. 1819; Cathe. Simms   13 BA-32
Hinds, William; 11 Dec. 1808; Barbara Copenhager   13 BA-5
Hines, Hugh; 15 Oct. 1807; Susanna Comper (15 FR-3231 gives date
     as 14 Oct.)   01 FR-1137
Hines, John; 11 July 1811; Rebas Travers   13 BA-13

```
Hines, Solomon; 13 Dec. 1820; Rosanna Grau          11 BA-39
Hines, Wm.; 25 March 1817; Eliza Burgess            13 BA-28
Hingery, Jacob; May 1806; Mary Myers                02 WA-80
Hink, Joseph; 30 Oct. 1808; Eliza M. Oliver         21 BA-7
Hinkel, Hennrich; 1802; Marg. Ditsch (or Titsch)    02 WA-72
Hinkle, Jesse; 23 Sept. 1819; Mary Ann Folk         08 AL-50
Hinkley, Edward; 27 Dec. 1820; Hannah Hargrove      21 BA-9
Hinks, William; 21 Oct. 1813; Mary Dent             11 BA-23
Hinnerickle, Jacob; 18 June 1804; Elizabeth Broudy  09 BA
Hinton, Abijah John; 18 Dec. 1808; Jane Mastin      02 BA-7
Hintze, Carl, widower; 5 July 1802; Henrietta Habliston, nee
     Machaux                                        07 BA-67
Hipkins, Charles G.; 16 Nov. 1818; Elizabeth Gorsuch 11 BA-33
Hipsley, Solomon; 5 Jan. 1815; Providence Orsler    08 BA
Hirchman, Jared; 14 Jan. 1818; Mary McCallister     14 BA-437
Hirsh, Martin; 6 Oct. 1811; Elizab. Scharr          14 BA-429
Hisong, John; 8 Nov. 1803; Rebecca McMahon          09 AL
Hissey, Archibald; 7 April 1803; Mary Butler        03 BA-426
Hissey, Charles; 1 Oct. 1801; Elizabeth Robinson    03 BA-407
Hitchcock, Nathaniel; 25 June 1811; Elizabeth Bowers 09 BA
Hitselberger, Anthony; 26 Feb. 1801; Apolonia Drexell 14 BA-401
Hitselberger, [Peter]; 12 [May?] 1807; Margareta Norbeck
                                                    39 BA-19
Hitselberger, Jacob; 11 April 1818; Hanna Haas      14 BA-437
Hitselberger, Jacob; 28 July 1816; Elizabeth Shorb  16 BA-39
Hitt, Andreas; 9 Feb. 1808; Sarah Meiers            07 BA-306
Hitzelberger, Baltasar; 11 May 1811; Barbara Schwartz 39 BA-26
Hixenbaugh, Henry; 8 Nov. 1803; Eleanor Madden (07 AL-274 gives
     the groom's name as Hixenbough)                04 AL-1
Hizz, Lewis; 30 May 1820; Esther Robison            30 BA-109
Hobbs, George; 5 Nov. 1803; Prudence Hammersley (see also
     02 BA-32)                                      03 BA-435
Hobbs, Horatio; 23 Feb. 1816; Anna Head             04 FR-18
Hobbs, Jno.; 5 March 1803; Mary Minnich             14 BA-414
Hobbs, Nicanah; 22 May 1805; Ainsey (?) Gray        09 BA
Hobby, John; 5 March 1801; Mary Stansbury           09 BA
Hoblitzel, George; 19 Nov. 1812; Sally McDermot     08 AL-51
Hoblitzel, Henry; 7 May 1812; Margaret Carlton      08 AL-51
Hoblitzel, John; 9 Nov. 1801; Peggy Quary           03 AL-613
Hobnutt, George; 21 Jan. 1818; Mary Porter          17 BA-19
Hobson, Joseph (s. of Joseph and Ann); 18 d. 3 mo., 1813;
     Rebeckah Talbott (dau. of John and Mary)       03 SF
Hoburg, John; 1 July 1811; Eliz. Wright             14 BA-429
Hoburg, Richard; 1 Dec. 1810; Eliza Rice            14 BA-428
Hockly, Walter L.; 28 Oct. 1810; Juliana Conaway    11 BA-16
Hodge, John; 9 Aug. 1803; Elizabeth Bramble         09 BA
Hodgkins, Thomas S.; 22 Dec. 1803; Elizabeth Smith  03 AA-120
Hodgkinson, John; 23 July 1820; Ann Skillman        11 BA-38
Hoeck, Andrew; 6 April 1804; Cath. Reim             14 BA-416
Hoey, John; 29 Oct. 1807; Keziah Brine              11 BA-11
Hoey, Thomas; 27 April 1805; Catherine Dunagan (see also
     03 BA-493)                                     02 BA-35
Hof (?); Joh. Heinrich; April 1807; Mary A-[page torn] 02 WA-82
Hoff [Roff?], David; Dec. 1809; Maria Miller        39 BA-23
Hoffard, John; 30 March 1812; Elizabeth House       06 FR
Hoffman, David; 7 Aug. 1817; Susan Williams         14 BA-436
Hoffman, David; 24 March 1803; Elizabeth Jempe      03 AL-613
Hoffman, Frederick; 1804; Elizabeth Socks           03 WA
Hoffman, Frederick W.; 28 Nov. 1816; Mary D. Lieuthaut 16 BA-46
Hoffman, Fried.; Dec. 1803; Elis. Peter             02 WA-75
Hoffman, Fried'k; 11 April 1805; Maria Funk         14 BA-418
Hoffman, George; 25 Jan. 1801; Mary Kent            09 BA
Hoffman, George; 26 feb. 1805; Henriette Rogers     11 BA-5
```

Hoffman, George; 30 Oct. 1808; Mary Shirly (15 FR-323 gives
    bride's name as Shirley)   01 FR-1137
Hoffman, George; 4 May 1819; Mary Smith   30 BA-109
Hoffman, Geo. Henry; 20 Aug. 1820; Sarah Sappington   13 BA-35
Hoffman, Henry; Nov. 1816; Susanna Garver   02 WA-102
Hoffman, Henry W.; 28 April 1818; Margareth Kemp   06 FR-1328
Hoffman, Jacob; Aug. 1820; Polly Bowser   02 WA-117
Hoffman, John; 23 Jan. 1811; Susannah Wengant   11 BA-18
Hoffman, John; 24 Sept. 1815; Sarah Dells   13 BA-23
Hoffman, John; 10 Jan. 1820; Maragarete Ann Peterson   16 BA-96
Hoffman, Lorenz; 15 May 1814; Nancy Smith   14 BA-432
Hoffman, Nelson; 1 Sept. 1818; Elizabeth Lemplin   06 FR-1328
Hofheins, Georg; March 1802; Magd. Fritsch   02 WA-73
Hofman, Gotlieb; 30 Oct. 1809; Sally Hurly   14 BA-226
Hofman, Johan Casper; 22 June 1817; Elizabeth Deller   07 BA-310
Hofman, Mich.; Nov. 1803; Maria Kau   02 WA-75
Hogan, John; 6 May 1811; Ellin Smith   03 BA-502
Hogg, Charles; 29 Oct. 1807; Arey Eagleston   09 BA
Hogg, Charles; 19 Nov. 1812; Margaret Bowers   11 BA-20
Hogg, James; 26 May 1812; Eliz'h Watson   13 BA-7
Hogins, Ruben; 8 Dec. 1807; Mary Klebsattel (See also 15 FR-322)
                                                       01 FR-1127
Hogmeyer, Daniel; May 1802; Marg. Hu(?)gert   02 WA-73
Hogner, John; 15 May 1815; Esther Rundels   13 BA-21
Hogthorp, Edward, widower; 11 Oct. 1801; Barbara Hock (or Hook)
    widow (both of Fells Point)   15 BA-158
Hohn, Jacob; April 1819; Rebecca Russell   02 WA-113
Hohns, James; 24 March 1808; Sarah Bretton   13 BA-3
Holbrooks, Wm.; 7 July 1804; Martha Wood   09 BA
Holden, Jos.; 9 Dec. 1807; Pleasance Brant   14 BA-423
Holdom, Conrad; 25 Sept. 1820; Mrs. Frances Manno (or Manro)
                                                       37 BA-153
Holdt, Aaron; 29 July 1815; Catherine Ewalt   11 BA-25
Holl, Henry; April 1814; Christiana Barchtel   02 WA-100
Holland, Henry; 7 Sept. 1809; Mrs. Rosanna McCormick   31 BA-66
Holland, James; 27 Sept. 1818; Nancy Fuller   13 BA-32
Holland, Joseph; 28 March 1818; Elizabeth Heller   17 BA-19
Holland, Wm.; 25 Dec. 1808; Cath. Francis (See also 15 FR-323)
                                                       01 FR-1137
Hollands, Wm.; 28 May 1809; Nancy Gillett   13 BA-6
Holle, Anthony; 16 July 1820; Elizabeth Mason   16 BA-102
Hollenbaugh, John; 19 March 1803; Mary Green   23 BA-2
Hollinger, William; 29 June 1815; Sarah Hughes   17 BA-11
Hollings, John; 26 Dec. 1813; Ellen Clemens   09 BA
Hollingsworth, Horatio; 1 Jan. 1818; Emily Caroline Ridgely
                                                       03 BA-602
Hollingsworth, Isaac; 17 April 1804; Cassandra Divens (33 BA-43
    gives date of marriage as 1 April 1805)   01 BA-10
Hollingsworth, Isaac; 24 Jan. 1815; Ruth Edwards Stansbury
                                                       11 BA-22
Hollingsworth, John; 19 Jan. 1803; Ruth Hatton   05 HA-1
Hollingsworth, John; 13 Dec. 1812; Marg't A. Fulwener 13 BA-15
Hollingsworth, Robert, (of Harf. Co. s. of Nathaniel [Robert?]
    and Abigail); 2 d. 11 mo., 1809; Elizabeth West (dau. of
    Thomas and Elizabeth) (See also 05 SF)   02 SF-111
Hollingsworth, Samnuel; 15 Oct. 1816; Allen Maria Moale
                                                       03 BA-507
Hollingsworth, Thomas (s. of Nathaniel and Abigail Green
    Hollingsworth); 21 d. 10 m., 1819; Elizabeth Garrett (dau.
    of Jonah and Esther)   05 SF
Hollingsworth, Thos. H.; 21 Dec. 1820; Mary Ann Keetch 13 BA-36
Hollins, John; 7 Jan. 1819; Mary Ann Cannon   16 BA-78
Hollins, Wm.; 9 Jan. 1810; Eliza Bowly   03 BA-501
Hollis, James; 9 Dec. 1813; Rebecca Ridgely Risteau   03 BA-505

```
Holliway, Hezekiah; 13 Sept. 1803; Harriet Kimble        05 AA-3
Hollyberey, Johnn; 31 Jan. 1805; Margaret Poland         03 AL-613
Holmes, Mr.; 12 April 1819; Miss Boyd                    12 BA-159
Holmes, Almoran; 22 May 1817; Adelia Reynolds            21 BA-9
Holmes, Henry; Feb. 1806; Charlotta Swad (or Swerd)      02 WA-80
Holmes, John; 8 June 1802; Lavinia Richardson            02 SM-185
Holmes, John Glen; 17 Sept. 1815; Henrietta Cassel       06 FR-1323
Holmes, Joseph; 28 March 1802; Ann Woolly                03 BA-415
Holmes, Landrum; 1 May 1814; Mary Goldthright            11 BA-22
Holmes, Richard; 16 April 1818; Elizabeth Richardson, both of
   Caroline Co.                                          02 TA-44
Holmes, William; 17 Nov. 1803; Maria Crow (see also 02 BA-33)
                                                         03 BA-435
Holmes, William B.; 24 March 1811 (by Rev. Roberts); Sarah
   Dallas                                                17 BA-8
Holston, Hamilton R.; 19 June 1817; Sarah Walker         05 BA-240
Holt, Lawrence O.; 12 Jan. 1802; Sarah Oden              03 MO-118
Holter, George; 25 March 1819 Anna Maria Ramsburg        06 FR-1329
Holtz, Jacob; 20 Oct. 1812; Susanna Frige (Fiege)        06 FR-1318
Holtz, Michael; 12 Nov. 1809; Marg. Strehlman            01 FR-1127
Holtzapfel, Daniel; 11 Oct. 1808; Elizab[eth] Kern (See also
   15 FR-322)                                            01 FR-1137
Homer, Daniel; 27 Dec. 1812; Margaret Mantz              15 FR-326
Honey, Amos; 9 May 1801; Susannah Wall                   11 BA-3
Honeywell, Stephen; 16 July 1812; Mary Magdalen Carre (dau. of
   Joseph Maria Carre and Madeline Deschard Carre)       15 BA-302
Hoober, Jacob; 5 June 1810; Betsy Ridge (See also
   01 FR-1137)                                           15 FR-324
Hood, Georg Walther; 24 May 1807; Susanna Gibbs          07 BA-305
Hood, Thomas; 10 Aug. 1805; Mary Murray                  03 BA-494
Hoof, Michael; Sept. 1807; Mary Benned                   02 WA-84
Hoohard, John; 24 March 1817; Agnes Murray               05 BA-239
Hook, Andrew; 24 March 1803; Susanna Rosensteel          15 BA-180
Hook, Ferdinand, widower; 21 April 1805; Eleanor Kean, widow
                                                         15 BA-217
Hook, Frederick; 28 June 1810; Elisabeth Fishpaw         09 BA
Hook, Jos.; 11 Nov. 1815; Ann Conn (Cohn)                13 BA-23
Hook, Josiah; 3 Oct. 1816; Sophia Spedding               13 BA-30
Hook, Thomas; 24 Feb. 1820; Sarah Dorsey                 11 BA-36
Hook, William S.; 28 Jan. 1802; Letitia Ripper           03 BA-412
Hooker, Jno.; 3 Dec. 1807; Mary Mumma                    14 BA-423
Hooper, Abraham; Aug. 1820; Mary Stewart                 02 WA-117
Hooper, Amos; 13 May 1819; Belinda Cook                  11 BA-34
Hooper, John; 12 July 1802; Mary McKeel                  01 DO-41
Hooper, John; 18 June 1803; Anne Light                   03 BA-429
Hooper, Nicholas; 15 March 1803; Mary Ridgely            12 AA-2
Hooper, Thomas; 2 April 1816; Eliza Dodson               13 BA-24
Hooper, Wm.; 22 Dec. 1811; Sarah Hooper                  11 BA-18
Hooper, William; 1 June 1812; Margaret Wells             15 BA-300
Hooper, William E.; 20 Jan. 1818; Susan Slacum           02 DO
Hoot, Samuel; 5 May 1807; Elizabeth Griffith (See also 15 FR-320)
                                                         01 FR-1136
Hoover, Adam; Aug. 1802; Heddy Donere                    02 WA-73
Hoover, Daniel; 11 Feb. 1815; Cath. Lammott              14 BA-433
Hoover, Jacob; 9 May 1815; Susan Newhouser               13 BA-21
Hoover, Jacob; Oct. 1818; Elizab. Poorman                02 WA-111
Hoover, Jacob; 9 Jan. 1820; Elizabeth Harshman (16 FR-76 gives
   bride's name as Hashman)                              03 FR-60
Hopewell, James, Jr.; 2 Jan. 1803; Elizabeth Cissell     02 SM-185
Hopkins, David; 20 Sept. 1818; Hannah Greenleaf (blacks)
                                                         19 BA-72
Hopkins, Ephraim; 21 Oct. 1802; Mary Morgan              33 BA-16
```

```
Hopkins, Evan (son of John and Elizabeth); 25th d. 1 mo., 1810;
     Elizabeth Hopkins (dau. of Joseph and Elizabeth [Gray]
     Hopkins                                         01 SF
Hopkins, George; 18 Dec. 1806; Sarah Brikhud        30 BA-108
Hopkins, Gerrard; 29 Sept. 1801; Patience Hopkins   06 AA-1
Hopkins, Gerard (s. of Jos. and Elizabeth); 14 d. 10 mo., 1804;
     Henrietta Snowden (dau. of Samuel and Elizabeth) 01 SF
Hopkins, Gerard (s. of Joseph and Elizabeth); 23 d. 12 mo., 1813;
     Mary Gover (dau. of William and Sarah)          01 SF
Hopkins, James; 14 April 1806; Rachel Grounfield    02 BA-3
Hopkins, Jeremiah; 28 Oct. 1802; Mary Stoneall      09 BA
Hopkins, Dr. Joel; 30 Oct. 1817; Harriet E. Beard   21 BA-9
Hopkins, Jno.; 15 April 1816; Rachel Ball           14 BA-435
Hopkins, John (of BA, s. of John and Elizabeth, both dec.); 10
     d. 6 m., 1818; Rebecca C. James (dau. of Joseph and w.
     Mary)                                           12 SF-70
Hopkins, Joseph; 28 March 1804 (AA Co.); Sally Duvall 40 BA
Hopkins, Nicholas; 7 Oct., 1817; Margaret Morrison  09 BA
Hopkins, Richard; 20 Nov. 1817; Mary Ann Gover      13 BA-29
Hopkins, Sol.; 5 April 1810; Ann Chapman            13 BA-9
Hopkins, Thomas (s. of Thomas and Sarah); 24 d. 5 mo., 1810;
     Elizabeth Edmondson (dau. of William and Sarah) 07 SF-15
Hopkins, William; 27 June 1802; Mary Blunt          03 AA-120
Hopkinson, Francis; 7 May 1808; Mary Hewitt         03 BA-498
Hoplitz, Jacob; 10 Jan. 1805; Elizabeth Riley       07 AL-274
Hoppe, Justus; 24 March 1813; Ann Eliza Wadsack     14 BA-31
Hoppel, George; 1 Jan. 1818; Ann Kelley             14 BA-437
Hopwood, Robert; 10 Nov. 1802; Mary Ann Walther     15 BA-174
Horine, John; Oct. 1806; Barbara Shrader            02 WA-81
Horman, Henry; 18 Nov. 1817; Ann Thiemann           17 BA-17
Horner, Francis (?); 10 April 1803; Biddy Fitzgerald 34 BA-1
Horner, Samuel; 12 Feb. 1804; Mary McFarland        03 MO-119
Horner, Thomas; c.1804; Sarah Simmons               34 BA-2
Hornet, Thomas R.; 9 Feb. 1811; Mary Ann Cager      11 BA-18
Horney, Samuel; 30 Dec. 1819; Mary Richardson       17 BA-22
Horney, Thomas; 24 Oct. 1801; Mary Milburn          03 BA-409
Horrell, John; 23 Nov., 1803; Elizabeth Reynolds    03 AA-120
Horsey, William; 7 Aug. 1806; Henry Langford        02 BA-4
Horstman, Henri; 26 May 1807; Catherine Garret      31 BA-23
Horta, Frederick; 15 Sept. 1811; Jane Winer         03 BA-503
Horton, James; 15 Dec. 1808; Elizabeth Diffenderfer 09 BA
Hose, Jacob;Feb. 1818; Elizab. Fauckler             02 WA-108
Hose, Philip; Oct. 1806; Margaret Huiret            02 WA-81
Hossefros, John; 23 Sept. 1817; Sarah Hambleton     32 BA-314
Houck, Math.; March 1807; (N) (N)                   02 WA-82
Houck, Michael; 12 Nov. 1811; Cath. Smith           02 WA-91
Houck, Sam'l; Jan. 1807; Jane M'Gowan               02 WA-81
Houer, Daniel; 27 Dec. 1812; Marg. Mantz            01 FR-1137
Hough, Edward Stabler, of BA (s. of Samuel and Ann of Loudoun
     Co., VA); 16 d. 12 mo., 1807; Sarah Atkinson (dau. of Joseph
     and Rachel of AA Co.)                           12 SF-1
Hough, Robert (s. of Joseph and Mary); 29th day, 3 mo., 1804;
     Rachel Hopkins (dau. of Johns and Elizabeth)    01 SF
Hough, W. H.; 16 Jan. 1817; Mary Ann Chambers       13 BA-27
House, James; 17 Sept. 1801; Susanna Harlan         03 BA-407
House, Jesse; 3 Feb. 1819; Cathe. Grover            13 BA-34
House, John; 12 Oct. 1815; Sidney Hall              14 BA-434
Houser, Ezra; 31 March 1819; Elizabeth Waltz        08 AL-53
Housman, Adam; 20 oct. 1818; Ann Gines              32 BA-322
Houston, James; 10 Aug. 1811; Augusta Chambers      03 KE-13
Hovey, Dominicus; 15 Dec. 1808; Ann Johnson         02 BA-7
How, Elias; 3 Sept. 1818; Mary Robinson             13 BA-31
Howard, Benjamin C.; 24 Feb. 1818; Jane Gilmor      05 BA-240
Howard, Brice; 2 June 1817; Barbara Tevis           08 BA
```

Howard, Henry; 11 March 1802; Rachel Hargrove   09 BA
Howard, Henry; 15 Nov. 1804; Eleanor Woods (both natives of
   Ireland)   15 BA-211
Howard, Ignatius; 27 Jan. 1814; Mary Barnes   02 WA-99
Howard, James; 3 Oct. 1820; Sophia G. Ridgely   03 BA-605
Howard, John; 6 April 1802; Mary Harrison Sewell   05 HA-2
Howard, John; 14 Oct. 1813; Lydia Jones   11 BA-21
Howard, John; 27 Feb. 1816; Pamelia Bond   11 BA-26
Howard, John; 15 Aug. 1816; Mary Grimes   13 BA-26
Howard, Jonathan; Sept. 1819; Lydia Castle   02 WA-114
Howard, Joseph; 5 Aug. 1815; Henrietta Young (both slaves
   belonging to Christopher Armat)   16 BA-23
Howard, Thomas; 24 March 1813; Mary Ann Jones   09 BA
Howard, Thomas; 15 Oct. 1815; Mary Ann Beedle   11 BA-25
Howard, Thomas W.; 26 March 1807; Eliz. Crabb (See also 02 MO)
                                                       01 PG
Howard, William; 25 March 1806; Susanna Joy   02 SM-187
Howe, Samuel; 9 Nov. 1815; Sophia Dixon   17 BA-13
Howel, Henry; 30 Jan. 1806; Jain [Jane: 15 FR-318] Head
                                                       01 FR-1136
Howell, Abraham P.; 4 Jan. 1816; Mary Weddington   11 BA-26
Howell, David; 28 April 1803; Susannah Jones   03 AL-613
Howell, Israel (s. of Stephen and Sarah); 3 d. 10 mo., 1805; Mary
   Smith (dau. of John and Sarah)   03 SF
Howell, John; 15 May 1819; Sarah Alcorn   17 BA-22
Howell, William (s. of John, dec., and Ann of West Nottingham
   Hundred, CE Co.); 13 d. 8 mo., 1801; Hannah Pugh (dau. of
   John and Rachel, dec., of East Nottingham Twp., Chester
   Co., PA)   06 SF
Howell, Wm.; 20 Oct. 1812; Frances Hall   03 BA-504
Hower, George; April 1818; Elizab. Diehl   02 Wa-109
Howk, Adam; April 1819; Julian Mayhugh   02 WA-113
Howland, John M.; 30 Nov. 1816; Maria H. Livingston   13 BA-27
Howlet, John; 19 Aug. 1814; Catherine Lowry   03 BA-506
Howlet, John; 20 Aug. 1814; Cathe. Lowry   13 BA-19
Howlett(?), John; 28 June 1804; Betsy Smith   33 BA-40
Hoxton, Dr. John J.; 18 May 1820; Margaret C. Gover   37 BA-153
Hoy, Alex.; c.1803; Fanny Basford   07 AA-3
Hubbard, William; 26 April 1806; Frances Harwood   21 BA-6
Hubbert, John; 13 Dec. 1810 (by Rev. Robert Roberts); Sarah
   Wise   17 BA-8
Huber, Henry; 7 Oct. 1804; Eleanor Browdy   14 BA-417
Huber, Henry; 14 Aug. 1805; Cath. Snyder   14 BA-418
Huchins, John; 29 Oct. 1818; Sarah Ellis   17 BA-20
Huddel, Joh.; April (?) 1803; Elis. Schwartz   02 WA-74
Hudson, George; 27 Aug. 1801; Elizabeth Clayton   27 BA-1
Hudson, John; 26 (Dec.?) 1807 (by Rev. Henry Smith); Elizabeth
   (Rien?)   17 BA-6
Hudson, Thomas Hunt; 13 Jan. 1802; Margaret Bulger   03 BA-412
Hueston, James; May 1818; Mary Shimer   02 WA-109
Huff, Abraham (s. of Abraham and Phebe); 28 d. (?) mo., 1801 (or
   1804); Nancy Webb (dau. of... [illeg.])   11 SF-88
Huffard, Solomon; 17 Oct. 1815; Polly Powell   06 FR-1323
Hufnagle, Matthias; 21 May 1805; Elizabeth Schartin (or
   Schaitin)   39 BA-17
Hugg, Benjamin; c.1804; Cassandra League   34 BA-2
Hugg, Richard; 17 Sept. 1808; Mary Underwood   13 BA-4
Huggins, James; 30 Jan. 1802; Sally Barrett   05 HA-3
Hughes, Aquila; 26 April 1804; Ann Statia Gefford   33 BA-40
Hughes, Christr.; 17 Dec. 1811; Laura Smith   13 BA-14
Hughes, Edward; 1813; Eleanor E. Ayton (See also 02 MO)
                                                       01 PG
Hughes, Gideon (s. of Elias and Hannah); 27 d. 11 mo., 1806;
   Rebecca Dillon (dau. of Moses and Hannah)   02 SF-102

```
Hughes, Henry; 3 Nov . 1808; Clements Thompson        09 BA
Hughes, Hugh; 6 May 1802; Sarah Burton                14 BA-412
Hughes, Hugh C. P.; 6 Sept. 1818; Mary Ludwige        32 BA-322
Hughes, Jesse; 3 June 1801; Sarah Harmonson Waters     01 SO
Hughes, John; 7 Oct. 1806; Juliana Susanna Bensowsky Weisenthal
                                                      03 BA-496
Hughes, Joseph; 14 Feb. 1808; Ann Haislet             31 BA-38
Hughes, Joseph; 1814; Margaret Corcoran               05 FR-6
Hughes, Peter; 8 June 1814; Kitty Price               03 BA-506
Hull, George; 24 Nov. 1808; Anne Slaughter            03 BA-499
Hull, James; 29 April 1820; Ann Derumedor             03 BA-604
Hull, John. See John Hall.
Hull, Silas; 30 June 1811; Hannah Waggoner            03 AL-614
Huls, Moses; 11 Aug. 1812; Frances Scrog              13 BA-14
Hulstine, Mich'l; 27 March 1810; Sarah Cole           13 BA-9
Hultz, Henry Frederick; 15 June 1820; Martha Ann Brown 13 BA-41
Hultz, Peter; 31 Aug. 1809; Catha. Coe                03 BA-500
Humberston, George; 25 Feb. 1812; Lydia Winebrenner   03 AL-614
Humbert, Mich'l; 10 Sept. 1803; Mary Bossert (See also
     01 FR-1136)                                      15 FR-315
Hummel, Jacob; 22 June 1815; Maria Leybrand           07 BA-309
Humphreys, Kerr; 21 March 1805; Violet Boyd           03 BA-493
Humphreys, Thomas; 12 Nov. 1805; Sarah Burgess        11 BA-7
Hungeford, Wm. B.; 23 July 1804; Ann Holland (See also
     01 FR-1136)                                      15 FR-316
Hunt, Caleb (of Brownsville, Fayette Co., PA, son of Joshua and
     Esther); 1 d. 5 mo., 1816; Rhoda Matthews Bartlett (widow of
     Joseph Bartlett, and dau. of Mordecai and Ruth Matthews)
                                                      02 SF-130
Hunt, Dawson; 22 Sept. 1815; Eve Porter               17 BA-11
Hunt, Elisha (of Fayette Co., PA, s. of Joshua, dec., and
     Esther); 12 d. 12 mo., 1806; Mary Hussey (dau. of Riccord.
     dec., and Miriam of York Co.)                    09 SF
Hunt, Jesse; 29 Aug. 1815; M. Yundt                   30 BA-109
Hunt, John; 22 Jan. 1804; Ann Bell                    29 BA-2
Hunt, Joseph (s. of John and Rachel of Delaware Co., PA); 13 d.
     11 mo., 1806; Rebecca Reynolds (dau. of Henry and Mary of
     CE Co.)                                          06 SF
Hunt, Walter S.; 14 Sept. 1815; Barba S. Nichols      13 BA-22
Hunt, William; 4 Feb. 1812; Rebecca Everhart          06 FR-1317
Hunteman, (N); 22 Nov. 1804; (N) Heil                 14 BA-417
Hunter, Alexander I.; 18 April 1820; Ellen Fernour    32 BA-328
Hunter, David; 8 Sept. 1817; Frances Thomas           17 BA-17
Hunter, Alexander; 12 Feb. 1802; Ann Thompson         09 BA
Hunter, John; 6 Oct. 1803; Elizabeth Adams            05 BA-234
Hunter, John; 6 Nov. 1806; Rebecca Stephens           05 BA-235
Hunter, John; 28 Nov. 1809; Martha Hillen             15 BA-277
Hunter, William; 15 Nov. 1801; Ann Hunter             15 BA-159
Hunter, William; 19 Dec. 1809; Mary Norris            14 BA-427
Huntley, Augustus; 14 Feb., 1812; Mary Schevaly       03 BA-503
Huntzman, John; 24 May 1804; Mary Smith               09 BA
Hurley, John; 3 Jan. 1808; Milly Offutt (See also 02 MO)
                                                      01 PG
Hurley, Joseph; 5 Nov. 1802; Mary Slacum              01 DO-41
Hurly, John; July 1819; Elizab. Staunton              02 WA-113
Hurly, Levin; 26 Nov. 1811; Eliz. Stottlemeyer        02 WA-92
Hurpthal, Ferdinand; 8 March 1808; Dorothea Karthaus  14 BA-423
Hurst, Bennett; 10 April 1817; Luisa Gordon           17 BA-16
Hurst, Elijah; 18 April 1816; Polly Kelly             14 BA-435
Hurst, William; 23 Feb. 1820; Rebecca Tarner          07 BA-312
Hurt, Henry; 2 Oct. 1817; Blanche Geogian             11 BA-32
Hurt, Samuel; 27 March 1808; Mary Ann Leary           13 BA-3
Hurxthal, Lewis; 15 June 1813; Caroline Harthaus      09 BA
Husband, Samuel Emlen; 16 Oct. 1801; Rachel Snowden   03 BA-408
```

Husbands, James; 26 June 1804; Margaret Galleher   05 HA-1
Husbands, Joseph (s. of Joseph, dec., and Mary); 8th d. 1 mo.,
    1801; Sasrah Brown (dau. of Freeborn and Mary)   11 SF-80.
Husler, John; 22 June 1809; Rachael Foreman   11 BA-14
Hussey, Emmion; 5 Dec. 1816; Lydia Fisher   14 BA-436
Hussey, Geo., Jr.; 22 Sept. 1812; Sarah Preston   13 BA-15
Hussey, Isaac; 29 Aug. 1816; Elisab. Cromer   14 BA-435
Hussey, William; 15 May 1817; Eliza Smith   17 BA-16
Hussman, Johann; 1801; Cath. Cow   02 WA-72
Hust (?), Shadrack; 21 Aug. 1803; Nancy Turner   06 BA-3
Huster, Gottlieb; 25 Sept. 1806; Elizab. Bush   14 BA-420
Huston, Thomas; 10 March 1801; Fanny G. Evans   09 BA
Hutchings, Jesse; 24 Jan. 1805; Jemima Galloway   01 BA-10
Hutchings, Thomas; 29 Jan. 1801; Ann Clarke   02 SM-185
Hutchins, Bennett; 13 March 1814; Ann Hutchins   01 SM-64
Hutchins, Geo. M.; 20 Jan. 1814; Nancy Brown   13 BA-18
Hutchins, John; 29 Dec. 1818; Sarah Ellis   17 BA-18
Hutchinson, James; 22 May 1814; Sarah Meekins, both of Dorset
    Co.   02 TA-43
Huthins, Samuel; 29 June 1808; Mareb Johnson   09 BA
Hutton, Arthur; May 1817; Susanna Kuhns   02 WA-105
Hutton, Daniel; 3 March 1803; Ann Carback   09 BA
Hutton, John; 17 July 1805; Eliza Suffield   03 BA-494
Hutton, John (s. of Thomas and Katherine); 17 d. 10 mo., 1820;
    Sarah Mason Johnson (widow of James Johnson and dau. of John
    and Ann Howard Mason)   05 SF
Hutton, Jos.; 30 July 1812; Rachel Kingsley   13 BA-14
Hutton, Richard; 10 Oct. 1816; Frans. Larrimore   13 BA-26
Hutton, William; c.1802; Elizabeth Nowell   09 AA-2
Hutton, William; 11 Dec. 1802; Rachel Crandell   03 AA-120
Hyatt, John; 4 Feb. 1819; Ann Roberts   11 BA-35
Hyde, George, Jr.; 21 Oct. 1816 (?); Catherine Butcher 08 AL-55
Hyland, Nathan; 9 Aug. 1803; Mary Fihd (15 FR-315 gives bride's
    name as Find)   01 FR-1136
Hyne, James; 13 Sept. 1801; Sally Silk   03 BA-406
Hynson, Nich's; 12 Nov. 1807; Elizab. Ziegler   14 BA-423
I'Anson, Richard M.; 29 May 1817; Mary Ryan   37 BA-150
Ijams, Plummer; 2 March 1815; Marian Montgomery   06 FR-1322
Iman, Emmanuel; 26 July 1816; Barbara Sites   08 AL-55
Immel, Jacob; 7 May 1811; Susanna Barnett   02 WA-90
Inglebright, Jno.; 30 July 1808; Susanna Star   14 BA-424
Ingles, Abraham; 10 June 1811; Charity Prawbaugh   07 BA-308
Ingleson, Robert; 19 June 1819; Mary Oger   03 BA-603
Inglis, Rev. James (Pastor of the First Presb. Church, Balto.);
    25 Nov. 1802; Jane Swan Johnston (of Alexandria) 05 BA-233
Inglis, John; 24 Dec. 1818; Rebecca Neville   37 BA-151
Inglis, Thomas; 14 Aug. 1804; Barbara Say   03 BA-491
Ingman, Henry; 6 Dec. 1802; Jane Morrison   03 AL-613
Ingram, James; 16 June 1815; Aby Waller   09 BA
Ingram, John; May 1808; Anna Moor   02 WA-85
Inloes, Abram; 14 Dec. 1813; Sarah Crawford   13 BA-18
Inloes, John; 25 July 1807; Elizabeth Gibson   02 BA-5
Inloes, Thos.; 14 May 1809; Rebecca Spencer   13 BA-6
Inright, Thomas; 4 Jan. 1803; Margaret Roach   03 BA-424
Insley, Theophilus; 13 Feb. 1819; Mary McCatlle   11 BA-34
Ireland, Edward; 19 Dec. 1811; Susannah Cheesman   02 BA-36
Ireland, Edward; 16 Aug. 1819; Deborah Owings Moale   03 BA-604
Ireland, Thomas R., 2 Dec. 1806; Sarah Mackall   02 SM-187
Ireland, Wm. H.; 1804; Mary Truman   13 AA-2
Irelent, Richard; 22 July 1816; Elizabeth Eden   11 BA-27
Ireson, Richard M.; 29 May 1817; Mary A. Snyder   02 BA-37
Irvin, Andrew; June 1807; Sarah Dillon   02 WA-83
Irvin, Gerard; 8 Aug. 1812; Eliza Eckels   13 BA-17
Irvin, James; July 1803; Elis. Barnes   02 WA-75

Irvin, John; Aug. 1817; Lea Irvin   02 WA-106
Irving, Rev. Thomas P.; 30 Dec. 1816; Bridget Phillburn
                                                     01 WA-200
Irwin, Andrew; 18 July 1812; Hannah Wilson   09 BA
Irwin, Henry, widower; 7 July 1807; Sarah Mackie, widow
                                                     15 BA-263
Isaac, John H.; 2 April 1801; Elizabeth Moore   09 BA
Isaminger, George; Jan. 1819; Susanna Adams   02 WA-112
Isburn, Washington; 28 March 1802; Sarah Wilson   14 BA-412
Isenberger, Nicholas; Sept. 1818; Jane Roxbury   02 Wa-110
Iser, Enoch; 22 July 1819; Rebecca Kelley   08 BA
Iser, Joseph; 2 March 1813; Margaret Ann Lewis   11 BA-21
Isler, John J.; 28 May 1815; Sarah Taylor   16 BA-20
Israel, Beal; 14 Nov. 1811; Ann Fitch   13 BA-13
Israel, Jacob; 17 Aug. 1809; Eliz'h Read   13 BA-8
Itneyer, John; Aug. 1807; Cath. Christian   02 WA-83
Ittenire, George; 17 March 1812; Elizab. Bealer   02 WA-90
Ivory, Thomas; 6 Jan. 1804; Elizabeth Pearce (or Peonce)
                                                     05 AA-4
Izuardi, Andrfew (native of Bilbao, Spain); 5 Feb. 1810; Ann
    Paterson   15 BA-278
Jacks, James; 4 April 1818; Susanna Massey   11 BA-28
Jackson, Abraham; 31 July 1810; Anne Turner   03 BA-501
Jackson, Alexander; 20 March 1820; Harriot Craig   37 BA-153
Jackson, Bolton; 17 Nov. 1817; Frances Jane Grant   05 BA-240
Jackson, Cesar (belonging to Richard Dorsey); 25 Nov. 1813;
    Kesiah Cole (belonging to Charles Carroll, Jr.) 15 BA-319
Jackson, Daniel; 5 Nov. 1816; Providence Griffin   09 BA
Jackson, Edward; 12 Jan. 1809; Harriot Myers   13 BA-5
Jackson, Elisha; 11 July 1804; Sarah Green   09 BA
Jackson, Henry; 9 Feb. 1805; Mancy Powel   15 FR-317
Jackson, Jacob; 1 Nov. 1804; Elizabeth Poland   03 AL-613
Jackson, Jacob; 1 Oct. 1812; Mary Tracey   02 WA-95
Jackson, James; 2 Aug. 1803; Eleanor Moore   21 BA-5
Jackson, James; 9 Aug. 1809; Bertha (or Bethia) Moore 05 BA-236
Jackson, John; 4 April 1801; Mary White   15 AA-1
Jackson, John; 7 June 1802; Ann Farmer   17 BA-1
Jackson, John; 1 Jan. 1805; Cassandra Bowen   09 BA
Jackson, John; 1 Oct. 1812; Phoebe Jackson   13 BA-15
Jackson, John; 14 Jan. 1813; Margaret Wise   11 BA-20
Jackson, John; 20 Aug. 1818; Malinda Joyce   09 BA
Jackson, Joseph; 14 Feb. 1804; Mary Robinson   36 BA-2
Jackson, Nathaniel; 26 Nov. 1820; Jane Shillingsburg 17 BA-23
Jackson, Richard; 7 April 1812; Jane Donaldson   15 BA-197
Jackson, Robert; 29 July 1819; Mary (Ann) Platt   37 BA-152
Jackson, Samuel; 1 Dec. 1804; Ann Jones (both of TA. Co.)
                                                     02 TA-39
Jackson, Samuel; 8 Oct. 1808; Rachel Poland   03 AL-614
Jackson, Samuel; 28 Nov. 1809; Ann Bromhall (both of VA.)
                                                     03 BA-500
Jackson, Thomas; 26 Oct. 1815; Martha Corporal   11 BA-26
Jackson, William; 14 May 1803; Mary Jamel   03 BA-428
Jackson, William; 3 Aug. 1807; Susannah Wilson   11 BA-11
Jackson, William M.; 4 July 1816; Maria Rook   14 BA-435
Jacob, (N); Sept. 1807; (N) (N)   02 WA-83
Jacob, (N); Oct. 1808; Elis. (N)   02 WA-86
Jacob, Georg; 3 Sept. 1807; Sarah Anna Reiser   07 BA-305
Jacob, Robert; 15 Feb. 1801; Ann Welsh   01 AA-68
Jacob, William; 21 March 1801; Kitty Nau (or New)   09 BA
Jacobs, Benjamin; 9 Nov. 1815; Massies Clark   09 BA
Jacobs, Corben; 27 Jan. 1817; Mary Rice   06 FR-1325
Jacobs, Gabriel; 21 Nov. 1805; Margaret Jackson   03 AL-613
Jacobs, George; 4 April 1805; Mary Myers   21 BA-6
Jacobs, Jacob; 19 Sept. 1802; Mary Spencer   03 AL-613

```
Jacobs, James; 28 Oct. 1810; Sarah Cook              13 BA-11
Jacobs, John; 25 Oct. 1812; Elizabeth White          06 FR-1318
Jacobs, Mathias; 14 Nov. 1809; Margaret Potter       03 AL-614
Jacobs, Samuel; 5 March 1816; Ann S. Pennington      02 BA-36
Jacobs, Septimus; 1 Jan. 1819; Sarah B. F. Taylor    13 BA-34
Jacobs, Willson; 26 Oct. 1807; Susanna Karg          14 BA-423
Jacson, Henry; 9 Feb. 1805; Nancy Powell             01 FR-1142
Jagle, Jacob; Nov. 1802; Elis. Wilson                02 WA-73
Jallifison (?), Francis Honore; 30 Jan. 1808; Elizabeth Philips
                                                     31 BA-37
James, Abraham; Jan. 1820; Sarah Stifler             02 WA-115
James, Dan'l; 15 Nov. 1802; Elis. Whitney            14 BA-413
James, David; 20 Sept. 1804; Charlotte Bradfield (See also
   15 FR-317)                                        01 FR-1142
James, Edward; Dec. 1817; Christiana Stuart          02 WA-107
James, Evin; 30 Aug. 1812; Lydia Wolf                03 AL-614
James, George; 22 Aug. 1802; Jane Shean              03 BA-419
James, George; 29 June 1805; Rachel Davis (see also 02 BA-35)
                                                     03 BA-494
James, Henry; 17 May 1810; Mary Starr                09 BA
James, Jesse; 7 May 1814; Mary Murphy                13 BA-19
James, John J.; 1 Oct. 1819; Sally P. Dore           01 SO-15
James, Jn. W.; 17 Oct. 1811; Mary Ann Bretton        13 BA-13
James, Peter; 17 Sept. 1816; Julie Anne Matthews (blacks)
                                                     17 BA-13
James, Robert; 10 May 1810; Mary High                13 BA-10
James, Sackner; 4 Dec. 1806; Elizabeth Kiner         02 BA-5
James, Thomas (s. of Isaac and Elizabeth of Fawn Twp.); 3rd d. 4
   mo., 1816; Martha Tomkins (of the same place, dau. of John
   and Sarah)                                        11 SF-116
Jameson, Charles; 30 Dec. 1806; Jane Beetle          02 BA-4
Jameson, Wm.; 16 Feb. 1809; Mary Thrift              13 BA-5
Jamison, John; 13 Oct. 1817; Mary Martin             05 BA-240
Janney, Abijah (of Alexandria, DC, s. of Israel of Loudoun Co.,
   VA, dec., and w. Pleasant); 16 d. 4 m., 1817; Mary Ellicott
   (dau. of John Mitchell and dec. w. Tacey)         12 SF-60
Janney, George (son of Jonas and Ruth); 31 d. 10, 1804; Susannah
   Boone (dau. of Isaiah and Hannah) (See also 10 SF)
                                                     01 SF
Janney, George F. (s. of Levin?, dec., and Mary); 16 d. 5 mo.,
   1816; Sarah H. John (dau. of Reuben and Lydia of Uwchlan
   Twp., Chester Co., PA)                            09 SF
Janney, Jacob (son of Jacob and Sarah); 2 d. 7, 1807; Hannah
   Hopkins (dau. of Philip and Mary)                 01 SF
Janney, Jonathan (of Loudoun Co., VA, s. of Israel and Anne); 16
   d. 5 mo., 1810; Elizabeth McPherson (dau. of Isaac of Balto.
   Town and Elizabeth)                               12 SF-5
Janney, Joseph (son of Joseph and Hannah); 2 d. 7, 1812;
   Elizabeth Hopkins (dau. of Elisha and Hannah)     01 SF
Jansen, Joannes; 15 April 1804; Catharina Topferdin  39 BA-17
Janson, Henricus; 9 Sept. 1806; Adilia Keller        39 BA-19
Janvier, Jos.; 24 Aug. 1820; Deborah Neal            13 BA-35
Jarbo, Varnel; 17 May 1802; Mary Hunt                06 BA-2
Jarboe, Henry; 17 March 1812; Eleanor Crampton       06 FR-1317
Jarratt, Jesse; 29 March 1804; Eliz. Bosley          36 BA-2
Jarret, Charles; 14 Oct. 1812; Justine Gouran French 09 BA
Jarrett, James; 30 April 1807; Henrietta fforset (?) (both of
   Dorset Co.)                                       02 TA-40
Jarrett, Samuel; 28 July 1809; Amelia Simpson        11 BA-15
Jarvis, Amos; 11 July 1820; Mary Dixon               13 BA-41
Jarvis, Aquila; 14 Dec. 1820; Matilda Christopher    13 BA-42
Jarvis, James; 10 March 1803; Eliz. Linch            03 MO-118
Jarvis, John; 25 Oct. 1812; Sarah Charleson          17 BA-9
Jarvis, Joseph; 20 July 1809; Sarah Parker           13 BA-6
```

```
Jarvis, Joseph; 10 Oct. 1811; Eliza Liggitt         13 BA-13
Jarvis, Phineas; 22 March 184; Sarah Kyser          13 BA-18
Jarvis, Solomon; 1 April 1813; Margaret Martin       11 BA-21
Jarvis, W. H.,; 16 June 1814; Eliza Bell             13 BA-19
Jason, John; 10 June 1813; Theresa Overstreet        31 BA-151
Jay, Sam'l; 16 May 1812; Sarah Rogers                13 BA-16
Jeancard, John Matthew Francis (son of Peter and Mary Esianas
     Jeancard); 8 April 1806; Mary Magdalen Berenger (dau. of
     Honore and Magd'n Crevellier Berenger)          15 BA-237
Jefferis, Samuel (s. of William and Priscilla of PA); 16 April
     1807; Hannah Townsend (dau. of Joseph and Mary, dec.)
                                                     09 SF
Jeffers, James Harris; 27 Aug. 1818; Cathe. Browning 13 BA-31
Jeffers, John; 29 Nov. 1804; Jane Richmond           11 BA-4
Jeffrey, James (native of France); 19 Aug. 1801; Jane Jenkins
     (widow, native of Ireland)                      15 BA-155
Jeffris, Gravener; 8 Oct. 1805; Nancy Yundt          30 BA-108
Jeffry, Thomas; 18 March 1819; Elizab. Himel         14 BA-438
Jenepre (Jempe), Thomas; 24 March 1803; Ruth Coddington
                                                     03 AL-613
Jenifer, Thomas M.; 22 March 1802; Ruth Codington    01 AL-6
Jenkins, Benedict; 15 Jan. 1817; Adeline Murphy      16 BA-49
Jenkins, Edward; 15 Feb. 1803; Ann Spalding          15 BA-177
Jenkins, Felix; 10 May 1814; Martha Coskery          16 BA-5
Jenkins, Francis; 12 Dec. 1819; Ann Hardy            16 BA-94
Jenkins, Frederick; 4 April 1820; Harriot A. Wells   16 BA-98
Jenkins, Henry; 17 Sept. 1809; Ann Harrison          15 BA-273
Jenkins, Job; 24 Jan. 1802; Mary Leakins (See also 15 FR-312)
                                                     01 FR-1142
Jenkins, John; 11 Feb. 1808; Charlotte Sparrow (See also 02 MO)
                                                     01 PG
Jenkins, Joseph; 30 july 1801; Elizabeth Howell      03 BA-404
Jenkins, Josias; 8 Oct. 1805; Elizabeth Hillen (dau. of John)
                                                     15 BA-228
Jenkins, Michael; 9 Jan. 1806; Ann Worthington       15 BA-234
Jenkins, Oswald; 10 April 1804; Sarah Pearce         01 BA-10
Jenkins, Sam'l; 13 July 1806; Sarah Lemmon           03 BA-495
Jenkins, Thomas; 28 Oct. 1815 (by Rev. Willey); Rebecca Ann Wood
                                                     17 BA-12
Jenkins, Thomas C.; 23 Jan. 1806; Elizabeth Gold     15 BA-235
Jenkins, Walter; 30 June 1801; Catherine Gillmeyer   15 BA-153
Jenkins, Walter; 14 Oct. 1816; Harriet Campbell      17 BA-15
Jenkins, William (native of CH Co.); 9 Nov. 1807; Ann Wells
     (native of Balto.)                              15 BA-256
Jenkins, William (s. of John and Elizabeth); 24 d. 2 m., 1820;
     Ruth Ann Neall (dau. of Francis and Susanna)    08 SF
Jenkinson, John (s. of Emanuel and Martha); 21 d. 3 mo., 1805;
     Sarah Parrott (dau. of Benjamin Parvin and Sarah)
                                                     08 SF
Jennings, Nathan; 16 Jan. 1817; Sarah Sleppy         20 BA-223
Jennings, Samuel; 23 Dec. 1820; Eliza Dowdill        03 BA-605
Jens, (N); 9 June 1812; Margaret Mitchell            04 FR-18
Jensen, Franciscus; Feb. 1807; Catharina Jane Grant  39 BA-20
Jeremiah, John; 22 Oct. 1817; Effe McClellan         11 BA-28
Jessop, Charles; 11 May 1812; Jemima G. Buck         13 BA-16
Jessop, Nicholas; 15 Dec. 1803; Ruth Welsh           21 BA-5
Jessop, Wm.; 31 Oct. 1811; Ann Wells                 13 BA-13
Jewel, George; 18 Nov. 1802; Mary Ridgaway           36 BA-1
Jewell, John; 3 Oct. 1810 (by Rev. Robert Roberts); Sarah
     Gregory                                         17 BA-8
Jewett, John (s. of Thaddeus and Ann); 16 d, 6 mo., 1808;
     Susanna Judge (dau. of Hugh and Susanna)        09 SF
Jillard, John; 20 Oct. 1804; Elizabeth Dillon        03 BA-492
Johannes, Wm. B.; 9 May 1816; Mary Callendar         14 BA-435
```

John, James; 23 July 1815; Anna M. Gardner   13 BA-22
Johnes, Thos.; 12 Aug. 1816; Eliza Suppers (Tuppers?)   13 BA-26
Johns, Francis; 10 Nov. 1818; Sarah Everett   17 BA-20
Johns, Isaac D.; 28 Feb. 1820; Susanna S. Laudenslager 07 BA-312
Johns, James; 11 Oct. 1812; Mary Clark   13 BA-15
Johns, Rev. John; 21 Nov. 1820; Juliana Johnson   02 FR-15
Johns, Leonard F.; 10 Feb. 1801; Margaret Williams   03 MO-117
Johns, Richard; 11 Aug. 1814; Sarah Fleetwood   17 BA-10
Johnson, Absolom; 18 May 1815; Ann Orell   17 BA-11
Johnson, Alexander; 24 June 1813; Margaret Smewin   09 BA
Johnson, Archibald; 1 Feb. 1807; Charlotte Cook   11 BA-10
Johnson, Baker; 2 Oct. 1810; Sophia Grundy   03 BA-501
Johnson, Charles Henry; 14 March 1819; Eliza Green   37 BA-152
Johnson, Christopher; 6 May 1802; Mary Gambrill   15 AA-2
Johnson, Edward; 14 Sept. 1809; Eliza Gray   03 BA-500
Johnson, Elijah; 27 April 1819; Hannah Barnett   13 BA-41
Johnson, Elisha; 25 May 1806; Anne Mills   03 AA-130
Johnson, Elisha S.; 16 Oct. 1815; Eleanor Worthington   11 BA-26
Johnson, Erasmus; 20 Sept. 1809; Anna Margaretha Huth   07 BA-307
Johnson, Fayette; 8 Jan. 1805; Elizabeth Cradock   01 BA-10
Johnson, Francis; May 1806; Mary Cleaton   02 WA-80
Johnson, Frederick (bel. to Henry Thompson); 4 Jan. 1817; Henny
    Williams (bel. to John Mertiacq)   16 BA-48
Johnson, George; 30 May 1816; Mary McClain   05 BA-239
Johnson, George; 17 June 1816; Eliz. Mokings (blacks)   17 BA-13
Johnson, George Wm.; 18 June 1816; Frances Walker   03 BA-507
Johnson, Hans; 11 Feb. 1807; Sarah McCausland   14 BA-421
Johnson, Henry; 2 Jan. 1805 (by Jno. Bloodgood); (N) (N) (list
    of marriages for blacks)   17 BA-5
Johnson, Henry (slave of Mrs. Stansbury); 18 July 1818; Phoebe
    (N) (slave of Dr. O'Connor)   32 BA-321
Johnson, Henry; 29 Dec. 1819; Christina Hannah   17 BA-22
Johnson, Jadwin (or Gideon); 1 July 1806; Margaret Fitzpatrick
                                                        31 BA-8
Johnson, James; 30 Aug. 1808; Kelister Roberts   13 BA-4
Johnson, James; 24 Dec. 1810; Catherine Baum   09 BA
Johnson, James; 6 April 1812; Julia Myers   15 BA-181
Johnson, James; 9 May 1814; Frances (N) (both free col'd)
                                                        16 BA-5
Johnson, James; 10 Aug. 1815; Prudence Lowry   03 BA-506
Johnson, James; 25 May 1820; Mary Ann Stevens   37 BA-153
Johnson, James; 9 Nov. 1820; Jan Lowe   08 BA
Johnson, Jas. J.; 30 May 1803; Elizab. Barry   14 BA-414
Johnson, John; 10 May 1807; Abigail Stevenson   13 BA-2
Johnson, John; 27 Aug. 1807; Marguerite Conner   31 BA-29
Johnson, John; 11 Feb. 1812; Ann Harding   06 FR-1317
Johnson, John; 6 June 1812; Mary Leatherwood   13 BA-17
Johnson, John; 14 June 1812; Elizabeth Sweeting   17 BA-9
Johnson, John; 10 Dec. 1818; Elizabeth McCliswe (?)   20 BA-223
Johnson, Jno. Peter; 11 Jan. 1806; Sophia Shane   14 BA-419
Johnson, Joseph; 6 Dec. 1805; Ruth Busby   09 BA
Johnson, Joseph; 25 June 1809; Jane Lee   13 BA-6
Johnson, Joseph; Feb. 1819; Elenor Hillary   14 FR
Johnson, Lewis; 26 June 1806; Sarah Jackson   09 BA
Johnson, Rev. Mathew; 6 Jan. 1820; Jane Jordon   38 BA
Johnson, Mathias; 11 June 1812; Jemima McGraw   01 DO-42
Johnson, Matthias; 27 May 1807; Margaret Watson   05 BA-235
Johnson, Nathan; 20 June 1817; Femby Hall (blacks)   17 BA-13
Johnson, Nicholas; 7 Dec. 1803; Ann Johnson   05 AA-4
Johnson, Peter; 22 Oct. 1808; Mary Gelwix   14 BA-425
Johnson, Peter P.; 16 May 1820; Adeline Smith   17 BA-23
Johnson, Richard; 9 Feb. 1802; Eleanor Johnson   18 BA-65
Johnson, Robert; 4 Nov. 1810; Bersheba/Bathsheba Hicks 03 BA-502
Johnson, Samuel; 3 April 1803; Betsy Thomas   09 BA

Johnson, Sam'l; 11 April 1810; Rachel Jacobs   13 BA-12
Johnson, Samuel; 12 June 1817; Marg't Anderson   13 BA-28
Johnson, Stephen; 7 May 1804; Sibby Jones   03 BA-490
Johnson, Stephen; 20 July 1815; Penda Jackson (both free col'd)
                                                      16 BA-23
Johnson, Thomas; 20 Feb. 1802; Sarah Philips   05 AA-2
Johnson, Thomas; 15 July 1815 (?); Adalina (N) (col'd) 11 BA-24
Johnson, William; 29 Oct. 1801; Mary Fakes   15 AA-1
Johnson, William; 27 March 1803; Mary Fleeharty   05 HA-3
Johnson, William; Sept. or Oct. 1804; Rebecca Boreing 23 BA-3
Johnson, William; 29 Oct. 1808; Jennet Sinclair   05 BA-235
Johnson, Wm. F.; 8 Oct. 1808; Elenor Humphry   13 BA-5
Johnston, Henry; 17 March 1820; Ann Peck (blacks)   19 BA-73
Johnston, Robert; 5 Jan. 1807; Catherine House   03 AL-614
Johnston, Solomon; 2 Nov. 1801; Catherine Snyder   21 BA-5
Johnston, William; 18 July 1804; Hannah Hews   09 BA
Johnston, William; 18 April 1819; Serena Redwood   09 BA
Johnston, William; 7 Oct. 1819; Kezia Richmond   20 BA-224
Joice, Henry; 24 Nov. 1803; Sarah Lovett   34 BA-1
Joice, Paul; (between 7 June and 4 July) 1813; Nelly Landigan
                                                      15 BA-311
Joice, Thomas; 12 Nov. 1801; Sarah Waller   09 BA
Joice, William; 10 Nov. 1808; Susanna Hanson   11 BA-13
Jones, Dr. (N); 10 April 1809; Sally Blake (both of QA Co.)
     (See also 02 TA-41)   01 QA-53
Jones, Abner (son of Evan and Susanna); 3 d. 3 mo. 1814; Maria
     Curtis (dau. of William and Martha [Hay]) (See also 05 SF)
                                                      02 SF-120
Jones, Abraham; 1802; Margaret Williams   07 AA-2
Jones, Abraham; 12 Oct. 1802; Honor McKinsey   21 BA-5
Jones, Abraham; 8 April 1804; Charity Stansbury   03 BA-490
Jones, Absolom; Aug. 1808; Magd. Dibert   02 WA-85
Jones, Amos; 18 Feb. 1806; Eliza Davis   03 BA-495
Jones, Archibald; 29 March 1803; Charity Myers   03 AL-613
Jones, Awbreay (widower); 27 Jan. 1801; Margaret Doran 15 BA-148
Jones, Barnes; 2 Aug. 1810; Eleanor Ashley   03 BA-49
Jones, Benj. W.; 27 Jan. 1802; Margaret Willson   03 MO-118
Jones, Caleb; 7 Jan. 1806; Elizabeth Bennett   02 SM-187
Jones, Charles; 30 March 1805; Eleanor Loid (02 BA-493 gives
     bride's name as Loyd)   03 BA-493
Jones, Daniel; 22 March 1804; Nancy Elliott   01 DO-41
Jones, Dennis; 30 May 1805 (02 BA-35 gives date as 27 May);
     Susanna Rubert   03 BA-493
Jones, Dorsey James; 9 April 1807; Mary Fisher   15 BA-248
Jones, Evan; 18 Feb. 1808; Sarah West (See also 02 MO) 01 PG
Jones, Ezekiel; 18 May 1802; Jemima Booze   01 DO-41
Jones, George; 18 March 1809; Emilia Dimbar   14 BA-425
Jones, George; 2 Aug. 1812; Frances Porter   11 BA-20
Jones, Henry; 19 July 1817; June Merson   17 BA-16
Jones, James; 16 April 1803; Nelly Addison (See also 02 BA-32)
                                                      03 BA-427
Jones, James; 9 May 1820; Anne Bernard   08 AL-57
Jones, Jeremiah; 23 Dec. 1800; Sarah Waters   15 AA-1
Jones, John; 7 Oct. 1802; Sarah Philips   05 AA-2
Jones, John; 18 Aug. 1808; Jane Carback   09 BA
Jones, John; 20 feb. 1809; Providence (N)   08 BA
Jones, John; 2 Jan. 1812; Sarah Cole   11 BA-18
Jones, John; 30 Sept. 1813; Jemima Woolrick   11 BA-23
Jones, John Le Roy; 5 Jan. 1805; Eliza Tillen   03 BA-492
Jones, John Nance; 14 Jan. 1819; Mary Ann Elise (?) Griffen
                                                      37 BA-152
Jones, Joseph; 6 Nov. 1800; Mary Clarke   15 AA-1
Jones, Joseph; 30 Sept. 1806; Susannah Alsrod   09 BA
Jones, Joseph; 12 Dec. 1815; Margaret Cullison   32 BA-306

```
Jones, Joshua; 23 Nov. 1809; Eliz'h Grubb           13 BA-8
Jones, Kinsey; 25 Oct. 1820; Alice Rowley (both col'd) 17 BA-23
Jones, Lewis; 9 Dec. 1802; Mary Baldwin             15 AA-2
Jones, Lewis; 23 Aug. 1815 Rebecca Brown            11 BA-24
Jones, Lloyd; 30 April 1814; Tracy Shorter (blacks) 09 BA
Jones, Lott; 27 Jan. 1803; Agy Hawkins              15 AA-2
Jones, Mahlon; 4 Nov. 1817; Ann Marriott            11 BA-28
Jones, Morris; 13 April 1809; Elizabeth Medtart     06 FR-1319
Jones, Philip; 31 July 1814; Mary Moore             06 FR-1321
Jones, Richard S.; 14 May 1816; Margaret B. Chew    03 AA-131
Jones, Robertson; 10 Sept. 1816; Mary Etchberger    13 BA-27
Jones, Samuel; 14 March 1805; Susanna Brady (See also 15 FR-317)
                                                    01 FR-1142
Jones, Samuel; 12 April 1819; Harriet Castle (with permission of
    the previous owners)                            16 BA-81
Jones, Thomas; 26 May 1803; Ann (?) Byer            34 BA-1
Jones, Thomas; 7 June 1804; Sarah Bowman            36 BA-2
Jones, Thomas; 12 Sept. 1805; Nancy Conelly         11 BA-7
Jones, Thomas; 13 Sept. 1805; Amelia Harrison (free blacks)
                                                    15 BA-227
Jones (?), Thomas; 28 Aug. 1806; Dolly Hasel        31 BA-11
Jones, Thomas; 14 Jan. 1808; Ann Jones              09 BA
Jones, Thomas; 22 June 1809; Mary Nailer            09 BA
Jones, Thomas; 15 Jan. 1818; Elizabeth Staly        06 FR-1327
Jones, Thomas; 23 April 1817; Margaret Jenkins      20 BA-223
Jones, Thomas B.; 18 March 1802; Nancy Lawrence (See also
    15 FR-313)                                      01 FR-1142
Jones, Thomas D.; 18 Oct. 1812; Olivia Edmondston   09 BA
Jones, Uria; 2 Dec. 1813; Ann Mincher               13 BA-17
Jones, William; 20 Feb. 1805; Catherine Roberts     09 BA
Jones, William; 17 June 1811; Sarah Bond            09 BA
Jones, William; 10 Nov. 1818; Margaret White        37 BA-151
Jones, Wm. R.; 31 Dec. 1801; Eliz. L. Richards      03 MO-117
Jones, Yearsley (s. of Abner and Hannah); 10th d. 12 m., 1807;
    Susanna Underwood (dau. of Nehemiah and Mary)   11 SF-122
Jonnes, John; 30 Nov. 1802; Rosanna Clear           03 BA-423
Jonnes, Joseph; Aug. 1813; Sus. Copenhaver          02 WA-97
Jonson, Thomas; 14 Dec. 1806; Jule Plummer (See also 15 FR-320)
                                                    01 FR-1142
Joquin, Joseph; 4 Dec. 1811; Mary Kelly             14 BA-429
Joray, John; 8 March 1806; Eliza Hammond            02 BA-3
Jordan, Charles; 31 Jan. 1816; Sarah Faulkner       03 BA-507
Jordan, Frederic; 19 April 1806; Margaret Willman   14 BA-420
Jordan, Henry; 1 Dec. 1808; Ann Herbert             14 BA-425
Jordan, James; 26 Jan. 1801; Elsey Buskirk          03 AL-613
Jordan, Joel; 21 July 1814; Hannah Sweeny           09 BA
Jordan, John; 13 Dec. 1813; Rachel Fulton           01 BA-11
Jordan, John; 12 Jan. 1815; Maria Elisabeth Afterheide (nee
    Minkin)                                         07 BA-309
Jordan, William; 18 March 1802; (N)(N)              06 BA-2
Joseph, Abraham; 7 Dec. 1816; Catherine Johnson     17 BA-15
Joseph, Peter; 10 Jan. (or Feb.) 1819; Mary Magdalene (N) (both
    people of color)                                16 BA-79
Journey, George; 14 Aug. 1808; Patience Jacobs      13 BA-4
Journey, John; 2 Feb. 1803; Doratha McDaniel        03 AA-120
Jubb, Richard; 18 Jan. 1810; Ruth Collins           13 BA-9
Judesind, John; 3 Nov. 1806; Maria Knip             14 BA-421
Judlin, Andrew Francis; 26 March 1812; Elisabeth (N) 11 BA-20
Judy, Jacob; 2 Oct. 1808; Elisabeth Calcloesir (See also
    15 FR-322)                                      01 FR-1142
Julon, William; 25 Aug. 1811; Cathen. Heffner       06 FR-1316
Junca, Bernard (widower, son of Robert Junca and Catherine Lacost
    Junca); 5 Dec. 1803; Emily Chevoleun (widow of the late
```

Martin Turel, dau. of Peter and Marg't [Chobat] Chevoliux
    [sic])   15 BA-191
Jung, Jacob; 15 Jan. 1818; (N) (N), widow   07 BA-311
Jung (?), William; 1806; Theresia Fader (?)   39 BA-19
Junge, Johann Abraham; 14 Dec. 1803; Rebecca Abrahams 07 BA
Jungling, Jacob (widower); 8 Dec. 1801; Susanna Schneidern
    (single)   01 CL-150
Jupiter, John. 6 April 1816; Jane Williams (blacks) 17 BA-13
Jurdan, William; 24 Jan. 1813; Hannah French   02 WA-96
Justice, Andrew; 14 April 1817; Maya(?) Russel   01 WA-200
Kaes, Mathias; 9 June 1807; Elisabeth Desilver (?) 39 BA-19
Kahler, Jacob; Jan. 1820; Mary Myers   02 WA-115
Kahm, Jacob; 27 Sept. 1812; Sarah Eakle   02 WA-95
Kahn, Christian; 5 July (or Aug.) 1813; Maria Myers 07 BA-309
Kahn, Daniel; 30 June 1814; Catherina Schally 07 BA-309
Kalbfus, Daniel; 29 Aug. 1815; M. Naerna   30 BA-109
Kalklosher, Imannuel; 5 Sept. 1806; Cath. Brim (See also
    15 FR-319)   01 FR-1145
Kalkman, Chas. Fred'k; 12 May 1808; Caroline Greipenheil
                                         14 BA-424
Kallress, Andrew; 26 Aug. 1803; Margaret Hanke 14 BA-415
Kaminsky, J. C.; 18 Oct. 1812; Martha Bayles 03 BA-504
Kannear, James; 28 April 1801; Ann Hays   03 BA-400
Kant, (?) org W.; Aug. 1806; Margaret Woltz 02 WA-81
Karrack, Joannes; 8 Jan. 1811; Magdalena Steinmetz (?) 39 BA-25
Katterman, Samuel; 1802; Mary Hockman   02 WA-72
Kauffman, Jona.; 28 May 1816; Phoebe Johnson 13 BA-25
Kauffman, Lenard; Aug. 1813; Mar. He(?)baugh 02 WA-98
Kaufman, Abraham; April 1819; Susanna Herr 02 WA-113
Kaufman, Christopher; 3 May 1817; Cathe. McDaniels 13 BA-28
Kaufman, John; 16 June 1812; Sarah Grubb 14 BA-430
Kays, Hugh; 27 Nov. 1805; Rachel McKinney 03 BA-495
Kayser, Samuel; 31 Dec. 1805; Hetty Poulk 09 BA
Keaf, George; 2 July 1801; Eliza Saunders 27 BA-1
Kealey, John; 25 May 1801; Anna Kearns 03 BA-401
Kean, Thomas; 3 Nov. 1801; Kitty Myers 27 BA-1
Keany, Martin; 27 April 1818; Ann Baggs 16 BA-67
Kearnes, Anthony; 25 Oct. 1813; Charlotte McDonald 15 BA-318
Kedge, John; 25 Jan. 1805; Mary Green 03 BA-492
Keefer, Christoph.; March 1807; Mary Schanck 02 WA-82
Keefer, Jacob; 10 Sept. 1818; Sophia Baer 06 FR-1328
Keefer, Peter; 9 Jan. 1813; Eva Gansaw (See also 15 FR-326)
                                         01 FR-1145
Keemle, Sam'l; 28 March 1815; Anna Maria Mather 21 BA-3
Keen, Aquila; 13 March 1816; Hannah James 09 BA
Keen, Jesse; 17 April 1814; Susan Perigo 11 BA-22
Keen, Samuel; 22 Dec. 1818; Elizabeth N. Roberts 16 BA-77
Keen, Thos.; 4 Aug. 1807; Catha. Berry 13 BA-2
Keenan, Charles; 29 Aug. 1815; Elizabeth Greene 16 BA-25
Keene, "Old" Daniel; 26 Dec. 1804; Betsy Watts "Very old;" (both
    of TA Co.)   02 TA-39
Keene, "Old" Daniel; May 1806; Peggy Tole (or Tate) (See also
    01 QA-52)   02 TA-40
Kenne, Daniel, Jr.; 27 Dec. 1806; Sally Tate 01 QA-52
Keene, Jesse L.; 25 Aug. 1807; Jannet Bryden 05 BA-235
Keene, John; 12 Feb. 1801; Sarah Dunnock 01 DO-40
Keene, Lawrence; 8 April 1808; Maria Martin 05 BA-235
Keene, Shadrach; 20 Jan. 1803; Sarah Robson 01 DO-41
Keener, Jacob; 24 May 1804; Nancy Johnson Jones (02 BA-33 gives
    the bride's name as Ann Johns)   03 BA-490
Keener, Jno.; 21 Nov. 1807; Mary Griffith 14 BA-423
Keener, Jno.; 21 Sept. 1809; Susan Yeiser 14 BA-226
Keesacker, Conrad; March 1807; Fanny Park 02 WA-82
Keetley, Thomas; 7 March 1806; Mary Burney 02 BA-3

Keever, Samnuel; 7 Jan. 1809; Elizabeth Lubstine   02 BA-7
Keeves, Arthur; Jan. 1816; Sarah Files   02 WA-101
Kehoe, John; 24 May 1817 (with lic.); Ann T (?)   16 BA-56
Keifel, Anthony, 29 May 1817; Sophia Kauder   07 BA-310
Keifel, Henry; 27 April 1820; Eliza Lingenfelter   14 BA-440
Keilholtz, William; 13 Feb. 1801; Molly Beckley   03 BA-398
Keirle, Matthew; 23 Nov. 1815; Charlotte Pindell   09 BA
Keith, Robt; 15 Jan. 1813; Letty Jordan   13 BA-15
Kell, Francis; 28 May 1816; Marg. or Mary D. Tucker   32 BA-309
Keller, Abraham; 21 March 1802; Susan Schreyer (See also
    15 FR-313)   01 FR-1145
Keller, Charles; 18 Jan. 1818; Charlotte Gantzang (15 FR-327
    gives bride's name as Jantzaung)   01 FR-1146
Keller, Christian; 11 Dec. 1815; Mary Kraher   14 BA-434
Keller, Conrad; 30 March 1815; Catherine Jordan   16 BA-17
Keller, Dan'l; Sept. 1807; Dorothy Bargman   02 WA-84
Keller, George; 15 Dec. 1816; Mrs. Lydia Zimmerman   06 FR-1325
Keller, Henrich; 26 Nov. 1805; Elizabeth Beisser   15 FR-318
Keller, Henry; 30 Aug. 1807; Nancy Eader (15 FR-321 gives bride's
    name as Fader)   01 FR-1145
Keller, Henry; 26 April 1808; Catharine Ourent   08 AL-58
Keller, Henry; May 1819; Martha M. Ford   02 WA-113
Keller, Jacob; 11 Oct. 1807; Rosina Daub (See also 15 FR-321)
                                                        01 FR-1145
Keller, Jacob; 5 March 1811; Charlotte Hoffman   06 FR-1315
Keller, Jacob; 31 March 1816; Catherine Heisle   06 FR-1324
Keller, John; 21 Aug. 1804; Catharine Albright   11 BA-3
Keller, Michael; 24 Nov. 1811; Eleonore Mills (See also
    15 FR-325)   01 FR-1145
Keller, Michael; 5 Nov. 1816; Mrs. Catherine Schaffner 06 FR-1325
Keller, Peter; April 1816; Mary Trovinger   02 WA-102
Kelley, James; 26 March 1801; Katey Jones   01 SO-15
Kelley, Nicholas; 22 July 1813; Elender Choate   08 BA
Kelley, William; 2 (or 26) Nov. 1803; Mary Mathewson   17 BA-3
Kelley, William; 20 Dec. 1810; Sarah Lynch   08 BA
Kelly, Christopher; 23 Oct. 1817; Ann McClain   17 BA-17
Kelly, Isaac; 2 April 1801; Drusilla Durbin   33 BA-28
Kelly, Isaac; 2 April 1801; Drusilla Durbin Nichols   33 BA-18
Kelly, Jacob; 20 June 1801; Sus. Ervin   02 WA-71
Kelly, James; 9 August 1807; Leathy Ann Bell   03 BA-497
Kelly, James; 21 July 1809; Sarah Stewart, widow   15 BA-170
Kelly, James; 1 March 1809; Sarah Kimble   03 BA-499
Kelly, James; 2 Dec. 1819; Jane Graham   20 BA-224
Kelly, John; 14 Dec. 1801; Mary Burney   03 BA-411
Kelly, Matthew; 21 June 1812; Harriet Wells   31 BA-126
Kelly, Patrick; 10 Nov. 1801; Bridget O'Connor (both natives of
    Ireland)   15 BA-158
Kelly, Patrick; 6 March 1810; Catherine, dau. of John Leady
                                                        15 BA-279
Kelly, Terence (native of Ireland); 15 Jan. 1810; Eleanor Crosby
    (widow, of BA Co.)   15 BA-278
Kelly, Thomas; 27 Aug. 1801; Jane McAllister   03 BA-405
Kelly, William; 26 Nov. 1803; Mary Mathewson   17 BA-3
Kelly, William; 18 April 1813; Eliza Law   13 BA-16
Kelser, William; 10 Dec. 1809; Ann Thompson (of HA Co.)
                                                        15 BA-277
Kelso, Joshua; 21 Feb. 1811; Sarah Hutchins   01 BA-11
Keltz, Georfge; 23 April 1812; Rebecca Reese   06 FR-1318
Keltzheimer, John; 20 June 1805; Sarah Burke   15 BA-221
Kemberley, William; 31 Dec. 1804; Eliza Webb   11 BA-5
Kemmitz, Florian; 3 Dec. 1803; Maria Maul   14 BA-415
Kemp, Abraham; 5 April 1812; Mary Brunner (See also 15 FR-325)
                                                        01 FR-1145

Kemp, Gilbert; 15 Oct. 1811; Rebecca Curfman (15 FR-325 gives
     bride's name as Cursman)   01 FR-1145
Kemp, John; 29 Oct. 1820; Ann Sawyer   37 BA-153
Kemp, Robert (s. of John, dec.); 20 d. 5 mo., 1801; Sarah Powell
     (dau. of Robert)   08 SF
Kemp, Thomas; 16 Aug. 1803; Sophia Hortsman (02 BA-32 gives the
     bride's name as Horstman)   03 BA-432
Kemp, Thomas; 15 Nov. 1809; Eliza Doyle   14 BA-226
Kemp, William; 22 Nov. 1809; Mary Kramer   14 BA-426
Kemperling, Michel; 1 Dec. 1808; Christina Nicholas 07 BA-306
Kempf, Peter (of Peter); 3 March 1801; Rachel Gater (See also
     15 FR-311)   01 FR-1145
Kempis, Abraham; 21 Nov. 1804; Ann Jonsen   14 BA-417
Kendle, James; Dec. 1820; Margaret Wherrett   02 WA-117
Kendle, Joseph; Oct. 1818; Peggy Rice   02 WA-111
Kenear, William; 7 (?) May 1812; Elizabeth Mines   09 BA
Kener, John; 28 Sept. 1815; Margaret Griffith   09 BA
Kennard, Thomas (s. of Levy and Ann, of Fawn Grove Twp.); 1st d.
     12 mo., 1813; Elizabeth Medcalf (dau. of Moses and Susannah)
                                                   11 SF-108
Kennard, William; 29 May 1806; Mary Ryan   11 BA-9
Kennedy, Dennis; 27 May 1813; Rachel Savage (widow) 15 BA-310
Kennedy, Ebenezer; 4 Nov. 1814; Rebecca Bennett   17 BA-10
Kennedy, Ezekiel; 7 July 1803; Mary Flinn   09 BA
Kennedy, Jno.; 23 Jan. 1812; Mary Somer   14 BA-429
Kennedy, John; 30 May 1815; Ann Williams   11 BA-24
Kennedy, John Fitzgerald; 29 Dec. 18901; Mercy Gray 03 BA-411
Kennedy, Michael; 1 Aug. 1816; Rebecca Price   13 BA-27
Kennedy, Thomas; 6 Dec. 1806; Ruth Wright   09 BA
Kennedy, William; 13 Aug. 1801; Sarah Boulden   03 BA-404
Kenny, Samuel; Oct. 1810; Margaret Hanna   02 WA-87
Kenny, William (native of Ireland); 13 July 1808; Betsy O'Leary
     (both of QA Co.) (See also 02 TA-41)   01 QA-57
Kenrick, Samuel; 16 Aug. 1813; Amelia Bramble   11 BA-23
Kenright, And'w; 23 July 1818; Marg't Fickds [sic] 13 BA-31
Kent, Robert; 3 Dec. 1802; Lucinda Atkinson   36 BA-1
Kenterwine, Chas.; 10 Dec. 1809; Mary Deerman   14 BA-227
Kentner, John; June 1818; Mary Dooble   02 WA-110
Kento, William; April 1817; Fanny Sprig   02 WA-104
Kephart, Peter; 15 Sept. 1816; Mary Peters   06 FR-1325
Kepheart, David; 17 Oct. 1802; Margaret Reister   23 BA-1
Kepler, Peter; 16 April 1807; Elizab. Schafer   01 FR-1145
Keplinger, Adam; 10 Sept. 1812; Magdal. Smutz   02 WA-95
Keplinger, Lewis; 25 Oct. 1813; Cath. Fitzwater (See also
     15 FR-326)   01 FR-1146
Kepner, John; 7 June 1806; Barbara Weisbach   30 BA-108
Ker, Dr. Samuel; 24 July 1816; Elizabeth Handy   03 SO
Kerby, Edw'd.; 9 Feb. 1814; Mariar K. Reese   13 BA-18
Kern, Frederick; 12 March 1805; Susan Christ (See also 15 FR-317)
                                                   01 FR-1145
Kern, Nicolaus; 1802; Mary Currel   02 WA-72
Kerns, John; 10 Jan. 1805; Mary Elliott   01 BA-10
Kerns, John; 2 Oct., 1806; Susannah Robb   09 BA
Kerr, David; 1 Nov. 1804; Maria Perry   01 TA-322
Kerr, James; 7 June 1803; Isabella Wilson   05 BA-233
Kerr, James; 11 June 1808; Mary Deale   15 BA-262
Kerr, John Leeds; 8 April 1801; Sarah H. Chamberlain 01 TA-322
Kerr, Robert; 9 Dec. 1806; Nancy Wenables   31 BA-16
Kershner, Abraham; 26 Jan. 1813; (N) Morgendale   02 WA-96
Kershner, Benjamin; Nov. 1807; Ez. Angony   02 WA-84
Kershner, Isaac; Feb. 1805; Eva Stortzman   02 WA-78
Kershner, Joseph; June 1820; Cath. Slice   02 WA-116
Kershner, Solomon; Aug. 1818; Elizab. Cole   02 WA-110

Kesler, John; 10 Nov. 1802; Mary Poley (See also 03 BA-422)
                                                    02 BA-32
Kesler, John Martin; 26 Sept. 1816; Sarah League   17 BA-15
Kesler, Peter; 3 Aug. 1805; Anna Schmitt (See also 15 FR-317)
                                                    01 FR-1145
Kessinger, Jacob; March 1807; Magd. Ga(?)   02 WA-82
Kessler, Christ'n; 19 July 1810; Mary Ann Miller   14 BA-427
Kessler, Jacob; 8 Dec. 1811; Elizab. Bohrer (See also 15 FR-325)
                                                    01 FR-1145
Kessler, John; 30 Aug. 1810; Elizab. Miller   14 BA-427
Kessler, William; 12 Dec. 1812; Margareth Titlow   06 FR-1318
Ketchen, Joel; 11 Feb. 1804; Sarah Hurst (of VA)   03 MO-119
Keyler, Peter; 16 April 1807; Elizabeth Schafer   15 FR-320
Keyper, John; 19 Nov. 1811; Christ. Bowert   02 WA-92
Keys, Stevenson; 23 Oct. 1817; Hannah Gregg   06 FR-1327
Keys, Bayley; 1 July 1818; Priscilla Taylor   05 BA-240
Keyser, John; 23 Aug. 1804; Catherine Greenwood   15 BA-207
Keyser, Samuel; 4 Jan. 1803; Mary Stowffer   09 BA
Keyser, Wm. W.; 9 July 1818; Eliza Fort   11 BA-33
Kidd, John; 3 Oct. 1813; Temperance Bosley   11 BA-21
Kidd, Samuel; 7 Jan. 1808; Pamela A. Sampson   02 BA-6
Kidney, Maurice; 28 Oct. 1808; Eleanor McCrofton   15 BA-266
Kiefer, Rev. Daniel; 9 April 1818; Elizabeth Sturm 07 BA-311
Kiefer, Henry; 10 April 1803; Elizab. Hohl (See also 15 FR-314)
                                                    01 FR-1145
Kiefer, Henry; 6 March 1808; Eliz. Goetzendanner (See also
    15 FR-314)   01 FR-1145
Kiefer, Samuel; 20 Dec. 1804; Mary Schoenholtz   01 FR-1145
Kiefer, Samuel; 20 Dec. 1804; Margaret Shonholtz   15 FR-317
Kielholtz, Philip; 9 June 1808; Elizabeth Disney   11 BA-2
Kiens, Michael; 19 Aug., 1805; Eliz. Schreyer   01 FR-1145
Kier, Joseph; 5 March 1812; Ann Price   11 BA-19
Kierfman, Henrich; 20 Dec. 1801; Cath. Dippel   15 FR-312
Kiernan, John; 8 Oct. 1818; Catherine McGrath   32 BA-322
Kilgore, John A. T.; 4 Dec. 1817; Ann Eliza Shelmerdine
                                                    20 BA-223
Killert, John A.; 1 Jan. 1809; Mary Ann Turner   02 BA-35
Killmun, Thomas; 8 April 1820; Elizabeth McCubbin 17 BA-22
Kilmer, John; 9 May 1802; Anna M. Gruble   30 BA-108
Kilpatrick, John; 18 June 1801; Rachel Collet   05 BA-9
Kilpatrick, Rob't; 18 June 1806; Jane Kelly   03 BA-495
Kimberly, Jacob; 8 Oct. 1815; Catherine Conn   08 AL-60
Kimberly, John; 23 April 1809; Eliza Burnes   13 BA-6
Kimes, Jacob; 30 June 1808; Jane Wycoff   08 AL-61
Kimes, John; 7 May 1806; Hanna Christman   08 AL-60
Kimes, Stephen; 19 Sept. 1805; Sarah Wyckoff   03 AL-613
Kimmel, Mich'l; 11 March 1802; Kitty Stouffer   21 BA-5
Kinard, Thomas J.; 27 Dec. 1818; Mary Ann Tanner (?) 17 BA-20
Kincade, James; 28 Sept. 1812; Barbara Kindell   13 BA-17
Kincade, Myers; 28 Feb. 1815; Cathe. Gardner   13 BA-20
Kincaid, George; 9 Oct. 1814; Ann Russell   17 BA-10
Kindle, Azariah; 14 Dec. 1802; Amelia Nicholson   03 MO-118
King, Anthony; 24 June 1802; Dorice Harttert   03 BA-417
King, Charles; c.1804; Elizabeth Hughes   34 BA-2
King, David; 10 Dec. 1807; Rachel Phelps (See also 15 FR-322)
                                                    01 FR-1145
King, Edward; 13 April 1802: he and his wife (unnamed) appeared
    before the registrar of the parish, acknowledged themselves
    to be man and wife, and requested to be registered as such
    in the journal   01 DO-40
King, Edward; 26 April 1804; Mary Welmor   02 SM-186
King, Edward; 10 May 1809; Mary Williams   13 BA-6
King, Georg; 11 June 1811; Susanna Earing   07 BA-308
King, George; 2 July 1809; Susanna Hamilton   03 AL-614

King, Geo.; 31 Oct. 1820; Sarah Jordan   13 BA-36
King, George Wilson; 25 Dec. 1814; Mary Gormly   11 BA-37
King, Gideon T.; 10 Oct. 1816; Louisa Bush   14 BA-436
King, James; 18 Dec. 1804; Elizabeth Jones (See also 02 BA-34)
                                                      03 BA-492
King, Jess; 13 Aug. 1818 (lic.); Elizabeth Hignot   11 BA-33
King, John; 2 April 1818; Hester B. Stanfer   13 BA-30
King, John; 16 April 1818; Catherine Baker   03 BA-603
King, John C.; 1 Jan. 1820; Louise J. Natalie La Lougs 16 BA-96
King, John S.; 11 July 1817; Eliza Reinhart   13 BA-28
King, Joseph, of Sussex Co., DE; 29 Nov. 1809; Eleanor (N) of SO
    Co., MD   02 TA-41
King, Joseph (of Balto. Town, s. of Thomas and Jane, late of
    Newcastle-upon-Tyne, Northumberland, Eng., dec.); 17 d. 12
    mo., 1817; Tacy Ellicott (dau. of Elias of Balto. Town and
    dec. w. Mary)   12 SF-64
King, Joseph; 16 Jan. 1820; Anne Walston   02 TA-44
King, Joshua (s. of Vincent, dec., and Mary of Little Britain
    Twp., Lancaster Co., PA); 13 d. 5 mo., 1802; Elizabeth
    Rogers (dau. of Thomas and Catherine of CE Co., MD)
                                                      06 SF
King, Joshua; 17 Oct. 1802; Ann Bohanan   02 SM-185
King, Richard; 25 March 1808; Elizabeth Ostrander   09 BA
King, Thomas; 16 Aug. 1801; Mary Malcomb   01 SO-15
King, Thomas; 14 Nov. 1808; Deborah Crawford   09 BA
King, Thomas; Feb. 1820; Catherine Donohoe   16 BA-17
King, William; 11 Jan. 1802; Eleanor Wilson   09 BA
King, William; 11 Dec. 1808; Martha Campbell   02 BA-7
King, William; 20 Sept. 1810; Marcho Green   08 BA
King, William; 24 Sept. 1818; Elizabeth Webb   17 BA-20
Kingon, James; Aug. 1817; Catherine Gan   02 WA-106
Kingsley, Samuel; 6 July 1815; Julia Ann Isly   09 BA
Kinkerly, John; 19 Aug. 1819; Corilla Wagers   06 FR-1330
Kinkle, Adam; Oct. 1816; Cath. Eichelberger   02 WA-103
Kinly, William; 11 Feb. 1802; Ann Spicer   03 AL-613
Kinnerman (?), Charles; 30 Jan. 1817; Sarah Ann Dorsey 20 BA-223
Kinsell, Enoch B.; Oct. 1817; Hannah Dillman   02 WA-107
Kinsey, Isaac (s. of Isaac and Mary); 2 d. 5 mo., 1804; Elizabeth
    Mason (dau. of James and Rachel)   02 SF-92
Kinsey, Levi; 23 July 1816; Mahala Balderston   0-9 BA
Kinsey, Mahlon (s. of Thomas and Margaret of London Grove Twp.,
    Chester Co., PA); 30 d. 11 mo., 1803; Ann Eastburn (dau. of
    Benjamin and Keziah of Little Britain Twp., Lancaster Co.,
    PA)   06 SF
Kinsey, Oliver (of London Grove, Chester Co., Penna., son of
    Isaac and Mary); 1 d. 6 mo., 1814; Ann Griffith (dau. of
    Abraham and Rachel)   02 SF-123
Kinsle, Fred. Benj. Otto; Dec. 1815; Mary Magd'l. Yomeg
                                                      02 WA-100
Kinsmore, Rich'd Sex; 19 Sept. 1804; Rebecca Yeiser   21 BA-5
Kintz, George; 15 Feb. 1813; Mary Krabel   15 BA-308
Kintz, Jacob; 4 Nov. 1805; Harriet Hudson   15 BA-231
Kirby, Cloudsberry; 6 Aug. 1812; Kitty Buckman   13 BA-14
Kirby, Cornelius; 9 Nov. 1816; Elizabeth Carpenter   13 BA-40
Kirby, James; 5 Sept. 1811; Jane Harvey   11 BA-17
Kirby, James M.; 22 Dec. 1803; Mary Milburn   02 SM-186
Kirby, John; 17 Jan. 1816; Sarah Grafflin   17 BA-12
Kirchhoff, Johanes; 13 Dec. 1801; Nancy Haftin   14 BA-411
Kirchner, Johan; 10 Feb. 1820; Chatarina Dreier   07 BA-311
Kirk, Aquila M. (of York Co., PA, s. of Caleb and Lydia); 27 d. 5
    m., 1818; Sarah Needles (of Balto. Town, dau. of Edward and
    w. Sarah, both dec.)   12 SF-69

Kirk, Erastus U. (s. of Caleb and Lydia, of York Co., Pa.); 1 d
   5 mo., 1816; Maria Matthews (dau. of Mordecai and Ruth)
                                                     02 SF-132
Kirk, George W.; 24 Nov. 1808; Rebecca Edes   14 BA-426
Kirk, Jacob (s. of Roger and Rachel of West Nottingham Twp.); 3
   d. 3 mo., 1803; Sarah England (dau. of John, dec., and
   Elizabeth of East Nottingham Hund., of CE Co., MD)
                                                     06 SF
Kirk, Rich'd; 3 Oct. 1802; Mary Kuntz   14 BA-413
Kirk, Roger (s. of Eli and Susannah of CE Co., MD); 15 d. 10
   mo., 1817; Anna Trump (dau. of Abraham and Jemima of the
   same place)   06 SF
Kirk, Samuel; 6 March 1817; Albina Powel   14 BA-436
Kirk, William (s. of Abner and Ann, dec., of West Nottingham
   Hund., CE Co., MD); 26 d. 3 mo., 1807; Elizabeth Haines
   (dau. of Job and Esther, dec., of the same place) 06 SF
Kirkham, Thomas; 21 Dec. 1803; Charlotte Betts   02 SM-186
Kirklane, Alexander; 12 April 1816; Agnes Quail   11 BA-30
Kirns, Michael; 19 Aug. 1805; Elizabeth Schreyer   15 FR-318
Kirrik, Thomas; 11 Oct. 1807; Phebe Carrothers   01 FR-1145
Kirshaw, John; 11 Nov. 1819; Pricala Kirshaw   01 CA-61
Kirwan, Matthew; 23 Feb., 1803; Catherine Foxwell   01 DO-41
Kirwan, Thomas; 25 March 1807; Catherine Woolford   01 DO-41
Kiser, George; 18 Feb. 1802; Elizabeth Chenowith   23 BA-1
Kisler, Mathias; 12 May 1811; Christina Lester   07 BA-308
Kissinger, Jacob; Oct. 1816; Margaret Beard   02 WA-103
Kistler, David; 15 Aug. 1808; Araminta Mercer   11 BA-12
Kitchard, David; 1 March 1801; Mary Charitor   03 BA-398
Kites, Jno.; 6 Aug. 1812; Eliz. Anderson   14 BA-430
Kitten, John; 18 June 1810; Rachel Tyson   15 BA-280
Kiwer, Jacob; 9 Dec. 1802; Charlotte Grof   15 FR-313
Klassen, Charles; 16 Nov. 1815; M. Smith   30 BA-109
Klein, Gottlieb; 3 March 1816; Maria Barrow   14 BA-435
Kleindienst, Joh.; 18 May 1807; Maria Capito   14 BA-422
Kleinert, Frederick; 3 Feb. 1813; Cath. Wylie   01 FR-1145
Kleinert, Frederick; 21 Feb. 1813; Catherine Wigle 15 FR-326
Kleinhaus, George; 15 Oct. 1807; Clara Sherr   14 BA-423
Kleis, William; 9 Feb. 1817; Susannah Heffner   06 FR-1326
Kleiss, Johannes; 21 Feb. 1802; Ann Wheateroft   15 FR-313
Kleisz, John; 21 Feb. 1802; Ann Wheatcroft   01 FR-1145
Klenan, Jacob; 20 Aug. 1806; Cath. Smith   14 BA-420
Klerie, Jacob; 20 March 1817; Catharine Headinger   07 BA-310
Kline, Henry; 24 May 1801; Eliz. Hens   22 BA-410
Kline, Henry; Nov. 1810; Rebecca M'Ginnis   02 WA-88
Kline, Philip; Nov. 1816; Catherine Showman   02 WA-103
Klingman, George; 7 Dec. 1802; Ann Clopdore   36 BA-1
Klock, Diedrich; 15 Oct. 1811; Christina Kleinhaus 14 BA-429
Klockgetter, Deidrich; 13 Feb. 1816; Charlotte Standly 14 BA-435
Klunk, Peter; 16 June 1807; Elizabeth Kintz   15 BA-250
Knable, Leonhard; 1805; Julia Lyser   02 WA-77
Knapp, Thomas; 18 Feb. 1806; Harriet Greenfield   17 BA-6
Kneepen, Ludwig Joh.; 31 Oct. 1805; An. (N) Lins   14 BA-419
Knepper, John; Aug. 1816; Susannah Davis   02 WA-102
Knidle, Jonathan; July 1819; Barbara King   02 WA-113
Knight, Abraham; 23 April 1811; Nancy Robinson   09 BA
Knight, Geo. W.; 5 July 1810; Mary Vochell   13 BA-10
Knight, Isaac (s. of Israel and Sarah; 25 d. 9 m., 1811;
   Julianna Maria Thomas (dau. of Samuel and Anna) 01 SF
Knight, John; 28 Sept. 1820; Sarah M. Laughlin   13 BA-35
Knight, John M.; 8 Nov. 1811; Mary Parks   11 BA-17
Knight, Joseph; 12 Nov. 1809; Sarah Furst   03 BA-500
Knight, Joshua; 23 Aug. 1816; Mary Henry   14 BA-435
Knight, Nathaniel; 8 May 1803; Elizabeth Hoyle   21 BA-5
Knight, Peregrine; 30 Jan. 1816; Sarah G. Forrest   05 BA-239

```
Knight, Thos.; 5 July 1819; Elizab. Kavin              14 BA-439
Knighton, Keese; 1803; Rachel Parrish                 07 AA-3
Knighton, Thomas; 9 Dec. 1815; Margaret Patton        11 BA-25
Knipe, Lawrence; 7 June 1802; Elizabeth Jackson       17 BA-1
Knoat, Joh.; 28 April 1801; Eliz. Schroeder           14 BA-409
Knobloch, Fred'k; 5 May 1806; Mary Augsperg           14 BA-420
Knod, Jacob; Dec. 1802; Elis. Hammond                 02 WA-74
Knode, Henry; April 1807; Mary Warner                 02 WA-83
Knodel, Georg; 1804; Cath. Weldy (02 WA-76 gives bride's name as
     Welty)                                           02 WA-77
Knodel, Joh.; Nov. 1803; Barbara Long                 02 WA-75
Knodle, (N); Dec. 1807; Sus. Wolford                  02 WA-84
Knop, John; 26 Sept. 1811; Maria Zoller               07 BA-308
Knot, Adam; 1 June 1802; Barbara Fiechelin            14 BA-412
Knouf, Greenbury; 10 Oct. 1815; Susan Dertzebach      06 FR-1323
Knowles, John; 15 Aug. 1811; Reba Safford             13 BA-13
Knowles, Thomas T.; 10 March 1807; Ann McConnell      02 BA-5
Knox, Edgar (?); 1819; Mary Corkril of TA             02 TA-44
Knox, James; 7 Feb. 1812; Charlotte Snider            02 WA-93
Knox, James; 20 Dec. 1818; Sarah Hayes                13 BA-32
Knox, John; 1 May 1801; Jane Wilson                   03 BA-400
Knox, John; 23 Dec. 1818; Margareth Sails             06 FR-1329
Knox, Joseph; 18 June 1820; Catherine Yeast           14 FR
Knup, Abraham; 25 June 1812; Margaretha Laronetto, widow
                                                      07 BA-308
Knupp, Abraham; 14 Nov. 1802; Katharina Wilhelmina Kall
                                                      07 BA-67
Koblentz, Daniel; 17 Dec. 1807; Cath. Stockman (See also
     15 FR-32)                                        01 FR-1145
Koblentz, John; 20 Oct. 1801; Mary Baulus (See also 15 FR-312)
                                                      01 FR-1145
Koch, Georg; 29 March 1814; Cath. Dreppert            14 BA-432
Koch, Henry; 23 April 1805; Eleonore Hummer (See also 15 FR-317)
                                                      01 FR-1145
Koch, Johanes; 25 Sept. 1803; Juliana Keim            14 BA-415
Kochler, Lewis; 30 March 1820; Catharine Troutman     08 AL-62
Koenig, Frederick; 16 April 1805; Marg. Brunner (See also
     15 FR-317)                                       01 FR-1145
Kohhaus, Frederic; 24 Oct. 1808; Mary Harrington      14 BA-425
Kohlenberg, Frederick; 10 Oct. 1813; Ann Nessmith     06 FR-1319
Kohler, Andrew; 1804; Polly Bower                     02 WA-76
Kohler, Georg; 14 March 1802; Margaret Hagen          14 BA-412
Kohlstadt, Benj'n; 7 July 1814; Elizab. Keener        14 BA-433
Kolb, Romer; 22 June 1817; Caroline Cauffman          06 FR-1326
Koller, Georg; 13 Oct 1807; Elisabeth Schweitzer      07 BA-305
Koller, Henry; 26 Nov. 1805; Eliz. Beisser            01 FR-1145
Koller, Philip; 8 April 1813; Susanna Brown           06 FR-1319
Kollness, Andrew; 26 Aug. 1803; Margaret Hanke        25 BA-3
Koneeke, Richard H. (?); 21 Dec. 1815; Rebecca Y. Sewell
                                                      20 BA-222
Konig, Fred'k; 9 Dec. 1802; Maria Mayer               14 BA-413
Konig, Georg; 25 Sept. 1812; Magdalena Wilkinson      14 BA-430
Konig, Joh.; Jan. 1801; Maria Becker                  02 WA-70
Konig, John; 1 April 1804; Margaret Life              30 BA-108
Konike, Jno. Godfrey; 2 Oct., 1802; Catherine Shidle  21 BA-5
Koogle, Christian; 5 March 1820; Frany Horine         16 FR-76
Konner, Frederick; 15 March 1807; Mary Clock          30 BA-109
Koon, Daniel; 24 Nov. 1808; Mary Work                 13 BA-5
Koon, Daniel; 10 Oct. 1811; Mary Arnsbarger           02 WA-91
Koon, William; 19 Nov. 1812; Sarah Heck               02 WA-96
Koons, Jacob; Oct. 1810; Eliz. Zacsarias              02 WA-88
Koontz, Henry; 11 Nov. 1806; Hannah Neff              03 AL-614
Koontz, Henry; 2 Dec. 1819; Julian Wiseman            16 FR-76
Koontz, Jacob; 6 Feb. 1816; Dorcas Aynels             08 AL-63
```

Kooper, John; 13 June 1803; Ann Light   02 BA-32
Korns, Charles; 5 Feb. 1815; Catharine Uhl   08 AL-63
Koush, Andrew; 28 Feb. 1811; Betsy Biddle   02 WA-89
Kraber, Henry; Oct. 1816; Catherine Brown   02 WA-103
Kracht, Fred'k; 3 Nov. 1801; Johanna Amelung   25 BA-2
Kraft, Christian; 25 Jan. 1820; Elizab. Bauer   14 BA-440
Kraft, Jac.; 26 Jan. 1812; Rosanna Deshong   13 BA-14
Kraft, Michael; 2 May 1807; Elisab. Morick   14 BA-421
Krail, Jno. Gotlieb; 28 Jan. 1812; Elizab. Geney   14 BA-429
Kramer, Fred'k; 1 April 1812; Mary Bell   13 BA-7
Kramer, Johan; 15 Dec. 1807; Elisabeth Beilefeld   07 BA-306
Krantz, John D.; 20 April 1815; Catherine Erter   06 FR-1322
Kraul, Conrad; 6 Aug. 1807; Rhode Oberra   14 BA-422
Kraus, Lawrence; 1 May 1801; Marg't Mintze   14 BA-409
Krauth, John; 3 Sept. 1818; Susanna Keller   06 FR-1328
Krebbs, Samuel; 13 March 1809; Sarah Edgely   13 BA-6
Krebs, Wm.; 7 Sept. 1820; Harriet Houser   14 BA-440
Krehmer, Frederick; 25 March 1806; Cath. Berk (15 FR-319 gives
     bride's name as Berck)   01 FR-1145
Krehmer, Henry; 9 Sept. 1806; Barbara Berg (See also 15 FR-319)
                                                         01 FR-1145
Kreis, Daniel; Sept. 1817; Susanna Kroeber   02 WA-106
Kreisz, Peter; 4 Oct. 1801; Susan Ludy (See also 15 FR-312)
                                                         01 FR-1145
Kremer, Frederick; 1 April 1809; Polly Steinbeck   03 BA-499
Krepel, Jacob; 28 feb. 1802; Cath. Schober (See also 15 FR-313)
                                                         01 FR-1145
Krepps, John; Jan. 1817; Frances Herr   02 WA-104
Krepps, William; Nov. 1816; Mary Russell   02 WA-103
Kretschmer, Wm.; 25 May 1819; Wilhelmina Maurer   14 BA-439
Kretsinger, George; July 1803; Dolly Ederberg (?)   02 WA-75
Kretzer, Leonard; June (?) 1804; Hanna Parry   02 WA-76
Krieg, Philip; 1802; Mary Clein   02 WA-72
Kriger, Daniel; 11 Sept. 1806; Elisabeth Brodbeck   15 FR-319
Kriger, Fredericus; 17 May 1807; Margareta Screiber   39 BA-19
Kriver, Jacob; 9 Dec. 1802; Charlotte Grof   01 FR-1145
Krofft, Wm.; 2 Nov. 1816; Achsah Hush   13 BA-40
Krug, Peter; 19 Oct. 1809; Elizabeth Weishgart (both single)
                                                         01 CL-150
Krumbein, John (Johannes); 10 June 1806; Sophia Weber (See also
     15 FR-319)   01 FR-1145
Kruse, Frederick; 3 Dec. 1811; Margareth Bowers   06 FR-1317
Kuch, George; 28 Oct. 1806; Catherine Hardin   08 AL-64
Kuger, Robert; March 1803; Scharlotta Geiger   02 WA-74
Kuhrech, Joh.; 12 April 1801; Cath. Wilhelm   14 BA-409
Kumer, Fred'k; 6 June 1801; Cath. Hartman   22 BA-410
Kummer, John; 10 June 1815; Elizabeth D. Clue   32 BA-304
Kunningham. See Cunningham.
Kunstler, Anton; 27 March 1817; Sally Fenner   17 BA-16
Kuntz, John; 11 Dec. 1819; Mary Prignon   07 BA-311
Kurfman, Henry; 20 Dec. 1801; Cath. Dippel   01 FR-1145
Kurtz, Benjamin; Sept. 1818; Ann Barnett   02 WA-110
Kurtz, Jacob; 24 Nov. 1818 (lic.); Mary Hammer   11 BA-35
Kurtz, Peter; Jan. 1801; Polly Bernolt   02 WA-71
Kush, Jonathan; Nov. 1810; Rebecca Kush   02 WA-88
Kysinger, Charles; March 1804; Elis. Eakle   02 WA-76
L'Corille, Jean (native of Bengal); 6 Jan. 1804; Justine (free
     negro woman from Martinique)   15 BA-196
L(?)gtel, Jacob; Jan. 1807; Mary Beard   02 WA-81
LaBarerre, Nicholas; 7 Nov. 18143; Sophia Bayer   16 BA-11
Labby, Lewis; 3 May 1806; Ann Perris   02 BA-3
Labord, Francis; 15 July 1813; Elizabeth Robinson   31 BA-153
La Boretille, Jean; 15 Feb. 1816; Marie Leclerc   16 BA-31
Labroquiere, Barney; 23 Dec. 1810; Diana Cables   09 BA

La Bruere, John Baptiste Henry (of La Rochelle, France); 4 Aug.
    1802; Armande Victoire Sophie Pattinel (widow of Bertrand,
    native of Havre de Grace)   15 BA-170
Lacey, Stephen; 20 July 1802; Hannah Godshaw   14 BA-413
Lack, John; 13 Dec. 1887; Elizabeth Stimmel   15 FR-322
Lacklin, Dennis; 11 April 1810; Eliza Appleby   11 BA-16
Lacy, Cephas S.; 2 Aug. 1810; Phoebe Wilson   13 BA-10
Ladman, Thomas; 12 June 1818; Mary Rhodes   01 QA-62
Ladman, Thomas; 12 June 1818; Mary Roads, both of QA Co.
                                                      02 TA-44
Laffore, John Emmanuel; 29 July 1812; Catherine Mage (widow)
                                                      15 BA-303
Lafitte, John; 29 Oct. 1818; Teresa Ladue   16 BA-76
Lainhart, Henry; 14 March 1820; Mrs. Mary Kline   37 BA-153
Lake, George; 4 Nov. 1802; Mary Slacum   01 DO-41
Lake, Jno.; 24 Nov. 1818; Eliza Riley   14 BA-438
Lamarle, Anthony (lawful son of Bernard Lamarle and wife Louise
    de St. Martin, native of Tarbes); 15 Feb. 1802; Mary Frances
    Galluchet (dau. of Eustache Galluchet and Mary Santaron;
    native of St. Domingo)   15 BA-163
Lamb, John; 2 Sept. 1802; Eleanor McDonald   09 BA
Lamb, John; 17 Feb. 1803; Mary White   12 AA-2
Lambden, Thomas; 23 May 1816; Ann Davis (dau. of Peter and
    Esther)   32 BA-308
Lambdin, Nicholas; 29 June 1815 (by Rev. Joshua Willey); Ann Hugg
                                                      17 BA-11
Lambe, James; 20 April 1816; Mary Kyser   13 BA-25
Lambert, Abraham; Feb. 1818; Rebecca Artz   02 WA-108
Lambert, Charles (age 27, free negro); 12 July 1806; Mary (?)
    (age 28, free negro)   31 BA-9
Lambert, Clement; 9 Dec. 1806; Mary Morrow   02 BA-5
Lambert, Thomas; 2 July 1810; Charlotte Sisseler   03 BA-501
Lambeth, William; 26 Dec. 1802; Elizabeth Carr   03 AA-120
Lambrecht, Georg; 7 Feb. 1804; Regina Spanseiler   15 FR-316
Lambrecht, Michael; 21 April 1816; Mary Metz   06 FR-1324
Lameter, Nany (?); 16 Feb. 1804 (by Rev. L. W. McCombes); Ruth
    Jones   17 BA-3
Lammot, Daniel; 8 July 1810; Mary Evans   21 BA-7
Lamore, Peter; 15 April 1801; Hetty Fairfax   9 BA
Lamply, John; 12 Jan. 1812; Eliza Evans   03 BA-503
Lancaster, Isaiah; 15 Oct. 1801; Anne Bluford   03 BA-408
Lancaster, John Henry (of CH Co.); 5 feb. 1807; Juliet Trenton
                                                      15 BA-246
Lancaster, Moses P.; 17 March 1801; Eliza Miller   11 BA-2
Lancy, Lewis; 14 Oct. 1820; Victoire Elizabeth Salve 03 BA-605
Lander, Benjamin; 29 Aug. 1814; Mary Burton   11 BA-22
Lander, George; 1 Oct. 1818; Julian Ann Mears   11 BA-33
Landing, William; 14 April 1803; Elizabeth Parker   03 AA-120
Landis, Christian; March 1819; Mary McCoy   02 WA-112
Landsbury, Shadrach; 15 Jan. 1817; Cath. Link   14 BA-436
Landstreet, John; 18 April 1810; Ann N. Orm   13 BA-12
Lane, George; 26 June 1812; Cath. Maloy   02 WA-94
Lane, Nathan; 9 Nov. 1809; Marg't Walker   13 BA-8
Lane, Richard; 25 Dec. 1803; Frances Cowman   03 AA-120
Lane, Thomas; 13 July 1811 (by Rev. Robert Roberts); Elizabeth
    Franklin   17 BA-8
Lane, William; 19 Aug. 1816; Dorothy Dudley   17 BA-15
Laneau, Constant; 30 Sept. 1804; Mary Mattereau   15 BA-209
Lang, Jonathan; 23 Feb. 1819; Sarah Troutmnan   08 AL-65
Langdon, Sylvester; 14 Sept. 1815; Eliza Kilpatrick   11 BA-26
Lange, Jacob; 26 Oct. 1806; Anna Elizabeth Britten   07 BA-305
Langford, Richard; 24 May 1801; Amelia Soper   03 MO-117
Langford, Samuel; 12 June 1803; Susanna Lane   09 BA
Langley, William G.; 19 May 1805; Ann P. Clayton   02 SM-186

```
Langenecker, Jacob; Nov. 1801; Nanzi Ryneberger      02 WA-72
Langrel, William; 21 May 1805; Elizabeth Haris       11 BA-6
Langrell, James; 1 Oct. 1805; Nancy Insley           01 DO-41
Langville, Wm.; 8 Jan. 1805; Nancy Current           03 MO-119
Langworthy, James Edward; 24 May 1804; Providence Norris
                                                     09 BA
Lannay, Peter; 27 May 1820; Jane Saillard            03 BA-604
Lanner, Joseph; 8 April 1809; Elizabeth Smith        02 SM-188
Lant, William; 9 March 1805; Eliz'th Switzer         15 BA-216
Lantz, Henry; Sept. 1810; Polly Schmutz              02 WA-87
Lanver, Jacob; Jan. 1818; Barbara Rohrer             02 WA-108
Lapalanche, Guillaume; 8 April 1817; Nanette Raubert 32 BA-312
Lapouraille, Peter; 9 Jan. 1819; Eugenie Rivoire     16 BA-78
La Reintree, John Louis Roy; 26 Dec. 1811; Catherine Neilson
                                                     05 BA-237
Larew, Jas.; 13 April 1808; Caroline Faus            14 BA-424
Larew, Jno.; 10 May 1808; Lisid Nagel                14 BA-424
Large, James (of Phila., PA, s. of Ebenezer Large, dec., and w.
      Dorothea); 25 d. 1 m., 1817; Elizabeth Poultney (dau. of
      Thomas of Balto. Town and w. Ann)              12 SF-58
Larkin, William; 9 Sept. 1818 (lic.); Mary Howser    11 BA-35
Larkland, Joseph; Sept. 1813; Eliz. Shiffler (?)     02 WA-98
Larner, Thomas; 30 Sept. 1818; Cath. McGee           16 BA-67
Laronet, Philip; 27 May 1806; Susanna Snyder         14 BA-420
Laroque, Francis; 17 March 1817; Sophia Legendre     21 BA-9
Laroque, John Michel; 23 Dec. 1817; Alexandrine Leroy 16 BA-62
La Rouet [dit], Jean Louis (free French negro); 8 Feb. 1808;
      Maria Magdelaine [dite Zeline]                 15 BA-259
Larpe (?), Greenbury; 19 Jan. 1804; Amelia Henshaw   05 AA-4
Larphear, John; 3 Feb. 1803; Else Carrs              14 BA-414
Larsh, Charles; 19 Oct. 1819; Rachel Richardson      11 BA-37
Larwood, John; 15 Dec. 1801; Ann Drummond            17 BA-1
Laska, John; 9 April 1816; Henry Robertson           13 BA-25
Lastly, John; 5 Jan. 1803; Martha Gill               14 BA-414
Lastly, John; 14 Jan. 1818; Mary Ann Dorman          37 BA-152
Late, Michael; 28 April 1812; Maria Roff             13 BA-7
Latham, Edward; 26 July 1804; Sarah Trapnell         09 BA
Latimer, James (of Phila.); 19 (Nov.?) 1809; Sophia Hoffman
                                                     03 BA-500
Latimer, James B,; 20 May 1817; Catherine H. Lyon    05 BA-240
Latimer, Randolph W.; 16 May 1816; Catherine B. Griffith
                                                     09 BA
Latswchower, George; June 1806; Eliz. Brandsletter   02 WA-80
Latton, Thomas; 13 Feb. 1806; Mary Brashears         03 AA-130
Lauber, Georg Mannes; 12 June 1805; Anna Maria Heye/Heyle
                                                     07 BA
Laudeman, frederic; 4 April 1816; Jane M. Harrison   02 BA-37
Lauder, John; 25 Feb. 1802; Ann Barton               09 BA
Laurence, James; 22 Feb. 1816; Jane Smoot            03 AA-131
Laurenson, Philip (native of England); 12 Oct. 1803; Margaret
      Whelan (dau. of Richard Whelan)                15 BA-187
Lavely, William; 9 Feb. 1804; Margaret Hammond       36 BA-2
Lavesky, John; 4 Sept. 1817; Sarah Russell           13 BA-29
Lavish, Joannes; 6 Oct. 1816; Mary Crow              39 BA-32
Lavitt, Capt. Abraham; 23 May 1820; Mary Barber      37 BA-153
Law, Henderson; 7 May 1807; Rebecca Patterson        11 BA-10
Law, Laws.; 18 Sept. 1807; Mary Black                13 BA-2
Law, Samuel B.; 28 Sept. (1817?); Hannah Sank        13 BA-39
Lawes, Thomas; 15 Jan. 1801; Nelly Long              01 SO-15
Lawrence, George; 2 May 1802; Ann Gardner            15 BA-166
Lawrence, James; 23 Nov. 1817; Margaret James        32 BA-317
Lawrence, Joseph; 2 May 1818p Sarah Hendrickson      11 BA-28
Lawrence, Moses; 5 March 1814; Ann Stone             11 BA-23
Lawson, Henry H.; 12 Dec. 1815; Priscilla Crane      11 BA-26
```

Lawson, Robert; 17 July 1818; Sarah Warner   21 BA-9
Lawson, Wm.; 27 Aug. 1803; Ann Duncan   36 BA-1
Lay, Henry; 27 June 1807; Sarah Slosser   11 BA-3
Laydam (Suydam), Jas.; 24 Dec. 1820; Rach'l R. Forest 13 BA-36
Layman, Jacob; 11 June 1819; Kitturah Moke   13 BA-40
Layport, John; 7 Feb. 1815; Catherine Lohr   08 AL-65
Layton, Charles; 19 Nov. 1803; Priscilla Wheatley   06 BA-3
Lazares, Abrahasm; 3 Feb. 1817; Elizabeth Cohen   17 BA-16
Lea, Thomas, Jr. (s. of Thomas and Sarah of Newcastle Co., DE);
    18 d. 11 mo., 1812; Elizabeth Ellicott, Jr. (dau. of George
    and Elizabeth of BA)   12 SF-32
League, Thomas; 4 Jan. 1801; Ann Bull   09 BA
League, Wm.; 14 April 1816; Elizab. Emerson   14 BA-435
Leahy, John; 16 May 1815; Mary Carran   16 BA-19
Leahy, Maurice; 17 May 1810; Cath. McDermott   15 BA-280
Leak, Norris; 13 March 1810; Margaret Owings   31 BA-76
Leakin, Thomas I.; 2 May 1813; Mary L. Little   05 BA-237
Leamon, John; Nov. 1808; Cath. Delinger   02 WA-86
Leary, Peter; 31 Jan. 1813; Eliza. Hagaman   14 BA-431
Leas, John; 23 April 1807; Margaret Stevens   15 FR-320
Leas, John; 9 June 1811; Susan Gregory   11 BA-16
Lease, Henry; 30 April 1811; Lydia Cadwalider   02 WA-89
Lease, Nicholas; 30 Jan. 1820; Catherine Zieler   06 FR-1330
Leasure, Elijah; 6 Oct. 1811; Susanna Miller   02 WA-91
Leather, George; 14 Nov. 1811; Elizabeth Leshhorn   06 FR-1317
Leather, John; 20 Dec. 1814; Elizabeth Leather   06 FR-1321
Leather, John, of G.; 7 Nov. 1816; Susannah Leather 06 FR-1325
Leatherborrow, William; 18 April 1801; Deborah Thompson
                                                     05 BA-9
Leatherbury, Levin; 6 Sept. 1819; Elizabeth Leatherbury
                                                     01 SO-15
Leatherbury, Samuel; 18 Dec. 1818; Mary Done   01 SO-15
Leatherman, John; 17 Nov. 1808; Eva Gaugh   15 FR-323
Leatherwood, John; 8 Oct. 1812; Sarah Meek   13 BA-15
LeBauge, Stephen; 10 Aug. 1815; Felicity Rose Victor 32 BA-304
Lebon, Charles; 20 July 1816; Marceline Dumas   13 BA-51
Lebren, Solomon; 19 Aug. 1817; Mary Frances Benguet 32 BA-314
Lebrou, Anthony; 13 May 1804; Ally Coughlin   15 BA-202
Lebrun, Anthony; 1 Nov. 1819; Marie Clement   16 BA-92
Lechleiter, Adam; 30 Nov. 1820; Elizabeth Powell   16 FR-76
Lechlider, Peter; 11 March 1813; Nancy Swope   06 FR-1319
Leckey, Hugh; 24 Feb. 1803; Eleanor Carey   05 BA-233
Le Clair, Joseph; 2 May 1805; Celina Lassaurius (both free
    mulattoes)   15 BA-218
Leclaire, Louis Sebastian; 23 Sept. 1817; Maria Regina Pere
                                                     16 BA-57
Lee, Abraham; 4 May 1820; Sarah Roberts   11 BA-37
Lee, Andrew; 14 Aug. 1808; Mary Tillman   14 BA-424
Lee, Benedict; 23 April 1818; Catherine Wayman   11 BA-33
Lee, Charles; 12 March 1805 (by Jno. Bloodgood in list of
    marriages for blacks); Priscilla Bond   17 BA-5
Lee, Cornelius (or Geo.); 13 Nov. 1818 (lic.); Mary Start
                                                     11 BA-35
Lee, Edward; 24 May 1816; Susan Seare   17 BA-12
Lee, George; 28 Jan. 1802; Mary Rogers   03 BA-412
Lee, George; 2 March 1808; Mary Gray   02 BA-6
Lee, George; 6 April 1809; Eliza Burton   13 BA-5
Lee, George; 26 May 1810; Sarah Wilson   13 BA-12
Lee, George; 19 March 1812; Jane Merryman   11 BA-20
Lee, James; 24 Dec. 1811; Margaret Wells   03 AL-614
Lee, James A.; 23 April 1816; Catherine M. Coskery   16 BA-33
Lee, James H.; 8 Oct. 1818; Maria Cook   13 BA-40
Lee, John; 26 Feb. 1809; Margaret Ebert   08 BA
Lee, John; 25 Sept. 1820; Elis. McKelden   13 BA-35

```
Lee, Jones; 24 Dec. 1820; Darkey (slaves)           16 BA-106
Lee, Joseph; 16 April 1804; Elizabeth Ramsey        02 BA-33
Lee, Joseph; 25 Jan. 1810; Rebecca Wortley Oats     03 BA-501
Lee, Joshua; 20 April 1806; Susanna Stansbury       03 BA-495
Lee, Lamach; 7 July 1803; Anna Dunbar               02 SM-186
Lee, Lewis (slave of S. Chase); 22 Nov. 1805; Nancy Wilkinson
                                                    03 BA-494
Lee, Lewis; 4 July 1819; Susan Colliman             14 FR
Lee, Nicholas; 6 Dec. 1803; Mary Clarke             09 BA
Lee, Philip; c.1802; Lucy Waters                    12 AA-1
Lee, Ralph; 16 Jan. 1812; Elizabeth Smithson        01 BA-11
Lee, William; 19 Nov. 1801; Mary Dickinson          09 BA
Lee, William; 2 Oct. 1809; Mary Lee Holliday        15 BA-273
Leef, Johnzee; 27 Jan. 1819; Mary Ann Dyers         17 BA-21
Leeke, Nicholas; 22 July 1802; Hannah Busk          09 BA
Leeke, Richard; 9 Nov. 1809; Elizabeth French       09 BA
Leepe, Adam; 9 Sept. 1819; Charlotte Brown          13 BA-33
Leer, George; 12 Nov. 1807; Susan Doll              15 FR-321
Lefeber, Jacob; 1 May 1804; Mary Jackson            15 FR-316
Le Febre, Jean brutus; 2 Jan. 1819; Ann Thompson    03 BA-603
Legg, William; 1 Jan. 1817; Hester Bishop           13 BA-39
Leggett, David; 6 Oct. 1808; Jane Wallace           13 BA-5
Legh, Abraham; 14 April 1816; Margaret Foster       17 BA-012
Lego, Benjamin; 2 April 1806; Elizabeth York        33 BA-41
Legrand, Thos.; 12 Nov. 1816; Mary Tull             13 BA-26
Legtmyer, Georg Aug.; 5 Feb. 1820; An. Cath. Raab   14 BA-440
Lehman, Henry; 13 Feb. 1814; Lydia Hohr             06 FR-1320
Lehman, Nicolaus; 6 Dec. 1812; Elisabeth Gibson     07 BA-308
Lehman, Nicolaus; 1 Oct. 1816; Margaretha Gibbs     07 BA-310
Leinen, Chris.; 19 Feb. 1809; C. Comfort            30 BA-109
Leister, Shipley; 5 May 1814; Mary Walton           13 BA-19
Leiter, Abraham; Jan. 1801; Mary Houser             02 WA-71
Leitner, Christoph; 28 Dec. 1815; Eliza Price       14 BA-434
Leitner, George; 26 March 1804; Ann Hunt            14 BA-416
Leitner, James; 9 March 1816; Susannah Poole        06 FR-1324
Leitner, Michael; 7 Oct. 1807; Delia Tracey         14 BA-422
Leloup, Lewis Francis (son of the late Louis Laloup and Jane
     Defrene); 7 Dec. 1805; Maria Antoinette Sophia Delarue (dau.
     of Lewis James Julian Delarue and the late Elizabeth
     Legourx)                                       15 BA-231
Lemaitre, Rene; 2 Feb. 1815; Christina Williams     32 BA-303
Lemmar, William; 18 Dec. 1805; Sarah Roberson       03 MO-119
Lemmon, John; 30 April 1801; Cathertine Birgine     09 BA
Lemmon, John; 4 Aug. 1804; Nancy Thompson           03 BA-491
Lemmon, John; 14 Sept. 1806; Phebe Wilson           03 BA-496
Lemmon, John; 8 Oct. 1811; Christiana Lusby         31 BA-111
Lemmon, Richard; 25 May 1809; Deborah Barry         13 BA-6
Lemmonier, Alexander Louis; 7 Feb. 1809; Mary Sophia Waters
                                                    03 BA-499
Lemon, William; 5 Feb. 1805; Ally Burns             15 BA-215
Lendsay, Abraham; 1804; Abigail Stuart              02 WA-75
Lennahan, James; 11 March 1802; Margaret Hassett    15 BA-164
Lenninger, Wm.; 5 Aug. 1817; Ann Redmond            13 BA-28
Lenox, William K.; 23 Nov. 1810 (by Rev. Robert Roberts); Mary
     McCarty                                        17 BA-8
Lerew, James; 1 March 1804; Sarah Todd              03 BA-490
Leruith, Philip; 22 July 1809; Mary Weller          03 BA-500
Lescure, W. A.; 12 Jan. 1819; Rebecca Woods         13 BA-34
Lesfauries, John Francis (son of John Martin Lesfauries and
     Radegonde Richer Lesfauries); 3 June 1802; Juliet Frances
     Elizabeth Cressionier de Beauplan (dau. of [N] Consonnier de
     Beaupolan and Radegonde Duvernis Cresonnier de Beauplan)
                                                    15 BA-167
Lesh, Georg; 20 Oct. 1807; Johana Heinrich          14 BA-423
```

```
Lesh, Hieronymus; 1 May 1801; Maria Simon              14 BA-409
Lester, Jno.; 14 Nov. 1812; Elizabeth Courtenay        03 BA-504
Lestley, John; 1 Aug. 1805; Sarah Hawkins              09 BA
L'Estrange, Joseph; 18 June 1801; Sarah Gihan          03 BA-401
Letherbury, Thos.; 21 May 1812; Mary Forwood           13 BA-7
Letter, Thomas; 12 March 1803; Mary Norris             03 BA-426
Letton, Bruce; 22 Sept. 1803; Harriot Moore            03 MO-118
Leudon (?), Joshua; 6 Oct. 1811; Cath. Sleigh          02 WA-91
Leve, George; 22 Dec. 1804; Jemima Fish                03 BA-492
Lively, John S.; 11 Nov. 1813; Pheobe Ann Skelton      20 BA-222
Leventon, Jacob of Moses; 1804; Elizabeth Whiteley     07 SF-8
Leventon, Jacob (s. of Moses and Ann, both dec.); 18 d. 5 mo.,
    1814; Esther Swiggett (dau. of Johnson and Mary)   07 SF-24
Levering, Aaron; 29 Nov. 1814; Ann Eliza Cave          09 BA
Levering, Francis; 6 Nov. 1806; Charlotte Elliot       02 BA-4
Levering, Jesse; 20 Jan. 1803; Sarah Brown             05 BA-233
Levering, John; 11 Feb. 1802; Ann Laureson             09 BA
Levering, Nathan; 21 Sept. 1802; Susanna Dentz         09 BA
Levering, Thomas (son of Griffith and Hannah); 21 d. 12, 1814;
    Rachel Ann Scholfield (dau. of Jos. L. and Susanna)
                                                       01 SF
Leverton, Jacob (s. of Moses and Ann); 23 d. 5 mo., 1804;
    Elizabeth Whiteley (dau. of Anthony and Sophia)    07 SF
Levi, Abraham; 23 Dec. 1804; Cath. Wigle               15 FR-317
Levi, Benjamin; 6 Aug. 1816; Rachel Simmonds Harson    17 BA-15
Levick, William (of Kent Co., DE; s. of William and Susanna); 19
    d. 5 mo., 1808; Hannah Bruff (dau. of Christopher and Mary)
                                                       08 SF
Levin, (Sol. Birckhead); 15 Nov. 1809; Charlotte A. Alexander
                                                       03 BA-500
Levy, David; 12 April 1820; Elizabeth Meyers           06 FR-1331
Levy, Jacob F.; 19 Nov. 1804; Anne Maggs               03 BA-492
Levy, Joseph; 31 Oct. 1816; Margaret Jones             17 BA-15
Lewes, Benedict; 6 July 1805; Elizah Conway            03 BA-494
Lewis, Benedict; 6 July 1805; Elizabeth Conway         02 BA-35
Lewis, Benjamin; 12 March 1807; Elizabeth Bockover     15 FR-320
Lewis, Edward; 13 Nov. 1806; Priscilla Reynolds        03 BA-496
Lewis, George; 22 March 1809; Hannah Sinck             02 BA-7
Lewis, Isaiah; 3 April 1804; Elizabeth Kertich         02 BA-33
Lewis, Job; 27 Nov. 1809; Mary Ann Harvey              02 BA-7
Lewis, John (slave); 17 May 1817; (N) (N) [illegible]  16 BA-52
Lewis, John (s. of John and Grace); 10 d. 9 m., 1818; Esther
    Fussell (dau. of Bartholomew and Rebecca)          05 SF
Lewis, John; Feb. 1819; Mary Sul[tz]er                 14 FR
Lewis, Lewis D.; 18 June 1812; Cathe. McGowan          13 BA-9
Lewis, Nathaniel; 27 Jan. 1803; Elizabeth Gent         23 BA-2
Lewis, Richard; 28 July 1804; Margaret Adams           21 BA-8
Lewis, Samuel; 11 Dec. 1808; Eliza C. Holliday         02 BA-7
Lewis, Thomas W. H.; 13 July 1801; Elizabeth Moss      05 AA-1
Lezear, Henry; 26 May 1813; Martha Beal                15 FR-327
Libbah, Jonathan; 24 Sept. 1801; Rebecca Ingrum        03 BA-407
Lichlider, Conrad; 24 Dec. 1812; Ally Patterson        15-FR 326
Lichte, Jacob; 17 April 1804; Gartraut Meyer           14 BA-416
Lichty, Henry; Aug. 1807; Mary Wallich                 02 WA-83
Lickleter, Henry; 9 Dec. 1819; Maria McAfee            04 FR-19
Liday (?), Henry; by 30 Oct. 1802; Delilah Hays        12 FR
Liddard, Moses; 28 Jan. 1818; Rachel Stewart           17 BA-19
Ligan, Stephen; 3 June 1815; Mary Olive Hull           16 BA-22
Light, John; 3 Jan. 1804; Mary Pearson                 05 BA-234
Light, William; 30 Oct. 1815; Elizabeth Hynes          09 BA
Lighter, John; 17 March 1812; Cath. Lighter            02 WA-93
Lighter, Samuel; 31 Jan. 1811; Cath. Myntz             02 WA-89
Lighthiser, Henry; 25 Nov. 1806; Sarah Fountz          14 BA-421
Lighthiser, Joshua; 13 May 1805; Kitty Gardner         14 BA-418
```

```
Lightner, James; Dec. 1812; Elizabeth Bray          06 FR-1318
Lightner, Jno.; 12 May 1813; Mary Camper            14 BA-432
Lille, Elijah C.; 18 Aug. 1808; Elizab. Booth       14 BA-424
Linck, Fried.; 4 Sept. 1806; Patty White            14 BA-420
Linck, Geo.; Jan. 1809; Martha Linck                02 WA-86
Lindenbergher, (N); 10 Dec. 1801; Rebecca Hebb      02 SM-185
Lindergreen, Henry; 19 May 1803; Cath. Williams     14 BA-414
Lineweaver, Casper; 18 May 1812; Eliza Burkhart     06 FR-1318
Lindsey, Andrew; 22 Jan. 1809; Harriet Spedding     13 BA-5
Ling, Joseph; 19 July 1819; Mary Goodall            37 BA-152
Ling, Robert; 16 June 1803; Ann Bilson              09 BA
Lingenfelter, James; 17 May 1807; Eliza Freeman     13 BA-2
Lingfelter, Nicolaus; 31 March 1801; Cathrina Sauers (both
    single)                                         01 CL-149
Lingford, John; 24 April 1806; Anne Mattocks        03 BA-495
Lininger, Conrad; Feb. 1802; Barbara Fink           02 WA-72
Link, Henry; 10 April 1817; Hanna Clark             14 BA-436
Link, John; 2 Nov. 1819; Lucy Filler                06 FR-1330
Linnott, John D.; 22 Aug. 1809; Catherine Doyle     15 BA-271
Linsey, Daniel; 20 Oct. 1803; Sarah Marsh           05 AA-3
Linste[ad?], Thos.; 27 (?) 1803; (N) (N)            03 MO-118
Linterman, Henry; 2 Sept. 1816; Mary Bell           06 FR-1325
Linthicum, Ezekiah; 27 Oct. 1801; Mary Hickman      03 MO-117
Linthicum, Frederick; 1 Dec. 1801; Rachel Mackelfresh 03 MO-117
Linthicum, Hezekiah; 10 May 1802; Sarah Jacob       15 AA-2
Linthicum, William; 26 Nov. 1808; Ellen Lowry       15 BA-266
Linthicum, Zachariah; 1 Nov. 1803; Anna Clagett     03 MO-119
Linton, Edward; 20 Nov. 1808; Sarah Ellison         15 FR-323
Linton, James; 1 Jan. 1807; Mary Lantz              15 FR-320
Linton, Washington; 12 Nov. 1818; Elizabeth Spanseller 06 FR-1329
Linton, Zachariah; 13 Feb. 1817; Susan Ramsburg     06 FR-1326
Linvill, Jas. M.; 6 Jan. 1813; Maria Lory           13 BA-15
Liony (?), Gaspard; 10 Oct. 1811; Cecily Rechard    31 BA-112
Lippe, Joseph; 18 Oct. 1812; Catharina Stephen      39 BA-28
Lippo, Jacob; 19 Feb. 1818; Susannah Miller         08 BA
Lippott, John Jacob; 15 Sept. 1803; Ann McManamy    09 BA
Lirp, John; 28 Oct. 1813; Deborah Jackson           03 BA-505
Liser, Jonathan; April 1817; Judith Keiser          02 WA-104
Litchfield, Charles; 27 June 1802; Christianna Case 15 AA-2
Litle, John (s. of Washington, DC, dec., and w. Hannah); 19 d. 6
    m., 1816; Sarah Sinclair (dau. of Robert of Balto. Town and
    w. Esther)                                      12 SF-52
Litle, Richard M. (son of Jno. and Hannah); 26 d. 12 m., 1810;
    Elizabeth Talbott (dau. of Joseph and Anne) (See also 1
    0 SF)                                           01 SF
Litten, James; Oct. 1817; Sarah Blair               02 WA-106
Littig, Frederick Shaffer; 17 Feb. 1820; Hannah Williams Pitt
                                                    17 BA-22
Little, Charles; 22 April 1816; Susan Remington     32 BA-308
Little, David; 10 Oct. 1819; Elizabeth Hargrove     04 FR-19
Little, George; 4 Aug. 1818; Ann Jacquett           17 BA-19
Little, Jacob; 13 Oct. 1816; Ann Dorothy Willins    06 FR-1325
Little, Jeremiah; 31 Dec. 1812; Amelia Apsby        11 BA-20
Little, Joseph; 10 Nov. 1808; Eliza Spicer          13 BA-5
Little, Peter; 19 May 1816; Catherine Levely        21 BA-8
Littlejohn, George Walter; 4 Aug. 1811; Elizabeth Gittinger
                                                    04 FR-17
Litzinger, Henricus; 4 Sept. 1811; Sale (?) Norris  39 BA-26
Litzinger, Joseph; 12 Feb. 1803; Matilda Wright     09 BA
Liverpool, Seymour (free negro); 21 Nov., 1820; Mary Ann Sopher
    (also free)                                     32 BA-330
Livers, Anthony; 5 May 1803; Priscilla Wickham      15 BA-182
Livers, James; 10 June 1802; Sarah Wheeler          15 BA-168
```

Livingston, Robert Leroy (of N. Y.); 2 July 1811 (at Greenhill,
    PG Co.); Ann Marie Digges   15 BA-289
Lizear, Elijah; 13 April 1817; Ann Joce   11 BA-32
Lloyd, William; 23 Dec. 1810; Maria Rusk   09 BA
Lobholt, P.; 18 Oct. 1807; Catherine Brooks   30 BA-109
Locher, Henry; March 1804; Rebecca Branner   02 WA-76
Lock, George; 28 Oct. 1813; Mary Fogle   06 FR-1320
Lock, Philip; 8 Nov. 1814; Elizabeth Wolf   06 FR-1321
Lock, Sam'l; 24 Nov. 1814; Eliza Harris   13 BA-20
Lock, Will'r; 14 Jan. 1808; Eliza Debrin   13 BA-3
Lockerman, Edward; 19 Nov. 1803; Fanny Carr   03 BA-435
Lockwood, Crandle E.; 6 March 1817; Ruth Cably 14 BA-436
Loga, John J. B.; 10 Dec. 1807; Clarissa Ball 14 BA-423
Logan, Jno. B.; 26 Aug. 1813; Mary Ann Bryson 21 BA-7
Logan, Joseph; 16 March 1812; Polly Powel   11 BA-20
Logan, Lloyd; 4 Feb. 1802; Rachel Duvall   15 AA-2
Logan, Michael; 24 Oct. 1805; Phebe Cary   11 BA-7
Lohr, George; 14 March 1815; Margaretha Rinehart 08 AL-67
Loiset, John; 2 May 1812; Margaret Wilson   31 BA-124
Loker, William; 31 Dec. 1805; Janett Thompson 02 SM-187
Loman, Emory; Jan. 1805 (by Jno. Bloodgood); Mary Hasheim
                                         17 BA-4
Long, Abraham; 13 Sept. 1806; Mary Thomas   09 BA
Long, Adam; April 1816; Marth. Beck   02 WA-101
Long, Arnold; 18 Nov. 1819; Julia Hush   13 BA-33
Long, Benjamin; 1 June 1802; Ann Athey   03 AL-613
Long, Benjamin; 15 Sept. 1807; Sarah Husher   03 AL-614
Long, Cornelius B.; 6 April 1806 (by Leonard Cassell); Elizabeth
    Hammond   17 BA-6
Long, David; 31 Aug. 1815; Rebecca West   11 BA-26
Long, David, of KY.; 13 Aug. 1819; Henrietta Elzey 01 SO-15
Long, David; March 1820; Mary Gletner   02 WA-116
Long, Henry; 17 Aug. 1809; Eliza Ann Gittings 01 BA-9
Long, Jacob; 27 Sept. 1818; Aplone Jasman   14 BA-437
Long, James; Aug. 1807; Eva Eversole   02 WA-83
Long, John; Jan. 1881; Elisab. Sensel   02 WA-108
Long, Peter; Jan. 1819; Rosanna Moudy   02 WA-112
Long, Robert Carey; 24 Jan. 1809; Ann Hamilton 15 BA-267
Long, Rosamond [sic]; 9 Aug. 1803; Ruth Ricketts 03 AL-613
Long, Sewell; 10 Nov. 1801; Elizabeth Salmon 10 BA-1
Long, Silvanus; 8 April 1802; Susana Brown   14 BA-412
Long, Thomas; 3 Feb. 1801; Mary Kennedy   14 BA-409
Long, Thomas; 12 Nov. 1801; Mary Sollers   09 BA
Long, William; 3 April 1804; Esther Leford or Siford 03 Al-613
Long, William; 24 Dec. 1806; Mary Reptkie [sic] 11 BA-10
Longley, Samuel; 5 July 1810; Margaret Berger 14 BA-227
Longshore, Jonathan; 30 Aug. 1804; Hannah Davidson (See also
    10 AL)   07 AL-274
Longshore, Stephen; 30 Aug. 1804; Hannah Davidson 04 AL-2
Lony, Samuel; 9 June 1803; Elizabeth Barton   34 BA-1
Lonybell, David; April 1805; Sus. Fasenacht   02 WA-78
Loof, John H.; 4 Feb. 1819; Eliza M. Hackley 11 BA-33
Loop, John; 15 Aug. 1820; Magdalena Bell   06 FR-1331
Loore, Mich'l B.; 27 Aug. 1814; Sarah Holland 11 BA-22
Loran, Thomas; 19 June 1806; Ruth Winters   15 BA-239
Lord, John; 7 Sept. 1804; Elizabeth Wheeler   23 BA-3
Lord, Joseph L.; 29 March 1818; Fanny Douglas 05 BA-240
Lorelius, Joseph A.; 8 Feb. 1806; Polly Reese 14 BA-419
Lorentz, Joseph; May 1809; (N) Stiger   39 BA-22
Loring, Elpalet; 29 Jan. 1807; Sarah Cublay   31 BA-17
Lorite (?), John; 20 Nov. 1803; Sarah Carman   06 BA-3
Lormor, Samuel; 18 April 1803; Mary Caswell   03 BA-427
Lory, Teire; 24 Nov. 1806; Anna Jenny Nelson 09 BA
Lottee, Laurence; 6 June 1816; Elizabeth Clark 11 BA-30

```
Lottee, Laurence; 6 June 1816; Elizabeth Clark          11 BA-31
Loughrety, John; 25 Dec. 1803; Ann Higgins              15 BA-194
Love, Bennet; 23 April 1809; Elizabeth Gilbert          01 BA-11
Love, Friend; 31 July 1814; Constant Taylor             17 BA-10
Love, George; 22 Dec. 1804; Jamima Fish                 02 BA-34
Love, James; 18 Oct. 1810; Marg't Morris                13 BA-17
Love, Dr. John (widower); 19 Nov. 1819; Ann Legg (widow)
                                                        16 BA-90
Love, Joseph; 7 July 1816; Catherine Barton             03 BA-507
Loveall, Enoch; 28 Sept. 1803; Lucy Brown               23 BA-2
Lovell, John; 5 April 1804; Mary Appold                 03 BA-491
Lovell, William; 12 Oct. 1805; Lilly Meekins            02 BA-2
Lovet, Charles; 22 Oct. 1803; Joanna Kennedy            15 BA-188
Low, Dennis; 27 June 1808; Elizabeth Eckle (both of Balto. Co.)
                                                        15 BA-263
Low, Henry; 30 Jan. 1816; Eliza Hinton                  13 BA-24
Low, John; 27 Aug. 1807; Barbara Wickel                 15 FR-321
Low, Rufus; 31 May 1820; Sarah Ruckel                   13 BA-35
Lowderman, Frederick; 24 July 1804; Sarah Lewis         03 BA-431
Lowdermilk, Peter; 8 Dec. 1801; Catherine Recknor       03 AL-613
Lowe, Adam B.; 26 Sept. 1816; Eliz. B. Fletcher         13 BA-026
Lowe, Bradley; 28 Sept. 1819; Adelaide Vincendiere      04 FR-19
Lowe, James; 11 July 1802; Elizabeth Mullikin           15 AA-2
Lowe, John; 1 6 June 1802; Lydia Danielson              15 AA-2
Lowe, John; 22 May 1817; Ann Gosnell                    08 BA
Lowes, Tubman (s. of Henry and Esther); 11 March 1801; Ann Hitch
  (dau. of Joshua and Mary)                             01 WI
Lowman, John; Nov. 1802; Mary Tom                       02 WA-73
Lowman, Emery; 3 Aug. 1809; Sarah Brooks                13 BA-8
Lowman, Emery; 5 Dec. 1811; Mary Chaney                 13 BA-14
Lowman, John; 30 July 1811; Mary Bush                   02 WA-90
Lowman, James; March 1819; Sarah Stineburg              02 WA-112
Lowman, Michael; April 1805; Sarah Nelson               02 WA-78
Lowman, Paul; Jan. 1811; Regina Holtzapple              02 WA-88
Lowne (?), John; 30 April 1817; Sarah Robinson          21 BA-9
Lowrig, Francis; 3 May 1816; Mary Hoffhand              07 BA-310
Lowry, Bartholomew; 4 March 1813; Susana Lobstein       14 BA-431
Lowry, John; 22 Oct. 1801; Hannah Maidwell              03 BA-409
Lowry, Joseph; 12 June 1804; Mary Coleman               15 AA-3
Lowry, Robert; 28 April 1808; Matilda Murphy            02 BA-6
Lowry, Robert; 3 Oct. 1815; Eliza Holmes                16 BA-27
Loxley, Edw'd; 23 April 1809; Rosetta Gray (free blacks)
                                                        03 BA-499
Loyd, John; 25 Sept. 1803; Mary Ry                      03 BA-434
Loyd, William; 10 Dec. 1803; Lyda Chandler              23 BA-3
Luberg, John; 21 March 1813; Dorothea Shoemaker         14 BA-431
Lucas, John; 3 Sept. 1820; Elizabeth Riley              37 BA-153
Lucas, Joshua; 14 Jan. 1808; Catherine Hostetter        03 BA-498
Lucas, Peter; 9 June 1811 (by Rev. Robert Roberts); Ann Mathews
                                                        17 BA-8
Lucas, Samuel; 25 June 1809; Nancy McCormick, both of Caroline
  Co.                                                   02 TA-41
Lucas, Samuel; 29 May 1820; Mary Benson                 17 BA-23
Lucas, Seth; 17 Sept. 1816; Harriet Sands               14 BA-435
Lucas, Stephen; 29 May 1808; Sally Keene, both of Caroline
                                                        02 TA-41
Luckbaugh, John; 7 Sept.. 1813; Mary McCoy              15 BA-315
Luckie, Will'm. A.; 30 March 1807; Jane Ward            21 BA-6
Lu[ckin], Antonius; 26 Sept. 1813; Anna Schwartz        39 BA-29
Ludden, Lemuel; 6 June 1815; Margaret McDonough         05 BA-238
Ludley, Isaac; 30 Dec. 1817; Harriet Norwood            13 BA-29
Ludwig, Joannes; April 1807; Rachel Fullweiler          39 BA-19
Ludwig, Jno.; 5 March 1809; Mary Ledinger               14 BA-425
Ludy, John; Feb. 1820; Susanna Moggins                  02 WA-115
```

```
Lufley, George; 25 Jan. 1808; Nancy Foxwell           14 BA-423
Lukenbill, Peter; 14 June 1804; Elizabeth Worman      15 FR-316
Lukens, Jacob (s. of Benjamin and Alice); 1 d. 7, 1801; Tace
    Parson (dau. of John and Rebecca) (See also O5 SF)
                                                      02 SF-79
Lukes (?), Jesse; 25 Feb. 1802; Polly Isenberg        10 FR
Lukins, Samuel, M.D.; 18 d. 9 m., 1807; Elizabeth Briggs
                                                      10 SF
Lunch, Peter; 5 Jan. 1818; Martha (or Margaret) Fitzpatrick
                                                      32 BA-317
Lund, John; 28 July 1803; Rebecca Harrison            09 BA
Luneberry, John; 22 Nov. 1807; Salley Curley          31 BA-34
Lurty, Thomas; 21 Oct. 1806; Margaret Shadrack        02 SM-187
Lusby, James; c.1802; Elizabeth Nagle                 12 AA-1
Lusby, John; 12 Aug. 1817; Sarah Nowland              01 CE
Lusby, Thomas R.; 30 Sept. 1820; Lucinda D. M. Kay    16 BA-104
Lutz, Adam; 15 April 1811; Sarah Hehl                 06 FR-1315
Lutz, Jacob; 18 July 1805; Barb. Ehring               14 BA-418
Lutz, Valentin; 14 Jan. 1808; Catherina Wolf          07 BA-306
Lutze, George; 5 May 1801; Henrietta Hopke            14 BA-409
Lyles, David C.; 9 Dec. 1817; Ann Dunbar              13 BA-29
Lyles, Sabritt; 1804; Elenner Gades (?)               07 AA-4
Lymas, Charles; 10 Sept. 1818; Phebe Clark            05 BA-241
Lynch, Abraham; 22 July 1806; Elizabeth Jones         02 BA-4
Lynch, James; [prob. Dec. 1814]; Martha Clarke        16 BA-13
Lynch, John; 8 Nov. 1803; Mary Hunter (see also 02 BA-33)
                                                      03 BA-435
Lynch, John; 3 Dec. 1812; Barbara Kurtz               15-FR 326
Lynch, Stephen; 13 July 1802; Priscilla Joy           02 SM-185
Lynch, Thomas; 18 July 1805; Elizabeth Hebb           02 SM-187
Lynch, Thomas; 27 March 1817; Barbara Moore           13 BA-28
Lynch, William; 31 Dec. 1805; Ann Bean                02 SM-187
Lynes, James; 21 Jan. 1804 (by Rev. L. W. McCombes); Helena
    Miller                                            17 BA-3
Lyon, Benjamin; 20 Aug. 1803; Rachel Davis            03 MO-118
Lyon, Jno.; 17 April 1802; Priscilla McKinstry        14 BA-412
Lyon, Will; 12 May 1814; Mary Bull                    13 BA-19
Lyon, William; c.1804; Mary Tucker                    34 BA-2
Lyons, Jacob; 17 June 1802; Jane Moses                03 AL-613
Lyons, Michael; 1 March 1802; Mary Russell            15 BA-164
Lyons, Mordecai; 23 July 1802; Mary Bausman           09 BA
Lyons, Thomas; 29 July 1811; Sarah Ann Staley         02 WA-90
Lytle, Thos.; 15 Dec. 1812; Mary Grover               03 BA-504
Lytle, Thomas; 24 April 1817; Charity McComas         11 BA-27
Lyvet, Louis Hyppolite; 27 March 1817; Amelia DeChamp 21 BA-9
Maass, Adam; 7 Feb. 1807; Mary (Charles) Collins      14 BA-421
Macht, Daniel; 7 Sept. 1815; Phoebe Blessing          06 FR-1323
Macken, Bernard; 1 Nov. 1820; Ann Sharkey             16 BA-104
Mackey, James H.; 29 Feb. 1819; Caroline P. Donaldson 13 BA-34
Mackey, John, Jr.; 28 June 1819; Ann Mary Henry       16 BA-83
Mackey, Michael; 16 Aug. 1801; Elizabeth Eisel        15 BA-155
Macknight, James (native of Ireland); 18 Aug. 1803; Elizabeth
    McGoveran (widow)                                 15 BA-185
Madden, Eli; 1 Aug. 1803; Kitty Martin                03 BA-432
Madden, Eli; 21 May 1804; Eliza Moore                 03 BA-490
Madden, Joseph; 19 Nov. 1801; Susanna Sparrow         03 MO-117
Madden, Walter; 2 Sept. 1802; Eliz. Mudd              03 MO-118
Madder, Wm.; 19 March 1818; Nancy Brown               03 BA-603
Maddigan, Paul; 3 Feb. 1805; Bridget Campbell (both natives of
    Ireland)                                          15 BA-214
Maddin, John; 23 March 1802; Susannah Magruder        03 AL-613
Madera, Johannes; 23 Aug. 1803; Theresia Gebeler      15 FR-315
Madera, John; 23 Aug. 1803; Theresia Gebeler          01 FR-1152
Madira, John; 20 Jan. 1819; Rachel Russell            13 BA-34
```

```
Madore, Francis; 9 April 1815; Elizabeth Rice        08 AL-69
Magaurin, James C.; 28 Nov. 1811; Elizabeth Fox      15 BA-293
Magee, Aquila; 6 June 1820; Mary Blizard             11 BA-36
Magee, John; 10 Oct. 1813; Mary Magan                15 BA-317
Magee, Rob't.; 23 Nov. 1804 (See also 02 BA-34); Susanna
    Brooks                                           03 BA-492
Mager, John Ludolph; 22 Oct. 1818; Dorothea Erbss    14 BA-438
Magnass, John; 7 Aug. 1806; Catherine Ball (See also 15 FR-319)
                                                     01 FR-1153
Magrain, Thomas; 22 Jan. 1804; Mary Conroy           15 BA-198
Magruder, Benj.; 6 Nov. 1814; Anna Prouh [sic]       03 BA-506
Magruder, Burgess; 18 May 1820; Margaret Neff        08 AL-69
Magruder, Dennis; 6 May 1814; Rebecca B. Claggett    03 BA-505
Magruder, Edward; 7 Aug. 1803; Jane Ayton            03 MO-118
Magruder, Geo.; 31 March 1801; Anna Turner           03 MO-117
Magruder, James Trueman; 6 Dec. 1803; Elizabeth Ann Magruder
                                                     03 AA-120
Magruder, Richard B.; 27 April 1809; Maria Stricker  05 BA-236
Magruder, Samuel; 12 March 1801; Eliz. Hawkins       03 MO-117
Magruder, Thomas C.; 1812; Mary Ann Magruder (See also 02 MO)
                                                     01 PG
Magruder, Warren; 3 Nov. 1803; Hariot Holmes         03 MO-119
Maguire, Edward; 28 April 1806; Mrs. Catherine Faharty 31 BA-6
Maguire, John; (betw. 14 July and 18 Aug.) 1803; Alice Maguire
                                                     15 BA-185
Maguire, William I.; 16 April 1818; Margaret Stenton 32 BA-319
Mahony, Nathan; 18 April 1811; Catherine Butcher     06 FR-1315
Maidwell, John; 12 Feb. 1813; Kezia Jones            11 BA-21
Main, John; 21 March 1805; Susanna Balzell (15 FR-317 gives
    bride's name as Baltzel)                         01 FR-1152
Maine, John; 24 Dec. 1807; Susan Maine (See also 15 FR-322)
                                                     01 FR-1153
Mains, James; 30 Aug. 1804; Sarah Johnson            09 BA
Mainster, Jacob; 6 Jan. 1808; Sally Wilkinson        21 BA-6
Maizo, John; 5 Nov. 1816; Mary Bie                   09 BA
Major, Charles; 22 Aug. 1820; Mary Thomas French     03 BA-604
Major, Jeremiah; 19 May 1814; Susan Miller           14 BA-433
Mallenhauer, Joseph; 5 Sept. 1808; Elizab. Voight    14 BA-424
Maller, Carl; 14 April 1803; Catherine Brunner       15 FR-314
Mallet, Francis Destaing (age 23, from St. Domingo, son of the
    late Francis Mallet and Magd'n Pisten); 19 May 1805;
    Catherine Genevieve Decout (age 20, dau. of John Decout and
    Genevieve Faustine Le Goadre)                    15 BA-219
Mallinger, Jacob; 9 March 1815; Charlotte Cook       14 BA-433
Mallonee, Emmanuel; 25 May 1806; Rachel Mathews      09 BA
Mallonee, William; 17 Oct. 1807; Martha Tudor        11 BA-11
Mallory, Henry S.; 8 June 1820; Ellen B. Hawkins     11 BA-38
Mallory, John; 7 July 1809; Mary Lawrence            02 BA-7
Mallory, John; 24 July 1817; Elizabeth Lockerman     02 BA-37
Malloy, Charles; 19 Nov. 1816; Mary McLaughlin       32 BA-311
Malmsteadt, Olof; 26 June 1805; Polly (02 BA-35 gives bride's
    name as Mary) Boyd                               03 BA-494
Malock, John; 16 Dec. 1818; Harriet Maciffe          17 BA-20
Malone, Daniel; April 1806; Rosanna Murry            02 WA-80
Malonee, George; 11 Jan. 1806; Mary Marsh            09 BA
Malott, Daniel; 1804; Susana Bleu                    02 WA-76
Malott, Peter; Dec. 1810; Susanna Eisenberger        02 WA-88
Malott, Thomas; March 1807; Mary Albert              02 WA-82
Maloy, Patrick; 30 May 1813; Susanna Curtain         15 BA-311
Malsby, David (s. of John, dec., and Mary); 2nd d. 10 m., 1806;
    Mary Coale (dau. of Samuel and Lydia)            11 SF-94
Man, John; 13 Jan. 1814; Sarah Brown                 13 BA-39
Man, Stephen L.; 7 Sept. 1820; Mary Coffin           11 BA-38
Man(?)es, Charles; 6 Dec. 1803; Eleanor Abercrombie  17 BA-3
```

Mandevel, Tobias; 11 Sept. 1805; Tareshea Trippolet   03 BA-494
Manele, Henry; Sept. 1813; Eliz. Beckenbaugh   02 WA-98
Maniger, John; Sept. 1803; Eva Pence   02 WA-73
Manlove, William; 11 Feb. 1806; Rachel Dailey   03 BA-495
Mann, Frederic; 31 Oct. 1816; Mary Parr   14 BA-436
Mann, Frederic; 22 April 1819; Maria Young   14 BA-439
Mann, James; 29 March 1818; Kitty King   11 BA-28
Manner, Gregory; 17 Aug. 1816; Mary Smith   17 BA-15
Mannican, Dennis; 20 Nov. 1813; Bridget Carroll   14 BA-431
Manning, Bartholomew; 27 Jan. 1820; Elizabeth Duane   16 BA-97
Manonesky, Joh.; Jan. 1809; Cath. Kuharich   14 BA-425
Manro, John; 10 Nov. 1815; Ann Maria Wilson   17 BA-12
Mans, Andrew; 1811; Eliz. Lowe   01 PG
Mansburger, Daniel; Oct. 1805; Hannah Jones   02 WA-79
Mansel, Henry; 8 Aug. 1801; Rachel Olster   14 BA-410
Mansen, Harman; 24 July 1817; Nancy Berrum   17 BA-16
Mansfield, Alexander; 8 July 1817; Sarah Moore   16 BA-55
Mansfield, John (of Old England); 25 Nov. 1809; Mary B. Smith
     (dau. of Gen. Samuel Smith)   03 BA-500
Mansfield, John; 28 Oct. 1811; Jane McCausland   02 BA-36
Mansfield, R'd; 2 Feb. 1807; Marg't McCullogh   03 BA-497
Manson, Henry; 12 Feb. 1807; Sarah Kemp   02 BA-5
Mantle, Levi; 5 Dec. 1805; Sarah King   03 BA-495
Mantz, Cyrus; 26 March 1818; Eliza Kuhn   06 FR-1328
Mantz, Ezra; 6 Dec. 1807; Mary Ritchie   01 FR-1153
Manuel, Augustus; 29 April 1802; Elizabeth Millerman   09 BA
Manus, Charles; Dec. 1803 (by Rev. L. W. McCombes); Cheney or
     Clara (or Eleanor) Abercrombie   17 BA-3
Manville, Joseph; 6 Nov. 1818; Deborah Banton (See also 17 BA-20)
                                                       17 BA-18
Maragan, Michael; 19 Dec. 1801; Nancy Keatinge   03 BA-411
Marcher, George H.; 10 June 1819; Elizabeth Wilson   09 BA
Marden, Spencer; Dec. 1817; Martha St. Claire   02 WA-107
Mare, William; 5 May 1805; Jane Bell   11 BA-6
Margaret, John; 6 Jan. 1814; Anna Dob (widow)   07 BA-309
Marin, Michael; 23 March 1806; Jane Gallaher   03 BA-495
Maris, George; 25 Aug. 1818; Mary Deagan   19 BA-72
Mark, Michael; 18 May 1807; Mieze Koch   14 BA-422
Markel, Samuel; 6 April 1813; Amelia Schley   15 FR-327
Markell, Jacob; 28 March 1816; Sophia Schly   01 FR-1153
Markell, John; 4 Nov. 1813; Catherine Mantz (See also 15 FR-326)
                                                       01 FR-1153
Markell, Samuel; 6 April 1816; Amelia Schly   01 FR-1153
Marker, Jno.; 26 Feb. 1817; Eliz. Rheim   14 BA-436
Marker, Joseph; Nov. 1817; Sarah Barringer   02 WA-107
Marker, William; May 1819; Mary Ann Sheetz   02 WA-113
Markle, Jesse D.; 12 Sept. 1819; Mary Armstrong   14 BA-439
Marks, Henry A.; 18 April 1818; Sterling Rose   03 BA-603
Marr, Alexander; 24 May 1807; Thamer Kessington   11 BA-10
Marrell, Thomas; 17 Sept. 1801; Elizabeth Jones   10 BA-1
Marriott, Elisha; 23 Jan. 1814; Ann Tool   13 BA-18
Marriott, John H.; 21 Sept. 1815; Kitty Humphrey   13 BA-22
Marriott, Joshua; 30 April 1818; Henrietta Warfield   13 BA-31
Marrow, John; 25 June 1818; Mary Thomas   06 FR-1328
Marrow, William; 22 April 1802; Eleanor Mulhorn   14 BA-412
Marrs (?), Andrew; 1811; Eliz. Lowe   02 MO
Marsden, James; 15 March 1819; Achsah Brooks   20 BA-223
Marsh, Gail; 1 June 1809; Marg't. Mask   13 BA-6
Marsh, Joel; 9 March 1811; Elizabeth Mills   06 FR-1315
Marsh, John; 19 April 1806; Catharine Madden   15 BA-238
Marsh, Jonathan (s. of John and Margaret); 30 d. 4 m., 1806;
     Levinah Naylor (dau. of John and Mary)   02 SF-100
Marsh, Nathaniel; 5 Oct. 1811; Margaret Cullison   11 BA-17
[Marsh, William]; 8 Sept. 1809; [Elizabeth] Harris   39 BA-23

Marsh, William; 30 Nov. 1820; Dicey Bowlings   08 BA
Marshall, Clement; 30 April 1809; Leah Jenking   09 BA
Marshall, Francis; 24 [June or July] 1815; Nancy Ralph 32 BA-304
Marshall, Jacob; 28 March 1813; Sophia Schley   15 FR-327
Marshall, John; 1 Feb. 1803; Lucretia Shields   03 AA-120
Marshall, John; 6 Oct. 1818; Mrs. Tacy Tebo   37 BA-151
Marshall, John (of Va.); 3 Feb. 1820; Elizabeth Maria Alexander
                                                       03 BA-604
Marshall, John B.; 22 June 1815; Sarah Crouch   11 BA-26
Marshall, Robert; 5 Jan. 1804; Mary Fox   05 AA-4
Marshall, Thos. I.; 3 Oct. 1816; Mary Gibson   17 BA-15
Marsily, Charles; 27 Feb. 1804 (by Rev. L. W. McCombes); Leah
   Goforth   17 BA-3
Mart, Matthaus; 2 feb. 1802; Elizabeth Mart   01 CL-150
Marteny, Geo.; Jan. 1818; Mary Cox   02 WA-108
Martin, (N); 6 Sept. 1812; (N) Thomas (See also 15 FR-326)
                                                       01 FR-1153
Martin, Benjamin; 6 Feb. 1810; Hopewell Hebb   02 SM-188
Martin, David; 12 Oct. 1813; Elizabeth Kille (?)   06 FR-1319
Martin, Edward; 22 March 1807; Margaret Thomas (his first wife)
                                                       01 TA-325
Martin, Edward; 2 June 1812; Lucretia Thomas (his second wife)
                                                       01 TA-325
Martin, Ezekiel; 9 Aug. 1804; Vialetta Shenton   01 DO-41
Martin, Francis Augustin DuBois; 4 Dec. 1820; Catherine Juhit
   Soutz   16 BA-106
Martin, George; 9 Oct. 1808; Mary Fowler   09 BA
Martin, Henry; 30 July 1811; Mary Hemm   02 WA-90
Martin, Jacob; 28 Nov. 1809; Sophia Rohr (See also 15 FR-324)
                                                       01 FR-1153
Martin, Jacob; Oct. 1818; Elizabeth McClure   02 WA-111
Martin, James; 16 Dec. 1802; Milly Price   03 BA-424
Martin, James; 12 March 1811; Sarah Walton   17 BA-8
Martin, James; 21 Dec. 1815; Jane Eugenie Valette   16 BA-29
Martin, James; 2 Oct. 1817; Delia Wattles   20 BA-223
Martin, James H.; 7 Jan. 1820; Louisa Caroline Wood   11 BA-34
Martin, John; 23 July 1801; Mary Reading (See also 06 BA-1)
                                                       11 BA-03
Martin, Jno.; 6 Oct. 1801; Sarah Daugherty   14 BA-410
Martin, John; 1804; Nancy McLane   13 AA-1
Martin, John; 7 Oct. 1804; Phebe Hilton   11 BA-4
Martin, John; 10 April 1810; Sarah Ravenscroft   03 AL-614
Martin, John; 19 March 1812; Maria McConkey   13 BA-14
Martin, John; 9 May 1816; Mary Woodman   06 FR-1324
Martin, John B.; 14 Jan. 1808; Eliza Flemming   05 BA-235
Martin, John J.; 19 March 1801; Maria A. Villard   09 BA
Martin, Joseph; 20 Sept. 1804; Amelia Lawrence   15 BA-209
Martin, Joseph; 20 June 1815; Catherine Polkenhu (?)   20 BA-222
Martin, Peter; 24 March 1808; Catherine Allender   02 BA-6
Martin, Peter; 8 July 1816; Charlotte Kohlenburg   06 FR-1324
Martin, Peter; 18 Sept. 1816; Mary [John]   32 BA-310
Martin, Thomas; May 1810; Susanna Karnes   02 WA-87
Martin, Thos.; 28 Aug. 1817; Ann Price   13 BA-29
Martin, Thomas; 28 Jan. 1819; Ann Hill   01 SO-15
Martin(?), Wm.; 3 June 1811; Eliz. Harrison   14 BA-428
Martin, Wm.; 16 April 1812; Ann Carrick   13 BA-7
Martin, William; Oct. 1816; Jemima Long   02 WA-103
Martin, Young; 17 Nov. 1810; Isabella Carr   05 BA-236
Marvin, Edward; 11 Sept. 1806; Sarah Ford   03 BA-496
Marye, Vincent Auguste (native of France, son of Francis Marye
   and Catherine Durend); 9 Nov. 1809; Louise Reynaud
   Chateaudun (native of St. Domingo, dau. of John Baptiste
   Lenourd de Chateaudun and Margaret Louise Charpentier)
                                                       15 BA-275

Masberg, Andrew; 8 April 1819; Letha Padgett   06 FR-1329
Masberg, David; 15 June 1815; Sarah Riggs   06 FR-1322
Masberg, John; 4 Jan. 1814; Catherine Kurtz   06 FR-1320
Masemore (?), Jacob; 4 Sept. 1804; Catherine Gosover 23 BA-3
Mashaws, Otto; 1 July 1804; Catherine Loll   30 BA-108
Mashett, John; 6 April 1805; Susanna Alexander   03 BA-493
Maskelly, [Patrick]; 24 March 1818; [Ann] Morgan   32 BA-319
Mason, David; 12 May 1805; Ann Fitzgivens   09 BA
Mason, George (s. of Benjamin and Sarah of Little Britain Twp.,
     Lancs. Co., PA); 21 d. 1 mo., 1808; Tabitha Paxson (dau. of
     Joseph and Mary of East Nottingham Twp., Chester Co., PA)
                                                      06 SF
Mason, Henry; 26 April 1804; Rachel Isor   09 BA
Mason, Henry (free negro, s. of Henry and Mildred); 26 Oct. 1800;
     Annastesey (negro woman belonging to Robert Combs; dau. of
     James, a negro man bel. to Mrs. Smith, and his wife Louisa,
     who bel. to Clement Norris)   03 SM
Mason, John; 4 Dec. 1806; Catherine Hertick   02 BA-5
Mason, John; 22 Oct. 1807; Sophia Slaughter   03 BA-497
Mason, John; 24 Oct. 1820; Frances Patterson   11 BA-36
Mason, Peter; 3 July 1817; Mary Carpenter   05 BA-240
Massey, Jesse; 29 Nov. 1801; Hannah Welsh   09 BA
Matchett, Richard; 13 Sept. 1812; Ann Woods   13 BA-14
Mathers, James; 13 April 1807; Sarah Townes   03 BA-497
Mathews, John; 24 April 1806; Catherine Fink   03 AL-614
Mathias, Joseph; 14 Dec. 1817; Priscilla Gerry   32 BA-317
Matley, Martin; 7 Sept. 1801; Sarah Grable   03 BA-406
Matlock, Jno.; 23 Nov. 1811; Mina Kisler   14 BA-429
Matlock, Jos.; 18 June 1815; Louisa Coats   13 BA-21
Matter, Jacob; 3 Dec. 1815; Elizabeth Doll   06 FR-1323
Matter, Johannes; 9 Sept. 1806; Christine Becker   15 FR-319
Matter, John; 9 Sept. 1806; Christina Becker   01 FR-1153
Matthews, Elias; 13 May 1809; Susanna Keplinger   14 BA-426
Matthews, Francis (widower); 18 Dec. 1809; Catherine Walsh
     (widow)   15 BA-277
Matthews, George W.; 19 Oct. 1818; Mary Matthews   11 BA-35
Matthews, Henry; 2 Jan. 1816; Mary Erhart   06 FR-1323
Matthews, James; 15 Nov. 1801; Elizabeth Fowler   10 BA-1
Matthews, James; 14 March 1813; Susannah Beyerle   06 FR-1319
Matthews, Nicolaas; 22 May 1810; Elisabeth Miller   07 BA-30
Matthews, Thomas (son of Thomas and Ann); 7 d. 12 mo., 1803;
     Sarah Hopkins (dau. of Philip and Catherine)   02 SF-87
Matthews, Thomas; 16 June 1807 (by Rev. Thomas 1. Budd); Ann
     Bartlett   17 BA-6
Matthews, Thomas L.; 9 May 1810; Hart. Bussey   13 BA-12
Matthews, William (son of Thomas, dec., and Rachel); 29 d. 1 m.,
     1800; Rebecca Price (dau. of Benjamin and Temperance, both
     dec.)   02 SF-76
Matthews, William; 4 June 1811; Rachel Rigby   09 BA
Matthews, William; 25 March 1819; Emily Rose   11 BA-35
Matthiot, George; 23 June 1808; E. Strammel   30 BA-109
Mattingly, John; 16 July 1820 (with mutual consent of their
     parents); Ann Magers   06 AL-157
Mattox, John; 24 Dec. 1807; Arabella Galloway   09 BA
Mattox, Thomas; April 1805 (by Jno. Bloodgood); Jemima Hammond
                                                      17 BA-4
Mattox, William; 12 March 1807; Susannah Grimes   09 BA
Mattox, William; 21 Nov. 1819; Susan Robertson   13 BA-33
Matzebaugh, Daniel; 29 Nov. 1812; Barbara Zimmerman   02 WA-96
Maudy, Jacob; March 1807; Polly Vanthree (?)   02 WA-82
Maugens, Joseph; 21 March 1820; Sarah Horine   16 FR-76
Maul, George; April 1818; Mary Meller   02 WA-109
Maulden, John; 22 April 1812; Martha Welsh   13 BA-7
Maulsby, Israel D.; 9 Feb. 1806; Jane Hall   01 BA-10

```
Maun, Joseph; 30 Oct. 1802; Sarah Holly              02 SM-185
Maxwell, George; c.1804; Rebecca Harriot Derrington  34 BA-2
Maxwell, John Yeoman; 27 Jan. 1814; Martha Byard     11 BA-23
Maxwell, Robert; 19 April 1803; Elizabeth Rogers     01 BA-10
Maxwell, William; 26 March 1801; Mary Willis         09 BA
May, Amos; 5 Dec. 1802; Frances Allisander           06 BA-3
May, Daniel S.; Oct. 1806; Elis. Flexon              02 WA-31
May, John Russell; 9 Feb. 1819; Elizabeth Barnhouse  16 BA-80
May, Samuel; 28 Dec. 1815; Eve Harlis                08 AL-71
May, Thomas; 11 July 1813; Ann Huler                 07 BA-309
Mayer, Jacob; 10 May 1820; Louisa S. C. Dannenberg   14 BA-440
Mayer, Joh.; July 1806; Phillipina Merckel           02 WA-81
Mayhew, William; 1 May 1817; Nancy Ann Dashiell      17 BA-16
Maynard, Foster; 17 Oct. 1811; Synthia Parsons       11 BA-17
Maynard, Quinsey; April 1814; Mary Murray            20 BA-222
Maze, James; 8 June 1820; Mary Wertinbaker           16 FR-76
M'Abee, Cassaway; Dec. 1810; Margaret Isenberger     02 WA-88
McAldin, Robert; 9 Dec. 1812; Fanny Wolfington       13 BA-15
McAlister, (N); 29 Jan. 1815; Ann Waters (both of QA Co.)
                                                     01 QA-53
McAllister, (N); 29 Jan. 1815; Ann Waters, both of QA 02 TA-43
McAllister, Christopher; 10 July 1805; Margaret Morton (see also
    02 BA-35)                                        03 BA-494
McAllister, John; 29 April 1802; Mary Miller         03 BA-416
McAllister, Richard; 5 July 1807; Mary Brannon       15 BA-251
McAllister, Rev. Richard; 16 Aug. 1820; Jane Barry   17 BA-22
McAllister, Rob't; 3 Dec. 1808; Mary Bray            14 BA-425
McAtee, Clement; 11 June 1801; Rebecca Thomas        22 BA-410
McAuley, William; 28 Sept. 1819; Rebecca Blatchley   13 BA-40
McBlair, Michael; 9 June 1802; Pleasant Goodwin      28 BA-1
McBride, Bernard; 14 Nov. 1806; Ann McClagherty (both natives of
    Ireland)                                         15 BA-243
McBride, Edward; 21 Jan. 1808; Ann Callaghan         15 BA-259
McBride, Edward; 23 July 1811; Sarah Havette         04 FR-17
McBride, John; 18 Aug. 1805; Elizabeth Winters       15 BA-225
McBriedy (?), Anthony; 12 May 1810; Sally Willis     14 BA-427
McCafferty, John; 30 June 1814; Elizabeth French     09 BA
McCallister, James B.; 28 June 1808; Sarah Dickey    05 BA-235
McCallister, John; 21 Aug. 1809; Sarah Mallet        02 BA-7
McCan, Henry; 26 Oct. 1818; Mary Cunningham          32 BA-322
McCan, Patrick; 21 Feb. 1811; Eleanor Miller         15 BA-285
McCandless, James; 25 Dec. 1803; Marg't March        21 BA-5
McCann, James; 13 Dec. 1815; Ann Roach               21 BA-8
McCann, Thomas; 16 May 1809; Elizabeth Norris (See also
    15 FR-323)                                       01 FR-1153
McCannon, James; 4 March 1817; Mary Sellers          13 BA-27
McCardell, Wm.; 4 Nov. 1813; Margaret Powlas         02 WA-98
McCarder, John; Aug. 1806; Nellie McCool             02 WA-81
McCardle, Henry; 24 Feb. 1811; Patty Chory           15 BA-285
McCarter, James; 28 April 1814; Mary Lemmon          13 BA-18
McCarty, Archibald; 12 Jan. 1812; Mary Ferby         03 AL-614
McCarty, Archibald; 30 April 1817; Sarah Ann Holland 16 AA-35
McCarty, Patrick; 26 Jan. 1803; Mary Roney (natives of Ireland)
                                                     15 BA-176
McCary, Hugh; 2 March 1807; Mary McLaughlin          31 BA-19
McCaskey, Edward; 22 Sept. 1820; Mary Jones          13 BA-41
McCaughlin, Irvine; 16 Dec. 1815; Deborah Duffield   03 BA-507
McCauley, Jas.; 19 April 1806; Jane Glenn Bird       03 BA-495
McCauley, William; 12 April 1804; Levina Gambrill    15 AA-3
McCauly, Caleb; 3 Feb. 1814; Ann White               09 BA
McCausland, Alexander; 8 Feb. 1816; Jane McCleary    08 AL-79
McCeney, Benjamin; 1802; Susanna Simmons             07 AA-2
McClain, Archibald; 13 Aug. 1815; Jane Murphy        11 BA-24
McClain, Daniel; Dec. 1810; Rosanna Lowman           02 WA-88
```

McClain, Elias; Dec. 1810; Betsy Herson   02 WA-88
McClain, Thomas; 1805; Rebecca Carline   02 WA-78
McClanachen, Michael; 25 Aug. 1809; Susanna McClery (15 FR-323
     gives month as April)   01 FR-1153
McClanagan, Sam'l; Sept. 1807; Rebb. Long   02 WA-84
McClary, Edward; 28 Sept. 1817; Mary Caughey   32 BA-315
McClary, Peter; 3 May 1820; Hannah Huston   08 AL-77
McClaskey, Wm. E.; 30 May 1811; Sarah Dare   14 BA-428
McClatchel, Jno.; 16 Dec. 1805; Marg't Hook   14 BA-419
McClean, Elias; 8 Aug. 1813; Mary Steiger   03 BA-505
McClean, John; 26 Sept. 1809; Ellen Holland   13 BA-8
McCleave, William; 4 Aug. 1808; Sarah Sibery   09 BA
McClellan, Andrew; 1 March 1811; Mary Danskin   13 BA-9
McClellan, William; 24 Dec. 1816; Elizabeth Gadd   20 BA-223
M'Cliery, John; Dec. 1815; Eleanor Hooper   02 WA-100
McClish, Archibald; 11 March 1819; Catherine Green   37 BA-152
McCloskey, Charles; 28 April 1816; Catherine Dougherty 16 BA-34
McCluard, Wm. G.; 19 Feb. 1810; Mary Finch   13 BA-11
McClung, William; Sept. 1808; Elis. Reitenauer   02 WA-85
McComas, Charles; 31 Jan. 1813; Nancy Study   11 BA-20
McCombs, Lawrence; 26 Nov. 1801; Mary Elis.   27 BA-1
McConkey, Jesse; 19 March 1812; Prisc. Bull   13 BA-6
McConkey, Wm.; 24 Nov. 1818 (date of lic.); Tabitha Morsell
                                                       11 BA-34
McConklin, Charles William; 2 June 1815; Margaret Chase
                                                       16 BA-20
McConnell, Robert; 8 Jan. 1809; Eleanor Burn   05 BA-236
McCormick, John; 1 Sept. 1804; Mary Leary (both natives of
     Ireland)   15 BA-208
McCormick, Michael; 30 Sept. 1801; Ann Monday   15 BA-157
McCormick, Stephen; 23 June 1802; Nanny Kennedy   14 BA-412
McCormick, William; 8 March 1801; Martha Montgomery   03 BA-398
McCoush, James; Nov. 1810; Susanna Ditch   02 WA-88
McCoy, Archibald; 13 Jan. 1803; Jane Campbell   03 BA-412
McCoy, Daniel; 29 Oct. 1805; Patsey Cadle   17 AA
McCoy, Daniel; 21 April 1807; Mary Hendricks   31 BA-17
McCoy, James; 19 March 1811; Eliz. Avey   02 WA-89
McCoy, James; 2 Dec. 1819; Eliz. Clark   13 BA-34
McCoy, Jehosophat; 19 Nov. 1816; Elizabeth Peirce   11 BA-31
McCoy, John; 22 March 1803; Mary Fuller   14 BA-414
McCoy, Joseph (s. of Andrew and Mary, both dec.); 17 d. 2 mo.,
     1803; Ann Hicks (dau. of James and Mary)   09 SF
McCoy, Samuel; 16 June 1816; Magdalena Heilholtz   05 BA-239
McCra, Edward; 11 Sept. 1806; Jane Porter   02 BA-4
McCrea, Robert; 29 March 1816; Maria Sterley   05 BA-239
McCreadon, Isaac; 30 Dec. 1802; Lydia Puntney   09 BA
McCrey, John; Oct. 1806; Ketty Fenceler (or Fenuler)   02 WA-81
McCridey, Isaac; 9 July 1816; Mary Brown   20 BA-222
McCristal, John; 1 Oct. 1819; Mary [Hoeg]   32 BA-325
McCrossen, James; 12 Nov. 1807; Sarah Barr   15 BA-257
McCubbin, John; 22 Sept. 1803; Eleanor Ridgely   09 BA
McCubbin, John Henry; 21 Oct. 1802; Ann Merriken Jones 03 BA-422
McCubbin, Lloyd; 3 Oct. 1802; Nancy Ridgely   15 AA-2
McCubbin, Nicholas Z.; 18 Jan. 1801; Rachel Rawlings   01 AA-68
McCubbin, William; 19 May 1803; Ruth Cromwell   05 HA-3
McCubbin, Wm.; 12 Nov. 1809; Catha. Grimes   03 BA-500
McCue, Edward; 19 Oct. 1809; Sarah Seigar   13 BA-8
McCue, Edward M.; 25 Nov. 1815; Jane Crag (widow)   16 BA-30
McCuen, John; 15 Aug. 1809; Rebecca Spencer   03 AL-614
McCullam, Mathew; 11 Sept. 1803; Elizabeth Segister   34 BA-1
McCuller, James; 29 May 1812; Julianna Woodruff   11 BA-19
McCulloch, Alexander; 1 Jan. 1801; Sarah Spicer   05 BA-11
McCulloch, James; 15 Sept. 1808; Elizabeth White   05 BA-235
McCulloh, James W.; 29 Dec. 1818; Susan Latimer   03 BA-603

McCurday, Robert; 16 Nov. 1807 (by Rev. Henry Smith); Sarah
  Hurst   17 BA-6
McCurdy, John; 17 Dec. 1815; Eliza Dorsey   09 BA
McCurdy, Jonathan; 30 May 1814; Tabitha Wittid   14 BA-433
McCurley, Hugh; 5 Nov. 1818; Sophia Henry   11 BA-33
Macey, William; 5 June 1816; Sarah McLaughlin   03 BA-507
Macully, James; 23 March 1814; Sarah Duley   09 BA
McDade, Charles; 28 Nov. 1819; Catherine Webster   06 FR-1330
McDade, Peter; 4 Sept. 1806; Bridget McCray   03 BA-496
McDaniel, John N. B.; 24 Nov. 1808; Margaret Barry   15 BA-266
McDavid, Daniel; 20 Dec. 1804; Rebecca Busy (See also 15 FR-317)
                                                           01 FR-1152
McDermott, Henry; 1 March 1813; Susan McElvainer   15 BA-308
McDermott, Peter; 22 Jan. 1814; Bridget McDermott (both natives
  of Ireland)   15 BA-307
McDermott, Stephen; Feb. 1814; Ann Bell   16 BA-2
McDevitt, Isaac; 6 May 1817; Mary Ann Larkins   06 FR-1326
McDole, Robert; 15 Sept. 1806; Sarah Donally   02 BA-4
McDonald, Cornelius; 11 May 1814; Rachel White   16 BA-6
McDonald, Henry; 29 Jan. 1815; Catherine Roche   32 BA-303
McDonald, Hugh; 9 Oct. 1803; Mary Buckley   15 BA-187
McDonald, James; Nov. 1814; Grace McHenry   16 BA-12
McDonald, John; 4 Jan. 1818; Margaret Coulter   16 BA-62
McDonald. John; 22 Sept. 1818; (Della?) Rand   17 BA-20
McDonald, Patrick; 13 March 1815; Catherine Faherty   16 BA-16
McDonald, Peter; 14 May 1803; Rachel Sherman   03 BA-428
McDonall, Hugh; 1 Oct. 1815; Susan McGuire   32 BA-305
McDonnell, John; 29 Dec. 1813; Deborah Chamberlain   09 BA
McDonnell, Henry; 1 Aug. 1808; Helen Dempsey   15 BA-264
McDonogh, Joseph; 3 July 1808; Rebecca Hageman   09 BA
McDonogh, Patrick; 15 March 1810; Cath. Timon   15 BA-279
McDonogh, Peter; 13 Feb. 1804; Cecily Trole (both natives of
  Ireland)   15 BA-199
McDorman, Lewis; 26 May 1814; Nancy Arkman   01 SO-15
McDormet, George; 23 Aug. 1813; Sarah Hughes   05 BA-237
McDowell, Hugh; 1 Aug. 1807; Eleanor Clarke   09 BA
McDowling, Henry; 15 Nov. 1802; Sarah Johnson (See also
  03 BA-422)   02 BA-32
McElfresh, Wm.; 21 Dec. 1802; Sarah Linthicum   03 MO-118
McElherin, Duncan; 12 Aug. 1810; Nancy Narguy   03 BA-501
McElligott, Pierce G.; 7 Oct. 1813; Catherine Sorenson 31 BA-159
McEnnis, John; 24 June 1803; Abigail Dunlevy (both of Fells
  Point)   15 BA-184
McEvers, Daniel; 16 Jan. 1802; Ursula Otts   28 BA-1
McFaden, Daniel; 1 Nov. 1816; Elizabeth Whitson   11 BA-31
McFadon, Charles; 27 Nov. 1806; Jane McClellan   15 BA-244
McFadon, Hugh; 14 Feb. 1804; Hannah McBride (both natives of
  Ireland)   15 BA-199
McFadon, John; 3 Feb. 1802; Rose Roney   15 BA-162
McFadon, Samuel; 21 May 1818; Eliza King   20 BA-223
McFarlon, Patrick; 16 June 1804; Ann McCarty   15 BA-204
McFaul, Eneas; 30 Dec. 1818; Mary Ann Collins   16 BA-95
McGakee, James; 1 Nov. 1806; Nancy Groat   14 BA-421
McGarigan, Francis; 8 April 1802; Nancy Fisher   14 BA-412
McGarithy, John; 4 Sept. 1817; Sarah Wheeler   11 BA-32
McGarman, Robert; 7 May 1804; Nancy McNamara (see also
  02 BA-33)   03-BA-490
McGarrety, Nicholas; 18 Jan. 1804; Mary England (of HA Co.)
                                                           15 BA-187
McGawly, Thomas; June 1818; Marg't Hartman   02 WA-110
M'Gewe, Hugh; Nov. 1817; Maria Miller   02 WA-107
M'Gee, Patrick; 20 Sept. 1812; Elizabeth Strawbridge   15 BA-304
MacGill, Thos., Jr.; 25 Feb. 1817; Elizabeth Simmons   03 BA-602

McGiverin, Patrick; 7 April 1802; Ann Martin (both natives of
    Ireland)   15 BA-165
McGlanan, James; 19 May 1811; Mary Grant   31 BA-100
McGlassan, James Wm.; 3 May 1819; Christiana Rhine 14 BA-439
McGlaughlin, James (alias John); 26 Sept. 1808; Agnes McNealy
                                                    03 BA-498
McGlennan, James; 2 March 1815; Susan Millerion   16 BA-16
McGowan, Barney; 7 Sept. 1801; Ann Smith   15 BA-155
McGowan, James; 17 March 1817; Eliza Brown   13 BA-28
McGrath, Miles; 23 June 1808; Sarah Middleton   39 BA-21
McGrath, Richard (native of Ireland: 1 Aug. 1805; Mary Duffield
                                                    15 BA-224
McGuech, Andrew; 22 April 1809; Mary Nelson   05 BA-236
McGuider, Francis; 10 Dec. 1818; Rosetta Jones (col'd) 11 BA-33
McGuire, John; 18 Nov. 1810; Cath. Connell   15 BA-283
McGuire, Philip; 19 Nov. 1820; Harriet Latchaw   112 BA-38
McGurk, John; 4 Sept. 1813; Martha Dickson (both of Baltimore)
                                                    15 BA-314
McHan (?), Barnaby (?); 30 April 1816; Elizabeth McGee 16 BA-34
McHenry, Daniel William; 23 June 1812; Sophia H. Ramsay
                                                    05 BA-237
McHenry, Francis D.; 1 Dec. 1804; Fanny Moren   03 BA-492
McHenry, Francis D.; 20 Nov. 1817; Milcah Owings   20 BA-223
McHenry, Jno.; 14 Nov. 1813; Martha Hall   03 BA-505
McHenry, John; 7 Dec. 1819; Juliana Elizabeth Howard 03 BA-604
McHugh, James; 18 Aug. 1801; Mary Young   27 BA-1
McIntire, James; 7 Jan. 1808; Susanna Recknor   03 AL-614
McIntire, John; 2 July 1801; Elizabeth Hall   03 BA-402
McIntire, John; 3 Nov. 1803; Lilly Ann Atmore   05 BA-234
McIntire, John; 19 Sept. 1818; Lean Ligget   17 BA-20
McIntire, William; 10 Dec. 1804; Sarah Westbury   11 BA-4
McIntosh, Hector; 2 Aug. 1803; Jennet McKensie   03 BA-432
McJilton, Daniel; 23 March 1805; Sally Rhode   11 BA-5
Mack, Benjamin; 13 Feb. 1803; Mary Bronam   12 AA-2
Mack, Frederick; 8 Jan. 1801; Martha Simmons   03 AL-613
McKain, John; Nov. 1806; Elis. Flora   02 WA-31
McKannon, Michael; 6 July 1802; Martha Garrett   33 BA-15
McKay, Benjamin; 27 Jan. 1807; Susanna Anderson   02 SM-187
Mackay, John; 21 March 1815; Nancy Hunter   03 BA-506
Mackay, John; 28 Nov. 1819; Jane Westcol   37 BA-152
McKay, William; 9 May 1801; Mary Grimes   09 BA
McKean, Alex'r; 1 Sept. 1816; Frans. Griffith   13 BA-27
McKee, Charles; 27 April 1815; Eliza. Wells   13 BA-21
McKee, Cornelius; 6 Nov. 1817; Mary Handley   16 BA-60
McKee, Joseph; Sept. 1813; Mary Pierson   02 WA-98
Mackelfresh, Joseph H.; 7 Jan. 1808; Nancy Aikens   09 BA
McKend (?), Nathan; 21 Aug. 1801; Mary Thompson   14 BA-410
M'Keney, Jabez; 4 Nov. 1813; Milhey Windel   02 WA-98
McKenny, Charles; 16 April 1811; Mary Saffron   31 BA-99
McKensie, James; 16 Oct. 1802; Eleanor Burrows   05 BA-233
McKensie, Normand; 10 Sept. 1805; Susan Burrows   21 BA-6
McKenzie, Alexander; Nov. 1804 (by Jno. Bloodgood); Mary Ruth
    (See also 40 BA)   17 BA-4
McKenzie, Richard; 17 June 1810; Elizabeth Spealman 03 AL-614
McKenzie, Samuel; 7 Nov. 1819 (?) (after the parties received a
    dispensation from Archbishop Carroll for being related in
    blood in the second degree); Henny McKenzie   06 AL-157
McKerley, Alex'r; 6 May 1813; Sarah Nicholson   21 BA-7
McKesson, James; 2 Oct. 1806; Mary Finly (See also 15 FR-319)
                                                    01 FR-1153
McKew, Daniel; 27 Oct. 1801; Harriott Williams   10 BA-1
Mackey, John; 13 Dec. 1814; Elizabeth Thorp   11 BA-22
Mackey, Michael; 16 Aug. 1801; Elizabeth Eisel   15 BA-155
Mackey, William; 24 Dec. 1818; Harriet Alloway   11 BA-35

McKim, Isaac; 15 Dec. 1808; Ann Hollins   03 BA-499
McKinly, Wm.; 21 Jan. 1808; Ann Walton   13 BA-3
McKinnel, James; 23 April 1801; Mary Creagh   15 BA-151
McKinny, Samuel; Dec. 1810; Sarah Wilkinson   02 WA-88
McKinsey, Alexander; 3 April 1805; Fanny Nasel (02 BA-35 gives
     groom's name as McKenzie and bride's first name as Frances)
                                                  03 BA-493
McKinsy, Alex'r; 14 Dec. 1805; Maria Lamb   14 BA-419
McKivan, Charles; 8 Aug. 1809; Elizabeth Thompson 02 BA-7
McKnight, Thos.; 17 Nov. 1811; Mary Denmead   03 BA-503
McKoy, Asia; 12 May 1813; Amelia Lanham   06 FR-1318
McKoy, Stephen; 29 May 1820; Sarah Williamson   20 BA-224
McKray, Patrick; 23 Jan. 1817; Margaret Makers   16 BA-48
McLanahan, James; 8 Sept. 1818; Eliza Tenant   03 BA-603
McLaran, John; 11 Dec. 1805; Ann Moore   15 BA-230
McLaughlin, Andrew; 16 Jan. 1820; Frances Ann Boarman 19 BA-73
McLaughlin, Francis; 24 July 1814; Ann Haley (widow) 16 BA-8
McLaughlin, Francis; 18 May 1820; Nancy Busk   32 BA-329
McLaughlin, George; 23 Oct. 1817; Margaret Dixon 04 HA
McLaughlin, John; 4 April 1805; Eliz'th Culliston 15 BA-217
McLaughlin, Paul; 12 Jan. 1819; Sarah Trott   17 BA-21
McLaughlin, Peter; 2 March 1813; Mary Senseney   14 BA-431
McLaughlin, Robert; 22 Oct. 1807; Mary Donan   11 BA-11
McLeod, John; 31 Dec. 1804; Rebecca Coulson   15 BA-214
McLitten, Daniel; 22 Aug. 1810; Margaret Hoyle   08 AL-81
McLure, John; 15 July 1818; Elizabeth Moore   17 BA-19
M'Luy, Patrick; 1804; Mary Lehn   02 WA-77
McMahon, Charles; 17 Oct. 1815; Ann R. Fenlater   11 BA-25
McMechen, Charles; 16 Nov. 1808 (by Rev. Leonard Cassell); Patty
     Miller   17 BA-6
McMechen, David, Esq.; 22 Oct. 1803; Margaret Carroll (dau. of
     Daniel Carroll of Mt. Dillon)   15 BA-188
McMechen, John; 4 Dec. 1820; Alice Gibbins   13 BA-42
McMechen, Samuel; 19 June 1817; Eliz'th Smith   19 BA-72
McMechens, Jos.; 30 May 1816; Eliza Ann Potee   13 BA-25
McMillin, William; 16 Dec. 1819; Rebecca Davis   20 BA-224
McMullan, John, of Caroline Co.; 17 May 1808; Susan Tubman of
     Dorset Co.   02 TA-41
McMullen, (N); 20 June 1814; (N) Miles   05 FR
McMullen, John; 19 Nov. 1803; Nancy Hayden   03 BA-435
McMullen, Nathaniel; 14 July 1803; Modest Trepannier 15 BA-184
McMullen, Timothy; 12 Jan. 1814; Mary Davidson   16 BA-1
M'Nab, Robert; 7 June 1804; Ann Montgomery   05 HA-1
McNabb, James; 20 Jan. 1817; Mary Flannagan   32 BA-312
McNalty, Patrick; 1 Jan. 1807; Nancy Dwyer   31 BA-17
McNamara, Levin; 27 April 1802; Mary Robertson   01 DO-40
McNamee, Patrick; 27 July 1814; Anna McCrosson   31 BA-177
McNamoo, George; Jan. 1801; Marg. Springer   02 WA-71
McNeal, Arthur; Jan. 1809; Elis. Bayer   02 WA-86
McNeal, John; 11 Feb. 1802; Sarah Childs   09 BA
McNeal, Roger; May 1802; Cassandra Lynch   33 BA-14
McNeale, John; 1 July 1806; Elizabeth Wilson   05 BA-234
McNeil, John; 22 June 1819; Mary Kemp Allen   37 BA-152
McNelly, Barney; 5 Sept. 1801; Margaret Thompson 03 BA-406
McNill, John; 1801; Precilla Cohill   02 WA-72
McNulty, Edward; 25 Aug. 1819; Elizabeth Clogherty 16 BA-86
McNulty, John (widower); 15 Nov. 1809; Catherine Cloherty
     (widow)   15 BA-276
Macon, Charles; 26 Aug. 1807; Maria Theophile (free mulattoes
     from the Island of Martinico)   15 BA-253
McPherson, Angus; 19 July 1814; Henrietta Cohen   13 BA-19
McPherson, Charles; 9 Nov. 1809; Ann Stevenson   02 BA-7
McPherson, Joh.; Jan. 1801; Elis. Lesler   02 WA-70
McPherson, John; 16 Oct. 1817; Mary Waters   20 BA-223

McPherson, W.; 10 Nov. 1818; Eleanor Shock   13 BA-32
McPherson, Wm.; 7 Oct. 1812; Ann Berry   14 BA-430
McPhial, Daniel; 7 May 1805; Rachel Wood   11 BA-6
McRay, Benjamin; 21 Aug. 1817; Susan Rinker   02 BA-37
McSweeny, Paul; 2 June 1802; Harriet Hammond   15 BA-167
McSweeny, Paul; 24 June 1818; Ann Scott   16 BA-70
McTaggard, Hugh; 23 March 1820; Catherine Johnson   11 BA-37
McTibbals, Auzi; 7 Jan. 1819; Susan Gwinn   05 BA-241
McWilliams; Alexander; 26 Aug. 1806; Ann Tabbs   02 SM-187
Mead, Benjamin; 28 Nov. 1820; Louisa Aulia Russell 11 BA-37
Mead, Uriah; 1 Sept. 1803; Ann Sears   03 AA-120
Mead, Walter; 11 Aug. 1803; Elizabeth Breeze   03 AA-120
Mean, Richard; 21 March 1805; Mary Bailey   02 BA-35
Measel, Jacob; 3 July 1814; Nary Ann Heffner   06 FR-1321
Mecarterd, Alexander; 16 Dec. 1804; Esther Parslerp 30 BA-108
Mecham, John (s. of Francis and Naomi); 21 d. 10 m., 1818;
    Hannah Tucker (dau. of David and Elizabeth Ely Tucker)
                                                    05 SF
Medcalf, Abner P. (s. of Abraham and Mary, both dec., of Balto.
    City, MD); 15 d. 9 mo., 1819; Mary Richards (dau. of Thomas
    and Hannah of W. Nottingham Hund., CE Co.)   06 SF
Medcalf, John D.; 6 Jan. 1801; Catherine Willie   05 AA-1
Medcalf, Richard; 5 April 1801; Susannah Gwinn   01 AA-68
Medler, John M.; 19 June 1811; Christine Richstein 14 BA-428
Medley, John; 10 (?) June 1802; Keziah Rathell   03 BA-417
Medtart, Joshua; 21 March 1816; Mary Ann Shultz   14 BA-435
Meek, Aaron; 14 Feb. 1804; Priscilla Mitchell   15 AA-3
Meek, James; 23 Feb. 1804; Mary Maccubbin   05 AA-4
Meek, Western; 13 Nov. 1800; Susanna Perkins   15 AA-1
Meek, William; 6 June 1805; Ann Wisby   11 BA-6
Meekins, John D.; 9 July 1805; Polly Griffith   02 TA-39
Meekins, John D.; 3 May 1808; Nancy Lynch   02 TA-40
Meeks, James; 12 Nov. 1815; Ruthy Ann McCeu   32 BA-306
Meginny, Edward; 7 April 1816; Elizabeth Hunt   17 BA-12
Mehl, Johanes; 4 July 1815; Cath. Groff   14 BA-433
Mehn, Adam; 24 Nov. 1804; Cath. Kemp (15 FR-317 gives bride's
    name as Cath. King)   01 FR-1152
Meissemer, Jacob; 3 Nov. 1801; Mary Schlicher   01 FR-1152
Meissemer, Jacob; 3 Nov. 1801; A. Marg. Schlicher   15 FR-312
Melcher, Frederic; 20 March 1804; Marg't Courtenay 03 BA-490
Melchers, Frederick Philip; 19 March 1803; Margaret Courtnay
                                                    02 BA-33
Mellemy, Daniels; 28 Jan. 1806; Elizabeth Spicer   03 AL-613
Mellinger, Jacob; 4 April 1806; Susanna Augustin   14 BA-420
Meloney, Clement, (of Sussex Co., DE, s. of William and Sophia);
    20 d. 1 mo., 1802; Ann Barton (dau. of William, dec., and
    Elizabeth)   07 SF-2
Meloney, William, (of Sussex Co., DE; s. of William and Sophia);
    24 d. 12 mo., 1801; Celia Wright (dau. of James and Sarah of
    Caroline Co.)   07 SF-1
Melony, Jeremias; 16 Aug. 1808; Mary Moser (See also 15 FR-322)
                                                    01 FR-1153
Melony, John; 9 Feb. 1804; Sarah Gill   23 BA-3
Melony, William, Jr., (s. of William of Sussex Co.,, DE, and dec.
    w. Sophia); 22 d. 11 mo., 1815; Mynta Swiggett (dau. of
    Johnson Swiggett of same Co., and dec. w. Mary) 07 SF-29
Meloy, Philip; 25 Feb. 1803; Catherine Trumpore   09 BA
Melvin, George W.; 29 June 1815; Rosina Graff   14 BA-433
Menchy, David; 29 May 1808; Mary Varris (15 FR-322 gives bride's
    name as Norris)   01 FR-1153
Menew, Thomas; 18 Nov. 1802; Mary Summers   15 AA-2
Mentzer, Conrad; Sept. 1813; Barbara Binkly   02 WA-98
Mercer, Bartholomew; 12 Nov. 1803; Temperance Dorrington (see
    also 02 BA-33)   03 BA-435

Mercer, Isaiah; 25 April 1810 (by Rev. Robert Roberts); Priscilla
    Scott   17 BA-8
Mercer, Wm.; 14 Sept. 1811; Nancy Grimes   03 BA-503
Mercke, George; 15 Oct. 1818; Cath. Lintamore   14 BA-437
Merdick, William; 25 June 1803; Mary Cadren   03 BA-429
Meredith, Benjamin; 30 Dec. 1802; Sarah Martin   34 BA-1
Meredith, Jonathan; 30 Oct. 1806; Hannah Haslett   05 BA-235
Meredith, Thomas; 5 March 1810; Maria Spalding   15 BA-179
Meredith, William; 10 Feb. 1803; Margaret Piet   03 BA-425
Meredith, William; 24 April 1803; Mary Farmer   06 BA-3
Mering, Johannes; 13 Jan. 1801; Catherine Glarin   01 CL-149
Merota. See Miroth.
Merrick, Ezekiel, of QA; 18 Jan. 1812; Polly Plummer of DE
                                                           02 TA-41
Merriden, William; 19 Nov. 1815; Mary Pinkerton   03 BA-507
Merrideth, Benj.; 24 Nov. 1815; Eliza Smith   13 BA-23
Merrideth, John; 1 Aug. 1811; Marg't Eddis   13 BA-13
Merriken, James; 16 June 1808; Catha. Forman   03 BA-498
Merriken, John; 2 Oct. 1806; Eliza Sleppey   03 BA-496
Merriken, William; 29 Nov. 1803; Elizabeth Chaney (see also
    02 BA-33)   03 BA-436
Merritt, Caleb; 6 Aug. 1819; Susan Baker   13 BA-33
Merritt, Henry; 18 June 1801; Rachel Hawkins   03 BA-401
Merritt, Jarvis; 30 june 1816; Juliann Waters   08 BA
Merritt, Trustin; 7 Jan. 1801; Peggy Bryan   14 BA-408
Merryman, B.; 23 Nov. 1819; Mary Ann Short   03 BA-604
Merryman, Elijah E.; 20 Sept. 1804; Cassandra Dye Harvey
                                                           09 BA
Merryman, George; 13 July 1818; Eleanor Coleman   32 BA-320
Merryman, Job; 1 April 1819; Marg't Levely   13 BA-32
Merryman, Nicholas, of Elijah; 16 Dec. 1802; Charlotte
    Worthington (01 BA-65 gives date as 10 Dec.)   01 BA-9
Mertengel, Hermanus; 14 Feb. 1808; Catharina Dreikseler
                                                           39 BA-21
Mertz, Daniel; 20 Sept. 1818;; Elizabeth Kurfman   06 FR-1329
Messenheimer, Peter; 21 Dec. 1801; Barbara Rheinland   01 CL-150
Messerly, George; Dec. 1801; Mary Schafer (See also 01 FR-1152)
                                                           15 FR-312
Messick, Ezekiel (of QA Co.); 18 Jan. 1812; Polly Plummer (of
    the Delaware)   01 QA-53
Metcalf, James; 17 Feb. 1817; Eliza Matthews   06 FR-1326
Metler, Isaac; 22 March 1801; Maria Heinert   01 CL-149
Metstruff, Johann; 6 Feb. 1806; Anna Kromer   07 BA-305
Mette, Henry; 21 June 1805; Margaret Barrot   14 BA-418
Mettee, Andrew; c.1808; Mary Roe   13 BA-38
Mettee, Joseph; 16 Nov. 1820; Ann McDermott   14 BA-440
Mettee, Leonard; 25 Dec. 1813; Ann Chamberlain   14 BA-432
Mettee, Martin; 8 Oct. 1818; Elisab. Howard   14 BA-437
Mettinger, Christoph A.; 16 March 1819; Sophia Toy   14 BA-438
Metyr, Joseph; 9 March 1810; Mary Conner   11 BA-15
Metz, William; 27 May 1816; Mrs. Lydia West   06 FR-1324
Metzger, John; 7 Sept. 1813; Elisabeth Gelli   07 BA-309
Meyer, Andrew; 24 March 1803; Dorothy Hassefratz   15 BA-180
Meyer, Chas.; 18 June 1803; Polly Wagner   14 BA-414
Meyer, Charles J.; 7 Septr. 1805; Anne Davidson   03 BA-494
Meyer, Friderich Wilhelm; 16 Aug. 1806; Salome Miller   07 BA-305
Meyer, Friedrich; 4 July 1802; Mary Lohrman   14 BA-413
Meyer, George; 18 April 1804; Betsy Wagoner   14 BA-416
Meyer, George; 6 June 1804; Mary Fleming   14 BA-416
Meyer, John Christian; 2 Nov. 1801; Ann Catherine Sugers
                                                           03 BA-410
Meyer, Solomon; 19 May 1808p; Eliza Shane   14 BA-424
Meyer, Wm.; 13 Nov. 1804; Maria Hanson   14 BA-417
Meyers, Geo.; March 1809; Nanzi Welty   02 WA-86

Meyers, Henry; 18 Nov. 1816; Emily Mantalden   14 BA-436
Meyers, Jacob; April 1803; Eliz. Meyers   02 WA-74
Meyers, Jerome Marry; 29 Dec. 1809; Mary Griffin   14 BA-427
Meyers, Joh.; Feb. 1803p Becky Parks   02 WA-74
Meyers, William; 1804; Cath. Carver   02 WA-77
Mezzick, Baptist; 14 Oct. 1801; Mary Johnson   06 BA-2
Miades, Joseph; 1 Oct. 1819; Eliz'th Ridgely   19 BA-73
Michael, Christopher; 21 March 1807; Cath. Grof (See also
     15 FR-313)   01 FR-1152
Michael, Daniel; betw. Sept. 1815 and Oct. 1820; Naomi Gilbert
                                                        07 HA
Michael, Hein.; 18 Jan. 1801; Sus. Gallatin   14 BA-409
Michael, Henrich; 12 Nov. 1809; Maria Gernan   15 FR-324
Michael, Henry; 12 Nov. 1809; Mary Gernan   01 FR-1153
Michael, Wilhelm; 2 Aug. 1809; Elizabeth Schenck   15 FR-324
Michael, William; 22 Aug. 1809; Eliz. Schecnk   01 FR-1153
Michael, William; 6 Oct. 1812; Sarah Potter   03 AL-614
Micheau, John; 5 Aug. 1816; Letitia Andea E. McCaskey 17 BA-15
Michel, John; 3 May 1818; Margaret Achenbach   07 BA-311
Mick, Charles 17 Sept. 1818; Elmira Boyce   17 BA-19
Middleton, Henry; 23 Nov. 1803; Mary Millard   14 BA-415
Middleton, John; 4 May 1820; Catherine McManus   16 BA-100
Middleton, Moses; 12 Nov. 1805; Mary Kennedy   02 BA-2
Miercken, David; 6 June 1802; Eleanor Harrison   09 BA
Milburn, Jeremiah; 12 Dec. 1808; Drayden McClelland   02 SM-188
Milchsack, John; 2 July 1818; Caroline Leninsay   14 BA-437
Mildurs, Aquila; 6 April 1806; Elizabeth Frowbright   30 BA-108
Miles, Archibald; 4 Dec. 1819; Susan Otto   14 BA-439
Miles, John; 1 Aug. 1816; Ann Waugh   16 BA-39
Miles, Samuel; 28 Aug. 1802; Rachel Voer   14 BA-413
Miles, Samuel; 20 June 1805; Elenor Rowland   11 BA-6
Miles, Stanislaus F.; March 1818; Cath. Clark   02 WA-109
Millar, Walter M.; 1 Aug. 1816; Ann M. Denny   02 BA-37
Millard, Samuel; c.1802; Margaret Bull   03 AA-120
Miller, Abraham; April 1808; Mary Zeller   02 WA-85
Miller, Alex'r; 29 April 1809; Mary Kepler   14 BA-426
Miller, Andrew; 24 May 1806; Elizabeth Shady   02 BA-3
Miller, Andrew; 28 Sept. 1809; Charlotte Johnson   02 BA-7
Miller, Arnold; 1801; Anna Jury   02 WA-72
Miller, Augustus; 18 June 1815; Ann Sumwalt   13 BA-21
Miller, Baltzer; April 1820; Rebecca Schriber   02 WA-116
Miller, Charles; 30 July 1817; Augustinia Richards   32 BA-313
Miller, Christ.; Aug. 1807; Cath. Reidenauer   02 WA-83
Miller, Christian; 23 April 1806 (by Rev. Leonard Cassell);
     Lucretia Barnes   17 BA-6
Miller, Daniel; Nov. 1816; Elizab. Newcomer   02 WA-103
Miller, Daniel; 15 May 1817; Mary Fox   06 FR-1326
Miller, David; 28 July 1803; Sarah Myer   03 AL-613
Miller, David; 14 Dec. 1812; Mary Getzendanner (15 FR-326 gives
     date as 17 Dec.)   01 FR-1153
Miller, Franciscus; 21 July 1808; Henrietta Tylman   39 BA-21
Miller, Fred'k; Jan. 1818; Barbara Miller   02 WA-107
Miller, George; 17 Jan. 1801; Cassander Mager   09 BA
Miller, George; 1802; Nanzi Thompson   02 WA-72
Miller, George; 4 Jan. 1804; Martha Marshall   02 BA-33
Miller, George; 20 June 1807; Hannah Mumford   14 BA-422
Miller, George; 24 May 1808; Mary Shafer (See also 15 FR-322)
                                                       01 FR-1153
Miller, Geo.; 29 May 1812; Sarah Smith   13 BA-16
Miller, George; 28 June 1812; Margaret Parkinson   03 AL-614
Miller, George; 1 Jan. 1815; Margaretha Croney   07 BA-309
Miller, George; 9 June 1815; Christiana Cole   20 BA-222

Miller, George H.; 7 March 1810; Charlotte Anton Miller
                                                      14 BA-427
Miller, George W.; 14 Feb. 1809; Harriot Jacob   02 BA-35
Miller, Henry; Nov. 1801; Cath. Shnyder or Shuyler   02 WA-72
Miller, Henry; 12 Oct. 1809; Maria Rigeas   14 BA-226
Miller, Henry; 26 Sept. 1815; Catherine Meyer   07 BA-311
Miller, Henry O.; 16 Nov. 1819; Ann S. Parker   20 BA-223
Miller, Howard; 3 Feb. 1801; Elizabeth Marriott   15 AA-1
Miller, Jacob; Aug. 1802; Cath. Werner   02 WA-73
Miller, Jacob; 10 May 1806; Elizabeth Swan   14 BA-420
Miller, Jacob; 6 July 1806; Mary Edwards   03 AL-614
Miller, Jacob; 1 Jan. 1807; Nancy Ricketts (See also 02 MO)
                                                      01 PG
Miller, Jacob; March 1814; Susanna Artz   02 WA-99
Miller, Jacob; March 1820; Nancy Strite   02 WA-116
Miller, Jas.; 12 Dec. 1811; Ann M. Godman   13 BA-14
Miller, James; 21 March 1813; Ann Maria Elms   09 BA
Miller, Johan; 15 Oct. 1820; Jane Degroft   07 BA-312
Miller, John; 1 Jan. 1801; Ann Hinton   15 AA-1
Miller, John; 31 Jan. 1801; Cath. Frick   14 BA-408
Miller, John; c.1802; Eliz'th Turner   03 AA-120
Miller, Jno.; 1 March 1802; Elizab. Dries   14 BA-412
Miller, John; 22 July 1802; Margaret Cooper   09 BA
Miller, Jno.; 6 Jan. 1804; Christina Hoffer   14 BA-416
Miller, Jno.; 27 Feb. 1804; Wilhelmina Busch   14 BA-416
Miller, John; 25 Sept. 1804; Ellen Handling   05 BA-234
Miller, Joh.; 1805; Elis. Shane   02 WA-77
Miller, John; 1 Oct. 1809; Catherine Jacobs   03 AL-614
Miller, John; 9 Sept. 1810; Nancy Young   13 BA-10
Miller, John; 4 Nov. 1811; Jane Colling   03 BA-503
Miller, John; 28 Feb. 1812; Sally Herring (See also 15 FR-325)
                                                      01 FR-1153
Miller, John; 31 March 1812; Elisab. Snyder   02 WA-93
Miller, John; 3 Dec. 1812; Anne Davis   09 BA
Miller, John; 13 Dec. 1812; Margaret Hawken   02 WA-96
Miller, John; 13 May 1813; Sus. Kreps   02 WA-97
Miller, John; 5 Dec. 1813; Cath. Powlas   02 WA-99
Miller, John; 14 Aug. 1817; Susannah Kerr   06 FR-1326
Miller, John; Feb. 1818; Cath. Cranmer   02 WA-108
Miller, John; March 1818; Mary Halfestine   02 WA-108
Miller, John; 7 July 1818; Margaret Lainhart   13 BA-40
Miller, John C.; 17 Oct. 181; Anna Schoenmaker   15 BA-292
Miller, John Nicolaus; 13 Feb. 1812; Elizabeth Christin
                                                      07 BA-308
Miller, John W.; 24 Feb. 1817; Ann Catherine Kolb   06 FR-1327
Miller, John W.; Jan. 1819; Harriot H. Patton   02 WA-112
Miller, Joseph (?); April 1808; Marg. Everly   02 WA-85
Miller, Lewis; 24 Feb. 1807; Patsy Kensy (15 FR-320 gives bride's
    name as Hensy)   01 FR-1153
Miller, Martin; 12 April 1818; Susannah Snook   06 FR-1328
Miller, Mat.; 7 May 1812; Milcah Miller   13 BA-7
Miller, Merritt; 18 Dec. 1814; Ann Scott   01 CR-272
Miller, Michael; 3 July 1813; Elizabeth Wigel   06 FR-1319
Miller, Michael; 21 Sept. 1816; Sarah Durgan (?)   17 BA-15
Miller, Michael; 19 Nov. 1818; Isabella Giese   17 BA-20
Miller, Nich's; 10 Aug. 1810; Eliza'h Carmichael   03 BA-501
Miller, Peter Arnold; Dec. 1803; Elis. Gass   02 WA-75
Miller, Philip; 7 July 1807; Mary McDonald   03 AL-614
Miller, Philip; 28 Oct. 1816; Elizabeth Jones   16 BA-43
Miller, Robert; 20 Sept. 1801; Sarah Boges   30 BA-108
Miller, Robert; 27 Dec. 1801; Elizabeth Butler (both free
    negroes)   15 BA-160
Miller, Robert; 16 April 1811; Cath. Kouch   02 WA-89
Miller, Robert; 24 Nov. 1814; Juliana Cowen   31 BA-185

Miller, Samuel; Oct. 1816; Elisab. Kershner   02 WA-103
Miller, Thomas; 20 Feb. 1803; Margaret Sappington   15 AA-2
Miller, Thomas; 4 July 1820; Elisab. Hennig   14 BA-440
Miller, Thomas; 14 Nov. 1820; Sarah Miller   01 CR-272
Miller, Valentine; 3 Nov. 1818; Elizabeth Fillbron 14 BA-438
Miller, Walter H.; 9 June 1812; Sarah Scott   01 CR-272
Miller, Wilhelm; 13 April 1802; Maria Blumenschein 01 CL-150
Miller, William P.; 11 Nov. 1819; Mary Ann Elliott 03 BA-604
Milleran, Jacob; 10 Sept. 1817; Mary Brensinger   14 BA-436
Millerson, Samuel; 14 Sept. 1809; Merab Lowe   08 BA
Millifield, William; 20 Jan. 1815; Catherine McGraw 17 BA-10
Milliman, George; 24 May 1807; Sarah Voss   13 BA-2
Million, Joseph (native of Grenoble, son of Francis and Mary
    Thomas Million); 2 Nov. 1805; Mary Magdalene Bartholomee
    (dau. of Philip Joseph Bartholomee, native of Artibonite,
    St. Domingo)   15 BA-230
Millium, Moses; 1 March 1820; Mrs. Sarah Leeman   37 BA-152
Mills, Archibald Spence; 15 Nov. 1803; Eleanor Sollers (See also
    02 BA-33) Eleanor Sollers   03 BA-435
Mills, Chs. H.; 8 July 1812; Eliza Powlas   13 BA-17
Mills, Ezekiel; Oct. 1812; Mary Ann Sands   03 BA-504
Mills, Henry; 2 Oct. 1802; Penny Hopkins   09 BA
Mills, William; April 1804 (by Rev. L. W. McCombes); Margaret
    (Mary) Snyder   17 BA-3
Mills, William; 18 April 1816; Mary Eliza Darley 16 BA-32
Milwater, Thomas; 15 June 1816; Henrietta McWeedon 02 BA-37
Minchin, Humphrey; 2 June 1803; Margaret Guttro (02 BA-32 gives
    her name as Guthron)   03 BA-428
Mines, Atticus; 16 Dec. 1805; Rachael Myers (colored) 21 BA-6
Minks, Andrew; 6 Feb. 1818; Margaret Matthews   14 BA-437
Minling, William; 20 Jan. 1817; A. Risinger   30 BA-109
Minnich, John; 17 May 1819; Frederica Eichenbrod 14 BA-439
Minnich, Michael; 9 May 1814; Mary Ann Hull   14 BA-433
Minskey, Sam'l; 6 April 1809; Ann MacCubbin   03 BA-499
Mirdick, William; 25 June 1803; Mary Cadren   02 BA-32
Miroth, Joannes [Merota]; 19 (?) 1807; Susanna Miller 39 BA-20
Miskelly, Hugh; 30 June 1817; Elizabeth [Falconer] 32 BA-313
Mitchel, John; 26 Dec. 1801; Elenor King   15 AA-2
Mitchel, Washington; 24 Dec. 1808; Mary Grevey (?) 14 BA-425
Mitchell, James W.; 11 April 1814; Ann Maria Price 16 BA-3
Mitchell, Jas.; 6 March 1802; Caroline Greby   14 BA-412
Mitchell, John; 25 Sept. 1813; Mary Ann James   15 BA-317
Mitchell, John; 22 July 1819; Frances B. Sweatman 21 BA-9
Mitchell, Joseph; 12 Dec. 1803 at Easton, Kent Co.; Sophia
    Granger   15 BA-192
Mitchell, Matthew; 7 Jan. 1807; Ann Peacock   17 BA-6
Mitchell, Richard B.; 5 Oct. 1809; Elizabeth Bedford 05 BA-236
Mitchell, Robt.; 21 Aug. 1807; Phebe Bell   14 BA-422
Mitchell, Sam'l; 7 Dec. 1809; Susan Lemmon   13 BA-8
Mitchell, Shadrick; 9 Dec. 1820; Mary Frazier   13 BA-42
Mitchell, Thomas; 20 May 1804 (by Rev. L. W. McCombes); Rebecca
    Ann Greenwood   17 BA-3
Mitchell, William; 19 July 1801; Polly Bell   15 AA-1
Mitten, William; 20 July 1817; Mary Goslin   06 FR-1326
Mitzgar, Wm.; 15 Nov., 1814; Marg't Kreber   13 BA-20
Mix, James; 12 July 1803; Anne Aitken   03 BA-430
Mix, Louis; 13 April 1815; Rebecca Patterson   11 BA-25
Moale, Robert North; 2 July 1801; Frances Owings (see also
    18 BA-65)   01 BA-9
Moan, Richard; 21 March 1805; Mary Bailey   03 BA-493
Moats, Joseph; Nov. 1817; Hannah James   02 WA-107
Mockeboy, Kinsey; 27 Dec. 1810; Ann Jordan   05 BA-236
Moffit, John; 28 Jan. 1815; Mary Glenn   03 BA-506
Moffitt, James; 21 Jan. 1818; Ann Roache   03 BA-602

```
Moke, John; 14 Nov. 1818 Elizabeth McClain         11 BA-35
Molan, Walter; 26 Nov. 1818; Harriet Bridge        32 BA-323
Molen, Noble; 25 Dec. 1817; Sarah Bibbins          06 FR-1327
Moles, Micajah; 1 Sept. 1805; Elizabeth Leckler    15 BA-226
Mollen, Peter; 20 Oct. 1816; A. Fowble             30 BA-109
Molloy, James; 13 Nov. 1804; Mary Wills            15 BA-211
Moloney, James; 5 May 1818; Barbara Adelsperger    05 FR-21
Molter, Francis; 18 Dec. 1806; Jean Rose Dew       21 BA-6
Molvey, Andrew; 4 Oct. 1803; Diana Jimson          01 FR-1152
Molvey, Andrew; 4 Oct. 1803; Diana Johnson         15 FR-315
Momoro?, Nicholas (native of Besancon in Franche-Comte); 28 Jan.
    1801; Ann Allaert                              15 BA-148
Mong, (N); 1804; Sus. Funk                         02 WA-77
Mong, Jacob; Feb. 1809; Marg. M'Millon             02 WA-86
Monghler, Christ.; 1801; Cath. Crow                02 WA-72
Monks, John; 25 Feb. 1805; Sarah Rebecca Lewis     33 BA-41
Monmonier, Francis; 21 June 1812; Susan Boyle      31 BA-126
Monny, Robert; Dec. 1803 (by L. W. McCombes); Elizabeth Holmes
                                                   17 BA-3
Monsarrat, David; 7 July 1803; Ann Weaver          21 BA-5
Monsrey (?), Robert; 19 Dec. 1803; Elizabeth Holmes 17 BA-3
Montgomery, Alexander; 17 April 1801; Nancy Walton 03 BA-399
Montgomery, Andrew; 4 May 1820; Priscilla Laws     17 BA-22
Montgomery, Nath.; 21 Jan. 1810; Barbara Bradford  21 BA-7
Montgomery, William; 1 Feb. 1820; Mary Ann Butler  04 HA
Montooth, Wm.; 22 Dec. 1810; Marg't Hannan         03 BA-502
Moody, Edward; 26 Aug.1815 (by Joshua Wells); Margaret Willis
                                                   17 BA-11
Moody, Ira L.; 15 April 1813; Nancy Cromwell       14 BA-431
Moody, Isaac; 27 July 1815; Mary Elliott           03 BA-506
Moog, George; 1 Jan. 1804; Mary Banks              14 BA-416
Mooney, Edward McFarlane; 2 Aug. 1820; Elvira Savage 16 BA-103
Moor, George W.; 1 Sept. 1805; Margaret Hussey     11 BA-6
Moore, Bernjamin P. (of TA Co., s. of Robert of Easton, TA Co.,
    and dec. w. Mary); 21 d. 5 m., 1817; Mary Hopkins (dau. of
    Gerard T. of Balto. Town and w. Dorothy)       12 SF-62
Moore, Chas.; 21 Nov. 1816; Esther Clarke          13 BA-27
Moore, Charles; 25 Feb. 1819; Louisa Hughes        06 FR-1329
Moore, Covington; 7 May 1807; Hetty Anderson       02 BA-5
Moore, George; 28 Jan. 1819; Margareth Haller      06 FR-1329
Moore, Henry; 7 Feb. 1811; Elsey Pearce            09 BA
Moore, Isaac; 27 May 1802; Rebecca McNamara        01 DO-41
Moore, James; 11 Dec. 1806; Margaret Fairbank      09 BA
Moore, James; 19 Sept. 1807; Hannah Pearson        13 BA-2
Moore, Jas.; 4 June 1812; Catha. Marion            03 BA-504
Moore, James; 7 Jan. 1816; Sarah Henson            06 FR-1323
Moore, John; 19 Jan. 1801; Margaret Maxwell        03 BA-397
Moore, John; 1 Aug. 1802; Eleanora S. Weybright    30 BA-108
Moore, John; 12 Dec. 1803; Eliza Wickham           03 BA-436
Moore, John; 30 Nov. 1819; Mary Ann Miller         17 BA-22
Moore, Moses (s. of Robert and Mary of Lancs. Co., PA); 19 d. 3
    mo., 1807; Hannah Brown (dau. of Elisha and Rachel of CE
    Co., MD)                                       06 SF
Moore, Nathan; 1 Feb. 1801; Eliz. Mantz            03 MO-117
Moore, Nicholas; 18 April 1803; Rachel Wilson      15 BA-181
Moore, Peter Dent; 8 April 1804; Louisa Stinger    03 MO-119
Moore, Robert; 25 May 1801; Belinda Slade          03 BA-401
Moore, Samuel; 9 June 1802; Peggy Hughes           03 BA-429
Moore, William; 31 Aug. 1801; Elizab. Donnaldson   14 BA-410
Moore, William; 3 Aug. 1817; Ann Stephens          17 BA-16
Moore, William; 11 June 1818; Maria [Manson]       32 BA-320
Moquet,. Michael; 18 May 1802; Annette de Clare (free French
    mulattoes)                                     15 BA-166
Moran, Gab'l; 23 July 1818; Maria Krebs            03 BA-31
```

```
Moran, James; 31 July 1817; Sophia Herbert            03 BA-602
Moran, William; 26 March 1818; Mary Holland           09 BA
Mordecai, Manuel; 4 June 1805; Charlotte Wilson (02 BA-35 gives
     date as 3 June 1805)                             03 BA-493
Morean, Francis; 14 Jan. 1819; Mary Ann Scroggs       14 BA-438
Moreat, James; 27 Feb. 1806; Jane Miles               02 BA-3
Morehead. James; 20 May 1817; Susan Worthington       17 BA-16
Morehead, Turner, Jr.; 12 May 1812; Martha C. Worthington
                                                      11 BA-19
Moreton, John; 14 Dec. 1815; Reba. Leapy              13 BA-23
Morfitt, Robert; 16 Feb. 1804; Sinah Griffith         23 BA-3
Morgan, Arthur; 7 June 1802; Nancy Lacaze             05 BA-233
Morgan, David; 24 Feb. 1801; Sally Squire             11 BA-2
Morgan, Edw.; 21 March 1808; Sarah Day                13 BA-3
Morgan, James Lee; 8 April 1802; Sophia, dau. of John Monks
                                                      33 BA-14
Morgan, Jesse; 16 May 1811; Sally Smith               09 BA
Morgan, Mordecai; 9 Dec. 1819; Rebecca Barker         17 BA-22
Morgan, William (Protestant); 23 April 1802; Mary Connor
                                                      15 BA-166
Morheiser, Philip; 28 July 1805; Magdalena Fogelgesing 15 BA-223
Moringer, Heinrich; Jan. 1801; Elis. Kind             02 WA-71
Morningstar, Philip; 24 Sept. 1811; Catherine Gunard  06 FR-1316
Morriell, Ezekiel; 4 Sept. 1806; Eva Gorades          14 BA-420
Morris, Anthony P. (of Phila., s. of Isaac and Sarah); 14th d. 9
     mo., 1820; Anne Husbands (dau. of Joshua and Margaret)
                                                      11 SF-124
Morris, Archibald; July 1819; Mary Holbert            02 WA-113
Morris, Jesse; c.1804; Eleanor Sater                  34 BA-2
Morris, John; 3 Feb. 1803; Dorcas Mitchell            15 AA-2
Morris, John; 19 Sept. 1811; Sarah Shevard            13 BA-13
Morris, John; 10 or 20 Nov. 1815; Anne Marie Wilson   17 BA-12
Morris, John B.; March 1817; Ann Maria Hollingsworth  03 BA-602
Morris, Morris; 31 Oct. 1819; Elizabeth Lusby         11 BA-36
Morris, Owen; 17 Aug. 1815 (by Joshua Wells); Mary Fowler
                                                      17 BA-11
Morris, William; 27 Jan. 1801; Mary Ross              09 BA
Morriset, Joseph; 27 Nov. 1810; Theresa Jarbo         31 BA-93
Morrison, James; 13 Oct. 1818; Frances Knout          05 FR-25
Morrison, James; 24 Oct. 1819; Joanna Lonnogan        16 BA-88
Morrison, James; Oct. 1820; Nancy Corse               02 WA-117
Morrison, John; 8 Oct. 1802; Margaret Hamilton        03 BA-421
Morrison, John; 8 Jan. 1807; Sarah Wheeler            03 BA-496
Morrison, John; 25 Oct. 1811; Sarah Monteith          03 BA-503
Morrison, Matthew; 17 June 1812; Biddy Cook (both col'd)
                                                      15 BA-299
Morrison, Neil; 25 May 1805; Ann McCoy (both natives of
     Ireland)                                         15 BA-220
Morrison, William; 16 Dec. 1802; Ann Edwards          09 BA
Morrison, William; 28 April 1807; Margaret Cloud      02 BA-5
Morrow, Isaac; 28 Dec. 1817; Marg't Wheelwright       13 BA-30
Morse, Charles H.; 19 Dec. 1815;; Sarah G. Quette     11 BA-24
Mortimore, John W.; 8 May 1815; Maria Smell           11 BA-25
Morton, Alexander; 21 March 1808; Martha Mathewson    05 BA-235
Morton, Henry; 28 Dec. 1820; Mary A. Bryant           22 BA-101
Morton, John; 27 July 1812; Ann Morton                09 BA
Mosby, James; 24 Jan. 1813; Mary McCarl               03 AL-614
Moser, John; 2 Sept. 1813; Mary Schott                14 BA-431
Mosher, James; 29 June 1817; Elizabeth Nickerson      05 BA-240
Moss, Brian; 29 July 1810; Bridget Feeny              31 BA-86
Moss, Charles; 6 Feb. 1812; Mary Wallbrook            31 BA-119
Moss, Christian; 16 Jan. 1817; Mary Patterson         11 BA-27
Moss, Stephen; 4 July 1803; Maria Lincke              14 BA-415
Mosure, William; 24 May 1812; Ann Brown               13 BA-7
```

```
Mott, Joshua (son of John and Mary); 30 d. 11, 1808; Rachel
  Mason (dau. of James and Rachel)                02 SF-109
Moudy, George; Feb. 1816; Eve Holtzman            02 WA-101
Moudy (?), Jacob; Feb. 1807; Polly Van Schneagel (?)  02 WA-82
Moudy, Michael; June 1807; Sus. (N)               02 WA-83
Moulionier, Louis; 21 May 1807; Marie Appolonissie Peniro (?)
  (free people of colour from St. Domingo)        15 BA-250
Mouse, Michael; Oct. 1813; Mary Manley            02 WA-98
Mouton, James; 31 March 1810; Hannah Holland       13 BA-12
Mowbrey, Henry E.; 17 Nov. 1818; Mary Bowen       11 BA-33
Moxley, John; 9 Sept. 1806; Frances Moxley        11 BA-9
Moyan, Edw.; 21 March 1808; Sarah Day             13 BA-4
Moyan, William; 20 Jan. 1814; Eliza Armstrong     13 BA-18
Moyer, Christian; Oct. 1819; Susanna Spigler      02 WA-114
Moyer, Peter; Dec. 1816; Elizab. Schlice¶         02 WA-103
Moyers, Fred.; July 1808; Sarah Moyers            02 WA-85
Much, Conrad; Nov. 1818; Cath. Sager              02 WA-111
Muir, James; May 1806; Marg. Locke                02 WA-80
Muler, Elia (?); Sept. 1801; Mary Furn            02 WA-72
Mullen (or Muller), George F.; 2 (?) Dec. 1813; Theresa Muller
                                                  14 BA-432
Mullen, John; 14 Jan. 1806; Ann Morgan (both natives of
  Ireland)                                        15 BA-234
Mullen, Jos.; 11 Jan. 1802; Barbara Schley (See also 15 FR-312)
                                                  01 FR-1152
Mullen, Patrick; 14 March 1801; Juliana Villerette 03 BA-398
Mullen, W.; 31 May 1818; Eliza Wrighter           13 BA-31
Muller, Lewis A. (or C.); 11 July 1809; Eliza Millard 14 BA-426
Mulley, James; 25 March 1802; Clementina Ritter   09 BA
Mullican, Archibald; 23 April 1805; Anna Matthews 03 MO-119
Mullican, Edward; 14 July 1818; Mary Hall         11 BA-33
Mullikin, Rignall; 28 Sept. 1815; Mary Eleanor Croxall 20 BA-222
Mullin, Stephen; 15 May 1812; Cathe. Haslen       13 BA-7
Mully, John; 17 Sept. 1801; Elizabeth Parks       09 BA
Mumma, Jno.; 16 Oct. 1802; Elizab. Andrews        14 BA-413
Mumma, Wm.; 24 Oct. 1815; Christina Rankert       14 BA-433
Mummey, Joshua; 13 July 1817; Maria C. Working    11 BA-31
Muncaster, Zachariah; 25 Sept. 1804; Harriot Magruder 03 MO-119
Muncks, Andreas; 5 Feb. 1818; Margaretha Mathews  39 BA-34
Munday, Thomas; June 1815 (or 1816); (N) (N) (col'd) 11 BA-24
Mung, Adam; Aug. 1806; Elis. Voltz                02 WA-81
Munn, Jno.; 5 Nov. 1807; Violet Handler           14 BA-423
Munnonnee, John; 14 Feb. 1803; Elizabeth Foard    09 BA
Munroe, Richmond; 1 Jan. 1816; Diana Edwards Dilworth 21 BA-9
Munter, Chas.; 29 Aug. 1819; Cath. Eiselin        14 BA-439
Murdock, James; 19 May 1818; Hannah Clouse        16 BA-68
Murphey, Bazil; 25 Feb. 1813; Opha Thomas         13 BA-16
Murphey, John; 23 June 1803; Mary Pickering       06 BA-3
Murphy, Archibald; 20 June 1801; Margery Maloy    03 BA-401
Murphy, Francis; 8 Feb. 1806; Hannah McClain      02 BA-3
Murphy, Isaac; 14 Nov. 1805; Mary Christie        03 BA-494
Murphy, John; 16 July 1817; Mary McGuire          32 BA-313
Murphy, John; 12 Nov. 1817; Ann Lewis             17 BA-17
Murphy, John N.; 12 May 1819; Sarah B. Miller     13 BA-33
Murphy, Samuel; 18 Dec. 1813; Rebecca McArter     06 FR-1320
Murphy, Stephen; 5 Dec. 1818; Ann Burnett         11 BA-35
Murphy, Thomas; 12 Dec. 1816; Jane Downey         06 FR-1325
Murphy, Thomas; 6 July 1819; Dorothy Etchburger   07 BA-311
Murra, James; June 1810; Marg't Baker             02 WA-87
Murray, Charles; 30 Dec. 1805; Jane Randolph      03 BA-3
Murray, Daniel; 8 Dec. 1808; Mary Dorsey          03 BA-499
Murray, Edward; 20 Dec. 1812; Mary Cushner        13 BA-15
Murray, Francis; 13 Aug. 1801; Ann Spear          09 BA
```

Murray, James; 18 Jan. 1816 (by Joshua Wells); Sarah Hatton
                                              17 BA-12
Murray, John; 2 June 1802; Mary Long   02 SM-185
Murray, John; 24 Nov. 1803; Sarah Gray   06 BA-3
Murray, Jno.; 7 June 1808; Ann Laughery   14 BA-424
Murray, John R.; 17 Feb. 1807; Harriet Rogers 03 BA-497
Murray, Mathew H.; 29 Oct. 1811; Marg't Schunch   14 BA-429
Murray, Michael; 30 April 1801; Nancy Maddux 01 SO-15
Murray, Nicholas; 1 Sept. 1808; Elizabeth Watson 05 BA-235
Murray, Richard; 9 June 1808; Anne Ross   15 BA-262
Murray, Thomas; 10 May 1813; Lydia Rutter   09 BA
Murrey, Michael; 14 Jan. 1813; Hannah McFadon (both natives of
     Ireland)   15 BA-307
Murry, John; 2 Jan. 1806; Susanna Randals   02 BA-3
Murry, Stephen; 23 Oct. 1803; Cath. Burall (15 FR-315 gives
     bride's name as Burrall)   01 FR-1152
Musgrove, Pet.; Jan. 1801; Cath. Iseminger   02 WA-71
Musket, John; 6 April 1805; Susanna Alexander 02 BA-35
Muskett, John; 9 Jan. 1806; Susanna Alexander 02 BA-3
Mussey, Asel; 22 Jan. 1805; Sarah Kizer   11 BA-5
Muth, George; 23 April 1820; Margaret Englis 14 BA-440
Muth, Philip; 31 July 1811; Louisa Becker   14 BA-429
Myer, Ezra; 24 Jan. 1813; Sophia Miller (See also 15 FR-326)
                                              01 FR-1153
Myer, Peter; 28 April 1808; Jane Fisher   03 AL-614
Myer, Philip; 19 May 1812; Julian Bell   03 AL-614
Myer, Thomas; 24 March 1818; Ann Ringgold   03 BA-603
Myers, Adam; 7 Aug. 1817; Eliz. Giger   14 BA-436
Myers, George; 5 Jan. 1809; Maria Barry   13 BA-5
Myers, Godfrey; 5 Feb. 1807; Cath. Eisell   15 BA-247
Myers, Henry; 17 July 1801; Julia Snook   03 AL-613
Myers, Henry; 4 Oct. 1804; Eliza Tall   03 BA-491
Myers, Henry; 25 May 1813; Mae Kephardt   02 WA-97
Myers, Henry; 20 June 1816; Mary Whenn   13 BA-25
Myers, Jacob; 22 April 1817; Rach'l Daughaday 14 BA-436
Myers, Jacob; March 1818; Elizab. Sheetz   02 WA-108
Myers, John; 9 Oct. 1804; Ann Eagen   15 BA-210
Myers, Jno. W.; 29 Nov. 1810; Cath. Burger   13 BA-11
Myers, Peter; June 1817; Amelia Binkley   02 WA-105
Myers, Philip; Aug. 1813; Eliz. Muse   02 WA-97
Myers, Samuel; 15 d. 4 mo., 1818; Pauline Iden   10 SF
Myers, Samuel; 2 d., 10 mo., 1813; Mary Frame 10 SF
Myers, Sam'l (s. of Jos. and Rachel); 24 d. 11, 1813; Mary Frame
     (dau. of David and Sarah)   01 SF
Myers, Wm.; 1 Jan. 1811; Ellen Warren   13 BA-11
Myler, John; 27 Jan. 1802; Unity Corry   03 BA-412
Myring, Joseph; 1 Nov. 1807; Susan Bussy   09 BA
Nabbs, William; 6 May 1810; Eliz'h Moor   13 BA-12
Nagel, Christ.; 15 June 1820; Elizabeth Macher   30 BA-109
Nailor, Geo.; 27 April 1809; Celecia Jacobs   13 BA-6
Nailor, Isaac; 1 Jan. 1801; Elizabeth Marsh   03 BA-397
Nailor, James; 5 June 1809; Sarah Parks   13 BA-6
Nants, John; 11 Feb. 1819; Ann Evans   09 BA
Nantz, John; 11 March 1818; Margaret Boyer   17 BA-19
Napp, Thomas; 20 Nov. 1809; Margaret Taylor   09 BA
Nase, Ambrose; Oct. 1808; Mary Wood   02 WA-86
Nash, And'w; 28 May 1810; Sarah McIntire   13 BA-12
Nash, Ephraim; 25 May 1806; Elizabeth Obrien 02 BA-3
Nats, William; 8 March 1808; Patsy Duley   08 AL-82
Naylor, Darby; 19 May 1810; Susanna Calts or Catts   09 BA
Neal, James; 17 April 1813; 15 April 1813; Mary Aubin 15 BA-310
Neale, John; 21 Dec. 1806; Susanna Eisell   15 BA-243
Neale, Joshua; 20 July 1819; Ann Morgan   04 SM

Neall, James (s. of Solomon of TA Co.); 22 d. 4 mo., 1801; Rachel
    Cox (dau. of Isaac)   08 SF
Nebling, Johanes; 27 June 1811; Sally Fisher   14 BA-429
Neebling, Peter; 31 Aug. 1820; Eliza Croker   03 BA-604
Needham, Asa; 3 Feb. 1820; Ann Eliza Lynch   11 BA-36
Needham, Christopher; 23 Aug. 1804; Jane Heartley 03 BA-491
Needles, Edward (s. of Tristram and Ann); 18 d. 4 mo., 1811;
    Elizabeth Troth (dau. of Samuel and Ann)   08 SF
Needles, John (of Balto., s. of Edward and Mary of TA Co.); 29
    d. 5 m., 1811; Eliza Matthews (dau. of Mordecai and Ruth)
                                                   02 SF-117
Needles, Tristram; 22 d. 12 mo., 1808; Susanna Matthews
                                                   08 SF
Needles, Tristram (s. of Tristram and Anna, both dec.); 21 d. 11
    mo., 1816; Sarah W. Nock (dau. of Joseph of Kent Co., DE,
    and Rachel)   08 SF
Needles, William; 24 d. 5 mo., 1810; Sarah Yarnall 08 SF
Neelan, Richard; 3 April 1810; Hannah Wilson   11 BA-15
Neeper, John; 17 Aug. 1820; Mary McLeen   03 BA-604
Neff, Fried.; April 1803; Elis. Schmidt   02 WA-74
Neff, George; 18 Feb. 1806; Margaret Hellmes   03 AL-613
Neff, George; 12 Dec. 1820; Margareth Hessong   06 FR-1331
Neff, John; March 1817; Rosanna Lorschbaugh   02 WA-104
Neff, Peter; 3 Oct. 1805; Nancy Sigler   03 AL-613
Neigh, Godfrey; 8 Oct. 1811; Nancy Katey   09 BA
Neil, William; 19 may 1815; Mary Ealer   03 BA-506
Neilson, Ignatius Michel; 30 April 1816; Luisa Nearry 39 BA-31
Neilson, Wm.; 12 July 1809; H. Welsh   30 BA-109
Nelms, Noah; 15 Jan. 1801; Mary Ann Lemmon   09 BA
Nelson, Basil; 8 Oct. 1812; Rosanna Ferguson   15 BA-305
Nelson, John; 31 March 1802; Jane McCulloch   09 BA
Nelson, John; 29 Feb. 1816; Salsbury Wiley   02 BA-36
Nelson, Samuel; 10 Aug. 1815; Rachel Cooper   17 BA-13
Nelson, William; 20 Dec. 1804; Hannah Hutchings   01 BA-10
Nenniger, John; 13 June 1810; Louisa Kohlstadt   14 BA-427
Nentine, John Gerard; 28 Aug. 1805; Ann Ubick   15 BA-225
Neptune, John; 27 March 1806; Anna Sigler   03 AL-614
Neptune, William; 15 Jan. 1801; Mary Poling   03 AL-613
Neptune, William; 1 Jan. 1811; Lydia Peeman   03 AL-614
Ness, Samuel; 20 Aug. 1818; Elizab. Small   14 BA-437
Netz, Peter; 26 March 1808; Eleanor Rallson   14 BA-424
Neuhaus, John; 8 Nov. 1809; Susanna Dries   14 BA-426
Neukirch, Henry; April 1805; Nancy Furry   02 WA-78
Neukirk, George; Feb. 1817; Polly Mondebaugh   02 WA-104
Nevit, John; 2 Jan. 1800; Susanna Multon   03 SM
Nevitt, William; 13 Sept. 1803; Rebecca Lovejoy   03 PG-1
Newall, John; 6 Feb. 1820; Sarah Vinn   16 BA-97
Newburgh, John; 16 Sept. 1812; Jane Scarlet   11 BA-19
Newcome, Jno.; 14 Sept. 1801; Nancy Jones   14 BA-410
Newcomer, Jacob; 8 Oct. 1801; Mary Black   15 BA-157
Newcomer, Martin; Feb. 1820; (N) Snavely   02 WA-115
Newcomer, Peter, Jr.; March 1820; Ann Good   02 WA-115
Newell, Perry (servant of William Hawkins); 25 Jan. 1816; Nelly
    War (?) (Free col'd girl)   16 BA-30
Newman, Abrsham; 1 June 1808; Laetitia Williams (both free)
                                                   31 BA-42
Newman, George H.; 21 Sept. 1820; Susan Buchanan   03 BA-605
Newman, Nehemiah Joshua Bates; 16 Dec. 1816; Susanna Campbell
                                                   08 AL-83
Newman, Thomas; 18 Sept. 1809; Catharina Towsans   07 BA-307
Newons, Thomas; 25 May 1806; M. Magd. Knauf (See also 15 FR-319)
                                                   01 FR-1157
Newton, John; 11 Nov. 1813; Eliza Townsend   11 BA-21

Newton, Nimrod; 11 Aug. 1818; Temperance Hynson   11 BA-34
Newton, William; 8 June 1820; Marie Gurt   17 BA-23
Ney, George; Aug. 1803; Sus. Knod   02 WA-75
Neymeyer, Hermann; 1 June 1804; Katharina Carpenter   07 BA
Nice, Frederick; 8 March 1807; Delila Stevens   11 BA-10
Niceart, George; May 1806; Mary Stiffler   02 WA-80
Nichol, Thos.; 14 April 1811; Rebecca Taylor   21 BA-7
Nicholas, Charles; 15 june 1815; Mary Teresa Marceline 16 BA-21
Nicholas, Jean; 17 April 1815; Melanie (N) (both French slaves)
                                                       16 BA-17
Nicholas, Jos.; 18 Sept. 1817; Mary Magdalen (both French: man
      white, woman black)   16 BA-56
Nicholas, Lewis; 22 Sept. 1804; Elizabeth Zebbne (See also
      02 BA-34)   03 BA-491
Nicholas, Matthias; Oct. 1819; Mary Poorman   02 WA-114
Nicholet, Julian; 30 Nov. 1818; Emily Von Bale   14 BA-438
Nicholls, Andrew; 9 Oct. 1817; Jane Dorman   17 BA-17
Nichols, Benj.; 5 Jan. 1802; Susanna Lowry (See also 15 FR-312)
                                                       01 FR-1157
Nichols, Pearson; 8 Oct. 1807; Sarah Ann Pratt   03 BA-497
Nichols, William; 13 March 1808; Mary Bond   08 BA
Nicholson, Benjamin; 15 Dec. 1803; Ann Long   05 AA-5
Nicholson, Christopher; 26 May 1804; Mary James   03 BA-491
Nicholson, Christopher; 12 Jan. 1818; Marg't Guppin   14 BA-438
Nicholson, Isaac; 30 Aug. 1804 (by Jno. Bloodgood, in list of
      marriages for blacks); Ann Williamson   17 BA-5
Nicholson, John; 4 April 1801; Mary Bateman   09 BA
Nicholson, John; 7 April 1801; Charity Fullfurt   15 BA-101
Nicholson, John; 14 Dec. 1809; Prudence Hilton   13 BA-8
Nicholson, Michael; 27 Nov. 1812; Nancy Conley   02 BA-36
Nicholson, Nicholas; 7 Jan. 1819; Ann Mitchell   13 BA-32
Nicholson, Patrick; 21 Dec. 1820; Jane Dougherty   32 BA-331
Nicholson, Thomas; 1 March 1807; Sarah Harwood   09 BA
Nicholson, Thos.; 2 May 1815; Mary Fauss   14 BA-433
Nickels, John; 13 Oct. 1803; Elizabeth Walter   03 BA-434
Nickerson, Lewis; 20 Aug. 1801; Elizabeth Vashon   09 BA
Nickison, James; Sept. 1817; Mary Snyder   02 WA-106
Nickles, John; 7 Nov. 1805; Catey Markee   08 AL-83
Nickolson, Nicolaus; 8 June 1810; Catherina Swears   07 BA-307
Nickson, Edward; 25 June 1817; Catherine Burns   21 BA-9
Nicole, William; 3 July 1803; Jennet Jackson   03 BA-430
Nicolls, Joseph; 12 Jan. 1818; Nancy McGargil   03 BA-602
Nicols, Henry; 14 May 1807; Sophia Breish (See also 15 FR-321)
                                                       01 FR-1157
Nicols, Henry; 21 May 1812; Sarah Hollyday (of Henry and Anna
      Maria)   01 TA-321
Nicols, Ninian Riley; 21 Sept. 1806; Barbara Smith Hunt
                                                       03 BA-496
Nicols, Noah; 13 Sept. 1807; Polly Daws   03 BA-497
Nicols, Peter; 1 Jan. 1804; Mary Evit   01 FR-1157
Nicols, Richard; 19 May 1803; Margaret Hudson (02 BA-32 gives
      bride's name as Margaretta)   03 BA-428
Nieghoff, Jacob; 3 Oct. 1820; Sarah Jaffry   14 BA-440
Nigh, Peter; Aug. 1810; Polly Smith   02 WA-87
Night, Ignatius; 1 Aug. 1820; Rachel Seabrooks   14 BA-440
Nightingale, Brister; 12 Nov. 1817; Esther Brown   17 BA-14
Nimmo, William R.; 7 Dec. 1818; Sidney E. Thornton   37 BA-151
Nind, Isaac; 15 June 1810; Sophia Folger   03 BA-501
Nisbet, Alexander; 24 Dec. 1807; Mary C. Owings   05 BA-235
Nix, Jno.; 11 May 1803; Barbara Schmelzle   14 BA-418
Nix, John; 26 Sept. 1803; Cath. Hoffman   14 BA-415
Nixdorf, Henry; 10 Feb. 1814; Susan Medtart   06 FR-1320
Noble, John Frederick; 16 June 1805; Hannah Cuddy   15 BA-221
Noble, Mark; 23 d. 9 mo., 1813; Mary Charles   07 SF-23

Noble, Mark, of NW Fork; 21 d. 11 mo., 1816; Elizabeth Meloney
    (dau. of William Meloney of Sussex Co., DE)   07 SF-30
Noble, Roswell; 25 Dec. 1813; Elizabeth Barrow   09 BA
Noel, John; 3 June 1816; Marie Volage (both natives of St.
    Domingo)   16 BA-36
Noel, Joseph; 17 Jan. 1807; Eliz. Woods   14 BA-421
Noles, William; Aug. 1808; Barbara Lowman   02 WA-85
Nolian (?), Christ.; Sept. 1802; Juliana Wagilly   02 WA-73
Noll (?), John; 30 July 1820; Mary Kelly (both free blacks)
                                                    04 SM
Nolte, Martin; 7 July 1805; Lisetta Casper   14 BA-418
Nolte, Stephanus; 25 June 1809; Anna Maria Peifer (widow of
    Kohler)   39 BA-22
Norman, B.; c.1803; Sarah Kirby   07 AA-3
Norman, Samuel; 13 Nov. 1804; Catherine Kribs   11 BA-4
Norris, Aquila; 10 Dec. 1809; Eleanor Norris   09 BA
Norris, Benjamin; 20 Dec. 1814; Susan Cockey   11 BA-22
Norris, Edward; 5 June 1806; Rachel Williaby   11 BA-8
Norris, Isaac; 13 Sept. 1810; Mary Smith   13 BA-10
Norris, Jacob; 24 May 1803; Henrietta Frick   14 BA-414
Norris, James; 24 Oct. 1802; Anne Collier   03 BA-422
Norris, Jas.; 15 Feb. 1816; Cath. Hahn   14 BA-435
Norris, Joel (s. of Benjamin and Ann); 27 d. 10 mo., 1808; Rachel
    Plummer (dau. of Joseph West and Mary)   03 SF
Norris, John Basil (age 54, son of Thomas and Susanna [Heard]
    Norris); 9 April 1801; Henrietta Norris (age 34, dau. of
    Philip and Monica [Stone] Norris)   03 SM
Norris, Nelson; 21 May 1816; Elizabeth Carnan   03 BA-507
Norris, Rhesa; 29 Oct. 1804; Susanna Dutton   05 HA-1
Norris, Robert H. (s. of Thomas and Ann); 13 d. 11 mo., 1817;
    Mary Morgan (dau. of Thomas and Sarah)   09 SF
Norris, Silas C.; 30 April 1817; Eliza March   03 BA-602
Norris, Wm.; 7 Aug. 1806; Sarah Hough Martin   03 BA-495
North, Edward; 26 July 1804; Prudence Wyles   21 BA-5
North, William; 22 Dec. 1807; Polly Pritchard   21 BA-6
Northcraft, James; 28 Jan. 1802; Rachel Fryer   03 MO-118
Norton, Stephen I.; 17 Sept. 1818; Mary Ann McDaniel 14 BA-437
Norwood. John; 14 May 1820; Margaret Samuels   17 BA-22
Norwood, Nicholas; 14 April 1818; Mary Choat   08 BA
Norwood, Samuel; 26 Dec. 1809; Henrietta Ridgely   13 BA-8
Nott, Joseph; 4 Feb. 1819; Sara Thornton   04 FR-18
Nottage, John; 13 Oct. 1811; Rachel Disney   09 BA
Notts, Geo.; 27 Aug. 1809; Elizabeth Sherman   03 BA-500
Noulson, Jos.; 28 Sept. 1811; Mary Ann Otridge   13 BA-13
Nouvell, Peter; 24 July 1813; Mary Holmes   15 BA-312
Nowell, James; Aug. 1810; Eliz. Malott   02 WA-87
Nowell, Will; 17 Nov. 1811; Mary Ann Lambert   02 WA-92
Noyes, John R.; 3 Feb. 1818; Mary Ann Adair   20 BA-223
Nuss, Jacob; 14 Aug. 1814; Polly Cantner   06 FR-1321
Nussbaum, Daniel; 26 Aug. 1810; Mary Sowers   15 FR-324
Nussbaum, Johannes; 22 Jan. 1804; Esther Burger   15 FR-316
Nussear, Jacob (widower); 18 Dec. 1803; Elizabeth Verley
    (widow)   15 BA-192
Nussear, Jacob; 16 Feb. 1806; Susanna Crouss   15 BA-236
Nusz, Ezra; 18 Feb. 1819; Sophia Metzger   06 FR-1329
Nuszbaum, Daniel; 26 Aug. 1810; Mary Sowers   01 FR-1157
Nuszbaum, John; 22 Jan. 1804; Esther Burger   01 FR-1157
Nuts, Henry; 18 Oct. 1810; Jane Richardson (free blacks)
                                                    03 BA-502
Oats, John; 30 Dec. 1802; Sarah Denton   09 BA
Ober, Jacob; 5 Aug. 1813; Mary Grice   08 BA
Oberholzer, Joh.; 20 Jan. 1801; Cath. Fitzgerald   14 BA-409
Oberhost, Friedr. Gotlieb; 29 March 1801; Maria Klein 14 BA-409

Oberhouser, Christian; 24 Aug. 1820; Tempy Seise (See also
    16 FR-76)   03 FR-60
Oberhuff, Frederick; 19 Nov. 1816; Hanna Opergraf   14 BA-436
O'Boyle, James; 15 Oct. 1807; Rhoda Hughes (See also 15 FR-321)
                                                            01 FR-1158
O'Brien, Henry; 30 March 1812; Betsy B. Smith   14 BA-430
O'Brien, J. (slave); 21 Oct. 1820; Emily Butler (free) 05 FR-36
O'Brien, John; 2 March 1819; Julia Carroll   03 BA-603
O'Brien, Michael; April 1820; Jane Graham   16 BA-99
O'Connor, James (age 23); 3 Aug. 1806; Sarah Morris (age 24,
    widow of the late John Angel)   31 BA-10
O'Connor, Thomas; 11 July 1805; Catherine Liddy   15 BA-223
O'Derfer, Henry; May 1817; Elizab. Hammond   02 WA-105
Odle, Abraham; 18 march 1813; Keturah Gean   08 BA
Odle, John; June 1814; Mary Carter   08 BA
Odle, Lot; 8 Oct. 1806; Elizabeth Frederick   03 AL-614
O'Donnell, Barney; 24 May 1802; Margaret Reed   15 BA-167
O'Donnell, Bernard (native of Ireland); 24 March 1811; Mary
    M'Kenny   15 BA-286
O'Donnell, Christopher Columbus; 8 Sept. 1813; Eleanor Pascault
                                                           15 BA-316

O'Farrell, Edward; 6 Sept. 1802; Elizabeth Nugent   15 BA-171
Offutt, Andrew; 20 April 1802; Eliz. Warfield   03 MO-118
Ogden, David; 11 Nov. 1810; Nancy Deems   13 BA-11
Ogden, John; 11 Aug. 1810; Eleanor McCann   15 BA-283
Ogden, John Wesley; 25 Dec. 1817; Nancy Ogden   20 BA-223
Ogden, Nathan I.; 25 May 1815; Catherine Spears   11 BA-24
Ogden, Thomas; 1802; Clarissa Ogden   07 AA-2
Ogen, Lawrence; 5 Oct. 1820; Jane Maybee   04 FR-20
Ogin, Peter; 1801; Jane Jinkins   02 WA-71
Ogle, Benjamin; 26 Feb. 1815; Loretta Livers   05 FR-9
Ogle, Joshua; 1 April 1802; Susannah Davis   03 AL-613
Ogleby, John; 12 Aug. 1811; Anna Bridigam   08 AL-84
O'Harra, Anthony; 20 Sept. 1806; Ann Ellis   02 BA-4
Ohlman, Heinr.; 19 Jan. 1810; Maria Scherer   14 BA-227
O'Hurt, John; 21 Nov. 1801; Catherine Sanfort   03 BA-410
Okley, Mi (?); 17 Oct. 1817; H[annah] Simmons   32 BA-316
Oldborn, John F.; 10 June 1801; Johanna Bright   17 AA
Olden, David; 25 July 1803; Susan Levy (See also 02 BA-32)
                                                           03 BA-431
Oldfield, Granville S.; 5 Aug. 1819; Ann Higinbotham   03 BA-603
Oldham, Thomas; 19 June 1809; Elizab. Lauch   14 BA-426
Oldham, William; 9 Sept. 1813; Susan (N) (both col'd)   15 BA-315
Oliver, John; 15 May 1807; Eliza Carey   03 BA-497
Olney, Benj'n Brown; 25 Jan. 1810; Elizabeth Hailer   03 BA-501
Olney, Thomas; 12 Nov. 1807; Catherine Miller   15 BA-257
O'Neal, Lawrence; 28 Aug. 1806; Nancy Galworth (See also 02 MO)
                                                           01 PG
O'Neale, Wm.; 6 May 1804; Anna Ball   03 MO-119
O'Neil, Jeremiah; 25 Nov. 1804; Harriet Keith   15 BA-212
Opperman, George L.; 27 July 1807; Justine Jordan   14 BA-422
Oram, John; 22 May 1801; Mary Duncan   09 BA
Oram, Samuel; 1 Sept. 1803; Charity Ledley   05 HA-3
Oram, William; 10 Jan. 1805; Chloe Crook Dallas   09 BA
Orchard, Thos.; 28 Nov. 1810; Rachel Van Horn   03 BA-502
Ord, George; 5 March 1804; Margaret Biays   05 BA-234
Orell, James; 7 Jan. 1813; Elizabeth Orell, both of Caroline
                                                           02 TA-42
Orem, John; 13 Aug. 1814; Marg't Ann Cross   13 BA-19
Orman (?), James; 9 Aug. 1807; Jane Warfield   17 BA-5
Orman, William; 22 Dec. 1820; Mary Schillknecht (See also 16
    FR-76)   03 FR-61
Orme, Jesse; 19 Nov. 1801; Lydia Anderson   15 AA-2
Orme, Patrick; 24 Dec. 1801; Mary Sedwell   10 FR

Oroux, Francis; 2 Feb. 1815; Eliza Preston   16 BA-14
Orr, Andrew; 5 July 1813; Mary Sweeny   11 BA-21
Orr, James; 5 July 1816; Marg't. Haskley   13 BA-26
Orr, John; Oct. 1805; Sarah Arnold   02 WA-7
Orr, William; 17 Dec. 1801; Eliz. Macklewain   03 MO-117
Orrick, Nicholas; 17 Nov. 1803; Susanna Keener   26 BA-1
Orsler, Paoli; 27 June 1815; Sophia Weller   06 FR-1322
Orstler, Edward; 3 July 1808; Charity Bond   08 BA
Ort (?), Adam; Jan. 1807; Bezi Weisman   02 WA-81
Ort, Matthias; 17 Oct. 1802; Katharina Miller   07 BA-67
Ort, Wilhelm; 9 Sept. 1811; Sally Jewell   14 BA-429
Ortner, Jacob; 6 Nov. 1820; Margareth Malamboe   06 FR-1331
Ortner, John; 24 Dec. 1818; Sophia Shop   06 FR-1329
Osborn, Elisha; 30 July 1804; Hannah Birkhead   33 BA-40
Osborn, Thomas; 15 Dec. 1808; Kitty Groundfield   02 BA-7
Osborn, William; 29 May 1817; Elizabeth Coles   05 BA-240
Osburn, Alex'r.; 15 July 1812; Martha James   13 BA-17
Osterday, Michael; Sept. 1802; Magd. Dagenhert   02 WA-73
Ostertag, Christian; 20 Sept. 1807; Nancy Landes (15 FR-321 gives
     bride's name as Lander)   01 FR-1158
Osthoff, Andrew; 8 Aug. 1805; Mary Wedsack   14 BA-418
Ostman, Sam'l; 8 Aug. 1820; Cath. Konighauser   14 BA-440
Oswald, John; 1801; Eva Gerver   02 WA-71
Ott, Adam; Aug. (?) 1803; Betzi Weisman   02 WA-75
Ott, George; 11 June 1818; Mary Leather   06 FR-1328
Ott, John; 27 Oct. 1806; Ann Ritchie (See also 15 FR-319)
                                                    01 FR-1158
Ott, Philip; 17 Sept. 1801; Marg. Gernhardt (See also 15 FR-312)
                                                    01 FR-1158
Ottesen, Jacob (native of Denmark); 4 Nov. 1805; Desiree Bourges
     (native of Bordeaux)   15 BA-230
Ourant, John; 7 Jan. 1804; Rachel Hewitt   06 FR
Oursler, Alexander; 1 April 1804; Hellen Daugheday 23 BA-3
Oursler, John; 15 March 1804; Elizabeth Manning   23 BA-3
Ovaire (?), John Fra's; 15 April 1807; Catherine Newcomer
                                                    15 BA-248
Ovenberger (?), John; Sept. 1813; Mar. Eakle   02 WA-98
Overpeck, Jacob; 16 Nov. 1811; Sarah Trout   02 WA-92
Owelfield, Martin; 20 Aug. 1818; Mary Romane   13 BA-31
Owen, Kennedy; 18 Dec. 1806; Agnes Riddell   03 BA-496
Owen, Thomas; 1 Sept. 1808; Elizabeth Foss   30 BA-109
Owens, George; 19 Jan. 1806; Mary Owens   02 SM-187
Owens, George; 3 April 1806; Susanna Greenwell   02 SM-187
Owings, Beale; 8 Sept. 1813; Eleanora B. Magruder   03 BA-506
Owings, Israel; 16 Dec. 1802; Sarah Mummy   14 BA-413
Owings, Jesse; 10 Dec. 1801; Hannah Wood   03 MO-117
Owings, John; 15 Feb. 1806; Margaret McAllister   15 BA-235
Owings, John; 7 April 1818; Cath. Alter   14 BA-437
Owings, Joshua; 1811; Eleanor Worthington   01 PG
Owings, Joshua W.; 1811; Eleanor Worthington   02 MO
Owings, Levi; 27 June 1811; Elizabeth Gardiner   09 BA
Owings, Levin; 23 July 1805; Achsah Owings   14 BA-418
Owings, Nicholas; 12 Dec. 1805; Margaret Parker   11 BA-7
Owings, Peter; March 1812; Eliza Winters   03 BA-503
Owings, Richard; 15 De.c 1812; Elizabeth Manro   09 BA
Owings, Thomas Beale; 11 Aug. 1803; Ann Johnson   01 BA-10
Oxford, Charles; 24 May 1801; Elizabeth Trumpow   03 BA-400
Packard, Elisha; 11 April 1811; Harriet Dillahaye   03 BA-502
Packer (or Parker), George; 2 Jan. 1802; Ann Palmer 14 BA-411
Padgett, Richard; 26 Feb. 1811; Mary Masberg   06 FR-1315
Page, John; 9 Dec. 1806; Charlotte Caton   09 BA
Paine, Joseph; 30 Jan. 1820; Sophia Copenhafer   04 FR-19
Pairpoint, Samuel; 11 Sept. 1806; Margaret Waul (See also
     15 FR-319)   01 FR-1160

Paisly, Thomas; (betw. 3 July and 4 Aug.) 1802; Mary Wilde (both
    natives of Ireland)					15 BA-169
Paistley, Thomas; 8 June 1802; Sarah White			09 BA
Palfrey, John; 14 March 1811; Ann James			03 BA-502
Palmatary, John H.; June 1808; Eliza Presbury			21 BA-7
Palmer, Christian; June 1819; Elizab. Bargan			02 WA-113
Palmer, Henrich; 11 April 1805; Maria Sinn			15 FR-317
Palmer, Henry; 11 April 1805; Mary Sinn			01 FR-1160
Palmer, Peregrine; 4 Feb. 1813; Ann Cole			02 WA-96
Pane, John; 17 Oct. 1816; Catherine Keller			06 FR-1325
Papion, John; 20 Sept. 1804; Marg't Bradberry			03 BA-491
Parish, Isaac; 15 March 1813; Sophia Parmer			17 BA-9
Parish, Joshua; 1 Jan. 1811; Eliz. Glenn			14 BA-428
Parish, William; 10 Nov. 1803; Mary Ann Crutchley		03 AA-120
Parish, Wm.; 11 Jan. 1816; Elizabeth Ball			05 BA-239
Parisot, Johann Baptiste; 20 July 1819; Eliza Wilhelmina
    Betefuhr					07 BA-311
Parker, Charles; 20 March 1815; Maria Pidgeon			03 BA-506
Parker, Edward; 14 July 1806; Martha Brown			14 BA-420
Parker, George; 2 Jan. 1802; Ann Palmer			14 BA-411
Parker, George; 18 Aug. 1810; Jane Busey			US
Parker, Isaac; 6 June 1805; Sarah Roberts			11 BA-6
Parker, James; 9 Jan. 1814; Catherine Kimmerly			08 AL-85
Parker, John; 27 Dec. 1804; Mary Pritchard			03 AL-613
Parker, Peter; 23 Jan. 1808; Sally Johnson			01 WO
Parker, Peter; 15 July 1812; Elizabeth Chesney			21 BA-7
Parker, Robert; 30 Oct. 1808; Elenor Mushberger		13 BA-5
Parker, Thomas; 10 Aug. 1801; Peggy Natherman			03 BA-404
Parker, Thomas; 31 May 1805; Elizabeth Foster			02 BA-35
Parker, Thomas; 2 June 1805; Elizabeth Foster			03 BA-493
Parker, Thomas; 19 June 1806; Rachael Wilkerson		11 BA-9
Parker, Thomas; 7 May 1809; Mary Rimmon			09 BA
Parkerson, Robert; 2 June 1816; Margaret Horner		17 BA-12
Parkes, Abraham; 29 Dec. 1811; Sarah Wright			05 BA-237
Parket, John; 5 Aug. 1805; Sidney Trownson			03 BA-494
Parkinson, Abraham; 1801; Sarah Taylor			07 AA-1
Parkinson, Jacob; Sept. 1812; Mary Keller			03 AL-614
Parks, Abraham; 14 Aug. 1803; Sarah Wright			03 BA-432
Parks, David; 18 Jan. 1801; Mary Brodie			03 BA-397
Parks, Frederick; 2 July 1807; Mary Buck			09 BA
Parks, James; 5 Nov. 1807; Kitty Hughes			09 BA
Parks, John; 25 Oct. 1806; Elizabeth Chamgion			09 BA
Parks, Thomas; 22 April 1819; Catherine Malcolm		11 BA-35
Parmele, J. H.; 29 Sept. 1816; Priscilla Horne			05 BA-239
Parr, John; 16 Sept. 1802; Mary Talbot			09 BA
Parr, William; 25 Aug. 1812; Martha Willis			14 BA-430
Parrish, Zebulon; 3 Aug. 1820; Clarissa Kelley			08 BA
Parrott, Thomas; 23 Jan. 1816; Rebecca Hutchins		03 AA-131
Parrott, William; 11 April 1815; Nancy Usher			13 BA-21
Parry, Joseph; 13 Nov. 1808; Eliza Heartly			03 BA-499
Parsons, Jno. D.; 7 Jan. 1817; Marg't. Etchberger		14 BA-436
Parsons, Jos.; 24 Jan. 1813; Marg't Shark			13 BA-16
Parsons, Thomas (of Tal. Co., s. of Joseph and Elizabeth); 29 d.
    5 m. 1811; Mary Price (dau. of Daniel and Elizabeth)
							02 SF-116
Parsons, Thomas D.; 25 May 1819; Henrietta Swager		09 BA
Partridge, William; 1 April 1806; Rosanna Wilmer		33 BA-41
Pascal, Peter; 17 Dec. 1815; Eliz. Marshall			03 BA-507
Pascault, Francis; 7 April 1817; Nancy Smith			32 BA-312
Pascault, Francis; 29 Dec. 1817; Catherine D. Hood (of AA Co.)
							16 BA-61
Pash, William; July 1808; Mary Ana Dowell			02 WA-85
Passey, William; 17 Feb. 1803; Ann Croxall			34 BA-1

Passmore, Andrew M. (son of Elisha and Ruth, both dec., of W.
    Nottingham Hund., CE Co.); 9 d. 11 mo., 1820; Judith Wilson
    (dau. of Samuel and Pheba of the same place)   06 SF
Passmore, John (of Lancaster); 18 Dec. 1809; Eliza Alexander (of
    Balto.)   03 BA-500
Pasture, Charles; 12 July 1812; Biddy Cain   15 BA-302
Pate, James; 7 July 1802; Mary McEvers   03 BA-413
Patrick, Hugh; 28 March 1810; Ann Love   13 BA-12
Patrick, James; Nov. 1807; Esther Lester   02 WA-84
Patrick, James; 15 Oct. 1812; Elizab. Bowhain (?) (See also
    15 FR-326)   01 FR-1160
Patrick, Sam'l. C.; 3 March 1805; Mary Kipp   03 BA-495
Patrick, William; 26 Jan. 1801; Eve Foupan   09 BA
Patterson, Arch'd; 4 Sept. 1809; Nancy Burns   13 BA-8
Patterson, Benjamin; 14 Dec. 1820; Juliet McComas   11 BA-38
Patterson, Edward; 20 April 1815; Sidney Smith   05 BA-238
Patterson, George; 15 Dec. 1811; Mary Ann Eagleston   11 BA-18
Patterson, Jas. Jno.; 30 July 1805; Ann Broom Dalrymple
                                                         03 BA-494
Patterson, John; 11 April 1806; Mary McCrea   15 BA-237
Patterson, John; 5 April 1810; Marg't Hines   13 BA-9
Patterson, John; 24 Dec. 1811; Ruth Eliz. Thomson (See also
    15 FR-325)   01 FR-1160
Patterson, Jno.; 17 Sept. 1812; Rebecca Tudor   14 BA-430
Patterson, John; 3 Aug. 1815; Sarah Catts   11 BA-24
Patterson (?), John; 6 May 1820; Catherine Fitzpatrick   32 BA-328
Patterson, Jno. W.; 3 Oct. 1816; Mary Brown   13 BA-26
Patterson, Joseph; 14 June 1809; Mary Taylor   11 BA-14
Patterson, Joseph W.; 30 Dec. 1817; Charlotte G. Nicols
                                                         03 BA-602
Patterson, Nathaniel; 13 April 1813; Catherine Meyerhoffer
                                                         06 FR-1319
Patterson, Robert; 1 May 1806; Mary Ann Caton (dau. of Richard
    Caton, Esq., of Brooklandwood, Balto. Co.)   15 BA-238
Patterson, Thos.; 26 July 1810; Martha Merrideth   13 BA-10
Patterson, William; 21 May 1804; Jane McJilton   14 BA-416
Patterson, William, Jr.; 21 Feb. 1804; Nancy Gittings   03 BA-490
Patterson, William; 15 May 1809; Ann McAllister   03 BA-499
Patterson, William; 1 Aug. 1811; Zoa Abell   11 BA-17
Patterson, William; 6 Aug. 1815; Sally Long   17 BA-13
Patterson, William (s. of James and Jane); 22 d. 1, 1817; Beulah
    Nixon (dau. of Samuel and Susannah) (See also 10 SF)
                                                         01 SF
Patterson, William; 20 May 1819; Martha Ward   11 BA-34
Pattison, James; 8 Dec. 1802; Elizabeth LeCompte   01 DO-41
Pattison?, John; 6 May 1820; Catherine Fitzpatrick   32 BA-328
Pattison, Thomas; 3 April 1809; Mary Cook (or Cross?)   31 BA-57
Patton, James; July 1810; Sarah Christ   02 WA-87
Patton, James; 21 April 1816; Rebecca Joiner   05 BA-239
Paugh, John; 16 April 1805; Ann Shipling   03 AL-613
Paugh, Michael; 12 March 1811; Sarah Davis   03 AL-614
Paugh, Nichelus; 2 Sept. 1802; Sarah Bray   03 AL-613
Paul, David; 15 April 1816; Marg't. McGowan   13 BA-26
Paul, Peter; 15 March 1804; Elizabeth Merril   02 BA-33
Paulsgrove, Henrich; Dec. 1802; Elis. Wagner   02 WA-74
Pauly, John; 15 March 1810; Anna Kilmor   30 BA-109
Pawson, Mat.; 30 July 1807; Mary Matilda Brevitt   13 BA-2
Paxton, Joseph; 5 Sept. 1819; Susanna Dennis   08 AL-85
Peacock, Elijah; 15 Aug. 1815; Nancy Houck   06 FR-1322
Peacock, Thomas; 4 July 1813; Eleanor McGlellan (both natives of
    Ireland)   15 BA-312
Peal, James; 3 April 1806; Ruth Neptune   03 AL-614
Pearce, Joshua; 3 Jan. 1802; Mary Bisset   10 FR

Pearce, William; 28 Nov. 1815, by Elder Joshua Wells; Ann
   Armstrong   17 BA-12
Pearcy, Henry; 1 March 1812; Hanna Dietz   14 BA-430
Pearse, Wm.; 4 May 1805; Mary Jackson   03 BA-493
Pearson, Dan'l; 5 Nov. 1809; Precilla Carr   13 BA-8
Pearson, Joseph; 18 May 1809; Mary Wells   14 BA-426
Pease, Jordan (?); 13 Sept. 1803; Ann Ammons   14 BA-415
Peck, Henry; 8 Nov. 1808; Eliza Culverwell   13 BA-5
Peck, Jacob; 11 May 1818; Harriot Faber   11 BA-28
Peck, John; 5 Jan. 1812; Susan Miller   02 WA-92
Peck, John Spotwood; 9 June 1803; Anne Wilson   03 BA-429
Peck, William; 9 Nov. 1820; Elizabeth Croney (col'd)   37 BA-153
Peck, William T.; Dec. 1817; Margaret Brannan   02 WA-107
Peckman, Joseph; 22 Sept. 1812; Mary Fultz   02 WA-95
Peduzo, Peter; 19 Oct. 1820; Catherine Harryman   32 BA-330
Pees, Jno. H.; 26 April 1802; Kitty Hooper   14 BA-412
Peirce, Edward; 15 Aug. 1815; Harriot McLoughlin   17 BA-13
Pelby, William; 16 Oct. 1815; Rosally Brown   05 BA-238
Pell, Thomas H.; 19 Dec. 1816; Elizabeth Clarke   11 BA-31
Pelsch, Anthony; 11 July 1818; Mary Maheny   16 BA-84
Pelther (?), Francis; 9 Feb. 1809; Mary Kisler   15 BA-268
Pembrooke, Thomas; 19 Oct. 1806; Winefred Dunbarr   02 SM-187
Pembrooke, Thomas; 7 Nov. 1809; Mary McKay   02 SM-188
Pendleton, Daniel; 27 April 1815; Lavina I. Ford   11 BA-24
Penman, John; 20 May 1815; Catherine O'Connor   16 BA-19
Penn, Benjamin; 26 March 1803; Cath. Hockl(e)y (See also
   15 FR-314)   01 FR-1160
Penn, Edw'd; 17 March 1812; Marg't Taylor   13 BA-14
Penn, Edward; 17 Aug. 1815; Rachel Coillins   13 BA-39
Penn, George; 26 July 1818; Margaret Gabell   13 BA-40
Penn, Jacob W.; 26 July 1807; Mary Holland   13 BA-2
Penn, John; 19 Nov. 1803; Polly Sisler   14 BA-415
Penn, William; 7 March 1809; Clara Tarlton   02 SM-188
Pennell, George; Dec. 1801; Marg. Martin   02 WA-72
Penniman, William; 10 July 1819; Henrietta Griffith   22 BA-101
Pennington, Elijah; 15 Dec. 1801; Elizabeth Lewis   15 AA-2
Pennington, Elijah; 25 July 1804; Rebecca Stinchcomb   05 AA-4
Pennington, Josiah (s. of Daniel and Martha); 20 d. 6 mo., 1811;
   Deborah Talbott (dau. of John and Mary)   03 SF
Pennington, Levi; 6 May 1804; Wealthy Jones   15 AA-3
Pennington, Robert; 17 Aug. 1805; Elizabeth Mayson   11 BA-6
Pennington, William; 21 Oct. 1803; Ann Little   05 AA-3
Pennington, Wm.; 28 May 1811; Eliz. Horn   14 BA-428
Penrice, Thos.; 10 Aug. 1809; Mary Ann Jones   03 BA-500
Penston, James; 21 Jan. 1804; Mary Burke   15 BA-198
Pentz, Dan'l; 13 Aug. 1815; Charlotte Seltzer   14 BA-434
Pepper, Jacob; 12 Jan. 1819; Ann Auld   17 BA-21
Percival, James; 25 Oct. 1820; Jane Martin   11 BA-38
Peregoy, Caleb; 27 Oct. 1817; Mary Croney   11 BA-28
Perigo, James; 30 March 1816; Catherine Willis   08 BA
Perigo, James; 21 Dec. 1817; Eliza Smith   13 BA-30
Perigoy, Benjamin; 3 Oct. 1816; Elizabeth Cunningham   09 BA
Perill, Basil; 28 Feb. 1802; Susan Steal (See also 15 FR-313)
                                                        01 FR-1160
Perine, David M.; 1 March 1818; Mary Glenn   03 BA-603
Perine, Richard; 4 March 1813; Nancy Edmondson   11 BA-21
Perkins, Elisha; 8 Jan. 1819; Eleanor Buel   13 BA-34
Perkins, William; 6 Jan. 1801; Susanna Bateman   02 CH
Perrigo, Joseph; 16 Aug. 1817; Rebecca Briggs   17 BA-17
Perrill, Samuel; 23 July 1811; Mary Atkins   06 FR-1316
Perrite, Nathan; 25 March 1806; Christina Stump   08 AL-86
Perry, Benj.; 2 Feb. 1804; Eliz. Magruder   03 MO-119
Perry, Elbert; 4 Feb. 1806; Rebecca Magruder (See also 02 MO)
                                                        01 PG

Perry, Jeremiah; 23 Sept. 1810 by Rev. Robert Roberts; Sarah
    Britenoder 17 BA-8
Perry, John; 28 feb. 1820; Mary Ann Wilkins 03 BA-604
Perry, William; 20 May 1819; Elizabeth Kable 06 FR-1330
Perry, Zadie H.; 27 Feb. 1817; Hannah Jones 17 BA-16
Perygoy, Rob't; 24 July 1817; Ruth Perregoy 13 BA-28
Pessly, Gottlieb; 1804; Cath. Dutters 02 WA-76
Petee, James; 25 Feb. 1813; Sarah Maddon 02 BA-36
Peter, Henry; 26 June 1801; Nancy Forester 30 BA-108
Peterkin, William; 11 April 1803; Elizabeth Spenser (See also
    02 BA-32) 03 BA-426
Peters, Charles; 7 April 1816; Polly Stewart 06 FR-1324
Peters, Christian; 14 Jan. 1801; Baloti Rose 14 BA-409
Peters, Daniel; 31 Dec. 1801; Sally Raney 09 BA
Peters, Daniel; 1804; Rlis. Night 02 WA-77
Peters, John; 13 Sept. 1803; Rachel Mills (See also 02 BA-32)
03 BA-433
Peters, John; 14 Nov. 18111; Mary Landrick (both people of
    colour) 15 BA-293
Peters, Michael; 29 Sept. 1816; Ann Grayble 06 FR-1325
Peters, Rees; 3 April 1806; Ann Welsh 11 BA-8
Peters, Richardus; 25 April 1819; Christina Emerich 39 BA-36
Peterson, George (native of Denmark); 11 June 1801; Sarah
    Hannan 15 BA-153
Peterson, Israel; Dec. 1810; Nancy Falker 02 WA-88
Peterson, Jas.; 4 Dec. 1802; Eliz. Willstaff 14 BA-413
Peterson, John; 31 Dec. 1803; Elizabeth German 15 BA195
Peterson, John; 18 May 1819; Ann Lawrey 14 BA-439
Peterson, Nich's; 26 Sept. 1808; Charlotte Downes 14 BA-425
Petro, Clovis; 6 Feb. 1815; Eliza Joseph Delion (both people of
    colour, both natives of St. Domingo) 16 BA-15
Petry, Philip; May 1806; Elis. Hogmire 02 WA-80
Petterson, Alexander; 19 July 1807; Priscilla Stevens 01 CE
Pettus, John; 24 Oct. 1803; Grace Anderson 03 BA-434
Peyton, John Smith; 9 Jan. 1816; Mary Carrere 16 BA-48
Peywnett (?), Joseph; 13 July 1806 (by Rev. Leonard Cassell); Ann
    Richards 17 BA-6
Pfaltz, Wm.; 19 Oct. 1808; Maria Grebe 14 BA-425
Pfeiffer, Nicholas; 3 July 1803; Barbara Deal 07 BA
Pharon, John Lewis; 14 Sept. 1809; Eugenia Boisson (people of
    colour from St. Domingo) 15 BA-272
Phebus, Peter; 30 Aug. 1820; Elizabeth Gardner 04 FR-20
Phelps, Gardiner; 5 Oct. 1814; Elizabeth Hague 0-9 BA
Phelps, Greenbury; 22 May 1804; Kitty Poulet (02 BA-33 gives
    bride's name as Pould) 03 BA-490
Phelps, James; 6 Jan. 1818; Eliza Lawrenson 13 BA-30
Phelps, Joseph; 1801; Catherine Thompson 06 AA-1
Phelps, Joshua; 16 April 1816; Alicia Inglesby 32 BA-308
Phenix, Thomas; 16 Nov. 1814; Jane Dawson 03 BA-506
Philips, Henry; 8 June 1801; Marg. Tubman 22 BA-410
Philips, William; 17 Aug. 1812; Jane Cramton (See also 15 FR-325)
01 FR-1160
Philips, Zachariah; 28 Dec. 1803; Margaret Granger 15 BA-194
Phillips, Ephraim; 3 April 1801; Sarah Howard 11 BA-2
Phillips, Isaac; 6 June 1801; Anne Goldthwait 03 BA-401
Phillips, Isaac, Jr.; May 1817; Ann B. Sweeting 20 BA-223
Phillips, Nathaniel; Aug. 1804 (by Jno. Bloodgood); Mary Ann
    Logan (See also 40 BA) 17 BA-4
Phillips, Paul; 11 Oct. 1806; Jemima Smith 11 BA-8
Phillips, Samuel; 21 Feb. 1804; Sarah Keene 01 DO-41
Phillips, Thomas; 25 July 1811; Mary Eichelberger 06 FR-1316
Phillips, William; 9 May 1805; Elizabeth Robinson 05 BA-234
Phillips, William; 12 Oct. 1803; Ann Parkinson 02 BA-7

Phillips, William (s. of John and Lydia of Kennett Twp., Chester
    Co., PA); 12 d. 11 mo., 1812; Ann Trimble (dau. of James and
    Sarah of East Nottingham, CE Co., MD)   06 SF
Philpot, Charles; 26 Dec. 1816; Ruth Delmar   17 BA-15
Phipps, Thomas; 17 June 1808; Elizabeth Ballentine   05 BA-235
Phips, Nathaniel; c.1802; Ann Phifas   07 AA-2
Pice, Richard; 1 Dec. 1801; Elizabeth Coats   30 BA-108
Pick, Henry; 23 July 1811; Rach'l Lindenberger   13 BA-13
Pickering, Jacob; 24 June 1815; Ann Conelly   14 BA-433
Picket, Levi; 20 Aug. 1808; Mary Brown   14 BA-424
Pickett, John; 27 May 1802; Eliza Ray   06 BA-2
Pickins, Samuel; 16 Nov. 1818; Mary Ann Clarke   17 BA-20
Picks, Nic.; 3 March 1807; Cath. Nentz   14 BA-421
Pidgeon, Isaac (of Campbell Co., VA, s. of William and Rachel of
    Belmont Co., OH); 29th d. 3 mo., 1808; Sarah Warner (dau.
    of Croasdale and Mary)   11 SF-100
Pien, Friederich; 9 April 1813; Philippina Maurer   07 BA-309
Pier (?), William; Nov. 1810; Rebecca Goodwin   02 WA-88
Pierce, Benj'n.; 13 Oct. 1812; Kitty Read   13 BA-15
Pierce, James; 29 July 1801; Martha Shaw   10 BA-1
Pierce, Thomas; May 1816; Jane French   02 WA-102
Pierel, John; 21 July 1810 (with dispensation because of the
    impediment of affinity; Emilia Chevoilleau (both natives of
    the Island of St. Domingo)   15 BA-282
Pierpoint, Joseph; 13 Sept. 1801; Martha Noel (See also 11 BA-3)
                                                       06 BA-1
Piers, George; 7 July 1816; Margaret Brend (free negroes)
                                                       32 BA-309
Pifer, Philip; 16 Aug. 1812; Rachel Brangel (See also 15 FR-325)
                                                       01 FR-1160
Pike, Adm.; 2 May 1810; Reba Davidson   13 BA-12
Pilch, John; 1 July 1801; Mary Donovan   03 BA-402
Pilch, Samuel; 21 Jan. 1804; Elizabeth Errickson   02 BA-33
Pinckney, Wm., Jr.; 29 Nov. 1813; Jane B. Hammond   03 BA-505
Pindell, Lewis; 21 March 1816; Catherine Cole   13 BA-39
Pindell, Richard; 31 Dec. 1807; Jane Ensor   09 BA
Pindell, Rinaldo; 6 July 1815; Eleanor Pindell   03 AA-131
Pindle, Stephen W.; 30 Sept. 1815; Mary Smith   27 BA-8
Pinelle, Joshua; 19 April 1803; Catherine Walker   09 BA
Pines, John; 10 Oct. 1816; Catharine Jones   09 BA
Pinky, Gottlieb; April 1805; Barb. Shenk   02 WA-78
Pinto (?), Joseph; 29 Aug. 1811; Sarah Gibson   31 BA-109
Piper, Philip; 15 Sept. 1807; Mary Mincher   11 BA-11
Pirkeson, John; 10 Oct. 1809; Nancy Storm   08 AL-87
Pitman, John; 27 Nov. 1811; Cathar. Aldray   02 WA-92
Pitt, Joseph; 7 Jan. 1802; Elizabeth French   17 BA-1
Pitt, Richard; 14 April 1801; Anne Berry   03 BA-399
Pitt, Thomas; 30 July 1815 (by Elder Joshua Wells); Catherine
    Isabella Herring   17 BA-11
Pitts, John; 28 Jan. 1802; Ediff Bosley   23 BA-1
Pitts, Thos.; 2 May 1802; Betsy Woodln   14 BA-412
Plaster, Israel; 4 April 1801; Sarah Long   01 So-15
Pleasants, John P.; 19 May 1816; Mary Hall   03 BA-507
Ploughman, Ephraim; 4 Jan. 1816; Elizabeth Brown   09 BA
Plowden, Henry (s. of Ed.); 1 Jan. 1800; Eddy (N)   03 SM
Plowse, Capt. John (of England); 15 Sept. 1819; Marg't Emery
                                                       03 BA-604
Plummer, John; 7 Jan. 1816; Nancy Plummer   06 FR-1323
Plummer, John; 23 June 1816; Nancy Corkrill (both of QA Co.)
                                                       01 QA-53
Plummer, John; 23 June 1816; Nancy Corkrill; of QA   02 TA-43
Plummer, Joseph P. (s. of John, dec., and Johanna); 13 d. 3 mo.
    1806; Susanna Husband (dau. of Joseph, dec., and Mary)
                                                       09 SF

Plummer, Richard; 9 Feb. 1814; Margaret Danison   05 AA-4
Plummer, Samuel (s. of Yate and Artridge [Waters]); 23 d. 4 mo.,
    1801; Margaret Wood (dau. of Thomas and Susanna)   03 SF
Plummer, Samuel (s. of Abraham and Sarah); 25 d. 3 mo., 1802;
    Priscilla Plummer (dau. of Yate and Artridge [Waters])
                                                         03 SF
Plunket, Alex'r; 30 March 1812; Elenor McDole   13 BA-6
Pochon, Charles Adrien Marie Francois, Jr.; 27 May 1819; Eulalie
    Maillet Lacoste Godfroi   16 BA-82
Pochon, Charles F.; 16 Feb. 1815; Harriet Phillips   16 BA-16
Pocock, John; 2 April 1816; Henrietta Krouse   13 BA-25
Poe, Jacob; 4 Jan. 1803; Bridget Kennedy   05 BA-233
Poffenberger, Andrew; Sept. 1816; Amelia Smith   02 WA-102
Pogue, John G.; 14 Jan. 1819; Mary A. Jones   20 BA-223
Poits, Isaac (s. of William and Caroline); 22 d. 6 mo., 1803; Ann
    Edmondson   07 SF
Polance, Basil; 24 Jan. 1801; Polly Lee (people of color)
                                                         09 BA
Poland, Carabene; 3 Oct. 1805; Susannah Jacobs   03 AL-613
Poland, John; 18 April 1805; Nancy James   08 AL-613
Poland, John; 30 Sept. 1811; Emely Baylis   02 WA-91
Poland, Roger; 10 Sept. 1804; Ann Dickson   03 AL-613
Poles, James; 23 March 1808; Ann B. Medcalf   13 BA-3
Polen, Aaron; 29 Sept. 1815; Catherine Miller   08 AL-87
Poling, Martin; 2 Feb. 1804; Esther Beavers   03 AL-613
Poling, Peter; 26 Feb. 1801; Ann Hixenbaugh   03 AL-613
Polk, David; 14 Oct. 1817; Sophia Smith   05 BA-240
Polk, William R. Gillis; 25 Feb. 1801; Hetty Sitler   09 BA
Polkinhorn, Henry; 10 April 1804; Catherine Askew   05 BA-234
Pollard, George; 4 Sept. 1803; Mary Munhollen   03 BA-433
Pollitt, William; 22 Oct. 1815; Emilia Warden   11 BA-24
Pollock, Oliver (widower, of Carlisle, Northumberland Co., PA);
    2 Nov. 1805;; Winifred Ann Dardy (widow)   15 BA-229
Pollock, Sam'l; 12 Dec. 1818; Mary Ann Delnet   14 BA-438
Polsen, Stephen; 27 May 1806; Caroline Lemont   02 BA-4
Polton, Thomas; 6 Oct. 1812; Susanna Yieldhall   15 BA-303
Poncett, Lewis; 19 Dec. 1805; Catherine Rosse Ducasse   09 BA
Pool, George; c.1808 (definite date not given); Sarah Rowles
                                                         13 BA-33
Pool, James; 12 Dec. 1816; Mary Ann McFadin   11 BA-31
Pool, Jonas; 12 March 1819; Barbara Feekley   13 BA-34
Pool, Philemon; 7 Aug. 1810; Sarah Dritt (See also 15 FR-324)
                                                         01 FR-1160
Pool, Walter; 11 Dec. 1808; Margaret Wolf (See also 15 FR-323)
                                                         01 FR-1160
Pool, Wm. Holder; 20 April 1806; Rebecca Foster   03 BA-495
Poole, Martin; 26 June 1817; Mary Clogherty   16 BA-54
Poole, Rezin; 26 April 1804; Nancy Hance   14 BA-416
Poole, Thos.; 6 Dec. 1807; Jane Gwinn   13 BA-3
Poor, Charles M.; 4 July, 1809; Elizabeth Roberts   05 BA-236
Poor, Dudley; 14 May 1814; Deborah H. O'Donnell   05 BA-238
Poor, John H.; 7 Aug. 1815; Jane E. Taylor   05 BA-238
Poor, Samuel; 21 July 1808; Mary Naclon   02 BA-6
Poorman, Abraham; June 1816; Mary Fox   02 WA-102
Pope, Elijah; 16 Sept. 1812; Ann Gladdell   13 BA-17
Pope, George; 12 Nov. 1812; Margreta Keens   39 BA-28
Pope, Jno.; 16 May 1808; Elizabeth Moore   14 BA-424
Pope, William; 1 Jan. 1815; Catherine Kelly   06 FR-1321
Popp (or Stopp), George; 16 Nov. 1819; Mary Lohr   08 AL-87
Poppe, Henrich; 6 June 1815; Marie Diefenberger   07 BA-309
Porter, Alexander; 18 April 1801; Sarah Honeycomb   09 BA
Porter, Benjamin; 1 Sept. 1805; Sarah Tomson   09 BA
Porter, Charles (age 68); 10 April 1803; Polly Fry (age 20)
                                                         03 MO-118

Porter, Charles; 20 Dec. 1808; Cassandra Gassaway   13 BA-5
Porter, Denton; 4 March 1806; Kitty Heiter (See also 02 MO)
                                                          01 PG
Porter, Isaiah; 1812; Hannah Braddock (See also 02 MO) 01 PG
Porter, John; 5 March 1801; Sarah Daley   03 BA-398
Porter, John; July 1808; Elis. Kealhouse   02 WA-85
Porter, Michael; 28 Oct. 1804; Mary Spedden   09 BA
Porter, Peregrine; 24 April 1806; Mary Biddeson   09 BA
Porter, Peter; 22 July 1817; Elizabeth Walker   17 BA-14
Porter, Ralph; 11 Oct. 1803; Bethiah Cunningham   05 BA-234
Porter, Robert; 26 Oct. 1803; Mary Cowan   33 BA-40
Porter, Thos.; 2 May 1805; Eleanor McNeale   03 BA-493
Porter, William; 20 July 1803; Jane Pannel   05 BA-234
Porter, Thomas; 7 Nov. 1819; Mary Sapp   06 AL-157
Porter, William; 6 Dec. 1815; Elizabeth Uhldrick   11 BA-26
Ports (?), Isaac; 1803; Ann Edmondson   07 SF-6
Posey, Adrian; 15 Aug. 1815; Margaret Byrne (widow)   16 BA-24
Posey, Nathaniel; 9 Oct. 1812; Margaret Kemp (See also 15 FR-326)
                                                          01 FR-1160
Posey, Walbert B. (of QA Co.); 26 May 1807; Susan Coots (?) or
     Cook (?) or Coats (?) (01 QA-52 says Coats)   02 TA-40
Poster, Thomas; 7 Nov. 1805; Eleanor Salter   11 BA-7
Poston, John; 5 July 1801; Nancy Clarke Hines   03 BA-418
Potee, Isaac; 7 Dec. 1817; Maria Thompson   13 BA-29
Potee, Peter; 10 Feb. 1820; Mary Young   13 BA-41
Potee, Sutton; 11 April 1810; Hannah Maggal   13 BA-12
Poteet, Jesse; 17 Nov. 1811; Ann Taylor   09 BA
Poteet, William; 16 Feb. 1818; Mrs (N) Greenfield   04 HA
Potter, Charles (free negro); 27 Dec. 1806; Margaret Somerfield
     (free negro)   31 BA-16
Potter, David; 8 Oct. 1815 (by Elder Joshua Wells); Rachel
     Lambert   17 BA-11
Potter, Martin; 20 Sept. 1816; Susanna Miller   09 BA
Pottinger, Thomas B.; 8 June 1815; Isabella Hodson   03 BA-506
Pouchard, Jean Philippe; 14 Aug. 1816; Susanna Junca (Junea?)
     (both natives of France)   16 BA-41
Pouder, George; 15 Feb. 1816; M. Fowble   30 BA-109
Pouder, John; 14 Nov. 1802; Catherine Kneisla   30 BA-108
Pouder, Leonard; 13 Dec. 1807; Mary Greenbach   30 BA-109
Poulson, Gerhard; 6 Nov. 1814; Eliz. Newman   14 BA-433
Poulson,. John; 3 Jan. 1802; Susannah Knight   10 FR
Poulson, Martin; 5 June 1806; Elizabeth Taylor   03 BA-495
Poultney, Samuel (s. of Anthony and Susanna [Plummer]); 1 d. 10
     mo., 1812; Elizabeth Wright (dau. of Joel and Elizabeth
     [Farquhar])   03 SF
Poulton, John; 7 Oct. 1820; Elizabeth Haslup   13 BA-41
Powel, William; 31 Oct. 1801; Mary Davidson   09 BA
Powel, William; 2 Oct. 1817; Phoebe Burckhardt   06 FR-1327
Powell, Howell; 26 Sept. 1804; Phebe Owings   29 BA-2
Powell, Howell, Jr. (s. of Howell and Ann); 17 d. 11 mo., 1813;
     Elizabeth Needles (s. of William and Elizabeth)   08 SF
Powell, John; April 1818; Nancy Bowers   02 WA-109
Powell, John B.; 12 Jan. 1802; Maria Howard   09 BA
Powell, Patrick; 3 April 1810; Elizabeth Arenberg, widow
                                                          39 BA-24
Powell, Samuel; 26 April 1820; Maria C. I. Shaffner (See also
     16 FR-76)   03 FR-60
Powell, William; 11 May 1806; Elizabeth Hair   09 BA
Powell, Wm.; 4 May 1809; Elizabeth Blake   03 BA-499
Power, John; 26 Oct. 1816; Cornelia Redgrave   16 BA-43
Power, Michael; 5 Nov. 1818; Elisa Hanson   32 BA-323
Power, Thos.; 21 July 1808; Mary Farrell   03 BA-498
Powers, Michael; Sept. 1812; Esther Thompson   20 BA-222
Powles, Joh.; May 1805; Juliana Deutch   02 WA-78

Pracht, Frederick; 3 Nov. 1801; Johanna Amelung   14 BA-411
Pratt, Jacob; 13 June 1802; Catherine D'Walt   03 BA-417
Pratt, John H.; 14 June 1804; Matthew Linvill   09 BA
Pravail, John; 2 Oct. 1806; Amelia Bussy   11 BA-9
Prentice, Amiee; 12 April 1806; Nancy Smith   14 BA-420
Presbury, Greenbury; 28 June 1803; Sarah Davis   05 HA-3
Preston, John; 24 Dec. 1801; Jane Warningham   03 BA-411
Preston, Joseph (s. of William and Mary of Octorara Hund., CE
   Co.); 18 d. 10 mo., 1815; Rebecca Reynolds (dau. of Jacob
   and Esther of W. Nottingham Hund., CE Co.)   06 SF
Preston, W.; 5 Feb. 1818; Susan Dukey   13 BA-30
Price, (?); May 1814; Cath. Gruber   02 WA-100
Price, Abraham; 13 April 1804; Patty Rose   09 BA
Price, Abraham; 13 Jan. 1813; Sarah Hammond   02 WA-96
Price, Archibald; 15 April 1807; Ann Hammett   02 SM-188
Price, Archibald; 31 Dec. 1804; Sarah Hebb   02 SM-186
Price, Beal; 22 May 1805; Mary Richardson   09 BA
Price, David; 17 Sept. 1820; Susan Providence Porter   08 BA
Price, Elijah (son of Mordecai and Rachel); 31 d. 10, 1804; Sarah
   Kittlewell (dau. of John and Margaret)   02 SF-94
Price, Emanuel; Nov. 1810; Sarah Price   02 WA-88
Price, Francois; 26 Aug. 1801; Ann Porter   01 TA-327
Price, George; 25 Dec. 1805; Henrietta Nicols   01 TA-327
Price, Hanable (?); 1 Nov. 1804 (by John Bloodgood, in list of
   marriages for blacks); Rebecca Williams   17 BA-5
Price, Henry; 20 Aug. 1801; Rosetta Ucum   03 BA-405
Price, Howel; 1 Oct. 1805; Elizabeth Cole   03 BA-494
Price, Israel (s. of Samuel and Ann); 18 d. 3 mo., 1813; Martha
   Davis (dau. of John and Mary)   09 SF
Price, James of TA; 12 Feb. 1801; Mary Richardson, of Caroline
   Co.   03 TA-71
Price, James; 15 May 1812; Ritta Price, both of TA Co.   02 TA-42
Price, Jared M. (son of Samuel and Frances); 16 d. 5 m., 1820;
   Sarah Matthews (dau. of Eli and Mary)   02 SF-140
Price, Jarret; 20 June 1801; Hannah West   22 BA-410
Price, Jehu (son of Samuel, Jr., and Frances); 12 d. 11, 1817;
   Susanna Matthews (dau. of Thomas and Ann)   02 SF-134
Price, Jeremiah; 29 July 1802; Ann Weatherston   02 SM-185
Price, Jesse; 29 Feb. 1816; Eleanor Cooper   13 BA-24
Price, John (son of Samuel, Sr., and Ann); 30 d. 11, 1803; Mary
   Matthews (dau. of William and Ann)   02 SF-90
Price, John; 19 Oct. 1806; Sarah Frey   13 BA-38
Price, John; 13 May 1812; Rach'l Jane (?)   13 BA-16
Price, John C.; 7 Feb. 1820; Rachel Benson   08 BA
Price, John R.; 19 Nov. 1811; Cathe. Euler   13 BA-13
Price, Mordecai (son of Samuel, Sr., and Ann); 2 d. 6, 1802; Mary
   Dillon (dau. of Moses and Hannah)   02 SF-83
Price, Philip (of Phila., s. of Benjamin Price of West Twp.,
   Chester Co., PA, and W. Ruth); 31st d., 8 mo., 1815;
   Elizabeth Coale (dau. of Isaac and Rachel)   11 SF-114
Price, Richard; 11 March 1810; Susanna Gwynne   08 AL-88
Price, Thomas T.; 30 July 1818; Elizabeth Keighler   03 BA-603
Price, William; 9 June 1803; Eliz'th Turner   05 HA-3
Price, William; 25 May 1806; Margaret P. Sears   21 BA-6
Price, (Little) William, miller; 17 June 1810; Becky Bourne
      02 TA-41
Price, William; 14 May 1818; Sarah Duckett   01 WA-201
Prickett, John H.; 1 July 1810; Mary Holmes   13 BA-10
Prig, Carvill Hall; 9 Nov. 1819; Christina Wheeler   04 HA
Pringle, Mark Udney; 18 April 1809; Catha. James   03 BA-499
Printiss, John G. B. B.; 4 Dec. 1802; Ann Kilman (?)   05 AA-3
Prints, Gaspar (native of Hungary); 2 May 1805; Maria Mihfar (?)
      15 BA-279
Pritchard, Elijah; 11 July 1818; Ann Todd   11 BA-19

Pritchard, Robert; 24 April 1802; Mary Dunbar   03 BA-416
Pritchard, Samuel; 10 Jan. 1819; Lavina Wrie   11 BA-37
Pritchard, William; 9 Oct. 1806; Eliza Hutton   03 AA-130
Prither, James; 10 Sept. 1811; Letha Greenwell   02 WA-91
Pritt, Benjamin; 4 Feb. 1813; Barbara (?)ourman   02 WA-96
Proctor, James; 14 June 1804; Cath. Suter   14 BA-41
Proctor, William (s. of Stephen and Rebecca, both dec.); 16 d. 11
    mo., 1809; Anna Wilson (dau. of John and Deborah) 09 SF
Proebsting, Theodore C.; 4 Oct. 1811; Frances Bohn   14 BA-429
Proscoe, David C.; 19 June 1817; Mary Ann Edwards   01 WA-200
Proser, Peter; 9 Oct. 1808; Henrietta Pierce   13 BA-5
Prosper, James; 2 May 1815; Eliza Dupre   11 BA-26
Prosper, Thomas; 28 Aug. 1806; Elizabeth Binger   02 BA-4
Protean, Peter; 24 March 1808; Catha. Hughes   03 BA-498
Proten, Peter; 28 Aug. 1804; Mary Mull   03 BA-491
Proud, John G.; 25 Oct. 1804; Eliza Sophia Coale   03 BA-492
Proud, Wm. T.; 9 Dec. 1813; Mary A. W. Coale   03 BA-505
Prout, Jas. (free black); 26 Aug. 1805; Ruth Harden (free
    mul'o)   03 BA-494
Prout, John W.; 11 Nov. 1817; Henrietta Anderson   03 BA-602
Prow, Jno. L.; 10 Dec. 1809; Eliza Weaver   13 BA-8
Pue, Caleb; 2 March 1816; Emily Dorsey   11 BA-026
Pue, Jesse; 13 Feb. 1805; Mary Wells   09 BA
Pugh, David; 13 Sept. 1815; Hester S. Munday   14 BA-434
Pulcifer, John H.; 7 Oct. 1806; Margaret Blanch   02 BA-4
Pumphrey, Eben'r.; 28 Feb. 1810; Rachel Shisly   13 BA-12
Pumphrey, Reason; 4 April 1802; Ann Stevens   15 AA-2
Pumphrey, Zachariah; 17 May 1802; Elizabeth Boon   15 AA-2
Purcell, William; 22 Jan. 1801; Rebecca Ray   15 AA-1
Purdy, James; 31 May 1801; Elizabeth Purdy   01 AA-67
Purdy, John; 4 Dec. 1817; Caroline Pickersgill   19 BA-72
Pufield, Thos.; 6 Aug. 1809; Ann Bensel   03 BA-500
Purfois, Adam; 15 March 1820; Catherine Stewart   37 BA-153
Purnell, Richard W.; 9 Nov. 1817; Ann Harris   13 BA-29
Pursey, John; 9 Dec. 1805; Mary Jenny (See also 15 FR-310)
                                                        01 FR-1160
Purviance, James; 15 June 1801; Polly Schaeffer   03 BA-401
Purviance, Robert; 8 Sept. 1812; Frances Young   05 BA-137
Putshaar, Martha [sic]; 14 Nov. 1801; Kitty Hillan   14 BA-411
Quail, Walter; 12 June 1812; Anne Miller   13 BA-17
Quarry, Edward; 5 Feb. 1816; Sarah Campbell   16 BA-31
Queen, Basil; 28 April 1814; Ann Queen (both col'd, formerly the
    property of the White Marsh)   16 BA-5
Queen, Edward; 23 Oct. 1817; Elizabeth Butler (both free col'd)
                                                        16 BA-59
Queen, Edward; 7 May 1818; Libby Wilson (both free col'd)
                                                        16 BA-68
Queen, William; 18 Sept. 1817; Amelia Wilson (both free col'd)
                                                        16 BA-56
Quig, James; 28 Dec. 1818; Mary Cahoor   03 BA-603
Quigley, Andrew; 11 July 1810; Margaret Bevins   15 BA-281
Quigley, James; 24 Jan. 1809; Ann Campbell   15 BA-267
Quinlan, Michael; 10 April 1803; Elizabeth Reaton   15 BA-181
Quinlan, Patrick; 6 Oct. 1808; Mary Gammell   31 BA-50
Quinlin, Marcus; 26 March 1810; Jane Langley   13 BA-9
Quinn, Charles (native of Ireland); 2 July 1812; Frances
    Laramore (both of Q. A. Co.)   01 QA-53
Quinn, Charles (native of Ireland); 12 July 1812; Frances
    Larremore, both of QA   02 TA-42
Quinn, John; 26 Aug. 1806; Maria Leakin   03 BA-496
    Quinn, Patrick (native of Ireland, now in Fred. Co.); 2
    Sept. 1816; Mary McAllister   15 BA-303
Raab, J. Philip; 22 March 1808; Ann Sandford   14 BA-424
Rabb, John; 2 June 1812; Marg. Baer   01 FR-1164

Rabbett, Henry; 6 June 1805; Anne Wilburn   03 MO-120
Radcliffe, John; 8 Nov. 1814; Sarah Beach   07 BA-309
Rady, Lewis; 24 Dec. 1803; Cath. Beetle   14 BA-415
Raffo, Manuel; Oct. 1812; Mary S. Deshats   03 BA-504
Ragan, John; Oct. 1810; Amelia Harry   02 WA-87
Ragin, Simon (slave); 19 May 1812; Dorothy Shorter (free colored
   woman)   15 BA-298
Raine, Thomas; 25 July 1805; Charlotte Craven (see also 33 BA-43)
                                                     01 BA-10
Raines, John; 31 March 1808; Elizabeth Oyston   09 BA
Rambergh, Henry; 21 Dec. 1820; Elizabeth Coblentz   16 FR-76
Ramsay, Charles; 26 July 1807; Sarah Hutchison   02 BA-5
Ramsberg, Casper; 25 April 1816; Elizabeth Snoke   06 FR-1324
Ramsberg, Christian; 25 Aug. 1813; Catharine Baulus 15 FR-327
Ramsberg, John P.; 26 Nov. 1818; Ann M. Kuhn   06 FR-1329
Ramsbergh, Henry; 21 Dec. 1820; Elizabeth Coblentz   03 FR-61
Ramsey, Axel; 1 Sept. 1818; Frances Biley (?)   17 BA-19
Ramsey, Robt; 3 Sept. 1815; Adelia Smith   14 BA-434
Ramsey, William (s. of Andrew and Jemima of West Nottingham
   Hundred, CE Co.); 15 d. 11 mo., 1815; Sarah Reynolds (dau.
   of Richard and Rachel of North Susquehanna Hund., CE Co.)
   06 SF
Rancrist, Alexander; 7 Oct. 1817; Elizabeth Alcock   17 BA-17
Rand, Wm.; 25 Dec. 1810; Lilly Lovell   03 BA-502
Randall, Aquila; 29 Dec. 1801; Dorcas Gorsuch   03 BA-411
Randall, Bale; 22 Nov. 1803; Betsy Fugate   34 BA-1
Randall, Isaac; 22 July 1801; Elizabeth Barrick   10 BA-1
Randall, Jacob; 3 Dec. 1817; Mary Wolf   13 BA-29
Randall, James; 20 May 1806; Susanna Olliworth   02 BA-3
Randall, John; 9 Dec. 1802; Caroline Killen   36 BA-1
Randall, Robert; 3 Jan. 1809; Teresa Baker   15 BA-267
Randall, Stephen; 28 Sept. 1813; Harriet Campbell   05 BA-237
Randle, Elisha; 27 Dec. 1804; Sarah Mercer   11 BA-5
Randle, William; 29 Jan. 1803; Mary Pierce   14 BA-414
Randol, John C.; 15 July 1815; Ann Jarvis   11 BA-26
Rankin, Matthew; 1802; Nancy Schmith   02 WA-72
Rankin, Samuel; 17 June 1819; Amelia Bryson   05 BA-241
Raphil, Peter, of Wheatlesburgh, DE; 15 April 1801; Betsy
   Hutchins, of Caroline Co.   03 TA-72
Rapp, Frederick T.; 10 Feb. 1808; Ann Dail   02 BA-6
Ratthell, Solomon; 7 Nov. 1801; Elizabeth Dirth   03 BA-410
Raus, John C.; 17 July 1820; Elizab. Sauerwein   14 BA-440
Raven, Isaac; 23 June 1803; Nancy Galloway   09 BA
Raven, Thomas; 28 Jan. 1802; Jane Long   09 BA
Ravenscroft, Thomas; 12 Aug. 1806; Mahala Dawson   03 AL-614
Rawlings, Benja.; 5 May 1807; Ann Sellman   03 BA-497
Rawlings, James; 19 June 1804; Sarah Richardson   03 MO-119
Rawlings, James; 29 Oct. 1807; Eliza Shaw (free negroes)
                                                     09 BA
Rawlings, James; 1 June 1809; Catherine Ghequit   11 BA-14
Rawlings, John; 4 June 1807; Priscilla Jolly   09 BA
Rawlings, Thomas; 15 Jan. 1804; Tabithy Donelson   15 AA-3
Rawlins, William; 1801; Elizabeth Riderlich   06 AA-1
Ray, George; 5 March 1807; Sarah Robertson (See also 02 MO)
                                                     01 PG
Ray, John; 29 Oct. 1816; Eliza Iser   13 BA-26
Ray, Richard; 9 July 1815; Mary Ann Marten   13 BA-22
Raye, Samuel C.; 5 Oct. 1813; Elizabeth Stewart   11 BA-23
Read. Charles (s. of Jacob and Ann of AA Co.); 16 d. 3 mo., 1809;
   Betty Fisher (dau. of Samuel and Susanna)   09 SF
Read, Dennis; 1 Jan. 1801; Rachel Wills   09 BA
Read, Dr. Jno. M.; 9 Nov. 1802; Mary Ann Clark   03 MO-118
Read, Robert; 9 April 1815; Frances Blades   17 BA-11

Read, Thomas; 7 July 1803; Polly Kershner (see also 04 AL-1;
     09 AL)   07 AL-274
Read, William; 18 Jan. 1819; Lydia Maria Fenn   05 BA-241
Readly, George; 17 Feb. 1808; Mary Thompson   17 BA-5
Ready, Jno.; 17 Sept. 1801; Elizabeth Rutter   14 BA-410
Ready, Wm.; 21 June 1810; Eleanor Thornton   13 BA-10
Ream, George; 21 Jan. 1813; Cath. Eliz. Stamen   14 BA-431
Reany, Henry; 17 Feb. 1820; Eve Schally   14 BA-440
Rearden, Richard; 31 March 1804; Mary Kelly   09 BA
Reardon, John; 16 April 1816; Elizabeth Squires   11 BA-27
Reason, Sam'l; 5 Nov. 1818; Mary S. Stevens   13 BA-32
Reberg, Lewis; 25 Jan. 1806; Sophia Rodeman   14 BA-419
Reblogel, Fried.; Dec. 1805; Cath. Bowman   02 WA-79
Recand, Thos.; 23 May 1812; Ann Shipy   13 BA-16
Recoe, George; 6 June 1804; Grace Buckler   14 BA-416
Reddell, Geo.; 8 July 1819; Eliza Arnold   13 BA-33
Redding, Geo.; 21 March 1816; Mary Fusselbaugh   13 BA-24
Redding, John; 6 Jan. 1803; Sophia Piper   36 BA-1
Reddish, Thomas; 1 Jan. 1806; Rachel McDaniel   02 BA-3
Redeford, Jesse; 23 Jan. 1811; Martha Shortel   11 BA-18
Reder, Frederick; 6 Jan. 1818; Rachel Foster   06 FR-1327
Redgrave, John; 1 May 1817; Elizabeth Hoffman   05 BA-240
Reding, William; 4 April 1814; Henrietta Lewis   03 BA-505
Redman, Barnabas; 16 April 1801; Sally Marshall   09 BA
Redman, Benjamin; 19 Aug. 1803; Hellen Bean   02 SM-186
Redman, Zachariah; 7 Sept. 1815; Penny Mattingly   01 SM-64
Redmond, Isaac; 23 June 1804; Isabella Julian   13 BA-4
Reed, Alex'r; 12 Feb. 1819; Eliza Whitelock   13 BA-32
Reed, Amos; 6 Oct. 1808; Grace Blackburn   09 BA
Reed, Benj.; 27 Nov. 1810; Sally Burneston   13 BA-11
Reed, David; 3 March 1808; Eliza McClary   13 BA-3
Reed, Dennis; 1 Jan. 1801; Rachel Wells   09 BA
Reed, Isaac; 6 Sept. 1803; Margaret Dunning   34 BA-1
Reed, Jacob; 10 May 1820; Elizabeth Rendel   07 BA-312
Reed, Joh.; 11 July 1801; Hanna Huett   02 WA-71
Reed, John D.; 17 July 1802; Ruth Underwood   06 BA-2
Reed, Joseph; 15 March 1809; Ann Carroll   13 BA-6
Reed, Joseph; 22 Dec. 1811; Mary Irvine   03 BA-503
Reed, Ninian; 23 April 1811; Mary Shank   02 WA-89
Reed, Thomas; 17 May 1812; Delia Roberts   13 BA-7
Reed, Wm.; 15 Nov. 1803; Margaret Hardy   03 BA-435
Reeder, Alex'r; 11 March 1816; Mary Ann Fowler   03 BA-507
Reeder, Frederick B.; Dec. 1818; Susanna Watts   02 WA-111
Reekins, Joseph; 5 May 1803; Elizabeth Ommalein   15 BA-181
Reel, John; Sept. 1804; Holdy Toneray   02 WA-77
Reese, Frederick; 12 July 1812; Mary Hutson   11 BA-19
Reese, George; 1 Dec. 1804; Margaret Webb   14 BA-417
Reese, Henry; July 1819; Catherine Beard   02 WA-113
Reese, John; 8 Oct. 1811; Susanna Staley   01 FR-1163
Reese, John L.; 14 Feb. 1812; Jemima Sanks (See also 15 FR-325)
                                                        11 BA-19
Reese, Thomas L. (of Balto. Town, s. of John E., dec., and Ann);
     24 d., 11 m., 1813; Mary Moore, Jr. (dau. of Thomas of BA
     and Mary) (19 SF gives date as 1812)   12 SF-40
Reese, Thos. S.; 22 May 1817; Matilda Barney   13 BA-28
Reese, Wm.; 5 Nov. 1818; Charlotte White (blacks)   19 BA-72
Reeve, George; 6 June 1804; Mary Fleming   25 BA-4
Reeves, Alexander H.; 17 Feb. 1820; Mary Ann Bishop   17 BA-22
Reeves, John; 11 June 1803; Abiel Allen   03 BA-429
Reeves, Nicholas; 9 Jan. 1817; Sarah Shilling   09 BA
Reeves, Robert D.; 16 June 1805; Helen Webb   02 SM-187
Reginold [Reginotte], Ambrose; 11 Sept. 1820; Elizabeth Shays
                                                        39 BA-38

Reginotte. See Reginold.

Regnier, Charles Louis; 6 Dec. 1815; Francoise Dana (both French
   col'd)   16 BA-29
Rehm. See Renner
Reib, Henry; 6 Oct. 1803; Margaret Froget   34 BA-1
Reich, Jacob; 2 April; 1812; Catherine Crumbaugh 06 FR-1317
Reich, Philip; 5 May 1811; Anna M. Creager   06 FR-1316
Reid, Jacob; 16 May 1820; Susannah Jacobs   06 FR-1331
Reid, John; 2 June 1805; Harriet Keene   01 DO-41
Reid, Zachariah; 22 Feb. 1816; Latty Reid   06 FR-1323
Reidel (or Reindel), Gottlieb; 11 Oct. 1808; Hana Spies
                                      14 BA-425
Reidenauer, Isaac; Dec. 1815; Cath. Sturtzman   02 WA-100
Reidenauer, Matthias; Nov. 1817; Elizab. Hunt   02 WA-107
Reidenauer, Nicholas; Dec. 1818; Cath. Holtzman 02 WA-111
Reider, Francis Lennox; 18 Feb. 1820; Maria Hemmel 39 BA-38
Reigard, Philip; 13 May 1813; Sophia Diefendorfer 07 BA-309
Reihle, Friedr.; 18 Apr. 1820; Christina Hanger 14 BA-440
Reiley, Wm. R.; 7 May 1805; Elizabeth Anderson (See also
   02 BA-35)   03 BA-493
Reinagle, Alexander; 20 Sept. 1803; Ann Duport 05 BA-234
Reineman, Christoph.; 21 July 1808; Dorothea Frelinger 14 BA-424
Reinhart, George; 17 Oct. 1803; Susanna Schmitt (See also
   15 FR-315)   01 FR-1163
Reintzel, John; 25 Sept. 1804; Elizabeth Waughop 02 SM-186
Reisinger, George; 5 May 1808; Mary Mackenheimer 14 BA-424
Reistein (?), George; 21 Jan. 1801; Cath. Batga   14 BA-409
Reister, John; 20 Dec. 1801; Eleanor Chapman   23 BA-1
Reiston, Robert; 20 Nov. 1817; Sarah M. Bowen   13 BA-29
Reitenauer, Jacob; Oct. 1808; Marg. (?)   02 WA-86
Reitenouer, Adam; Aug. 1802; Elis. Stephan   02 WA-73
Reitenour, Joh.; Dec. 1803; Dorothea Fink   02 WA-79
Reiter, George; 13 Feb. 1804; Dorothea Koch   14 BA-416
Reiter, Ludwig; 2 July 1810; Johanna Little   07 BA-307
Reitz, Frederick; 30 April 1806; Elizabeth Everstine 08 AL-90
Reitz, Frederick; 13 Feb. 1816; Catherine Weber 08 AL-90
Reitz, Thomas; 27 April 1813; Elizabeth Valentine 08 AL-90
Remington, James; 12 June 1802; Frances Richardson 09 BA
Remmer, Moses; 24 July 1802; Hannah Rutledge   09 BA
Remmick, William; Nov. 1817; Abigail Talbert   02 WA-107
Remsberg, Christian; 26 April 1808; Mary Schnoock (See also
   15 FR-322)   01 FR-1163
Remsperger, John (or Johannes); 8 Feb. 1803; Hanna Murphy (See
   also 15 FR-314)   01 FR-1163
Remsperger, John (or Johannes); 31 Dec. 1805; Mary Durst (See
   also 15 FR-318)   01 FR-1163
Renaud, Francis; 24 Oct. 1816; Elizabeth Meyer   32 BA-310
Renner, George; Jan. 1803; Christ. Sauer   02 WA-74
Renner, Jacob; Aug. 1802; Mary Grieger   02 WA-73
Renner [Rehm], Joannes; 1 Oct. 1806; Christina Wattman 39 BA-18
Renner, John; 26 Oct. 1811; Letitia Flanigan   04 FR-18
Renno, Richard; 28 Aug. 1802; Rebecca Turner   09 BA
Rennous, John; 25 March 1819; Susannah Grice   08 BA
Renshaw, Thomas; 25 Nov. 1818; Elizabeth Clearum 11 BA-33
Rent, Christ'n; 30 Jan. 1802; Barb. Small   14 BA-411
Rentze, Heinrich; 20 Sept. 1810; Wilhelmina Weber 07 BA-307
Reppert, George; 30 Aug. 1808; Hanna Satzinger   14 BA-424
Reppert, Ludwig; 14 Oct. 1803; Regina Gebler   14 BA-415
Rescaniore, Peter (son of Joseph Rescaniore and Louise Esport
   Rescaniore, native of Vira, Dept. of Lariege); 5 Aug. 1805;
   Magd'n Philippine Antoinette Tardieu (dau. of John Bapt.
   Jos. Tardieu and Mary Magd. O'Coin Tardieu, native of
   Jeremie in the Island of St. Domingo)   15 BA-224
Resh, Jacob; Nov. 1807; Mary Holl   02 WA-84
Resin, Thomas; Nov. 1807; Anna Gray   02 WA-84

Ressow, Michael; 19 July 1818; Jane Lynch   08 BA
Reten (?), William; 13 May 1819; Rebecca Mahaney   22 BA-101
Rettig, John; 10 Jan. 1802; Mary Hindor   09 BA
Reubaugh, John; 16 June 1806; Mary King   11 BA-9
Reubell (or Reubelt), John James (native of Colmar, son of John
     James Reubell and Mary Ann; Adjutant General in the Service
     of the French Republic); 25 Aug. 1803; Esther Pascault (dau.
     of Lewis Felix Pascault and his wife Mary Ann Magdalen)
                                                         13 BA-185
Revell, John; 12 Oct. 1815; Charlotte Frazier Shahanasey
                                                         05 BA-238
Revell, Thos.; 3 Dec. 1807; Sarah Revell   14 BA-423
Reyburn, Thomas Goodwin; 3 Nov. 1811; Alicia Clarke   15 BA-292
Reynolds, Brian; 31 May 1802; Mary Phenix   03 BA-417
Reynolds, Collin; 9 Sept. 1802; Delilah Smith   09 BA
Reynolds, David; 25 March 1802; Luesia Fowler   02 SM-185
Reynolds, Henry; 1804; Leah Ann Deibert   03 WA
Reynolds, Huston; 20 Sept. 1804; Margaret Loughton   03 AL-613
Reynolds, Isaac; 23 Nov.1807; Mary Huffman   14 BA-423
Reynolds, James; 14 Feb. 1801; Ruth Imbert (Sse also 03 TA-71)
                                                         01 QA-43
Reynolds, Jas.; 19 Nov. 1802; Cath. Schally   14 BA-413
Reynolds, James (s. of Jacob, dec. and Esther of West Nottingham
     Hundred, CE Co., MD): 6 d. 11 mo., 1813; Ann Moore (dau. of
     Joseph and Mercy of the same place)   06 SF
Reynolds, John; 23 June 1818; Barbara Forney   05 BA-240
Reynolds, Dr. John; 11 May 1819; Maria Sprigg   01 WA-202
Reynolds, Levi (s. of Samuel and Isabel, dec., of Colerain Twp.,
     Lancs. Co., PA); 12 d. 3 mo., 1801; Mary Kirk (dau. of
     Timothy and Lydia, dec., of West Nottingham Twp., Chester
     Co., PA)   06 SF
Reynolds, Lewis; 18 Nov. 1818; Eliza Councilman   11 BA-35
Reynolds, Patrick; 30 Dec. 1802; Honor Conner   15 BA-175
Reynolds, Richard Barnard (s. of Joseph and Rachel) of West
     Nottingham Twp.); 16 d. 4 mo., 1812; Esther Sidwell (dau. of
     Job, dec., and Rebecca)   06 SF
Reynolds, Samuel; 13 April 1804; Eleanor Reynolds (See also
     15 FR-316)   01 FR-1163
Reynolds, Samuel (s. of Samuel and Isabel, dec., of Colerain
     Twp., Lancs. Co., PA); 2 d. 5 mo., 1804; Anne Reynolds (dau.
     of Henry and Elizabeth of the same place)   06 SF
Reynolds, Sam'l; 25 Sept. 1816; Eliz. Gantz   14 BA-436
Reynolds, William; 11 Feb. 1806; Letita Osborn, both of QA Co.
     (See also 02 TA-40)   01 QA-52
Reynolds, Wm. Holland; 3 Dec. 1811; Mary Reynolds   13 BA-14
Rhoad, John; 1 June 1813; Margaret Lynch   06 FR-1319
Rhodes, Daniel; 26 Oct. 1806; Mary Recknor   03 AL-614
Rhodes, Eli; 19 Nov. 1812; Pricela Hobbs   13 BA-15
Rhodes, Jacob; 6 Sept. 1804; Sarah Reckner   03 AL-613
Rhodes, Jeremiah; 20 (?) April 1806; Betsy Orell (?) (both of
     Caroline Co.)   02 TA-40
Rhodes, Jeremiah; 20 April 1811; Rachael Seth (both of QA Co.)
     (02 TA-11 states he was of Caroline Co.)   01 QA-53
Rhodes, Lewis; 7 May 1801; Ann Oral, both of Caroline   03 TA-72
Rhodes, Philip; 10 April 1817; Sarah Milliman   11 BA-27
Rhodes, Zachariah; 31 July 1810 (by Rev. Robert Roberts); Harriet
     Cunningham   17 BA-8
Rial, George; 9 Dec. 1819; Sarah Harrod (both free col'd)
                                                         16 BA-93
Ribble, Peter; 31 Jan. 1807; Margaret Clair   02 BA-5
Ricand, John; 14 Dec. 1813; Mary Hoffman   13 BA-39
Rice, Arthur; 3 Aug. 1806; Elizabeth Connell   15 BA-240
Rice, George; 29 Jan. 1801; Elizabeth Doxey   02 SM-185
Rice, James; 8 Jan. 1818; Elizabeth Titlow   15 FR-327

```
Rice, John; Dec. 1819; Elizab. Hertzog            02 WA-115
Rice, William; 16 Jan. 1806; Elizabeth Steele     02 BA-3
Rice, Wm.; 4 March 1812; Mary Scott               21 BA-7
Richard, Francis Theodore (native of Paris); 10 June 1804; Ann
    Bennan (native of Baltimore)                  15 BA-204
Richards, Aquila; 2 Feb. 1806; Elizabeth Reed     09 BA
Richards, Benedict; 19 Sept. 1819; Isabella Ebsworth  17 BA-22
Richards, Benjamin; 28 Sept. 1804; Grace Taylor (free blacks)
                                                  03 BA-491
Richards, David; 1 Dec. 1801; Ann Lacy            03 AL-613
Richards, George; 9 Feb. 1804; Lucy Riley (See also 04 AL-2;
    10 AL)                                         07 AL-274
Richards, Jacob; 16 Nov. 1819; Catherine Easterday  06 FR-1330
Richards, John Custis; 15 Nov. 1810; Mary Thomas  09 BA
Richards, Jonathan; 6 Oct. 1802; Hester Adams     09 BA
Richards, Joseph; 15 Aug. 1816; Mary Clarke       17 BA-15
Richards, Sam'l; 1 Nov. 1811; Mary Long           13 BA-13
Richards, Timothy; 30 May 1802; Charlotte Griffin  09 BA
Richardson, Alexander; 7 Oct. 1804; Mary Collins  11 BA-4
Richardson, Charles; 19 Jan. 1819; Julianna Smith  17 BA-21
Richardson, Daniel; 24 Aug. 1805; Rebecka Love Jones  11 BA-6
Richardson, David; 29 Jan. 1811; Elizabeth Lynn   03 AL-614
Richardson, Edward; 16 Oct. 1806; Rachel Lee      11 BA-3
Richardson, Edward M.; 1 May 1819; Hannah Jones   11 BA-37
Richardson, Ignatius; 15 Nov. 1806; Ann Colvin    02 BA-4
Richardson, John; 27 Feb. 1814; Elizabeth Inloes  11 BA-23
Richardson, Joseph; 19 May 1801; Dorcas Mackall   02 SM-185
Richardson, Joseph; 3 March 1819; Mrs. Oril       02 TA-44
Richardson, Robert; 30 April 1817; Margaret Reardon (both res.
    of HA Co.)                                     16 BA-52
Richardson, William; 25 Nov. 1806; Jane Green     02 BA-4
Richardson, William; 11 Nov. 1807 (by Rev. Henry Smith); Mary
    Inducet                                        17 BA-6
Richardson, William; 7 Sept. 1809; Rachel Blueford  03 BA-500
Richers, William; 8 Oct. 1807; Catherine Lynard   15 BA-255
Riches, Rufus; Dec. 1815; Mary Crunkleton         02 WA-100
Richmond, Geo.; July 1817; Mary Colyer            02 WA-105
Richmond, Henry; 3 Dec. 1807; M. Yundt            30 BA-109
Richtenspate, Herman; 18 Jan 1801; Eliz. Kirk     14 BA-409
Richter, George; 5 March 1809; Eleanor Rust       05 BA-425
Rickard, Simon; 24 Nov. 1813; Mary Sanbower (?)   06 FR-1320
Rickenbaugh, Martin; April 1818; Mary Lewis       02 WA-109
Ricketts, Benj.; 20 April 1819; Reba Waters       13 BA-34
Ricketts, Ignatius; 2 July 1805; Margaret Poland  03 AL-613
Ricketts, Rezin; 14 Jan. 1819; Mary Magd. Stear   14 BA-438
Rickey, Anthony; 17 Dec. 1816; Ann Hullison       32 BA-311
Rickhard, John; 1 Jan. 1811; Hetty Hutchinson     03 BA-502
Riddle, Moses; 11 Feb. 1806; Mary Ball            03 AL-613
Riddle, William; 13 Sept. 1804; Margaret Mark (02 BA-34 gives
    bride's name as Marks)                         03 BA-491
Ridenhour, Frederick; 25 June 1804; Charlotte Thomas  03 AL-613
Ridenour, Fred.; 30 June 1811; Susana Houer       02 WA-90
Ridenour, John; 14 Feb. 1813; Elizab. Goll        02 WA-96
Ridenour, John; 4 Nov. 1819; Catherine Frendle    01 WA-202
Ridenour, Martin; July 1813; An. Eliz. (N)        02 WA-97
Rider, Arthur; 7 Oct. 1802; Rose O'Neal           03 BA-421
Rider, Thomas; 19 May 1816; Margaret Black        09 BA
Riders, David; 12 Aug. 1814; Ann Orr (?)          20 BA-222
Ridesel, Franciscus; 8 July 1810; Magdalena Yannaway  07 BA-307
Ridgell, Jonathan; 20 Jan. 1801; Polly David      02 SM-184
Ridgely, Charles (of Hampton); 21 (?) Sept. 1809; Maria Campbell
                                                  03 BA-500
Ridgely, Charles Sterett; 11 April 1804;1 Elizabeth Ruth
    Hollingsworth                                  03 BA-490
```

```
Ridgely, David; 12 April 1814; Julia M. Woodfield        17 BA-10
Ridgely, Jno.; Oct. 1812; Prudence Gough Carroll         03 BA-504
Ridgely, John Williams; 7 Nov. 1818; Isabella Folger     11 BA-35
Ridgely, Lott; 24 Dec. 1801; Polly Williams              15 AA-2
Ridgely, Nicholas; 4 Oct. 1804; Rebecca Croxall          11 BA-3
Ridgely, Nicholas Greenbury; 30 July 1801; Elizabeth Eichel-
     berger                                              03 BA-404
Ridgely, Noah; 27 Jan. 1803; Hannah Lee                  15 AA-2
Ridgely, William; 10 Feb. 1803; Nancy Woodward           15 AA-2
Ridgely, William A.; (c.1 March 1814: date of marriage not given
     but this is the date of the marriage immediately preceding);
     Elizabeth Dumeste                                   05 BA-237
Ridgway, Aquilla; 3 May 1817; Sophia Dove                13 BA-38
Ridley, John; 4 April 1802; Amelia Powers                09 BA
Ridnower, Nepolan; 19 Jan. 1813; Mary Bruher             02 WA-96
Rieley, Edward; 10 Jan. 1815; Mary West                  13 BA-20
Riely, John; 29 May 1817; Miltada (?) Carter             11 BA-27
Rieman, Henry; 30 Dec. 1807; Mary Jones                  30 BA-109
Rier, Frederick: 25 March 1819; Sarah Raabe              17 BA-21
Riley, John; 22 Oct. 1817; Martha Taylor                 11 BA-28
Rigby, Henry; 26 March 1812; Cary Ann Maydwell           09 BA
Rigdon, John E.; 20 Oct. 1808; Ann Orrick                11 BA-12
Rigel, Richard; 29 Jan. 1805; Elizabeth Bruce            02 SM-186
Riggans, Israel; 15 Sept. 1811; Sophia Wolford           13 BA-13
Riggert, John; 30 April 1809; Deborah Moreton            09 BA
Rigges, Edmund; (Feb.?) 1806; Elis. Robey                02 WA-80
Riggin, James; 26 Oct. 1815 (by Elder Joshua Wells); Rhoda
     Clare                                               17 BA-11
Riggins, James; 19 Dec. 1813; Rachel Evrits              09 BA
Riggins, Levi; 10 Dec. 1801; Elizabeth Peirce            09 BA
Riggs, Elijah; 19 Sept. 1801; Elizabeth Ready            27 BA-1
Riggs, Geo. W.; 18 Jan. 1803; Eliza Robertson            03 MO-118
Riggs, George; 28 Jan. 1813; Mary Gibbs                  20 BA-222
Riggs, George W.; 2 July 1820; Reba. Norris              13 BA-35
Riggs, Reuben; 12 Feb. 1805; Mary Thomas                 03 MO-119
Right, James; 3 Feb. 1803; Mary Wilds                    09 BA
Rigney, John; 22 June 1806; Sophia Heisley (See also 15 FR-319)
                                                         01 FR-1163
Riley, David; 15 July 1819; Elizabeth Swenson            11 BA-35
Riley, (Geo)rge; 1810; Mary Richards                     01 PG
Riley, Joseph; 11 May 1805; Mary Driscoll                03 BA-493
Riley, Michael; 21 Aug. 1819; Martha I. Kreider          16 BA-86
Riley, [Geo?]rge; 1810; Mary Richards                    02 MO
Riley, Peter; 7 Aug. 1802; Charlotte Cooper              14 BA-413
Riley, Ralph; 23 Sept. 1805; Mary Andrews                14 BA-418
Riley, Terence (widower); 6 or 7 Feb. 1817; Susanna Higgins
     (widow)                                             16 BA-50
Riley, Thomas; 6 Nov. 1818; Mary Ann Brewer              11 BA-35
Riley, Warrick; 10 Aug. 1820; Mary Nutter                03 BA-604
Riley, Wm.; 24 July 1812; Nancy Williams                 14 BA-430
Rimmer, Isaac; 16 Sept. 1802; Sarah Sinclair             09 BA
Rimmer, Peter; 30 Jan. 1816 (by Elder Joshua Wells); Mary Smith
                                                         17 BA-12
Rimmer, William; 20 Dec. 1804; Achsah Ingle              09 BA
Rineford, Hugh; 26 Jan. 1819; Rebecca Allen Daffer       17 BA-21
Rinehart, Jacob; 28 March 1819; Gertrude Buckham         08 AL-93
Rinehart, Jonathan; June 1817; Susanna Bovey             02 WA-105
Riner, George; July 1818; Peggy Marker                   02 WA-110
Ring, David; 29 Aug. 1820; Sophia Cath. Benteen          14 BA-440
Ring, Frans.; 3 March 1816; Eliza Burtge                 13 BA-24
Ring, George; 3 June 1805; Cath. Smith                   03 BA-493
Ring, Thomas; 28 May 1806; Elizabeth Jones               02 BA-4
Ringer, Daniel; 23 Dec. 1819; Catherine Alexander        03 FR-60
Ringer, Solomon; 1 Nov. 1803; Jane Biddle                15 FR-315
```

Ringgold, Benjamin; 24 Oct. 1816; Sarah Gray   02 BA-37
Ringgold, James W.; 3 Nov. 1818; Ann W. Comyges   02 KE-320
Ringgold, William; 14 June 1801; Polly Blake (See also 03 TA-72)
                                                       01 QA-43
Ringoun, Solomon; 1 Nov. 1803; Jane Ridle   01 FR-1163
Risingson, Henry; 21 Nov. 1815; Achsah Clark   13 BA-39
Rister, George; 22 Aug. 1817; Mary Ann Lewis   17 BA-13
Riston, George; 26 Nov. 1816; Margaret Hermange   16 BA-45
Ritchie, Jno.; 26 May 1801; Cath. Hartman   22 BA-410
Ritchy, Henry; 20 Dec. 1804; Mary Spohn (See also 15 FR-317)
                                                       01 FR-1163
Riter, Christ'n; 20 Jan. 1806; Elizab. Hix   14 BA-419
Riticker, Jacob; 27 July 1815; Sophia A. Glendenin   06 FR-1322
Ritter, Adam; 31 Oct. 1811; Catherine Martin (See also 15 FR-325)
                                                       01 FR-1164
Ritter, Jacob; 7 Feb. 1802; Mary Wiest (See also 15 FR-313)
                                                       01 FR-1163
Ritter, Jacob; 14 June 1807; Anne Weck   07 BA-305
Ritts, Joseph; 1801; Elis. Grove   02 WA-72
River, Peter; March 1819; Elizab. Rouck   02 WA-112
Roach, James; 15 Feb. 1820; Hannah Barrickman   39 BA
Roach, John; 1 Dec. 1812; Biddy Kelly   31 BA-140
Roach, John; 20 July 1820; Joanna Landegrin   16 BA-103
Roach, Joseph; 30 Dec. 1819; Henrietta Medcalf   37 BA-152
Roach, Robert; 27 Jan. 1814; Cath. Miller   02 WA-99
Roache, Alexander; 28 Aug. 1808; Mary Owings   31 BA-48
Roadanser, Henry; 24 Dec. 1812; Polly Carson (See also 15 FR-326)
                                                       01 FR-1164
Roany, Hugh; 10 July 1820; Eleanor Murphy   16 BA-101
Robb, Jno.; 5 Nov. 1808; Achsa Bull   14 BA-425
Roberts, Charles; 5 June 1817; Hetty Lurnmaux   05 BA-240
Roberts, Edward; 20 Jan. 1820; Elizabeth Burns   08 AL-94
Roberts, Francis; 14 July 1803; Elizab. Korgh   14 BA-414
Roberts, George; 6 June 1805; Elizabeth (N) (free Negroes)
                                                       15 BA-220
Roberts, Henry; 20 June 1810; Catherine Austi   09 BA
Roberts, John (s. of Richard and Mercy [Betts]); 31 d. 3 mo.,
    1803; Sarah Russell (dau. of John and Hannah)   03 SF
Roberts, Jonah; 9 June 1819; (Mrs.) Ellen McQuillon   37 BA-152
Roberts, Jonathan; 16 April 1805; Wilhelmina Baugher   14 BA-418
Roberts, Jos.; Jan. 1816; Marg't Rager   02 WA-101
Roberts, Joseph; 8 April 1819; Elizabeth Hammond   17 BA-21
Roberts, Owen; 1 Sept. 1813; Margaret Gould   11 BA-21
Roberts, Richard (s. of Richard and Mercy [Betts]); 20 d. 5 mo.,
    1813; Ann Plummer (dau. of Samuel and Mary)   03 SF
Roberts, Richard (s. of Richard and Mercy [Betts]); 19 d. 4 mo.,
    1820; Sarah Hibberd (dau. of Joseph and Jane [James])
                                                       03 SF
Roberts, Samuel; 20 June 1812; Hannah Davis   02 WA-94
Roberts, Thos.; 16 May 1705; Louvet Kemp   03 BA-493
Roberts, Thomas Henry; 16 July 1811; Sarah Jane Jackson Campbell
                                                       21 BA-7
Roberts, Wm.; 24 March 1812; Cath. Duvaldt   13 BA-6
Roberts, Zachariah; 3 Aug. 1806; Anne Brown   03 BA-495
Robertson, Daniel; 11 Feb. 1806; Sarah Greenfield (See also
    02 MO)   01 PG
Robertson, Daniel; 18 Sept. 1815; Ann Shorter   32 BA-305
Robertson, George; 30 Dec. 1802; Hatty (?) Blunt   05 AA-2
Robertson, George; 25 June 1805; Sarah Wheeler Livers (widow)
                                                       15 BA-222
Robertson, John; 13 June 1801; Alice Keith   03 BA-401
Robertson, John; 7 Jan. 1812; Mary Harry   02 WA-92
Robertson, John; 25 May 1812; Patty Morross   13 BA-16
Robertson, John; 3 May 1814; Susannah Craig   20 BA-222

```
Robertson, Robert; 7 April 1801; Elizabeth Ross        09 BA
Robertson, Thomas; 13 Jan. 1803; Louizear Fairbrother  05 AA-3
Robertson, Thos.; 21 Feb. 1815; Harriott Shaeffer      13 BA-20
Robertson, William; 1 April 1807; Mary Branghan        01 DO-41
Robertson, William; 1813; Harriott Cooke (See also 02 MO)
                                                       01 PG
Robertson, William B.; 11 Dec. 1806; Ann B. Thomas     02 SM-187
Robins, John L.; 12 Jan. 1818; Ellen Ann Brown         09 BA
Robins, Zina; 14 Nov. 1818; Mary White                 17 BA-20
Robinson, Abraham; 24 Aug. 1805; Susanna Oler          14 BA-418
Robinson, Alexander; 21 Jan. 1806; Elizab. Reddy (See also
   15 FR-318)                                           01 FR-1163
Robinson, Alexander; 27 March 1807; Margaret Miller (See also
   15 FR-320)                                           01 FR-463
Robinson, Andrew; 16 May 1810; Mary Anderson           14 BA-427
Robinson, Chas.; 24 Feb. 1802; Cath. Keens             14 BA-411
Robinson, Henry; 6 May 1813; Isabella Maxwell          03 BA-505
Robinson, James; 22 Nov. 1806; Sarah Bradford          11 BA-9
Robinson, James; 28 Sept. 1809; Sarah Miller (See also 15 FR-324)
                                                       01 FR-1163
Robinson, James S.; 18 Aug. 1818; Mary Rogers          11 BA-33
Robinson, John; 1 April 1803; Mary Smith               29 BA-1
Robinson, John; 15 April 1806; Margaret Winter         03 AL-614
Robinson, John (free negro); 27 April 1806; Sarah Thomas (dau. of
   Thomas and Monica) (free negroes)                   31 BA-6
Robinson, John; 21 Oct. 1807; Bursheba Clarke          17 BA-5
Robinson, John; 23 April 1815; Betsey Coleman          21 BA-8
Robinson, Joseph; 14 April 1802; Ann Steel             09 BA
Robinson, Joseph; 19 June 1803; Kesiah Bantrum         06 BA-3
Robinson, Joseph; 13 Oct. 1808; Catha. Miller          03 BA-498
Robinson, Joseph; 312 May 1812; Sarah Kemp             17 BA-9
Robinson, Joshua (of William); 20 Jan. 1805; Mary Carter
                                                       09 BA
Robinson, Nic.; 21 March 1816; Sarah Heath Stewart     03 BA-507
Robinson, Richard; 6 Dec. 1807; Nancy Norris           21 BA-6
Robinson, Thomas; 21 May 1801; Elizabeth Selby         15 AA-1
Robinson, Thomas; 21 Sept. 1813; Mary Kelly            31 BA-158
Robinson, Walter; 7 Sept. 1809; Elizabeth Miller (See also
   15 FR-324)                                           01 FR-1163
Robinson, Wm.; 10 Feb. 1802; Deborah James             28 BA-1
Robinson, William; 7 July 1806; Jane Warnick           03 AL-614
Robinson, William; 11 June 1807; Susanna Lakee         09 BA
Robison, John; 18 June 1820; Mary Ann Yong             04 FR-20
Roboson, Richard; 2 Feb. 1804; Margaret Pierpoint      14 BA-416
Roche, Jesse; 24 April 1819; Caroline Ridgway          13 BA-34
Roche, William H.; 3 Dec. 1819; Amelia Austin          16 BA-93
Rochester, Joseph; 22 June 1815 (by Joshua Willey); Anne Elbert
                                                       17 BA-11
Rochin, John; 19 Nov. 1816; Sartah Fowler              13 BA-27
Rockell (?), Thomas; 24 June 1802; Ara Conaway         05 AA-2
Rockhold, Chas.; 22 Aug. 1811; Margaret Bowers         14 BA-429
Rodd, (N); 27 Dec. 1814; Ruth (N)                      11 BA-21
Roddy, James; 28 Feb. 1808; Eleanor Roney              31 BA-38
Rodenmeyer, George; 5 July 1810; Mary Bamberger        14 BA-427
Rodgers, John; 24 Dec. 1820; Elizabeth Nolan (or Molom?)
                                                       04 HA
Rodley, Robert; 15 Oct., 1807; Eliza Swindell          13 BA-3
Rodriguez, Don Miguel Adalid (native of Buenos Aires); 24 July
   1813; Aimee Marie Francois Rosella Milhau (native of
   Wilmington, Delaware)                               15 BA 313
Roe, David; 18 Jan. 1819; Mary Golden                  13 BA-32
Roe, Peter; 4 Sept. 1806; Mary Stiles                  02 BA-4
Roff, David. See David Hoff.
Rogan, Charles; Jan. or Feb. 1812; Margaret Byrnes     15 BA-295
```

Roger, Andrew Lewis; 1 Nov. 1803; Marg't Hinckes   03 BA-434
Rogers, Alexander; 15 Oct. 1801; Delia Christie (dau. of
    Gabriel)   33 BA-13
Rogers, Alexander; 23 March 1815; Hannah Barry   20 BA-222
Rogers, Charles; 19 May 1801; Sarah Hopkins   09 BA
Rogers, David; 14 April 1816; Mary Allen   17 BA-12
Rogers, Elisha; 16 Dec. 1802; Mary Gordon   34 BA-1
Rogers, George; 18 Jan. 1810; Elizabeth Neale Ford   05 BA-236
Ro[g]ers, Henry; 6 Dec. 1804; Elizab. Deetz   14 BA-417
Rogers, Hiram; 27 Dec. 1814; Ann Broadbetts   09 BA
Rogers, John; 2 Feb. 1812; Sarah Rosensteel   15 BA-295
Rogers, John; 26 Oct. 1813; Sarah Tilyard   11 BA-23
Rogers, John; 14 Dec. 1814; Eliza Kithcart   20 BA-222
Rogers, Joshua; 19 June 184; Elizabeth Hutton   09 BA
Rogers, Joshua; 18 Dec. 1817; Margaret Vass   09 BA
Rogers, Nicholas L.; 28 May 1801; Hannah McAllister   09 BA
Rogers, Richard; 11 July 1803; Phoebe Miller (See also
    02 BA-32)   03 BA-430
Rogers, Richard; 31 Oct. 1816; Margaret Boyle   16 BA-44
Rogers, Thomas; 25 Nov. 1802; Elizabeth Howard (See also
    02 BA-32)   03 BA-423
Rogers, William; 15 May 1806; Lydia Quick   03 AL-614
Rogers, William; 2 March 1818; Ann Moore   16 BA-65
Rogers, William; 2 April 1818; Mary Sweetser   11 BA-33
Rogers, William; 27 July 1819; Matilda Mackey   16 BA-85
Rogge, Charles; 26 Oct. 1817; Magdalen Eisler   16 BA-59
Roggers, Robert; 7 Sept. 1809; Eliz'h King   13 BA-8
Roh, Michael; 29 March 1807; Elizab. Griffith   14 BA-421
Rohr, Andrew; 11 May 1807; Elizab. Gall   14 BA-42
Rohr, Jacob; 26 March 1807; Elizabeth Hauer (See also 15 FR-320)
                                                        01 FR-1163
Rohr, Matt.; 1804; Cath. Mack   02 WA-77
Rohrer, Daniel; 1802; Mary Kuntz   02 WA-72
Rohrer, Henry; July 1813; Mar. Hedrick   02 WA-97
Roht, George; 18 March 1806; Salome Bossert   01 FR-1163
Roland, Abraham; June 1810; Eliz. Funk   02 WA-87
Roles, Richard; 1 Nov. 1801; Rachel Watkins   10 BA-1
Rollings, William; 5 Feb. 1807; Ann Hughes   09 BA
Rollins, Isaac; 21 Aug. 1804; Hannah Haryman   09 BA
Rollins, William; 10 June 1815; Maria Johnson   17 BA-13
Rolloson, Jos.; 24 Aug. 1817; Mary Burns   13 BA-29
Romaine, Alexis (native of Lyons in France); 19 March 1803;
    Ursula Surpix (?), widow Poivier (native of Marseille,
    France)   15 BA-179
Romer, Frederick; April 1805; Elis. Smith   02 WA-78
Romich, John; 9 May 1816; Eleonora Lare   06 FR-1324
Roney, James; 10 April 1803; Bridget Ward   15 BA-180
Roney, Patrick; 30 Nov. 1808; Elizabeth King   03 BA-499
Roney, William; 12 Sept. 1809; Alice McBlair   05 BA-236
Ronswell, Georgius; 12 April 1819; Christina [Krepbell]
                                                        39 BA-36
Roof, Andr.; 24 March 1808; Eliza Janaway   13 BA-3
Rook, Joshua; 13 May 1817; Catherine Rhodes   13 BA-28
Roop, Peter; 15 Dec. 1817; Rosina Price   03 BA-602
Root, John; 26 March 1812; Cath. Moore   02 WA-93
Rosanna, Dominic; 27 Oct. 1811; Mary Ann Johnston   31 BA-113
Rose, George; 3 July 1815; Teresa Deale   16 BA-22
Rose, George; Sept. 1817; Cath. Serbey   02 WA-106
Rose, Henry; 14 April 1807; Casandria Hardins (See also
    15 FR-320)   01 FR-1163
Rose, John D.; 30 April 1806; Elizabeth Mitchell   11 BA-9
Rose, John P.; 27 Aug. 1808; Caroline Hague   09 BA
Rosenberg, Lewis; 27 (Dec. 1807 or Jan. 1808) (by Henry Smith;
    Ann Blades   17 BA-6

Rosenmiller, Lewis; 30 April 1804; Rebecca Porter   14 BA-416
Rosensteel, Henry; 9 Feb. 1817; Marg't Ryland   16 BA-50
Roseensteel, William; Jan. 1810; Eliza Graham   39 BA-23
Roskapf, Jacob; 18 Oct. 1819; Cath. Piek (Pilk?)   14 BA-439
Ross, Aaron; 15 April 1819; Catherine Gilliss   16 BA-81
Ross, Angus; 27 April 1806 (by Leonard Cassell); Elizabeth
    German   17 BA-6
Ross, Aquila; 22 Sept. 1804; Elizabeth Howell   14 BA-417
Ross, Daniel; 27 Jan. 1811; Mary Hay   13 BA-11
Ross, Geo.; 28 May 1815; Mary Carter   13 BA-21
Ross, Henry; 23 May 1809; Sarah Burke   03 BA-499
Ross, John; 19 Aug. 1807; Mary Bradenbaugh   21 BA-6
Ross, Wm. G.; 16 April 1818; Mary T. Heusler   16 BA-65
Rosse, James; 17 Feb. 1814; Elizab. Harrold   14 BA-432
Rosse, John; 23 Feb. 1819; Eleanor Dougherty   32 BA-324
Rossel, Hugh; Feb. 1807; Anna Webb   02 WA-82
Rostman (?), Peter A.; 3 March 1811 (by Rev. Robert Roberts);
    Sarah Moore   17 BA-8
Rote, Jno.; 16 July 1812; Sarah Darmy   14 BA-430
Rotermund, Diederich; 28 Dec. 1808; Wilhelmina Schmachlenbergr
    (widow)   07 BA-306
Roth, Georg; 18 March 1806; Salome Bossert   15 FR-318
Roth, John; 9 May 1805; Ann Dorney   14 BA-418
Rothe, Wilhelm; 21 May 1807; Ann Catherine Osterlohr   07 BA-305
Rothrock, Jacob; 27 Aug. 1807; Eva Russel (See also 15 FR-321)
                                                         01 FR-1163
Rothrock, Jacob; 6 Oct. 1807; Elizabeth Drew (See also 15 FR-321)
                                                         01 FR-1163
Rothrock, Philip; 19 June 1811; Mary Wineman   14 BA-428
Rouls, David; 18 Oct., 1807; Charlotte Benson (blacks) 21 BA-6
Rousch, Martin; 26 June 1817; Margaret Patton   01 WA-200
Rouse, Jas.; 12 April 1804; Cath. Millard   14 BA-416
Roushkolb, Samuel; 26 Jan. 1812; Sarah Miller   02 WA-92
Rouster, Louis; 19 Oct. 1815; Elizab. Rawlings   11 BA-25
Routzang, Jacob; 9 Jan. 1820; Catherine Flook (16 FR-76 gives
    bride's name as Flock)   03 FR-60
Row, John; 26 Jan. 1804; Catherine Wirt (See also 10 AL)
                                                         07 AL-274
Row, John; 13 May 1813; Mary Boswell   06 FR-1319
Row, Michael, Jr.; 19 Sept. 1815; Polly Marker   06 FR-1323
Row, Thomas; 12 Feb. 1802; Elizabeth MacCreery   03 BA-413
Row, William; 19 Dec. 1820; Margaret Jenkins   17 BA-23
Rowe, Henry; April 1818; Sarah Zimmerman   02 WA-109
Rowe, John; 26 Jan. 1804; Catherine Wirt   04 AL-2
Rowe, John; 26 April 1810; Sarah Woolf   08 AL-96
Rowe, Philip; 26 Dec. 1807; Charlotte Creusa (Cromb or Holcomb)
                                                         03 BA-498
Rowland, Christian; Oct. 1817; Barbara Bear   02 WA-106
Rowland, Edward; 27 Oct. 1816; Jane Smith   14 BA-436
Rowland, Samuel; Aug. 1816; Lydia Harden   02 WA-102
Rowland, Thomas; 27 Feb. 1803; Eleanor Harrison   03 AA-120
Rowlee, Israel; 18 March 1806; Rachel Williams   09 BA
Rowles, John; 2 March 1815; Eliza Kerr   13 BA-20
Rowles, Jno. C.; Sept. 1812; Sterling Lankford   03 BA-504
Rowles, Joshua L.; 7 Jan. 1819; Harriet Donaldson   03 BA-603
Rowles, Rezin; 9 June 1803; Sophia Meyer   14 BA-414
Rowley, Edward; 22 May 1802; Charlotte Woodward   03 BA-416
Royal, Yahinara (?); 19 Jan. 1815; Kitty A. P. Hawkins 13 BA-20
Royston, John Scott; 25 Sept. 1803; Elizabeth Coon   35 BA-1
Ruark, Samuel; 13 July 1807; Mary Trott   31 BA-27
Rudenstein, Jno. M.; 5 Nov. 1807; Marg't Raab   14 BA-423
Rudolph, Ferdinand; 21 July 1808; Mary Gongh (?)   14 BA-424
Rudy, Christian; 7 May 1820 (N) Alexander (See also 16 FR-76)
                                                         03 FR-60

```
Rudy, Emanuel; 9 Sept. 1818; Sarah Westeberger        01 WA-201
Ruff, Daniel; 31 Dec. 1801; Hannah Maffitt            33 BA-18
Ruffner, John; 20 June 1817; Elizabeth Long           01 WA-200
Rummell, Thos. A.; 14 Jan. 1810; Mary Hosler          13 BA-9
Rumsey, Charles H.; 19 Dec. 1820; Caroline B. Howard  33 BA-47
Runkle, George; 30 Jan. 1812; C. Steneke              30 BA-109
Runner, Henrich; 13 Nov. 1808; Elisabeth Thomas       15 FR-323
Runner, Henry; 13 Nov. 1808; Elizab. Thomas           01 FR-1163
Ruppert, John; 24 Dec. 1802; Charlotte Alberson       14 BA-413
Rush, Benjamin; 11 July 1801; Rachel Daughaday        03 BA-402
Rush, Francis; 7 Nov. 1809; Nancy Colin               03 AL-614
Rush, Rich'd; 11 May 1808; Eliz. Grimes               14 BA-424
Rush, Samuel; 22 July 1802; Martha Dean               09 BA
Rusk, Jno.; 15 Oct. 1808; Barbara Kaufman             14 BA-425
Rusk, Paul; 6 April 1820; Patience Stinchcomb         13 BA-41
Rusk, Samuel; 2 Jan. 1819; Rachel Thompson            13 BA-34
Rusk, Thomas; 12 Nov. 1818; Barbara Waggoner          09 BA
Russel, Alexander; 7 Jan. 1819; Ann Degooff           11 BA-35
Russel, Charles; 14 Dec. [prob. 1806]; Margaret Guy   02 BA-5
Russel, James; 31 Jan. 1816; Milcah S. Browning       11 BA-26
Russel, Patrick; 29 June 1815; Mary [Larner]          39 BA-30
Russel, Philip; 8 Aug. 1819; Ann Maria Coleman        19 BA-73
Russel, William M.; 8 Dec. 1819; Mary Ann Curry       14 BA-439
Russell, Abel (s. of John and Hannah); 24 d. 11 mo., 1808;
   Elizabeth Roberts (dau. of John and Rebecca)       03 SF
Russell, Alex'r; 14 Feb. 1810; Lovinia Dynes          13 BA-11
Russell, Charles; 13 Sept. 1806; Margaret Guy         02 BA-4
Russell, Charles; 10 May 1811; Hebe Conrad            15 BA-287
Russell, George; 1 April 1809; Polly Nobbs            11 BA-13
Russell, John (s. of John and Hannah); 18 d. 5 mo., 1809; Ann
   Hughes; (dau. of Jesse and Elizabeth)              03 SF
Russell, John; [date not given: after 13 Oct. 1812]; Marie
   Brady                                              15 BA-306
Russell, John D.; 28 Aug. 1818; Mary Ann Kenny        16 BA-73
Russell, Thos.; 21 Sept. 1809; Nancy Montgomery       03 BA-500
Rutherford, Benjamin; 8 Feb. 1814; Sophia Schell      06 FR-1320
Rutledge, Abraham; 11 May 1809; Margaret Magan [Magaw?]
                                                      14 BA-426
Rutledge, Edward; 27 April 1802; Susanna Wilson       01 BA-9
Rutledge, Thomas; 17 May 1804; Sarah Gorsuch          06 HA-1
Rutles, Thos. B.; 27 Feb. 1816; Eliza McL. Rutter     13 BA-24
Rutter, Geo.; 1 Oct. 1805; Polly Pierpoint            14 BA-418
Rutter, John; 5 June 1817; Margaret Cronmiller        11 BA-27
Rutter, Richard; 16 July 1803; Elizabeth Kimmell      09 BA
Rutter, Robert; 12 Sept. 1819; Catherine Barron       16 BA-87
Rutter, Valentine; 7 May 1801; Mary Rusk              14 BA-409
Ryan, James; 6 May 1807; Mary Hilford                 03 BA-497
Ryan, Peter; 17 Nov. 1812; Margaret Williams          14 BA-431
Ryan, Thomas; 3 June 1813; Nancy Hanna                09 BA
Ryan, William; 3 Nov. 1801; Thamer Wayman (15 FR-312 gives date
   as 6 Nov.)                                         01 FR-1163
Ryan, William; 21 July 1808; Cath. Gormley            14 BA-424
Rye, Henry; 8 Dec. 1814; Ann Smith                    06 FR-1321
Rymer, John; March 1804; Rosey Montreese              02 WA-76
Rymon, Philip; 25 May 1806; Nancy Alloway             09 BA
Sabbelee, Thomas; 23 Nov. 1809; Maria Von de Hoff     39 BA-23
Sable, John; 5 April 1810; (by Rev. Robert Roberts); Catherine
   Ole                                                17 BA-8
Sackrider, Dan'l W.; 14 Feb. 1805; Mary Adair         21 BA-6
Sadler, Jos.; 27 June 1816; Marg't Lines              13 BA-25
Sadler, Thos.; 19 Dec. 1819; Ann Maria Forister       13 BA-34
Sadtler, Philip B.; 8 Dec. 1812; Cath. Sauerwein      14 BA-431
Saffell, Hezekiah; 8 Sept. 1804; Lydia Davis          03 MO-119
Saffield, Chas.; 17 April 1809; Mary Kennedy          14 BA-426
```

```
Saffield, Joshua; 29 Jan. 1803; Ruth McCoy              15 AA-2
Saffield, [Or]lando; 1813; Deborah Saffield             01 PG
Saffield, Orlando [or Oratio]; 1813; Deborah Saffield   02 MO
Sager, Jacob, Jr.; Aug. 1819; Mary Newcommer            02 WA-114
Sailer, John; Nov. 1810; Eliz. Miller                   02 WA-88
Sailes, George; 23 Jan. 1817; Margareth Jacobs          06 FR-1325
St. Clair, James; 19 Jan. 1806; Pososhe(?) Pocock       09 BA
St. Clair, John; 18 April 1802; Charity Saunders        33 BA-14
St. Clair, Moses; 29 Sept. 1809; Ann Blaney             01 BA-11
St. Clair, Will; May 1806; Mary Empig                   02 WA-80
St. Victor, Armand B.; 11 May 1815; Eliza Ann Giles     03 BA-506
Salge, Conrad; 26 June 1804; Hannah F. Sandels          14 BA-417
Salinave, James; 2 Dec. 1819; Ann Catherine Privatory   32 BA-326
Salman, Chas.; 30 Jan. 1816; Eliza Ann Wyant            14 BA-435
Salsbury, Clark; 20 Sept. 1818; Ellinor H. York         17 BA-19
Sampson, David; 29 July 1806; Belinda Satiswait         02 BA-4
Sampson, Francis; 15 Aug. 1802; Matilda Baxter          03 BA-419
Sampson, George; 7 July 1801; Pamelia Haregrove         09 BA
Sampson (?), Thistle; 23 Oct. 1806; Susannah Tomlinson  03 AL-614
Samuels, Samuel; 4 March 1813; Wilhelmina Lobstein      14 BA-431
Samuels, Thos.; 18 Nov. 1811; Nancy Dougherty           03 BA-503
Sanbower, Michael; 21 Dec. 1820; Elizabeth Carnes       02 FR-16
Sander, Valentine; 5 March 1802; Sophia Fay             14 BA-412
Sanders, Benedict I.; 4 March 1819; Sally Scharr        14 BA-438
Sanders, Benj'n.; 22 Dec. 1807; Polly Geese             14 BA-423
Sanders, Edward; 3 April 1801; Harriet Williams         11 BA-2
Sanders, Geo.; 10 Feb. 1805; Elis. Locher               02 WA-78
Sanders, John; 28 May 1801; Anne Seabright              03 BA-401
Sanders, John; 24 July 1817; Priscilla Stout            16 BA-55
Sanders, Jos.; 1 May 1812; Sarah Fisher                 13 BA-16
Sanders, Tho.; 14 April 1811; Elizabeth Morton          21 BA-7
Sanderson, Aaron; 26 May 1805; Margaret O'Connor        15 BA-220
Sanderson, William P.; 14 May 1807; Elisabeth Lederman  15 FR-320
Sanderson, Wm. R.; 14 May 1807; Elizab. Lederman        01 FR-1171
Sandforth, Leon; 8 Aug. 1816; Eliza Johns               13 BA-26
Sands, Benjamin; 3 March 1803; Rebecca Hook             09 BA
Sands, Samuel; 22 April 1819; Sarah Buckler Innis       09 BA
Sanford, Joseph; 29 July 1801; Rachel Davis             09 BA
Sank, Elijah; 25 Dec. 1817; Mary Ann English            13 BA-30
Sank, Martin; 25 March 1817; Marg't A. McCarter         13 BA-23
Sank, Nicholas; 3 Feb. 1801; Peggy Benson               03 BA-398
Sankey, W.; 21 May 1818; Bridget Horner                 13 BA-31
Sanks, Corbin; 7 Nov. 1820; Eliza Nicholls              11 BA-37
Sanner, Jonathan; 22 June 1802; Frances Dunbar          02 SM-185
Sansberg, John; 16 Aug. 1815; Ann Eve Bendon (widow)    16 BA-24
Sansort, Richard; 21 Nov. 1806; Nancy Misix             30 BA-108
Sap, Jno.; 21 Aug. 1806; Sarah Boswell                  14 BA-420
Sapp, Daniel; 3 Feb. 1819; Elizabeth Baine              17 BA-21
Sapp, Fred'k; 26 Dec. 1801; Mary Fifer                  14 BA-411
Sapp, Henry; 16 June 1808; Elizabeth Trapnell           09 BA
Sapp (Lapp?), Joseph; 21 Jan. 1802; Elizabeth Starner   03 AL-613
Sapp, Oliver; 11 March 1813; Mary Overy                 14 BA-431
Sapp, William; 25 Sept. 1813; Sarah Harrison            14 BA-431
Sappington, Nathaniel; 8 Feb. 1801; Mary Taylor         15 AA-1
Saprevort, Richard; 25 June 1816; Ann Pero              17 BA-12
Sargentt, James; 20 July 1806; Martha Esbay             09 BA
Sarney, Michael; 21 Jan. 1819; Jane Green               32 BA-324
Sauer, Georg; 28 Nov. 1812; Helena Metzger              07 BA-302
Saunders, Jabez; 30 June 1809; Susannah Lamden          11 BA-14
Saunders, John; 11 April 1802; Elizabeth Fletcher       17 BA-1
Saunders, Thomas; 25 April 1816; Margaret Holland       16 BA-33
Sauner (Zohner?), Jno. G.; 30 Sept. 1819; Eliz. Keilholz
                                                        14 BA-439
Savage, Hugh; 25 Nov. 1816; Sarah Curran                16 BA-46
```

Savage, Patrick; 14 June 1804; Rachel Wise   15 BA-204
Saville (Laville), John; 29 March 1814; Araminta Savington
                                                    13 BA-18
Savin, Richard; 3 Nov. 1816; Car. Dorry Augustine   14 BA-436
Savin, Thos. S.; 11 Dec. 1810; Sarah Dennison   13 BA-11
Savington, William; 23 July 1812 (by Rev. Ryland); Frances
    Garrettson   17 BA-9
Saylor, Frederic; Aug. 1818; Susanna Thomb   02 WA-110
Saylor, Frederick; 25 April 1816; Ann Seirer   16 BA-35
Scarf, Jno.; 25 May 1809; Elizab. Rawles   14 BA-426
Schaaf, Peter; 18 March 1804; Eliz. Reidenauer (See also
    15 FR-316)   01 FR-1171
Schade, John; 31 Oct. 1820; Elizab. Gruber   14 BA-440
Schaeffer, John A.; 24 Oct. 1811; Elizabeth Baltzer 06 FR-1316
Schaff, Thomas; 4 July 1815; Rachael Matthews   06 FR-1322
Schaffer, Fred'h Y.; 21 Nov. 1815; Louisa C. Kurtz 14 BA-434
Schaffer, John; 2 Nov. 1817; Elizabeth Sultzer   06 FR-1327
Schafner, Jacob; 2 Jan. 1803; Phebe Weber (See also 15 FR-313)
                                                    01 FR-117
Schanck, Abrah.; May 1806; Nancy Rest   02 WA-80
Scharer, Johannes; 29 March 1801; Cathrina Heidern 01 CL-149
Scharff, George; 3 March 1807; Mary Tarr   14 BA-421
Schaub, Christian; 31 Aug. 1803; Mary Eller (15 FR-315 gives
    bride's name as Maria)   01 FR-1171
Schaub, John; 4 Aug. 1817; Elisabeth Bauer   07 BA-311
Scheeler, Christian; 13 Nov. 1803; Mary Bowser   15 BA-191
Scheeman (or Schneemann), John Andrew Christopher; 21 April 1803;
    Hannah Brache   03 BA-427
Schelly, Peter; July 1804 (by Jno. Bloodgood); Eleanor Griffin
    (See also 40 BA)   17 BA-4
Schelman, Adolphus; 19 Aug. 1810; Elizabeth Weber   39 BA-25
Schemel, Henry; Nov. 1808; Elis. Poffenberger   02 WA-86
Schenck, Philip; 17 Dec. 1808; Sophia Chamberlain   14 BA-425
Schickenhelm, George; 19 March 1805; Cath. Leas (See also
    15 FR-317)   01 FR-1171
Schiller, Christopher; 26 Nov. 1812; Rebecca Buschen 07 BA-308
Schindel, Philip; March 1808; Cath. Hide   02 WA-85
Schindler, Daniel; 10 May 1808; Elisabeth Riess   15 FR-322
Schister, Joh.; Dec. 1805; Peggy Lang   02 WA-79
Schlagel, John; Oct. 1808; Sus. Gelwickes   02 WA-86
Schleg, Johannes; 8 June 1802; Cathrina Kesselring (both single)
                                                    01 CL-150
Schleicker, Peter J.; 16 Oct. 1812; Hanna C. Kleinhaus 14 BA-431
Schleigh, John; Dec. 1819; Mary Artz   02 WA-115
Schley, Henry; 28 Oct. 1817; Maria Warrall   19 BA-72
Schley, Jacob; 4 June 1818; Anna P. Jones   05 BA-240
Schlosser, George; 23 Jan. 1814; Phebe Gough   06 FR-1320
Schlusselberger, Martin; 30 June 1805; Elizabeth Henskey
                                                    39 BA-18
Schmactamberg, John; 30 Aug. 1801; Wilhel(mina?) Weck 30 BA-108
Schmal, Johan; 23 July 1809; Louisa Rossmeier   07 BA-307
Schmecke, Wm.; 26 Sept. 1810; Polly Wilcox   14 BA-227
Schmedicke, J. Carl; 20 Jan. 1818; Sally Thomas   14 BA-437
Schmekpeffer, Rudolph; 3 Sept. 1806; Martha Fray   14 BA-420
Schmid, Friederich Christian; 22 Jan. 1818; Wilhelmina Rottermund
    (widow)   07 BA-311
Schmidt, Adam; 2 Sept. 1806; Jane Williams   14 BA-420
Schmidt, Andreas; 13 Sept. 1812; Marg. Burkitt   14 BA-430
Schmidt, Ferdinand; 19 May 1802; Sarah Waters   14 BA-412
Schmidt, Jas.; 20 April 1808; Cath. Mellinger   14 BA-424
Schmidt, Johan David; 27 Aug. 1820; Sarah Ihlen   14 BA-440
Schmidt, Lud. Fred'k; 6 Feb. 1818; Susan Light   14 BA-437
Schmidt, William L.; 30 April 1805; Maria Furnival (See also
    03 BA-493)   02 BA-35

Schminoke, George; 10 Nov. 1814; Anna Tschudy   07 BA-309
Schmit, George; 24 May 1801; Mary Pish (15 FR-311 gives bride's
    name as Pisch)   01 FR-1170
Schmit, John; 14 May 1804; Charlotte Brunner   01 FR-1171
Schmitt, David; 19 Aug. 1804; Susan Grebill   01 FR-1171
Schmitt, George; 9 Aug. 1807; Mary Bastian   01 FR-1171
Schmitt, Joseph; 26 Nov. 1807; Sybilla Tofler (See also
    15 FR-321)   01 FR-1171
Schmitt, Peter; 24 Aug. 1805; Mary Gandis (15 FR-318 gives
    bride's name as Maria Yandis)   01 FR-1171
Schnauber, George; 21 Aug. 1801; Elizab. Keller   14 BA-410
Schnebly, John; March 1819; Eliza. Kealhoffer   02 WA-112
Schneeman, John Andrew Christopher; 20 April 1803; Hannah
    Bracke   02 BA-32
Schneider, [Frederic] Rodolphus; 22 June 1818; Ann Theresa
    Hondorf   39 BA-34
Schneider, Herrman; 23 March 1807; Rebecca Fletscher   07 BA-305
Schneider, Johan; 8 Nov. 1816; Hannah Merfield   07 BA-310
Schneider, John James; 16 Feb. 1805; Mary Genevieve Le Roy (both
    residents of Fells Point)   15 BA-215
Schneider, Michael; 13 Jan. 1803; Delilah ingman   15 FR-313
Schneider, Philip; Aug. 1802; Cath. Herhans   02 WA-73
Schneider, Wm.; 23 Oct. 1802; Mary Cline   25 BA-2
Schnell, Nicholas; 26 April 1807; Mary Kamerling   30 BA-109
Schnertzell, George; 9 Jan. 1803; Marg. Mohler (See also
    15 FR-323)   01 FR-1171
Schnider, Michael; 13 Jan. 1803; Delila Ingman   01 FR-1171
Schober, John; 18 Oct. 1808; Lydia Schmit (See also 15 FR-323)
                                                       01 FR-1172
Schofstall, George; Jan. 1801; Ann Simpson   02 WA-70
Scholl, Henry; 22 Dec. 1811; Christina Fiege   06 FR-1317
Schoolfield, Joseph L. (s. of John and Rachel); 27 d. 8 mo.,
    1812; Mary Russell (dau. of John and Hannah)   03 SF
Schott, Jacob; 26 Nov. 1815; Harriet Davidson   14 BA-434
Schotten, John; 4 May 1820; Maria Jackson   14 BA-440
Schrader, Heinrich; Feb. 1803; Christ. Schin   02 WA-74
Schreiber, Abraham; 17 Oct. 1803; Marg. Lederman (See also
    15 FR-315)   01 FR-1171
Schreiber, Henry; 24 April 1803; Cath. Hauck (See also 15 FR-314)
                                                       01 FR-1171
Schroder, Henry; 26 April 1809; Mary Williams   14 BA-426
Schroder, Ludwig; 12 Nov. 1815; Maria Reily (widow)   07 BA-310
Schroeder, Georg; 8 March 1807; Hanna Geiger   14 BA-421
Schroeder, Henry; 17 Oct. 1809; Henrietta Maria Ghequiere (dau.
    of Charles)   15 BA-274
Schrote, Matthias; 27 June 1818; Everline Davidson   13 BA-40
Schroy, John; 24 Sept. 1811; Rachel Domer   02 WA-91
Schryer, Gotlieb; 25 Oct. 1810; Dolly Hanna   14 BA-228
Schuck, Adam; 10 April 1816; Barbara Brooks   14 BA-435
Schuck (Shuck), John; 6 Feb. 1806; Maria Dull   08 AL-99
Schuck, Solomon; 1 Oct. 1805; Eliz. Kuntz (See also 15 FR-318)
                                                       01 FR-1171
Schumacher, Mauritius Antonius; 3 Feb. 1810; Anna Maria Knecht,
    widow of Hanshue (?)   39 BA-37
Schunck, Jacob; 9 April 1816; Elizabeth Wilhelm   09 BA
Schuy, Joh.; May 1805; Sus. Guthig   02 WA-78
Schwab, Joh.; May 1803; Cath. Schwab   02 WA-75
Schwab, John; Nov. 1806; Milly Horly   02 WA-81
Schwarer, Geo.; 9 July 1812; Ketura Walls   13 BA-14
Schwartz, Casper; 19 Oct. 1802; Sus. Oliver   14 BA-413
Schwartz, Thomas; March 1803; Barb. Wolf   02 WA-74
Schwarzauer, Daniel; 18 Sept. 1801; Eliz. Heims   14 BA-410
Schwatge, August; 28 April 1802; Cath. Geisenderfer   14 BA-412
Schweitzer, Conrad; 19 March 1808; Mary Hausman   14 BA-423

Schweitzer, Johan; 16 Nov. 1808; Elizabeth Miller   07 BA-306
Schweitzer, Michael; 14 Sept. 1817; Sophia Britton   07 BA-311
Schwerd, Conrad; Jan. 1801; Elis. Hye   02 WA-71
Schwertz, Francis Philip; May 1818; Charlotte Gruber   02 WA-109
Scofield, Issacher; 4 mo., 1802; Edith Marshall   10 SF
Scofield, Joseph; 1812; Mary Russell   10 SF
Scott, Abraham; 21 Sept. 1807; Margaret Leitheyer   14 BA-422
Scott, Abraham; 27 Oct. 1816; Eliza Rodner   13 BA-40
Scott, Beckington; 5 Dec. 1820; Julianna F. Miller   01 CR-272
Scott, Benjamin; 7 Aug. 1805; Ann Dougherty (widow)   15 BA-224
Scott, Frederick; 6 Jan. 1820; Marker Baker   13 BA-41
Scott, George; 4 Dec. 1800; Margaret Cole   15 AA-1
Scott, Jacob; 9 April 1807; Elizabeth Overy   03 BA-497
Scott, John; 30 May 1801; Henrietta Smith   03 BA-401
Scott, John; 26 May 1807; Nancy Pickett   11 BA-121
Scott, John; 3 Dec. 1807; Nancy Divers   13 BA-3
Scott, John L.; 11 March 1813; Rosanna Connall   15 BA-309
Scott, Richard; 29 Sept. 1817; Elizabeth Brown   17 BA-17
Scott, Samuel; 17 April 1808; Mary Biscoe   02 SM-188
Scott, Samuel (son of William and Sarah); 7th d. 12 mo., 1820;
    Elizabeth Kinsey (dau. of isaac and Rachel)   02 SF-138
Scott, Solomon; 21 May 1816; Leonora Page   01 CR-272
Scott, Thos.; 5 Oct. 1815; Mary Dixon   13 BA-23
Scott, Thomas; 24 Oct. 1815; Henrietta Flemmin   11 BA-25
Scottin, Stephen; 24 d., 1 mo., 1816; Ann Foulkes   10 SF
Scotton, Stephen (s. of John and Ruth); 24th d. 1 mo., 1816; Ann
    Foulke (dau. of Asher and Alice)   01 SF
Scrivener, Edward; March 1818; Mary Carey   02 WA-108
Scrivenor, John; 18 April 1809; Elizabeth Brown   09 BA
Scuffham (?), William; 18 May 1809; Mary Goliace (?)   31 BA-61
Seaderburg, Nicholas; 26 Dec. 1815; Elizab. Peters   14 BA-434
Seamer, Joseph; 12 Dec. 1811; Mary English   15 BA-294
Sears, Caleb; 14 Feb. 1802; Charity Mullikin   15 AA-2
Sears, James F.; 3 Dec. 1818; Maria C. Coe   03 BA-603
Sears, Joshua; 18 Jan. 1806; Elizabeth Taylor   05 FR
Sederburg, Truls (?); 6 Nov. 1804; Elizab. Snell   14 BA-417
Sedwick, Benjamin; 20 Oct. 1807; Eleanor White (See also 02 MO)
                                                           01 PG
Seekamp, Albert; 8 Sept. 1806; Sophia Volkman   14 BA-420
Seford, William; 18 Feb. 1802; Susannah Jones   03 AL-613
Segeser,George; 29 Nov. 1810; Cath. Clarke   14 BA-428
Seguin, Casimir (age 23, with consent of his mother, Ma (?) Azane
    Seguin, widow); 14 Jan. 1804; Ar (?) Ann Morangues (age 20,
    with consent of her father Stephen A (?))   15 BA-197
Seguin, Peter; 28 July 1814; Clara Eleonor Lamotte   31 BA-177
Seguins, A (?) Claude; 17 Nov. 1818; Rachel Charlotte Jones
                                                           16 BA-76
Seibert, Daniel; 9 June 1808; Ann Britain   13 BA-4
Seidenstricker, Joh.; 1804; Magd. Springer   02 WA-77
Seider, Wm.; 23 Oct. 1802; Mary Cline   14 BA-413
Seister, Wm.; 14 Nov. 1815; Eliz. Weaver   02 WA-100
Selby, (N); 1810; Sarah Davis (See also 02 MO)   01 PG
Selby, Brice; 8 Oct. 1801; Catherine Marker   03 MO-117
Seldon, William Boswell; 22 Nov. 1802; Charlotte Colegate
                                                           03 BA-423
Segus (or Selguy), John Baptist; 23 Sept. 1817; Margaret
    Barbine   16 BA-56
Sell, Bernard; 12 July 1810; Margaret White, widow   39 BA-25
Seller, Jno.; 21 Aug. 1802; Susanna Schaun   25 BA-2
Sellers, James; 16 Sept. 1804; Marie E. Thurston   11 BA-3
Sellers, William; 11 Aug. 1816; Elizabeth Mumford   06 FR-1324
Sellman, Thomas; 28 Oct. 1806; Susanna Smoot   03 AA-130
Sellman, Vachel; 6 May 1803; Rachel Owings   23 BA-3
Selser, Jacob; 4 Sept. 1810; Marie Creider   07 BA-307

Selsitzel, George; 28 March 1801; Susanna Freeman   03 BA-399
Seltzer, Lewis; 21 Dec. 1815; Elizab. Nippert   14 BA-434
Senger, John; March 1819; Hanny Steffy   02 WA-112
Senseny, Jacob; 27 Oct. 1811; Eliz. Johnson   14 BA-429
Seth, Jacob; 6 Oct. 1814; Mary Wilcox (both of QA Co.) (See also
    02 TA-43)   01 QA-53
Sever, Philip; Oct. 1816; Sarah Ohr   02 WA-103
Seward, Elisha; 24 June 1807; Mary Ann Underwood   11 BA-11
Seward, Thos.; 24 Dec. 1815; Susanna Minetree   13 BA-24
Sewell, Benjamin; 23 May 1819; Mary Smith   11 BA-37
Sewell, John; 1 March 1804; Lydia Baldwin   15 AA-3
Sewell, Jno.; 29 Dec. 1810; Elizab. Garey   14 BA-428
Sewell, Richard; 29 Dec. 1814; Susan Hughes   11 BA-22
Sewell, William H.; 15 Feb. 1803; Rebecca Lewis   05 HA-3
Sexton, Charles; 16 April 1801; Peggy Fisher   09 BA
Seybert, (N); 4 Aug. 1812; Mary (N)   02 WA-94
Seybert, Michael; 16 Jan. 1812; Elizab. Bruer   02 WA-921
Seyster, Michel; 1 May 1801; Jane Rogers   03 AL-613
Shade, George; 13 Aug. 1818; Hannah Deering   16 BA-73
Shade, John; 18 Sept. 1813; Elizab. Dries   14 BA-431
Shade, Martin G.; 22 Aug. 1816; Mary Ann Miller   02 BA-37
Shaefer, George; 16 Feb. 1812; Elisabeth Remsberg   15 FR-325
Shafer, Daniel; Sept. 1817; Elizab. Gettner   02 WA-106
Shafer, George; June 1807; Bezi Muse   02 WA-83
Shafer, George; 16 Feb. 1812; Eliz. Remsberg   01 FR-1172
Shafer, Jacob; Aug. 1813; Christ. Kauffman   02 WA-98
Shafer, Jacob; 1 March 1819; Louisa Popp   14 BA-438
Shafer, John; 12 May 1812; Rebecca Welty   02 WA-94
Shafer, Ludwig; 3 Aug. 1806; Jane Howard   14 BA-420
Shafer, Peter; 1804; Cath. Dreytel   02 WA-77
Shaffer, Jacob; 28 Oct. 1813; Mary Wycoff   08 AL-100
Shaffer, John; 19 Feb. 1810; Susan Dunnan   13 BA-11
Shaffield, William; 29 Sept. 1801; Elizabeth Wescot   03 BA-407
Shaker, Geo.; 10 May 1803; Mary Hauk   14 BA-414
Shally, John; 7 Feb. 1801; Elis. Hofflich   14 BA-409
Shanck, Jacob; 1804; Cath. Dutterow   02 WA-77
Shane, Henry; 11 Nov. 1805; Mary Almony   09 BA
Shane, Joseph; 156 Sept. 1808; Elizabeth Krebs   11 BA-13
Shank, Daniel; 24 Dec. 1811; Mary Hoffman   02 WA-92
Shank, George; 15 March 1814; Cath. Adams   02 WA-99
Shank, Henry; 30 April 1812; Barbara Ann Crumbaugh   06 FR-1318
Shank, Jacob; 24 Dec. 1812; Polly Beckenbaugh (See also
    15 FR-326)   01 FR-1172
Shanklin, Robert; 17 March 1804 (by Rev. L. W. McCombes); Eliza-
    beth Bosley   17 BA-3
Shanks, Capt. William; 2 April 1820; Charlotte Howell   37 BA-153
Shannon, David; 25 Nov. 1813; Fanny Sheetz   02 WA-98
Shannon, Joseph; Aug. 1817; Elizab. Artz   02 WA-106
Shaphans, Sebastian; 27 Jan. 1803; Elizabeth Brown   15 BA-176
Shaphard, Geo.; 17 Oct. 1816; Elizabeth Whiteford   03 BA-508
Sharon, James; 16 March 1808; Marg. Findley (See also 15 FR-322)
                                                          01 FR-1171
Sharp, Charles; 9 Oct. 1819; Mary O'Connor   20 BA-224
Sharp, John; 22 Jan. 1807; Susanna Hay   17 BA-5
Sharp, John; 12 April 1814; Cath. Keesaere   02 WA-100
Sharp, Thomas; 24 May 1801; Sarah Clyne   22 BA-410
Sharper, Wm.; 15 March 1802; Henrietta Rothers   14 BA-412
Sharpless, Daniel; 9 July 1812; Russy Knotts   03 AL-614
Sharpless, Jesse; 13 Sept. 1804; Sarah Neptune   03 AL-613
Sharty, Daniel; 23 Dec. 1819; Catharine Ringer   03 FR-60
Shartz, Daniel; 23 Dec. 1819; Catherine Ringer (See also
    16 FR-76)   08 FR-413
Shaw, Edward; 26 Aug. 1820; Martia Dawson   17 BA-23
Shaw, George; 4 June 1807; Ruth Hawkins   03 AL-614

```
Shaw, George; 4 April 1819; Eliza A. Robinson        02 AA
Shaw, Isaiah; 8 Feb. 1813; Ellen Grimes              13 BA-16
Shaw, James; 26 Oct. 1808; Eliza Anglin              13 BA-5
Shaw, John; 23 Oct. 1806; Charity Ricketts           03 AL-614
Shaw, John H.; 25 Nov. 1819; Ann Keene               02 DO
Shaw, Joshua; c.1804; Mary Williamson                34 BA-2
Shaw, Joshua; 5 June 1817; Margaret Smith            17 BA-16
Shaw, Richard; 28 July 1817; Mary Todd               17 BA-16
Shaw, Richard; 30 Nov. 1820; Sarah Ann Flemming      37 BA-153
Shaw, Samuel; 3 Sept. 1805; Rachel Woolf             09 BA
Shaw, Samuel; 21 April 1810; Susanna Leinhart        09 BA
Shaw, Thomas; 21 July 1814; Sophia Morris            06 FR-1321
Shaw, William; 9 Oct. 1804; Ann Waddell              03 AL-613
Shaw, William; 23 Sept. 1813; Mary Ann Gordon        03 BA-505
Shaw, William C.; 8 May 1817; Ann Maria Usher        03 BA-602
Shawn, Peter; 24 March 1804; Margaret Wallis         15 FR-316
Sheanerman, John; 26 June 1809; (N) Purrusall        30 BA-109
Shears, Michael; 7 Sept. 1804; Phebe Mail (See also 03 BA-491)
                                                     02 BA-34
Sheaves, Robert; 11 May 1813; Jane Young             11 BA-21
Sheckton, Daniel; Nov. 1820; Mary Emmert             02 WA-117
Sheehy, John; 21 Feb. 1814; Hetty Willis             16 BA-2
Sheetz, Jacob; March 1816; Mary Sheetz               02 WA-101
Sheetz, Joseph; 26 Nov. 1801; Ruth Owings (See also 18 BA-65)
                                                     01 BA-9
Sheetz, Joseph; Sept. 1818; Anne Horine              02 WA-111
Sheffel, Fried.; 26 Dec. 1803; Cath. Mette           14 BA-415
Shekel, Richard; 23 Nov. 1808; Tempy Boreing         13 BA-3
Sheldon, James; 15 Nov. 1812; Sarah Barnes           09 BA
Sheldon, John; 8 March 1812; Margaret Barnes         09 BA
Shell, Ezra; 16 Nov. 1815; Margaret Deshan           14 BA-434
Shell, Jno.; 18 Sept. 1806; Margaret Michael         14 BA-420
Shelly, William; 17 Sept. 1818; Martia Cheston       32 BA-321
Shelton, John; 26 Dec. 1805; Mary McComas            09 BA
Shenton, Denis; 13 May 1813; Any Shenton, both of Dorset Co.
                                                     02 TA-42
Shenton (?), Thomas; 14 Nov. 1804; Rosa Pickering (both of Dorset
    Co.)                                             02 TA-39
Shenton, William; 19 May 1814; Margaret Phillips, both of Dorset
    Co.                                              02 TA-43
Shepalander, Nicholas; 31 March 1808; Sarah Jones    02 BA-6
Shephard, James; 13 Jan. 1812; Hannah Hall           02 WA-92
Shepherd, Basil; 30 July 1802; Elizabeth M (?)       05 AA-2
Shepherd, John; 20 Oct. 1803; Elizabeth Barnes       05 BA-234
Shepherd, John; 15 April 1804; Mary Owens            03 AA-130
Shepherd, Philip; 15 June 1810; Delia Goulding       11 BA-15
Sheppard, David; 19 May 1816; Barbara Weaver         14 BA-436
Sheppard. William (of FR Co., MD. s. of Solomon and Susanna); 20
    d. 5 mo., 1813; Ruth Fisher (dau. of Samuel and Susanna)
                                                     09 SF
Sherbert, Benjamin; 9 Jan. 1816; Ann Hutton          03 AA-131
Sheredine, John; 1805; Ann Allen                     33 BA-43
Sheredine, John; 18 April 1805; Ann Allen            01 BA-10
Sherley, Samuel; 1 Aug. 1801; Maria Jung             15 FR-312
Sherley, Samuel; 2 Aug. 1801; Mary Jung              01 FR-170
Sherlock, William; 20 Oct. 1802; Margaret Lovet      02 BA-32
Shermadine, Thos.; 20 May 1815; Ann Burgett          13 BA-21
Sherman, Lewis; 9 Feb. 1817; Ann Campfer             09 BA
Sherry, Charles; 4 Oct. 1812; Eliza Gambrell         13 BA-15
Sherwood. Samuel; 14 June 1820; Johanna Forrester    17 BA-23
Shettleford, Lewis; 5 Aug. 1815; Mary Curtain        03 BA-494
Shields, Benjamin; 10 Oct. 1805; Sarah Johnson       03 AA-130
Shields, Bernard; 16 Oct. 1806; Sus(anna) Donovan (See also
    15 FR-319)                                       01 FR-1171
```

Shields, James; 23 March 1801; Elizabeth Thomas   33 BA-13
Shields, Solomon; 29 March 1807; Chlora (Ohlora) Gray   03 BA-497
Shields, William; 4 April 1802; Hannah Somerwell   03 BA-415
Shields, William; 1 Dec. 1808; Kitty Waldren   02 BA-7
Shields, William; 26 Dec. 1811; Harriet Butler   09 BA
Shillin, Philip; 6 Oct. 1804; Abigail Omansetter   03 BA-491
Shilling, John; 1 Jan. 1802; Sally Wishard   09 BA
Shilling, John; 28 April 1811; Mary Dusing   02 WA-89
Shilling, Philip; 6 Oct. 1804; Abigail Omansetter   02 BA-34
Shilling, Philip; 21 March 1816; Sarah Simpson   09 BA
Shimer, Ezekiel; 8 Sept. 1805; Zanedin Jones   03 AL-613
Shimer, isaac; 2 Aug. 1802; Ann James   03 AL-613
Shindler, Daniel; 10 May 1808; Eliz. Riesz   01 FR-1171
Shipham, George; 2 Sept. 1801; Polly Hall   01 SO-15
Shipley, Adam; 8 Aug. 1802; Ruth Crisman (See also 18 BA-65)
                                                         01 BA-9
Shipley, Charles; 26 Aug. 1802; Priscilla Gorsuch   23 BA-1
Shipley, Ezekiel; 19 March 1812; Charlotte Peck   09 BA
Shipley, George; 13 Feb. 1814; Elizabeth McGreger   13 BA-39
Shipley, Joshua; 10 Aug. 1809; Nancy Greenwood   03 BA-500
Shipley, Joshua; 6 Feb. 1820; Catherine Doran   04 HA
Shipley, Peter; 12 May 1816; Elizabeth Bell   13 BA-39
Shipley, Robert; 13 Sept. 1818; Sarah Dimmitt   08 BA
Shipley, Zachariah; 10 Sept. 1808; Milcah Gardiner   03 BA-498
Shirrick, Jacob; 11 Aug. 1808; Harriet Divers   14 BA-424
Shiret, Jno. P.; 24 Sept. 1818; Sarah Seagar   14 BA-437
Shisler, Wilhelm; 2 July 1805; Maria Willstink   14 BA-418
Shissler (?), Paul; 7 Oct. 1811; Elizab. Alter   02 WA-91
Shivers, John; 4 Nov. 1810; Eliz'h Merryman   13 BA-11
Shmith, David; July 1805; Mary Wolaschlager   02 WA-79
Shmith, James; 1804; Elis. Seibert   02 WA-77
Shmith, Tho.; Jan. 1801; Marg. Hogmier   02 WA-70
Shoat, Ostin; 14 Feb. 1802; Amei Ford   24 BA-1
Shock, George; 10 Oct. 1815; Elizabeth Hutchings   32 BA-305
Shock, George; 31 Aug. 1820; Masha Reddison   11 BA-38
Shoemaker, David; 10 Oct. 1816; Mary Sumwalt   13 BA-26
Shoemaker, Edward; 2 Nov. 1819; Jane Falls   16 BA-90
Shoemaker, Ellick; 4 Nov. 1811; Maria Sullivan   14 BA-429
Shoemaker, George; 24 Nov. 1808; Rachel Walton   13 BA-5
Shook, Charles; 27 Feb. 1805; Priscilla Ball   03 MO-119
Shook, Jacob; 1 Sept. 1803; Mary Stonecipher   03 AL-613
Short, David; Nov. 1807; Mary Pence   02 WA-84
Shortridge, John; 18 Feb. 1810; Sarah Oram   13 BA-9
Shote, George; 24 Dec. 1815; Marg't Reed   14 BA-434
Shott, Augustin; 13 May 1805; Margaret Scharr   14 BA-418
Shouers, Emanuel; 4 Nov. 1811; Hannah Lindsay   02 WA-91
Shoun, James; 6 Jan. 1807; Elizabeth Hefner   15 FR-320
Showecker, William; March 1820; Nancy Slice   02 WA-116
Showers, Thomas R.; 25 March 1818; Charlotte McClellan   20 BA-223
Shown, Peter; 24 March 1804; Margaret Wallis   01 FR-1171
Shraiter, Daniel; 5 Feb. 1801; Cath. Leyer   14 BA-409
Shreck, (N); April 1804; Cath. Campple   02 WA-77
Shreider, Frederick; 13 April 1801; Violet Wilson   03 BA-399
Shreve, Thomas (s. of Caleb and Grace); 5th d. 11 mo.,   1801; Ann
     Hopkins (dau. of Johns and Elizabeth)   01 SF
Shriber, Jacob; 21 June 1810; Rebecca Ridge (See also
     01 FR-1172)   15 FR-324
Shriver, Daniel; Nov. 1820; Elizab. Grosh   02 WA-117
Shriver, Henry M.; 28 Feb. 1811; Mary Blair   03 Al-614
Shriver, Jacob; 2 Dec. 1813; Ann Shekels   13 BA-17
Shriver, Philip; 5 Nov. 1821; Barbara Hamersley   06 FR-1317
Shroeder, Jno.; 6 March 1808; Margaret Rosel   21 BA-6
Shrrtz [sic], John; 15 April 1811; Polly Yeakle   02 WA-89
Shryock, David; 9 Nov. 1815; Sarah Wilson   02 WA-100

Shryock, George; 9 May 1816; Elizabeth Flore   06 FR-1324
Shryock, Valentine; 6 Aug. 1816; Elizabeth Stimmel   06 FR-1324
Shuck, Peter; 10 Sept. 1818; Rebecca Bobst   06 FR-1328
Shuderland, A.; 29 March 1807; Mary Buck   30 BA-109
Shuebridge, Jno.; 10 Nov. 1818; Eliz. Weis   14 BA-438
Shugars, Zachariah; 22 June 1811; Sarah Binkley   02 WA-90
Shugart, John; Oct. 1818; Mary Reed   02 WA-111
Shultz, Jno.; 13 July 1815; Alley (Bohmar) Palmer   14 BA-434
Shultz, John; Feb. 1819; Elizab. Smith   02 WA-112
Shultz, Jno. Jacob; 15 Sept. 1812; Sally Steel   14 BA-430
Shultz, Nicholas; July 1820; Elizab. Shank   02 WA-116
Shulze, Wm. L; 22 May 1805; Mary Jones   14 BA-418
Shuman, Peter; April 1819; Molly Herr   02 WA-113
Shuman, Samuel; April 1819; Christiana Newcomer   02 WA-113
Shurley, John (of FR Co.); 9 May 1816; Margaret Jones 16 BA-35
Shurkey, Michael; 7 Sept. 1819; Elizabeth Donnelly   16 BA-87
Shute, Henry; 9 Aug. 1804; Elizabeth Asher   09 BA
Shutterly, David; 12 May 1818; Jemima Lewis   11 BA-28
Sides, Jacob; 11 July 1815; Susan Cline   14 BA-434
Sidwell, Richard (s. of Abraham and Hannah of East Notingham
     Twp., Chester Co., PA; 8 d. 6 mo., 1820; Mary Griffith (dau.
     of William and Alice of E. Nottingham Hund., CE Co., MD)
                                                      06 SF
Siebman, Christian; 5 Nov. 1809; Sarah Wiggand   14 BA-426
Siemsen, John Jacob; 21 April 1816; Eleanor McConnell 05 BA-239
Sifton, William; 26 Nov. 1815; Eliz. Thompson   11 BA-24
Sigler, Jacob; 4 Dec. 1816; Mary Brown   11 BA-31
Sigler, Michael; 14 July 1805; Susanna Eller   01 FR-1171
Sigler, Peter; 31 Aug. 1809; Susanna James   03 AL-614
Sigler, William; 12 Feb. 1806; Grace James   03 AL-613
Silence, Richard; 2 Jan. 1817; Susanna League   17 BA-15
Silvers, Edward; Sept. 1818; Mary Locker   02 WA-110
Silverthorn, Henry; 9 Dec. 1819; Julia Ann Norris   13 BA-34
Silvey, Anthony; 18 Feb. 1818; Catherine Martin   17 BA-19
Silvey, Anthony; 18 July 1818; Catherine Martin   17 BA-18
Simer, Peter; Nov. 1807; Cath. Cost   02 WA-84
Simering, John; 9 March 1815; Susanna Kempler   14 BA-433
Simering, Peter; 30 March 1815; Eve Houstman   14 BA-433
Simes, Thomas; Dec. 1803; Mary Miller   02 WA-75
Simmon (or Simmor), Earl; 30 Sept. 1816; Magdalen Hintz
                                                      07 BA-310
Simmons, Bazil; c.1801; Ann Wyvill   07 AA-1
Simmons, Isaac; c.1801; Ann Childs   08 AA-1
Simmons, Jacob; 28 March 1812; Eliz. Drury   02 WA-93
Simmons, Joh.; 18 Feb. 1802; Catherine Dunckler   15 FR-313
Simmons, John; 28 Feb. 1802; Cath. Dunkler   01 FR-1171
Simmons, John; 29 Nov. 1804; Rosanna Stafford   01 DO-41
Simmons (?), Martin; 5 Sept. 1816; Elizabeth Randall 17 BA-15
Simmons, Peter; 29 March 1807; Catherine Jacobs (See also
     15 FR-320)   01 FR-1171
Simmons, Richard; 30 Jan. 1806; Agnes Hardesty   03 AA-130
Simmons, William; 23 Sept. 1804; Matilda Tillard   03 AA-130
Simmons, William; 2 Dec. 1805; Mary Hall   03 AA-130
Simms, Jos.; 23 May 1819; Eliza Fite   13 BA-33
Simms, William; 18 Jan. 1817; Eliza McCoy   11 BA-31
Simon, David; 13 March 1801; An. Maria Walter   14 BA-409
Simon, Peter; 23 Jan. 1802; Rachel Harman   14 BA-411
Simond, Andrew; 10 June 1807; Ann Pearse   09 BA
Simons, James; 15 Jan. 1811; Sarah Browning   14 BA-428
Simonson, Jno.; 31 May 1808; Margaret Keener   14 BA-424
Simpers, Benjamin; 30 April 1818; Sophe Insor   08 BA
Simpkins, Abel; 1 Dec. 1805; Rebecka Burns   08 AL-104
Simpson, Charles; 15 March 1812; Cathe. Stewart   13 BA-14
Simpson, John; c.1803; Elizabeth Ford   11 AA-1

```
Simpson, John; 15 Sept. 1809; Jane Kuyt              02 BA-7
Simpson, John; 19 July 1810; Agness Bartlett         13 BA-10
Simpson, John; 20 March 1818; Sarah Davis            03 BA-603
Simpson, Rezin (?); 2 Aug. 1801; Mary Gordon (See also 01 AL-5
                                                     03 AL-613
Sims, Robert; 25 Jan. 1819; Elizabeth Brown          17 BA-21
Sims, Thomas; 23 June 1801; Sarah Manly              03 BA-402
Sin, Henry; 23 Nov. 1804; Catherine Bier             30 BA-108
Sinclair, Alexander; 22 Nov. 1812 (by Rev. Ryland); Alice
    Cockey                                           17 BA-9
Sinclair, John; 28 Nov. 1811; Mary McColdon          02 BA-36
Sindal, John; 22 Jan. 1816; Mary Daugherday          11 BA-26
Sindall, John; 29 June 1815; Elizabeth Richards      09 BA
Singer, Fred.; Feb. 1806; Molly Reitenower           02 WA-80
Sinley, Alexander; 3 Oct. 1812; Margaret McDaniel    09 BA
Sinnot, James; 12 June 1808; Ann Doyle               31 BA-43
Sinser, Jesse; 4 Dec. 1817; Margaretr Burgoyne       09 BA
Sinstack, Henry; 21 Sept. 1819; Elizabeth Dyer       04 FR-18
Sintler (?), George; 12 Feb. 1803; Nancy Long        09 BA
Sior (Sion?), Benjamin; 17 March 1814; Sarah Utrim   13 BA-18
Sislar, Jno.; 8 April 1801; Kitty Will               14 BA-409
Sisnop, Adam; 13 April 1806; Catherine Brown         07 BA-305
Sisson, Martin; 22 Aug. 1816; Mary Beard             13 BA-27
Sitler, Abraham; 5 Aug. 1806; Corneli(a?) Welsh      07 BA-305
Sitler, Jacob, Jr.; 2 Dec. 1804; Rebecca Morris      09 BA
Sittlemyer, Jonathan; 2 Dec. 1819; Elizabeth Wyant   07 BA-811
Sittler, Benjamin; 5 April 1801; Catherine Switzer   30 BA-108
Sittler, James; 2 Jan. 1817; Catherine Waller        17 BA-15
Skinner, James; 23 July 1804; Sarah Clarke           03 BA-431
Skinner, James; 14 March 1816; Mary Pollard          13 BA-24
Skinner, Thomas; 9 Nov. 1819; Eleanor B. Rencher     01 SO-15
Skipper, John; 28 April 1803; Elizabeth Herring      23 BA-2
Slade, John; 2 March 1803; Elizabeth Hutchings       01 BA-10
Slater, James; 1 Sept. 1811; Rebecca Davis           11 BA-17
Slater, Richard; 24 Dec. 1801; Sarah Joice           09 BA
Slates, John; 1 Oct. 1811; Elizabeth Rose            06 FR-1316
Slawter, Nathan; 11 May 1809; Marg't Black           13 BA-6
Sleasman, Geo.; 17 Nov. 1811; Cath. Hintz            02 WA-92
Slee, John; 29 March 1810; Mary Tipton               13 BA-9
Slicer, Samuel; 8 Sept. 1807; Fuessa Sanford         03 AL-614
Slicer, Walter; 30 May 1811; Mary Bruce              03 AL-614
Slicer, Walter; 12 Nov. 1812; Priscilla Beall        08 AL-104
Sligh, Thomas; 7 Sept. 1815; Ann Richards            13 BA-22
Sloan, Archibald; Oct. 1817; Margaret Kephart        02 WA-106
Sloan, John; 28 March 1820; Mary Ann Milhoun         11 BA-36
Sloan, William I.; 4 Feb. 1819;' Margaret Newman     11 BA-35
Slough, Wm.; 12 Sept. 1811; Sarah Dugan              13 BA-13
Sly, Christianus; 9 April 1806; Maria Ludgen         39 BA-19
Slye, John (s. of Samuel and Anne); 24 Dec. 1801; Martha
    Buckingham                                       01 CA-64
Smady, John; 2 Nov. 1820; Mary Lane                  16 BA-105
Small, Moses; 28 Nov. 1816; Mary Cure (col'd)        11 BA-31
Small, Rodey, 22; 12 July 1806; Betty McKanan        31 BA-9
Smallwood, (N); 1804; Peggy Dowell                   02 WA-75
Smallwood, Geo.; 16 Sept. 1815; Juliet Jarber        05 BA-238
Smallwood, Joseph; 24 Jan. 1804; Rachel Frazier      15 AA-3
Smallwood, William; 6 Nov. 1806; Ann Kaufman         14 BA-421
Smell, Peter; 12 Sept. 1807; Rachel Little           13 BA-2
Smick, Peter; 26 Dec. 1805; Elizabeth Warner         09 BA
Smidt, Peter; 3 June 1806; Margaret Mark             02 BA-4
Smiley, Peter; 9 July 1816; Cath. Walters            16 BA-38
Smiley, Peter; 15 April 1817; Elizabeth Gillmeyer    05 FR-16
Smith, Abraham; 12 Sept. 1801; Elizabeth Bernan      27 BA-1
```

Smith, Absalom; 25 June 1812; Margaret Nusbaum (See also
    15 FR-325)   01 FR-1172
Smith, Adam; 13 Aug. 1801; Elizabeth Platton   03 BA-404
Smith, Adam; 17 Feb. 1811; Sarah Grayble   06 FR-1315
Smith, Amos (s. of Samuel and Rachel); 30 d. 7 mo., 1801;
    Rebeckah West (dau. of Thos. and Elizabeth) (See also 05 SF)
                                                  02 SF-81
Smith, Andrew; 3 July 1803; Elizab. Zollers   14 BA-414
Smith, Andr.; 7 May 1815; Cathe. Vaunce   13 BA-21
Smith, Bartholomew; 29 Jan. 1807; Eleanor Bean   02 SM-187
Smith, Caleb; 25 April 1801; Permelia Ensor   09 BA
Smith, Caleb; 15 April 1806; Martha Harper   14 BA-420
Smith, Charles; 24 Feb. 1810; Tabitha Sollers   09 BA
Smith, Cyrus; 29 Nov. 1819; Jane Cath. Hanna   14 BA-439
Smith, Dan'l; 22 July 1807; Elizab. Small   14 BA-422
Smith, Daniel; March 1816; Cath. Woleslager   02 WA-101
Smith, Daniel; April 1816; Peggy Harrow   02 WA-101
Smith, David; 13 Nov. 1803; Levina Paugh   03 AL-613
Smith, Dennis A.; 23 Dec. 1802; Elizabeth T. Presbury 34 BA-1
Smith, Eli; 9 March 1819; Mary Peck   13 BA-32
Smith, Eli; 18 March 1819; Phoebe Zimmerman   13 BA-40
Smith, Ellick; 18 Oct. 1806; Sarah Pellom   02 BA-4
Smith, Frederick W.; 19 Feb. 1815; Marriann Parker 03 BA-506
Smith, George; 18 Aug. 1803; Mary Rogers   34 BA-1
Smith, George; 8 Feb. 1806; Martha Sharp   02 BA-3
Smith, George; 31 Dec. (1806?); Rebecca Howard (the marriage is
    entered between two others dated 25 and 26 July 1807)
                                                  02 BA-5
Smith, Geo.; 15 Aug. 1815; Augusta Wheeler   13 BA-22
Smith, Geo.; 27 June 1816; Frances Smith   13 BA-25
Smith, George; Nov. 1816; Susanna Foderell   02 WA-103
Smith, George; 6 April 1820; Susan Felby   14 FR
Smith, Henry; 19 Oct. 1807; Elizabeth Danall   11 BA-11
Smith, Henry; 7 Dec. 1815; Jane McThowen   05 BA-238
Smith, Henry; 31 Jan. 1816; Harriet Daniels   02 BA-36
Smith, Henry; 17 June 1819; Mary Jackson   19 BA-72
Smith, Henry C. W.; 17 April 1817; Mary Ensminger 01 WA-200
Smith, Isaac (s. of Isaac and Sarah of Chester Co., PA); 5th d.
    12 mo., 1807; Margaret Coale (dau. of Samuel and Lydia)
                                                  11 SF-106
Smith, Isaac; 19 Sept. 1815 (by Elder Joshua Wells); Cecelia
    Grover   17 BA-11
Smith, Jacob; 30 Dec. 1806; Elizabeth Rogers   03 BA-496
Smith, Jacob; 31 March 1808; Ana Harman   30 BA-109
Smith, Jacob; 14 May 1811; Rebecka Groves   03 AL-614
Smith, Jacob; 13 Feb. 1812; Delia Wildeman   14 BA-429
Smith, Jacob; April 1816; Mary Bruner   02 WA-101
Smith, Jacob Giles; 20 March 1804; Sarah Evans   02 BA-33
Smith, James; 13 Jan. 1801; Ann Price   02 SM-184
Smith, James; 21 Oct. 1805; Sarah Gooding   14 BA-419
Smith, James; 9 Feb. 1806; Amelia Greson (both of QA Co.)
                                                  02 TA-40
Smith, James; 5 Nov. 1806; Margaret McGrath (widow; both natives
    of Ireland)   15 BA-243
Smith, James; 15 Sept. 1808; Cecelia Clarke   02 SM-188
Smith, James; 8 Dec. 1816; Sarah Overhulty [Overholtz?]
                                                  13 BA-27
Smith, James; 28 April 1817; Bridget Byrnes   32 BA-312
Smith, James B.; 14 Dec. 1820; Louisa Smith   11 BA-38
Smith, Job; 15 April 1807; Ann King   02 SM-188
Smith, Job I.; 31 May 1810; Julian Butler   31 BA-81
Smith, Jno.; 12 May 1802; Mary Arnest   14 BA-412
Smith, Jno.; 1 Feb. 1804; Sarah Ervin   14 BA-416
Smith, John, Jr.; 11 Aug. 1804; Frances Toon   02 BA-34

Smith, John; 28 Nov. 1805; Sarah Parks   09 BA
Smith, Jno.; 8 Dec. 1805 (by Jno. Bloodgood; in list of marriages
    for blacks); Priscilla Hawkins   17 BA-5
Smith, John; 12 May 1808; Margaret Toner   15 BA-261
Smith, John; 21 May 1810; Eliz'th Quinn   15 BA-280
Smith, John; 26 Sept. 1813; Mary Foucke   01 FR-1172
Smith, John; 10 Feb. 1814; Rebecca McNallen (McNalton)   07 BA-309
Smith, John; 18 June 1815; Sarah Walker   17 BA-13
Smith, John; 16 May 1816; Grace Emery   02 BA-37
Smith, John; 16 Nov. 1816; Eliza Wright   17 BA-15
Smith, John; 18 Oct. 1817; Henrietta Durgin   17 BA-17
Smith, John; March 1818; Elizab. Hammer   02 WA-109
Smith, John; June 1818; Christiana First   02 WA-110
Smith, John; 12 Dec. 1819; Catherine Rhode (See also 16 FR-76)
                                                         03 FR-60
Smith, John; 13 Aug. 1820; Mary Google (16 FR-76 gives bride's
    name as Koogle)   03 FR-60
Smith, John A.; 26 Sept. 1813; Maria Faucke   15-FR 326
Smith, Jno. Edw'd; 7 July 1812; Susanna Jeffers   03 BA-504
Smith, John M.; 30 Dec. 1803; Ann Mounsey (See also 03 BA-437)
                                                         02 BA-33
Smith, John S.; 1 Feb. 1819; Mary Mitchell   17 BA-21
Smith, Joseph; 8 Oct. 1801; Elizabeth Dew   27 BA-1
Smith, Joseph; 29 Nov. 1802; Eliz. Beltz   14 BA-413
Smith, Joseph; Oct. 1808; Mary Swope   02 WA-86
Smith, Joseph; 7 March 1816; Henrietta Barney   14 BA-435
Smith, Jos., Jr.; 20 April 1815; Rach'l Stevenson   13 BA-21
Smith, Joshua; 26 March 1812; Cath. Koons   02 WA-93
Smith, Joshua; 12 Aug. 1817; Maria Rhodes (both of QA. Co.) (See
    also 02 TA-43)   01 QA-62
Smith, Louis Richard; 1 Dec. 1820; Elizabeth Jenkins   16 BA-106
Smith, Martin; 19 March 1815; Elizabeth Simon   06 FR-1322
Smith, Math.; 1801; Barb. Bachtel   02 WA-72
Smith, Nathaniel; 24 June 1807; Sarah Eisell   15 BA-251
Smith, New; 25 Dec. 1817; Betsy Care (colored)   02 BA-37
Smith, Nicholas 13 May 1802; Martha Caldwell   05 BA-233
Smith, Nicholas; 6 Sept. 1804; Anne Clarke   03 BA-491
Smith, Nich's; 14 May 1808; Susanna Bernhard   14 BA-424
Smith, Patrick; 7 June 1813; Margaret Beatty (both natives of
    Ireland)   15 BA-311
Smith, Pernel; 24 May 1805; Ann Gilberthorp (See also 03 BA-443)
                                                         02 BA-35
Smith, Philip; c.1803; Marg. Gardner   07 AA-3
Smith, Richard; 25 Jan. 1802; Ann Clark   14 BA-411
Smith, Richard; 9 Oct. 1808; Regina Staab   15 BA-265
Smith, Richard; Oct. 1812; Elizabeth Durgen or Dwigen   03 BA-504
Smith, Rich'd Brooke; 11 Sept. 1803; Sarah Letton   03 MO-118
Smith, Robert; 29 Jan. 1806; Margaret Hargrove   15 BA-235
Smith, Robert; 20 July 1812; Nancy Thrash   13 BA-17
Smith, Samuel (s. of Henry and Martha of Washington Co., PA); 21
    d. 6 mo., 1804; Ann Brown (dau. of William and Elizabeth,
    dec.)   09 SF
Smith, Samuel; 3 Sept. 1808; Margaret Coal   09 BA
Smith, Samuel; 7 Nov. 1817; Mary Hissey   05 BA-240
Smith, Seth (s. of Samuel and Rachel; of Southfolk, Loudon Co.,
    VA); 22 d. 4 m., 1813; Ann Churchman (dau. of Edward and
    Rebecca of HA Co., MD)   02 Sf-119
Smith, Solomon; 10 May 1812; Sarah Fogle   06 FR-1318
Smith, Stoughton; 24 Oct. 1810; Sally Riggin   03 SO
Smith, Thomas; 1803; Marg't Clark   07 AA-3
Smith, Thomas; 20 Dec. 1803; Ann Doxey (or Dorsey)   02 SM-186
Smith, Thomas; 21 May 1804; Mary Ann Griffith   09 BA
Smith, Thomas; 11 Aug. 1808; Cath. Bartel   14 BA-424
Smith, Thos.; 22 Dec. 1816; Sarah Robinson   21 BA-8

```
Smith, Thomas; 2 July 1818; Mary Mowbray              17 BA-19
Smith, Thomas; 20 Jan. 1819; Susanna Rhodes           01 QA-62
Smith, Thomas; 20 Jan. 1819; Susanna Roads            02 TA-44
Smith, W. B.; 30 Dec. 1817; Isabella Thornbury        13 BA-30
Smith, Walter; 1 Nov. 1808; S. Hoffman                30 BA-109
Smith, Warren; 17 Feb. 1820; Mary Thomas (See also 16 FR-76)
                                                      03 FR-60
Smith, William; 25 Feb. 1802; Delilah Hissey          03 BA-414
Smith, William; 4 June 1803; Elizabeth Hague          02 BA-32
Smith, William; 13 April 1807; Sarah Wilkerson        13 BA-2
Smith, Wm.; 11 Nov. 1808; Else Murphy                 14 BA-425
Smith, Wm.; 18 March 1813; Sarah Hete                 21 BA-7
Smith, William; 7 March 1814; Mary Drury              03 AA-131
Smith, William; Dec. 1816; Nancy Frazier              02 WA-103
Smith, William; 2 Sept. 1818; Elizabeth Widerman      13 BA-40
Smith, William; 1 Oct. 1818; Rebecca Smith            11 BA-33
Smith, William; 24 Jan. 1820; Susan Unsworth          17 BA-23
Smith, William Henry; 18 May 1815; Mary Butler        09 BA
Smith, William I.; 16 Nov. 1820; Eliza Chalmers       11 BA-38
Smith, William N.; 15 Oct. 1815; Elizabeth Errickson  03 AA-131
Smith, Winston D.; 17 Dec. 1818; Sarah Coleman        13 BA-32
Smithers, Robert; 21 April 1815; Ann Spicer           17 BA-11
Smothers, Dan'l; 14 April 1805; Mary McCain           21 BA-6
Smothers, Elisha; c.1802; Ally Alsop                  07 AA-2
Smull, Jacob; 27 Dec. 1814; Margaret Gardner          09 BA
Smyth, Joseph; 11 June 1819; Catherine McGlown        37 BA-152
Snauffer, George; 2 April 1815; Darky Thomas          06 FR-1322
Snell, Thomas; 11 Oct. 1804; Ruth Valentine           11 BA-4
Snider, Chr. L.; 26 May 1812; Eliz'h R. Berry         13 BA-7
Snider, George; 16 Feb. 1802; Susanna Fout            23 BA-1
Snoke, Adam; 2 April 1816; Nancy Cockerle             06 FR-1324
Snook, John; 25 Aug. 1811; Harriet Gittinger          06 FR-1316
Snook, William; 31 Aug. 1802; Margaret Myers          03 AL-613
Snow, Freeman (of Boston); 10 June 1806; Eleanor Lee (of
    Balto.)                                           15 BA-234
Snow, Freeman; 17 July 1817; Rebecca Lowry            20 BA-223
Snow, Isaiah; 29 June 1815 (by Joshua Willey); Mary Bradford
                                                      17 BA-11
Snow, Jethro; 14 Jan. 1808; Eliza Smith               02 BA-6
Snow, John; 15 Oct. 1816; Mary Bevens                 02 BA-37
Snow, Zedekiah; 17 Aug. 1801; Elizabeth Lee           09 BA
Snowden, Samuel (s. of Samuel); 1 d. 12 mo., 1796; Elizabeth
    Cowman (dau. of John)                             01 SF
Snuggross, Wm.; 9 Aug. 1811; Margaret Forbes          14 BA-429
Snyder, Adam; July 1805; Marg. Brucks                 02 WA-79
Snyder, Daniel; 3 May 1812; Darky Thought             02 WA-94
Snyder, George; 1804; Jane Wallace                    02 WA-75
Snyder, George W.; 4 May 1810 (by Rev. Robert Roberts); Ruth
    Ferrall                                           17 BA-8
Snyder, Jacob; 23 Aug. 1812; Mar. Bryan               02 WA-95
Snyder, Jacob; 23 Dec. 1818; Mary Carmack             06 FR-1329
Snyder, John; 6 June 1803; Margaret Parker            06 BA-3
Snyder, John; 1 Nov. 1806; Harriott Webb              09 BA
Snyder, John; Aug. 1818; Elizab. Hose                 02 WA-110
Snyder, John; 5 April 1820; Eliza Spry                11 BA-36
Snyder, Lenhard; 29 Sept. 1812; Rebecca Spitznagle    02 WA-95
Snyder, Leonard; Nov. 1818; Rebecca Charlton          02 WA-111
Sohn, Conrad; May 1817; Ann Christian                 02 WA-105
Solomon, Benjamin; 31 Jan. 1802; Henrietta Pryse      09 BA
Solomon, Joseph; 24 Jan. 1804; Betsey Quarry (See also 07 AL-274;
    10 AL)                                            04 AL-2
Solomon, William; 13 Oct. 1819; Ann Simmons           27 BA-152
Solomon, Wm.; 2 April 1820; Eliza Myers               14 BA-440
Somerville, Henry N.; 26 Dec. 1815; Rebecca M. Tiernan 16 BA-30
```

```
Somerville, Richard; 10 May 1810; Cath. Nice           14 BA-427
Sonder, George; 7 Jan. 1802; Elizab. Emich             14 BA-411
Sonstrom, Manglist; 14 Sept. 1801; Polly Cooper        14 BA-410
Sonyes, Christian; 13 March 1801; An. Maria Walter      14 BA-409
Soslater (?), Gabriel; 7 Feb. 1806; Julian Waskey       33 BA-41
South, John; Dec. 1818; Barbara River                   02 WA-111
South, William; March (?) 1804; Cath. Brouchmeyer       02 WA-76
Southcomb, Cary; 30 June 1818; Alisanna C. Ford         17 BA-19
Southern (?), John; 10 Feb. 1813; (N) Driscoll          31 BA-143
Southgate, John; 2 Oct. 1810; Fanny P. McCausland       09 BA
Soyster, John; June 1807; Hany Camerer                  02 WA-83
Spafford, Samuel; 5 March 1806; Ann Alderson            02 BA-3
Spaguette, Peter; 6 Feb. 1810; Julia (last name not given)
                                                        31 BA-77
Spahm, (N); (June?) 1804; Susana Miller                 02 WA-76
Spalding, John; 24 Feb. 1819; Lydia Parton              09 BA
Spalding, Rd.; 21 Jan. 1813; Maria Sower                03 BA-504
Spalding, Stanislaus; 31 Oct. 1803; Eleanor Snowden (dau. of Col.
     Francis Snowden)                                   15 BA-189
Spangler, Joseph; 13 March 1814; Polly Smith            02 WA-99
Spann, John; 6 Jan. 1807; Elizab. Hefner                01 FR-1171
Spanseiler, Jacob; 6 Dec. 1814;; Catherine Shobe        06 FR-1321
Spanseiler, John; 26 Aug. 1806; Eliz. Lambrecht         01 FR-1171
Spark, Will, ([s.] of Sol.); 17 Sept. 1816; Ann E. Warham
                                                        02 QA-66
Sparks, Aquila N.; 25 Aug. 1816; Dorcas Conway (?)      32 BA-310
Sparks, William; 22 Oct. 1812; Henny Callechane (both of TA Co.)
                                                        02 TA-42
Sparrow, Daniel; 22 June 1802; Deborah Williams         05 AA-2
Sparrow, John; 1 Oct. 1815; Ann Griffith                03 AA-131
Sparrow, Thos.; 31 Jan. 1805; Sarah Sparrow             03 MO-119
Sparrow, William; 21 March 1802; Eliza Campbell         03 MO-118
Speak, George; 21 May 1803; Elisab. Pumphrey            14 BA-414
Speake, Thomas; 15 Sept. 1805; Mary Lawrence            15 BA-227
Spealman, Jacob; (1808); Polly Erb                      03 AL-614
Spear, James; 19 Dec. 1820; Maria Penston               16 BA-106
Specht, Conrad; 20 Jan. 1807; Cath. Harriott (See also
     15 FR-320)                                         01 FR-1171
Speck, (N); Nov. 1807; Christ. Geishwa                  02 WA-84
Speck, Henry; 26 Jan. 1812; Ann Wright                  14 BA-429
Speck, John H.; 28 March 1820; Angelica Bennett         37 BA-153
Speck, Martin; Oct. 1810; Nancy Speigler                02 WA-87
Speck, William A.; 10 march 1818; Cecily Peak           32 BA-318
Spedden, Lieut. Robert, U. S. N.; 9 Sept. 1817; Mary Ann
     Thompson                                           02 BA-37
Speeden, Edw'd; 17 May 1818; Eleanor Reese              13 BA-31
Spencer, Abel; 29 Sept. 1818; Charlotte McDonnell       11 BA-13
Spencer, James; 8 Dec. 1816; Ann Brooks                 13 BA-27
Spencer, John; Sept. 1817; Nancy Simpkins               02 WA-106
Spencer, John; 14 Sept. 1819; Leah Handy Guy            01 SO-15
Spencer, Jos.; 30 June 1814; Frances Matchett           13 BA-19
Spencer, Robert; 23 Aug. 1815; Susan McLaughlin         13 BA-22
Spencer, Thomas; 11 June 1801; Mary Nabb                33 BA-18
Spencer, William; 6 Oct. 1812; Ann Larghuge             03 AL-614
Spengler, Joh.; May 1804; Rebb. Lurenfelder             02 WA-76
Spenser, Jess; 27 Oct. 1811; Catherine Hansell          03 AL-614
Sperry, John; 27 Oct. 1818; Ann Augusta Fox             03 BA-603
Spessard, Daniel W.; 1804; Mary Ann Hartel              03 WA
Spessart, John; April 1814; Cath. Stover                02 WA-99
Spessart, Peter; Sept. 1802; Cath. Weaver               02 WA-73
Spicer, Aaron; 11 Aug. 1803; Elizabeth Walls            02 SM-186
Spicer (or Sticer), Nathaniel; 6 April 1802; Susanna Hoffman
                                                        03 AL-613
Spicey, Samuel L.; 23 Nov. 1815; Rosanna Carrick        16 BA-29
```

```
Spies, Johann P.; 16 July 1805; Margaretha Tschudi      07 BA
Spieser, Fried'k; 4 Oct. 1803; Margaret Bentz           14 BA-415
Spigler, John; Sept. 1820; Matilda Young                02 WA-117
Spiker, Adam; 5 Dec. 1811; Ann Reckmore                 03 AL-614
Spiker, Henry; 7 Sept. 1806; Elizabeth Miller           03 AL-614
Spiker, Michael; 7 April 1801; Mary Koonts              03 AL-613
Spilman, James; 29 Jan. 1815; Maryan Bergman [or Barrickman]
                                                        39 BA-30
Spilman, Peter; 15 June 1803; Nancy Clark               34 BA-1
Spilman, Thomas Frank; 19 May 1818; Hannah Barrickman   16 BA-69
Spinks, Alexander; 5 Oct. 1815; Charlotte Heston        11 BA-26
Spitz, David; 3 Jan. 1804; Temperance Bray              03 AL-613
Spitzenberger, William; 26 Aug. 1818; Catherine Bell    06 FR-1328
Spitznagel, Joh.; 30 June 1801; Barb. Meyers            02 WA-71
Spelich, Georg; 22 May 1809; Catharina Konig            07 BA-306
Sponseiler, Johan; 26 Aug. 1806; Elisabeth Lambrecht    15 FR-319
Sponseiler, John; 18 May 1812; Sarah Conrad             06 FR-1318
Spoon, Elias; 20 Aug. 1809; Mary Baltzel (15 FR-324 gives bride's
     name as Maria)                                     01 FR-1172
Spoon, Elias; 27 Aug. 1812; Polly Keller (15 FR-326 gives date as
     27 Oct. 1812)                                      01 FR-1172
Sporke, John Gerhard; 01 Jan. 1801; Anna Miller         14 BA-408
Spottiswood, John; 8 June 1803; Ann Wilson              02 BA-23
Sprecher, George; May 1816; Mary Houck                  02 WA-102
Sprecher, Philip; Feb. 1820; Cath. Houck                02 WA-115
Sprigg, Thomas; 26 April 1803; Harriot Minstry          02 BA-32
Spring, Adam; 14 May 1807; Elizab. Shnutz (15 FR-320 gives
     bride's name as Schantz)                           01 FR-1171
Spring, Franciscus; 23 March 1806; Barbara Befler       39 BA-19
Spring, Jacob; 16 June 1801; Susanna Schmitz (See also 15 FR-311)
                                                        01 FR-1170
Sprinstien, Abraham; 28 Jan. 1819; Margaret DeRochbrun  11 BA-33
Sprols, Andrew; 10 April 1802; Mary Hill                21 BA-5
Sprostun, Samuel; 30 March 1814; Jane Marriott          16 AA-21
Sprung, Georg; 2 Aug. 1812; Christiana Hasin            07 BA-308
Spurier, Wm. Thomas; 12 Sept. 1815; Guliet Spurrier     13 BA-22
Spurrier, Beale; 7 March 1804; Ann Askew                02 BA-33
Squires, Charles Clover; 11 May 1810; Maria M. Hay      13 BA-12
Stabler, James P. (s. of William and Deborah); 30 d. 12 mo.,
     1816; Elizab. Gilpin (dau. of Bernard and Sarah)   01 SF
Stabler, James Pleasants (s. of William and Deborah); 10 mo.,
     1816; Elizabeth Gilpin                             10 SF
Stabler, Stephen (s. of Thomas and Margaret of Stanton, New
     Castle Co., DE); 11 d. 5 mo., 1809; Sarah Reynolds (dau. of
     Henry and Mary of North Milford Hund., CE Co.)     09 SF
Stabler,  Thomas P. (s. of William and Deborah); 26 d. 6 mo.,
     1813; Eliza P. Brooke                              01 SF
Stabler, Thomas Pleasants (s. of William and Deborah); 2 d. 6
     mo., 1813; Elizabeth Pleasants Brooke              10 SF
Stabs, Jacob; 4 Feb. 1812; Catherine Blessing           06 FR-1317
Stack, Charles; 22 Jan. 1820; Belinda Wells             03 BA-604
Stackpole, John; 18 March 1802; Mary Preston            03 AL-613
Stackus, Sol.; 5 June 1814; Chrisa. Stardley            13 BA-19
Stacy, George W.; June 1819; Julian McCowly             02 WA-113
Stacy, Matthew; 5 Nov. 1801; Jane Fletcher (See also 18 BA-65)
                                                        01 BA-9
Stacy, Thomas (s. of Francis and Sarah Stacy from Portsmouth, N.
     H.); 22 Dec. 1805; Catherine Liddell (widow of late John
     Liddell)                                           15 BA-232
Staeler, Philip; 7 June 1803; Catherine Overhof (widow, Lutheran
     by profession)                                     15 BA-183
Stafford, John; 15 Oct. 1809; Mary Sigler               03 AL-614
Stafford, Samuel; 29 Nov. 1808; Adelaide (N) (free negroes)
                                                        31 BA-53
```

```
Stafford, William J.; 5 June 1811; Mary Laudeman       14 BA-428
Stafford, William Josephus; 2 Oct. 1805; Mary Whipple  03 BA-494
Stahl, Simon; Feb. 1803; Cath. Stempfle                02 WA-74
Stahly, Frederic; 31 Jan. 1809; Elizab. Shafer (See also
    15 FR-323)                                         01 FR-1172
Stahly, George; 4 April 1805; Cath. Stahly (See also 15 FR-317)
                                                       01 FR-1171
Stake, Peter; 26 July 1812; Rosanna Moudy              02 WA-94
Staley, Daniel; 7 March 1812; Sarah Thornborough       02 WA-93
Staley, John; 20 Nov. 1817; Elizabeth Giese            06 FR-1327
Staley, Stephen; 27 Sept. 1818; Mary Lively            01 WA-201
Stall, Samuel; 24 March 1808; Patty Potter             13 BA-4
Stallings, Henry; 24 Dec. 1812; Elizabeth Stansbury    09 BA
Stallings, Isaac; 8 Oct. 1812; Mary Carback            09 BA
Stallings, Thomas; c.1801; Mary Poole                  08 AA-1
Stallings, Thomas; 23 Jan. 1816; Ann Lambeth           03 AA-131
Stallions, James; 20 Oct. 1801; Elizabeth Dunnock      01 DO-40
Stallions, Richard; 19 Nov. 1816; Jane Wroe            20 BA-223
Stallions, Samuel; 24 March 1808; Patty Potter         13 BA-4
Staly, Abraham; 19 Feb. 1811; Elizabeth Schaeffer      06 FR-1315
Stamp, Elie; 25 March 1819; Ellen Brannon              01 WA-202
Standiford, John; 7 Jan. 1810; Delia Hutchings         01 BA-11
Standiford, Lloyd; 17 Nov. 1812; Mary Hindon           01 BA-11
Stanfield, John; 12 Dec. 1811; Nancy Barnes            01 DO-41
Stanford, Michael (native of Ireland); 21 May 1807; Catherine
    Jackson (native of VA)                             15 BA-250
Stankey, George; 1 Feb. 1818; Elizabeth O'Donley       01 CE
Stanley, James(?) R.; 9 Sept. 1809; Rosetta (or Rosanna) McCann
                                                       31 BA-66
Stanly, Joseph; 12 Feb. 1814; Margt Rohrbach           14 BA-431
Stanly, William; 27 Sept. 1802; Mary Ann Rutter        09 BA
Stansbury, Augustus; 25 Dec. 1813; Margaret Young      09 BA
Stansbury, Benjamin; 14 Sept. 1812; Sarah Swopsed [sic]
                                                       11 BA-19
Stansbury, Chalep (?); 30 Nov. 1815; Mary Boring       08 BA
Stansbury, Daniel; 8 May 1817; Susanna L. Morand       09 BA
Stansbury, Darius; 29 Sept. 1803; Polly Holland        34 BA-1
Stansbury, Ephraim; 3 Jan. 1805; Elizabeth Phipps      09 BA
Stansbury, George; 8 April 1802; Elizabeth Sollers     09 BA
Stansbury, Isaiah; 27 Aug. 1815; Mary Lane             08 BA
Stansbury, Jacob; 19 May 1818; Margaret Lemmons        03 BA-605
Stansbury, John; 5 Sept. 1818; Sarah S. Pearce         17 BA-19
Stansbury, John E.; 15 March 1802; Ann Proctor         09 BA
Stansbury, John E.; 9 June 1819; Mrs. Frances Abbott   37 BA-152
Stansbury, Joseph; 19 March 1807; Elizabeth Pockerd (or Packard)
                                                       09 BA
Stansbury, Nicholas; 27 June 1805; Winifred Farrell (dau. of
    James and Mary)                                    15 BA-222
Stansbury, Robert D.; 12 Jan. 1819; Anne Kerr          37 BA-152
Stansbury, Dr. T. A.; 11 Jan. 1815; Anne Biays         05 BA-238
Stansbury, Thomas; 20 Dec. 1801; Elizabeth Skelton     03 BA-411
Stansbury, William; 11 April 1805; Susanna Buck        09 BA
Stansbury, William; 16 Feb. 1808; Ellen K. Gilder      11 BA-13
Stansbury, William; 1 Aug. 1820; Rebecca Bosley        12 BA-159
Stansbury, William; 12 Sept. 1820; Mary Ortner         06 FR-1331
Stansbury, William S.; 15 March 1819; Maria Norwood    20 BA-223
Stansfield, Benjamin; 23 May 1809; Elizabeth Upton     08 BA
Stanton, James; 31 Dec. 1812; Sarah Gardiner           02 WA-96
Staples, Chas.; 27 June 1816; Margaret Rhea            14 BA-435
Staples, Robert; 20 Sept. 1801; Ruth Jalland           03 BA-407
Stapleton, Edward; 16 Oct. 1817; Elizabeth (N)         09 BA
Stapleton, John; 31 Aug. 1816; Mary Matthews           17 BA-15
Stapleton, Joseph K.; 9 July 1801; Eleanor Cannon      09 BA
Stapleton, Joshua; c.1804; Harriet Tashew              34 BA-2
```

Stapleton, Robert; 4 April 1805; Sidney Thompson   11 BA-5
Starks (?), Joseph (slave of Mr. Lawrence); 18 July 1819; Genie
  Adams (mulatto)   32 BA-325
Starling, Aaron; 3 June 1813; Elizabeth Rudisel Kusick 31 BA0151
Starling, Zachariah; 30 July 1816; Elizabeth Parry   17 BA-15
Starr, Charles W. (s. of John and Mary, dec., of Philadelphia,
  PA); 4 d. 11 mo., 1819; Elizabeth Wilson (dau. of John and
  Catherine of East Nottingham Twp., Chester Co., PA)
                                                      06 SF
Starr, John; 27 April 1805; Mary Ann Shilling   09 BA
Starr, Joseph; 10 April 1802; Margaret Nowers   21 BA-5
Starr, William; 16 Dec. 1802; Rebeckah Richardson   34 BA-1
Start, William H.; June 1807; Cath. Henry   02 WA-83
States, David; 17 Nov. 1805; Catha. Hickman   03 BA-494
Staton, Robert; 29 Nov. 1803; Elenor Murphy   03 BA-436
Staufer, Daniel; 11 April 1803; Eleanor Yauler (See also
  15 FR-314)   01 FR-1171
Stauffer, Jno.; 14 Nov. 1805; Ann Stitcher   14 BA-419
Stauffer, Joseph; 9 Aug. 1801; Cath. Kroneisz (See also
  15 FR-312)   01 FR-1171
Stautz, Leonhard; May 1805; Cath. Bashor   02 WA-78
Staylor, George; 15 April 1819; Mary Walton   16 BA-81
Staylor, Henry; Feb. 1818; Ann Ellen [Rife]   39 BA-34
Staylor, John; 7 Jan. 1817; Mary Dougherty   16 BA-48
Staylor, Philip Jacob; 26 March 1809; Sophia Orban   15 BA-269
Staylor, William; 24 April 1808; Ann Maxfield   15 BA-261
Stear, George; 25 Jan. 18096; Nancy Sharey   14 BA-419
Steel, John; 1 May 1807; Achsah White   11 BA-10
Steel, Robert; 9 march 1813; Esther Long   02 WA-97
Steele, John; 11 April 1819; Maria H. Hinchman   32 BA-324
Steele, John N.; 30 Sept. 1819; Anne O. Buchanan   01 WA-202
Steele, Thomas; 22 Dec. 1811; Mary Bainer   15 BA-295
Steele, William; 24 April 1802; Ann Vaughan   09 BA
Steerman, Richard; 17 Oct. 1815; Anne Ring   08 AL-109
Steese, Henry; July 1817; Susanna Murphy   02 WA-105
Steever, George; 17 Sept. 1808; Mary Weaver   14 BA-424
Steffler, Jacob; 4 May 1820; Susannah Waldeck (See also 16 FR-76)
                                                      03 FR-60
Stegman, John H.; 30 June 1801; Nancy Culberson   03 BA-402
Stehly, Jacob; 1 Nov. 1803; Eliz. Widerich (See also 15 FR-316)
                                                      01 FR-1171
Stein, George; 3 May 1809; Cath. Wilderman   14 BA-426
Stein, George; 24 Dec. 1816; A. M. Hammer   14 BA-436
Stein, Jacob; Jan. 1801; Cath. Schuck   02 WA-71
Stein, Johannes; 12 Dec. 1802; Elizabeth Gleiss   15 FR-313
Stein, John; 12 Dec. 1802; Eliz. Gleisz   01 FR-1171
Stein, Joh.; Jan. 1803; Peggy Frankenberger (or Trautenberger)
                                                      02 WA-74
Stein, Peter; April 1805; Anna Lowman   02 WA-78
Stein, Peter; 1 Dec. 1816; Sophia Lauzatteln   07 BA-311
Steinbrecker, Gunrod; Jan. 1803; Cath. Shrader   02 WA-74
Steinbrenner, Philip; 19 March 1807; Christina Sauter (See also
  15 FR-328)   01 FR-1171
Steiner, Abraham; Aug. 1807; Sarah Stover   02 WA-83
Steiner, Heinrich; 20 May 1806; Rachel Murrye   15 FR-319
Steinhart, Christopher; 6 April 1815; Margaret Wight 11 BA-25
Stembler, Jno.; 20 Oct. 1807; Sarah Lees   14 BA-423
Stemforth, John; 7 Feb. 1813; Ann Christian   14 BA-431
Stempel, Anthony; 23 March 1809; Margaretha Locher   07 BA-306
Stenson, William (widower); 3 Nov. 1806; Mrs. Martha Eccleston
                                                      15 BA-242
Stephe, George; Nov. 1808; Maria Rinden   02 WA-16
Stephens, Christ.; Oct. 1805; Sara Bob   02 WA-79

Stephens, Sothy; 12 Nov. 1803; Eleanor Waugh (See also 04 AL-1;
    09 AL)   07 AL-274
Stephens, William; 20 Oct. 1804; Charity Cottrage   11 BA-4
Stephenson, John; 17 July 1803; Eleanor Harrison   03 AA-120
Sterbel, Jno. P.; 17 July 1802; Barb. Bader   14 BA-413
Sterratt, James; 14 Sept. 1809; Maria Harris   05 BA-236
Sterret, Andrew; 16 April 1801; Henrietta Steel   03 BA-299
Sterret, James; Feb. 1807; Sus. Grubb   02 WA-82
Steuart, Edward; 1 or 7 Dec. 1817; Maria Reiman   17 BA-17
Steven, Dan'l; 7 June 1814; Sarah Smith   13 BA-19
Stevens, Ezekiel; 8 March 1814; Elizabeth Brookover   06 FR-1320
Stevens, Henry; 21 May 1807; Elizabeth Creamer   09 BA
Stevens, James; 30 March 1815; Mary A. Rigart   11 BA-22
Stevens, James H.; 7 Feb. 1813; Ann Owings   09 BA
Stevens, Robert; 12 Sept. 1802; Mary Hare   03 BA-420
Stevens, William; 13 March 1813; Mary Jackson   17 BA-9
Stevens, Wm.; 10 May 1818; Maria Bowers   14 BA-437
Stevenson, Benjamin; 15 Oct. 1811; Eliza Grimes   06 FR-1316
Stevenson, Henry; 25 Sept. 1817; Mary B. Waters   13 BA-29
Stevenson, Isaiah; 25 May 1815; Ella Hopkins   11 BA-26
Stevenson, Nathan;; (date not given); Elizabeth Stevenson
                                                             13 BA-38
Stevenson, Sater; 3 Dec. 1815; Hester Picket   13 BA-39
Stevenson, Zachariah; c.1804; Sarah Stevenson   34 BA-2
Steward, Levin; 25 June 1815; Henrietta Stinchcomb   13 BA-22
Steward, Thomas; 7 Jan. 1801; Ann Jacobs   01 FR-1170
Steward, William; 17 Feb. 1814; Catherine Lehman   06 FR-1320
Stewart, Godfrey; 4 Dec. 1817; Elizabeth Watts   03 BA-602
Stewart, Isaac; 16 Feb. 1817; Ann Brown (col'd)   11 BA-31
Stewart, Jas.; 7 April 1801; Jane Alexander   14 BA-409
Stewart, James; 2 Nov. 1815; Ann Shrote   14 BA-434
Stewart, James; 17 Nov. 1818; Sarah Hawkins   14 BA-438
Stewart, John; 18 April 1805; Rachel Stafford   11 BA-5
Stewart, John; 12 Nov. 1807; Mary Griffith   03 BA-497
Stewart, John; 12 April 1812; Elizabeth Robertson   13 BA-7
Stewart, John; 11 March 1813; Susan Jones   13 BA-16
Stewart, John; 1 Dec. 1816; Elizabeth Waddington   09 BA
Stewart, John Thompson; 31 May 1812; Mary Hicks   03 BA-504
Stewart, Jos.; 29 Oct. 1816; Eliza Frebick   13 BA-26
Stewart, Peter; 21 Sept. 1802; Susanna Daughaday   06 BA-2
Stewart, Thomas; 7 feb. 1801; Ann Jacobs   15 FR-311
Stewart, Thomas; 16 March 1801; Mary McDowell   05 BA-13
Stewart, Thomas; 17 Dec. 1803; Elizabeth Benson   15 AA-3
Stewart, Thomas; 27 Dec. 1807; Sarah Barker   11 BA-13
Stewart, Thomas; 17 Oct. 1811; Sidney Helms   14 BA-429
Stewart, Walter; 1809; Eleanor Gray (See also 02 MO)   01 PG
Stewart, William; 17 Sept. 1801; Eliza Hagerty   09 BA
Stewart, William; 14 Dec. 1808; Mary Peckhend   13 BA-5
Stewart, Zachariah; 25 Aug. 1815; Julian Byard   13 BA-39
Stickney, John; 4 Feb. 1804; Mary Ann Grache   15 BA-198
Stieg[h]ler, Joannes; 12 April 1804; Magdalenas Folweiler
                                                             39 BA-17
Stiles, Michael; 16 Feb. 1807; Mary Burns   03 BA-4976
Stillwell, David; Sept. 1813; Mar. Fauch   02 WA-98
Stimmel, Abraham; 10 June 1806; Mary (or Maria) Lang (See also
    15 FR-319)   01 FR-1171
Stimson, Stephen; 27 May 1816; Ann Fletcher   17 BA-12
Stinchcomb, Beal C.; 12 April 1818; Eliza Swann   11 BA-28
Stinchcomb, George; 17 Dec. 1818; Catherine Crook   17 BA-20
Stinchcomb, John; 24 Feb. 1814; Eliza Foreman   13 BA-18
Stinchcomb, Thomas; 11 Feb. 1804; Sarah Phipps   05 AA-4
Stine, John; Jan. 1819; Magdalena Bovey   02 WA-112
Stine, Matthias; 17 March 1812; Elizab. Yokle   02 WA-93
Stinebaugh, George; Jan. 1817; Mary Sheller   02 WA-104

```
Stinebaugh, Philip; June 1819; Cath. Bowser          02 WA-113
Stinger, Fred'k; 18 Sept. 1809; Christiana Klat      14 BA-226
Stinger, John; 18 June 1818; Margaret Knott          14 BA-437
Stitcher, John; 18 March 1802; Sarah Clemens         14 BA-412
Stitcher, Peter; 30 April 1807; Cath. Fetty          14 BA-421
Stith, Griffin; 26 June 1817; Marg. Ann Wilmer       03 BA-602
Stocker, Jesse L.; 14 May 1815; Elizabeth Myers      11 BA-24
Stocker, Jesse L.; 30 Jan. 1817; Alice Murlnee [sic] 11 BA-27
Stocker, John; 6 Dec. 1804; Delia Boon               14 BA-417
Stocker, Zach'r; 3 June 1810; Maria Jaffray          13 BA-10
Stockman, George; 10 Jan. 1804; Eliz. Windbigler (See also
   15 FR-316)                                        01 FR-1171
Stockman, William; 17 Dec. 1819; Elizabeth Montgomery 06 FR-1329
Stockten, Francis P.; 17 Nov. 1817; Arabella Loney   03 BA-602
Stockton, Henry; 1 March 1810; Elizabeth Fox         09 BA
Stoll, Georg; 20 Dec. 1807; Maria Warner             07 BA-306
Stoll, George; 12 March 1816; Elizabeth Stein        06 FR-1324
Stoltz, Peter; June 1805; Elis. Schupp               02 WA-79
Stone, Adam; 26 July 1803; Eliza Tilden              21 BA-5
Stone, Andrew A.; 20 Jan. 1806; Margaret Stephens    14 BA-419
Stone, Francis; 14 Feb. 1804; Mima Lake              02 SM-186
Stone, John; 2 June 1803; Ann Guess                  03 AA-120
Stone, John; 30 June 1812; Sophia Gilbert (See also 15 FR-325)
                                                     01 FR-1172
Stone, Jno.; 19 Aug. 1819; Elizab. Forney            14 BA-437
Stone, Matthew; 20 Feb. 1820; Ann Askew              11 BA-34
Stone, Michael; 21 Dec. 1820; Ellen Tobin            32 BA-330
Stone, Richard; 28 March 1816; Marg't Mopps          13 BA-24
Stone, Wm.; 22 Oct. 1806; Jemima Chenoweth           03 BA-496
Stonebraker, John; 31 Jan. 1811; Naomi M'Coy         02 WA-89
Stonebraker, Sebastian; 16 April 1811; Anna Greenwell 04 FR-17
Stonebreaker, Christian; 5 April 1812; Jean Bettler  04 FR-18
Stonebrecker, George; Dec. 1808; Bezi Neff           02 WA-86
Stoner, Daniel; Sept. 1819; Marg. Fysinghasen        02 WA-114
Stoner, Henry; 16 April 1812; Susanna Haller         06 FR-1318
Stonff, Jno.; 13 Aug. 1801; Priscilla Messer         14 BA-410
Stopp (or Popp), George; 16 Nov. 1819; Mary Lohr     08 AL-111
Storm, James; 3 June 1817; Sarah Gillmeyer           05 FR-17
Storm, Peter; 13 Jan. 1811; Mary Haller              06 FR-1315
Stormbeck, Jacob; 19 March 1816; Ann Daley           14 BA-435
Storr, Jacob; Feb. 1808; Sarah Allison               02 WA-85
Story, John; 6 March 1811; Mary Shaw                 14 BA-428
Story, Robert; 8 March 1808; Cassandra Davis         02 BA-6
Stottlemeyer, Daniel; Nov. 1819; Hannah Racher       02 WA-114
Stottlemeyer, John; Nov. 1819; Susanna Wolf          02 WA-114
Stottlemyer, Nelson; July 1820; Hannah Pryor         02 WA-116
Stoufer, John; 21 March 1811; Barbara Welty          02 WA-89
Stouffer, Jacob; 27 Nov. 1816; Ann C. Tinges         13 BA-27
Stout, Jesse; 14 Sept. 1815; Mary Mortry             06 FR-1323
Stover, Philip; 27 Jan. 1802; Delia James            09 BA
Stradley, John; 12 May 1804 (by Rev. L. W. McCombes); Sarah
   Porter                                            17 BA-3
Strain, Thomas; June (?) 1804; Sarah Hamond          02 WA-76
Stran, Thomas P.; 20 April 1820; Ann Follen          17 BA-22
Strange, David; 4 Dec. 1817; Isabella Collins        13 BA-29
Strause, Jacob; Feb. 1820; Christiana Evy            02 Wa-115
Strawbridge, Robert; 29 Jan. 1804; Mary White (See also
   15 FR-316)                                        01 FR-1171
Stream, William; 29 June 1820; Jemima Hirl           06 FR-1331
Strebeck, Jno.; 4 June 1812; Harriet Waites          14 BA-430
Strebel, Jno. P.; 7 July 1802; Barb. Bader           25 BA-2
Streby, George; 9 Jan. 1812; Ellen McCubbin          11 BA-18
Street, Edward; 29 Dec. 1803; Jane Byus              01 DO-41
Street, Thomas; Feb. 1813; Catherine Merryman        01 BA-11
```

```
Streich, David; March 1805; Mary Schmidt              02 WA-78
Stremmel, Friedrich; 12 June 1803; Elisabeth Capito   07 BA-68
Stricker, Jno.,; 31 Aug. 1801; Elizab. Bryan          14 BA-410
Strider, Jno.; 17 May 1812; Charlotte Wheeler         14 BA-430
Stringer, Frederick; 24 Sept. 1801; Elizabeth Martin  09 BA
Stringer, Jacob; 29 Nov. 1810; Catherine Gray         09 BA
Stringer, John; 14 April 1801; Catherine Trevila      03 BA-399
Stringer, John H.; 15 Feb. 1813; Hollan Parker        09 BA
Stroll, Philip; Jan. 1801; Scharl. Studer             02 WA-71
Strong, David; April 1802; Mary Price                 02 WA-72
Stroud, Reece; 31 July 1819; Rebecca Richardson       11 BA-37
Stuart, Richardson; 1 July 1808; Sarah Glen Douglas   03 BA-498
Stubbin, Thomas (by Rev. Robert Roberts); 10 Aug. 1810; Ann
     Bourke                                           17 BA-8
Stubbs, Isaac (s. of Daniel and Ruth, dec., of Little Britain
     Twp., Lancs. Co., PA); 11 d. 6 mo., 1801; Hannah Brown (dau.
     of Jeremiah and Hannah of the same place)        06 SF
Stubbs, James; April 1812 (by Rev. Ryland); Rachel Gore
                                                      17 BA-9
Stubbs, Vincent (s. of Vincent and Priscilla of Little Britain
     Twp., Lancaster Co., PA); 5 d. 1 mo., 1820; Mary E. Haines
     (dau. of Joseph and Rebecca, dec., of West Nottingham Hund.,
     cecil Co.)                                       06 SF
Studdy, John; 7 May 1807; Nancy McCaskey              09 BA
Stump, Samuel; 10 June 1802; Martha Burrows Stone (see also
     18 BA-65)                                        01 BA-9
Stupor, Leonard; 21 May 1818; Rosanna Grieves         03 BA-603
Sturgess, Jonathan B., (widower); 12 May 1807; Mary Patterson,
     (widow)                                          15 BA-249
Sturgis, John; 21 May 1815 (by Joshua Willey); Susan Lowry
                                                      17 BA-11
Sturm, Leonhard; 24 Nov. 1807; Eliz. Sauter (See also 15 FR-321)
                                                      01 FR-1171
Sturmhaus, Harry; 27 Aug. 1801; Marg. Righter         14 BA-410
Sturtzman, Jacob; April 1820; Ann Jack                02 WA-116
Sturtzman, Peter; 26 Oct. 1815; Polly Holtzman        02 WA-100
Sturtzman, Samuel; Sept. 1819; Susanna Sturtzman      02 WA-114
Suinshine [sic], Michael; 16 April 1812; Rebecca Dorsey
                                                      11 BA-19
Sukes (?), Jesse; 25 Feb. 1802; Polly Isenberg        10 FR
Sulavin, John; 5 Aug. 1813; Mary Colen                08 BA
Sullins, Richard; 16 June 1805; Eliz. Eycof           01 FR-1171
Sullivan, Clement; 11 Sept. 1819; Rebecca Bowen       11 BA-34
Sullivan, Daniel; 3 March 1804; Margaret Williams     02 BA-33
Sullivan, Daniel; 28 June 1810; Bridget Cusic         31 BA-83
Sullivan, Dennis; 9 March 1817; Comfort Woodland      13 BA-28
Sullivan, John; 9 Feb. 1814; Matilda Dorsey           13 BA-18
Sullivan, John; 21 Feb. 1814; Abigail Robinson        11 BA-23
Sullivan, John; 7 Nov. 1820; Christina Bougham        16 BA-105
Sullivan, William; 1 April 1802; Elizabeth Collett    24 BA
Sully, Carl; 1 Jan. 1809; Marg't Dietz                14 BA-425
Sulzer, Michael; 4 May 1820; Mahala Thomas            06 FR-1331
Suman, Isaac; Sept. 1817; Margareth Haller            06 FR-1327
Suman, William; 5 Dec. 1816; Phoebe Haller            06 FR-1325
Sumblin (?), Francis; 5 Feb. 1801; Mary Crouch        05 AA-1
Summer, Abraham; 12 Nov. 1820; Catherine Main (See also 15 FR-76)
                                                      02 FR-61
Summer, Walter; 25 April 1805; Sarah Swearingen       03 MO-120
Summers, Archibald; 31 March 1803; Margaret Pain      03 MO-118
Summers, Felty; Oct. 1802; Rebecca Linton             02 WA-73
Summers, Jacob (of Christopher); 15 Feb 1820; Elizabeth Main (See
     also 16 FR-76)                                   03 FR-60
Summers, John; Jan. 1801; Elis. Petry                 02 WA-71
Summers, John; 27 Dec. 1803; Mary King (Ring?)        17 BA-3
```

Summers, Thomas; 25 Aug. 1801; Kilty Stewart   03 BA-405
Summers, William (of Caroline Co.); 1806; Dolly Dubman (of Dorset
   Co.)   02 TA-40
Summers, Wm. L.; 23 Oct. 1804; Louisa Ferguson   03 BA-492
Summers, William S.; 23 Oct. 1804; Louisa Ferguson 02 BA-34
Sumner, Henry P.; 29 June 1818; Frances A. Steele   03 BA-603
Sumwalt, George; 2 Aug. 1818; Elizabeth Chisholm   05 BA-240
Sumwalt, Geo. B.; 6 Aug. 1807; Jane Russell   13 BA-2
Sumwalt, John; 16 March 1809; Jamima Langdon   13 BA-5
Sumwalt, John L.; 21 Dec. 1816; Rachel Sparks   11 BA-31
Sumwalt, Philip; 22 Dec. 1816; Maria Parsons   17 BA-15
Sunderland, Bazil; c.1801; Priscilla Magnes (?)   08 AA-1
Sunderland, Benjamin; 11 March 1804; Elizabeth Kelly 09 BA
Sunderland, Daniel; 20 April 1814; Elizabeth Williams 16 BA-4
Sunderland, Zachariah; 16 Aug. 1804; Dorothy Wood   03 AA-130
Super, Joh.; 22 Feb. 1807; Charlotte Rorick   14 BA-421
Supple, Patrick; 16 Sept. 1819; Margaret Carr   16 BA-87
Survine, Daniel; 6 July 1820; Mary Petey   11 BA-36
Susex [sic], Jos.; 30 July 1820; Elize. Sesler   13 BA-35
Sutcrop, Chas.; 25 Jan. 1806; Charlotte Honsteen   14 BA-419
Suter, Jacob; 27 Aug. 1801; Maria Rossenmond   14 BA-410
Suter, Jacob; Oct. 1816; Elizab. Miller   02 WA-103
Suter, Jacob; 12 Feb. 1818; Prudence Saulsberry   13 BA-30
Suter, Jno.; 14 Feb. 1807; Sarah Dorsey   14 BA-421
Sutor, James; 20 May 1818; Nancy McCaffer   05 BA-240
Sutton, (N); 2 Nov. 1812; (N) Miller   02 WA-95
Sutton, Jno.; 16 April 1815; Sarah Price   14 BA-433
Sutton, Lewis; 1803; Martha Dorsey   07 AA-3
Suydam, Jas. See Laydam, Jas.
Swain, Benj'n; 22 Dec. 1810; Dories [sic] Green   14 BA-428
Swain, Freeman; 13 Sept. 1806; Eliza Thorn   02 BA-4
Swan, James; 27 Oct. 1818; Elizabeth Donnell   03 BA-603
Swan, Jno. S.; 12 Nov. 1818; Lydia Carson   13 BA-32
Swan, Zedekiah; 1809; Eliz. Manley (See also 02 MO) 01 PG
Swann, Isaac; c.1804; Ann Tasker   34 BA-2
Swann, Robert; 9 March 1820; Sophia A. Broadhag   08 AL-113
Swarpsted [sic], Nicholas; 9 Oct. 1808; Nancy Hammond 11 BA-12
Swarts, B.; 4 July 1816; Ann B. Caule   13 BA-25
Swarts, Ephraim; 25 Nov. 1806; Susanna Jones   33 BA-41
Swaving, Justus Gerardus; 12 March 1812; Elizabeth Toomes
                                                    09 BA
Swearingen, Van; 1812; Eliz. Green (See also 02 MO) 01 PG
Sweeny, Daniel, (widower); 12 Aug. 1810; Elizabeth Graham
                                                    16 BA-85
Sweeny, John; 8 Oct. 1815; Johanna Burke   03 BA-507
Sweeting, Benjamin; 15 Oct. 1811; Mary Boyle   02 BA-36
Sweeting, John; 16 Dec. 1819; Rebecca Spicer   13 BA-34
Sweeting, Thos.; 26 March 1809; Caroline Phillips   03 BA-499
Sweetland. William; 4 May 1802; Mary Ann Waggoner   17 BA-1
Sweetser, Samuel; 30 May 1818; Mary Ann Oldham   11 BA-28
Sw[au?]ger, John; 24 Aug. 1802; Catherine Shimer   03 AL-613
Swick, Charles; 15 Feb. 1816; Sarah B. Martin   17 BA-12
Swift, David; 7 Dec. 1803; Martha Roberts   33 BA-40
Swift, Joseph; 14 July 1803; Anne Wheeler Williams 03 BA-430
Swiger, George; 27 April 1806; Esther Sharpless   03 AL-614
Swiggett, Henry (s. of Johnson and Mary, dec.); 18 d. 11 mo.,
   1813; Deborah B. Shanahan (dau. of Jonathan and Margaret,
   both dec.)   08 Sf
Swiggett, Johnson; 17 d. 12 mo., 1817; Mary Ross   07 SF-36
Swiggett, Solomon (s. of Johnson and Mary); 23 d. 12 mo., 1818;
   Phama Charles (dau. of Henry and Mary)   07 SF-38
Swingle, Leonhard; April 1805; Prudence Brendlinger 02 WA-78
Switzer, Fred'k; 7 April 1804; Rhode Vaughan   14 BA-416
Switzer, Jacob; 5 Jan. 1802; Rachel Buckinham   14 BA-411

```
Switzer, [Joseph]; 8 June 1820; Julian Farrall         39 BA-37
Swope, Barnet; July 1818; Mary Bowman                  02 WA-110
Swope, Daniel; 11 Feb. 1813; Lucy Ellis                06 FR-1319
Sword, John; 13 Dec. 1808; Sarah Boult                 02 SM-188
Sword, Uriah; 23 Jan. 1806; Ann Welsh                  02 SM-187
Sykes, James; 30 Nov. 1815; Mary Brown                 13 BA-23
Symons, Evan; 20 Jan. 1803; Elizabeth Snears           06 BA-3
Tabbs, Benjamin; 18 Feb. 1806; Ellenor Aisquith        02 SM-187
Tabler, Christian; 18 May 1820; Barbara Tabler         06 FR-1331
Taggart, John; 1 Dec. 1806; Hannah Russell             08 AL-113
Tailley, Geo.; 20 July 1812; Eliz'h Patterson          13 BA-14
Talbort, Wilson; Sept. 1817; Nancy Hedge               02 WA-106
Talbot, Jesse; 1 d. 6 mo., 1808; Hannah Little         10 SF
Talbot, Richard; 27 Sept. 1810; Sarah Farriall         13 BA-10
Talbot, Thomas; 21 March 1816; Eleanor Beares          03 BA-507
Talbott, Allen (s. of Joseph and Mary [Farquhar]); 25 d. 11 mo.,
     1819; Mary Roberts (dau. of John and Rebecca)     03 SF
Talbott, Edward; 1 Nov. 1810; Elizabeth Reynolds       09 BA
Talbott, Elisha; 22 Jan. 1804 (by Rev. l. W. McCombes); Catherine
     Littig                                            17 BA-3
Talbott, John; 21 March 1814; Nancy Sewell             09 BA
Talbott, Thomas; 29 Jan. 1804; Mary Merryman           01 BA-10
Talbott, Vincent; 24 Feb. 1803; Mary Talbott           23 BA-2
Talley, John; Feb. 1818; Sarah Newcomer                02 WA-108
Taney, Ethelbert; 16 May 1820; Elizabeth Jarboe        04 FR-18
Tanney, Samuel; 16 Sept. 1815; Rebecca Gibbs           11 BA-26
Tapless, Michael; 11 Nov. 1817; Elizabeth McCue        11 BA-28
Tashpole, William; 21 Aug. 1816; Chartlotte Milford    17 BA-15
Task, Davis B.; 7 Feb. 1811; Marg't Calder             14 BA-429
Tate, Thomas; 19 June 1806; Angela (?) D. Emerson      03 AL-614
Tatersall, William; 26 Jan. 1801; Anne Henry           03 BA-398
Tavener, William; 18 Sept. 1806; Ellen Wheeler         03 BA-496
Taxpole, William; 31 May 1818; Eliza Boston            13 BA-31
Taylor, Benj.; 17 Jan. 1815; Sarah Howland             13 BA-20
Taylor, David; 10 Feb. 1818; Harriot VanHorne          17 BA-18
Taylor, Capt. G.; 9 Feb. 1802; Mary Ann Ridley         21 BA-5
Taylor, George; 21 Aug. 1817; Margaret Hopkins         17 BA-17
Taylor, Isaac; 12 April 1816; Lavinia Quail            11 BA-30
Taylor, Isaac P. (s. of John P. and Hannah); 21 d. 7 mo., 1814;
     Rebecca Plummer (dau. of William and Rachel [Morsell]
     Plummer                                           03 SF
Taylor, Jacob (s. of Jacob and Elizabeth, dec., of Sadsbury Twp.,
     Chester Co., PA); 12 d. 10 mo., 1814; Grace Trump (dau. of
     Abraham and Jemima of W. Nottingham Hundred, CE Co.)
                                                       06 SF
Taylor, James, (merchant); 13 Aug. 1804; Anne Williamson (dau. of
     David Williamson)                                 15 BA-207
Taylor, James; 12 April 1812; Cath. Burkitt            02 WA-93
Taylor, James; 16 Nov. 1815; Phoebe Logsdon            11 BA-25
Taylor, James; 1820; Ann McCann                        09 FR-101
Taylor, John, (of Alabama); 28 Oct. 1819; Fanny I. D. Owings
                                                       03 BA-604
Taylor, John; 27 July 1820; Sarah Ann Rutter           37 BA-153
Taylor, John B.; 7 Jan. 1809; Catheriue S. Spaulding   09 BA
Taylor, Jonathan; 21 Aug. 1807; Louisa Altherr         14 BA-422
Taylor, Joseph; 14 Jan. 1801; Sarah Ruppert            14 BA-408
Taylor, Joseph; 18 April 1818; Ruth Silvay             11 BA-28
Taylor, Joseph; 16 July 1818; Margaret Whiteman        20 BA-223
Taylor, Joshua; 19 March 1811; Lydia Richards          09 BA
Taylor, Lemuel; 26 April 1809; Deidamia Davis          11 BA-14
Taylor, Len'l, Jr.; 6 June 1815; Marg't Fowler         13 BA-25
Taylor, Levi; 18 Dec. 1817; Cathe. Ash                 13 BA-30
Taylor, Levin; 13 Oct. 1814; Elizabeth Cook            16 BA-10
Taylor, Levin; 22 Dec. 1814; Betsy Chaille             17 BA-10
```

Taylor, Loyd G.; 24 Jan. 1802; Mary E. Thornton   01 AA-71
Taylor, Menoah; 26 Feb. 1807; Elizabeth Williams   11 BA-10
Taylor, Reuben; 2 April 1809; Rachel Jones (col.)   02 BA-7
Taylor, Richard; 20 Jan. 1801; Rebecca Boyd   15 AA-1
Taylor, Robert A.; 6 June 1820; Mary Ann Schroeder   19 BA-73
Taylor, Samuel; 11 Feb. 1803; Sally Mumma   14 BA-414
Taylor, Samuel; 27 March 1804; Julia Walsley   33 BA-40
Taylor, Samuel; 7 May 1812; Polly Keifer   06 FR-1318
Taylor, Samuel; 13 June 1815; Ann Chalmers   11 BA-26
Taylor, Samuel; 30 May 1816; Elizabeth Stansfield   13 BA-39
Taylor, Samuel; 10 Aug. 1819; Maria Keene   37 BA-152
Taylor, Samuel (s. of Elisha and Elizabeth of West Notingham
    Hund., CE Co.); 8 d. 12 mo., 1819; Hannah Richards (dau. of
    Thomas and Hannah of the same place)   06 SF
Taylor, Thomas; 2 Dec. 1806; Ann White   02 BA-5
Taylor, Thos.; 24 Sept. 1808; Marg't Scanlaw   03 BA-498
Taylor, Thomas; 29 June 1815; Ann Cummins   13 BA-39
Taylor, William; 4 April 1803; Mary Berry   09 BA
Taylor, William; 12 April 1806; Ann Conner   02 BA-3
Taylor, William; 10 Aug. 1815; Sally Kennedy   32 BA-304
Taytum, Daniel; 6 Aug. 1801; Rosanna Handler   09 BA
Teal, Archibald; 15 Oct. 1803; Susanna Whitelock   14 BA-417
Teldray, Samuel; 1 June 1805; Alsia Cottrell   02 SM-186
Tenant, James; 11 April 1811; Polly Avey   02 WA-89
Tennar, John; 25 Aug. 1806; Sally Clark   05 BA-235
Tennhagen (or Feenhagen), Bernbard Henry (or Gervase Henry); 29
    Jan. 1818; Susanna Cercilla   32 BA-318
Tepton, Jarrett; 28 Jan. 1818; Martha McComas   11 BA-31
Teshy, John: 25 March 1804 (by Rev. L. W. McCombes); Mary Ann
    Jones   17 BA-3
Tessandier, John Bapt. (son of John Baptist Tessandier and
    Francis De Ruelle, native of Angouleme); 21 Aug. 1806;
    Louisa Monsarrat Leguay (widow Gouret, dau. of Peter M.
    Leguay and Elizabeth Bourot, native of Cap. Francois, St.
    Domingo)   15 BA-241
Tessier, Peter; 3 April 1809; Mary Jero   03 BA-499
Tettle, Richard; 9 March 1818; Elizabeth Talbott   17 BA-18
Thayer, Laban; 28 June 1817; Mary Ann Louis   17 BA-16
Theban, Henry; 18 Feb. 1816; Eliza Gamble   13 BA-24
Thelfalt, John Ludwig; 15 Nov. 1803; Anne Fisher   03 BA-435
Thiering, Henry; 17 Jan. 1811 (by Rev. Robert Roberts); Margaret
    Cooke   17 BA-8
Thistle, George; 26 Nov. 1801; Ann Boyar   03 AL-613
Thistle, Thomas; 20 Jan. 1803; Elizabeth Hoffman   03 AL-613
Thistle, thomas; 7 June 1805; Juliann Cresap   03 AL-614
Thoe, Merrichurch Llewkilling [sic]; 18 Dec. 1803; Dorothy
    Cummins   03 BA-436
Thomae, Hulfrich; 26 Sept. 1801; Rosina Hupfeld   14 BA-410
Thomas, Abraham; 31 Dec. 1812; Elizabeth Thomas (See also
    15 FR-326)   01 FR-1179
Thomas, Allen; 26 Nov. 1816; Eliza B. Dall   03 BA-408
Thomas, Argalis G. D.; 6 Nov. 1817; Rebeckah Shade   11 BA-28
Thomas, Benjamin; 24 Feb. 1811; Rosanna McChery   04 FR-17
Thomas, Daniel L.; 9 June 1807; Jane Olliphant   05 BA-235
Thomas, Ebenezer; 3 Oct. 182; Ann Boon   15 AA-2
Thomas, Edward; 11 April 1802; Barbara Corum   02 SM-185
Thomas, Edward; 25 Nov. 1806; Elizab. Thomas (See also 15 FR-320)
                                                       01 FR-1179
Thomas, Gabriel; 22 Sept. 1804; Sophia Todd (see also 02 BA-34)
                                                       03 BA-491
Thomas, George; 15 July 1810 (by Rev. Robert Roberts); Jane Cunn-
    ingham   17 BA-8
Thomas, Henrich; 24 Oct. 1809; Susan Schaefer   15 FR-324
Thomas, Henry; 24 Oct. 1809; Sus. Shafer   01 FR-1179

Thomas, Isaac; 1 Jan. 1804; Petty Burkins   36 BA-2
Thomas, Isaac (s. of Isaac and Eleanor); 23 d. 11 mo., 1809;
     Hannah Starr (dau. of Jonathan and Phebe)   03 SF
Thomas, James; 2 Sept. 1820; Elize. Kirkpatrick   13 BA-35
Thomas, Jeremiah; 1801; Cassey Williams   06 AA-1
Thomas, John; 13 Aug. 1801; Dorcas Morrow   03 BA-404
Thomas, Jno.; 7 April 1804; Dorothy Upperman   14 BA-416
Thomas, John; 26 Aug. 1804; Eleanor Bussey   23 BA-3
Thomas, Jno.; 3 Aug. 1805; Louisa Oler   14 BA-418
Thomas, John; 19 Sept. 1805; Cath. Carty (See also 15 FR-318)
                                                   01 FR-1179
Thomas, John; 22 Nov. 1806; Mary Dawson   02 SM-187
Thomas, John; 13 July 1815; Catherine Shenley   13 BA-22
Thomas, John; 21 July 1818; Eliz. Sophia Spurrier 03 BA-603
Thomas, Joseph; 22 April 1813; Mary Burton   09 BA
Thomas, Michael; Nov. 1802; Marg. Ogle   02 WA-73
Thomas, Mich.; Nov. 1805; Mary Painter   02 WA-79
Thomas, Mordecai (s. of John and Sarah); (?) th d. 4 mo., 1812;
     Sarah Pyle (dau. of Amos and Ruth)   11 SF-104
Thomas, Philip; 3 Dec. 1817; Frances Johnson   05 BA-240
Thomas, Philip William; 20 Nov. 1803; Julia Chisholm 03 AA-120
Thomas, Richard; 23 May 1811; Mary Jane Fagg   11 BA-16
Thomas, Robert (col'd); 4 Jan. 1816; Neely McClish 05 BA-239
Thomas, Sterling; 25 July 1811; Elizabeth Pentz   11 BA-15
Thomas, Thomas; 13 June 1803; Fanney Gore   06 BA-3
Thomas, William; 14 April 1806; Cath. Hauser (See also 15 FR-319)
                                                   01 FR-1179
Thomas, William; 16 Dec. 1815; Pheby Green   17 BA-13
Thomas, William; 20 March 1818; Matilda Onion   11 BA-28
Thompson, Alexander; 3 March 1810; Hannah Burnham 09 BA
Thompson, Alexander; 28 May 1815; Kezia Medley   11 BA-24
Thompson, Alex'r; 21 June 1817; Rachel Thorps   03 BA-602
Thompson, Alex'r; 29 July 1819; Mary Manes   13 BA-33
Thompson, Allen; 3 May 1812; Mary Nash   13 BA-7
Thompson, Andrew; 5 March 1805; Frances Day   33 BA-41
Thompson, Andrew; 8 De.c 1808; Ann Dillon   09 BA
Thompson, Charles; 14 Aug. 1806; Margaret Thompson (both of
     Sussex Co. Delaware)   15 BA-241
Thompson, Chas.; 7 Nov. 1817; Jane Orr   14 BA-436
Thompson, Edward; (poss. 22 Jan. 1807); name not given 17 BA-5
Thompson, Edward B.; 26 Sept. 1818; Margaret Green 11 BA-35
Thompson, Francis; 1 July 1807; Elizabeth Hanscomb 09 BA
Thompson, Henry; 12 Nov. 1803; Mary West   03 BA-435
Thompson, Hiram; 10 Nov. 1816; Ann Parsons   03 BA-508
Thompson, Ingree; 27 Aug. 1804; Elizabeth Smith   03 BA-491
Thompson, Israel P.; 27 March 1817; Angelica Robinson 05 BA-239
Thompson, James; 9 May 1807; Nancy Morris (both of Sussex Co.,
     Delaware)   02 TA-40
Thompson, James; 18 Feb. 1819; Cath. Schaub   14 BA-438
Thompson, James; May 1819; Judith Funk   02 WA-113
Thompson, John; 23 May 1801; Mary Smith   11 BA-3
Thompson, John; 15 Aug. 1802; Mary Bateman   03 BA-419
Thompson, John; 5 July 1805; Margaret Tilly   03 BA-495
Thompson, John; 13 March 1811; Marg't Coale   03 BA-502
Thompson, John; 26 Aug. 1812; Rach'l Vanhorne   13 BA-17
Thompson, John; 4 Nov. 1812; M. Kittys   30 BA-109
Thompson, John; 12 June 1817; Marg't Wright   13 BA-28
Thompson, John; 1 June 1820; Sarah A. Elderdice   13 BA-35
Thompson, John B.; 20 Jan. 1818; Ann Beam   03 BA-602
Thompson, John Hornan; 12 Aug. 1802; Rachel Gash   03 BA-419
Thompson, Joseph; 21 Jan. 1807; Rachel Waughop   02 SM-187
Thompson, Joseph; 4 Nov. 1819; Mariam (?) Dunn   18 BA-66
Thompson, Laurence; 21 Nov. 1816; Maria E. Boller 14 BA-436
Thompson, Richard; 11 Nov. 1807; Sarah Mackey   21 BA-6

```
Thompson, Samuel; 13 Jan. 1817; Sarah Brown          21 BA-8
Thompson, Samuel; 8 July 1819; Ann Lock              11 BA-35
Thompson, Stephen; 19 Dec. 1802; Fanny Edge          03 BA-424
Thompson, Stephen; 26 March 1815; Sophia Rusk        13 BA-21
Thompson, Thomas; 5 Nov. 1801; Mary Fownes           03 BA-410
Thompson, Thos.; 30 Sept. 1819; Mary Ann Allerder    13 BA-33
Thompson, Thos. F.; 15 April 1819; Mary Burven       13 BA-13
Thompson, William; 19 Sept. 1804; Sarah Button (see also
   02 BA-34)                                         03 BA-491
Thomson, John C.; 25 Feb. 1810; Margaret Winemiller (See also
   15 FR-324)                                        01 FR-1179
Thomson, Wm.; 21 Aug. 1806; Clara Waltman            11 BA-9
Thomson, William John; 6 Nov. 1820; Elvia Ann Crosby 16 BA-105
Thornton, John; 19 April 1804; Harriet Spicer (free mulattoes)
                                                     15 BA-201
Thornton, Joseph; 14 July 1802; Ann Crabber          09 BA
Thornton, Joseph; 22 Oct. 1808; Ally Brannon         11 BA-12
Thornton, Seagood; 3 April 1805; Sarah Heartley      03 BA-495
Thorpe, Jno.; 30 Oct. 1801; Rachel Brunton           14 BA-411
Thorpe, Wm.; 8 July 1807; Mary Rothrock              14 BA-422
Thrift, J.; 25 Aug. 1808; Jane Workman               13 BA-38
Thrift, Richard; 8 Oct. 1801; Mary Daws              33 BA-13
Throllas, Nathaniel; 23 July 1811; Barb. Kopler      06 FR-1316
Thrush, Nicholas; 2 June 1814; Rebecca Kanner        11 BA-22
Thruston, Charles M.; 5 Sept. 1820; Juliana Hughes   03 BA-604
Thumb, Dr. George; 12 Nov. 1818; Maria Warner        19 BA-22
Thurla, Richard; 25 May 1820; Mary Carroll           13 BA-35
Tice, George; 24 April 1803; Elizabeth Shade (See also 15 FR-314)
                                                     01 FR-1179
Tice, Henry; 25 Dec. 1806; Mary Beckwith (See also 15 FR-320)
                                                     01 FR-1179
Tice, John; Aug. 1817; Ann Eliza Stoner              02 WA-106
Tidings, Leonard; 6 Jan. 1814; Sus. Galbreath        14 BA-432
Tiernan, Patrick; 8 Sept. 1814; Ann Susanna Clarke, widow
                                                     16 BA-10
Tiffer, John; 1 July 1812; Eliza Rogers              13 BA-17
Tigdon, Eph'm; 8 May 1810; Mary Webster              13 BA-9
Tigler, Michael; 14 July 1805; Susanna Eller         15 FR-317
Tilden, Charles E.; 25 Aug. 1820; Mary E. Brown      02 QA
Tilden, Perry; 31 Jan. 1813; Mary Taylor             17 BA-9
Tilge, Heinrich; 5 Jan. 1818;; Helena Herz, widow    07 BA-311
Tilghman, Edward; 14 April 1818; Anne Maria Tilghman (both of QA
   Co.) (See also 02 TA-44)                          01 QA-62
Tilghman, Col. F.; 23 Sept. 1819; Louisa Lamar       01 WA-202
Tilghman, George; 21 Dec. 1819; Ann Eliza Lamar      01 WA-202
Tilghman, Jacob; 22 Oct. 1818; Rebecca Israel        08 BA
Tilghman, Matt; 10 Jan. 1802; Eleanor M. Rosier      01 QA-43
Tilghman, Matthew; 10 Jan. 1802; Eleanor Rozier      03 TA-73
Tilghman, Tench (son of Peregrine and Deborah); April 1807; Anna
   Margaretta Tilghman (dau. of Col.Tench and Anna Maria
   Tilghman)                                         01 TA-331
Tilghman, William; 20 June 1817; Martha Hall (both of QA Co.)
   (See also 02 TA-43)                               01 QA-62
Tilgman, Emanuel; Aug. 1806; Sarah Howard            02 WA-81
Tillard, John; 24 July 1817; Thomazine Craft         02 BA-37
Tilton, Jos.; 27 Nov. 1817; Marg't McPherson         13 BA-29
Timanus, Charles; 8 Feb. 1801; Jane Lester           09 BA
Timanus, Henry; 12 Feb. 1818; Mary Capito            14 BA-437
Timanus, John; 19 Oct. 1815; Eliza Wall              13 BA-23
Timothee, John; 16 Sept. 1817; Mary Sophia           32 BA-314
Tindle, Robert W.; 14 Nov. 1818; Elizabeth M. Gregory 11 BA-35
Tinges, Adam; 29 April 1804; Elizabeth Palmer        29 BA-2
Tinscum, Benjamin; 5 July 1801; Elizabeth Scantley   33 BA-13
Tinstrom, Peter; 21 April 1806; Catherine Haley      02 BA-3
```

```
Tipton, Aman; 1 July 1820; July Ann Plowman          11 BA-37
Tipton, Joshua; 4 Nov. 1813; Ruth Tye                08 BA
Tipton, Stephen; 21 Jan. 1819; Elizabeth Lynch       08 BA
Tisdale, Ruben; 9 Oct. 1817; Sarah Scudder           13 BA-29
Tillow, Adam; 3 Nov. 1811; Rebecca Hull              06 FR-1317
Tillow, John; 2 April 1811; Margareth Fogler         06 FR-1315
Tittle, Richard; 9 March 1818; Elizabeth Talbott     17 BA-19
Titus, W.; 23 June 1816; Reb'a. Gordon               13 BA-25
Tobin, James; 9 March 1805 (by Jno. Bloodgood); Elizabeth
     Lucans                                          17 BA-5
Tobin, John; 13 Sept. 1815; Mary Mullans             32 BA-304
Todd, Bernard; 14 Jan. 1802; Polly Green             09 BA
Todd, Christopher; 5 Sept. 1805; Susanna Sindle      09 BA
Todd, George W.; 28 Sept. 1803; Mary Merryman        23 BA-2
Todd, Samuel; 15 March 1813; Sarah Middleton (?)     17 BA-9
Todd, Thomas; 4 Oct. 1804; Rachel Clark              09 BA
Todhunter, Jacob; 14 June 1812; Polly Johns          06 FR-1318
Todhunter, Jos.; 11 Dec. 1810; E. Onion              30 BA-109
Toelle, Fred'k; 26 Jan. 1813; Sarah J. Rous          14 BA-431
Tolbert, Benjamin; July 1819; Malinda Hedge          02 WA-113
Tom, Jacob; Oct. 1810; Susan Arm(?)ey                02 WA-87
Tomlinson, Samuel; 7 July 1811; Polly Matthews       03 AL-614
Tompkins, William; 26 Dec. 1801; Ann Farr            02 CH
Toms, Jacob, Jr.; 12 Nov. 1820; Mary Flight          03 FR-61
Toms, Jonathan; Feb. 1819; Mary Markle               02 WA-112
Toms, William; Oct. 1805; Mary Staull                02 WA-79
Tone (?), Stephen; 15 Jan. 1801; Elizabeth Yieldhall 15 AA-1
Toner, Edward; 5 Nov. 1802; Mary C. McCormick (see also
     03 BA-422)                                      02 BA-32
Tongue, James; 9 June 1803; Ann Cowman               03 AA-120
Tongue, Walter I.; 19 Jan. 1809; Ann Linton          09 BA
Toogood, Edward; 22 May 1816; Nancy Peeterson        05 BA-239
Tookas, Peter; 2 Sept. 1817; Elizabeth Lee (both col'd)
                                                     16 BA-55
Toole, Fergus; 14 March 1805; Mary Faherty           15 BA-217
Toole, Peter; 8 Feb. 1816; Nancy McCleary            08 AL-115
Toon, Samuel; 2 April 1807; Elizabeth Bennett        02 BA-5
Tooth, Thos.; 22 Dec. 1812; Elis. Hooper             13 BA-15
Topken, Gerhart; 6 Dec. 1808; Johanna Pauli, widow   07 BA-306
Tott, John; 15 Dec. 1803; Elizabeth Wheat            15 AA-3
Totter, Daniel; 22 Aug. 1816; Nancy Parker           08 AL-115
Towel, Zacharia; 16 March 1820; Amelia Jones         14 BA-440
Tower, Gideon; 23 June 1814; Ann Hancock             13 BA-39
Townsend. Benjamin (of OH, s. of Joseph and Lydia of E. Bradford.
     Chester Co., PA); 18 d. 6 mo., 1807; Elizabeth Naylor (dau.
     of John and Jane, both dec.)                    09 SF
Townsend. Benjamin; 10 June 1819; Anna Maria Townsend 17 BA-22
Townsend, Granville L.; 29 Feb. 1820; Sarah Brown    03 BA-604
Townsend, Jonathan; 18 July 1807; Mary Willen        14 BA-422
Townsend, Jonathan; 16 July 1815 (by Joshua Willey); Rebecca
     North                                           17 BA-11
Townsend, Percy R.; 17 Jan. 1819; Ann Maria Duncan   19 BA-72
Towson, Joseph; 28 April 1814; Sarah Yundt           11 BA-22
Towson, Obadiah; 16 July 1812; Catherine Irvine      31 BA-130
Towson, Philemon; 18 April 1811 (by Robert Roberts); Catherine
     Cushman                                         17 BA-8
Towson, Philip; 3 March 1803; Ann Cockey             23 BA-2
Towson, Thomas; 17 Nov., 1803; Mary Butler           03 BA-435
Towson, Thos.; 16 Oct. 1816; Henrietta Grubb         14 BA-436
Toy, Ammael; 27 Aug. 1818; Sarah Gardner             05 BA-241
Toy, Joseph; 26 Feb. 1810; Sarah Owings              13 BA-11
Traber, Thomas; 9 Dec. 1804; Mary Zimmerman (See also 15 FR-317)
                                                     01 FR-1179
```

```
Tracey, Joseph; 1 Nov. 1804; Keziah Thompson        09 BA
Tracey, Peirce; 13 July 1805; Mary Wilson           09 BA
Tracey, Richard; 7 Aug. 1814; Mary Edwards          11 BA-22
Tracy, Alexander; 18 Sept. 1802; Mary Grimes        09 BA
Tracy, Peter; April 1807; Elis. Malone              02 WA-83
Tracy, William; 1804; Elizabeth Winterson           07 AA-4
Traden, Parker; 30 March 1801; Else Carnes          03 BA-399
Trail, Ashford; 29 Dec. 1803; Anne Sanders          03 MO-119
Trail, Edward; 1813; Harriet Fish                   01 PG
Traill, Nathan; 22 Dec. 1801; Susanna Buxton        03 MO-117
Trant, John; 14 April 1805; Marg. Schaun            01 FR-1179
Trates, John; 2 June 1816; Brid't. Harris           13 BA-25
Traut, Johannes; 14 April 1805; Margaret Schaum     15 FR-317
Traverse, Jeremiah; 13 Dec. 1804; Henny Martin      01 DO-41
Traverse, John; 24 April 1806; Susan Traverse       01 DO-41
Traverse, John, Jr.; 3 April 1816; Susan R. H. Moale  03 BA-507
Traverse, John Hicks; 18 June 1807; Mary Brooke     01 DO-41
Travis, Edward; 29 Aug. 1815; Mary Thompson         17 BA-13
Treage, Daniel; 15 Jan. 1807; Eliza Peachgood       03 BA-496
Tregs, Sam'l; 6 June 1817; Eliza Nicholson          13 BA-28
Tremell, John William; 1 Jan. 1814; Margaret Lawrence  31 BA-165
Trencle, Isaiah; 24 Dec. 1811; Mary Burke           03 BA-503
Tresler, Adam; 1 May 1808; Margarethe Barley        08 AL-115
Tress, Frans.; 19 June 1812; Ann Lee                13 BA-14
Trexil, Michael; 21 May 1816; Margaret Markel       14 BA-435
Trieger, Daniel; 11 Sept. 1806; Eliza Broadbeck     01 FR-1179
Trenton, Anthony; 12 Oct. 1807; Sarah Gray          09 BA
Trifird, Jas.; 13 Sept. 1805; Mary Thomas           03 BA-494
Triplet, John; 24 Feb. 1801; Terresia Marshall      03 BA-398
Tripolett, Edward; 12 Oct. 1817; Elizabeth Parker   08 BA
Trippe, Edward; 14 Sept. 1820; Ann Thompson         13 BA-35
Tritch, William; Jan. 1816; Marg't Kline            02 WA-101
Trollenburgh, William; 31 May 1802; Hannah Leader   06 BA-2
Trott, John; 1804; Elizabeth Prout                  13 AA-2
Trott, Zachariah; 6 April 1806; Eliz'th Bareford    03 AA-130
Trottenburgh, Wm.; 25 Dec. 1809; Sarah Williams     14 BA-427
Troup, David; 28 March 1812; Cath. Weaver           02 WA-93
Troup, Jacob; 20 Feb. 1811; Peggy Snyder            02 WA-89
Troup, John; Aug. 1808; Mary Snider                 02 WA-85
Trownson, George; 4 May 1802; Sidney Allen          03 BA-416
Troxell, Abraham; 22 April 1813; Sarah Amboucher    15 BA-310
True, Wm.; 2 April 1811; Julia Petit                02 WA-89
Truly, John; Nov. 1814; Susan Cromwell (both free col'd)
                                                    16 BA-12
Truly, Wm.; 15 June 1819; Nancy Anderson            19 BA-72
Trumbo, David S.; 14 Dec. 1810; Harriet Hallbrook   14 BA-428
Trunnell, David; 15 Jan. 1812; Rosa McManus         04 FR-18
Truslen, Sam'l; 1 Aug. 1815; Mary Flananday         13 BA-22
Tschudy, John; 3 May 1804 (by L. McCombes); Elizabeth Ford
                                                    17 BA-3
Tschudy, Samuel; 20 March 1817; Elizabeth Clemme    03 BA-602
Tubman, Capt. Charles; May 1816; (Mrs.?) Anne Keine, both of
     Dorset Co.                                     02 TA-43
Tubman, Richard. Jr.; 16 Aug. 1808; Miss Zippy Wallace, both of
     Dorset Co.                                     02 TA-41
Tubman, Richard. Sr.; 2 Aug. 1810; Polly Keene, both of Dorset
     Co.                                            02 TA-41
Tuck, Washington G.; 27 March 1814; Rachel S. Whittington
                                                    03 AA-131
Tuck, William A.; 25 May 1801; Cave Mullikin        15 AA-1
Tucker, Benjamin; 2 Aug. 1804; Ann Avis             09 BA
Tucker, George Crabtree; 31 Aug. 1815; Lunetta Martiacq
                                                    16 BA-26
Tucker, Hanson; 17 Oct. 1817; Mary Burk             14 BA-423
```

Tucker, Henson; 23 April 1815; Mary Ridley   13 BA-21
Tucker, James; 30 April 1811 (by Robert Roberts); Harriet Bond
                                                          17 BA-8
Tucker, John; 26 Feb. 1801; Lurena Rawlings   15 AA-1
Tucker, John; 23 Dec. 1804; Sarah Hardesty   03 AA-130
Tucker, John; 29 June 1818; (N) Guishard   17 BA-19
Tucker, Joseph; 30 Nov. 1819; Ann Young   11 BA-36
Tucker, Richard; 19 Dec. 1802; Lurena Tucker   15 AA-2
Tucker, Roger; 27 Dec. 1802; Anny White (See also 15 FR-313)
                                                          01 FR-1179
Tucker, Seaborn; 14 feb. 1804; Henrietta Wood   03 AA-130
Tucker, William; 2 Aug. 1801; Mary Ann Brewer   05 AA-1
Tucker, Wm.; 3 Sept. 1818; Eliza Lindsey   13 BA-31
Tucker, Zachariah; 16 Nov. 1802; Sarah Stewart   15 AA-2
Tuder, John (s. of William and Martha); 3 d, 6 mo., 1807; Phebe
     Morthland (dau. of Samuel and Susannah)   02 SF-106
Tuell (?), Martin; 4 Sept. 1810; Mary Roach   31 BA-89
Tull, Wm.; 29 Nov. 1818; Eliza Todd   13 BA-32
Tullins, Richard; 16 June 1805; Elizabeth Byloff   15 FR-317
Tumbleton, William; 26 May 1818; Elizabeth Ready   17 BA-19
Tunis, Charles; 17 June 1802; Harriet Coale   03 BA-417
Tunnill, Henry; 3 Jan. 1801; Elizabeth Hughes   03 BA-397
Turfield, Philip; 10 May 1814; Mary Greenwood   13 BA-39
Turner, Abraham; c.1801; Rachel Disney   08 AA-1
Turner, Caleb; 30 May 1808; Elizabeth Davis   14 BA-424
Turner, Isaac (of Cecil MM, KE Co., s. of Joseph and Sarah); 5th
     d. 5 mo., 1814; Sarah Massey (dau. of Isaac and Margaret)
                                                          11 SF-112
Turner, Isaac; 10 Nov. 1818; Elizabeth Brashears   06 FR-1329
Turner, Jacob; 7 Nov. 1801; Susannah Forrester   09 BA
Turner, John; 24 April 1803; Eliz. Herbein (See also 15 FR-314)
                                                          01 FR-1179
Turner, John; 30 Dec. 1811; Sarah Evans   02 WA-92
Turner, John; 6 Oct. 1815; Margaret Gwynn   03 BA-507
Turner, John D.; 6 July 1820; Adeline Holmes   13 BA-35
Turner, Jos.; 4 May 1816; Eliza Shekels   13 BA-25
Turner, Joseph; 15 Aug. 1810; Mary Green   14 BA-427
Turner, Joseph, Jr., (of Balto. Town, s. of Joseph of KE Co., and
     dec. w. Sarah); 21 d. 10 m., 1812; Rebecca Sinclair (dau.
     of John of Balto. Town and w. Elizabeth)   12 SF-30
Turner, Joshua; 22 Feb. 1803; Marg't Spear   21 BA-5
Turner, Richard; 28 May 1809; Mary Wills (See also 15 FR-323)
                                                          01 FR-1179
Turner, Samuel; Feb. 1807; Brainine S (?)   02 WA-82
Turner, Thomas; 12 Nov. 1801; Phebe Norris   33 BA-13
Turner, William; 23 July 1801; Margaret M'Kezzey   10 BA-1
Turner, Wm.; 14 Jan. 1807; Elisab. Huber   14 BA-423
Turtle, John; 18 March 1815; Barbara Lootz   14 BA-2
Turtle, William; 14 Aug. 1808; Mary Norris   13 BA-4
Tustis, Peter; 25 June 1819; Adelina Anna Blissett   08 AL-116
Tustle, John; 19 March 1815; Barba. Loots   13 BA-20
Tweedy, Samuel; 5 Dec. 1820; Ann Williams   13 BA-36
Twigg, Elias; Jan. 1816; Elizab. Cheney   02 WA-101
Tyler, William; 19 Oct. 1809; Harriet Murdock   02 FR-17
Tyler, Zebedee; 3 Dec. 1804; Rachel Williams   01 DO-41
Tylor, John; 3 Dec. 1807; Amelia Woodland (both of Dorset Co.)
                                                          02 TA-40
Tyson, Elisha (s. of Isaac and Esther); 22 d. 9 mo., 1814;
     Margaret Cowman (dau. of Jno. and Sarah)   01 SF
Tyson, Geo.; 28 March 1810; Hannah Bull   13 BA-12
Tyson, Henry; 4 June 1806; Mary Ann Mulkern   02 BA-4
Tyson, Jesse (s. of Isaac and Esther); 22 day, 5 mo., 1806; Sarah
     Ridgely (dau. of Henry and Anne)   01 SF
Tyson, Nathan; 29 Sept. 1801; Mary Randall   09 BA

Tyson, Nathan, Jr. (of Balto. Town, s. of Elisha and dec. w.
    Mary); 21 d. 9 m., 1815; Martha Ellicott (dau. of George of
    BA Co., and w. Elizabeth)   12 SF-45
Tyson, William (s. of Elisha and Mary); 26 d. 10 mo., 1803 at Elk
    Ridge; Elizabeth Ellicott (dau. of Jonathan and Sarah)
                                                        09 SF
Uhl, Andreas; 11 Feb. 1812; Catherine Banckert   07 BA-308
Uhl, George; 12 dec. 1819; Elizabeth Sturtz   08 AL-116
Uhler, Andrew; 19 April 1803; Polly Sullivan   23 BA-2
Uhler, Erasmus; 12 Sept. 1816; Cath. Hoffman   14 BA-435
Uhler, George; 19 July 1812; Barbara Good   14 BA-430
Uhler, Jacob; 3 June 1817; Ellender O'Donnell   08 BA
Uhler, Jno.; 23 May 1816; Priscilla Galloway   14 BA-435
Uhler, John; 12 Nov. 1816; Sary Kelly   08 BA
Umbaugh, Michael; 8 July 1819; Jane R. Herbert   01 WA-202
Underwood, John (of York Co., PA; s. of Nehemiah and Mary, both
    dec.); 8 d. 5 mo., 1814; Mary Clark (dau. of Israel and
    Amy)   02 SF-122
Underwood, William; c.1804; Mary Roach   34 BA-2
Underwood, Wm. B.; 2 Jan. 1803; Ruth Marschall   01 FR-1180
Underwood, William B.; 2 Jan. 1803; Ruth Marshall   15 FR-313
Undutch, Henry; 24 July 1817; Ann Hacke   13 BA-28
[Uneman], Adam; 13 Jan. 1818; Frederica Horn, widow   39 BA-34
Unger, (N); Dec. 1807; Sophia McClure   02 WA-84
Unglesbee, John; 14 Aug. 1817; Magdalen Daub   06 FR-1326
Updegraff, Ambrose (or York Co., PA, s. of Joseph and Susanna,
    dec.); 21 d. 5 mo., 1805; Rachel Hayward (of William and
    Sydney)   09 SF
Updegraff, Ambrose; 4 March 1813; Cath. Robison   02 WA-97
Upperco, Thomas; 30 Oct. 1817; Mary Jones   08 BA
Upperman, John; April 1804; Elis. Will   02 WA-76
Uptegraph, Joseph; 26 Feb. 1806; Hester Propick   03 AL-613
Upton, John; 4 April 1816; Susan Ann Stansfield   13 BA-39
Urnst, John; Sept. 1810; Eliz. Strickler   02 WA-87
Ury, Jeremiah; 25 June 1801; Levina Hoges   27 BA-1
Usher, James; 26 June 1803; Catherine Fitzgibbons   03 BA-429
Usher, Luke Noble; 28 April 1804; Harriet Anna Snowden 09 BA
Ute, John; 13 Nov. 1804; Sarah Matilda Webly   11 BA-4
Uthman, Anthony; 27 Dec. 1818; Cath. Slough   14 BA-438
Valentine, Adam; 29 March 1810; Elizabeth Raitz   08 AL-117
Valentine, David; Dec. 1802; Sus. Mayer   02 WA-73
Valentine, Frederick, Jr.; 16 Aug. 1812; Susanna Reitz 08 AL-117
Valentine, John; 21 Nov. 1809; Maria Reitz   08 AL-117
Valliant, John; 8 March 1804 (AA Co.); Mary Meek   40 BA
Valliant, John; 4 May 1809; Catherine Riley   11 BA-14
Van Beuren, Wm.; 16 Sept. 1811; Ann Billis   03 BA-503
Van Bibber, Washington; 19 May 1807; Lucretia Emory   03 BA-497
Van Buren, James; 29 June 1811; Catherine I. Nicholls   15 BA-288
Van Buskirk, Samuel; 8 May 1806; Ann Hull   03 AL-614
Vance, William; 17 June 1802; Anne Lowes   03 BA-417
Vancott, Platt; 6 Feb. 1819; Mary Ann Mitchell   13 BA-32
Vanharten, Gerhard; 13 April 1802; Hetty Kimel   14 BA-412
Vanhorne, John; 22 Dec. 1818; Nancy White   01 WA-201
Vanhorne, Samuel; 15 Feb. 1804; Alce Thomas   01 DO-41
Van Lassel, Peter; 6 July 1805; Catherine Baker   05 BA-234
Vanlear, Joseph; 19 Feb. 1801; Samuel McDaniel   09 BA
Vanleur, Joseph; 12 Jan. 1817; Sarah Moore   06 FR-1325
Van Praag, Solomon H.; 23 Dec. 1820; Hester Berand (?) Swaab
                                                        37 BA-153
Van Ripor, John; 19 Nov. 1818; Letitia McKee   37 BA-151
Van Riswick, John; 8 Dec. 1810; Catha. Amos   03 BA-502
Van Rooten, Peter; 30 June 1804; Caroline Mulonniere   15 BA-206
Vansant, Christ.; 8 Dec. 1811; Eliza Fenton   03 BA-503
Van Sant, Cornelious; 19 May 1803; Chatrine Kirby   34 BA-1

```
Vansant, John; 30 July 1812; Rhoda Crouds            13 BA-14
Vansant, Wm.; 11 June 1812; Sarah Hutler             13 BA-9
Vansant, William; 7 April 1814; Mary Saunders        11 BA-21
Varble, Math.; June 1807; Elis. Stauss               02 WA-83
Varon, Peter; 26 April 1813; Victorie Hansette       03 BA-505
Vasey, Edward; 16 June 1808; Sophia Deiter           13 BA-4
Vasley, Henry; 20 Jan. 1812; Mary Curry              03 BA-503
Vaspinto (?), Antoine; 9 Jan. 1810; Margaret Hutton  31 BA-72
Vaughan, Benjamin; 5 Aug. 1818; Susanna Naul         32 BA-321
Vaughan, Jeremiah; 26 Nov. 1807; Rebneckah Night     11 BA-12
Vaughan, Sherdine; 7 Oct. 1809; Susanna West         09 BA
Vaugn, William; 25 or 26 March 1815; Cath. Kline (?) 17 BA-10
Veale, John; 15 July 1816; Mary Leddy                16 BA-38
Veatch, Thomas; 10 Dec. 1801; Mary Self (See also 15 FR-312)
                                                     01 FR-1181
Veazey, James; 2 Jan. 1804 (by L. W. McCombes); Elizabeth
     Carroll                                         17 BA-3
Veazey, John; 30 July 1801; Hannah Clackner          09 BA
Veazy, Josiah; 2 Feb. 1819; Sarah Hines              11 BA-34
Venn, James; 3 Nov. 1811; Julia Johnson              11 BA-17
Vent, Christian; 12 Jan. 1811; Eliz. Birch           14 BA-428
Vermillion, James; 3 July 1815; Eliza Carter         11 BA-25
Verrow, John; May 1817; Eve Brunner                  02 WA-105
Vevers, John; 24 Dec. 1807; Mary Brannan             03 BA-498
Vickers, Charles; 19 Aug. 1819; Mary Hillman         13 BA-33
Vickers, Henry; 21 Dec. 1802; Aramintha Hart         14 BA-412
Vickers, John; 5 Sept. 1816; Elizabeth Griffin       17 BA-15
Vickers, Thomas, Jr. (s. of Thomas and Jemima); 1 d. 9 mo.,
     1819; Hannah P. Harmer (dau. of Amos and Elizabeth) (See
     also 10 SF)                                     01 SF
Victory, Daniel; 6 Oct. 1814; Winifred Donnally      31 BA-181
Vinard, Henry; 14 June 1813; Rachel Gothrop          09 BA
Vincent, John; 23 Sept. 1812; Nancy Campbell         05 BA-237
Vincent, Morris; 12 March 1810; Hannah Deakins       13 BA-12
Vinsatt, james; 21 Sept. 1805 (by John Bloodgood); Sarah Mackey
     (in list of marriages for blacks)               17 BA-5
Vintree, Francis; 23 Oct. 1908; Cath. Miller         14 BA-426
Vintree, Jacob; 29 Nov. 1806; Elizabeth Schrote      14 BA-421
Vissett, William; 2 May 1801; Cath. Sitler           14 BA-409
Vizze, William; 11 June 1808; Britanne Smallwood     15 BA-262
Vogel, Andreas; 27 Sept. 1801; Eva Heiner            01 CL-149
Vokel, Peter; 20 April 1808; Mehlle Gun (?)          39 BA-21
Vondermuhl?, Joseph; 19 Oct. 1820; Cath. Eliza Sharper 21 BA-9
Von Durnbury, Franciscus; 19 Feb. 1811; Maria Kreiter 07 BA-308
Von Hemechsen, Andrew J.; 20 May 1802; Cath. Yeiser  14 BA-112
Von Hollen, Christopher; 11 Feb. 1819; Annie Rickstein 14 BA-438
Vonkapff, B. John; 20 May 1804; Hester M. Didier     21 BA-5
Von Rossom, John; 19 Dec. 1819; Martia Mallony       32 BA-327
Vore, Isaac (of Fawn Twp., York Co., PA, s. of Jacob and Mary);
     13th d. 5 mo., 1807; Ruth Bond (dau. of Benjamin and Mary)
                                                     11 SF-102
Vore, Jacob; 9 d. 11 mo., 1814; Elizabeth Clark (dau. of Israel
     and Amy)                                        02 SF-125
Vore, Mordica (s. of Gideon and Mary); 23 d. 10 m., 1806; Mary
     Morris (dau. of Benjamin and Ann)               03 SF
Vosburgh, Abraham; 16 May 1820; Priscilla Roberts    17 BA-23
Votgs (?), Claas (?); 5 Dec. 1820; Eliz. Foy         14 BA-440
Vowell, John D.; 8 June 1815; Margaretta Brown       05 BA-238
Vurmears, William; 23 June 1803; Mary Edelen         03 PG-1
Wachope, Samuel; 28 July 1801; Rachel Davis          09 BA
Wachter, George; 27 March 1817; Maria Balzell        06 FR-1326
Wachter, Jacob; 29 March 1807; Mary Wiedrick         01 FR-1182
Wachter, Jacob; 29 March 1807; Maria Widerich        15 FR-320
Wachter, Jacob; 16 March 1813; Peggy Witterich       01 FR-1183
```

```
Wachter, Jacob; 16 March 1813; Peggy Ditterich        15-FR 326
Wachter, Michael; 12 Dec. 1820; Maria M. Wiest        06 FR-1331
Wachter, Samuel; 16 Feb. 1813; Susanna Stull          06 FR-1319
Wachter, Samuel; 13 Aug. 1818; Mary Stoll             06 FR-1328
Wade, Caleb; 1804; Arey Hall                          02 WA-76
Wade, Jesse; 7 Dec. 1804; Mary Flemming               03 MO-119
Wade, John; 3 Jan. 1811; Anne West                    01 PG
Wade, Philip; 19 Feb. 1818; Harriet Davis             03 BA-503
Wade, Thomas; 7 June 1808; Dorothea Furlong           02 BA-6
Wafer (?), James; 20 July 1817; Ann Kelly             32 BA-313
Wagely, Joh.; July 1806; Cath. Knedy                  02 WA-81
Waggener, Henry; 19 June 1816; Nancy Carey            11 BA-30
Waggoner, George; 5 May 1803; Catherine Brusebanks    06 BA-3
Waggoner, John; 3 Oct. 1811; Margaret Pageant         06 FR-1316
Wagner, Cornelius J.; 12 June 1811 (by Robert Roberts); Hannah
    Young                                             17 BA-8
Wagner, Fried.; 1808; Barb. Esons                     02 WA-71
Wagner, Jno.; 16 July 1806; Rebecca Barnes            14 BA-420
Wagner, Joannes; 21 Sept. 1820; Alice McCalister      39 BA-38
Wagoner, Daniel; 30 April 1811; Mary Murphy           04 FR-17
Wainwright, Samuel (of TA Co., s. of James and Elizabeth); 30 d.
    5 mo., 1810; Matilda Matthews (dau. of John and Leah)
                                                      02 SF-113
Wait, Thomas; 6 Jan. 1801; Alice Greedily             03 BA-397
Waites, Philip; 11 Jan. 1817; Elizabeth Cook          03 BA-602
Waites, Richard; 22 Oct. 1811; Eliza Bassett          21 BA-7
Waits, James; 27 Feb. 1811; Jane Cotts                11 BA-18
Walcot, Jesse; 25 Dec. 1818; Mary Pashes              13 BA-5
Walker, Arthur; 10 Sept. 1818; Jane Jones             14 BA-437
Walker, Christopher; 2 May 1802; Eliz'th Hambleton    09 BA
Walker, Cornelius; 31 Oct. 1802; Elizabeth Owings     09 BA
Walker, Ezekiel; 27 Aug. 1801; Marg. Smallwood        14 BA-410
Walker, Henry; Nov. 1817; Cath. Adam                  02 WA-107
Walker, Henry; 18 March 1818; Cynthia McGeath (?)     06 FR-1328
Walker, Isaac; 12 May 1812; Julia Foster              14 BA-430
Walker, John; 10 May 1806; Eliza Marrell              03 BA-495
Walker, John; 18 Oct. 1811; Polly Shultz              06 FR-1316
Walker, John; 11 April 1819; Catherine Wiest          06 FR-1329
Walker, Jno. P; 29 Aug. 1816; Sarah Chambers          03 BA-507
Walker, Joseph; 25 Dec. 1820; Ellen Stacy             19 BA-73
Walker, Peter; 24 Aug. 1811; Mary Hartnell (both natives of
    Ireland)                                          15 BA-289
Walker, Richard; 11 Jan. 1803; Ellen Bond             23 BA-2
Walker, Samuel; 5 Nov. 1812; Caroline Lee             03 BA-504
Walker, Samuel; May 1817; Eliza Dean                  02 WA-105
Walker, Thomas B.; 1 Feb. 1812; Elizabeth Finlas      09 BA
Walker, Thomas B.; 17 June 1812; Lucinda Dilworth     09 BA
Walker, Dr. Thomas C.; 17 Feb. 1818; Catherine Cradock 18 BA-66
Walker, William; 2 Feb. 1802; Susanna Chaires         09 BA
Walker, William; 1 May 1803; Elizabeth Kensell        34 BA-1
Walker, William; 21 Jan. 1809; Betsy Kramer           13 BA-38
Walker, William; 11 Nov. 1813; Sary Bell              08 BA
Walker, William (of Taney Town); 1 Aug. 1814; Mary Costigan
                                                      16 BA-9
Walker, Willson; 8 Oct. 1801; Deborah Prather         03 MO-117
Wall (?), John; 9 Nov. 1815; Cav. Willigmeyer         13 BA-23
Wall, Samuel; 2 July 1812; Mary Hamilton              09 BA
Wallace, Benja.; c.1804; May League                   34 BA-2
Wallace, George T.; 4 Jan. 1817; Rebeckah Horney      11 BA-27
Wallace, John L.; 23 May 1808; Mary Bingham           17 BA-6
Wallace, Joseph; 2 March 1802; Milley Ross            01 DO-40
Wallace, Richard; 30 July 1818; Lucy Potter Chaffinch 11 BA-32
Wallace, Solomon; 14 Sept. 1819; Ruth Stansbury       11 BA-37
Wallam, William; 30 May 1816; Emity Foreman           17 BA-12
```

```
Waller, William; 17 June 1819; Bridget D. Jones        01 SO-15
Wallich, Conrad; March 1805; Cath. Beard               02 WA-78
Wallich, George; 9 Feb. 1811; Elizabeth Spohn          06 FR-1315
Wallins, Joseph (widower); 10 March 1801; Elizabeth Johnson
     (widow)                                           15 BA-150
Wallis, Edward; 18 April 1812; Cervette Stephen        15 BA-297
Wallow, Abraham; 26 June 1817; Amey Chapman            21 BA-9
Walls, Ezekiel; 14 May 1807; Eliza Hays                13 BA-2
Walls, Frederick; 1 June 1817; Julia Ann Parks         11 BA-31
Walsh, Edward; 2 Aug. 1804; Rachel Sheppard            14 BA-417
Walsh, Elijah; 12 May 1803; Mary Stansbury             09 BA
Walsh, Jacob, Jr.; 24 June 1802; Margaret Yates        03 BA-418
Walsh, John; 21 June 1804; Mary Doyle (both natives of Ireland)
                                                       15 BA-205
Walsh, Michael (native of Ireland); 16 Oct. 1802; Rosanna Blott
     widow; native of Dunkirk)                         15 BA-173
Walsh, Philip; 14 Nov. 1802; Elizabeth Leever          36 BA-1
Walsh, Peter; 28 April 1816; Catherine Creek           16 BA-33
Walston, Thomas; 4 June 1801; Leah White               01 SO-15
Waltam, Charlton; 13 June 1816; Mary Hill              17 BA-12
Waltemeyer, Adam; 6 Oct. 1814; Rachel W. Pierpoint     09 BA
Walter, Fred'k; 9 July 1815; Anne E. Julian            13 BA-22
Walter, George B.; 29 Sept. 1814; Mary B. Waters       01 WI
Walter, Henry; 11 May 1807; Susan Hoss                 14 BA-422
Walter, Henry; 15 Jan. 1814; Eliz. Coppenhauer         14 BA-432
Walter, Jacob; 19 Nov. 1810; Mary Deagle               15 BA-284
Walter, Jacob; 24 Sept. 1820; Christina Cramer         06 FR-1331
Walter, John; 18 Dec. 1804; Eleanor Jenkins            15 BA-213
Walter, John; 1 Jan. 1805; Maria Cochran (02 BA gives date as 29
     Dec. 1804)                                        03 BA-492
Walter, Joseph; 21 Feb. 1803; Nancy Dean               03 BA-426
Walter, Joseph Louis; 5 June 1804; Anne Needle         15 BA-203
Walter, Josephus; 12 Jan. (?) 1808; Catharina Frank    39 BA-20
Walter, Philip; 21 Sept. 1808; Marg't Krause           14 BA-424
Walter, William; 18 Oct. 1810; Margaret Boyd           15 BA-283
Walterding, Joh.; 5 Oct. 1815; Elizab. Vollers         14 BA-434
Waltermayer, Philip; Dec. 1810; Barbara Wagely         02 WA-88
Walters, Alexander; 25 March 1806; Elizabeth Worthington
                                                       21 BA-6
Walters, Jacob Slate; 21 April 1811; Ann O. McNeal     08 BA
Walters, William; Dec. 1809; Susanna Bond              08 BA
Waltham, Charles; 9 May 1807; Cassander Jarman         09 BA
Waltham, Clement; 29 Jan. 1801; Alisanna Webster       33 BA-12
Waltman, William; 17 April 1808; Sarah Beckwaith       02 BA-6
Walton, Michael; 6 July 1801; Margaret Brown           03 BA-402
Wamlinger, Joannes; 3 Jan. 1808; Maria Schaffer        39 BA-20
Wane, John; 11 Dec. 1806; Elizabeth Ellicott           02 BA-5
Wann, Dan'l; 2 June 1812; Anne Lemare                  13 BA-17
Wann, John; 18 June 1818; Mary Newcommer               16 BA-70
Wantz, Esra; 6 dec. 1807; Maria Rithie (?)             15 FR-321
Ward, Hanson; 11 Jan. 1815; Elizabeth Black            08 AL-120
Ward, James (?); 16 Jan. 1812; Phebe Ougel             31 BA-118
Ward, James; 26 Feb. 1815; Elizabeth Finletter         11 BA-22
Ward, John; 3 Dec. 1818; Elizabeth Roberts             03 BA-603
Ward, John H.; 25 June 1815; Juliana Martin            16 BA-21
Ward, John Wesley; 13 Jan. 1807; Eleanor Greentree (See also
     01 PG)                                            02 MO
Ward, Joseph; 8 Dec. 1808; Permela (N)                 08 BA
Ward, Robert; c.May 1802; Catherine Spicknell          03 AA-120
Ward, Robert; 26 Feb. 1805; Elizabeth Perrin           09 BA
Ward, William; 1 Feb. 1801; Rebecca Murray             03 BA-398
Ward, William; 19 April 1802; Jane Jeffrey             09 BA
Ward, William; 21 April 1805; Mary Delany              15 BA-218
Ward, William; 20 April 1815; Ann B. Carson            11 BA-26
```

Ware, Spedden; 6 July 1804; Susan Abel   14 BA-417
Ware, Thomas; 19 Feb. 1815; Nancy Rummey   08 BA
Ware, William; 1 Nov. 1816 (or 1819); Elizabeth Blevins
                                                08 AL-120
Warfell; Jam's; Jan. 1803; Rachoal [sic] Dudd   02 WA-74
Warfield, (N); 9 Oct. 1808; Mary Dugan   01 PG
Warfield, Allen; 7 Oct. 1808; Mary Dugan   03 MO-121
Warfield, Basil W.; 2 Jan. 1806; Elizabeth Richman   11 BA-9
Warfield, Daniel; 9 Feb. 1819; Ann Mactier   05 BA-241
Warfield, Mesheck; 25 Dec. 1803; Rachel Cherick   15 AA-3
Warfield, Dr. Peregrine; 13 May 1806; Harriot Sappington (See
    also 02 MO)   01 PG
Warfield, Presly; 1 May 1813; Catherine Johnston (Sse also
    01 FR-1183)   15-FR 326
Warfield, Richard; 24 June 1802; Elizabeth Lucas   09 BA
Waring, Dr. Horatio Smith (of Charleston, S. C.); 2 Feb. 1813;
    Henrietta Higinbothom   03 BA-504
Warnecke, Michel; 18 May 1807; Beta Hormans   07 BA-305
Warner, Andrew E.; 25 June 1812; Dorothy Litzinger   09 BA
Warner, David; Aug. 1819; Elizab. Dugan   02 WA-114
Warner, Friederich; 14 July 1802; Sarah Tany   07 BA-67
Warner, Henry; 9 March 1808; Charlotte Arnold   14 BA-423
Warner, Jonathan (s. of John and Phebe Smith Warner); 10 d. 7 m.,
    1810; Sarah Brinton (dau. of Edward and Letitia Dilworth
    Brinton)   05 SF
Warner, Joseph; May 1807; Magd. Wright   02 WA-82
Warner, Silas (s. of Joseph and Ruth); 3rd d. 12 mo., 1807);
    Sarah Warnock (dau. of Philip and Mary, dec.)   11 SF-98
Warner, Thomas; 25 Oct. 1810; Mary Helms   03 BA-502
Warner, Thomas S.; 19 July 1802; Ruth Wilson   14 BA-412
Warner, Wm.; 19 Nov. 1804; Susanna Miltenberger   14 BA-417
Warnick, Joseph; 22 Oct. 1815; Elizabeth Fazenbaker   08 AL-120
Warnock, Samuel; 12 June 1808; Kezia Ross   03 AL-614
Warrell, Henry; 17 Dec. 1803; Mary Way   14 BA-415
Warren, George; 21 Nov. 1807; Elizabeth Allen   09 BA
Warren, Isaac; 19 Jan. 1804; Rosanna Mackmee   05 BA-234
Warren, Jno.; 30 July 1814; Cecilia Bann   14 BA-433
Warren, Natrum; 10 Nov. 1808; Martha Burney   02 BA-7
Warren, Thomas; 7 Dec. 1815; Nancy Pritchet   13 BA-23
Warren, William; 10 Sept. 1801; Mary Wedge   27 BA-1
Warren, Wm.; 13 Sept. 1804; Catherine Gribling   11 BA-3
Warren, William; 28 Aug. 1806; Ann Wignell   02 BA-4
Warrick, Guy; 13 April 1815; Elizabeth Buck (both free colored)
                                                16 BA-17
Warum, Isaac; 19 Dec. 1805; Catherine Warum   15 BA-231
Waserman, Jacob; 31 Aug. 1812; Elizab. Brosh (?)   02 WA-95
Washington, Chas.; 1 Oct. 1816; Ruth Harden   14 BA-436
Washington, Charles; 16 July 1818; Ruthy Prout   03 BA-603
Washington, Laurence; 20 Dec. 1812; June Willock   09 BA
Wasky, Christian; 21 May 1820; Margareth Thomas   06 FR-1331
Waterman, Irah (?); 14 Dec. 1820; Susannah Barton   08 BA
Waters, Azsel; 15 Oct. 1805; Cassandra Williams   03 MO-120
Waters, Edwin (of Balto., s. of Edward and Hannah); date not
    given; Sarah W. Brown (dau. of William and Elizabeth, dec.)
                                                09 SF
Waters, Horace; 28 Nov. 1816; Marg't Meyerhofer   13 BA-27
Waters, Horace W.; 19 Oct. 1820; Alverda Robinson   05 BA-243
Waters, Jacob; 10 Feb. 1820; Mary Ann Harrison   17 BA-22
Waters, James; 28 Aug. 1803; Mary Gardner   15 AA-2
Waters, John; 19 Nov. 1818; Ann Carson   13 BA-32
Waters, Joseph; Oct. 1804 (by Jno. Bloodgood); Mary Burrice
                                                17 BA-4
Waters, Joseph; 30 Oct. 1804; Mary Burrall   40 BA
Waters, Joseph; 17 Dec. 1810; Sophia Easom   21 BA-7

Waters, Michael; 25 Nov. 1804; Elizabeth Hoggins   15 BA-212
Waters, Nathaniel; 1809; Achsah Dorsey (See also 02 MO)
                                                        01 PG
Waters, Peter; 20 Jan. 1814; Tabitha Franklin   13 BA-18
Waters, Stephen; 1 April 1802; Mary Ann Brown   33 BA-14
Waters, Thomas; 10 March 1803; Sarah Devers   09 BA
Waters, William; c.1804; Ellen Dodd   34 BA-2
Waters, Wm.; 13 Dec. 1810; Alice Boomer   03 BA-502
Waters, Wm. D.; 1 Oct. 1817; Sarah Gettis   21 BA-9
Watkins, James; 9 June 1807; Mary Ann (?)   03 BA-497
Watkins, Nicholas J.; 7 May 1801; Rachel S. (?) Watkins
                                                        01 AA-68
Watkins, Vincent Jeoffrey; Sept. 1812; Elizabeth Aldridge
                                                        01 BA-11
Watkins, William; 7 Oct. 1819; Catherine Ketters   06 FR-1330
Watson, Coleman; 11 May 1813; Elizabeth James   21 BA-7
Watson, Henry; 16 June 1807; Catherine Ripple   03 BA-497
Watson, Isaac; 15 Dec. 1803; Sarah Howard   03 AA-120
Watson, John; 2 July 1809; Martha Staunton   13 BA-6
Watson, Joseph; 6 July 1809; Mebealo [sic] Storman   14 BA-426
Watson, Robert; 18 April 1815; Rachel Price   05 BA-238
Watson, Robert; 5 Oct. 1820; Mary White   13 BA-36
Watson, Silvester; 27 June 1815; Louisa G. W. Furnival 20 BA-222
Watson, William (s. of Joseph and Sarah, both dec., late of
     Cumberland Co., Old Eng.); 5th d. 3 mo., 1801; Martha Jay
     (dau. of Stephen and Hannah)   11 SF-84
Watson, Wm.; 7 Sept. 1806; Harriet Peasley   03 BA-496
Watson, William; 14 July 1810; Marg't Night   14 BA-427
Watson, William; 15 April 1815; Margaret Brogan   15 BA-279
Watstacum [sic], Saml; 24 Aug. 1815; Mary Day   13 BA-22
Watt, George; 7 Aug. 1817; Elizabeth Penn   06 FR-1326
Watt, James P.; 17 June 1810; Susannah Long   31 BA-83
Watts, Henry; 2 Feb. 1804; Rebecca Stansberry   15 AA-3
Watts, Joseph (Protestant); 13 Aug. 1801; Margaret Davis (He
     promised to allow his wife to educate their children in the
     Catholic Church)   15 BA-154
Watts, Richard B.; 22 Feb. 1803; Elizabeth Rawlings   15 AA-2
Watts, Thomas; 16 Jan. 1803; Polly Tarlton   02 SM-185
Waughop, Henry; 30 Sept. 1802; Sarah S. Watts   02 SM-185
Way, Andr.; 15 May 1809; Mary Mailder Pawson   13 BA-6
Way, Jacob; 1 July 1804; Mary Jung (See also 15 FR-316)
                                                        01 FR-1192
Way, John D.; 20 May 1819; Ann Green   37 BA-152
Way, Joseph; 26 Feb. 1801; Sally Simpson   11 BA-2
Wayne, Thomas; 20 Oct. 1811; Elizabeth Carson   11 BA-17
Ways, Brice; 19 Dec. 1808; Debora Driscoll (See also 15 FR-323)
                                                        01 FR-1183
Ways, Samuel; 18 May 1815 (by Joshua Wiley); Elizabeth Wise
                                                        17 BA-11
Wears, Samue; 26 June 1815 (or 1816); (Name not given) (col'd)
                                                        11 BA-24
Weatherly, Littleton; 3 Feb. 1803; Sarah Chenett   36 BA-1
Weathers, James; 1 March 1806; Mary Williams   09 BA
Weaver, Aquila; 23 Sept. 1815; Eliza Hammond   13 BA-22
Weaver, Dan'l; 29 Nov. 1810; Ellen High   13 BA-11
Weaver, George; 14 Aug. 1803; Eva Margaretha Brown   07 BA
Weaver, Heinrich; 3 Feb. 1813; Dorothea Macelroy   07 BA-309
Weaver, Jacob; 13 Sept. 1801; Mary Laterman   03 BA-406
Weaver, Jacob; 27 Feb. 1818; Elizabeth Reed   20 BA-223
Weaver, James; 7 April 1818; Mary Ann Jackson   21 BA-4
Weaver, John; 6 Aug. 1807; Cloe Boring   11 BA-11
Weaver, John; 8 April 1810; Reb'a Stinchcomb   13 BA-12
Weaver, Lewis; (date not given); Martha Smith   13 BA-38
Weaver, Lewis; 12 May 1801; Elizabeth Mofflen   05 AA-1

```
Weaver, Michael; Nov. 1802; Mary Spessert              02 WA-73
Weaver, Michael; 25 April 1815; Elizabeth Butler       06 FR-1322
Webb, Charles; 20 May 1819; Clarissa Legg              17 BA-22
Webb, George; Sept. 1807; Anna Allender                02 WA-84
Webb, Henry; 1 Oct. 1817; Elizabeth Robinson           03 BA-602
Webb, Jas.; 11 July 1811; Eliz. Cullidon               14 BA-429
Webb, John; 8 May 1806; Ketty Davis                    02 BA-3
Webb, Jonathan; 14 Jan. 1819; Hester Ann Crouch        09 BA
Webb, Nathaniel; Nov. 1820; Hariot Allender            02 WA-117
Webb, Pointon; Oct. 1819; Mary Webb                    02 WA-114
Webb, Samuel; 17 Nov. 1803; Sarah Hardy (?)            15 AA-3
Webb, William; 18 July 1805; Ann Seabright             15 BA-223
Webb, William; 31 Dec. 1806; Catherine White           15 BA-245
Webb, William; 7 Jan. 1816; Achsah Trapnall            09 BA
Weber, Henrich; 27 Dec. 1807; Sally Smith              15 FR-322
Weber, Henry; 27 Dec. 1807; Sally Smith                01 FR-1183
Weber, Johannes; 11 June 1809; Cath. Bossert           15 FR-323
Weber, John; 11 June 1809; Cath. Bossard               01 FR-1183
Weber, John; 23 Nov. 1809; Maryt Leeson                03 BA-500
Weber, Jno. C.; 12 July 1818; Cle (?) Charlotte Uthman 14 BA-437
Weber, Wilhelm; 11 July 1804; Nancy Hickman            07 BA
Webster, Hazen; 4 Aug. 1812; Mary Frazier              13 BA-14
Webster, John; 26 Oct. 1817; Mary Kline                06 FR-1327
Webster, John A.; 8 Feb. 1816; Rachel Biays            05 BA-239
Webster, Joshua (s. of William and Ann, dec., of Lancaster Co.,
   PA); 5 d. 7 mo., 1820; Hannah Reynolds (wid. of Stephen
   Reynolds, and dau. of Isaac and Mary Kinsey of BA Co.)
                                                       06 SF
Webster, Mich'l D.; 23 July 1815; Eliza Harris         13 BA-22
Webster, William; 29 Feb. 1804; Mary Hollis            33 BA-40
Wedekind, Johan; 3 Sept. 1808; Anne Wessel             14 BA-424
Wederstrande, Philemon; 25 Nov. 1813; Helen Smith      15 BA-320
Weeber, Wm; 23 March 1813; Mary Ann Chase              03 BA-505
Weed, Ezra; 7 Oct. 1819; Julian Grafford               11 BA-37
Weeden, Hora.; 28 July 1816; Rach'l Riggens            13 BA-26
Weedon, Richard; 15 Feb. 1801; Matilda Thomas          15 AA-1
Weekly, Thomas; 2 Sept. 1813; Susannah Drill           06 FR-1319
Weeks, Philip; 30 Jan. 1803; Susanna Fenton            03 BA-425
Weeks, Wm.; 20 Jan. 1812; Sophia Price                 13 BA-14
Weems, Geo.; 1 March 1808; Sarah Sutton                13 BA-3
Weems, James; c.1802; Elizabeth Ridgely                12 AA-1
Weems, James; 27 Sept. 1819; Rachel Mansfield          16 BA-88
Weems, John; 1804; Rachel Norman                       07 AA-4
Weems, John Compton; 19 Jan. 1804; Elizabeth Webster   03 BA-490
Weems, Thos.; 16 June 1818; Mary Fowler                13 BA-31
Weems, Wm.; 1804; Mary Lyles                           07 AA-4
Weems, William; 10 May 1804; Priscilla Sellman         03 AA-120
Weer, George; 28 Dec. 1802; Mary Jones (See also 02 BA-32)
                                                       03 BA-424
Weest, Jacob; 7 Sept. 1815; Susan Gebhard              01 FR-1183
Wehrly, Jonathan; 27 March 1815; Elizabeth Utz         14 BA-433
Weidemeier, Georg; 19 May 1818; Carolina Gerlach       07 BA-311
[Weimget], Daniel; 12 April 1818; [Ephalia] Millers    39 BA-34
Weinmiller, John; 9 April 1809; Cassandra Wart         15 FR-323
Weinmuller, John; 9 April 1809; Cassandra Wart         01 FR-1183
Weis, John; 18 May 1820; Louisa Mildue                 14 BA-440
Weis, William; 30 Oct. 1806; Barbara Ridgely           30 BA-108
Weise, Dr. Godfrey; 21 July 1819; Susanna L. Weise     21 BA-9
Wekson (or Wison), Mr.; 1 March 1814; Sally Burgin     07 BA-309
Welch, John; 14 May 1816; Mary Owens                   03 AA-131
Welch, Peter; 18 July 1816; Sharlott Gray              17 BA-13
Welch, William; 16 June 1813; Ann McLaughlin           04 HA
Welkenson, Joseph; 312 Aug. 1816; Ann Simms            13 BA-27
Well, William; 16 Nov. 1815; Jane Downes               11 BA-26
```

```
Welland, Nicholas; Jan. 1818; Margaret Dooble          02 WA-108
Weller, George; 25 Dec. 1804; Eva Zorn                 30 BA-108
Weller, George; 28 Feb. 1805; Susanna Zorn             14 BA-418
Weller, Rev. George; 8 July 1818; Harriet Caroline Birckhead
                                                       02 DO
Weller, Joseph; 12 Dec. 1819; Marg't Kines             13 BA-34
Welleslager, David; 16 May 1811; Christiana Charlotte Hasson
                                                       09 BA
Wellford, Robert Y.; 14 March 1815; Louisa Gittings    05 BA-238
Welling, William; 8 Dec. 1801; Catherine Winchester    03 BA-411
Welling, William; 1 Oct. 1804; Providence Dorty or Douty
                                                       11 BA-3
Wellington, Dix; 26 Nov. 1818; Mary Lee                17 BA-20
Wells, Danl.; 19 Nov. 1815; Cav. Frost                 13 BA-23
Wells, Elijah; 21 Aug. 1808; Jane Wolford              13 BA-4
Wells, Francis M.; 8 May 1810; Margaret Fisher         15 BA-280
Wells, Harrison V.; 23 March 1816; Mary Jeffers        09 BA
Wells, Isaac; 10 Oct. 1805; Susanna Miller             03 AL-613
Wells, Isaac; 23 June 1808; Elizabeth Davis            09 BA
Wells, Isaac; June 1820; Elizab. Herring               02 WA-116
Wells, James (of James); 4 June 1811; Nancy Poland     03 AL-614
Wells, John; 7 Nov. 1820; Susan Cookford               37 BA-153
Wells, Joshua; 22 Sept. 1812; Eve Reinecke             11 BA-209
Wells, Lewis; 10 March 1818; Ann Small                 05 BA-240
Wells, Nath'l.; 29 Aug. 1808; Sarah McCoy              13 BA-4
Wells, Nelson; 21 Oct. 1814; Mary Lee                  03 BA-506
Wells, Richard; 17 Feb. 1814; Rachel Deale             03 AA-131
Wells, Richard; 14 Feb. 1817; Catherine Murphey        11 BA-31
Wells, Thos.; 23 Nov. 1812; Mary White                 13 BA-15
Wells, William; 12 May 1807; Nancy Parlit              03 AL-614
Wells, William (of Wm.); 25 June 1811; Sarah Wells (dau. of
    James)                                             03 AL-614
Wells, William V.; 5 March 1806; Elizabeth Chalmers    11 BA-8
Welsh, Benjamin; 9 Feb. 1804; Ruth Drury               03 AA-120
Welsh, Dan'l; 7 Jan. 1815; Susan Eppart                14 BA-433
Welsh, Henry; 25 April 1815; M. Sharrer                30 BA-109
Welsh, James; 17 March 1801; Judith Crowder            03 BA-399
Welsh, James; 20 Nov. 1816; Elizabeth Adams            32 BA-311
Welsh, James; 18 Sept. 1817; Mary Renauld              32 BA-314
Welsh, John; 29 June 1805; Elizabeth Stockes           11 BA-6
Welsh, Jno.; 12 Dec. 1815; Betsy Johnson               14 BA-434
Welsh, Nicholas; 7 March 1809; Rachel Fleming (See also
    15 FR-323)                                         01 FR-1183
Welsh, Robert; 4 June 1806; Patty Sellman              03 BA-495
Welsh, Thomas; 26 Feb. 1811; Harriot Slicer            03 AL-614
Welsh, Thomas; 12 Jan. 1813; Elizabeth Pouder          30 BA-109
Welsh, Wm.; 30 May 1803; Polly Snyder                  14 BA-414
Welsh, William; 9 Aug. 1819; Mary Bard (widow of Lansberg)
                                                       39 BA-37
Welsh, William; 12 Dec. 1819; Ellinor Hall             16 BA-94
Welshofer, Heinrich; 2 April 1811; Maria Kerr          07 BA-308
Welt, Jacob; 15 June 1809; Henrietta Coleman           14 BA-426
Weltsner, AAntonius; 18 Jan. 1812; Maria Lowman        39 BA-27
Welty, David; 2 Nov. 1813; Mary Gehr                   02 WA-98
Welty, Jacob; Aug. 1810; Eliz. Holm                    02 WA-87
Welty, Jacob; 16 Feb. 1819; Hannah Knouff              05 FR-29
Welty, Joh.; Aug. 1802; Nancy Heller                   02 WA-74
Welty, John; March 1804; Sus. Hollom                   02 WA-76
Welzheimer, John; 19 Feb. 1809; Elizab. Schlosser      01 FR-1183
Wembell, George; 25 Dec. 1808; Ann Shilling            11 BA-12
Wendle, John; April 1806; Elis. Thornsburg             02 WA-80
Wendling, Joh.; Aug. 1806; Cath. Server                02 WA-81
Werdebaugh, John; 13 Nov. 1807; Amelia Ratien          14 BA-436
Werner, Daniel; 16 March 1815; Catherine Snyder        06 FR-1322
```

Werner, George; 25 Oct. 1812; Christina Heishman (See also
    15 FR-326)   01 FR-1183
Werner [Warner?], Joannes; 20 May 1810; Elizabeth Bergman
    [Barckman]   39 BA-24
Werner, John; 21 Nov. 1811; Eliz. Scheck   02 WA-92
Werner, John; 10 July 1819; Louisa Berner   30 BA-109
Wert, Levin B.; 6 Sept. 1807; Mary Jennings   13 BA-7
Wescott, William; 26 Dec. 1802; Elizabeth Foy   15 BA-175
Weskett, John; 12 July 1810; Barbara Midgett   09 BA
West, Abner; 3 Aug. 1803; Sophia Frazier   02 BA-32
West, Amos (of Balto., s. of Thomas and Elizabeth); 15 d. 4 mo.,
    1802; Elizabeth Coates (of Jonathan and Jane, dec.)
                                                         09 SF
West, Gassaway; 15 Aug. 1815; Catherine Brown   11 BA-24
West, Hugh; 18 Dec. 1802; Achsah Right   09 BA
West, James C.; 22 Feb. 1819; Susan McGee or McKee   32 BA-324
West, Jno.; 5 April 1801; Lydia Shuck   03 MO-117
West, Nich's.; 12 May 1814; Louisa Robertson   13 BA-19
West, Samuel H.; 2 May 1811; Catherine Bantz   05 BA-236
West, Thomas (of HA, s. of Nathaniel and Elizabeth, dec.); 21 d.
    1 m., 1818; Cassandra McCoy (of Balto. Town, dau. of Philip
    Coale and w. Ann, dec.)   12 SF-65
West, William; 25 May 1815; Eady Middletown   17 BA-11
Westbay, Thos.; 11 Sept. 1806; Sarah Buchup alias Bishop
                                                         03 BA-496
Westeberger, John; 5 May 1811; Eliz. Jones   02 WA-90
Westly, William; 24 Dec. 1801; Elenor Warfield   15 AA-2
Weston, Elijah Brownwell; 17 Sept. 1818; Diadewry Ewel   03 BA-603
Westz, Johann; 12 June 1803; Elisabeth Wolf   07 BA
Wethered; Levin; 16 July 1805; Eliza Ellicott   03 BA-494
Wetherly, Dick; 20 Oct. 1804; Hannah Lianee (on page of list of
    marr. of blacks)   17 BA-5
Whalen, Michael; 10 July 1806; Elizabeth Jones   17 BA-6
Whalen, William; 23 May 1819; Henrietta Horsey   09 BA
Whartenby, William T.; 24 Oct. 1817; Matilda Onion   17 BA-17
Wheat, Jesse; 25 Oct. 1804; Harriot Sappington   15 AA-3
Wheat, Jno.; 13 Dec. 1806; Clara Cole   14 BA-421
Wheatley, Bing (s. of William and Delitha of DO Co.); 30 d. 12
    mo., 1802; Rhoda Pool of John and Any [?])   07 SF
Wheatley, David; 26 Feb. 1802; Nancy Wrotten   01 DO-40
Wheatley, Richard P.; 31 Jan. 1807; Sarah Thatcher White
                                                         02 BA-5
Wheatley, Wm.; 9 June 1804; Mary Cashell   03 MO-119
Wheelan, William; 23 April 1801; Honor Hailes   09 BA
Wheeler, Benjamin; 30 Aug. 1818; Mary Ann Johnson   11 BA-33
Wheeler, Ignatius; 12 Nov. 1820; Elizabeth Morgan   04 SM
Wheeler, Isaac; 23 Dec. 1819; Mary Bernon   17 BA-22
Wheeler, Isaac; 13 Sept. 1819; Catherine Grove   06 FR-1330
Wheeler, James; 17 Oct. 1817; Elizabeth Simmons   11 BA-28
Wheeler, John; 15 Jan. 1805; Sophia Robinson   09 BA
Wheeler, Jonathan; 9 Oct. 1804; Mary Wharton (See also 02 BA-34)
                                                         03 BA-491
Wheeler, Joseph A.; 13 April 1820; Henrietta Green   04 HA
Wheeler, Robert; 11 Feb. 1812; Polly Kepner   14 BA-430
Wheeler, Robert W.; 13 July 1815; Mary James   09 BA
Wheeler, Solomon; 28 Oct. 1813; Ann Fleehart   11 BA-23
Wheeler, Thos.; 25 April 1805; Alice Blackbarr (02 BA-35 gives
    bride's name as Blackburn)   03 BA-493
Wheeler, Thomas; 21 Feb. 1811; Elizab. Brady   03 AL-614
Wheelock, James; 4 May 1818; Mary Robinson   03 BA-603
Whelan, David; 24 Feb., 1805; Sarah Maccubbin (dau. of Maj.
    Zachariah Maccubbin of BA Co.)   15 BA-216
Whelan, James; (after Oct. 1812); Mary Flaherty (both natives of
    Ireland)   15 BA-505

```
Whelan, Matthew; 1 March 1808; Eleanor Vize              15 BA-260
Whelan, Thos.; 7 Dec. 1806; Elizabeth Bickham            15 BA-244
Wherrett, Geo.; Sept. 1816; Sarah McIntosh               02 WA-102
Wherrett, John; 6 Jan. 1803; Sarah Armstrong             02 SM-185
Wherrett, Thos.; 24 Dec. 1815; Sarah Hickey              13 BA-24
Wherrett, William H.; 30 Aug. 1801; Mary Clarke          02 SM-185
Whetly, John; 6 May 1819; Catherine Blessing             06 FR-1330
Whip, John; 2 Nov. 1815; Catherine McLane                06 FR-1323
Whitaker, John; 24 Dec. 1805; Mary Thomas                02 BA-3
White, Alfred; 16 Jan. 1817; Mary W. Kitchen             13 BA-27
White, Benj'n.; 22 Feb. 1806; Mary Miller                14 BA-419
White, Dennis; 12 April 1804; Rebecca Herrick            15 BA-200
White, Francis Freeland; 25 April 1805; Anne Stringer    03 BA-493
White, Gideon; 4 Jan. 1801; Ruth Haslup                  15 AA-1
White, Henry; 8 Aug. 1811; Margaret Elder                05 BA-236
White, Henry; 13 March 1816; Eliz. Gersonderffer         05 BA-239
White, James; 11 Oct. 1803; Maria Chesley                02 SM-186
White, James; 28 April 1806; Mary Cole                   09 BA
White, James; 20 Jan. 1808; Elizabeth Hubbert            09 BA
White, James; 11 Dec. 1810; Mary Stewart                 09 BA
White, James G.; 24 Aug. 1820; Sophia Bowry              37 BA-153
White, Jehu; 24 Dc. 1815; Mary R. Rodgers                21 BA-8
White, John; 25 Dec. 1800; Mary White                    15 AA-1
White, John; 28 Oct. 1805; Cath. Iron                    14 BA-419
White, John; 8 April 1806; Sarah Bahon                   15 BA-237
White, Jno.; 7 March 1818; Elizab. Boss                  14 BA-437
White, Jno.; 4 March 1819; Elizab. Pearce                14 BA-438
White, John M.; 8 Aug. 1805; Ann Davis                   03 BA-494
White, John M.; 19 Sept. 1809; Eliza Dew                 02 BA-7
White, Joseph; 3 Oct. 1801; Sophia Smith                 09 BA
White, Joseph; 1 Feb. 1810; Harriott Ross                13 BA-9
White, Jos.; 13 Aug. 1810; Marg't Faris                  13 BA-10
White, Joseph; 30 April 1812; Susanna Robinson           09 BA
White, Joseph; 1 May 1815; Isabella Pinkney              03 BA-506
White, Joseph C.; 16 March 1805; Mary Jones              02 SM-186
White, Joseph C.; 2 June 1807; Elizabeth Matthews        11 BA-11
White, Lloyd; 8 Feb. 1802; Cath. Courtney (both natives of
     Ireland)                                            15 BA-162
White, Nicholas; 9 June 1807; Harriot Gibson             13 BA-4
White, Nicholas; 18 May 1817; Ann Price                  11 BA-31
White, Peter; 22 Jan. 1801; Mary Branzel                 02 SM-184
White, Rezin; 26 July 1804; Ann Neale                    05 BA-234
White, Robert; 5 Feb. 1802; Ann Thompson                 09 BA
White, Robert; 15 June 1820; Arlaidge Grimes             13 BA-35
White, Stephen (native of Baltimore); 16 Dec. 1806; Juliet Martin
     (native of St. Domingo)                             15 BA-245
White, Stevenson; 25 May 1820; Priscilla Hill Ridgely    03 BA-604
White, Thomas; 13 Nov. 1807; Mary Dannels                08 AL-122
White, Thomas; 23 Jan. 1812; Ann Hays                    09 BA
White, William; 11 March 1817; Jane Hoy                  03 BA-602
White, Wm.; 22 April 1817; Hagar Pugan                   13 BA-28
White, William; March 1818; Amelia Clinetage             02 WA-109
Whiteford, David; 17 Nov. 1801; Eliz. Calp               14 BA-411
Whiteford, David; 3 March 1814; Elizab. Hoffman          14 BA-432
Whiteley, Anthony; 23 d. 1 mo., 1812; Sarah Wright       07 SF-20
Whiteley, Byng, (s. of William); 1802; Rhoda Pool        07 SF-3
Whiteley, Daniel (s. of Anthony); 18 d. 3 mol, 1819; Celia
     Charles                                             07 SF-39
Whiteley, Isaac (s. of Anthony and Mary (dec.); 20 d. 12 mo.,
     1820; Lydia Anderson (dau. of James and Celia)      07 SF-40
Whitelock; Elisha; 30 June 1811; Susanna Adams           01 SO-15
Whithington, Samuel; 16 June 1814; Sally Wingat          17 BA-10
Whithington, William; 19 Aug. 1804; Sarah Welch          05 AA-4
Whitney, Ephraim; 26 March 1801; Elizabeth Le Gros       03 BA-399
```

```
Whitson, David; 12 Aug. 1812; Mary Marr              13 BA-17
Whitten, William; 21 April 1802; Ann Binnix          23 BA-1
Whittermore, John; 13 Nov. 1804; Nancy Moore         03 BA-492
Whittington, Benjamin; 10 Oct. 1816; Ann David       11 BA-27
Whittle, Jeremiah; 14 June 1804; Nancy Best          14 BA-417
Whittlesey, Stephen; 26 April 1808; Nisa B. Pattison 03 BA-498
Wichard, John; 19 March 1810; Mary Rice              08 AL-123
Wickersham, William; 15 Oct. 1811; Mary Ann Roache   31 BA-112
Wickler, Ehrenfield; 7 April 1803; Christ'n Spielman 14 BA-414
Wicks, Heinr.; 28 May 1807; Hanna Horn               14 BA-422
Widafelt, Jacob; 31 Dec. 1816; Ann Pease             16 BA-47
Widdifield, James; 11 July 1813; Ann Bain            11 BA-23
Widdington, Robert P.; 29 Aug. 1813; Mary Shute      09 BA
Widenstore, Jacob; 7 Jan. 1802; Elizabeth Caplinger  09 BA
Widerman, George; (date not given); Rebecca Smith    13 BA-38
Widrow, Samuel; 7 Feb. 1808; Mary Roberts            13 BA-3
Wiebert, Jacob; 6 Oct. 1806; Susana Goll             14 BA-420
Wien, Georg; 31 Aug. 1807; Mary Schmith              07 BA-305
Wien, Georg; 1 Feb. 1816; Elizabeth Heil             07 BA-310
Wier, Charles; 15 July 1806; Charlotte Fowler        09 BA
Wier, Henry; 2 Dec. 1802; Comfort Morris             35 BA-1
Wiest, Jacob; 7 Sept. 1813; Susan Gebhart            15-FR 326
Wigens, John H.; 24 Dec. 1812; Mary Whilson          14 BA-431
Wiggins, Henry; 11 April 1805; Charlotte Black (free colored)
                                                     03 BA-493
Wilarid, John; 20 March 1814; Elis. Troup            02 WA-99
Wilcearn, Thomas; 11 Feb. 1806; Eliza Funk           03 AL-613
Wilcoxon, (N); 1810; Susan Swearingen (See also 02 MO) 01 PG
Wilde, Michael; 5 Oct. 1802; Elizabeth Ann Coyne     03 BA-421
Wile, William; 24 Nov. 1811; Catherine Dorner        06 FR-1317
Wiles, James; 9 Feb. 1815; Elizabeth Hershberger     06 FR-1321
Wiley, John; 6 Feb. 1806; Mary Douglas               03 BA-495
Wiley, William; 4 Oct. 1812; Frances Brown (or Brewer) 17 BA-9
Wilhelm, Adam; 30 May 1816; Lydia Funk               14 BA-435
Wilhelm, Henry; 31 Aug. 1808; Marg. Heney            14 BA-424
Wilhelm, Peter; 22 Nov. 1812; Eva Smith (See also 15 FR-326)
                                                     01 FR-1183
Wilhelm, Peter; 14 Nov. 1816; Susanna Thompson       14 BA-436
Wilhelm, Philip; Aug. 1817; Rahannah Wellshantz      02 WA-105
Wilhide, Solomon; 25 Nov. 1817; Susannah Lehman      06 FR-1327
Wilhite, Henry; 6 April 1813; Mary Miller            06 FR-1319
Wilhite, Jacob; 22 Nov. 1813; Margaret Late          06 FR-1320
Wilie, John; 2 Aug. 1804; Ann Rickets                01 BA-10
Wilk, Peter; 24 Feb. 1801; Catherine Maguire         03 BA-398
Wilkie, Thomas; 24 Aug. 1803; Mary Story             06 BA-3
Wilkins, James; 6 April 1819; Mary Gosnell           13 BA-34
Wilkins, John; 19 Oct. 1809; Elizabeth Dorsey        11 BA-15
Wilkinson, John; 13 Feb. 1805; Susanna Wells         03 BA-492
Wilkinson, John; 28 Feb. 1806; Mary Toocart          11 BA-8
Wilkinson, Shubael; 24 Sept. 1802; Anne Morgan       03 BA-420
Wilkinson, Shubael; 6 June 1816; Eliza'h Harvey      03 BA-502
Willard, John; 10 Sept. 1811; Barbara Ridenour       02 WA-91
Willdanger, George; 2 Feb. 1806; Barbara Lang (See also
  15 FR-318)                                         01 FR-1182
Willeby, Charles; 13 April 1809; Ann Supenton        13 BA-6
Willer, Ezekiel; 24 Sept. 1818; Cath. Grimes         14 BA-437
Willerd, Julius; 6 Jan. 1803; Eleanor Danshine       09 BA
Willerman, Charles; 23 May 1801; Sarah Hilton        11 BA-3
Willer(n), Justus; 18 April 1810; Maria Elizabeth Korrebornk
                                                     07 BA-307
Willers, John; 28 July 1807; Julia Andoin            15 BA-253
Willess, Wm.; 29 Oct. 1815; Sarah Griffen            02 BA-36
Willey, Henry; 8 April 1802; Betsey Chilcoat         14 BA-412
Willey, Jno.; 9 July 1812; Ann Rohrback              14 BA-430
```

```
Willey, John; 5 Dec. 1808; Barbara Flug            01 FR-1183
Williai, Andr.; 28 Dec. 1813; Ann B. Reiman        13 BA-18
Williams, Abraham Ralph; 7 Sept. 1802; Mary Baxley 11 BA-3
Williams, Arnold; 6 Aug. 1816; Rebk. Morfil        13 BA-26
Williams, Bnej.; 15 April 1802; Ann Seiffel        21 BA-5
Williams, Benjamin; 12 Aug. 1802; Jane Hood        03 AL-613
Williams, Benjamin; 21 May 1811; Sarah Morton      05 BA-236
Williams, Bennet; 8 May 1817; Lydia Robertson      16 BA-52
Williams, Charles; 19 Feb. 1810; Rachel Gooding    13 BA-11
Williams, Cumberland D.; 15 Jan. 1816; Elizabeth Pinkney
                                                   03 BA-507
Williams, Elijah; 21 Jan. 1813; Rebecca Aras (See also 15 FR-326)
                                                   01 FR-1183
Williams, Elisha; 3 July 1814; Dorothy Hyson       13 BA-19
Williams, Ennion (s. of Isaac and Lydia); 23 d. 9 mo., 1818;
    Hannah Bartlett (dau. of Richard and Rebecca)  08 SF
Williams, Ezekiel; 14 March 1811; Nancy Rogers     17 BA-8
Williams, George; 3 April 1804; Mary Wherrett      02 SM-186
Williams, George; 14 Oct. 1804; Kitty Deil         11 BA-4
Williams, George (?); 23 June 1811; Ally Colgan     31 BA-103
Williams, George; 1 June 1815; Elizabeth B. Hawkins 05 BA-238
Williams, George; 25 Sept. 1816; Mary Ann Waters   17 BA-13
Williams, George; 2 July 1818; Eliza Bevans        37 BA-151
Williams, George; 16 July 1806; Elizabeth Fletcher 05 BA-234
Williams, Griffith; 26 Nov. 1817; Catherine Jones  20 BA-223
Williams, Isaac; 29 May 1802; Elizabeth Bevins     09 BA
Williams, Jacob; 29 Sept. 1802; Margaret England   10 FR
Williams, James; 7 May 1807; Elizabeth Savary      11 BA-10
Williams, James (servant of Col. John Dorsey); 2 Oct. 1808;
    Henrietta Gross (free; both colored)           02 BA-6
Williams, James; 28 Dec. 1811; Elizabeth Burrows   11 BA-18
Williams, Jeremiah; 29 Feb. 1804; Elizabeth Roberts 17 BA-3
Williams, John; 27 Aug. 1801; Mary Lovet           03 AL-613
Williams, John; 4 April 1805; Mary Butley          02 SM-186
Williams, John; 20 July 1805; Sophia Drawan (See also 02 BA-35)
                                                   03 BA-494
Williams, John; 25 Dec. 1806; Sarah Meritt (See also 02 MO)
                                                   01 PG
Williams, John; 18 March 1807; Susanna Ward        02 BA-5
Williams, John; July 1807; Elis. James             02 WA-83
Williams, John; 28 Aug. 1809; Elizabeth Green      15 BA-271
Williams, John; 7 June 1810; Nancy (?) Stevenson   17 BA-8
Williams, John; 23 April 1812; Elizabeth Wells (free people of
    color)                                         09 BA
Williams, John; 3 July 1814; Louisa Burk           11 BA-22
Williams, John; 27 Nov. 1817; Sarah Green          02 BA-37
Williams, John; 23 Sept. 1819; Mary Williams       11 BA-34
Williams, John Mason (the celebrated Anthony Pasquin); 12 June
    1817; Sarah Furber                             21 BA-9
Williams, John W.; 18 Feb. 1802; Elenor Duvall     15 AA-2
Williams, Jos.; 14 Dec. 1813; Patty Whitaker       13 BA-18
Williams, Joseph Sprigg; 17 Sept. 1809; Catherine Murray
                                                   15 BA-272
Williams, Lewis; 13 Feb. 1805; Eleanor Thomas      09 BA
Williams, Richard; 5 [May] 1816; Maria Ross        39 BA-31
Williams, Rich'd S.; 7 Sept. 1811; Elizab. Hate    14 BA-429
Williams, Robert; 14 April 1805; Sarah Harding     03 BA-493
Williams, Robert; 15 Sept. 1813; Elizabeth Yates   11 BA-23
Williams, Samuel; 1 Dec. 1817; Elizabeth Colston   02 DO
Williams, Thomas; 15 Aug. 1805; Mary Winks         03 BA-494
Williams, Thomas; 14 Dec. 1805; Ann Beadle         02 BA-2
Williams, Thomas; 9 Oct. 1808; Eleanor White (See also 15 FR-322)
                                                   01 FR-1183
Williams, Thos.; 1 Oct. 1812; Maria Kerr           13 BA-15
```

Williams, William (belonging to D. Bixler); 2 April 1809;
   Araminta (N) (belonging to William Winchester)   03 BA-499
Williams, William; 18 March 1810; Sarah Sinclair   09 BA
Williams, William; 14 Jan. 1818; Maria Cooper   17 BA-19
Williams, William E.; 23 April 1812; Susan F. Cooke   03 BA-504
Williams, Zachariah; 1 March 1805; Latitia Cooper   15 BA-216
Williamson, David; 1 Feb. 1814; Rebecca Tiernan   16 BA-1
Williamson, James; 24 Dec. 1801; Ann Plummer   06 BA-2
Williamson, John; 24 Feb. 1814; Mary Howland   20 BA-222
Williamson, William; 5 Jan. 1807; Rebecca Dixon   09 BA
Williard, Johannes; 9 June 1803; Maria Schaefer   15 FR-315
Williard, John; 9 June 1803; Mary Schafer   01 FR-1182
Willing, Josias; 3 (Sept.?) 1810; Mary Bankson   17 BA-8
Willing, Samuel L. P.; 18 Sept. 1817; Hannah Hussey   13 BA-29
Willis, George Griffin; 15 April 1806; Rbeecca Savell   03 BA-495
Willis, John; 23 Dec. 1802; Elanor Hill (03 BA-424 gives date as
   24 Dec.)   02 BA-32
Willis, Joshua; 24 April 1811; Mary Bowen   14 BA-428
Willis, Richard; 21 June 1803; Hannah Lowrey   06 BA-3
Willis, Robert; 15 March 1805; Jane H. Burk   11 BA-5
Willis, Wm.; 13 Sept. 1809; Margaret Reed   14 BA-226
Willoughby, Edward; 15 Dec. 1804; Betsy Moore (both of Caroline
   Co.)   02 TA-39
Willoughby, Joseph; Feb. 1816; Betsy Corkrill   02 TA-43
Wills, Michael; 12 Jan. 1812; Elizabeth Mahenny   06 FR-1317
Willson, Charles E.; 9 Nov. 1819; Mary Davis   17 BA-22
Willson, John; 1 June 1815; Penelope Lee   08 BA
Willson, Joseph; 28 Jan. 1810; Margaret Gallion (native of
   Ireland)   15 BA-278
Willy, John; 5 Dec. 1808; Barbara Flug   15 FR-323
Willy, William; 24 Oct. 1801; Mary Wright   14 BA-411
Willyard, Adam; 19 April 1814; Mary Hill   06 FR-1320
Wilmer, James J.; 20 March 1803; Letitia Day   05 HA-3
Wilmer, Samuel; 16 Aug. 1814; Jane H. Henrietta Farley (?)
                                                          03 KE-14
Wilmer, William; 21 Feb. 1804; Anna Ford   01 BA-10
Wilmot, Geo.; 19 Sept. 1815; Reba. Howland   13 BA-22
Wilson, Aaron; 14 May 1802; Jemima Taylor   14 BA-412
Wilson, Andrew; Feb. 1810; Rebecca Scarff   01 BA-11
Wilson, Benjamin; 6 May 1804; Ann Cunningham   09 BA
Wilson, Benjamin; 9 July 1806; Charlotte Briscoe (free colored)
                                                          11 BA-9
Wilson, Benjamin; 17 Nov. 1812; Ann Bates   05 BA-237
Wilson, Bottle; 28 Aug. 1801; Elizabeth Pratt   03 BA-405
Wilson, David T.; April 1816; Anne Mary Cramer   02 WA-101
Wilson, Dennis; 5 July 1812; Mary Phillips   01 DO-42
Wilson, Edward; 21 June 1814; Hannah Bond   11 BA-22
Wilson, Edward. (merchant, of Phila., s. of William and Mary,
   both dec., of Yeadon, Yorkshire); 15 d. 9 mo., 1814; Sarah
   Proctor (dau. of Stephen and Rebecca (both dec., of York,
   Great Brit.)   09 SF
Wilson, Edward M.; 8 June 1817; Sarah Linton   09 BA
Wilson, Geo.; 19 Dec. 1811; Mary Jones   03 BA-503
Wilson, George; 14 Aug. 1816; Maria Wickham   02 BA-37
Wilson, Henry; 7 July 1803; Elizabeth Morsell   14 AA-1
Wilson, Henry; 16 April 1804; Sophia Anderson   14 BA-416
Wilson, Horace; 7 April 1816; Eliza Coats   13 BA-25
Wilson, Isaac (of Belmont Co., OH, s. of Samuel and Rebecca of
   Bucks Co., PA, dec.); 14 d. 4 m., 1819; Ann McCoy (of
   Balto. Town, wid. of Joseph McCoy, and dau. of James Hicks
   [of HA Co., dec.] and w. Mary)   12 SF-72
Wilson, Jacob; 27 Sept. 1803; Frances Thomas   33 BA-40
Wilson, James; 13 June 1802; Catherine Shilling   09 BA
Wilson, James; 29 Sept. 1803; Isabella Allen   34 BA-1

```
Wilson, James; 4 Jan. 1807; Martha Ashby            03 AL-614
Wilson, James; 1 Oct. 1807; Frances Fisher          14 BA-422
Wilson, James; 9 Feb. 1809; Ann Mobley              11 BA-13
Wilson, James; 11 Jan. 1810; Elizabeth Cooper       09 BA
Wilson, James; Aug. 1813; Sarah Lincke (?)          02 WA-98
Wilson, James; 6 Nov. 1814; Cathe. Kempler          13 BA-19
Wilson, James; 19 d. 12 mo., 1816; Ann Poits        08 SF
Wilson, John; 2 May 1801; Sarah Tipton              09 BA
Wilson, John; 4 May 1802; Mary Hack                 30 BA-108
Wilson, John; 13 Jan. 1803; Susanna Alter           14 BA-414
Wilson, Jno.; 18 July 1803; Mary Ann Howard         14 BA-414
Wilson, John; 7 Feb. 1804; Alley Robinette          05 AL-2
Wilson, John (s. of William and Hannah); 23 d. 10 mo., 1806;
     Sarah Hopkins (dau. of Thomas and Sarah)       08 SF
Wilson, John; 12 Jan. 1808; Ann Colwell             11 BA-12
Wilson, John; 11 Sept. 1808; Nancy Lemmon           03 BA-498
Wilson, John; Jan. 1818; Sarah Hays                 02 WA-108
Wilson, John; betw. Sept. 1815 and Oct. 1820; Elizabeth Wilson
                                                    07 HA
Wilson, Johnzey; 5 March 1818; Rebecca Bryan        11 BA-28
Wilson, Joseph; c.1804; Catherine Miller            34 BA-2
Wilson, Joseph; 22 Oct. 1806; Mary Dalrymple        03 BA-496
Wilson, Joseph; 25 Dec. 1809; Margaret Johnson      14 BA-427
Wilson, Joseph; 8 Sept. 1810; Nancy Bowser (free blacks)
                                                    03 BA-501
Wilson, Joseph; 21 Dec. 1813; Mary Beard            02 WA-99
Wilson, Joseph H.; 3 Oct. 1815; Sarah E. Lawrence   03 AA-131
Wilson, Mathew; 23 March 1802; Hannah Green         14 BA-412
Wilson, Moses; 22 Dec. 1808; Polly Lemmon           13 BA-5
Wilson, Otho I.; 7 Sept. 1819; Ann Jones            03 BA-604
Wilson, Peter; 13 March 1817; Elizabeth Dugan       17 BA-16
Wilson, Richard; 10 Sept. 1816; Mary Gardner        03 BA-507
Wilson, Robert; 13 Dec. 1812; Maria Wilson          17 BA-9
Wilson, Robert; 3 April 1814; Mary Moody            09 BA
Wilson, Robert; Jan. 1817; Elizab. Caldwell         02 WA-104
Wilson, Robert; April 1818; Elisab. Summers         02 WA-109
Wilson, Rob't; 13 July 1819; Marg't Pendergrass     13 BA-33
Wilson, Robert, Jr.; Oct. 1820; Elizabeth Kelty     05 BA-243
Wilson, Robert Stephen; 19 April 1814; Ann Maria McCausland
                                                    09 BA
Wilson, Samuel; 14 Feb. 1819; Mary F. Gatchell      37 BA-152
Wilson, Thomas; 3 Jan. 1801; Elizabeth Garlick      09 BA
Wilson, Thomas (of QA Co.); 3 June 1806; Anna Maria Smith (of KE
     Co.) (See also 01 QA-52)                       02 TA-40
Wilson, Thomas; 16 July 1807; Anna Maria Blackburn  03 BA-497
Wilson, Thomas; 26 Oct. 1820; Hannah Houlton        03 BA-605
Wilson, William; 26 March 1801; Margaret Winstandley 33 BA-18
Wilson, William (of Third Haven, Caroline Co., s. of William and
     Hannah, dec.); 23 d. 3 mo. 1803; Sarah Swiggett (dau. of
     Jonson and Mary)                               07 SF
Wilson, William (s. of William, dec.); 23 d. 5 mo. 1804; Mary
     Bowers (dau. of John)                          08 SF
Wilson, William; 2 June 1806; Susanna Burgess       17 BA-6
Wilson, William; 14 Oct. 1807; Elisab. Hill         14 BA-422
Wilson, William, Jr.; 30 March 1815; Mary Knox      09 BA
Wilson, William Elson; 12 Nov. 1807; Eleanor Swearingen (See also
     02 MO)                                         01 PG
Wilt, Jacob; 26 May 1807; Margaretta Cline          07 BA-305
Wiltberger, Geo.; 7 Nov. 1816; Catherine Blair      03 BA-508
Wilyard, George; 11 June 1805; Susanna Koller (See also
     15 FR-317)                                     01 FR-1182
Wilzheimer, John; 19 Feb. 1809; Elisabeth Schlosser 15 FR-323
Wimmell, John; 28 March 1816; Lydia Shoemaker    13 BA-24
Wimsett, Samuel; 7 March 1802; Ann Arven      15 BA-164
```

```
Winand, Jacob; 8 Jan. 1805; Sidney Brown            03 BA-492
Winchester, Charles; 23 Dec. 1816; Elizabeth Pannell 03 BA-508
Winchester, David; 6 Nov. 1817; Sarah Forney         03 BA-602
Winchester, Samuel; 8 Oct. 1818; Fanny Mactier       05 BA-241
Winchester, Thos. E.; 19 March 1816; Ann Page        13 BA-24
Windbigler, Rich'd; 30 Nov. 1806; Eliz. Harriot (See also
  15 FR-320)                                         01 FR-1182
Windsor, Robert; 9 May 1805; Eliz. Thompson          03 MO-120
Winebrenner, Jacob; 6 June 1813; Sophia (N)          15-FR 326
Winebrenner, Jacob; 6 June 1814 (?); Sophia (N)      01 FR-1183
Wineburg, John; 4 Dec. 1817; Catherine Walker        06 FR-1327
Wineman, Henry; 28 Jan. 1801; Mary Smith             14 BA-409
Wingate, John; 13 Nov. 1804; Susanna Moore           14 BA-417
Wingert, John; 19 Nov. 1811; Cath. Rowland           02 WA-92
Winget, Thomas; 28 Jan. 1811; Elenor Young           11 BA-18
Wininger, Stephen; 28 or 29 Nov. 1817; Jane Locke    17 BA-17
Winkel, Frederick; 28 July 1802; Maria Sandel        14 BA-413
Winkelman, Thomas; 6 Nov. 1806; Nancy Tinder         09 BA
Winkler, Jno.; 3 Dec. 1806; Janet Adams              14 BA-421
Winks, John; 11 March 1813; Margaret Halfpenny       17 BA-9
Winn, Elisha; 19 Jan. 1817; Mary Robbnett            09 BA
Winstandly, John; 18 Aug. 1803; Cassandra Baker      33 BA-40
Winter, Benjamin; 10 Oct. 1820; Sarah Francis        13 BA-41
Winter, Henry; 17 Dec. 1803; Mary Dickin             14 BA-415
Winter, Joh.; March 1803; Elis. Reidenauer           02 WA-74
Winters, George; 11 July 1816; Elizabeth Neymeier    08 AL-126
Winters, Jacob; 12 Sept. 1811; Sarah Shriver         03 AL-614
Winters, Wm.; 15 Oct. 1811; Mary Keller              02 WA-91
Winterson, Benjamin; 1801; Ann Tucker                07 AA-1
Wirepach, John; 20 Nov. 1808; Rachel Lee             11 BA-12
Wirgman, Chas.; 21 Feb. 1805; Sarah Stewart Bowly    03 BA-492
Wirgman, Peter; 6 June 1811; Rebecca Bowly           03 BA-502
Wirt, James; 27 June 1810; Mary White                13 BA-12
Wirts, Jacob; 17 Nov. 1807; Lucy Brunner (See also 15 FR-321)
                                                     01 FR-1182
Wirts, Philip 27 Aug. 1806; Cath. Hasselbach         14 BA-420
Wise, Adam; 13 Sept. 1809; Polly Thomas              02 SM-188
Wise, Frederic; 17 Oct. 1818; Rachel Howard          14 BA-439
Wise, Frederick A.; 18 July 1815; Phebe A. Kenny     09 BA
Wise, George; 9 April 1808; Margaret Sinclair        14 BA-424
Wise, George; 24 Nov. 1813; Sophia Hammett           01 SM-64
Wise, Jacob; Nov. 1806; Emeally Moore                02 WA-81
Wise, Jesse; 17 Nov. 1818; Julia Ann Kingley         14 BA-438
Wise, Joh.; April (?) 1803; Christ. Keller           02 WA-74
Wise, John; 25 Aug. 1805; Mary Wise                  02 SM-187
Wisebach, Martin; 17 Oct. 1812; Hettie Leddie        14 BA-431
Wiseback, John; 13 June 1802; Mary Campbell          09 BA
Wisong, Isaac; 16 Jan. 1819; Elizabeth Baer          06 FR-1329
Wisotzky, Friederich; 11 Jan. 1809; Elizabeth Schmids 07 BA-306
Wissinger, George; 11 Oct. 1807; Elizabeth Lab (See also
  15 FR-321)                                         01 FR-1182
Witemore (?), Benjamin; 14 May 1801; Elizabeth Beall 15 AA-1
Witman, George; 13 March 1811; Mary Krebs            06 FR-1315
Witmer, Johan; 18 Nov. 1803; Elizabeth Schwartz      15 FR-315
Witmer, John; 28 Nov. 1803; Eliz. Schwartz           01 FR-1182
Witmer, John, Jr.; Feb. 1820; Rosanna Brewer         02 WA-115
Witney, Solomon; 5 Jan. 1813; Margaret Pate          05 BA-237
Witt, David; May 1819; Charlotte Weltz               08 AL-127
Witt, John; 2 June 1816; Catherine Wineland          08 AL-127
Wittenberg, Hein.; 16 Sept. 1804; Margaret Kibber    14 BA-417
Wittenberg, Wm.; 22 Jan. 1818; Dorothy Wilson        14 BA-437
Wittinton, Benjamin; 1804; Elizabeth Cowman          07 AA-4
Wittmer, Christian; 17 May 1801; Elizabeth Schili    01 CL-149
Wolf, Conrad; Aug. 1813; Sus. Potter                 02 WA-98
```

```
Wolf, George; Aug. 1820; Ann Elizab. Bowser            02 WA-117
Wolf, Henry; 23 Nov. 1804; Mary McCausland             14 BA-417
Wolf, Jacob; Aug. 1816; Sary Snyder                    02 WA-102
Wolf, Jacob; 18 May 1820; Rachel Lilley                08 BA
Wolf, John; Aug. 1813; Cath. Ward                      02 WA-97
Wolf, John; July 1817; Catherine Walper                02 WA-105
Wolf, Michael; 24 April 1815; Dorothea Schroder        14 BA-433
Wolf, Peter; 8 Feb. 1809; Mary(?) Hancock              14 BA-425
Wolf, Valentine; 30 Aug. 1803; Mary Rice               01 FR-1182
Wolf, William; 4 June 1816; Julie Ann Trexil           14 BA-435
Wolfe, Geo.; 8 Jan. 1815; Eliza Lenoss                 13 BA-20
Wolfe, Jacob; 27 Sept. 1810; Eliza Harner              03 BA-501
Wolfe, Sam'l; 21 Aug. 1817; Eliza Spicer               14 BA-436
Wolfernden, Charles James; 1 March 1818; Mary Lambert  06 FR-1328
Wolferz, Johann Abraham; 2 April 1804; Maria Juliana Reigel
                                                       07 BA
Wolff, James; 27 Dec. 1806; Massy Fitz                 09 BA
Wolff, Valentin; 30 Aug. 1803; Mary Rice               15 FR-315
Wolfkill, John; Sept. 1807; Elis. Reynolds             02 WA-84
Wolford, John; April 1816; Elizab. Bower               02 WA-101
Wolford, John; Nov. 1819; Ann Noll                     02 WA-114
Wolgamot, Samuel; 29 Sept. 1811; Mary Beard            02 WA-91
Wollender, Daniel; 1 May 1806; Eliz. Tate              14 BA-420
Wolslager, Jacob; 26 April 1801; Betsey Jurg           21 BA-4
Woltz, Joh.; March 1809; Leah Updegraff                02 WA-86
Woltz, Will; March 1809; Polly Simpkins                02 WA-86
Wonn, Horatio; 6 May 1816/7(?); Belinda Griffin        08 BA
Wood, David  (s. of Joseph, dec., and Catherine of West
    Nottingham Twp., Chester Co., PA); 9 d. 2 mo., 1803; Hannah
    Carter (dau. of Samuel and Ruth of the same place)
                                                       06 SF
Wood, Henry Hobbs; 29 July 1813; Rebecca Ruth          20 BA-222
Wood, James; 9 April 1801; Elizabeth Maxwell           33 BA-18
Wood, James; 18 Feb. 1817; Mary King                   11 BA-31
Wood, Jeptha; 8 April 1813; Harriot Lee                13 BA-16
Wood, Joel (s. of William and Mary); 21 d. 6 mo., 1804; Eliza-
    beth Poultney (dau. of Anthony and Susanna [Plummer])
                                                       03 SF
Wood, John; 11 Aug. 1805; Margaret Owes [sic]          03 AA-130
Wood, Jno.; 12 Nov. 1807; Barbara Miller               14 BA-423
Wood, John; 12 Nov. 1814; Sarah McCoy                  09 BA
Wood, John; 23 Nov. 1817; Elizer Steresman             13 BA-29
Wood, Joseph; 4 Feb. 1802; Elizabeth Hugg              17 BA-1
Wood, Joseph; 23 July 1802; Sarah Ward                 03 AA-120
Wood, Nathan (s. of Thomas and Susannah); 22 d. 1 mo., 1801;
    Margaret Waters (dau. of Samuel and Susanna)       03 SF
Wood, Richard; 26 Feb. 1801; Rachel Leatherwood        15 AA-1
Wood, Richard; 11 Feb. 1804; Rachel Stinchicum         15 AA-3
Wood, Robert; 20 Dec. 1803; Elizabeth Stephens         03 AA-120
Wood, Stephen C.; 8 July 1818; Hannah Totten           17 BA-19
Wood, Thomas, widower (s. of William and Margaret; 22 d. 4 mo.,
    1813; Sarah Russell Roberts, widow (dau. of John and Hannah
    Russell)                                           03 SF
Wood, William; 3 March 1804; Sarah Short               15 AA-3
Wood, William; 17 April 1817; Ann Ghent                05 BA-240
Wood, William Hawkins; 13 Oct. 1814; Mary Ann Kent     13 BA-19
Woodard, William; 26 Jan. 1804; Ellenor Pitcock        05 HA-1
Woodcock, Wm.; 11 June 1818; Amelia B. Davidson        13 BA-31
Woodland, Ezekiel; 24 Nov. 1819; Sarah Cox             37 BA-152
Woodland, John; 30 Oct. 1820; Cassandra Divers         13 BA-36
Woodland, William; 6 Oct. 1808; Elizabeth Davis        02 BA-7
Woodland, William W.; 7 May 1801; Polly Jones          09 BA
Woodring, Jacob; 30 July 1805; Catherine Erb           03 AL-613
Woodrough, Echibod; 14 Aug. 1808; Ruthy Awl            09 BA
```

```
Woods, John; 3 Dec. 1814; Margaret Griffith          31 BA-186
Woods, John D.; 1 March 1806; Elizab. Stauffer       14 BA-419
Woods, Luther; 26 Nov. 1812; Susn. Ominsche          13 BA-15
Woods, William; 22 June 1809; Elizabeth Gilbert      11 BA-14
Woodsides, Abraham; 26 Oct. 1802; Sarah Bailey       03 BA-422
Woodsworth, Alex'r; 9 Oct. 1817; Ann McGowan         13 BA-29
Woodward, Thomas; 7 Oct. 1816; Octava O. Roysel      11 BA-31
Woody, William; 12 June 1817; Ruth B. Atkinson       13 BA-28
Woodyear, Thomas; 16 Sept. 1817; Eliz'th Yellott     19 BA-72
Wooles, Stephen; 3 Feb. 1816; Maria Heny or Sleny    11 BA-26
Woolf, Joseph; 7 June 1801; Mary Springer            02 WA-71
Woolford, Thomas, M. D.,; 6 Jan. 1818; Margaret Le Compte
                                                     02 DO
Wooten, Richard (of SM Co., age c.30, s. of Joseph and Molly
    (Booth) Wooten); 3 Feb. 1801; Mary Tanna (age c.30, dau. of
    John and Ann [Anderson] Tanna)                   03 SM
Wootton, Dr. John; 17 June 1806; Betsy Lynn Magruder (See also
    02 MO)                                           01 PG
Work, Aron; 29 Sept. 1808; Cathe. Etchburger         13 BA-4
Workman, David; 18 Aug. 1812; Elizabeth Robertson    03 AL-614
Workman, David; 17 Jan. 1819; Elizabeth Bockholtz    39 BA-35
Workman, Isaac; 19 Nov. 1805; Catherine Anderson     03 AL-613
Workman, Isaac; 13 Feb. 1810; Lydia Merrill          03 AL-614
Workman, Jacob; 7 June 1807; Margaret Housel         03 AL-614
Workman, John;1 16 May 1809; Abigail Combs           03 AL-614
Worly, John; Aug. 1808; Eva Tise                     02 WA-85
Worman, William; 27 Jan. 1814; Susannah Wagner       06 FR-1320
Wornock, John; 25 Sept. 1810; Martha Wilson          03 AL-614
Worrel, Jonathan; 10 Sept. 1807; Harriet Garrettson  09 BA
Worthen, Francis; 9 June 1807; Elizabeth Drill (See also 01 FR-
    1182)                                            15 FR-321
Worthing, Raymond; 26 Sept. 1811; Sarah Slency       13 BA-13
Worthing, Thomas (s. of John and Priscilla, both dec.); 13th d.
    5 mo., 1816; Mary Husbands (dau. of Joshua and Margaret)
                                                     11 SF-117
Worthington, Brice John; 12 Oct. 1809; Ann Lee Fitzhugh
                                                     01 BA-11
Worthington, Charles; 16 Sept. 1802; Mary Todd       03 BA-420
Worthington, Charles; 1 March 1803; Susanna Johns    01 BA-10
Worthington, Charles; 17 April 1806; Hannah Yellott  01 BA-10
Worthington, Garrett G.; 4 Jan. 1820; Julia Price    37 BA-152
Worthington, Niclas I.; 4 Jan. 1816; Matilda Odle    08 BA
Worthington, William (s. of John and Priscilla); 12th d. 6 mo.,
    1816; Hannah Coale (dau. of William and Elizabeth)
                                                     11 SF-120
Worthington, Wm. G. D.; 6 Oct. 1810; Eliza Chaytor   03 BA-502
Wright, Allen, (s. of Joel, dec., late of FR Co., and Elizabeth);
    26 d. 10 mo., 1803; Phebe Heston (dau. of Joseph and Phebe
    of AA Co.)                                       09 SF
Wright, Daniel (s. of Lemuel, dec.,, and Elizabeth, of Caroline
    Co.); 19 d. 2 mo., 1801; Sarah Edmondson (widow of William,
    and dau. of John and Hester Register)            08 SF
[W]right, Ed., of Peter, of QA; 4 Jan. 1801; Pen Blake, dau. of
    J., of QA                                        03 TA-71
Wright, Elisha (s. of James and Sarah); 20 d. 12 mo., 1810; Adah
    Williams (dau. of William and Delilah)           07 SF-16
Wright, Hatfield; 20 d. 3 mo., 1817; Mary Wright     07 SF-35
Wright, Henry; 12 Jan. 1804; Mary Lusby              14 AA-1
Wright, Isaac (of FR Co., s. of Isaac and Elizabeth, dec.); 31
    d. 12 mo., 1801; Elizabeth Cox (dau. of William and Rachel)
                                                     11 SF-86
Wright, Jesse; 22 Oct. 1815; Nancy Fogle             02 WA-100
Wright, Jno.; 4 Nov. 1801; Mary Waller               14 BA-411
Wright, John; 18 Aug. 1803; Elizabeth Chesley Clarke 03 BA-433
```

```
Wright, John (of Caroline Co.); 24 Nov. 1804; Mary Conolly (of
    QA Co.)                                                  01 QA-52
Wright, John; 30 Aug. 1814; Sarah Horton                    13 BA-19
Wright, Jonathan, Jr., (s. of Jonathan and Susannah); 28 d. 9
    mo., 1814; Susannah B. Jones (dau. of Aquila and Elizabeth)
                                                             02 SF-124
Wright, Joseph; 17 July 1806; Mary Rose                     11 BA-9
Wright, Levin; 13 April 1802; Susan King                    01 DO-40
Wright, Mark; 22 Sept. 1810; Ann Lomey                      13 BA-10
Wright, Nathan; 28 April 1814; Mary Seadere                 13 BA-18
Wright, Nathaniel; 20 Oct. 1803; Sarah Harryman             09 BA
Wright, Peter; July 1806; Sus. Lefever                      02 WA-81
Wright, Peter (s. of John and Esther); 17 d. 2 mo., 1813; Mary
    Anderson (dau. of James and Celia)                      07 SF-21
Wright, Roger (s. of James and Sarah); 20 d. 12 mo., 1804; Mary
    Wright (dau. of James and Ann)                          07 SF
Wright, Thomas; 2 June 1808; Elizabeth Cooper               11 BA-12
Wright, Thomas; 3 Dec. 1811; Christianna Branneman          11 BA-18
Wright, Thomas; 28 March 1812; Martha Cromley               02 WA-93
Wright, W. J.; 22 Dec. 1814; Marg't Howard                  13 BA-20
Wright, William; 8 April 1804; Amelia Smithson              06 HA-1
Wright, William (s. of James and Sarah); 19 d. 2 mo., 1807; Celia
    Wright (dau. of Jacob and Rhoda)                        07 SF-13
Wright, William; 14 Dec. 1809; Susanna Neff                 03 AL-614
Wright, William; 18 May 1812; Mary Arnold                   14 BA-430
Wright, William; 28 Jan. 1818; Jane Crow                    17 BA-19
Wright, Willis (s. of John and Hester); 20 d. 11 mo., 1816;
    Hannah Wilson (dau. of James and Sarah)                 08 SF
Wrightman, John; 4 April 1819; Ann Maria Askew              11 BA-35
Wroe, Everitt; 21 July 1808; Mary Davis                     02 BA-6
Wroe, Everitt; 29 Aug. 1816; Euphemia Grey                  21 BA-8
Wroe, Samuel; 27 Nov. 1815; Maria G. Bowers                 14 BA-434
Wrosher, William; 22 June 1815; Rachel Cullings             09 BA
Wurstsorn, Philippus; 27 Aug. 1809; Sarah Baker, widow      39 BA-22
Wyant, Daniel; 26 June 1812; Cath. Shroder                  14 BA-430
Wyant, Peter; 16 Jan. 1803; Maria Maul                      07 BA-68
Wyckoff, William; 21 March 1805; Mary Hellemes              03 AL-613
Wycoff, William; 28 Aug. 1815; Catherine Michael            08 AL-129
Wynaert, Jacques; 16 July 1818; Francoise Delinott          16 BA-71
Wynn, Aaron; 3 Sept. 1808; Eliza Ann White                  14 BA-424
Wyvil, Robert; 28 March 1818; Ann Keene                     02 DO
Wyvill, Walter; 3 June 1811; Ann Wood                       03 AA-126
Yander, Simon; 8 Sept. 1812; Rebecca Trovinger              02 WA-95
Yardly, Richard; 16 Oct. 1808; Matilda Pasin (See also 15 FR-323)
                                                            01 FR-1186
Yates, Edward; 26 March 1816; Catherine Richards            06 FR-1324
Yates, John; 16 Nov. 1802; Rachel Henshaw                   03 BA-423
Yates, John; 15 Sept. 1803; Anne Mitchell                   03 BA-433
Yates, John; 23 May 1811; Bridget Fell                      15 BA-288
Yates, Robert; 3 July 1806; Mary Addison                    03 BA-495
Yates, William; 14 Jan. 1806; Elizabeth Crouse             02 BA-3
Yeager, John; 3 Oct. 1816; E. M. M. Hanson                  05 BA-239
Yeakly, John; Feb. 1803; Christ. Diederly                   02 WA-74
Yearby, Ab'm; 20 May 1810; Anna Handy or Hardy              15 BA-279
Yeiser, John; 27 May 1802; Eleanor A. Holliday (See also
    18 BA-65)                                               01 BA-9
Yellott, John; 1 May 1806; Rebecca R. Coleman (33 BA-43 gives
    bride's middle name as Ridgely)                         01 BA-10
Yeo, Benjamin; 21 Dec. 1801; Susanna Amos                   06 BA-2
Yerkes, Anth.; 9 March 1815; Sarah Richards                 13 BA-20
Yewell, Samuel; 29 March 1803; Deborah Miles (02 BA-32 gives
    date as 26 March 1803)                                  03 BA-426
Yewell, Samuel; 15 Nov. 1804; Elizabeth Burk                11 BA-4
Yieldhall, Joshua; 1 Jan. 1801; Mary Stewart                03 BA-397
```

Yieldhall, Samuel; 30 Nov. 1801; Rachel Benson   03 BA-411
Yoe, Benjamin S.; 5 Feb. 1807; Sarah A. Kershaw   01 CA-63
Yoe, Thomas B. (son of Thomas and Lydia, both dec.); 19 d. 10 m.,
    1820; Elizabeth Sherwood (dau. of William, dec., and
    Elizabeth   08 SF
Yontz, Benj.; 15 April 1811; Polly Hammond   02 WA-89
York, George; 26 July 1816; Rose (slaves)   03 BA-507
York, Gilbert; 26 April 1801; Mary Chilsom   33 BA-18
York (?), John; 1 Oct. 1816; Catherine Lambrecht   06 FR-1325
York, Joseph; 2 June 1806; Mary McManaman   09 BA
Yost, Joseph; 7 Oct. 1819; Ann Crist   14 BA-439
Yost, Mich'l; 13 July 1810; Cath. Simering   14 BA-427
Youler, George; Nov. 1816; Elizab. Bowers   02 WA-103
Young, Alexander; Jan. 1805; Ann Weeks   17 BA-4
Young, Alexander; 16 March 1805; Elizabeth Rowe   05 BA-234
Young, Charles; 9 Oct. 1806; Eleanor McMan   05 BA-235
Young, David; 17 Jan. 1813; Mary Ringer   06 FR-1319
Young, Duncan; 2 Nov. 1815; Elizabeth Weaver   11 BA-26
Young, George; 12 Nov. 1809; Barbara Whiteman   15 FR-324
Young, George; 21 Nov. 1809; Barb. Whiteman   01 FR-1186
Young, Jacob; Feb. 1818; Margaret Bowman   02 WA-108
Young, Jesse; 30 July 1805; Mary Brady   03 AL-613
Young, John; 27 Oct. 1801; Hannah (Hammal?) Moss   05 AA-1
Young, John; 23 June 1803; Mary Arnold   09 BA
Young, John; 24 March 1808; Elizabeth Christopher   02 BA-6
Young, John; 17 March 1811; Elizabeth Deitch   02 WA-89
Young, John; 4 Nov. 1819; Mary Bond   08 BA
Young, John I.; 25 Sept. 1816; Cornelis Ensor   17 BA-15
Young, Patrick C.; 9 May 1804; Jemima Summers   156 BA-202
Young, Richard; 10 Sept. 1807; Mary Cockran   11 BA-11
Young, Richard; 24 Nov. 1807; Jane Deal   17 BA-5
Young, Richard; 25 July 1816; Elizabeth Taylor   13 BA-40
Young, Robert (s. of William and Amelia, both late of KE Co.,
    dec.); 21 d. 4 mo., 1808; Rebecca Hussey (dau. of George and
    Rachel, dec., of Baltimore)   09 SF
Young, Robert; 19 March 1816; Lucinda Day   09 BA
Young, Samuel; 6 June 1809; Maria Kuntz   15 FR-323
Young, Samuel; Sept. 1818; Harriot Strain   02 WA-110
Young, Samuel; 17 Nov. 1818; Mary Morris   17 BA-20
Young, Thomas; 15 June 1806; Margaret Loker   02 SM-187
Young, Thomas; 13 April 1819; Sophia Holtringer   04 FR-18
Young, William; 14 June 1804; Mary Emmison (Emerson?)   03 AL-613
Younge, Fair; c.1801; Catherine Mead   08 AA-1
Younger, (N); 1810; Rebecca Collins (See also 02 MO)   01 PG
Younger, Jesse B.; 2 April 1819; Margaret Stewart   20 BA-224
Younger, Nehemiah; 10 Nov. 1803; Thiffy Taylor   05 AA-3
Younker, Francis; 10 Nov. 1807; Elizaberth Rosen   15 BA-257
Youston, Johan; 30 Jan. 1811; Wilhelmina Loudergoring   07 BA-308
Yundt, Leonard; 26 Sept. 1808; C. Kalbfus   30 BA-109
Yung, Samuel; 6 June 1809; Mary Kuntz   01 FR-1186
Zachary, William; 8 July 1819; Elisa Griggs   32 BA-325
Zadi, Johan Jost; 21 Dec. 1809; Margaretha Hildebrand   07 BA-307
Zane, Joseph; 14 July 1808; Eliza Hopkins   02 BA-6
Zeller, Joh.; 21 Aug. 1802; Susanna Shaun   14 BA-413
Zeller, Johannes; 15 April 1807; Elisabeth Wilfried   15 FR-320
Zeller, John; 15 April 1807; Elizab. Wilheid   01 FR-1187
Zentmayer, Jacob; 14 Dec. 1813; Mary Protzman   02 WA-99
Zevet, Thomas; 27 March 1816; Catherine Woodhand   03 BA-507
Ziegler, Adam; 21 May 1807; Rebecca Levi (See also 15 FR-213)
                                                        01 FR-1187
Ziegler, Geo.; 5 March 1801; Eliza Roberts   14 BA-401
Ziegler, Jno.; 11 June 1807; Maria Bender   14 BA-422
Ziegler, John; 3 Sept. 1808; Mary Rettig   14 BA-424
Zigler, Jno.; 7 March 1804; Ann Benkert   14 BA-416

```
Zimerman, John; 27 Oct. 1811; Rebecca Harr              06 FR-1316
Zimmerle, Jacob; 12 Sept. 1819; Mary North             08 AL-130
Zimmerly, John; 27 April 1802; Lucy Twigg              05 AL-1
Zimmerman, Christian; 1 Dec. 1814; Elizabeth Walter    06 FR-1321
Zimmerman, George; 22 June 1816; Sophia Trickell       13 BA-40
Zimmerman, Henry H.; 11 June 1818; Lydia Cullen        13 BA-39
Zimmerman, Jacob; 29 Oct. 1818; Amelia Steigars        09 BA
Zimmerman, John; 22 Aug. 1807; Ann Connelly (See also 15 FR-321)
                                                       01 FR-1197
Zimmerman, John; 10 Jan. 1808; Susannah Freeman        11 BA-13
Zimmern (?), Petrus; 22 Feb. 1809; Catherine Harvey    39 BA-23
Zingling, Christian; 1 Dec. 1808; Johanna Weber        07 BA-306
Zinsner, Fred'k; 22 June 1809; Louisa Bankert          14 BA-426
Zipperer, Christ'r Siegman; July 1820; Marg. Welsh     02 WA-116
Zitelman, Johanes; 18 May 1805; Hannah Wissick         14 BA-418
Zoachs, Francis; 20 May 1809; Elizabeth Miller         39 BA-21
Zoll, Peter; 9 Nov. 1806; Cath. Wirttenbacher (See also
     15 FR-320)                                        01 FR-1187
Zollickoffer, William; 17 Oct. 1817; Sarah Edwards     11 BA-28
Zolligofer, John; 15 April 1813; L. Ringgold           30 BA-109
Zorn, Christian; 17 May 1804; Mary Barton              14 BA-416
Zug, Frederic; 7 March 1815; Cath. March               14 BA-433
Zwick, Jno. Henry; 24 Oct. 1807; Cath. Meddinger       14 BA-423
```

MARRIAGES OF INDIVIDUALS WITH

NO GIVEN SURNAMES

```
Abraham (slave of Chas. Carroll of Carrollton); 1 Jan. 1803; Anna
     (slave of Chas. Carroll, Jr.)                     15 BA-175
Abraham; 17 Nov. 1803; Leny (blacks)                   14 BA-415
Abraham; 13 Dec. 1818; Lucina Harris (slaves, with cons. of their
     respective masters)                               16 BA-76
Adam (slave of Archibald Campbell); 22 May 1802; Nancy (slave of
     Robt. G. Harper)                                  15 BA-166
Allen (negro slave of Frederick Jenkins); 24 April 1817; Mary
     (free col'd)                                      16 BA-51
Anthony; 17 June 1819; Hannah (blacks)                 19 BA-72
Augustus (slave of Dr. James McHenry); 7 Nov. 1802; Rachel
     (slave of Robert Ridell)                          15 BA-193
Basil (bel. to Lewis Ford); 2 May 1819; Sarah (bel. to Joshua
     Neale)                                            04 SM
Benj.; 17 Aug. 1811; Susan (both slaves of Hugh Thompson)
                                                       03 BA-503
Bill (bel. to Chas. Carroll of Carrollton); 2 Oct. 1804; Darkee
     (bel. to Mr. Abner)                               16 BA-10
Brice; 19 May 1804; Patience (both slaves of Chas. Carroll of
     Carrollton)                                       15 BA-203
C. Salvator (?) (free negro); 4 Sept. 1811; Genie la Joye (in
     poss. of (N) Douet)                               31 BA-109
Charles (slave of D. Delozier); 14 April 1805; Eliza (Islave of
     Johnzee Sellman)                                  03 BA-493
Charles; 5 Sept. 1805; Violet                          17 BA-5
```

Charles (slave of Josias Stevenson); 19 Jan. 1806); Sarah (slave
	of (N) Hunter)					15 BA-235
Charles; 28 Feb. 1809; 28 Feb. 1809; Eliza Marr		13 BA-5
Clement (free mulatto); 16 Jan. 1810; Mary (free)	31 BA-77
Coffee (slave of Mr. Wm. Conway); 26 Dec. 1816; Nancy (slave of
	Mrs. Ridgely)					05 BA-239
Conrad; March 1807; Cath. Horny				02 WA-82
Cornelius; 28 Nov. 1801; Prudence (mulatto slaves of Walter
	Dorsey)						15 BA-159
Daniel (slave of Stanislaus Spalding); 14 Jan. 1804; Sarah (slave
	of William Jenkins)				15 BA-196
David; 5 Sept. 1813; Mary				11 BA-21
David; 2 April 1820; Jane (with permission of their respective
	owners)						04 HA
David; 9 Nov. 1820; Nelly (both about 60 years of age) 16 BA-105
Dominique; 6 Feb. 1805; Antoinette (both French blacks from St.
	Domingo)						15 BA-215
Dublin; 25 Sept. 1805; (N) Auckerman			17 BA-5
Edward; 24 Nov. 1807; Milly (slaves of Robert Patterson)
							15 BA-208
Enoch (slave of Robert North Carnan); 22 Oct. 1808; Cecily (slave
	of Richard Caton)				15 BA-265
Ephraim (slave of Abraham [Jussey?]); 11 Nov. 1815; Elizabeth
	Scott (free col'd)				16 BA-28
Frederick; 13 March 1808; Maria (slaves of W. L. Bowly)03 BA-498
Gabriel; 22 April 1802; Mary (free negroes from St. Domingo)
							15 BA-165
Garrett (slave); 28 Dec. 1818; Louise (free negro)	16 BA-77
George (bel. to Jos. Sterett); 1 March 1805; Mary Ann (bel. to
	Geo. Dugan)					03 BA-495
George; Nov. 1808; Cath. Seyers (?)			02 WA-86
George; 11 Jan. 1815 or 1816) (N) (N) (col'd)		11 BA-24
George; 14 July 1820; Kesiah (both col'd slaves)	16 BA-101
Gerard (negro slave of Richard Caton); 19 April 1802; Violet
	(negro slave of Phineas Bond)			15 BA-165
Hector; 28 Dec. 1807; Sally (slaves, m. with certificates of
	consent from their respective proprietors)	05 BA-235
Henry (slave of Jas. Piper); 15 Sept. 1808; Rachel (free negro)
							15 BA-264
Hyacinthe; 21 Aept. 1809; Mary Magdalen (widow Salmon) (free
	negroes from St. Domingo)			15 BA-273
Ignatius (c.38, negro bel. to Mr.Williams, s. of Matthew and
	Kate who are also owned by said Williams); 1 Feb. 1801;
	Sally (c.38, bel. to Mr. Williams, dau. of Prince [bel. to
	to Capt. Skelton] and his wife Diana [bel. to Mrs. Mary
	Lee])						03 SM
Isaac (free negro); 29 June 1804; Patty (negro slave of Mrs.
	Elizabeth Stirling)				15 BA-205
Isaac; 30 July 1814); Agnes (slaves of Joseph Doxy)	31 BA-177
Jackson; 12 Jan. 1815; Sarah (slaves)			03 BA-506
Jacob (negro slave of William B. Hawkins); 22 Feb. 1803; Sarah
	(negro slave of Miss Rebecca Matthews)		15 BA-178
Jacob; 3 Jan. 1804; Matilda Lambeth			03 AA-120
Jacob; 23 Feb. 1813; Sus. Rohrer			02 WA-97
Jacob; 15 Oct. 1815 (?); Jane (col'd)			11 BA-24
Jacob; 2 Nov. 1815; Diana (blacks, bel. to Mrs. Brownley)
							21 BA-8
James (slave of F. Bastin); 15 Jan. 1803; Rachel (slave of George
	Presstman)					15 BA-176
James (negro slave of R. G. Harper); 20 Dec. 1806; Margaret
	Stephenson (free mulatto)			15 BA-243
James; 22 Aug. 1815; Henny (servants to John Young)	22 BA-8
James; 4 June 1817; Agnes (bel. to Wm. Ducatel)		16 BA-54

Jarrett (free black); 7 Feb. 1819; Maria (slave of Mr. Reilly
04 SM
Jerry; 25 Dec. 1813; Polly (both bel. to Robert G. Harper)
15 BA-320
Joh.; March 1807; Millie Horly   02 WA-82
Joh.; June 1807; Sally M (?)   02 WA-83
John (negro slave of Pat Deagan); 18 April 1802; Priscilla (negro
slave of M. Ledue)   15 BA-165
John; 17 Dec. 1807; Ann Stuart   17 BA-5
John (negro slave of David Harris); 2 Dec. 1809; Prudence (free
woman of color)   15 BA-177
John; 4 June 1815; Grace (bel. to Margaret Caughey)   02 BA-36
John Antoine (c.35); 17 March 1808; Mary Saubret (widow of the
late Benedict Laplumie)   31 BA-39
John Baptist; 18 May 1809; Mary Therese (slaves, marr. with
permission of their owners)   31 BA-61
John Peter (commonly called Cupidon); 1 July 1807; Angele (negro
slaves of Mr. Rescamiere)   15 BA-251
Joseph (mulatto slave of Basil S. Elder); 17 Aug. 1806; Nancy
(negro slave of Geo. Rosensteel)   15 BA-241
Joseph (slave of Charles Chilton); 24 Sept. 1809; Patty (slave of
Susanna Abell)   03 BA-500
Joseph (bel. to Richard Frisby); 20 Nov. 1814; Letitia Sanson
(free col'd)   16 BA-11
Joseph (free black); 30 Sept. 1820; Leah Mary (slave) 16 BA-104
Lambert (free man); 24 May 1817; Henny (bel. to Chas. Carroll of
Carrollton)   16 BA-53
Lewis (free); 3 Sept. 1819; Catherine (slave of Mr. Rodrigues)
32 BA-326
Lewis (bel. to William Bristow); 30 April 1820; Jane (bel. to
Cornelius Davis)   04 SM
Lewis (bel. to Capt. J. Payne); 30 Jan. 1820; Elizabeth (bel. to
Mrs. Lidy Maryman)   04 SM
Lot (slave of Charles Carroll, Jr.); 18 April 1807; Betty (slave
of J. E. Howard)   15 BA-248
Louis; 1 Aug. 1810; Mary Catherine (with permission of her
owners)   15 BA-281
Louis (alias Amadis; slave of Rev. John Jesier?); 19 Nov. 1810;
Maria (slave of Mr. Marye)   15 BA-293
Michael; April 1816; Esther   02 WA-102
Michael; 14 Aug. 1817; Sillan   04 HA-1
Moses (slave of Wm. Craddock); 28 Sept. 1817; Fanny (slave of the
R. C. clergy)   01 CE
Nace (slave of Joseph Carr); 26 Dec. 1805; Cecily (slave of John
McIntire   15 BA-232
Nicholas (slave of Judge Nisbet); 4 Dec. 1818; Hagar (slave of
Mrs. Cockey)   05 BA-241
Paul; 16 Oct. 1805; Katy (slaves of Richard Caton   15 BA-265
Peter (man of Ed Wright); 1 Jan. 1801; Pen (bel. to John Blake)
01 QA-42
Peter; 2 March 1820; Milley (in presence of their [masters?])
32 BA-328
Philip (slave of Samuel Owings); 26 Nov. 1809; Polly/Mary (bel.
to Richard Caton)   15 BA-276
Philip (black man of Charles Carroll of C.); 19 July 1813;
Charity Joice (free black)   15 BA-312
Polydore; 7 Jan. 1816; Mary Ann (slaves)   03 BA-507
Richard (free negro); 30 May 1805; Henny (negro slave of David
Armour)   15 BA-220
Robert (negro slave of Jeremiah Booth); 10 June 1802; Henny
(negro slave of William Buckler)   15 BA-168
Robert; 3 July 1802; Fanny (both slaves of Wm. Evans) 15 BA-169
Robert (slave of Charles Drummond); 16 May 1803; Jenny (slave of
John F. Schwartze)   15 BA-182

Robert; 26 Dec. 1804; (N) Deshealds   17 BA-5
Sample; Sept. 1813; Bridget (both people of color) 15 BA-316
Samuel (black); 14 April 1807; Rachel (marr. with note from S.
    Braddock)   21 BA-6
Samuel (slave of William Patterson); 10 Aug. 1815; Sarah (bel. to
    Charles Carroll, Jr.)   16 BA-23
Samuel; 9 Feb. 1819; Sarah (blacks bel. to Lewis Booth of New-
    town)   04 SM
Samuel (free); 24 Sept. 1819; Mary (with permission of master)
                                                   04 HA
Simon; 1 June 1808; Adelaide (slaves of Me. Bounet) 31 BA-43
Stephen (bel. to Col. James Walker); 5 Aug. 1820; Sylvia (bel. to
    Capt. J. Briscoe)   04 SM
Thomas; 28 Nov. 1802; Harriet (slaves of Mr. Thomas Lee)
                                                   15 BA-174
Thomas; 28 April 1805; Mary (both slaves of John Kennedy)
                                                   15 BA-218
Thomas, slave of Mr. Green; 10 Dec. 1808; Mary, slave of John
    Hanson   01 CE
Thomas (slave of D. Delozier); 20 July 1809; Susan (slave of John
    Bolte)   03 BA-500
Thomas (slave of John Taggert); 16 Feb. 1806; Patience (serv. of
    Wm. Krebs)   03 BA-495
William; 18 Oct. 1806; Lucy (slaves of Richard Caton) 15 BA-242
William; 5 Jan. 1811; Becky (mulattos bel. to Charles Carroll,
    Jr.)   15 BA-284

ADDENDA

[Hoffman], Joannes; [12 Nov.]; Theresia Dreckseler   39 BA-33

[Hush], William; 30 Jan. 1816 (by lic.); Maria [Boughin]
                                                      39 BA-

Medley, Joseph; 14 June 1801; Lydia Smith   US

Yerk (?), John; 1 Oct. 1816; Catherine Lambrecht   06 FR-1325

INDEX

Included in this index are surnames of other relatives, of slave owners, and variant spellings of surnames. Middle names that might provide clues to family names have also been included. A surname may appear more than once on a page.

Coale, 25, 117,
147, 148, 169,
186, 203
Coaler, 41
Coates, 195
Coats, 120, 144,
146, 199
Cobb, 33
Coblentz, 149
Coburn, 51
Cocheran, 76
Cochran, 63, 190
Cochrane, 38
Cochron, 8
Cock, 71
Cockerie, 171
Cockey, 59, 137,
168, 184, 208
Cockran, 205
Coddington, 96
Codington, 96
Coe, 92, 163
Cofenay, 18
Coffin, 55, 117
Cohen, 110, 125
Cohill, 125
Cohn, 89
Cole, 16, 19, 28,
32, 61, 73, 76,
77, 85, 92, 94,
98, 102, 128,
140, 144, 147,
163,195
Colegate, 163
Coleman, 1, 115,
127, 156, 159,
171, 194, 204
Colember, 69
Colen, 178
Coles, 139
Colet, 103
Colgan, 198
Colim, 73
Colin, 159
Colins, 123, 177
Collett, 178
Collier, 16, 137
Colliflower, 51
Colliman, 111
Colling, 129
Collings, 81
Collins, 7, 15, 17,
19, 22, 51, 64,
99, 116, 142,
153, 205
Collison, 71
Colston, 28, 198
Colvin, 153
Colwell, 200
Colwin, 32
Colyer, 153
Combs, 2, 70, 75,
120, 203
Comfort, 111

Compher, 36
Comyges, 155
Conain, 19
Conaway, 1, 77, 87,
156
Conelly, 99, 144 99
Conkling, 80
Conley, 62, 136
Conn, 7, 89, 103
Connall, 163
Connell, 124, 129,
152
Connelly, 36, 41,
74, 76, 206
Conner, 31, 59, 97,
127, 152, 181
Connoll, 69
Connolly, 49
Connor, 132
Connoway, 73
Conolly, 204
Conovan, 65
Conrad, 159, 173
Conrod, 46
Conroy, 117
Conry, 51
Constable, 10
Constant, 37, 80
Constantine, 44
Conway, 112, 172,
207
Cook, 31, 56, 78,
80, 89, 95, 97,
110, 117, 132,
141, 146, 180,
189
Cooke, 33, 42, 69,
156, 181, 199
Cookford, 194
Cookson, 76, 85
Coon, 158
Cooper, 1, 5, 63,
66, 69, 76, 129,
135, 147, 154,
172, 199, 200,
204
Coots, 146
Copale, 182
Copenhafer, 139
Copenhager, 86
Copenhaver, 99
Copes, 71
Coppenhauer, 190
Corcoran, 92
Corkril, 106
Corkrill, 80, 144,
199
Cornu, 31
Corporal, 94
Correy, 59
Corry, 134
Corse, 132
Cortley, 9
Corum, 66, 181

Corwin, 1
Cosin, 36
Coskery, 96, 110
Cossel, 11
Cost, 167
Costello, 27, 37
Costigan, 189
Cottrage, 176
Cottrell, 181
Cotts, 189
Couchman, 55
Coughlin, 110
Coulson, 125
Coulter, 123
Councell, 27
Councill, 16
Councilman, 152
Coursey, 35
Courtenay, 112, 126
Courtnay, 126, 196
Cousins, 29
Cow, 59, 93
Cowan, 146
Cowen, 129
Cowman, 108, 171,
184, 186, 201
Cowning, 27
Cox, 5, 34, 63,
119, 135, 202,
203
Coy, 160
Coyne, 197
Crabb, 91
Crabben, 43
Crabber, 183
Crabbers, 5
Crabbin, 5
Craddock, 208
Cradock, 97, 189
Craft, 183
Crag, 122
Craig, 5, 6, 51,
57, 59, 94, 155
Cramer, 10, 25,
190, 199
Cramford, 78
Crampton, 31, 95
Cramton, 143
Crandal, 45
Crandell, 93
Crane, 57, 58, 109
Cranford, 25
Cranmer, 129
Crans, 67
Crasins, 50
Crate, 4
Craven, 149
Crawford, 5, 33,
53, 93, 104
Craycroft, 70
Crea, 21
Creager, 41, 151
Creagh, 125
Creamer, 176